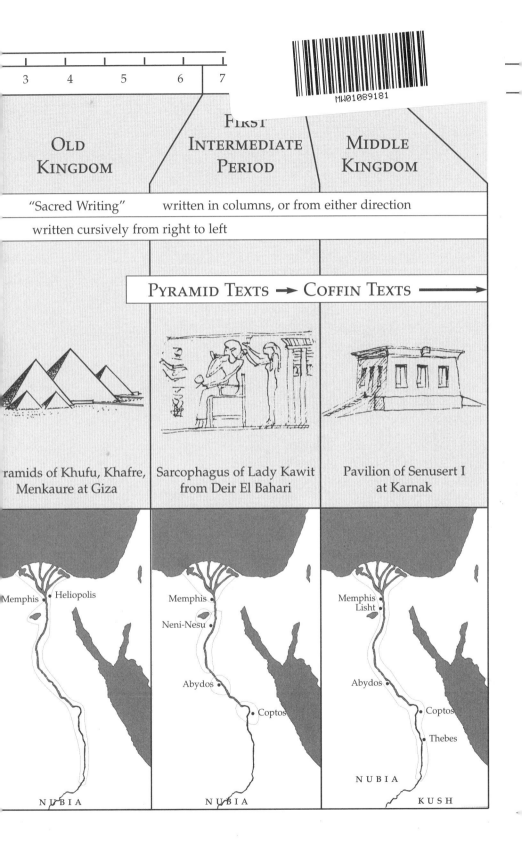

3	4	5	6	7

OLD KINGDOM

FIRST INTERMEDIATE PERIOD

MIDDLE KINGDOM

"Sacred Writing"   written in columns, or from either direction

written cursively from right to left

PYRAMID TEXTS → COFFIN TEXTS →

ramids of Khufu, Khafre, Menkaure at Giza

Sarcophagus of Lady Kawit from Deir El Bahari

Pavilion of Senusert I at Karnak

Memphis • Heliopolis

Memphis •
Neni-Nesu •
Abydos •
• Coptos
NUBIA

Memphis •
Lisht •
Abydos •
• Coptos
• Thebes
NUBIA
KUSH

ABRAHAM IN EGYPT

The Collected Works of Hugh Nibley: Volume 14

ABRAHAM IN EGYPT

Hugh Nibley
Second Edition

Edited by
Gary P. Gillum

Illustrations directed by
Michael P. Lyon

Deseret Book Company
Salt Lake City, Utah
and
Foundation for Ancient Research and Mormon Studies
at Brigham Young University
Provo, Utah

The Collected Works of Hugh Nibley
Volumes published to date:
Old Testament and Related Studies
Enoch the Prophet
The World and the Prophets
Mormonism and Early Christianity
Lehi in the Desert/The World of the Jaredites/There Were Jaredites
An Approach to the Book of Mormon
Since Cumorah
The Prophetic Book of Mormon
Approaching Zion
The Ancient State
Tinkling Cymbals and Sounding Brass
Temple and Cosmos
Brother Brigham Challenges the Saints

Library of Congress Cataloging-in-Publication Data

Nibley, Hugh, 1910–
  Abraham in Egypt / edited by Gary P. Gillum. — 2nd ed.
    p. cm. — (The collected works of Hugh Nibley : v. 14)
  Includes bibliographical references and indexes.
  ISBN 1-57345-527-X (hardcover)
  1. Book of Abraham — Criticism, interpretation, etc. I. Gillum, Gary P. II. Title. III. Series : Nibley, Hugh, 1910– Works, 1986; v. 14.
BX8629.B563N53 1999
289.3'2—dc21   99-24106
                                            CIP

Printed in the United States of America   72082-6466

10 9 8 7 6 5 4 3 2

Contents

Illustrations

Key to Abbreviations

ASAE   *Annales du service des antiquités de l'Égypte*
BAR   *Biblical Archaeology Review*
BE   *Bibliothèque égyptologique*
CdE   *Chronique d'Égypte*
CWHN *The Collected Works of Hugh Nibley*
IE   *Improvement Era*
JAOS   *Journal of the American Oriental Society*
JEA   *Journal of Egyptian Archaeology*
JEOL   *Jaarbericht van het vooraziatisch-egyptisch genootschap: Ex Oriente Lux*
JNES   *Journal of Near Eastern Studies*
JQR   *Jewish Quarterly Review*
OMRO *Oudheidkundige mededeelingen, uit het Rijksmuseum van Oudheiden te Leiden*
Or   *Orientalia*
PG   J.-P. Migne, ed., *Patrologiae Cursus Completus . . . Series Graeca*, 161 vols. (Paris: Garnier, 1857–66)
PL   J. P. Migne, ed., *Patrologiae Cursus Completus . . . Series Latina*, 221 vols. (Paris: Garnier, 1844–64)
PO   François Nau and René Graffin, eds., *Patrologia Orientalis* (Paris: Librarie de Paris, Firmin-Didot, 1903–)
RdE   *Revue d'Égyptologie*
REJ   *Revue des études juives*
RHR   *Revue de l'histoire des religions*

RT	*Recueil de travaux relatifs à la philologie et à l'archéologie égyptiennes et assyriennes*
TB	Babylonian Talmud
Wb	Adolf Erman and H. Grapow, *Wörterbuch der ägyptischen Sprache*
ZÄS	*Zeitschrift für ägyptische Sprache und Altertumskunde*

Foreword

It comes as no surprise that our greatest Latter-day Saint scholar, Hugh Nibley, would select Abraham as the subject of an important study. To Abraham belongs the distinction of being the only person in the Old Testament whom the Lord calls "my friend" (Isaiah 41:8; see also 2 Chronicles 20:7), or more literally, "my beloved friend."[1] This unique designation occurs in a part of the book of Isaiah which many moderns posit was written by a later author; however, the Book of Mormon not only establishes Isaiah as the true author,[2] but also recounts a unique endorsement of his writings by the resurrected Lord, who commanded his listeners to "search these things diligently; for great are the words of Isaiah" (3 Nephi 23:1).

Searching those great words reveals a second divine testimonial of Abraham and the continuing relevance of his life: "Hearken to me, ye that follow after righteousness, ye that seek the Lord: look unto the rock whence ye are hewn. . . . Look unto Abraham your father, . . . for I called him" (Isaiah 51:1–2). The singularity of the divine compliment here paid to Abraham is better appreciated after reading one noted scholar's assertion that the passage must have originally referred not to Abraham but to the Lord as the rock, a metaphor reserved elsewhere in scripture for the Lord himself.[3] But the Book of Mormon's quotation of this Isaiah passage follows the King James's nearly verbatim (2 Nephi 8:1–2), indicating that the traditional reading is correct: the Lord—the true Rock[4]—chose to use that same metaphor to describe Abraham, whom his descendants are commanded to remember.

Nephi's reward for remembering Abraham[5] included some of the same blessings that Abraham had received, like being led away from a wicked society—Jerusalem, which was about to be destroyed—to a promised land where Nephi and his faithful posterity continued to remember their forefather Abraham and his covenant[6] as they aspired ultimately to have their "garments spotless" so as to "sit down with Abraham" and his righteous posterity "in the kingdom of heaven" (Alma 5:24; 7:25; Helaman 3:30). Meanwhile back in Jerusalem in the second century B.C., Abraham was considered "a great father of many people: in glory there was none like unto him; who kept the law of the most High, . . . and when he was proved he was found faithful."[7]

Jesus seemed to confirm this tradition when he preached about the beggar Lazarus ascending to heaven—to "Abraham's bosom"—where he conversed with "father Abraham" (Luke 16:19–31). On another occasion when Jesus' audience resisted his teachings by boasting of their Abrahamic descent, he did not deny the importance of their claim but merely explained that notwithstanding their biological descent, they could not be true children of Abraham without "do[ing] the works of Abraham" (John 8:39). The apostle Paul would likewise emphasize that those works necessarily bring one to the Savior, for "if ye be Christ's, then are ye Abraham's seed" (Galatians 3:29). If the rabbis never accepted that premise, they at least did continue to remember Abraham as the outstanding example of one who had kept the commandments[8] and who "is said to have 'loved God' because he loved righteousness; this was Abram's love of God."[9]

Nor was Abraham any less regarded among the separatist Israelite community at Qumran during the time of

Christ, where those entering the covenant were exhorted to
follow the path of Abraham who "was accounted a friend
of God . . . and did not choose his own will."[10] At the same
time among the Alexandrian Jewish community (more popu-
lous than the entire Palestinian community), Abraham's life
was remembered as so congruent with divine law that he
was considered "himself a law and an unwritten statute."[11]

And some six centuries later in nearby Arabia, Muhammad claimed to restore the true religion of his forefather
Abraham, who as the very paradigm of submission (*Islam*)
to God was revered in the Qur'an as "indeed a model,
devoutly obedient to God, (and) true in faith."[12] To this day
Abraham is commonly referred to among his Muslim
descendants not just as Abraham but as "Abraham the
friend,"[13] echoing the Qur'an's statement that "God chose
Abraham as friend,"[14] or as more literally translated, "a
beloved friend."[15]

These impressive traditions uniformly attesting to
Abraham's righteousness help explain what the book of
Genesis does not: why this particular man was selected for
his pivotal role in God's plan for the human race. With
Abraham's entrance onto the stage of history comes an
abrupt shift of focus in the Genesis story, which, as scholars
note, had previously concerned itself with the broad scope
of mankind as a whole. But "all at once and precipitously
the universal field of vision narrows; world and humanity
. . . are submerged, and all interest is concentrated upon a
single man."[16] To use a modern analogy, the lens of the
Genesis camera that has been panning the landscape suddenly zooms in on one man and will thence occupy itself
exclusively with this individual and his descendants.

Why such a radical shift? Because what is promised to
Abraham extends far beyond personal benefit; he is told
that through him and his posterity all nations of the earth
will be blessed. As Nibley points out, Abraham embarks on

his momentous journey not just for himself but for all mankind, causing one writer to call him "the most pivotal and strategic man in the course of world history."[17]

With so much entrusted to Abraham, no wonder many readers are perplexed by the first incident in Genesis in which he speaks. Having obediently left his native country, Abraham arrives in the promised land only to find, ironically, that conditions there seem to threaten God's promise of worldwide blessing. "There was a famine in the land," Genesis reports, and "the famine was grievous" (Genesis 12:10). So grievous that Abraham was forced to leave the parched land of Palestine for the country the Greek historian Herodotus would rightly call "the gift of the Nile"— Egypt, where crops depended not on rainfall but on the annual flooding of the great life-giving river. Thus "Abram went down into Egypt to sojourn there" (Genesis 12:10). Referring to another part of the Abraham story in Genesis, one scholar has called it "fraught with background,"[18] a description equally applicable to the terse, nearly cryptic account of Abraham's sojourn in Egypt:

> And it came to pass, when he was come near to enter into Egypt, that he said unto Sarai his wife, Behold now, I know that thou art a fair woman to look upon: Therefore it shall come to pass, when the Egyptians shall see thee, that they shall say, This is his wife: and they will kill me, but they will save thee alive. Say, I pray thee, thou art my sister: that it may be well with me for thy sake; and my soul shall live because of thee. And it came to pass, that, when Abram was come into Egypt, the Egyptians beheld the woman that she was very fair. The princes also of Pharaoh saw her, and commended her before Pharaoh: and the woman was taken into Pharaoh's house. And he entreated Abram well for her sake: and he had sheep, and oxen, and he asses, and menservants, and maidservants, and she asses, and camels. And the Lord plagued Pharaoh and his house with great plagues because of Sarai

Abram's wife. And Pharaoh called Abram, and said, What is this that thou hast done unto me? why didst thou not tell me that she was thy wife? Why saidst thou, She is my sister? so I might have taken her to me to wife: now therefore behold thy wife, take her, and go thy way. And Pharaoh commanded his men concerning him: and they sent him away, and his wife, and all that he had. (Genesis 12:11–20)

One might expect that any ambiguities in this account would be read as Martin Luther chose to read them[19]—congruent with the widespread ancient tradition praising the exemplary goodness of Abraham's life. Surprisingly, many readers have seized upon this story as license to criticize the father of the faithful, calling him, for example, "a desperate man . . . act[ing] in prudential and unprincipled ways"[20] out of "cowardice and betrayal" and "with a brutal disregard for Sarai" in this "despicable ruse."[21] All in all, complain the critics, Abraham "never sank lower,"[22] and "no attempts should be made to try to justify or excuse what [he] did."[23]

Such zealous certainty in censuring Abraham appears curious in light of what scholars (including some of those same critics) observe about the difficulty of understanding the story. "How strange this is!"[24] "How different is the Abram of [this episode] from the trusting, obedient Abram of [before]!"[25] He seems to be "acting completely out of character"[26] in this "puzzling"[27] and "incongruous scene"[28] which "pose[s] a challenge" for anyone attempting to interpret the Abraham story.[29] Indeed, the episode is "a melange of the credible and the unexplained"[30] and "provides an extreme example of how little suggestion most of the patriarchal stories give the reader for any authoritative explanation and assessment of any occurrence,"[31] for it contains "some extraordinary gaps which have not been covered over."[32] In fact, some scholars insist that the original story contained additional information which has long since dropped out of the text.[33]

The significance of that missing information is hinted at by what the ancients understood about Abraham's experience in Egypt. "If Abram had not gone down to Egypt and been tested there," says an important Jewish source, "his portion would not have been in the Lord."[34] According to the learned Philo of Alexandria, it was by means of Abraham's sojourn in Egypt that "the nobility and piety of the man" were made manifest.[35] That Abraham's Egyptian experience not only vindicated his character but also confirmed his pivotal role in God's plan may be implied by the assertion of a prominent scholar, quoted by Nibley, who insists that "to the ancients . . . the encounter between Pharaoh and the traveler from Ur of the Chaldees seemed as a crucial event in the history of mankind."[36]

The lost knowledge of why that was such a crucial event was restored in the Book of Abraham, which reveals that it was the Lord who commanded Abraham to ask Sarah to feign being only his sister in order to preserve his life in Egypt (see Abraham 2:22–25). Then to further prepare Abraham for his journey, the Lord showed him the vastness and order of the cosmos, man's premortal existence, and the creation, in order that Abraham might teach these things to the Egyptians (Abraham 3:15). Although the book's narrative portion ends here, Facsimile 3 (the last of the book's three illustrations) presupposes a dramatic turn of events, for Pharaoh himself (who traditionally claimed exclusive possession of priesthood and kingship) actually recognizes Abraham as the true priest and king and ushers him onto the royal throne to instruct the sages of Egypt. This intriguing scenario is rendered all the more remarkable in light of Abraham's earlier experience in Ur where, as the Book of Abraham has already recounted, he had once lain bound on a sacrificial altar as Pharaoh's priest lifted the knife to slay

Abraham. Only divine intervention at the very last moment saved him (see Abraham 1:5–20). Nibley's insightful exploration of those ancient scenes helps us appreciate their historical uniqueness as well as their continuing relevance.

But the genius of the Book of Abraham is that interwoven through the description of those momentous events is a panorama of mankind's divine origin and potential. As literal spirit offspring of God (see Abraham 3:11–12), we are sent into mortality to be "prove[n] . . . to see if [we] will do all things whatsoever the Lord [our] God shall command [us]" (Abraham 3:25) so that we can "have glory added upon [our] heads for ever and ever" (Abraham 3:26). Parley Pratt noted that in Abraham's record "we see . . . unfolded our eternal being—our existence before the world was—our high and responsible station in the councils of the Holy One, and our eternal destiny."[37] The Book of Abraham even describes the road to that highest destiny: strictly obeying all God's commandments (see Abraham 3:25); diligently seeking righteousness and peace (see Abraham 1:2); making and keeping sacred covenants (see Abraham 2:6–13); receiving the priesthood and sacred ordinances (see Abraham 1:2 and Facsimile 2); building a family unit (Abraham 2:2); searching the scriptures (see Abraham 1:31); keeping journals and records (see Abraham 1:31); sharing the gospel (see Abraham 2:15); and proving faithful in the face of opposition (see Abraham 1:5–15 and Facsimile 1)—all works of Abraham, who is as much a model for Latter-day Saints as he was in ages past for those aspiring to be the people of God. "Do the works of Abraham," declared a revelation given through the Prophet Joseph Smith (D&C 132:32; see also 101:4–5).

One can appreciate, then, the profound joy among the early Saints of this dispensation at the coming forth of the Book of Abraham. On 19 February 1842, after helping set the type to print the first installment of the Book of Abraham,

Wilford Woodruff could hardly contain his exuberance as he recorded in his journal:

> Truly the Lord has raised up Joseph [Smith] the Seer of the seed of Abraham . . . & is now clothing him with mighty power & wisdom & knowledge. . . . to reveal the mysteries of the kingdom of God [and] to translate . . . Ancient records . . . as old as Abraham . . . , which causes our hearts to burn within us while we behold their glorious truths opened unto us.[38]

Wilford was hardly less effusive a month later when, after spending the day printing another installment of the book, he recorded:

> The truths of the Book of Abraham are truly edifying, great & glorious, which are among the rich treasures that are revealed unto us in the last days.[39]

Later that year when the Book of Abraham was first printed for the British Saints in the *Millennial Star,* the paper's editor, Parley Pratt, exulted:

> When we read the Book of Abraham with the reflection that its light has burst upon the world after a silence of three or four thousand years, during which it has slumbered in the bosom of the dead, and been sealed up in the sacred archives of Egypt's moldering ruins, . . . we are lost in astonishment and admiration. . . . The morning of celestial light has dawned.[40]

But just as the great Abraham has not escaped the criticism of the modern world, neither has the great latter-day restorer of his record, Joseph Smith, who has been accused of producing a story that departs radically from the biblical account and contains features similar to standard Egyptian texts. Ironically, as Nibley demonstrates, such objections are now proving to be the very points that overwhelmingly confirm the antiquity and authenticity of the Book of Abraham. For what the critics did not foresee was the emergence of numerous ancient sources—apocryphal, pseudepigraphical, Egyptian, and otherwise—that would collectively recount essentially the same story as that found in the Book of Abraham.

Nibley takes us on a grand tour of many of those sources, pointing out their remarkable parallels with the Book of Abraham and filling in much of the background that Genesis leaves out. In the process, Abraham comes alive for us as Nibley deepens our understanding and appreciation of the man whose extraordinary life still serves as a model for the saints. The morning of celestial light, Parley Pratt would say, shines yet brighter.

E. Douglas Clark

Notes

1. The Hebrew word derives from the verb *ʾāhaḇ*, "to love"; see Francis Brown, S. R. Driver, and Charles A. Briggs, *A Hebrew and English Lexicon of the Old Testament* (Oxford: Clarendon, 1980), 12–13; and G. Johannes Botterweck and Helmer Ringgren, eds., *Theological Dictionary of the Old Testament* (Grand Rapids, MI: Eerdmans, 1986), 1:99–118. The word also "implies a more intimate relationship than . . . the usual word for 'my friend/companion,'" so that God literally calls Abraham "him whom I loved," Christopher R. North, *The Second Isaiah: Introduction, Translation and Commentary to Chapters XL–LV* (Oxford: Clarendon, 1964), 97; or "my beloved" or "my beloved friend," as the passage is in fact translated in some versions both ancient and modern. The Septuagint has the Greek equivalent of "whom I have loved," while Aquila has the Greek equivalent of "my beloved." John D. W. Watts, *Isaiah 34–66*, Word Biblical Commentary, vol. 25 (Waco, TX: Word Books, 1987), 99; Westermann reads "whom I loved," in Claus Westermann, *Isaiah 40–66: A Commentary*, The Old Testament Library (Philadelphia: Westminster, 1969), 67; Gileadi reads "my beloved friend," in Avraham Gileadi, *The Literary Message of Isaiah* (New York: Hebraeus, 1994), 351; *The Emphasized Bible* reads "my loving one," in Curtis Vaughan, *Twenty-Six Translations of the Bible*, 3 vols. (Atlanta: American Home Libraries, 1967), 2478.

2. The numerous passages of Isaiah 40–66 quoted from the brass plates demonstrate that such passages are by no means postexilic but were actually part of the original book written by Isaiah.

3. P. A. H. de Boer, *Second-Isaiah's Message,* Oudtestamentische Studien, vol. 11 (Leiden: Brill, 1956), 58–67.

4. See, for example, Moses 7:53; 1 Nephi 15:15; 2 Nephi 4:30; 9:45; 18:14 (= Isaiah 8:14); Helaman 5:12; and Gerhard Kittel and Gerhard Friedrich, *Theological Dictionary of the New Testament* (Grand Rapids, MI: Eerdmans, 1968), 6:95–99.

5. In teaching his spiritually illiterate brothers, Nephi repeatedly refers to Abraham and his covenant, which, as Nephi points out, was received through Abraham's exemplary righteousness; see 1 Nephi 15:18–19; 17:35–40.

6. See 2 Nephi 29:14; Jacob 4:5; Alma 13:15; Helaman 8:16–17; 3 Nephi 20:25–27; Mormon 5:20; and see also Ether 13:11.

7. Ecclesiasticus [Sirach] 44:19–20 (Apocrypha, King James Version).

8. "Abraham," in *Encyclopaedia Judaica,* corrected ed., 2:115–17, citing numerous rabbinic sources, including this statement from 32a of the tractate Nedarim of the Babylonian Talmud: "No one occupied himself so much with the divine commandments as did Abraham."

9. *Lech Lecha* 76b, in *The Zohar,* 2nd ed. (London: Soncino, 1984), 1:260.

10. *Damascus Document* III.4, in Geza Vermes, *The Complete Dead Sea Scrolls in English* (New York: Penguin, 1997), 129.

11. Philo, *On Abraham* 46, in *Philo* (1935; reprint, London: Heinemann, 1966), 6:135.

12. Qur'an 16:120, in A. Yusaf Ali, *The Holy Qur'an: Text, Translation and Commentary* (Brentwood, MD: Amana, 1983), 688 (parentheses in original).

13. As I was emphatically reminded by a Kurdish taxi driver near the Turkish city of Urfa, which claims to be the birthplace of Abraham. See also Ali, *The Holy Qur'an,* 219 n. 634; and George Sale, *The Koran* (London: Warne, n.d.), 90 n. 2.

14. Qur'an 4:125, in Ahmed Ali, *Al-Qur'an* (Princeton: Princeton University Press, 1988), 90.

15. Qur'an 4:125, in Kenneth Cragg, *Readings in the Qur'an* (London: Collins, 1988), 92; so also in a note in Muhammad Asad, *The Message of the Qur'an* (Gibraltar: Dar Al-Andalus, 1980), 129 n. 144: "chose Abraham to be [His] beloved friend" (brackets in original).

16. Gerhard von Rad, *Genesis: A Commentary,* rev. ed. (Philadelphia: Westminster, 1972), 154.

17. Hugh W. Nibley, "A New Look at the Pearl of Great Price, *IE* 72 (January 1969): 30, quoting J. M. Adams.

18. Erich Auerbach, *Mimesis: The Representation of Reality in Western Literature* (Princeton: Princeton University Press, 1974), 12.

19. Luther's lengthy exegesis of the story includes the following observations: "When [Abraham] had to migrate from Canaan, he could have thought: 'Where is the promise that was given to me concerning this land, which I must leave now unless I want to perish from hunger with my people? Is this the way God does what He promises? Is this the way He concerns Himself about me?'" But Abraham "overcomes this trial by his patient hope for the future blessing. . . . You see here an outstanding example how faith is tried in the saints; and yet holy Abraham does not succumb." Finding famine in the promised land, yet "he knew for certain that he would not be permitted to return to the place from which he had departed, for he had been commanded by the divine Word to depart. . . . Attracted by the fertility of [Egypt], therefore, he sets out. . . . In earthly dangers reason has its place. . . . Hence this prudent householder, finding himself in danger, directs his destiny by reason and yet does not discard his faith. . . . Aware of the various dangers, he still looks only at the promise. He knows that it has been given to him and his seed and has, so to speak, been attached to his body. . . . Therefore he looks for every means of safety or self-defense, as though he were saying: 'I am not avoiding the death of this body if it thus pleases God; and yet the promise must not be wasted through negligence. . . . Therefore, my dear Sarah, do not say that I am your husband; say that I am your brother. Thus I shall remain alive through your favor. But as for you, do not have any doubt. You will experience the help of the Lord, so that nothing dishonorable may befall you; and I shall also help you in this regard as much as I am able, with prayers before the true God, who has promised that He will be merciful.' . . . Because Scripture often presents Abraham to us as a believing father and a perfect model of faith, I prefer to decide in favor of the opinion that here, too, his great faith is revealed rather than either that he sinned or that his faith succumbed in the trial." Jaroslav Pelikan, ed., *Luther's Works* (Saint Louis: Concordia, 1960), 2:289–90, 294. Luther's conclusion that Abraham knew that Sarah would be protected echoes an ancient tradition in the *Zohar* (a tradition of which Luther seems unaware) telling that Abraham made the request of Sarah only after "he saw an angel escorting her, who said to him: 'Fear not on her account, for the Holy One . . . hath sent me to protect her from every danger.'" Menahem M. Kasher, ed., *Encyclopedia of Biblical Interpretation: A Millennial Anthology, Genesis* (New York: American Biblical Encyclopedia Society, 1955), 2:130, quoting Zohar 3:52 (apparently *Lech Lecha* 81b–82a).

20. Walter Brueggemann, *Genesis,* Interpretation: A Bible Commentary for Teaching and Preaching (Atlanta: Knox, 1982), 128.

21. Joyce G. Baldwin, *The Message of Genesis 12–50: From Abraham to Joseph,* The Bible Speaks Today (Leicester, England: InterVarsity, 1986), 38–39.

22. H. C. Leupold, *Exposition of Genesis* (1942; reprint, Grand Rapids, MI: Baker, 1984), 1:425.

23. G. Ch. Aalders, *Genesis: Volume I* (Grand Rapids, MI: Zondervan, 1981), 274.

24. W. H. Griffith Thomas, *Genesis: A Devotional Commentary* (1953; reprint, Grand Rapids, MI: Eerdmans, 1983), 119.

25. Victor P. Hamilton, *The Book of Genesis: Chapters 1–17* (Grand Rapids, Mich.: Baker, 1990), 383.

26. Clyde T. Francisco, in *The Broadman Bible Commentary,* ed. Clifton T. Allen, rev. ed. (Nashville, TN: Broadman, 1973), 1:157.

27. Rabbi Joseph Telushkin, *Biblical Literacy: The Most Important People, Events, and Ideas of the Hebrew Bible* (New York: Morrow, 1997), 25; Eugene F. Roop, *Genesis,* Believers Church Bible Commentary (Scottdale, PA: Herald, 1987), 104.

28. Ronald Youngblood, *Faith of Our Fathers,* A Bible Commentary for Laymen (Glendale, CA: G/L Publications, 1976), 22.

29. Everett Fox, *In the Beginning: A New English Rendition of the Book of Genesis* (New York: Schocken, 1983), 49.

30. Bruce Vawter, *On Genesis: A New Reading* (Garden City, NY: Doubleday, 1977), 182.

31. Von Rad, *Genesis: A Commentary,* 168–69.

32. Brueggemann, *Genesis,* 129.

33. John J. Scullion, *Genesis: A Commentary for Students, Teachers, and Preachers,* Old Testament Studies, vol. 6 (Collegeville, MN: Liturgical, 1992), 112–13, agreeing with H. Gunkel and K. Koch.

34. *Lech Lecha* 83a, in *The Zohar,* 2nd ed. (London: Soncino, 1984), 1:276.

35. Philo, *On Abraham* 19, in *Philo,* 6:53. It was this same Philo who could not help but criticize the critics of another of Abraham's great-but-much-misunderstood actions, his offering of Isaac: "Quarrelsome critics who misconstrue everything and have a way of valuing censure above praise do not think Abraham's action great or wonderful." Ibid., 33, in *Philo,* 6:89.

36. Ben Zion Wacholder, "How Long Did Abraham Stay in Egypt?" *Hebrew Union College Annual* 35 (1964): 43.

37. Parley P. Pratt, "Editorial Remarks," *Millennial Star* 3/4 (August 1842): 70.

38. Scott G. Kenney, ed., *Wilford Woodruff's Journal: 1833–1893 Typescript* (Midvale, UT: Signature Books, 1983), 2:155, journal entry for 19 February 1842.

39. Ibid., 159, journal entry for 19 March 1842 (punctuation altered for clarity).

40. Pratt, "Editorial Remarks," 70–71.

Editor's Preface

Throughout his writings, but especially in *Abraham in Egypt*, Hugh Nibley implies that we all need to be doing the works of Abraham. Abraham's works should illuminate for all of us a spiritual stance in which light is victorious over darkness, good over evil, the meaningful over the insignificant, in which living is not acted out through a dark glass simply because we have failed to clean the glass, but because in our searchings we have not yet attained the clearest vision. While working on this volume the highest reward for me was the clearer vision I received from Nibley, mostly because he required that I clean the glass of my own perspective.

Nibley, for some time, requested that his earlier Egyptian works not be reprinted before his book *One Eternal Round* appeared. He was finally persuaded that his historical views on Abraham had value and gave us permission to proceed with the publication of a new edition of *Abraham in Egypt*. He felt, however, that some of his material from "A New Look at the Pearl of Great Price," published as a series in the *Improvement Era* from 1968 to 1970, should be incorporated into this second edition. Sections from that series appearing in this edition include "Appeal to Authority," "May We See Your Credentials," "Empaneling the Panel," "Second String," "Setting the Stage—The World of Abraham," "The Sacrifice of Isaac," and "The Sacrifice of Sarah."

No doubt Nibley has made statements and conclusions that some readers would like to have had modified or deleted. Editorially the decision was made that what Nibley originally said should, for the most part, remain the same. Readers who have differences of opinion will need to remember that even Nibley himself would rewrite many of his earlier books and articles to reflect newer insights or research findings. During the editing of this present volume, however, he was heavily involved in finishing his massive work on the hypocephalus (Facsimile 2 in the Book of Abraham), *One Eternal Round.* Therefore no effort has been made to systematically update Nibley's interpretations or transliterations in light of more recent research. Some changes have been made to bring the material in line editorially and stylistically with the other books in the Collected Works of Hugh Nibley and as the sources were thoroughly rechecked.

The source checking for this new edition was carried out meticulously. We have tried to make the sources accessible to the interested reader. Unfortunately, some of the sources cited in the original edition have proved impossible to find, mostly because the citations were made parenthetically with numbers that referred to a numbered bibliographic list; typographical errors in those numbers have made the sources difficult or impossible to find. In a few cases, we have retained the material without source citation for whatever value it may have for the reader; in those cases we have indicated in an endnote that the source was not found.

During the years it took me to edit *Abraham in Egypt,* the following people have participated in some spiritual experiences with me, provided valuable assistance, and earned my deepest gratitude: Professors John W. Welch, Stephen D. Ricks, and Don E. Norton for moral support and for checking the text; my secretaries Leann Walton and Valene Novak for entering footnotes on the computer; students Lourdes Chile, Anna Damien, Jeanette Decker, Alan Goff, Cristine Guajardo, Jan Lujan, Kaja Hall, Lynne Hall, Barney Madsen, and Jeyantha Ponnuthurai, for retrieving books from the library, checking references, proofreading the retyped manuscript, and doing other odd jobs; and the interlibrary loan staff of the Harold B. Lee Library, especially Kathleen Hansen and Carolin Crosby, for tracking down some very obscure references. John Gee was particularly helpful with the Egyptian sources, and Daniel B. McKinlay and Wendy H. Christian also assisted in source checking. Michael D. Rhodes shared his indispensable talent in Egyptian to check the hieroglyphics in the Coffin Texts, and Darrell Matthews lent his expertise by editing chapter 12. Michael P. Lyon has enhanced this edition of *Abraham in Egypt* with his meticulous illustrations based on his artistic talents and broad knowledge of the ancient world.

I would also like to acknowledge the assistance given me by the staff of the Foundation for Ancient Research and Mormon Studies (FARMS) at Brigham Young Unversity, especially Josi J. Brewer, Rebecca S. Call, Melissa E. Garcia, Paula W. Hicken, Mari Miles, and Art Pollard. Individuals who have contributed time and talents to the production of *The Collected Works of Hugh Nibley* include Janet Carpenter, Glen Cooper, Karen Dick, James Fleugel, Fran Clark Hafen, Andrew Hedges, Brent McNeely, Tyler Moulton, Phyllis Nibley, Kathy O'Brien, Matthew Roper, James Tredway, and Natalie Whiting. Final editorial and production work has been coordinated by Shirley S. Ricks and Alison V. P. Coutts at FARMS and the staff at Deseret Book: Jennifer Adams, Laurie Cook, and Richard Erickson. We acknowledge and thank L. Stephen and Annette Richards and Alan and Karen Ashton for their generous contributions in support of the *Collected Works of Hugh Nibley*. My family patiently supported me during many hours of working with the text at home, and for their understanding I am truly grateful. Finally, I am indebted to E. Douglas Clark for his insightful comments about Hugh Nibley and *Abraham in Egypt* provided in the foreword.

GARY P. GILLUM

Author's Preface to the First Edition

Two things which the great Egyptologist Adolf Erman would not tolerate in students or colleagues were *Phantasie* and *Romantik.* His was that "bacon and greens honesty" that Carlyle so admired in the Prussian character. From the positivists of the Berlin School, bacon and greens scholarship became the heritage and fare to this day of English and American Egyptology. No secrets from the Crypt, please! The student who suggests in class that some Egyptian might have known something of importance that we do not know instantly and infallibly activates the red light and the buzzer. In no other field have practitioners concentrated with fiercer intensity on the ordinary and the commonplace; their glory is to discover that the Egyptians after all bought and sold, ate and drank, had families, and gave parties, even as we do today—like everybody else, in fact: "As it was in the days of Noah . . ."

With that discovery, the student should be free to turn to more significant matters. Life is too short to devote years of study to learning that what went on with the Ancients was just more of the same; it is too short to let us live both our lives and theirs from day to day *unless* they have something to add to the story, something we do not have, something quite wonderful and unexpected. Of all people the Egyptians are most likely to supply us with such matter, and this is exactly what most of the schoolmen would deny us. From time to time a few eminent Egyptologists have commented with sorrow on the failure of their discipline to bring forth after many generations of toil a single really important discovery—the shovel alone will speak for them. They have robbed themselves, in their fierce jealousy of each other and the amateur, of untold riches—untold because no one has been allowed to examine them. Whatever cannot be explained in terms of our own everyday experience must be bypassed as an unsolved mystery or brushed aside as complete nonsense, preferably the latter, to keep the layman from meddling in a field where common ignorance places him on a common footing with the learned. This book is dedicated to the proposition that the Egyptians have something important and unexpected to communicate, and that such knowledge is to be found, among other places, in the Book of Abraham.

From the first, our no-nonsense scholars picked Joseph Smith for an easy mark; the man was just too uneducated to produce anything serious. To the question, Do you mind looking at what he actually produced? the answer was always, Yes, we do mind, our time is much too valuable for such nonsense. How do they know it is nonsense? Answer: It must be, coming from such an unlearned man. And so his work goes untested and unread.

Yet for one thing alone he commands the respect and awe of any who take more than a passing glance; that is the vast scope of his work. He has given us what purport to be original fragments (in inspired translation) of books of Adam, Enoch, Noah, Abraham, Moses, Zenos, and John, a full-scale epic from the "Separation" (from the Tower), also a thousand-year history of a lost civilization, an account of great complexity and detail. And all these things were given out as true history. Has any other modern author ever even remotely approached such a performance for sheer daring? But daring was the least part of it. The multitude of names,

places, institutions, and events and the powerful presentation, with its inexhaustible variety and rapid succession of
intensely dramatic situations, the manifest sincerity, the
clear purpose and meaning, the frightening relevance to our
own day, are only surpassed by the most remarkable feat of
all, which was getting the whole thing straight the first
time; there are no snags or loose ends discoverable to the
reader struggling desperately to follow all the threads that
Joseph Smith handles so adroitly. What more could scholars in a dozen fields ask for should they ever decide to run
exhaustive tests on him? And it is he who invites the test;
after 150 years these histories are still on public display
without the slightest apology or retraction of any of the
claims made for them in the beginning. If these writings are
fraudulent, the best possible way to get rid of them would
be to encourage the widest possible reading of them,
instead of which every effort has been made and is still
being made to keep people from reading them. To this day
the usual answer of the critics to the challenge has been simply to ignore it, contemptuously dismissing Joseph Smith's
unparalleled performance by comparing his lack of education to their own titles and degrees.

The purpose of the present book is to carry forward
beginnings made in my long series of articles in the *Improvement Era* and a book on the Egyptian Endowment, and in
the process to clarify the proposition that the critics up to
now have been exceeding their authority in maintaining
that the Book of Abraham cannot by the remotest possibility
have anything to do with the real Abraham or the real
Egypt. The reader is invited to join me in discovering how
little anyone today knows about either and how a good
deal of what we do not know may well have to do with
Abraham.

1

The Book of Abraham and the Book of the Dead

Just What Is the Problem?

"I, Abraham . . ." These words in the opening verse of Joseph Smith's Book of Abraham ring out like a trumpet blast challenging all comers to a fair field. They state the argument and set up the target. Is this an authentic autobiography of Abraham the Patriarch, or is it not? Let us not evade the issue by dismissing the proposition as too absurd to be taken seriously; if it is as impossible as it seems to modern scholars, let them please take a few minutes off to disabuse the public mind and explain it to the world. To date, not one critic has laid a finger on the Book of Abraham. Instead, they have all sought to discredit it by indirection, dwelling exclusively on the method and person by which they assume it was produced.

To discredit Joseph Smith, or anyone else, in the eyes of an uninformed public is only too easy, requiring but the observance of a few established routines in the art of public relations. That gets us nowhere honestly. What about the Book of Abraham? In it Joseph Smith has given us a straightforward and detailed narrative, whose boldness, ingenuity, and originality should excite the interest and command the

1

respect of anyone who has ever tried to write anything.
Even as a work of fiction it does not permit the reader to see
in it the production of some poor fool who had no idea of
what he was doing, completely befuddled as to his sources,
trying to squeeze a story out of a handful of perfectly meaningless Egyptian doodles. We invite the critics to use the great
advantage of their superior education and vast resource
material to produce anything like it. We will even allow
them full use of what they call Joseph Smith's *modus
operandi,* which they have so brilliantly suggested as the
explanation of how he really did it. And to assist them further, we offer at no extra charge another clue, a statement
by the great E. A. Wallis Budge that is all the more revealing for its frank hostility to the Prophet: "The letter press
[Joseph Smith's explanation of the Book of Abraham] is as
idiotic as the pictures, and is *clearly* based on the Bible, and
some of the Old Testament apocryphal histories."[1] As to
those apocryphal sources, why have all his other critics
overlooked them, insisting that the whole thing is "a pure
fabrication" and "simply the product of Joseph Smith's
imagination"? As we have already observed, what could
Joseph Smith have known about Old Testament apocryphal
histories? Budge was possibly the greatest authority of his
day on apocrypha, but that was because he spent his days
mostly in the British Museum among original manuscripts
to which nobody else had access. There were indeed a number of important apocrypha published in Budge's day—but
in the 1830s? Who has access to the apocryphal Abraham
materials even today?"[2] Now if Budge insists that the
Abraham story in the Pearl of Great Price is *clearly based* on
Old Testament apocryphal sources, that story deserves to be
treated with some attention. What? the relatively uneducated Joseph Smith using sources of which none of the
experts save only Budge, the most prodigiously learned and

productive Orientalist of his time, was aware? What a flattering accusation!

How is the book supposed to have been produced? By direct revelation, a method unsearchable and imponderable, which renders research along that line fruitless and pointless. But that is not to say for a moment that the Book of Abraham is beyond criticism—far from it! It can be tested as a diamond is tested—not by inquiring from whence it came, who found it, who owns it, how much was paid for it, where and when, who says it is genuine, and who says it is not, etc., but simply by subjecting it to the established and recognized jewelers' tests for diamonds. Or suppose, for example, that a newspaper reporter comes up with an "eyewitness account" of the sinking of the *Titanic,* and it later turns out that this witness never was on the *Titanic.* Does it follow that the account is a fraud? It does follow that the man's claim to have been on the ship is fraudulent, *but that is not the question.* His account may be accurate in the highest degree, based on careful research and scrupulous reporting by others; it may even have been compiled by someone else. Even less does it follow from his deception that there never was a *Titanic* and that the whole story of the sinking was a newspaper hoax. The whole issue rests on evidence taken from *other* sources, even as it must with the Book of Abraham.

In short, it is the Book of Abraham that is on trial, not Joseph Smith as an Egyptologist, nor the claims and counterclaims to scholarly recognition by squabbling publicity seekers, nor the provenance and nature of Egyptian papyri, nor the competence of this or that person to read them. The resounding charge in the headlines was that "the *Book of Abraham* is a pure falsification."[3] Joseph Smith is no longer with us; his reputation must rest on the bona fides of the book, *not* the other way around. By his own insistence, he was merely an implement in bringing forth the record, not its creator. We have stubbornly passed the real evidence by,

like the Purloined Letter, to investigate all manner of trivia:
Exactly how did the Prophet get the papyri? What difference does that make once we have them in our hands and
know that they are genuine? The Kirtland papers contain
clues to what was going on in Kirtland but tell us absolutely
nothing about Abraham.

Abraham's Autobiography

The original heading of the Book of Abraham, as published in the *Times and Seasons* for 5 March 1842, was "A
translation of some ancient Records that have fallen into our
hands, from the Catacombs of Egypt, purporting to be the
writings of Abraham, while he was in Egypt, called the
Book of Abraham, written by his own hand, upon papyrus."[4] Nine years later, when the text was printed in
England in the *Millennial Star* in 1851, the editor made
changes in the heading that have led to serious misunder-
standings ever since.[5] Indeed, it is a question whether the
Book of Abraham has suffered more damage from its
friends or from its enemies, for like other things Egyptian it
has exerted an irresistible attraction for everyone to get into
the act.

The 1851 heading still stands: *A Translation of some
ancient Records, that have fallen into our hands from the catacombs of Egypt—The writings of Abraham while he was in
Egypt, called the Book of Abraham, written by his own hand,
upon papyrus.* But note the significant omissions and inser-
tions. The words "purporting to be" are omitted, and in
their place is an imperious dash that brooks no nonsense—
it *is* the writing of Abraham. Joseph Smith, on the other
hand, informs us that the ancient records purport to be
writings of Abraham and proceeds to tell us what they contain. He had already demonstrated at great length his
power to translate ancient records with or without possession
of the original text (see D&C 7). As it stands, the statement

"written by his own hand, upon papyrus" comes as an unequivocal declaration of the editor, while it is actually part of the original Egyptian title: "called *the Book of Abraham, written by his own hand, upon papyrus*"—that was Abraham's own heading. This is important, since much misunderstanding has arisen from the assumption that the Joseph Smith Papyri were the original draft of Abraham's book, his very own handiwork. I discussed the sense in which the formula is to be understood some years ago:

> Two important and peculiar aspects of ancient authorship must be considered when we are told that a writing is by the hand of Abraham or anybody else. One is that according to Egyptian and Hebrew thinking any copy of a book originally written by Abraham would be regarded and designated as the very work of his hand forever after, no matter how many reproductions had been made and handed down through the years. The other is that no matter who did the writing originally, if it was Abraham who commissioned or directed the work, he would take the credit for the actual writing of the document, whether he penned it or not.
>
> As to the first point, when a holy book (usually a leather roll) grew old and worn out from handling, it was not destroyed but *renewed*. Important writings were immortal—for the Egyptians they were "the divine words," for the Jews the very letters were holy and indestructible, being the word of God. The wearing out of a particular copy of scripture therefore in no way brought the life of the book to a close—it could not perish. In Egypt it was simply renewed (*ma.w, sma.w*) "fairer than before," and so continued its life to the next renewal. Thus we are told at the beginning of what some have claimed to be the oldest writing in the world [the Shabako Stone], "His Majesty wrote this book down anew. . . . His Majesty discovered it as a work of the Ancestors, but eaten by worms. . . . So His Majesty wrote it down from the beginning, so that it is more beautiful than it

was before."[6] It is not a case of the old book's being
replaced by a new one, but of the original book itself continuing its existence in a rejuvenated state. No people
were more hypnotized by the idea of a renewal of lives
than the Egyptians—not a succession of lives or a line of
descent, but the actual revival and rejuvenation of a
single life.

Even the copyist who puts his name in a colophon
does so not so much as publicity for himself as to vouch
for the faithful transmission of the original book; his
being "trustworthy (*iqr*) of fingers," i.e., a reliable copyist, is the reader's assurance that he has the original text
before him. An Egyptian document, J. Spiegel observes,
is like the print of an etching, which is not only a work of
art in its own right but "can lay claim equally well to
being the original . . . regardless of whether the individual copies turn out well or ill." Because he thinks in
terms of types, according to Spiegel, for the Egyptian
"there is no essential difference between an original and a copy.
For as they understand it, all pictures are but reproductions of an ideal original."[7] . . .

This concept was equally at home in Israel. An interesting passage from the Book of Jubilees [a text unknown
before 1850] recounts that Joseph while living in Egypt
"remembered the Lord and the words which Jacob, his
father, used to read from amongst the words of Abraham."[8] Here is a clear statement that "the words of
Abraham" were handed down in written form from generation to generation, and were the subject of serious
study in the family circle. The same source informs us
that when Israel died and was buried in Canaan, "he
gave all his books and the books of his fathers to Levi his
son that he might preserve them and *renew* them for his
children until this day."[9] Here "the books of the fathers"
including "the words of Abraham" have been preserved
for later generations by a process of renewal. [Joseph's
own books were, of course, Egyptian books.]

In this there is no thought of the making of a new

book by a new hand. It was a strict rule in Israel that no one, not even the most learned rabbi, should ever write down so much as a single letter of the Bible from memory: always the text must be copied letter by letter from another text that had been copied in the same way, thereby eliminating the danger of any man's adding, subtracting, or changing so much as a single jot in the text. It was not a rewriting but a process as mechanical as photography, an exact visual reproduction, so that no matter how many times the book had been passed from hand to hand, it was always the one original text that was before one. . . .

But "written by his own hand"? This brings us to the other interesting concept. Let us recall that that supposedly oldest of Egyptian writings, the so-called Shabako Stone, begins with the announcement that "His Majesty wrote this book down anew." This, Professor Sethe obligingly explains, is "normal Egyptian usage to express the idea that the King ordered a copy to be made."[10] Yet it clearly states that the king himself wrote it. Thus when the son of King Snefru says of his own inscription at Medum, "It was he who made his gods in [such] a writing [that] it cannot be effaced," the statement is so straightforward that even such a student as W. S. Smith takes it to mean that the prince himself actually did the writing. And what could be more natural than for a professional scribe to make an inscription: "It was her husband, the Scribe of the Royal Scroll, Nebwy, who made this inscription"? Or when a noble announces that he made his father's tomb, why should we not take him at his word? It depends on how the word is to be understood. Professor Wilson in all these cases holds that the person who claims to have done the work does so "in the sense that he commissioned and paid for it."[11] The noble who has writing or carving done is always given full credit for its actual execution; such claims of zealous craftsmanship "have loftily ignored the artist," writes Wilson. "It was the noble who 'made' or 'decorated' his tomb," though one noble of the

Old Kingdom breaks down enough to show us how these claims were understood: "I made this for my old father. . . . I had the sculptor Itju make (it)."[12] Dr. Wilson cites a number of cases in which men claim to have "made" their father's tombs, one of them specifically stating that he did so "while his arm was still strong"—with his own hand![13]

Credit for actually writing the inscription of the famous Metternich Stele is claimed by "the prophetess of Nebwen, Nest-Amun, daughter of the Prophet of Nebwen and Scribe of the Inundation, 'Ankh-Psametik,'" who states that she "*renewed* (*sma.w*) *this book* [there it is again!] after she had found it removed from the house of Osiris-Mnevis, so that her name might be preserved."[14] The inscription then shifts to the masculine gender as if the scribe were really a man, leading to considerable dispute among the experts as to just who gets the credit. Certain it is that the Lady boasts of having given an ancient book a new lease on life, even though her hand may never have touched a pen.[15]

Nest-Amun hoped to preserve her name by attaching it to a book, and in a very recent study M. A. Korostovstev notes that "for an Egyptian to attach his name to a written work was an infallible means of passing it down through the centuries."[16] That may be one reason why Abraham chose the peculiar Egyptian medium he did for the transmission of his record—or at least why it has reached us only in this form. Indeed Theodor Böhl observed recently that the one chance the original Patriarchal literature would ever have of surviving would be to have it written down on Egyptian papyrus.[17] Scribes liked to have their names preserved, too, and the practice of adding copyists' names in colophons, Korostovstev points out, could easily lead in later times to attributing the wrong authorship to a work. But whoever is credited with the authorship of a book remains its unique author, alone responsible for its existence in whatever form.[18]

There is early evidence for this idea in Israel in the Lachish Letters from the time of Jeremiah in which the expression "I have written," employed by a high official, "must certainly," according to Harry Torczyner,[19] "not be meant as 'written by my own hand,' but may well be 'I made (my scribe) write,' as in many similar examples in the Bible, and in all ancient literature," even though the great man actually says he wrote it.

So when we read "the Book of Abraham, written by his own hand upon papyrus," we are to understand that this book, no matter how often "renewed," is still the writing of Abraham and no one else; for he commissioned it or, "according to the accepted Egyptian expression," wrote it himself with his own hand. And when Abraham tells us, "That you may have an understanding of these gods, I have given you the fashion of them in the figures at the beginning," we do not need to suppose that the patriarch himself necessarily drew the very sketches we have before us. It was the practice of Egyptian scribes to rephrase obscure old passages they were copying to make them clearer, and when this was done the scribe would add his own name to the page,[20] which shows how careful the Egyptians were to give credit for original work only—whatever the first author wrote remained forever "by his own hand."

The Fatal Clue

There is one piece of evidence that all by itself has sufficed for years to discredit the Book of Abraham in the eyes of the world. One does not have to be an Egyptologist (as many an Egyptologist has reminded us) to recognize that at least two of the facsimiles illustrating the Book of Abraham are familiar motifs from the Book of the Dead. And that has been enough to exonerate any critic from having to investigate the Abraham claims any further; if these pictures are simply well-known drawings from the Egyptian funerary literature, it is argued, they cannot possibly by any stretch of the imagination belong to Abraham, let alone have been executed to illustrate the particulars of his career. From Theodule Devéria in the 1850s to the critics of the 1950s, 1960s, 1970s, and 1980s, that has been the one definitive argument against the authenticity of the Book of Abraham, the one obstacle, pointed out again and again, that dwarfs all the others. So the first thing we should do is to show how neatly it has been removed by modern discoveries.

How does one go about testing the bona fides of such a document as the Book of Abraham? Since the great scholars of the Renaissance, no procedure has been better established or more thoroughly accepted than theirs: When any text is put forward as the genuine production of an ancient author of a given time and place, it remains only to compare the writing with documents known to be authentic coming from that same time and place and to weigh the points of conflict or agreement among them. In the case of the Book of Abraham, however, we find ourselves at a disadvantage, because there is no agreement among scholars today as to when Abraham lived—estimates now run all the way from the sixth century B.C. of John Van Seters to 2500 B.C. of some Ebla scholars. The situation is far from hopeless, however, for to make up for the absence of reliable dates to give us texts contemporary with Abraham, we possess a number of old and very valuable writings actually bearing the *name* of Abraham, which writings are just at present and for the first time coming under the serious scrutiny of specialists, who are busily comparing them far and wide in an attempt to fix their true sources. As a first step in their cooperative enterprise they have established one fact of singular interest, namely, that said *Abraham texts are closely related to the Egyptian Book of the Dead.* This certainly calls for closer scrutiny.

The Emergence of the Book of Abraham: The *Apocalypse of Abraham*

The position of the Book of Abraham today is much like that of the book of Enoch about 150 years ago. Ever since ancient times scattered clues, even sizable fragments, of a supposedly lost book of Enoch kept turning up, leading to much speculation and controversy as to whether there ever really was a book of Enoch.[21] It was only when one major text, the Ethiopian book of Enoch, known as *1 Enoch*, was brought to light early in the nineteenth century that scholars started looking seriously and putting together evidence that brought forth one version after another—Old Slavonic, Greek, Hebrew, Aramaic, etc.—of that same lost book of Enoch which had so long been viewed as a figment of Gnostic imagination. After all that, it turned out, the book of Enoch was real. So it is now with the Book of Abraham.

In hailing "the rediscovery of Apocalyptic" in the 1960s, Klaus Koch placed at the head of the list of pseudepigraphical writings (called "pseudo" only because they are not found in the biblical canon) as preeminent in both age and importance the *Apocalypse of Abraham* as preserved in the Old Slavonic texts.[22] Since the opening sentence of the work declares that "I [Abraham] was searching as to who the Mighty God in truth is," while the opening sentence of the Book of Abraham informs us that "Abraham, . . . desiring . . . to possess a greater knowledge," was seeking God earnestly (cf. Abraham 2:12),[23] natural curiosity prompts us at once to compare the two purported autobiographies of the patriarch, apparently produced in times and places so remote from each other, to see what further similarities they might contain.

In 1898, just a year after the *Apocalypse of Abraham* was published to the world by Bonwetsch, two Latter-day Saint students made the first English translation of the writing, which appeared in the first volume of the *Improvement Era*.[24]

The *Apocalypse of Abraham* belongs to a body of Abraham literature flourishing about the time of Christ. "The Book is essentially Jewish," wrote George H. Box, with "features . . . which suggest Essene origin." From the Essenes it passed, he suggested, "to Ebionite circles . . . and thence, in some form, found its way into Gnostic circles," though "Gnostic elements in our Book are not very pronounced."[25] Conventional Judaism and Christianity of a later day frowned upon it, as also was the case with the book of Enoch; hence "in its Greek and Semitic forms [the *Apocalypse of Abraham*] has, in fact, disappeared, only surviving in its Old Slavonic dress."[26] And although the Slavonic version goes back no further than the eleventh or twelfth century, ample controls attest to its remarkable faithfulness to the old vanished accounts,[27] which "can hardly be later than the first decades of the second century"[28] and may be older. The text, originally published in Russia in 1863, was first made known to the West in an 1897 edition of Bonwetsch; he produced a German translation in 1898, and in the same year the first—and for many years the only—English version appeared in the first volume of the *Improvement Era!* It is significant that it was the Latter-day Saints who first made the *Apocalypse of Abraham* available to the world in English, as it was they who first recognized the book of Enoch, in Parley P. Pratt's review of 1840, not as a worthless piece of apocrypha, but as a work of primary importance.[29] But while the book of Enoch suggested only the Book of Mormon to the Brethren, the *Apocalypse of Abraham* from the first brought to mind their own Book of Abraham. Brothers Edward H. Anderson and R. T. Haag, who made an excellent translation of Bonwetsch's German— remarkably close, in fact, to Box's "official" English version of 1919—detected in the text "many things of a character both as to incidents and doctrines that ran parallel with what is recorded in the Book of Abraham, given to the world by Joseph Smith."[30] They wisely contented themselves, however, with printing the text without commentary other than three or four passages in italics, trusting the Latter-day Saint reader to think for himself.

Let us quickly run through the *Improvement Era* text of the *Apocalypse of Abraham* to see what the translators mean by "parallels" to the Joseph Smith Book of Abraham, placing the two side by side without altering a syllable of either one.[31] We shall take the liberty to emphasize significant parallels by occasional italics and quote from the Box translation from time to time.

The *Apocalypse of Abraham* and the Book of Abraham Compared

Apocalypse of Abraham IV. "Hear, my father Terah . . . how shall they [your idols] help you or bless me?" And when he heard my words, he was very angry with me because I had spoken hard words against his gods.

Abraham 1:5. My fathers, having turned . . . unto the worshiping of the gods of the heathen, utterly refused to hearken to my voice. Abr. 1:7. They turned their hearts to the sacrifice . . . unto these dumb idols, and hearkened not unto my voice.

Ap. Abr. VII. Father Terah, let me make known to you the God who has created all these . . . and has now *found me* in the perplexities of my thoughts. O, would that God, through himself might reveal himself to us!

Abr. 2:7. For I am the Lord thy God; I dwell in heaven; the earth is my footstool. Abr. 2:12. Thy servant has sought thee earnestly; now I have *found thee.*

Ap. Abr. VIII. While I thus spake to my father Terah, in the court of my house, the *voice* of a *Mighty One from Heaven* came from a *fiery cloud* saying and calling: ". . . get you out of his house." . . . And . . . as I went out . . . *he was burned,* and his house, and all that was in it, even to the earth of forty ells.

Abr. 2:6–7. But I, Abraham, and Lot . . . prayed unto the Lord, and *the Lord* appeared unto me, and *said* unto me: Arise, and take Lot with thee . . . away out of Haran. . . . *I dwell in heaven;* . . . I cause the *wind and the fire to be my chariot.* [Note the common motifs: He is talking to a member of the family when he is ordered by the Lord to leave, and Lot's place is burned. Note how the *Apocalypse of Abraham* has converted the figure of the *wind* and the *fire* as God's chariot into "the voice of a Mighty One from Heaven . . . from a *fiery cloud.*" Also, the various lurid legends about the burning of Terah's house, of Nehor, of all the people, etc., betray the common practice of literalizing ancient metaphors.]

Ap. Abr. VIII (Box). The voice . . . from . . . a fiery cloud-burst, saying . . . : "Abraham, Abraham, . . . Thou art seeking in the

Abr. 1:1–2. Abraham, . . . desiring also to . . . possess a greater knowledge . . . and desiring to receive instructions, . . . and to understanding of thine heart the God of Gods and the Creator; I am He."

keep the commandments of God. Abr. 2:12. Thy servant has sought thee earnestly; now I have found thee. [This is the theme on which both Abraham histories open.]

Ap. Abr. IX. "Abraham, Abraham!" I answered: "Here am I." And he said, "Behold it is I, be not afraid, for I am before the world was, a strong God who created even before the light of the world. [Box: "I am before the worlds, and a mighty God who hath created the light of the world."] I am your shield and your helper. Go hence . . . bring me a pure sacrifice. And in this offering I will show you the Aeons, and reveal to you that which is secret; and you shall see great things never before beheld by you; for you have loved to seek me, and I have called you my friend. . . . I will show *you the Aeons which have been wrought by my word*, and firmly established, created and renewed."

Abr. 3:11. Thus I, Abraham, talked with the Lord, face to face . . . and he told me of the works which his hands had made. Abr. 3:21. I dwell in the midst of them all; I now, therefore, have come down unto thee *to declare unto thee the works which my hands have made*, wherein my wisdom excelleth them all, for I rule in the heavens above, and in the earth beneath, . . . *thine eyes have seen* from the beginning.

Ap. Abr. IX (Box). Then *a voice* came to *me* speaking twice: *"Abraham, Abraham!"* . . . *"Behold,* it is I; fear not, for I am before the worlds. . . . I am a shield over thee, and *I am thy helper."*

Abr. 1:16. And his *voice was unto me: Abraham, Abraham, behold,* my name is Jehovah, and I have heard thee, and have *come down to deliver thee.*

Ap. Abr. X (Box). I heard the voice of the Holy One speaking: "Go, Jaoel [Box, note 5: . . . The name *Yahoel* (Jaoel) is evidently a substitute for the ineffable name of *Yahweh*] and by means of my ineffable Name raise me yonder man, and strengthen him (so that he recover) from his trembling." And the angel came, whom He had sent to me, in the likeness of a man, and *grasped me by the right hand* and set me upon my feet. . . ."I am called Jaoel by Him who moveth with that which existeth with me on the seventh expanse upon the firmament. . . . Stand up, Abraham! Go without fear; . . . [I am he who hath been commissioned to loosen Hades, to destroy him who stareth at the dead]."

Abr. 1:15–16. And the angel of his presence stood by me, and immediately unloosed my bands. And his *voice* was unto me: . . . behold, *my name is Jehovah.* Abr. 1:18. Behold, I will *lead thee by my hand.* [In the Book of Abraham this is the theme of Abraham's deliverance from the altar. The expressions "loose the bands of Hades" and "him who stareth at the dead" signify the nature of the deliverance and are both typically Egyptian, the latter of which Box finds quite bizarre. Facsimile 1 is a very proper illustration to the story.]

Ap. Abr. X. "Arise, Abraham, with courage, go with joy and gladness. I am with you, for the Eternal One has prepared for you honor everlasting, . . . for behold I am *set apart with you* and with *the generations which have been before prepared,* out of you; and with me [Jehovah], Michael blesses you forevermore."

Abr. 3:22–23. Now the Lord had shown unto me, Abraham, the *intelligences that were organized before the world was;* and among all these there were many of the noble and great ones. And God . . . stood in the midst of them, and he said: These I will make my rulers; . . . and he said unto me: Abraham, *thou art one of them;* thou wast chosen before thou wast born.

The visit of the pair Jehovah and Michael to Abraham to raise him up and instruct him recalls like experiences of Adam and Moses, which we have discussed elsewhere.[32] This is apparent from the following sections:

Ap. Abr. XII. [Next Abraham as he sacrifices on the altar is accosted by Satan (Azazel), who is rebuked and cast out by the angel. After which a *dove* carries Abraham aloft to heaven to view the wonders of the universe]: He [the angel] said unto me: ". . . I ascend upon *bird's [dove's] wings to show you that which is in heaven, and upon the earth,* and in the sea, and in the abysses,

Cf. Moses 1:24. When Satan had departed from the presence of Moses, . . . Moses lifted up his eyes unto heaven, being filled with the *Holy Ghost.* Moses 1:27. And . . . Moses *cast his eyes and beheld the earth, yea, even all of it.* Moses 1:37. And the Lord God spake unto Moses, saying: *The heavens, they are many.* Abr. 3:12. And he said unto me: My son, . . . behold *I will show you all* in the underworld, and in the Garden of Eden and its rivers, and in *the fullness of the circuit of the whole world; for you shall behold all."*

these. And he put his hand upon mine eyes, and I saw those things which his hands had made, which were many; and they multiplied before mine eyes, and I could not see the end thereof.

Ap. Abr. XII. Behold the *altar* upon the mountain to *offer the sacrifice.* . . . But the turtle *dove* and the *dove* give to me, for I ascend upon bird's wings to *show you that which is in heaven,* and upon the earth . . . and in the *fullness of the circuit* of the whole world.

Cf. Abr. Fac. 2, fig. 2. Holding the key of power also, pertaining to other *planets;* as revealed from God to Abraham, as *he offered sacrifice* upon an *altar,* which he had built unto the Lord. Fac. 2, fig. 7. [It is the *dove* who gives Abraham the key.]

In Section XIII (Box), Satan appears to Abraham while he is sacrificing and commands his obedience. Abraham, perplexed, asks the angel (also present), "What is this my Lord?" and the angel tells him, "This is ungodliness, *this is Azazel* [Satan]." Satan has threatened to possess *the bodies* of Abraham's posterity, and the angel rebukes him: "For God . . . hath not permitted that the bodies of the righteous should be in thy hand." He then casts Satan out, telling him that God has placed enmity between him and Abraham: "Depart from this man! Thou canst not lead him astray, because he is an *enemy* to thee, and of those who *follow thee* and love what thou willest," i.e., the spirits that follow Satan.

Ap. Abr. XV (Box). [During the sacrifice the angel] took me with the right

Moses 1:24–25. Moses lifted up his eyes unto heaven, being filled with

hand and set me on the
right wing of the *pigeon* . . .
and he bore me to the bor-
ders of the *flaming fire,* and
we ascended as with many
winds to the heaven.

Ap. Abr. XV (Box). And I
saw . . . a strong light, . . .
and lo! in this light . . .
many people of male
appearance, all *(constantly)*
changing in aspect and
form, running and being
transformed.

Ap. Abr. XVII (Box).
[Continuing the theme of
processing the worlds,
Abraham calls upon the
Lord]: El, El, El—El, Jaoel!
[addressing him as the
creator who organized the
world]: Who *dissolveth* the
confusions of the world
. . . *renewing* the age of the
righteous! . . . Accept my
prayer and be well-
pleased with it, likewise
also the sacrifice which
Thou hast prepared Thee
through me who *sought*
Thee! Accept me favour-
ably, and shew me, and
teach me, and make

the *Holy Ghost.* . . . And . . .
he beheld his glory again.
Moses 1:27. and beheld the
earth, yea, even all of it.
Abr. 2:7. I cause the *wind*
and the *fire* to be my
chariot.

Moses 1:38. And as one
earth shall *pass away,* and
the heavens thereof even
so shall *another come;* and
there is *no end* to my
works, neither to my
words.

Abr. 2:12. Thy servant has
sought thee. Abr. 1:2.
desiring . . . to possess a
greater knowledge.

known to Thy servant as
thou hast promised me!
[Box, note 7, quotes *Genesis
Rabbah* 78:1: Every morning
God *created a new* angel host
and these cantillate a new
song before Him and *then
disappear.* (This ceaseless
processing of the worlds is
an ancient teaching.)][33]

Ap. Abr. XIX. And a voice
came to me. . . . And it
said: "Behold the expanse
under the plain *upon which
you now stand.*"

Abr. 3:3–4. And the Lord
said unto me: . . . all those
which belong to the same
order as that *upon which
thou standest.* . . . according
to the time appointed unto
that *whereon thou standest.*
Abr. 3:6. . . . the set time of
the earth *upon which thou
standest.* [The expression
upon which thou standest
also appears in verses 5
and 7.]

Ap. Abr. XIX. And as he still
spoke, behold the expanse
opened itself, and below
me the heavens. And I saw
upon the *seventh firmament*
upon which I stood, a
spreading, fiery light
[Kolob?], and dew, and a
multitude of angels, and *a
power of invisible glory over
the living beings.* . . . And I

Abr. 3:2–3. And I saw the
stars, that they were very
great, and that one of them
was *nearest unto the throne
of God;* and there were
many great ones which
were near unto it. . . . *These
are the governing ones;* . . . I
have set this one to govern
all those which belong to
the same *order* as that upon

looked downward . . .
upon the sixth heaven. . . .
And behold also upon this
firmament was no other
power except that of the
seventh firmament. . . .
And the voice commanded
that the sixth heaven
should disappear, and I
saw the *powers* of the stars
of the fifth heaven *whom
the elements of earth obey.*
Ap. Abr. XX (Box). As the
number of the stars *and
their power,* [so will] I make
thy seed a nation.

Ap. Abr. XXI. He said to me:
"Now look beneath your
feet upon the plane and
recognize the *pre-formed*
creature upon this firma-
ment, and the beings
thereon; and the aeons *prepared before." Ap. Abr.* XXII.
And I said: "Primeval One,
Strong One, what is this
picture of the creature?"
And he said to me: "This is
my will in relation to that
which has a being *in the
Council,* and it became
pleasing before me, and
then afterwards *I com-
manded them* through my
word. And it came to pass

which thou standest. Abr.
3:9. Kolob is set nigh unto
the throne of God, to *govern*
all those planets which
belong to the same *order* as
that upon which thou
standest. Fac. 2, fig. 1.
Kolob . . . first in government. fig. 2. Stands next to
Kolob, . . . the next grand
governing creation. fig. 5.
This is one of the *governing*
planets also . . . through the
medium of . . . the *governing
power,* which *governs fifteen*
other fixed planets or stars.

Abr. 3:22–23. Now the
Lord had shown unto me,
Abraham, the intelligences
that were *organized before
the world was;* and among
all these there were many
of the noble and great
ones. And God saw these
souls that they were good,
and he *stood in the midst of
them,* and he said: *These I
will make my rulers;* for he
stood among those that
were spirits. Fac. 2, fig. 1.
Kolob, signifying the first
creation, nearest to the
celestial, or the residence
of God.

that as many as I had
authorized to exist, before
portraid [*sic*] in this picture,
and had *stood before me pre-
created*—as many as you
have seen."

Ap. Abr. XXII. And I said:
"Ruler, Strong One, Thou
Who Wast Before the
World, Who are the multi-
tude in this picture, on the
right hand and on *the left?*"
And He said to me: "...
These for judgment and
order; those for vengeance
and destruction at the end
of the world. But those on
the right side of the picture are the people chosen
for me, *separated from the
peoples of Azazel [Satan].*
These are those which I
have prepared to be born
through you and to be
called my people."

Ap. Abr. XXII (Box). This is
my will with regard to
those who exist in the
(divine) world-council,
and it seemed well-
pleasing before my sight,
and then afterwards I gave
commandment to them
through my Word.

Abr. 3:25–28. And we will
prove them herewith. ...
And they who keep their
first estate shall be added
upon; and they who *keep
not their first estate* shall
not have glory in the same
kingdom. ... And the
Lord said: Whom shall I
send? And one answered
like unto the Son of Man:
Here am I, send me. And
another answered and
said: Here am I, send me.
And the Lord said: I will
send the first. And the second was angry, and kept
not his first estate; and, at
that day, *many followed
after him.*

[Counsel and discussion is
the theme.]

Ap. Abr. XXII (Box). "They are the people *set apart* for me. . . . These are they whom I have ordained to be born of thee and to be called My People."

Abr. 3:23. And God . . . stood in the midst of them, and he said: These I will make my rulers. . . . Abraham, thou art one of them; thou wast *chosen* before thou wast born.

Ap. Abr. XXII. And I said: "Primeval One, Strong One, what is this *picture* of the creature?" *Ap. Abr.* XXIII. Behold also in the *picture* him who led Eve astray; and behold the fruit of the tree. . . . And I looked about in the *picture,* and my eyes rested upon the side of Paradise [he then saw the Garden of Eden drama presented in a sort of moving picture].

Abr. 1:12, 14. And that you may have a knowledge of this altar, I will refer you to the *representation* at the commencement of this record. . . . That you may have an understanding of these gods, I have given you the *fashion* of them in the *figures* at the beginning. Abr. 5:13. In the time that thou eatest thereof, thou shalt surely die. Now I, Abraham, *saw* that it was after the Lord's time.

Ap. Abr. XXV. I saw there the likeness of an idol of wrath, *an image* made of material like unto that which my father had made. . . . Before it stood a man, and he worshipped it, and there was an altar opposite, and *boys* were butchered upon it in full view of the *idol.* [The Lord explains that this

Abr. 1:7. They turned their hearts to the sacrifice of the heathen in offering up their *children* unto these dumb *idols,* and hearkened not unto my voice, but endeavored to take away my life by the hand of the priest of Elkenah. Fac. 1, fig. 2. [The same picture showing Abraham in his youth on the altar.]

represents the defilement of the priesthood, "but the image which you see is my wrath."]

Ap. Abr. XXVI [Abraham after beholding the drama of the creation and fall]. And I said: "Primeval One, Strong One, *wherefore hast thou decreed that it should be so?* Give me again testimony of it." And He said: . . ."Hearken, Abraham: as the decree [will] of your father was within him, and as *your will is in you, so also is the will of my decree in me."*

Moses 1:30–31. And . . . Moses called upon God, saying: Tell me, I pray thee, *why these things are so,* andby what thou madest them? . . . And the Lord God said unto Moses: *For mine own purpose* have I made these things. Here is wisdom and it *remaineth in me.*

Ap. Abr. XXVII. "Rather the dispensation of the just is seen in the image of kings and those who judge with righteousness, *whom I before created to be rulers* among them; from these proceed men who guide the destinies of all whom you have seen, and which have been made known to you."

Abr. 3:23. And God saw these souls that they were good, and he stood in the midst of them, and he said: *These I will make my rulers;* for he stood among those that were spirits, and he saw that they were good; and he said unto me: Abraham, thou art one of them; thou wast chosen before thou wast born.

Ap. Abr. XXVIII–XXIX (Box). One hour of the age—the same is a hundred years. . . . And I said:

Fac. 2, fig. 1. The measurement according to celestial *time,* which celestial time signifies one day to a

"O Eternal [Mighty One]!
And how long *a time* is an
hour of the Age?" . . . And
do thou reckon and under-
stand and look into the
picture.

cubit. Abr. 3:4. One revolution was a day unto the
Lord, . . . it being one
thousand years according
to the time appointed unto
whereon thou standest.

In both our Abraham texts, Abraham is referring to a
certain picture or diagram to explain the organization of
time and space in the universe.

Ap. Abr. XXIX. "Hear,
Abraham, the man whom
you have seen derided
and smitten, and again
worshipped, that is the
Salvation (Pardon) from
the heathen to the people
which is to come of thee,
in the last days—the
twelfth hour of the *aeon of
wickedness.* But in the
twelfth year of my aeon of
the last days, I will raise
up this man which you
saw from your seed, out of
my people, and him shall
all follow. . . . Before the
aeon of righteous com-
mences to grow, my judg-
ment cometh over the dis-
solute Gentiles."

Abr. 3:27. And the Lord
said: Whom shall I send?
And one answered like
unto the Son of Man: Here
am I, send me. Cf. Moses
7:46–47. And the Lord
said: It shall be in the
meridian [12th hour] of
time, in the *days of wickedness* and vengeance. And
behold, Enoch saw the day
of the coming of the Son of
Man.

Ap. Abr. XXX (Box). But
while He was still speak-
ing, *I found myself upon the*

Moses 1:9–10. And the
presence of God withdrew
from Moses, that his glory

earth. And I said: "O Eternal [Mighty One] I am no longer in the glory in which I was (while) on high, and what my soul longed to understand in mine heart *I do not understand."*

Ap. Abr. XXXI (Box). And then I will sound the trumpet . . . and . . . summon my despised people from the nations and I will burn with *fire* those who have insulted them . . . and I have *prepared them* . . . for the fire of Hades and for ceaseless flight to and fro through the air, . . . for *I hoped that they would come to me,* and not have *loved and praised the strange (god),* and not have *adhered to him.* . . . (Instead) they have forsaken the mighty Lord.

was not upon Moses. . . . And as he was left unto himself, *he fell unto the earth. . . . And he said* unto himself: Now, for this cause I know that man is nothing, which thing *I never had supposed.*

Moses 7:38. A prison have I *prepared for them.* Moses 7:33–34. And unto thy brethren have I said, and also given commandment, that they should love one another, and that *they should choose me, their Father;* but behold, they are without affection, and they hate their own blood. And the *fire* of mine indignation is kindled against them. Moses 7:37. *Satan shall be their father,* and misery shall be their doom.

The *Testament of Abraham*

Along with the *Apocalypse of Abraham* goes a companion piece, the *Testament of Abraham.* "With the Testament of Abraham," wrote Box in 1919, "there is a certain affinity, and this work, like our Apocalypse, may be of Essene origin."[34] The oldest texts of the Testament are Greek and were first edited by Montague R. James in 1892. He described the work as "a second century Jewish-Christian writing composed in

Egypt."[35] Subsequent studies have tended to push the date back. In 1973 Mathias Delcor wrote: "There is no Christology, and traces of christianizing are few and superficial," while a "number of elements point to Egypt as the place of origin." As he sums it up, "We have, then, at the heart of the *Testament of Abraham*, a midrashic account, developed in Egypt from the LXX [Septuagint, or Greek translation], embellished by traditions from the Palestinian Targum, written in Therapeutic circles around the turn of the era."[36] In September 1972, a symposium was held in Los Angeles under the auspices of the International Congress of Learned Societies in the Field of Religion to discuss "The *Testament of Abraham* and Related Themes." Out of this emerged in 1976 a volume of studies[37] relating the *Testament of Abraham*, as Box had the *Apocalypse*, to a large number of Testaments, or Ascensions, or Assumption texts centering around the basic theme of the holy man taken to heaven, teaching his family and his followers on his return, and leaving his blessing or testament with them. A perfect example of this once-thriving genre is the first chapter of the Book of Mormon—the Testament of Lehi. The most significant contribution of the Los Angeles conference was the general recognition of and emphasis on the strong *Egyptian* influence in the *Testament of Abraham*.

"Most recently," writes George Nickelsburg Jr., "the suggestion of *Egyptian* origin has been spelled out in considerable detail in a Strasbourg doctoral dissertation [1971] by Francis Schmidt."[38] He "compares [the *Testament of Abraham*] with judgment scenes in two late Egyptian documents: The *Book of the Dead of Pamonthes* (A.D. 63 [other and much older texts would have done as well]) and *The Tale of Satni-Khamois* (A.D. 50–100)."[39] I have already discussed the latter work in the light of the Joseph Smith "Sen-sen" Papyrus.[40] On a basis of an "aggregate of parallels, Schmidt finds evidence for a tentative conclusion that [the *Testament of Abraham*] used an Egyptian judgment scene as its model."[41]

The picture, that is, as well as the text—a drawing from the Egyptian Book of the Dead—was the inspiration for the *Testament of Abraham!*

Other scholars at the conference also called attention to the Egyptian elements in which the book abounds.[42] The further we look, the less scope there is for originality on the part of the Therapeutae of Palestine, with whom originality was never a strong point. They certainly did not invent the idea that Abraham wrote an autobiography while he was in Egypt, for in the book of *Jubilees,* written, according to R. H. Charles, between 109 and 105 B.C. and put forward as "a revelation from God to Moses,"[43] we learn that Joseph in Egypt "remembered the Lord and the words which Jacob, his father, used to read from amongst the words of Abraham, that . . . sin will be recorded against [the wicked] in the eternal books, . . . and Joseph remembered these words."[44] This, written in the second century B.C., makes it certain that the idea of a *Testament of Abraham* was not first dreamed up in the second century A.D. but must be much older. The same tradition is referred to in the Joseph Smith book of Enoch (1830), wherein sinful men and women were confronted with a record of their deeds in a book of remembrance written "according to the pattern given by the finger of God" (Moses 6:44–47).

It should be observed in passing that most editors of the Abraham texts are aware of a tendency of Enoch motifs to turn up in Abraham's writings, and of Moses to surface from time to time as the editor of both—a phenomenon, which we cannot pursue here, conspicuous in the Pearl of Great Price. Box's observation on the subject may suffice at present: "We conclude, then, that the Book [the *Apocalypse of Abraham*], substantially as it lies before us, is a Jewish and Essene production, like the related *Testament of Abraham.* . . . We have reached the stage when Enoch has fallen into the background, and Abraham, like Moses, has become the centre of mystic lore."[45] The "mystic lore" that binds the three together is, according to Box, "the initiation of Abraham into the heavenly mysteries,"[46] centering around Abraham's sacrifice (Genesis 15) and the rites of the *temple,*[47] whose destruction he finds to be "the central point of the picture."[48] In other words, we are dealing in the apocryphal books of Abraham with Abraham's endowment as conveyed in an Egyptian idiom.

The manuscripts of the *Testament of Abraham* are late, the earliest (Greek) one being no older than the thirteenth century. But their contents reveal matter from much earlier times, and it has been the consensus of scholars from the first that the material comes from Essene or related circles, from around the first centuries B.C. and A.D. That was a time, we know now, of immense activity in the copying and transmission of sacred writings: there is hardly an apostle, prophet, or patriarch for whom we do not now possess an apocalypse or testament from that milieu. But that does not mean, as is commonly assumed, that the writings *originated* in that setting; the pious sectaries devoted immense time and energy to the copying and study of these texts precisely because they held the original writing in such veneration and awe. Though the scribes are often moved to embellish or explain, they are the last people in the world to forge or invent holy scripture. Speaking of an old Rumanian text of the *Testament of Abraham,* Moses Gaster, its editor, wrote, "The stories, however, came originally from the poetical East, with its fantastic imagery, and amidst the influence of similar pictures of olden times."[49] That was the official explanation of the whole literature in the last century when texts were relatively few and far between, but today we ask, If it is all the work of unbridled Oriental imaginations, why do thousands of texts from many lands and many centuries, instead of bursting with infinite variety of invention and imagination, persist in nothing more than telling the same stories over and over again? For example, the Rumanian text in question, though in an exotic language from an out-of-the-way people and from four manuscripts no later than the eighteenth century, is actually a very good Abraham source. Comparing it with the Old Slavonic text, Gaster wrote: "The complete Slavonic text (400 years older) is distinguished from our present one only by some unimportant features, and therefore points to a common and more ancient source."[50] Here is a Falasha text of the *Testament of Abraham* "probably derived from a Christian-Ethiopic text" (of the fourteenth to fifteenth centuries), which in turn was taken from an Arabic version, which in turn had been translated from the Coptic, taken from a Greek version that in the fourth century belonged in a collection, "The Treasury of Knowledge," kept at Alexandria by the famous Athanasius, the Greek version having been taken from a Hebrew or Aramaic original.[51] One would expect, after all that time and wandering, to find a pretty wild hodgepodge of stuff in the African Falasha dialect, but it is nothing of the sort. It is a perfectly sober, straightforward account, very close indeed to the *Testament of Abraham* that we are about to consider. As ever more ancient sources turn up, nothing is more conspicuous than their total *lack* of invention or imagination—the wild, unbridled Oriental imagination, to which nineteenth-century German scholarship appeals to explain everything, simply did not exist. The *Testament of Abraham*, instead of being dreamed up in the sober, bookish societies of Therapeutae wholly dedicated to returning to the pure ancient source and order of things, now shows signs of going back long before them to an origin of "hoary antiquity." After viewing many texts from many times and places, all telling the same story, one emerges with the conviction that there was indeed one Abraham story. If Joseph Smith is going to get away with anything, he must stick fairly close to it.

Before comparing the *Testament of Abraham* with the *Apocalypse of Abraham*, it will be instructive and mandatory to compare the two different ancient versions of the former, the long text (Recension A) and the short (Recension B), to demonstrate the general reliability of texts even when they differ, by showing the manner in which the scribes would embellish a story without departing from the essential plot.

Recension B.III. [The party were greeted] about 3 stades from the city [by] a great tree having 300 branches, resembling a tamarisk.

Recension A.III. Beside that road there stood a cypress-tree, which at God's order called out in a human voice.

B.III. And the tears of Michael fell into the basin, and became a precious stone.

A.III. And the tears of the Archistrategos [Chief Leader of the Hosts] dropped into the basin, into the water of the wash-stand, and became precious stones.

B.VIII. [In the other world Adam] would weep and then laugh, and the weeping exceeded the laughter seven times. B.VII. [Abraham is told his body will remain upon the earth until *seven thousand* aeons are fulfilled; then all flesh will arise.]

A.XI. [Adam would weep and tear his hair and then rejoice and be happy], For among *seven thousand* is hardly to be found a single just and uncorrupted soul which is saved.

B.X. Then Michael took Abraham upon a cloud, and led him to "the paradise," [where he witnessed the heavenly law court in session.]

A.XX. [God to Michael:] Take my friend Abraham, then, to the paradise. [Thus this story ends. Rec. B has a different ending.]

B.XI. [The Judge is Abel and the one who convicts the wicked is] the scribe of righteousness, Enoch [who keeps the books].

A.X. [There is no mention of Enoch or Abel in this episode or elsewhere.]

B.XII. Then the Lord God spoke to Michael saying, "Turn Abraham back to his house again and don't let him make the tour [circle] of the whole creation, for he does not pity the sinners."

A.X. And forthwith there came a voice from heaven to the Archistrategos, speaking thus: Command the wagon [Heb. *merkavah*] O Michael, Chief Leader of the Hosts, to stop and turn Abraham back lest he see all the *oecumene* [Gk.; there is a marked Egyptian syntax in this passage].

B.XIV. On that day died the servants of Abraham, through fear of Death.

A.XVII. [When Death entered the house of Abraham], because of the exceeding sharpness and savagery [of his appearance] there died about 7,000 male and female servants.

Thus we see that it is sometimes A who embroiders, and sometimes B, but there is no doubt that they are telling the same story. Now let us take this *Testament of Abraham* and compare it with the Old Slavonic *Apocalypse of Abraham*. We soon detect that they are quite different works, but that they contain much material in common. While the *Apocalypse* is Abraham's autobiography, written by himself during his lifetime, the *Testament* begins with the story of his death— it is a true Book of the Dead, dealing with the vicissitudes of the soul from the painful experience of dying to the ultimate exaltation and eternal lives in the realms above. Yet though the two texts deal with different periods in Abraham's life, they both have the same theme—the initiation of Abraham into the heavenly mysteries. In the closing lines of the *Testament,* God the Father says, "Take, then, my friend Abraham to the garden [lit. paradise—Gk. *eis ton paradeison*], where the tents of my righteous ones and the resting places [Gk. *monai*—lit. overnight stops, Lat. *mansiones*] of Isaac and Jacob are *in his bosom.*"[52] In his earlier cosmic tour in the same book Michael "took Abraham on a cloud, and led him to paradise," the heavenly court.[53]

Books of the Dead

The title *Testament* applied to the writings of an ancient patriarch, prophet, or apostle is frequently interchangeable with that of *Ascension* or *Assumption*. All three titles are valid for the basic scenario—the ascension to heaven or cosmic tour of the hero, with his return to earth to reveal the mysteries in an apocalyptic prophetic sermon that concludes with a farewell testament. The hero bids farewell to the earth more than once—Enoch being the classic example. Why must he go to heaven twice? To anticipate: in the Abraham literature it is quite clear that his first ascension, departing from a sacrificial altar, is to the place of "horror of great darkness" (Genesis 15:12); the mounting up amid smoke and flames to heaven was his own sacrificial death, making his return to earth a type and shadow of the resurrection.

Countless reports have been preserved of individuals

declared clinically dead, who tell of being conducted elsewhere by spirit guides before being allowed to return to
earth. Whether or not the many instances of such collected
by Dr. Raymond Moody[54] are scientifically demonstrable
events, the fact is that many human beings have reported
them as actual experiences, and there is no reason why this
should not have been so anciently. In the earliest Christian
account of Lazarus's return from the dead, the *Gospel of the
Twelve Apostles*,[55] the event is accepted as absolute proof of
the resurrection, as it is also in a wealth of legends about
later saints.[56] The place of the theme in the mysteries has
been made clear by Geo Widengren,[57] and who does not
know the tale of Er the Armenian from the last book of
Plato's *Republic?*

   Recent studies of the sacrifice of Isaac dwell on the paradoxical nature of the event.[58] The hero dies, but he does not
die. He is saved at the last moment by the providential
appearance of a substitute; yet because it is the *last* moment
and he has allowed himself to be bound (the Akedah), he
receives full credit for having offered his life, even as does
Abraham on the occasion for showing his willingness to
sacrifice his son: "For now I know that thou fearest God,
seeing thou has not withheld . . . thine only son from me"
(Genesis 22:12). In the Book of Abraham it is Abraham himself who is rescued from the altar at the last moment, and a
substitute—the priest—is slain in his place; the ancient tradition has it that Abraham willingly suffered himself to be
placed on the altar to atone for any sins of his own that may
merit death.[59] Then there is Sarah, who makes the same
supreme sacrifice by her intention to remain true to her
husband to the end, risking her life by mortally offending
Pharaoh on his other lion couch,[60] only to be delivered at the
last moment by an angel sent in response to her prayers and
Abraham's.[61] Some learned authorities among the Jews
insisted that Isaac actually was sacrificed, his soul mounting

up in the flames after the knife had done its work,[62] only to return as an earnest of resurrection. Even without that turn of events, the atoning sacrifice of the ram in a sense restores him to life.[63]

In the *Testament of Abraham,* the angel who comes to fetch Abraham's soul, in order to calm his terrified victim, explains to him that he appears to each person as that person is mentally prepared to see him, his commonest form being that of deadly serpents[64] or the familiar seven-headed dragon, a well-known Egyptian image that the angel explains as a metaphor: Because "for seven ages I devastate[d] the world, . . . therefore I showed you the seven dragons' heads."[65] Because of Abraham's righteousness, his grim summoner is commanded by God to alter his ordinary aspect completely, from that of death and horror to one of life and glory.[66] This abrupt change from the theme of eternal death to the theme of eternal life, a true resurrection of the dead, goes back to the earliest Egyptian funerary rites, as Joachim Spiegel has shown in his study of the Pyramid Texts of Unas, the last king of the fifth dynasty.[67] The point is clearly brought home in an earlier episode of the Abraham story where Abraham is entertaining the same angel and his two heavenly companions at dinner. The unblemished calf that he serves to them, after being eaten, "arose again and sucked its mother happily."[68] In the final episode of the book, Abraham begs the angel to restore to life all the servants of his household, who have been frightened to death by the fearful aspect of the visitor, and the angel obliges— the resurrection of the patriarch's entire staff (seven thousand male and female servants in the long version) takes place on the spot.[69]

The resurrection theme is equally conspicuous in both the *Apocalypse* and the *Testament.* Both are Books of the Dead, since both follow the fearful process from the last illness to the resurrection. In both, a shining figure repeatedly descends from heaven to take the hero away with him. There can be little doubt as to what the departure really is. In the *Testament* the luminous man takes the sun and moon from Isaac's own head, which, we are told, signifies the deaths of Abraham and Sarah, while the rays of the departed luminaries remain with their son.[70] In the next section God rebukes Abraham for wanting to escape "the mystery of death," and as he stubbornly refuses to accompany the heavenly messenger, God relents and says he is sending his angel to make things as easy as possible for the patriarch.[71] In the *Apocalypse,* we find much the same situation as the angel says: "Let not my countenance nor my speech frighten you. . . . Go with me, and I will go with you to the visible sacrifice, and I will go with you *eternally* to the sacrifice which is visible. Be of good cheer and go!"[72] In the *Testament,* to postpone the dread journey Abraham suggests a preliminary run: First, he suggests, "I wish to see the whole of the inhabited world and all the creations which you established. . . . Then, if I depart from this life I shall be without sorrow."[73] In the *Apocalypse* this preliminary journey has as its starting point a sacrificial rite during which Abraham himself is horribly afraid.[74] The angel says: "Behold the altar upon the mountain . . . the dove give to me, for I ascend upon bird's wings to show you that which is in heaven, and upon the earth, . . . the circuit of the whole world; for you shall behold all."[75] "At sunset, behold there was smoke as from a furnace. . . . And the angel took me by the right hand [and] carried me to the border of the fire-flame. And we arose as by many winds to heaven. And I spoke to the angel: '. . . I cannot see, since I have become so weak that my spirit faints.'"[76] (This is something like a description of the death experience in the Tibetan Book of the Dead.) In the *Testament,* Michael took Abraham "in a chariot of the [flaming] Cherubim right up to the vault of heaven, and drove him above the cloud (along with) 60 angels; and Abraham sailed in his vessel [Gk. *ochema* or container] over the whole inhabited world."[77] Both accounts make much of the fiery terrors of the beyond, both celestial and punitory:

Testament. A.XII. He was still speaking these things to me, when behold, two fiery angels, driving myriads of spirits (through the wide gate). . . . Between the gates stood a terrible throne, like awesome crystal in appearance, flashing like fires of lightning. And upon it was seated a marvelous man, even like the sun, like the Son of God.	*Apocalypse* XVII–XVIII. He was still speaking, when behold, fire surrounded us, and a voice was in the fire. . . . And as the fire was lifted, I saw beneath the fire a flaming throne. . . . And behold an indescribable light encompassed a fiery multitude.

There is much more to the same effect in both versions, and both give a description of the heavenly court of judgment, which has been readily associated by scholars with the Egyptian psychostasy scenes. Worth noting is *Apocalypse* XVIII: "beneath the throne, [Abraham saw] four fiery, living beings; . . . one was like a lion, one like a man, one like an ox, and one like an eagle." These are the four canopic figures that appear before the throne of judgment in Joseph Smith Papyrus III—the "Psychostasy" scene—and also beneath the altar bed in Facsimile 1, and as in Facsimile 2, figure 6, correctly explained in this context as representing "this earth in its four quarters" (fig. 1). To find these four old friends at home in the *Apocalypse of Abraham* is another undeniable link between the Book of Abraham and the Book of the Dead. Though the four heads are not always the same—e.g., the head of an ox instead of an ape—it is always the same unmistakable quartet (fig. 2).[78]

Figure 1. Joseph Smith informs us that these four images in Facsimile 1 represent various idolatrous gods (A). They can also represent "this earth in its four quarters" in Facsimile 2 (B).

Another thing that makes it clear that we are dealing with the sacrifice *of* Abraham in the *Apocalypse* is the meddling role of Satan in the story. In the stories of Abraham on the altar and in the sacrificial fire of the Chaldees, Satan does his best to trick Abraham into doing things his way,[79] much the same as in the *Apocalypse* XIII–XIV, and Abraham rebukes and frustrates him; the same thing happens in the story of the sacrifice—*by* Abraham—of Isaac on the altar on the mountain, where Satan tries alternately to expedite and to prevent the offering.[80]

In both the *Testament* and the *Apocalypse*, Abraham is not only given an instructional tour of the universe, but also spends most of the time *among the hosts of the dead*, viewing their afflictions and being greatly concerned about their problems. The true "friend of man" to the end, he is determined to do what he can for the dead, sinners though they are, to get them the best possible settlement, and he urgently enlists the assistance of Michael in the project.[81] He is among the dead and is working for the dead—more evidence that he has passed to the beyond.[82] He is able to effect his plan because his compassion is shared, and surpassed, by that of the glorious man on the throne, the judge, who is no other than Adam, the parent of them all, "the most wondrous man who is decked out in such glory and who weeps sometimes and mourns, and other times he rejoices and is happy"[83]—as the wicked or the righteous pass before him. No stern and relentless judges here, but merciful and loving parents.

Nothing could express more clearly, in the Egyptian manner, the idea that Abraham both died and was delivered from death than Sections X and XI of the *Apocalypse of Abraham* as rendered by Box:

> I looked hither and thither, and lo! there was no breath of a man, and my spirit was affrighted, and I became like a stone, and fell down upon the earth, for I had no more strength to stand on the earth. And while I was still lying with my face up on the earth, I heard the voice of the Holy One speaking: "Go Jaoel [Box, n. 5: "evidently a substitute for the ineffable name of Yahweh"] and by means of my ineffable Name raise me yonder man, and strengthen him. . . . And the angel came, whom He had sent to me, in the likeness of a man, and grasped me by the right hand, and set me upon my feet. . . . I am he who hath been commissioned to loosen Hades, to destroy him who stareth at the dead. . . . Stand up, Abraham! Go without fear; be right glad and rejoice; and I am with thee! . . . And with me [Jehovah] Michael blesseth thee forever. And I rose up and saw him who had grasped me by the right hand and set me upon my feet: and the appearance of his body was like sapphire, and the look of his countenance like chrysolite, and the hair of his head like snow and a golden sceptre was in his right hand. And he said to me, . . . I will go with thee, until the sacrifice, visible, but after the sacrifice, invisible forever.[84]

This passage may be compared with Moses 1:9–10: "And Moses was left unto himself. And as he was left unto himself,

B.

Figure 2. The four beings shown in figure 1 appear in Ezekiel 1 and Revelation 4 as symbols of the majesty of God. One of the earliest Christian examples is this wooden door panel (at the left) from the fifth-century Roman church of the martyr St. Sabina, who is being crowned in the lower portion (A). Though early arrangements varied, by this time the figure of a man represented the gospel of St. Matthew (1), the bull, St. Luke (2), the lion, St. Mark (3), and the eagle, St. John (4). Like the four winds of classical art, their wings fill the space around the victory wreath where Christ returns in glory between Alpha and Omega. The heads of the four beasts also appear on this Coptic liturgical metal fan (B), one of a pair. They were used by Christians in Egypt to fan the eucharist on the altar and symbolized the wings of the cherubim on the ark of the covenant as well as the six-winged seraphim of Ezekiel.

he fell unto the earth. And . . . it was for the space of many hours before Moses did again receive his natural strength." At this point Satan tries to get Moses to worship him, but he is rebuked and cast out. "And it came to pass that when Satan had departed from the presence of Moses, that Moses, . . . calling upon the name of God, . . . beheld his glory again" (Moses 1:24–25).

Professor Box was puzzled by the expressions above, "commissioned to *loosen Hades*, and to destroy him who *stareth* at the dead."[85] They strongly suggest Egyptian usage, where to "loosen" Hades means to break its power,[86] and he "who stareth at the dead" may be a sinister god of the underworld mentioned in the Book of the Dead as "the Starer who is not seen" (*ʿSt mʾirt n maa.tw.f*). The description of the delivering angel compares his parts with precious minerals—sapphire, chrysolite, gold—in the manner in which the Horus-hawk as the delivering messenger-bird (*nḏty*, the Rescuer, fig. 3) is described in the Book of the Dead, including one of the Joseph Smith Papyri,[87] and in the Coffin Texts.[88] That hawk was compared with the angel of deliverance in Facsimile 1, figure 1, of the Book of Abraham.[89] Also, we must not overlook the role played by certain birds in getting Abraham to heaven in the *Apocalypse* (fig. 4).[90] Jan Zandee has pointed out that the owner of a Coffin Text (or Book of the Dead) could ritually identify himself with the Horus-Hawk in the special capacity of a messenger between heaven and earth.[91]

Look upon This Picture—and on This

At the outset of their journey, the angel promises to show Abraham what is "in the fulness of the whole world and its *circle*—thou shalt gaze in (them) all."[92] Accordingly, he saw the pattern of the heavens, "the firmaments, . . . the creation foreshadowed in this expanse, . . . the age prepared according to it. And I saw beneath the sixth heaven, . . . the

Figure 3. Joseph Smith identified this messenger bird (A) from Facsimile 1 as "The Angel of the Lord." In Facsimile 2 the bird (B) can represent the "sign of the Holy Ghost unto Abraham, in the form of a dove." Among the hypocephali that contain this scene, most feature hawk-headed serpents with legs (C), while some take the form of a hawk-headed man (D).

earth and its fruits, and what moved upon it . . . and the power of its men. . . . And I saw there a great multitude— men and women and children, [half of them on the right side of the picture] and half of them on the left side of the picture."[93] "And I said . . . 'Who are the *people* in this picture

Figure 4. In this fourteenth-century manuscript painting of a Slavonic *Apocalypse of Abraham,* the angel Yahoel (also known as Metatron or Enoch) seizes a fearful Abraham by the wrist and shows him the wonders of the heavens. Though the angel is winged, they both ascend on the wings of eagles, as described in the text.

on this side and on that?' And he said to me: 'These which are on the left side are . . . some for judgment and restoration, and others for vengeance and destruction. . . . But these which are on the right side of the picture, . . . these are they whom I have ordained to be born of thee and to be called My People.'"[94] "And I looked and saw: lo! the picture swayed and [from it] emerged, on its left side, a heathen people, and they pillaged those who were on the right side."[95]

Note that Abraham was shown all these things in a *picture*, a graphic representation of "the whole world in its circle," in which the human race, "God's people and the others," confront each other beneath or within the circle of the starry heavens, on opposite halves of the picture. To the classical scholar, this evokes one of the most ancient and venerable images of antiquity, to which Dr. Schmidt has duly called attention,[96] namely, the famous Shield of Achilles, as described by Homer in book 18 of the *Iliad* (fig. 5).

It was a great round (Gk. *antyx*) shield,[97] with a conspicuous rim around the outside,[98] representing the celestial ocean (fig. 6).[99] It was covered with designs of deep significance (Gk. *iduiesi prapidessin*),[100] designating earth, sea, and sky, including the sun, moon, and constellations,[101] in their relative positions and motions.[102] Human society was also indicated, divided into two parts,[103] one, a community at peace, the other at war. The former are engaged in religious rites and festivals, marriages, dancing, and music and games, with housewives relaxed and happy watching from their doors;[104] there is a solemn but lively law court in session in the town square, with freedom of speech and a great prize for the wisest.[105] A long idyllic poem describes the happy agrarian life, enjoying the fruits of the earth in its seasons in a peaceful and prosperous kingdom.[106] The other city is at war, besieged on two sides by armies that are already quarreling over the expected loot, even while the besieged are laying deadly ambush for them.[107] What a fine sight as they go forth in their splendid armor! But presently the fine sight becomes a nightmare, an orgy of slaughter on both sides, as Eris (Strife, Contention) and Confusion enter the fray while Fate in a blood-soaked robe runs about spreading havoc and butchery.[108]

The pictures are equally lurid and inspiring in Homer's and in Abraham's accounts. While Abraham is repeatedly invited to inspect and ask about "the world and its circle,"[109] Homer refers us to an equally tangible design placed on a round shield. Those who protest that it is extravagant if not impious to look for ties between the Father of the Faithful and the pagan Homer may be referred to the earliest and most revered of ancient Christian apologists, Justin Martyr himself, who sees in the Shield of Achilles a most obvious borrowing from the book of Genesis, explaining the coincidence by suggesting that Homer became acquainted with Moses' cosmic teachings while he was visiting Egypt. For him the shield "proves that the poet [Homer] incorporated into his own work many things from the sacred history of the Prophets; first of all the account of the Creation in the Beginning as given by Moses, 'In the beginning God created the heaven,' etc. Having learned these things in *Egypt*, and impressed [pleased] by what he [Moses] had written about the origin of the cosmos, he depicted it in the Shield of Achilles, with Hephaestus [the Smith] in the role of the Creator of the world."[110] Schmidt concludes that "in the

Figure 5. We have only two surviving examples from the ancient world of attempts to illustrate Homer's description of the many scenes depicted on the divine shield. Both are marble plaques dating from the time of Augustus and may have adorned the libraries of private homes. The enlargement (A) from the center of an illustrated cycle of the Trojan War (B) shows that the goddess Thetis has brought the shield from heaven to give to her son Achilles. The encircling zodiac of the revolving heavens starts at her right hand with Aries and moves counterclockwise to Pisces, just as the explanations on the outer panels read through the alphabet down from the upper left and up on the right. The horizontal panels in the shield show a surprising similarity to the divisions of Facsimile 2, which may have been drawn around the same time. Unfortunately we cannot see many details of the scenes or recognize who is seated in the center. To emphasize the importance of the shield, the sculptor placed it in the center of his composition, as if to say its message was an epitome of the entire epic.

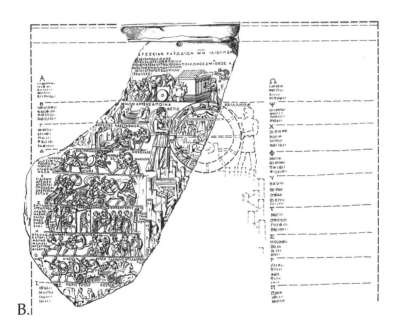

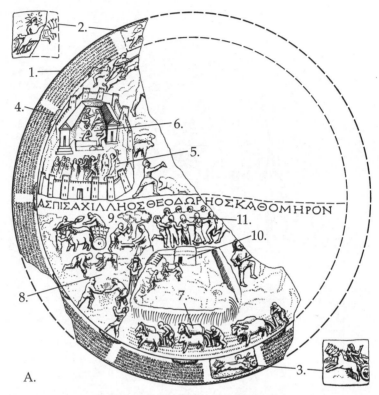

Figure 6. This seven-inch-wide marble disk (A) may have been used as a papyrus weight on the desk of someone who enjoyed reading Homer. The sculptor has tried to crowd in as much as possible on this convex side while still making it recognizable. The encircling cosmic ocean (1) was indicated by small chiseled waves. The sun-god Helios (2) drives his four-horsed chariot at the top while the moon goddess Selene (3) is at the bottom. The band of the zodiac (4) surrounds the edge of the inhabited world. A marriage procession (5) with flutes, harps, and dancers winds its way through the city. The law court (6) is convened within a three-sided portico. Three yoke of oxen (7) are busy plowing while a plowman pauses to drink. Harvesters (8) reap in a field while others tie the sheaves and a heavily loaded grain wagon moves to the barn. A couple (9) prepares a meal under a tree. A vineyard (10) surrounded by a hedge has a winepress within. Ten revelers celebrating the harvest (11) dance in a circle. The missing half would have shown the city at war and its besieging armies. Remarkably, the artisan has included Homer's entire description of the shield in tiny letters on panels all around the rim so one could read it and find the visual counterpart in Theodorus's reconstruction on top of the shield.

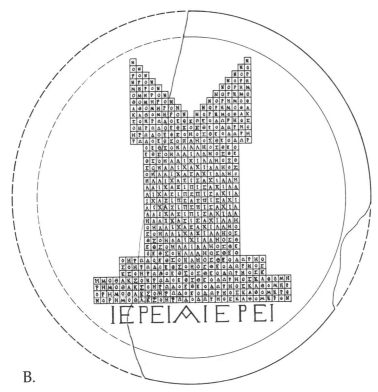

B.

The flat side of the disk has the outline of a four-horned altar containing an elaborate letter diagram (B). It is a type of word game, where one needs to find the center in order to riddle it out. A pattern of concentric squares of the same letter is thus soon perceived, with the letter A in the very center of the altar and surrounding disk. One can read out to the four directions—a connection with the symbolism of the four-horned altar. It is a rephrase of the artist's signature from the other side:

ΑΣΠΙΣ ΑΧΙΛΛΗΟΣ ΘΕΟΔΟΡΗΟΣ ΚΑΘ ΟΜΕΡΟΝ

Shield of Achilles, by Theodorus, according to Homer

Below the altar is another wordplay in large letters. It can be read both left to right and right to left with the letter A in the center. All three elements—altar, letter pattern, and palindrome—come together on the disk's central axis. The palindrome reads:

ΙΕΡΕΙΑ ΙΕΡΕΙ

The Priestess, to the Priest

The meaning, if there is one, may be obscure, but the overall idea of these letter squares comes from Egypt, where the priests enjoyed making sacred puns on the axis of symmetry of their inscriptions.

Testament of Abraham, the vision of the world in the picture
on the shield would be like the mythical presentation [trans-
lation] of a philosophic problem."[111]

The Classics student may well be disturbed at the far-
fetched comparison of Homer's Hephaestus, the crippled,
semicomic figure at the forge (fig. 7), with the Creator of the
universe; though not acceptable by Western standards, it
provides strong support for Justin's belief in its Egyptian
source, for Khnum, the prehistoric Egyptian smith—and
workshop—god, equated by the Greek-speaking Egyptians
with Hephaestus, is also the Creator of the world. Such
broad hints should have led Dr. Schmidt, having gone so
far, to search for an Egyptian equivalent of Abraham's and
Homer's circular maps. He would not find it in the usual
illustrations to the Book of the Dead—which is perhaps
why he missed it—but it is to be found in a much rarer type
of document, always closely associated with the same,
namely the *hypocephalus,* that round cushion placed under
the head of the sleeping dead to keep him or her in touch
with the universe. Abraham's and Homer's pictures are
actually drawn out for us in the Book of Abraham, Facsimile 2 (fig. 8). This too is a crowded representation of the
cosmic drama, containing within its circular rim the
"designs of deep significance" that indicate the starry heavens in their times and seasons, and showing by cunning,
half-abstract figures the circle of the universe and what is in
it—or so at least Joseph Smith explained it, though there are
no conventional indications of heavenly bodies in the drawing, as there are in other hypocephali (fig. 9). Most conspicuous is the division into two antithetical halves, the one the
reverse or mirror image of the other. The top two-thirds are
solar in nature, showing the great orbs of light in the upper
heavens and their times and degrees, amidst symbols of
patriarchal creativity and governance, as is explained by the
captions. The lower third of the circle is the reverse or mirror

Figure 7. In this wall painting from Pompeii, the crippled Hephaestus holds his hammer and displays the finished shield on his anvil to an alarmed Thetis. The sword, greaves, and breastplate are at their feet, but the mysterious designs on the shield capture not only our attention but also that of Achilles' mother. A winged figure, perhaps the personification of Destiny, hovers behind her and points out the inescapable fate of her son as shown in the stars. We can dimly make out an undulating serpent, the constellation Draco, running through the center of the shield and surrounded by the signs of the zodiac.

Figure 8. This is the original 1842 facsimile by Reuben Hedlock. In the *Apocalypse of Abraham* the hero is shown a round picture filled with symbolic figures and divided into opposing halves. The picture, representing the cosmos, was presented to him when he was carried up to heaven on the wings of a bird (see here, Fac. 2, fig. 7) to behold a theophany—God sitting upon his throne. Other features of the hypocephalus are touched on in this book, but the object has never received the attention it deserves.

image of the other. There the earth forces, the female powers of creation, are in evidence, as represented "in the lower regions," as the *Testament of Abraham* XXI describes it. It is the dark underworld of the womb (the Hathor-Cow dominates), while the upper half is conspicuously solar, as many students of hypocephali have observed.[112]

Figure 9. Encircled by five-pointed stars, a god holds up the night boat of the sun as it moves from the western horizon on the left through the underworld, or Duat, to the east and sunrise on the right.

In both the Abraham apocrypha and Homer, we are shown a high council in session in high and far-off times. The bard[113] takes us to a holy complex, an assembly place with a sacred stone circle in the middle: "And the Elders were seated upon shining stones in a holy circle," with scepters of inspired utterance in their hands, while the concerned citizens were gathered all around, passionately taking sides as two men debated a matter of blood money and whether it had been properly paid. Here, surely, are the

makings of a full-blown Greek tragedy, with the protago-
nists divided over the perennial issue of guilt and blood
atonement, while the chorus of humanity argues both sides.
Two gold talents lay in the midst of the circle as the reward
for whoever among them should speak with the truest and
most exact discernment.

In the *Apocalypse of Abraham* it is the "divine world-
council" that he sees,[114] a theme we have treated elsewhere.[115]
The Lord explains to Abraham, "And it came to pass whatever I had determined to be, was already planned before-
hand in this picture [council], and it stood before me ere it
was created." It, too, was divided in discussion: "And I said:
O Lord, mighty and eternal! Who are the people . . . on this
side and on that?" They were, he was told, on the one side
"the multitude of the peoples which have formerly been in
existence and which are after thee destined, some for judgment . . . and others for vengeance and destruction at the
end of the world"—i.e., they were to come to earth after
Abraham. "But these which are on the right side of the
picture—they are the people set apart for me of the peoples
with Azazel [i.e., living in the wicked world]. These are they
whom I have ordained to be born of thee and to be called
My People."[116]

The scene does not appear in the facsimile, but is
vividly presented in the *text* of the Book of Abraham:

> Now the Lord had shown unto me, Abraham, the
> intelligences that were organized before the world was;
> and among all these were many of the noble and great
> ones; And God . . . stood in the midst of them, and he
> said: These I will make my rulers; for he stood among
> those that were spirits, . . . and he said unto me:
> Abraham, thou art one of them; thou wast chosen before
> thou wast born. And there stood one among them that
> was like unto God, and he said unto those who were with
> him: We will go down . . . and we will make an earth
> whereon these may dwell. . . . And the Lord said: Whom

shall I send? And one answered: . . . Here am I, send me.
. . . And the Lord said: I will send the first. And the second was angry, and kept not his first estate; and, at that
day, *many followed* after him. (Abraham 3:22–24, 27–28)

This drama meets us repeatedly in Egyptian literature
as the classic confrontation between Horus and Seth in the
presence of the assembled gods at the creation or New
Year.[117] It is nowhere more completely at home than in the
Book of the Dead;[118] but perhaps the most remarkable version, and the closest to the Book of Abraham with respect
both to the council in heaven and the creation story that follows, is that of the so-called Shabako Stone, which many
scholars have held to be the oldest religious text in the
world. In it we are told how "there was a great assembly of
the gods, and a controversy between Horus and Seth. The
Great God forbade them to quarrel and the difference
was settled," but only for a time.[119] After a while "Geb was
troubled in his heart, . . . and so he gave his whole heritage
to Horus, the son of his son, his Firstborn."[120] Stage directions here specify that "Geb shall address the entire assembly of the gods: I have chosen thee [pointing to Horus] to be
the Opener of the Ways, thee alone. [He points to Horus:]
My inheritance belongs to this my heir, let it go to the son
of my son, let it go to . . . the Opener of the Ways, my First
Born, who leads the way," etc.[121] There follows a description
of the planning of the creation in the presence of "Ptah the
Great who presides as the mind and the mouth of the Great
Council of the Gods."[122] Finally all was done as it was
ordered: "So it was said: He who begot Atum and the other
Gods, is Ptah; all things came forth from him, all food, all
nourishment, all good things. . . . And after all things were
created by his Word Ptah was pleased with all."[123] Of this
passage Sethe observed that it "vividly recalls the Biblical
Creation story,"[124] even more vividly, we may add, than in
the Book of Abraham.

The hypocephalus in the Book of Abraham has much to teach us. For the present we must confine our attention to the strong bond it establishes between the figure of Abraham and the symbolism of the Egyptian mysteries. We have just indicated that the thematic matter and overall design of Facsimile 2 have important features in common with the "picture" of the world shown to Abraham in the *Apocalypse of Abraham*. No less significant is the context in which the two presentations are set forth. It was, in all accounts, as Abraham "offered sacrifice upon an altar" (explanation of Facsimile 2, figure 2) that he was overcome with a "horror of great darkness" (Genesis 15:12) and his spirit mounted up to the heavens to behold a theophany, the sight of God seated upon his throne in glory, and to be instructed in the mysteries of the cosmos. Almost the same thing happens to Moses in Joseph Smith's companion piece to the Book of Abraham (as in other apocalypses—Enoch, Adam, etc.), where Moses, after being overwhelmed by Satan and knowing "the bitterness of hell" as paralyzing fear overcame him, was presently rescued and "lifted up his eyes unto heaven, being filled with the Holy Ghost, . . . and, calling upon the name of God, he beheld his glory again" (Moses 1:24–25).

In the Old World accounts the hero is taken up to heaven by a dove; in the Joseph Smith revelations, it is by the Holy Ghost. The two are strikingly brought together in Abraham's cosmic chart (Facsimile 2), which has as its central theme the theophany, a design which does not depict but "*represents* God sitting upon his throne, revealing through the heavens the grand Key-words of the Priesthood; as, also, the sign of the Holy Ghost unto Abraham, in the form of a dove" (explanation of Facsimile 2, figure 7). So there you have the whole situation—the dove that takes one to heaven is the Holy Ghost, who also instructs and teaches "through the heavens," "revealing . . . the grand Key-words . . . as, also, the sign" by which alone supernal knowledge can be conveyed. It is exactly the same scenario in the Abraham apocrypha as in the Joseph Smith Book of Abraham.

So the Book of Abraham is right at home in the world of the *Apocalypse* and *Testament of Abraham*. And those texts in turn are full of Egyptian matter, which is so generally accepted that no long demonstration is necessary. A few salient points in which the *Testament* shows its Egyptian affinities may be mentioned (fig. 10): (a) the psychostasy, the weighing of the soul in court by a pair of scales (a fine example is the Joseph Smith Papyrus III);[125] (b) the Stone of Truth in the wash-basin;[126] (c) the various appearances of death, e.g., viper, asp, cerastes, many-headed fire-serpent[127] (so in the Metternich and Anchnesneferibre stelae); (d) the Two Ways[128]—an Egyptian funerary book that has that title; (e) the nets of Hades from which the victim prays to escape;[129] (f) ordeal by fire (Letopolis); (g) the triple-crown (the Egyptians have many) with specific mention of the crown of justification;[130] (h) the final ritual embrace of the father;[131] (i) father and mother as sun and moon; (j) lingering rays of glory after the departure of the same;[132] (k) ascent to heaven in bird-form (the human-headed *Ba*); (l) man, woman, serpent, and tree; (m) punishment of the damned—fire, whips, swords, knives, etc., chopping blocks; and (n) wrapping of the dead in linen, unguent, and perfume, intact until the third day.

There is a common type of funerary stela which the Egyptians were wont to set up before the entrances to their tombs and which served to identify the grave owners, call them to the remembrance of the living, and establish ties between the spheres in which the soul may live. The top of these modest monuments is usually rounded and presents some of the same motifs appearing on the round hypocephali such as our Facsimile 2. Thus the stela of one Imi-is (fig. 11), its half-circle top displaying the solar disk and the

Figure 10. Egyptian parallels. One of the earliest examples (c. 1380 B.C.) of the psychostasy scene is from the Book of the Dead of Iouya (A). The priests stood on this alabaster pedestal (B) to be purified before officiating in the temple at Karnak. From the tomb of Thutmosis III (see fig. 13, p. 67); the five-headed serpent protects the king's body in its coils. The details from an Akkadian cylinder seal (c. 2200 B.C.) on the right shows two gods spearing a seven-headed dragon of chaos (C).

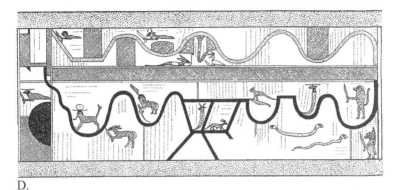

D.

E.

This map from the Middle Kingdom Book of the Two Ways portrays the two different routes for the soul: by water above and by land below (D). Also from Iouya's Book of the Dead, his *Ba* escapes from the clap-net below, guided by a human-headed Anubis. A large temple bas-relief (c. 300 B.C.) shows the Pharaoh Ptolemy X and three gods pulling the clap-net closed, trapping not only birds and cattle, but four bound captives kneeling within (E).

F.

G.

H.

I.

The doorways lead to the fires prepared to incinerate the damned (F). The first example (G) of the triple Atef crown is late Ptolemaic, while the next is from the great gateway (c. 550 B.C.) at Pasargadae, a Persian citadel over twelve hundred miles from Egypt. The third drawing shows the deceased praising the crown of justification, a depiction influenced by Greek laurel crowns. The god Horus encircles King Qa-hedjet in this bas-relief, one of the earliest examples (c. 2650 B.C.) of the divine embrace (H). The inscription explains that Horus the god speaks to Horus the king. The earliest example of the royal title "Son of the Sun" (I) is found on the base of a statue of Khafre, builder of the pyramid adjacent to the Great Pyramid.

Rays from the sun permeate the heavenly boat and shine on the mummy beneath (J). The deceased leaves his tomb as his *Ba* flies up to heaven (K). Ani can turn his back on the bloody knife and chopping block because his head is firmly tied on to his body as a reward for his righteousness (L). The lower register shows the naked body of the deceased being carried forward by an animated lion couch to Anubis who will start wrapping the corpse; above Anubis leans over the completed mummy (M).

Figure 11. The stele of Imi-is displays the typical round-headed top of Egyptian funerary monuments.

outspread wings that signify the expanse of the heavens (cf. Facsimile 2, figure 4), begins the inscription by distributing the owner's complex being in various realms: his "*Ba* in heaven in the presence of Osiris, his *mummy* [written with a seal and glory-sign] among the exalted [glorified] ones, . . . his *heir* flourishing on earth in the presence of Geb, upon his throne in the presence of the living, his *name* perpetuated upon the mouth of those who live after him by virtue of the *Book of Passing through Eternity.*"[133]

The funeral stele of Imi-is is thus like the *Apocrypha* and the Book of Abraham, an autobiography announcing his ascension and leaving a testament for the instruction of the writer's posterity, who will go on telling his story. Next follows a description of the ordinance of the Opening of the Mouth, a preparation for later resurrection,[134] which leads directly to the cosmic tour:

> You rise up to heaven unrestrained; your arm is unhindered. You descend to the *Dat* [underworld] and are not detained there but proceed on the way of the gods of the Horizons. You make your place with the Westerners; you circulate in the heavens in their *khabasu* [another reading: "in their time (or moments)"]; you circumambulate the stars of the lower heavens. You travel as the messenger of the Lords of the Horizon, you join the company of those in the land of the gods [Ḥrt-nṯr]. You unite with the Lord of Eternity when he makes his course by day, and with the Lord of Changelessness [*djt*] when he enters the night. This land welcomes you as a noble one of the airs [in flight].[135]

Here is the motif of Abraham's journey to heaven upon his death. The reference to the subject as one at home in the air reminds us, of course, of the visit of the dead to the upper worlds as or with a bird. Also recognizable is the emphasis on circumambulation and the dual nature of the realms visited, with the same sun-god entering alternately into the day-world and night-world, the themes also of the Abraham apocrypha, the cosmic pictures shown to Abraham by his messenger, and our Facsimile 2.

Of particular interest is the mention of the *khabasu* (*ḥȝbȝs.w*). A famous text on the coffin of a daughter of Psammetichus II calls upon certain *khabasu* in Heliopolis to witness the birth of one who will "take the helm" of government and "reason [*wadj*] with you, ye star-reckoners, concerning the secret teachings of the great court [*ws.t*] of the gods," and who will also receive Osiris into his "Ship of a Thousand."[136] What is that all about? According to the *Wörterbuch*, these "Khabasu in Heliopolis" (1) are the *expanse* of the starry heavens as observed from Heliopolis [by the Great-Seer] and (2) provide the *reckoning of time* at the New Year; (3) their name is written with the ideogram of a *ship*, signifying, for some reason (4) that "its soul is a *thousand*-fold," (5) the thousand referring specifically to the "collectivity of the starry hosts" (fig. 12).[137] Let us turn for a moment to that interesting session of school at the court of Pharaoh depicted in Facsimile 3 of the Book of Abraham in which we are told that the teacher on the throne is Abraham "reasoning upon the principles of Astronomy, in the king's court," and take just long enough to point out the sort of thing Abraham is teaching and being taught. According to the astronomical chart which he has provided in Facsimile 2, there is a ship (figure 4), which, we are told, does indeed (1) specify "the collectivity of the starry hosts," or as Joseph Smith puts it, "answers to the Hebrew word *Raukeeyang*, signifying expanse, or the firmament of the heavens"; it also (2) provides the reckoning of time, "answering to the measuring of . . . time"; also the ship (3) signifies here (d) that "its soul is a thousand-fold," since, according to Joseph Smith, it is "also a numerical figure, in Egyptian signifying one thousand." Expanse, starry heavens, a ship, a thousand, time reckoning—it is all there, with Pharaoh's court as the

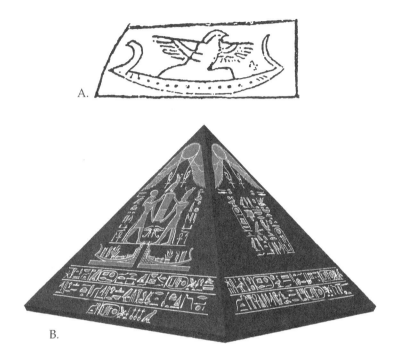

Figure 12. Joseph Smith tells us that this figure (A) "answers to the Hebrew word *Raukeeyang,* signifying expanse, or the firmament of the heavens." Of the forty-three royal pyramids in Egypt, only three fragmentary capstones from the Middle Kingdom have survived. Both of the inscribed ones have the word *khabasu* on the north side, indicating its great importance in describing the circumpolar stars. This capstone (B) of polished black granite belonged to Pharaoh Khendjer (c. 1750 B.C.), whose Asiatic name is of Syrian or Palestinian origin. The most elaborate side on the left with its two *Wdȝ.t* eyes faced east to behold the beauty of the rising sun. The inscription above says that the pharaoh is beloved of Re Horakhty and Atum of Heliopolis, gods of the rising and setting sun. Below, two boats of the sun, prow to prow, symbolize the moment of transition from the underworld of the dead to the sunrise of life (see fig. 15, p. 81, and the hypocephali in fig. 20, p. 135).

seminar where one who "takes the helm" reasons upon the
principles of astronomy.[138]

Here again we have the motifs of Abraham's heavenly
journey as set forth in the Abraham apocrypha, as also in
the text and facsimile (with explanation) of the Book of Abraham, and in other Egyptian ritual and funerary sources,
such as the stele of Imi-is.

The rationale for the Egyptian drawings given in the
Book of Abraham is also worth noting, since it is the very
same reason the Egyptians give for illustrating the mysteries with odd-looking drawings. When Abraham tells us,
"And that you may have a knowledge of this altar, I will
refer you to the representation at the commencement of this
record" (Abraham 1:12), or "that you may have an understanding of these gods, I have given you the fashion of them
in the figures at the beginning" (Abraham 1:14), he is following the Egyptian practice as evidenced, for example, in
the great book of mysteries known as the Amduat: "The
nature of this thing is to be seen drawn on the south wall of
the hidden chamber" (short version 4th hour, 5th hour,
end);[139] "This secret thing . . . is to be seen completely set
forth in a representation on the south wall of the hidden
chamber" (6th Hour);[140] "This thing can be seen explained
in a drawing on the north side of the secret room in the
Duat" (8th Hour), etc.[141] In the long version such examples
are legion (fig. 13).

How can all this be mere coincidence? Again and again
the setting, the characters, and the plot in this strange series
of dramas are the same. We ask the candid reader, if you
were given a free hand to write your own Book of Abraham, without merely paraphrasing the Bible, how would
you, living in the backwoods America in the mid-1830s,
have fared? Can one blame the Mormons for refusing to
applaud when people who could not come within a thousand miles of Joseph Smith's performance go about busily
declaring that he did it all with wires and mirrors? The evidence that has led the experts in the past ten years to recognize the closest ties between the old Abraham apocrypha

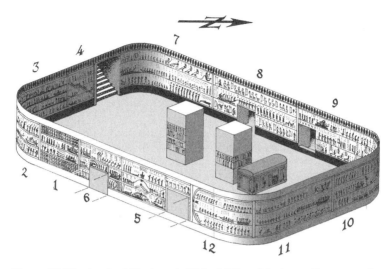

Figure 13. The tomb of Thutmosis III (c. 1450 B.C.) is the earliest example of the Amduat recorded in the Valley of the Kings. It is as though a great scroll were unrolled around the walls (seen here as transparent) of his "Room of Gold," protecting him; his red quartzite sarcophagus is carved in the form of a great cartouche, the protective circle of the sun. He joins the sun-god in his journey through each of the twelve hours of the night, as described on his walls.

and the Egyptian Book of the Dead, especially with references to the pictures in the latter, effectively eliminates the one argument against serious reading of the Book of Abraham. Now the shoe is on the other foot: How was Joseph Smith to know that an authentic Abraham apocryphon should not be *without* visible affinities to the Book of the Dead?

Notes

1. Letter from E. A. Wallis Budge to James W. Barclay, published in Junius F. Wells, "Scholars Disagree," *IE* 16 (1913): 342.

2. Hugh W. Nibley, "A New Look at the Pearl of Great Price," *IE* 72 (January 1969): 27.

3. Cf. Wallace Turner, "Mormons Debate Egyptian Papyri," *New York Times*, 15 July 1968.

4. "The Book of Abraham," *Times and Seasons* 3 (1842): 704.

5. *The Pearl of Great Price; being a choice selection from the revelations, translations, and narrations of Joseph Smith, first prophet, seer, and revelator to the Church of Jesus Christ of Latter-day Saints* (Liverpool: Richards, 1851), title page.

6. Kurt H. Sethe, *Dramatische Texte zur altägyptischen Mysterienspielen* (Leipzig: Hinrichs, 1928), 20.

7. Joachim Spiegel, "Typus und Gestalt in der ägyptischen Kunst," *Mitteilungen des deutschen Instituts für ägyptische Altertumskunde in Kairo* 9 (1940): 160.

8. *Jubilees* 39:6, in *The Apocrypha and Pseudepigrapha of the Old Testament*, ed. Robert H. Charles, 2 vols. (Oxford: Clarendon, 1976), 2:70.

9. *Jubilees* 45:16, in ibid., 2:76 (emphasis added).

10. Sethe, *Dramatische Texte*, 20.

11. John A. Wilson, "The Artist of the Egyptian Old Kingdom," *JNES* 6 (1946): 239–40.

12. Ibid., 243.

13. Ibid., 240.

14. Constantin E. Sander-Hansen, *Die Texte der Metternichstele* (Copenhagen: Munksgaard, 1956), 7:48 (emphasis added).

15. Ibid., 7:48–49.

16. Dimitri Meeks, review of *Pisty Drevnevo Egipta [Les scribes de l'ancienne Égypte]*, by M. Korostovstev, *RdE* 19 (1967): 191.

17. F. M. Theodor de Liagre Böhl, "Babel und Bibel (Pt. II)," *JEOL* 17 (1964): 134–35.

18. Hugh W. Nibley, "As Things Stand at the Moment," *BYU Studies* 9/1 (1968): 74–78.

19. Harry Torczyner, *The Lachish Letters, Lachish I* (London: Oxford University Press, 1938), 81.

20. Siegfried Schott, ed., "Das Buch vom Sieg über Seth," in *Urkunden mythologischen Inhalts*, vol. 6, part 1, of *Urkunden des ägyptischen Altertums*, ed. Kurt Sethe and Heinrich Schäfer (Leipzig: Hinrichs, 1929), 3.

21. Hugh W. Nibley, "A Strange Thing in the Land: The Return of the Book of Enoch," in *Enoch the Prophet*, CWHN 2 (Salt Lake City: Deseret Book and FARMS, 1986), 91–103.

22. Klaus Koch, *Ratlos vor der Apokalyptik* (Gütersloh: Verlagshaus, 1970), 16.

23. George H. Box, *Apocalypse of Abraham* (New York: SPCK, 1918), 35.

24. G. Nathanael Bonwetsch, "The Book of the Revelation of Abra-

ham," trans. Edward H. Anderson and R. T. Haag, in *IE* 1 (August 1898): 705–14, 793–806.

25. Box, *Apocalypse of Abraham*, xxi (preface).

26. Ibid., xxii–xxiii.

27. Ibid., xxi–xxiv.

28. Ibid., xvi.

29. Nibley, "A Strange Thing in the Land," in *Enoch the Prophet*, *CWHN* 2:111.

30. Bonwetsch, "Book of the Revelation of Abraham," 705.

31. Ibid., 709–14, 793–804.

32. Hugh W. Nibley, *The Message of the Joseph Smith Papyri: An Egyptian Endowment* (Salt Lake City: Deseret Book, 1975), 7–19.

33. See ibid., 59–60.

34. Box, *Apocalypse of Abraham*, xxxi.

35. George W. E. Nickelsburg, ed., *Studies on the Testament of Abraham* (Missoula, MT: Scholars Press, 1976), 9.

36. Ibid., 19.

37. Ibid., passim.

38. Ibid., 32.

39. Ibid.

40. Nibley, *Message of the Joseph Smith Papyri*, 177.

41. Nickelsburg, *Studies on the Testament of Abraham*, 33.

42. Ibid., 29–40.

43. Charles, *Apocrypha and Pseudepigrapha of the Old Testament*, 2:6–7.

44. *Jubilees* 39:6–87, in ibid., 2:70.

45. Box, *Apocalypse of Abraham*, xxiii–xxiv.

46. Ibid., xxiii.

47. Ibid., xxiv–xxv.

48. Ibid., xv–xvi.

49. Moses Gaster, "The Apocalypse of Abraham," *Society of Biblical Archaeology Transactions* 9 (1893): 197.

50. Ibid.

51. Wolf Leslau, trans., "Testament of Abraham," in *Falasha Anthology* (New Haven: Yale University Press, 1951), 94–95.

52. Recension A.XX, in Michael E. Stone, trans., *The Testament of Abraham: The Greek Recensions* (Missoula, MT: Society of Biblical Literature, 1972), 54–57 (Nibley's translation).

53. Recension B.X, in ibid., 77.

54. Raymond Moody, *Life after Life: The Investigation of a Phenomenon— Survival of Bodily Death* (Simons Island, GA: Mockingbird, 1975).

55. Eugene Revillout, ed. and trans., *Evangeliae XII Apostolorum*, in *PO* 2:136–44.

56. Hugh W. Nibley, "Evangelium Quadraginta Dierum," *Vigiliae Christianae* 10 (1966): 1–24; reprinted as "Evangelium Quadraginta Dierum: The Forty-day Mission of Christ—The Forgotten Heritage," in *Mormonism and Early Christianity, CWHN* 4 (Salt Lake City: Deseret Book and FARMS, 1987), 10–44.

57. Geo Widengren, *The Gnostic Attitude*, trans. Birger A. Person (Santa Barbara, CA: Institute of Religious Studies, 1975), 14–18.

58. Nibley, "A New Look at the Pearl of Great Price," *IE* 73 (March 1970): 84–94; reprinted in this volume as chapter 7, "The Sacrifice of Isaac."

59. Ibid., 85; in this volume, p. 322.

60. Nibley, "A New Look at the Pearl of Great Price," *IE* 73 (April 1970): 79–95; reprinted in this volume as chapter 8, "The Sacrifice of Sarah."

61. Ibid., 80; in this volume, pp. 346–47.

62. Nibley, "A New Look at the Pearl of Great Price," *IE* 73 (March 1970): 89; in this volume, pp. 328–29.

63. Ibid., 87–88; in this volume, pp. 326–28.

64. Recension A.XVII–XVIII, B.XIII–XIV, in Stone, *Testament of Abraham*, 44–49, 82–85.

65. Recension A.XIX, in ibid., 51.

66. Recension A.XVIII, B.XIII, in ibid., 48–49, 82–83.

67. Joachim Spiegel, "Das Auferstehungsritual der Unaspyramide," *ASAE* 53 (1955): 339–44, 378–80, 393.

68. Recension A.VI, in Stone, *Testament of Abraham*, 15.

69. Recension A.XVII–XVIII, B.XIV in ibid., 48–49, 84–85.

70. Recension A.VII, in ibid., 14–17.

71. Recension A.VIII, in ibid., 18–21.

72. Box, *Apocalypse of Abraham*, 49–50.

73. Recension A.IX, in Stone, *Testament of Abraham*, 23.

74. Box, *Apocalypse of Abraham*, 50–51.

75. Ibid., 55–56.

76. Ibid., 56–57.

77. Recension A.IX, in Stone, *Testament of Abraham*, 22–23.

78. Nibley, "A New Look at the Pearl of Great Price," *IE* 72 (August 1969): 82–86.

79. Ibid., 79–80.

80. Nibley, "A New Look at the Pearl of Great Price," *IE* 73 (March 1970): 86; in this volume, pp. 324–25.

81. Recension A.XIII–XIV, B.IX–XI, in Stone, *Testament of Abraham*, 32–39, 74–81.

82. Nibley, "A New Look at the Pearl of Great Price," *IE* 73 (January 1970): 57–59.

83. Recension A.XI, in Stone, *Testament of Abraham*, 27.

84. See Hugh W. Nibley, "To Open the Last Dispensation: Moses Chapter 1," in *Nibley on the Timely and the Timeless* (Provo, UT: BYU Religious Studies Center, 1978), 7–15; reprinted in *Enoch the Prophet, CWHN* 2:159–67.

85. Box, *Apocalypse of Abraham*, 47–48.

86. *Wb*, 1:578.

87. Nibley, "A New Look at the Pearl of Great Price," *IE* 71 (February 1968): 40e–f.

88. Coffin Text 312.

89. Nibley, "A New Look at the Pearl of Great Price," *IE* 72 (July 1969): 108–10.

90. Box, *Apocalypse of Abraham*, 50–53.

91. Jan Zandee, "Sargtexte, Spruch 75," *ZÄS* 99 (1972): 60.

92. Box, *Apocalypse of Abraham*, 51.

93. Ibid., 66–67 (brackets in original).

94. Ibid., 68–69.

95. Ibid., 74 (brackets in original).

96. Francis Schmidt, "Le monde à l'image du bouclier d'Achille: sur la naissance et l'incorruptibilité du monde dans le 'Testament d'Abraham,'" *RHR* 185 (1974): 123.

97. Homer, *The Iliad* XVIII, 478–80.

98. Ibid., 479.

99. Ibid., 606.

100. Ibid., 480–81.

101. Ibid., 483–86.

102. Ibid., 487.

103. Ibid., 490.

104. Ibid., 491–95.

105. Ibid., 503–9.

106. Ibid., 541–605.

107. Ibid., 509–22.

108. Ibid., 535–40.

109. Cf. Box, *Apocalypse of Abraham*, chaps. 15–27.

110. Justin Martyr, *Cohortatio ad Graecos (A Hortatory Address to the Greeks)* 28, in *PG* 6:293.

111. Schmidt, "Le monde à l'image du bouclier d'Achille," 125.

112. Philippe-Jacques de Horrack, "Hypocephalus of the Louvre," *BE* 17 (1907): 156.

113. Homer, *Iliad* XVIII, 497–508.

114. Box, *Apocalypse of Abraham*, xxii.

115. Hugh W. Nibley, "The Expanding Gospel," in *Nibley on the Timely and the Timeless*, 23–33; reprinted in *Temple and Cosmos: Beyond This Ignorant Present, CWHN* 12 (Salt Lake City: Deseret Book and FARMS, 1991), 178–94.

116. Box, *Apocalypse of Abraham*, 69.

117. *The Contendings of Horus and Seth*, in Alan H. Gardiner, *Late Egyptian Stories* (Brussels: Fondation Égyptologique Reine Elisabeth, 1932), 37–60; Schott, "Buch vom Sieg über Seth," 7–17.

118. See Book of the Dead 17.

119. Sethe, *Dramatische Texte*, 23.

120. Ibid., 27–28, col. 10c–12c.

121. Ibid., 28, col. 13a–18a.

122. Ibid., 47, col. 48–52a.

123. Ibid., 66, col. 58.

124. Ibid., 68.

125. See Nibley, "A New Look at the Pearl of Great Price," *IE* 71 (February 1968): 40b–c.

126 Nibley, *Message of the Joseph Smith Papyri*, 122–23.

127. Recension A.XVII, in Stone, *Testament of Abraham*, 46–47.

128. Ibid., A.XI, in ibid., 24–25.

129. Nibley, *Message of the Joseph Smith Papyri*, 215.

130. Ibid., 228–29.

131. Ibid., 241–44.

132. Ibid., 159–61; Recension A.VII, in Stone, *Testament of Abraham*, 16–17.

133. Walter Wreszinski, "Das Buch vom Durchwandeln der Ewigkeit nach einer Stele im Vatikan," *ZÄS* 45 (1908): 114 (Nibley's translation of the Egyptian throughout).

134. Nibley, *Message of the Joseph Smith Papyri*, 106–10.

135. Wreszinski, "Buch vom Durchwandeln der Ewigkeit," 117.

136. Constantin E. Sander-Hansen, *Die religiösen Texte auf dem Sarg der Anchnesneferibre* (Copenhagen: Levin and Munksgaard, 1937), 36–37.

137. *Wb*, 3:230.

138. Sander-Hansen, *Religiösen Texte*, 37, renders the text: "Seht doch, Ihr ḫꜣbꜣs.w von Heliopolis . . . Der Gott is geboren worden . . . einer, der das Ruder greifen kann. Osiris A. wird mit auch richten [*wadj*] gemäß dem Geheimnis welches in der Halle der Götter ist, und den Osiris in seinem Schiff der 1000 bis zu seinen beiden Köpfen mitnehmen, damit er darin zum Himmel aufsteigt und zum Gegenhimmel fährt." Cf. Facsimile 2, the two-headed figures and the lower half of the circle which is the upside-down *Gegenhimmel*. The *Wörterbuch*, 3:230, renders *khabasw* as

lamps or lights; ḫȝbȝs.w means *"tausendfalt ist ihre Seele"* (her soul is a thousandfold), signifying the collectivity of the *Sternenhimmel* (starry heaven). Raymond O. Faulkner, *A Concise Dictionary of Middle Egyptian* (Oxford: Griffith Institute, 1964), 184, says *Khabas* is the starry sky; in E. A. W. Budge, *An Egyptian Hieroglyphic Dictionary*, 2 vols. (New York: Ungar, 1960), 1:530, it means "star or luminary." Heinrich K. Brugsch, *Hieroglyphische-Demotisches Wörterbuch*, 7 vols. (Leipzig: Hinrichs, 1867–80), 3:1068, refers to the temple lamp; the verb means to gather together, collect, as a light or lamp; it represents the stars at the New Year.

139. Erik Hornung, *Das Amduat: Die Schrift des verborgenen Raumes*, 3 vols. (Wiesbaden: Harrassowitz, 1963–67), 1:62–96.

140. Ibid., 97–166.

141. Ibid., 134–62.

2

Joseph Smith and the Sources

The Help That Came Too Late

It should be clear, by now, that there is a real relationship between the Book of Abraham, the *Apocalypse of Abraham*, and the *Testament of Abraham*. The Old Slavonic *Apocalypse of Abraham* was first published in 1863 and the (Greek) *Testament* in 1895. Here there can be no question of convenient rabbis popping out of the woodwork with timely hints and proddings to help the Book of Abraham along. (The definitive study on that subject was made by Professor Louis C. Zucker of the University of Utah, from whom we learn that Joseph Smith's first Hebrew teacher, Professor Joshua Seixas, arrived in Kirtland on 26 January 1836 and spent only two months there.)[1] During those months, however, he was quite close to the Prophet, who had a good chance for some really first-class tutoring. But Seixas not only arrived too late to supply the first chapters of Abraham, but would have been the last man in the world to do so. For he was strictly a conservative Jew, and his sessions with Joseph and the Brethren were closely confined to the translation of the Bible and not to flights of apocalyptic fancy. Zucker notes that up until that time, Joseph Smith had no need of conventional scholarship in making translations:

"Until 1835, Joseph had been content to translate by transcendental intuition. . . . The 'New Translation' of the New Testament was finished in February, 1833, and five months later, the Old Testament also. Joseph never laid claim to having in those years a knowledge of Hebrew or Greek." What? Translate the whole Bible without knowing the languages? It was a special kind of translation, as we have been at pains to insist all along, which, as Professor Zucker puts it, "purported to be no other than a 'revision'"; and he quotes B. H. Roberts: "What he did was to revise the English . . . Bible under the inspiration of God."[2]

Then, at the end of 1835 we find "the Mormon high elders . . . determined to study Hebrew." This puzzles Zucker. "Why was it Hebrew and not Greek?" he asks, since "Is not Mormonism, above all, a Christ-centered religion?"[3] The answer is partly that they had just obtained Egyptian papyri, and the Egyptian connection is all with the Old Testament. Immediately they started looking around for a teacher, and early in 1836 Seixas arrived on the scene just in time: the Hebrew words used in explaining things to Abraham's descendants appear in the Book of Abraham in the Sephardic accent of Professor Seixas, a Jew of Portuguese extraction. This would indicate that parts of the translation were completed while he was still there, in early 1836. With a real savant on hand, the Brethren were now in business as scholars: It was then that they decided to undertake the "Egyptian Alphabet and Grammar." But Joseph Smith's study with "the precise scholarly" Seixas, though it may have been adequate to give him a good start in reading the Bible, "did not," as Zucker observes, "confirm Joseph Smith in the ways of scholarship."[4] How fortunate! This is the whole issue with the critics today, but the ways of scholarship would have gotten nowhere with Egyptian in those days; moreover, they had been quite expendable in the Prophet's many earlier translations—how long would it take the ways of scholarship to produce a Book of Mormon? But for all that, the ways of scholarship do have an irresistible appeal to the curiosity and vanity of the race, and, as we have seen, the Brethren were duly impressed and fell to with a will. The sudden abandonment of their ambitious projects is matched by the equally sudden and complete "silence about the Seixas family, and silence about Hebrew"; after 27 March 1836, the former simply disappeared from sight, and Hebrew "was never taught again to the Mormons in Kirtland."[5]

If Joseph Smith definitely did not get the apocalyptic material in the Book of Abraham from Seixas, Professor Zucker thinks he can explain it as part of the Prophet's Christian heritage: "In theology, Mormonism, like Christianity, derives in part from the Jewish apocalyptic literature; but apocalypse is a fitful, minor force in normative Judaism," and we can be sure that Seixas viewed it as adversely as did Professor Zucker himself.[6] But what our informant overlooks is that Christianity absorbed its Jewish apocalyptic elements anciently, as part of the original message, as an abundance of recent manuscript discoveries makes disturbingly clear both to conventional Christianity and normative Judaism, *equally* upset and offended by Jewish apocalyptic. The books of Revelation and Daniel are authentic Jewish apocalyptic, to be sure, and never more fervidly studied than in Joseph Smith's day; but they are not the substance of the Book of Abraham—for that one must go to far more recondite sources than any known to conventional Jewish or Christian scholarship.

One can illustrate this by some of Professor Zucker's own observations on the vagaries of Joseph Smith's name-giving. Thus he notes that Mahujah and Mahijah of the Joseph Smith book of Enoch are "off-biblical names," which at best "resemble 'Mehujael' in Genesis 4:18."[7] But now the name of Mahujah turns up in the oldest version of the book of *Enoch*, that found in Qumran Cave 1 and first published in 1976, in which Mahujah is the central figure of a strange little story that is found nowhere else in the now large and growing ancient Enoch literature *except* in the Joseph Smith Enoch history contained in the book of Moses, where the man Mahijah goes to the place Mahujah as the hero of the *same* little story.[8] Zucker also notes that of course Adam does not mean "many," as Joseph Smith says it does, in Moses 1:34 (Joseph would hardly need Seixas to tell him that!); but now a number of recent studies have shown that archaic Atum-Adamu means "many" in a very special and impressive sense, as the one who contains in himself the being of all who have gone before and the seed of all who are to follow after.[9] Finally, Zucker would explain the name Baurak Ale as rendered by Joseph Smith as a clumsy attempt to derive a proper name from the Hebrew word for blessing, *bərākāh*,[10] apparently completely oblivious to the amply documented fact that Bārāq-ʾĒl, "God's Lightning," was an important epithet for Enoch, which is just how Joseph Smith uses it.[11] If the learned Professor Zucker did not recognize that ancient title, who could have given it to Joseph Smith? Even the most cooperative rabbi in Joseph's day could have been of little help in putting him on to the *Apocalypse of Abraham*, for example, a text discovered in 1863 and written not in Hebrew but in Old Slavonic. We are reminded of the Sarah episode in the *Genesis Apocryphon:* Place it beside the Book of Abraham account and it fairly screams plagiarism. Here is something the critics could really crow about if it were not for that one disturbing little detail: The *Genesis Apocryphon* was not discovered until 1947—more obfuscation![12]

Summary of Study since 1967

Before proceeding further it may be well to take a brief glance backward at some of the terrain we have already

covered in a swarm of articles appearing between 1967 and
1970. Our first step was to show that the men of 1912 in
their haughty and perfunctory replies to Bishop Franklin S.
Spalding's leading questions never gave Joseph Smith or
the Book of Abraham a hearing.[13] They considered both
beneath them, agreed in calling the whole thing a fraud
(though they agreed in little else), and asked to be excused.[14]
In reply to their repeated charges that the three facsimiles
in the Book of Abraham are perfectly ordinary Egyptian
funerary motifs depicted innumerable times,[15] it can be
readily shown by comparing large numbers of such documents that the Joseph Smith papyri differ in significant
points from all the others, so much so that Egyptologists
have often complained that the Mormons have deliberately
redrawn them—an accusation that the discovery of some of
the originals disproved.[16] Heretofore most of our attention
has gone to Facsimile 1, of which the church now possesses
the original (fig. 14).[17] It is full of quite unique features such
as the crocodile, the "pillars of heaven," the hieroglyphic
cryptogram framing it, peculiar aspects of the human figures, the lotus stand, etc.,[18] all of which imply (without
necessarily proving) the presentation of a special dramatic situation; peculiarities of the drawing supply further evidence
that the artist was trying to tell a particular story.[19] From
first to last, the whole thing represents *ritual*, a sacrificial
scene.[20] It was time to bring Abraham into the picture. The
past hundred years have seen the publication of a wealth of
nonbiblical but very ancient stories about Abraham, most of
them fairly recent discoveries, the rest long despised by normative Judaism and ignored by scholars but at last receiving serious attention in some quarters.[21] The dominant
theme of these stories is the jealousy of a great king who
fears for his priesthood and kingship—both threatened by
Abraham—from the time Abraham's birth is foretold by the
king's wise men to the time the king finally recognizes the

Figure 14. In 1842 when Reuben Hedlock published the Book of Abraham in the *Times and Seasons,* he made a true facsimile of the original papyrus by tracing it on thin paper; he then pasted it facedown on the woodblock and painstakingly cut through the paper and carved into the wood to remove all the white areas. When inked and printed, his wood-cut gave a faithful reproduction of the original. A comparison of the two images shows how accurate he was and that his other facsimiles are similarly reliable.

true God, after an unsuccessful attempt to put Abraham to death on an altar.[22] Being placed on the altar at the urging of the king's courtesans, Abraham prays for deliverance, an angel of the Lord appears, and at the last moment the altar is overthrown and the erstwhile sacrificing priest becomes the victim.[23] The Book of Abraham thus has the support of the legends, but where does Pharaoh come in? Abraham's royal rival, usually designated as Nimrod, is definitely identified with Pharaoh in the oldest versions of the story.[24]

Among hundreds of Egyptian lion-couch scenes resembling Facsimile 1 are some found in the tombs of great kings that have become the object of special study (fig. 15); they are only incidentally funerary in nature and depict the dramatic climax of the Sed festival of Egypt, the moment at which the king, overcome by the evil power of Seth, lies helpless on the couch, which is simultaneously deathbed, embalming table, and bed of deliverance and rejuvenation.[25] In actual practice the person on the couch was a substitute for the king and was really sacrificed; according to the legends, Abraham was chosen to be such a substitute, and after his miraculous delivery (the priest being killed in his place with the overthrow of the altar), he also took the king's place in sitting upon his throne.[26] In the Sed rites the royal person is resurrected from the lion couch to mount the throne as the king for a new period of years.[27] Abraham goes through all of this as a substitute, according to the Abraham traditions *and* the Book of Abraham, the whole thing being at the same

Figure 15. In the tomb of Ramses VI (c. 1150 B.C.), this painting on the ceiling before the tomb chamber depicts the resurrection of the king as Osiris from the lion couch, where he is shown emerging from his mummy wrappings. The *res* sign above him means to be awake, vigilant. Beneath the couch are the symbols of his divine kingship: various crowns (including the Atef), clothing, and weapons such as the two crossed arrows (see fig. 97, p. 598) and the white stone-headed mace (see fig. 96, p. 597). The king then ascends to heaven to join the winged sun protected by the two uraei. On the left he is introduced by a goddess to Re-Horakhty, the god of the rising sun, and on the right to Atum, the god of the setting sun. The solar boats are joined at the prow by the *sema*, symbol of unification and reconciliation. Since the king's mummy would have rested just a few yards away on a real lion couch within a golden shrine, this painting expressed eloquently the belief that he would literally rise from the dead to be an eternal king and join the gods in their never-ending journey through the heavens.

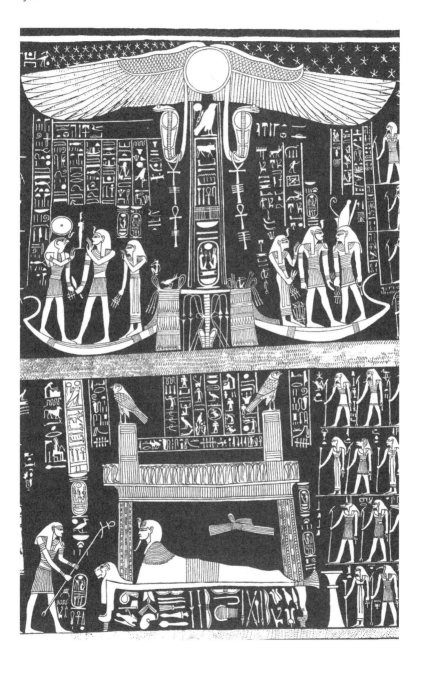

time in strict conformity with the Egyptian Sed rites as well as the well-established practice in other lands (we have called it the Procrustes Cycle).[28] The substitute motif in the Abraham traditions has quite recently come in for serious study by scholars who see in the sacrifice of Isaac a royal substitute rite of the Canaanites as well as of Israel.[29] As in the case of Abraham, the sacrifice is arrested by an act of sudden divine intervention supplying yet another substitute—the ram in the thicket. We have shown that the sacrifice of Sarah follows the same pattern, as confirmed by the newly discovered and very old *Genesis Apocryphon* of the Dead Sea Scrolls: Sarah must go to Pharaoh's bed—a lion couch—where she prays fervidly for deliverance (though it is Abraham's prayer that receives the most attention), which happens when at the last moment an angel arrives and Pharaoh is smitten and helpless—he ends up confessing the superiority of Abraham's God and loading the patriarch, and especially Sarah, with royal gifts.[30]

This is enough to indicate that the story of Abraham told in the Book of Abraham has the support of very ancient tradition and that both have peculiar ritual ties with Egypt, confirmed by recent studies of actual Egyptian practice. Facsimile 1 is a symbolic representation of the little-known but well-attested sacrifice of Abraham—not Isaac. All of which bids us take the Book of Abraham seriously, even while it raises many interesting questions.

Stirred by Professor Zucker's study, the student may well ask, Who put Joseph Smith's Abraham so completely into the ancient picture? The recent investigations into nonbiblical Abraham material by Geza Vermes (1961), Robert Martin-Achard (1969), George W. E. Nickelsburg, and others (a symposium of scholars in 1972–1976)[31] quite overlook many of the sources we cited in our *Improvement Era* series of 1968–70. Having no access to their studies, how could Joseph have known about the forgotten sources even they ignore?

In 1968 a Jewish rabbi wrote *A Critical Analysis of the Book of Abraham in the Light of Extra-Canonical Jewish Writing,* a Ph.D. dissertation in which he draws upon the *Talmud,* Josephus, *Jubilees,* and *Sefer Yetzirah* for the life of Abraham, but overlooks all the other sources.[32] And you expect Joseph Smith to use them? Even Robert C. Webb, in chapter 8 of his *Joseph Smith as Translator,* is impressed only by the *contrast* between the Book of Abraham and the noncanonical sources available to him—he too apparently knows nothing of that large but neglected body of Abraham literature that is now coming to light.[33]

The first important collection of Abraham texts was begun by Adolph Jellinek in his *Bet ha-Midrasch,* starting in 1856, a work so rare in the West that I had never seen a copy of it until its reprinting in Israel in 1967. In 1859 Bernhard Beer's *Leben Abraham's* made sources hitherto completely unknown to scholars available, and extensive and important Arabic sources were first published by Heinrich Schütz-inger in 1961.[34]

Going through a list of Abraham sources with their dates of publication is one way of showing how recent most of the stuff is and how highly improbable it is that Joseph Smith could have made use of any of it: *Genesis Apocryphon* (1956); *Apocalypse of Abraham* (1863); various *Ma'aseh Abraham* (Arabic text discovered by Tischendorff, which follows ben Asher's *Commentary on the Pentateuch*);[35] Ka'b al-Akbar, *Qiṣaṣ Ibrahim Abinu* (1920); *Sefer ha-Yashar* (1923); Pseudo-Philo's *Biblical Antiquities* (1898); *Jubilees* (1859); *Cave of Treasures* (1883); *Testament of Abraham* (1892); Bar Hebraeus, *Chronography* (1923). References in the *Talmud,* Mishnah, Pirkê de Rabbi Eliezer, etc., are few and scattered, while exotic Arabic sources all published late, e.g., the *Brethren of Basra,* 'Antar, Tha'labi, etc., are out of the question. The *Midrash* recalls the sacrifice of Abraham,[36] but in a form that no one without a clue would recognize, as we have shown elsewhere.[37] Classical writers known in Joseph Smith's day contain brief references to Abraham, consulting which the reader may judge for himself whether he made any use of them: Eusebius, *Praeparatio Evangelica;*[38] St. Augustine, *The City of God;*[39] *Clementine Recognitions* (1854);[40] and Philo, *De Abrahamo* (very disappointing).[41]

Absurd as it seems to labor a point as obvious as Joseph Smith's ignorance of a literature that has always been recondite and is still largely unknown even to experts on Abraham, it has been nonetheless necessary because of the growing practice of assuming offhand that Joseph must after all have had access to this and that apocryphal source whenever such a source strongly confirms some statement of his—a phenomenon that occurs with disturbing frequency. And so we find his learned critics swinging perilously between two extremes, issuing withering comments on his gross and disgusting ignorance on one page only to accuse him of deep and recondite researches on the next. The desperate resort of summoning uniquely erudite and cooperative rabbis to appear whenever he needs them requires us first to discover any such prodigals of learning in the America of his day—or any other. The most eminent Abraham authorities of the present day have assured me that Joseph Smith's story of the sacrifice of Abraham simply reveals his ignorance of the Bible, in which, according to them, he has got the sacrifice of Isaac all mixed up.

Ebla Changes Things

Everything must wait upon Ebla today. At that ancient site in northern Syria in the last week of digging in 1975 a library of over fifteen thousand cuneiform tablets was discovered. More tablets—sixteen hundred of them—were added in the following year, and who knows what is yet to turn up, for fully ten years before the great discovery the searchers were digging "within one yard of the library room, but were not alerted to it by a single tablet."[42] So much for the argument of silence. For all these years nobody had any idea where Ebla was—it was just another city mentioned in the Babylonian archives far to the south. And suddenly it emerges as the capital of a mighty empire. Nor has any ancient record besides the Bible ever mentioned Abraham's five "cities of the plain"; such silence put the whole Abraham story in doubt: "In its heyday the older criticism became quite skeptical about this material, writing it off as legend of no historical worth."[43] Those were the same critics who dismissed the Book of Abraham with a contemptuous glance and flick of the hand. But now in the Ebla records the mysterious cities of the plain emerge in an everyday business document, waiting for the traveler, as large as life on the very route that Abraham was supposed to have followed.[44] And along with them there is another city specifically called "Ur in Haran." "An especially intriguing notice," write the editors of the *Biblical Archaeology Review,* "is a reference to 'Ur *in* Haran.' Does this mean that the Ur from which Abraham originally came was near Haran rather than a thousand miles further away in southern Mesopotamia where 'Ur of the Chaldees,' is supposedly located?"[45] We have noted elsewhere how the Abraham legends and traditions strongly favor that northern as against the southern Ur, a theme to which we shall return presently.[46] The name of Jerusalem also appears in the tablets, which abound with biblical matter. Thus the discoverer of the tablets, the Roman archaeologist Giovanni Pettinato, calls the place "Canaanite Ebla" and notes that this big city of over a quarter of a million had a king called Eber and referred to its god as both Ya and El. In fact, in one tablet a man changes his name from Mika-il to Mika-ya, thus adding a new dimension to the long controversy over which was Israel's special God—Yahweh or El.[47] The kings at Ebla were "anointed," "their governors were called

Figure 16. Franklin Spencer Spalding
1865–1914

'judges,'" and their prophets were *nabi'tūm* (Akkadian).[48]
All of which reminds us of Israel. Long ago when "the
Egyptian and Mesopotamian texts thrust Israel into a real
world," the picture of Abraham as the simple wandering
shepherd should have been erased, though artists and
Sunday School teachers still cling to it.[49]

The Appeal to Authority[50]

Of all attacks on Mormonism undertaken beneath the
banners of science and scholarship, the great campaign of
1912 conducted by the Right Reverend Spalding (fig. 16),
Episcopal bishop of Utah, was the one that should have succeeded most brilliantly. Carefully planned and shrewdly
executed, it enlisted the services of the most formidable
roster of scholars that have ever declared against Joseph
Smith as a prophet, while at the same time loudly professing

feelings of nothing but affection and esteem for the Saints and a real desire to help them find the light in a spirit of high-minded dedication to truth at all costs.

Bishop Spalding's grand design had all the ingredients of quick and sure success but one, and if in spite of it the Pearl of Great Price is still being read, it is because the bishop failed to include in his tremendous barrage a single shell containing an item of solid and relevant evidence. If he had any other ammunition than names and credentials, he never used it—he hurled at the Mormons a cannonade of titles and opinions, and nothing more. "The authority of experts in any line of research is always accepted without question unless there is grave reason to doubt their conclusion. There was no such reason here."[51] And who is talking? Spalding's number one expert, a young man who had just got his degree (*not* in Egyptology)—*he* tells us that we must accept his verdict "without question" because he is an expert and sees no reason to doubt his conclusions. This is what we mean by authoritarianism.

But then, who would ever have thought in 1912 that any other kind of ammunition would be necessary? What was there to say after the official voice of scholarship had spoken? The Mormons did what they could. They pointed out that equally great authorities had been proven wrong about the Bible time and again.[52] They called attention to the brevity and superficiality of the expert's comments: "This 'inquiry,'" wrote Webb, "has been no inquiry at all in any real sense. . . . [It] presents merely a medley of opinions. . . . It furnishes absolutely no assistance to . . . [the] reader."[53] They noted that the judges approached their task in a thoroughly hostile state of mind.[54] When an editorial in the Church newspaper pointed out in the most reserved and respectful language that there were indeed some rather obvious contradictions and discrepancies in the views of the experts, and that the Mormons might at least be permitted to ask for "a stay of final judgment," since (as B. H. Roberts expressed it) "these questions that depend on special scholarship are questions that require time and research . . . and the conclusions of the learned in such matters are not as unchangeable as they seem,"[55] the *New York Times* exploded with indignation: "The *Deseret Evening News* spent its entire editorial page reviling scholars and scholarship."[56] One did not talk back to recognized scholars—it just wasn't done.

The *Deseret News* editorial in question pointed out that the Mormons had some years before already anticipated Bishop Spalding's investigations by making inquiries on their own among leading British Egyptologists, which "at least serves to show that we have not been lax, nor afraid to learn from whatever light the wisdom of the world might throw upon the illustrations of the Book of Abraham and their translation by the Prophet Joseph."[57]

Two days earlier an editorial in the *Deseret News* made a clear statement of policy: "The Latter-day Saints court inquiry, such as this. They want to know the truth, and only the truth. There is no important issue that they are not glad to face, whether presented by friend or foe."[58] And in the discussion that followed, the Mormons proved their good faith and sincerity by printing in the pages of the *Improvement Era* the letters of Bishop Spalding and his supporters, without deletion and without comment, along with those of the Latter-day Saints defending Joseph Smith.

There was no such dialogue in the non-Mormon periodicals in which Dr. Spalding published, including his own Utah newspaper, the *Utah Survey;* in spite of his constant protests of impartiality and intellectual integrity, only his own and like opinions ever appeared there.[59]

The Mormon writers, moreover, never claimed any such religious immunity as might have been conceded to Joseph Smith as a spiritual leader, but always insisted on arguing the case on its merits: "I allow the bishop all his claims to the dire results to 'Mormonism,'" wrote B. H. Roberts, "if he can, to the point of demonstration, make his case good against Joseph Smith as a translator."[60] Bishop Spalding's scholarly band, on the other hand, most emphatically *did* claim immunity—to question them was to "revile" that noble thing called scholarship, and that was the secret of their strength.

When Dr. S. A. B. Mercer, a hustling young clergyman who ran interference for the bishop throughout the game, summed up the case for the prosecution, his argument made a perfect circle: "The failure of the Mormon replies," he wrote, "is explained by the fact that the unanimous opinion of the scholars is unassailable. In the judgment of the scholarly world, therefore, Joseph Smith stands condemned of self-deception or imposition."[61]

Who said that the Mormon reply had "failed"? Mercer did, to be sure. Here we see the great convenience of permitting the attorney for the prosecution to act as judge. Dr. Mercer announces that the Mormon replies to him and his colleagues have failed—because he says so. And what he says must be so because his colleagues agree with him.

When the Mormons pointed out that there was anything but unanimous agreement among the colleagues, Mercer sternly overruled them, explaining that where any ordinary person might find the disagreements rather obvious, "to the expert there is here no discrepancy."[62] Only one had to be an Egyptologist to see it that way. That is why when B. H. Roberts was pressing Dr. Mercer pretty hard, the latter overruled him too, with the observation that the source of the difficulties in the case of Mr. Roberts "is to be found in the fact that the writer is a layman in things Egyptian."[63] What Mercer's explanation amounts to, as R. C. Webb observes, is the argument, in effect, that scholars in his department can make no mistakes,[64] or, in Mercer's own words, that their opinions are "unassailable." How can one discuss an "unassailable" opinion? One can't—that is just the point: the issue is closed; no debate is intended or possible.

In his final letter, Dr. Mercer divides the opposition into three classes: "First, intelligent and fair-minded Mormons," namely those who do not challenge the scholars in any way; second, "biased Mormons (perhaps unconsciously)," that is, Mormons guilty of pro-Mormon leanings, including B. H. Roberts, John A. Widtsoe, John Henry Evans, and Janne M. Sjodahl—in fact, all who have presumed to question the verdict of the experts. Fortunately for Mercer, all their remarks can be summarily stricken from the record, since they are "very ignorant in respect to the subjects they pretend to criticize"—it is not for them under *any* circumstances to talk back; they are all out of order. Dr. Mercer's third class is "biased and ignorant gentiles," being any such as may be inclined to give ear to the Mormon replies.[65]

And so the Doctors must be allowed to sit in judgment on their own case because no one else is qualified; and if they should happen to decide in favor of themselves, why, there is just nothing we can do about it, since their expertise is far beyond the reach of the layman, placing them in fact at "the intellectual summit of the universe" by the ancient professional mystery of "autodeification in the order of knowing."[66]

In the Spalding discussion "the prosecution rests its case on the reputations and standing of its witnesses."[67] "In compiling the pamphlet," wrote the bishop in his summing-up, "I made no claim to a knowledge of Egyptology. I merely wrote an introduction to the opinions of scholars. In a matter of this kind most of us must form our judgment from the opinion of competent experts."[68] Thus he echoes the opinion of his number one expert, cited above, who gracefully returns the compliment, noting that, after all, it was the good bishop's opinion that in the end would settle all disputes: "The advisers of the Bishop proved to his satisfaction" that glaring contradictions of the judges did not really exist, "that there were no such differences. . . . The apparent discrepancies were proved to be not real."[69] Thus Spalding's chief adviser declares that his advisers, by satisfying the bishop that all was well, had brought the issue to its final and satisfactory conclusion, binding all thinking men to accept and share his opinion.[70]

Thus reassured, Bishop Spalding proceeded to demolish R. C. Webb: "We feel that we should be in a better position to judge the value of the opinions of Robert C. Webb, Ph.D. . . . if we were told definitely who he is. . . . If Dr. Talmage . . . would inform us what the author's real name is, where he received his degree, and what academic position he holds, we should be better able to estimate the value of his opinions."[71] Here it is again: The bishop is not interested in Webb's arguments and evidence, but in his status and rank—considerations that are supposed to bear no weight whatever with honest searchers after truth—*Nullus in verba!* What on earth have a man's name, degree, academic position, and, of all things, opinions, to do with whether a thing is true or not?

In this case the answer is—everything. Dr. Mercer frankly admits that he and the other scholars "did not seem to take the matter very seriously," and devoted very little time to it indeed: "The haste was justified in the minds of the scholars by the simplicity of the task. Even less time could have been expended."[72]

Elsewhere he explains the perfunctory treatment of the whole thing: "They probably felt as I did, that their time was too valuable to spend on such scientific work as that of Joseph Smith's guesses."[73] Whatever the reason, they never intended to do any real work, but depended entirely on their credentials to see the thing through.

May We See Your Credentials?[74]

If the knowledge of Egyptologists is greater today than it was in 1912, their authority is less, for it is doubtful whether any living scholar could or should ever hope to enjoy the enormous prestige of a Petrie, Meyer, Breasted, von Bissing, or Sayce. But the appeal is still as much as ever to authority, and that is why it is now high time that somebody ask the question that has never been raised yet, namely, just how well equipped Dr. Spalding's illustrious jury really were, individually and collectively, to make a pronouncement on the Book of Abraham. That, after all, is the crux of the whole business, and it will remain so as long as it is assumed that whoever knows most about a subject must have all the answers. Bishop Spalding's boast was that he had made "an extensive inquiry among the scholars of the world" and had enlisted the services of leading scholars throughout the civilized world, his work being thus an anthology of opinion of authoritative scholars, "judgments of the world's greatest Egyptologists."[75] At no time did the Mormons or anyone else ever challenge the right of the committee to its claims to learned preeminence. "I took no issue with the Egyptologists," wrote Dr. John A. Widtsoe. "I shall not allow myself to be drawn into any discussion of the meaning of Egyptian hieroglyphics, which you have agreed to make clear to us."[76]

The big question of the authenticity of the Book of Abraham is one that must be broken down into many smaller questions, and the questions that will occur to various investigators differ greatly, depending on their various lines of approach. An Egyptologist will ask questions that would never occur to a layman, a Bible student will ask questions that one indifferent to the Bible would never think to ask, and a believer will ask questions that mean little or nothing to an unbeliever. Among such questions, that of the competence of any jury to judge of the inspiration of the Pearl of

Great Price is entirely irrelevant. Whatever competence any such jury may have is bound to appear inevitably in the nature of the questions *they* ask and the answers they supply. But since in this particular case the board of experts asked no questions(!), and since the professional standing of its members turned out to be not merely the principal but the *only* support for the Spalding thesis, the question of their competence, no matter how impertinent or embarrassing it might be, cannot be avoided. It is one question that should have been asked before all others, and it so happens that it is also the one question that nobody ever asked.

If "in a matter of this kind [as Spalding puts it] most of us must form our judgment from the opinions of competent experts," the question for all to keep in mind at all times is whether or not the experts have bridged the gap between our world and the world of Abraham. That gap may not be as wide today as it was half a century ago, but it is just as absolute. This is no paradox. Traveling in the "red rock country," one sometimes comes upon an abrupt canyon with sheer walls hundreds of feet high and must either turn back or seek to find the head of the canyon and go around it. This can make a trip to Canyonlands a very frustrating experience. It makes little difference whether the walls that drop off at our feet are one hundred or one thousand feet high, and it makes no difference at all whether the big gap is fifty feet wide or a mile across—in either case you are stopped cold.

So it is with the Book of Abraham. We either have the knowledge requisite to understanding it all the way or we do not, and we would be just as far from the mark in claiming such knowledge today as the scholars were in 1912. Knowing a lot is not enough: we have heard moving stories of wandering Arabs who have died of thirst in the night only a few feet from water. It makes no difference how far one has come or how near one may be to the water—he

who has not gone all the way cannot drink. None have discoursed more eloquently than the Egyptologists themselves
on their perennial predicament, which is that though they
may be much nearer their goals than they once were, like
the benighted Arab they have no means of knowing how
much nearer or even whether they have been moving in the
right direction or not. Their uncertainty is echoed in a
remark of de Rougé: "Champollion had to contend all his
life against lively and obstinate opposition. He died, and
scholarship stood still for twenty-five years," for the great
man's critics "did not even have the courage to profit by his
discoveries."[77] The whole history of Egyptology is, as Maspero observed from time to time, a warning against that
peculiar overconfidence that is born of a safe and timid conformity. And it is doubtful if any other Egyptologist ever
exemplified more fully the predicament of the specialist in
that field than Professor S. A. B. Mercer.

As we have seen, the Bishop's right-hand man throughout the controversy was the "Rev. Prof. C. A. B. Mercer
[Spalding got the initials wrong], Ph.D., Western Theological Seminary, Custodian Hibbard Collection, Egyptian
Reproductions."[78] The 32-year-old Mercer (fig. 17), with his
shiny new two-year-old Ph.D. degree from Munich, had
just transferred from a seminary in Kansas to the one in
Chicago, there to become "Professor of Hebrew and the
Interpretation of the Old Testament."[79] It was Mercer who,
after the others had withdrawn, encouraged his superior to
carry on: "In this particular case I think you are right in following up what you have already done; and I shall be glad
to help you as far as my time will permit."[00] Interestingly
enough, in 1956 Mercer sold his splendid Egyptian library,
the fruit of a long lifetime of diligent collecting, to Brigham
Young University at a price that can only be described as
generous.

Of all Bishop Spalding's helpers, Dr. Mercer was by far

Figure 17. Samuel Alfred Browne Mercer
1879–1965(?)

the hardest on the Mormons. Had he taken any other position than that of absolute certainty of his own sufficiency
and fierce and unrelenting denunciation of Joseph Smith, to
whom he conceded not the slightest glimmer of sense or
integrity, Dr. Mercer would not have been the legitimate target he is, or invited by way of rebuttal examination of his
boasted competence, for never was there a man who was
more sure of his scholarship, more wholeheartedly dedicated to the learned establishment as such. The young semi-
narian is quite intoxicated with the importance of being a
recognized scholar; he never lets us forget that he is a
scholar speaking with the authority of scholarship. Above
all, he prides himself on competence as a linguist. "I speak
as a linguist," he wrote in 1912, "when I say that if Smith
knew Egyptian and correctly interpreted the facsimiles
which were submitted to me, then I don't know a word of

Egyptian."[81] "Any pupil of mine who would show such absolute ignorance of Egyptian as Smith does, could not possibly expect to get more than a zero in an examination in Egyptology."[82] "If he [Dr. Widtsoe] knew anything about linguistic work of the nature of hyerogly[p]hics he would not ask such a question, for any ancient linguist knows that the unanimous testimony of eight scholars is the same as that of eighty and eight."[83] Any linguist knows nothing of the sort, but what a production Dr. Mercer makes of it!

When in 1953 a zealous collector of anti-Mormon tidbits asked Professor Mercer whether he still maintained his position as of 1912/13, the doctor replied by letter, "I am sure that my views on the subject have not changed, because the translation was so clear-cut."[84] Still harping on translation, the "clear-cut" translation—and nobody had translated a word! In dealing with the Mormons, Mercer clings to the linguistic issue because it is there alone that he has the Mormons at a complete disadvantage. "This will be a purely literary and scientific test. . . . The scholars felt that linguistically . . . the subject was not worth much of their valuable time. . . . They condemned it purely on linguistic grounds. . . . The animus evident . . . is purely because of linguistic, and not because of religious reasons," etc.[85] The translations were absolutely wrong in every detail, Mercer had declared, and he should know, since "many documents from all Egyptian periods . . . can be read with comparative ease."[86]

The Mormons, whom Mercer dismisses as mere "laymen in things Egyptian," need not feel too badly under the lash of his scorn, however, for Mercer's own colleagues, including the foremost Egyptologists of the time, were not spared his withering rebukes, nay, even fellow members of the Spalding committee do not escape his two-edged sword of science and scholarship.

When the great Breasted, Mercer's teacher, published

his *Dawn of Conscience,* one of the freshest and most original works ever written about Egypt, Mercer, as editor and reviewer of the short-lived journal *Egyptian Religion,* could only report, "There is very little that is new revealed in this book," and chided its author for "excessive use of superlatives, . . . which cannot fail to irritate a bit, especially when some of the superlatives are not justifiable."[87] Mercer never explains why the superlatives are not justified, unless it is because true, sound, cautious scholars are never guilty of using superlatives. He objects to Breasted's dating of an important document as "an example of too many assumptions by him," justifying his criticism not by contrary evidence but by the sage and learned platitude that "origins and borrowings are very difficult things to determine and establish." He should have thought of that when he so lightly brushed the facsimiles aside. Dr. Mercer cautions us that in reading the work of Breasted "the student must be on his guard against the results of an enthusiasm, legitimate in itself, but not always helpful in attempting to arrive at sound conclusions."[88] All very patronizing, very much the cautious scientist and scholar. He tells us that Breasted's "'messianism' cannot be found in the Egyptian texts no matter how sympathetically they may be studied and interpreted. Breasted has done his best to find it, but the reader may be left to judge of his success."[89]

Again, instead of doing any real work in showing where Breasted is wrong, Mercer leaves the decision with the reader—an odd procedure indeed for one who worships authority and merely tolerates the layman. As in his dealings with the Mormons a decade earlier, Mercer in his reviews in *Egyptian Religion* rarely gives the reader anything to go on but his opinion—but when it is his opinion against that of a giant like Breasted, what are we to think?

In another review Dr. Mercer criticized S. H. Hooke for employing exactly the same method in defense of "patternism" that Mercer himself had recommended in attacking the Pearl of Great Price: "After formulating his theory Hooke gets six scholars, experts in their own department of Oriental research, to try to illustrate or prove his theory." This method he finds altogether too "imaginative" and untrustworthy.[90] But was it not Mercer himself who only a short time before had insisted that "the unanimous opinion of the scholars is unassailable," and that "the practical agreement of eleven admittedly competent Orientalists" should be final proof, and that "the unanimous testimony of eight scholars is the same as that of eighty and eight"? Speaking exactly as if he were attacking the Mormons, Mercer notes that Professor Blackman "strikes a deadly blow at the 'pattern' theory of the editor" by suggesting that "the original 'pattern' was not a product of Egypt but an importation thither."[91] Yet Egyptian origin is not an essential condition to the pattern theory at all— Mercer has missed the point, but how familiar his scolding sounds! Shortly before this, Mercer had dismissed in two sentences Alfred Jeremias's truly remarkable work, *Der Kosmos von Sumer,* with crushing finality: "Of course, Dr. Jeremias has his own special and peculiar ways of interpreting ancient cosmic ideas."[92] Of course, indeed—that is just what made Jeremias a great scholar, but for Mercer it is the unpardonable sin of deviating from the respectable conventions of the establishment: no explanations are indicated; Mercer dismisses Jeremias with a magisterial wave of the hand.

He is even more patronizing in dealing with Arthur Weigall, who had been the inspector general of antiquities for the Egyptian government since 1905, with an impressive list of important archaeological publications to his credit. "Weigall's academic preparation did not enable him to enter very deeply into the more intricate problems of editing and translating texts and commenting upon them. . . .

His lack of training in philology led him into serious difficulties."[93] Always the language business. More serious is his casual dismissal of the work on Egyptian religion of one of the greatest of all Egyptologists, Hermann Junker: "But, curiously enough," says Mercer, speaking of Junker's fundamental thesis, "he believes he has found evidence to prove a primitive belief in one great world god. This to my mind shows a complete misunderstanding of the nature of primitive thought and understanding."[94] Just where has the great Junker failed? "His idea of a primitive universal god in ancient Egypt [is] an idea which really has no foundation in fact."[95]

This is a very serious challenge indeed, but Dr. Mercer does not bother to show us what the real factual foundation is; against Junker's solid and original work he is content to place the opinions of contemporary anthropology.[96] We may excuse him for thrusting aside W. O. E. Oesterley and T. H. Robinson's famous *Introduction to the Books of the Old Testament* as practically worthless;[97] but when he chides the immortal Adolf Erman for negligence in his specialty we wonder if he may not be going too far: "Like many other Egyptologists who have written on this subject, Erman uses such a term as 'monotheism' in a very loose sense, without defining what he understands by 'monotheism'"—though Erman had written a whole book on the subject. Mercer is good enough to explain that *he* believes in modern, *scientific* monotheism, whatever that is.[98]

The last of the auxiliary troops to rush to Dr. Spalding's assistance when he found himself entangled in the contradictory statements of the other experts was Professor George A. Barton. And how does Dr. Mercer deal with Dr. Barton? Of his *Semitic and Hamitic Origins,* the Reverend Mercer writes, "All such collections of deductions, possibilities and probabilities are doomed by nature to be superceded," and this particular book "contains too many fanciful as well as bold deductions for its destiny to be otherwise."[99] In dealing with Egypt in particular, according to Mercer, Dr. Barton "has very often fumbled very badly." "Throughout the book there are far too many hypotheses without adequate foundation; . . . the reader must be on his guard to check every statement, and especially all words and phrases in Egyptian, Coptic, etc. . . . As to French, German and English the misprints and errors are legion."[100] He recommends that any future edition of the book "should be rigorously revised" and states that "for students of Semitic origins the book will be found to be of considerable value, when used with caution. The same cannot, however, be said in the case of students of Egyptian origins."[101] As ever, Mercer plays up his role as that of super linguist and Egyptologist. Barton's worst offense, however, is that when he comes to treat the Sumerian flood story he does not ever refer to Mercer's work on the subject; and though he mentions Mercer's own work on Babylonian religion, "he could not have read the book which he so lightly brushes aside."[102]

Shortly after the Spalding affair Dr. Mercer made his first solid contribution to Egyptology. With dramatic detail he reports in the *Recueil de Travaux* how "during the summer of 1912 when the writer was in a quiet New England town," he discovered a collection of Egyptian antiquities brought hither by Lt. Commander Gorringe in 1879 but since ignored for the keeper was in no way "scientifically interested in Egyptian antiquities."[103] The prize piece was a long inscription, which had been known from another but damaged fragment that had been translated in 1905 by Ali ben Kemal.

Mercer's great discovery allowed him to supply the complete text, which Kemal did not have. But in furnishing the missing lines Mercer simply sent in a photograph, without any translation or commentary. This is remarkable. He had understandingly begged off where the poorly copied hieroglyphics of the Pearl of Great Price were concerned, but here was his first great chance to shine as a linguist and a scholar. This thing was his discovery, and it was the practice and privilege of Egyptologists who discovered texts to publish them in the *Recueil de travaux* with their own translations and commentaries. But never a word of translation or commentary from Mercer. He had room for a long description of the document and a picturesque account of how the inscription was found, with the usual pompous references to science and scholarship, but as to the linguistic aspects of the thing—complete silence. In the same spirit of dash and caution, Dr. Mercer, in his last rebuttal against the Mormons, noted in passing: "It might be added that also on the basis of the few easier hieroglyphics which were copied correctly, the Prophet's interpretation is found incorrect."[104] But true to form he never indicated what those few correctly copied hieroglyphics were or what they said. Instead, he assures us that "many proofs of the correctness of his [Mercer's] conclusions *could* be furnished if desired,"[105] and lets it go at that. Indeed, we have been unable to find a translation by Mercer of any Egyptian writing that had not already been translated and published by someone else.

When Isaac Russell, a non-Mormon, put in a word in defense of the Book of Abraham, Mercer was quick to light into him. "A man who will . . . jumble up opinions of thirty years ago with the corrected views of recent years, cannot escape contradicting himself and being considered by any scholar a dilettante of the worst type."[106] Forty years later the same Mercer was being taken to task by the reviewers for being hopelessly dilettantish and out of date in *his* scholarship, but even in his youth his buoyant confidence in his linguistic powers led him to extend himself far beyond the bounds of prudence. Within a decade of blasting the Book of Abraham, Mercer had published, among other things, translations and commentaries of Egyptian, Aramaic,

Greek, and Latin texts bearing on the Bible (1913),[107] an Ethiopian liturgy (1915),[108] Sumero-Babylonian sign lists (1918),[109] a translation of an Egyptian grammar (1920),[110] an Ethiopic grammar (1920),[111] an Assyrian grammar (1921),[112] and books on the Babylonian and Assyrian religion (1919)[113] and Egyptian religion (1919).[114] We know of no savant, including even the immortal Athanasius Kircher, who has ever equaled such a performance for sheer daring.

The reader may be interested to know how Mercer's efforts were accepted by the learned world. Only two years after 1912 Mercer brought out a work on an Ethiopian liturgy, of which F. Praetorius, the world leader in the field, wrote: "The writer's knowledge of the Ethiopian language is at present, however, totally inadequate. The numerous errors of translation which he commits provide the reader at times with real comic relief."[115]

If Mercer keeps at it, however, "it may be possible for him at a later date to get out a critical edition instead of just a photograph . . . and to answer some of the questions which he has here dealt with prematurely."[116] In other words, Mercer bites off more than he can chew.

Fifteen years later Mercer was still having difficulty following the advice of Praetorius, for Henry S. Gehmann, in reviewing his Ethiopic text of Ecclesiastes, notes that as long as Mercer is merely reproducing the text all goes well, "but in his further discussion of the Ethiopic version he is not so fortunate, . . . and he makes statements which upon analysis are seen to be contradictory or at least not clear."[117]

In 1929 Mercer published an ambitious book on Egyptian religion that was reviewed by Hermann Kees, a leader in that field: "It is superficially written and in many passages one comes upon familiar ideas of Maspero [to whom the book was dedicated]. But because Maspero never lost contact with the real world of Egypt one is all the more disturbed by the lack of any smell of Egyptian earth."[118] "To uphold his theories . . . Mercer must schematize mercilessly [*grausam schematisieren*]"; his reconstruction of the beginnings is "a peculiarly artificial picture," and to explain the distribution of the cults of Egypt "Mercer must invent the most remarkable migrations."[119] Kees notes that "the unnatural way in which things are constructed" is "typical of this whole school of inventing religious history." Kees refers to his own classic work, *Totenglaube der Ägypter,* as "a book with which Mercer is of course [*freilich*] not acquainted." He takes note of "Mercer's peculiar way of putting questions and his naive and off-hand conclusions."[120]

Our own impression after working for some years among Dr. Mercer's books and notes is obligingly put into words by an Egyptologist whom few may challenge: "The book is pleasant [*nett*] to read . . . but it brings no advance,"[121] for, "granted that Mercer has taken the trouble to read and cite all sorts of things, the whole thing is done in a disturbingly superficial way [*bedenklich oberflächlich*]."[122] What Mercer's work does give us of value, Kees decides, is "unfortunately" a demonstration "of how urgent is the necessity for anyone who wishes to undertake the study of Egyptian religion and especially of its beginnings, first of all to handle at firsthand the raw materials presented by the local cults of the land and by its topography . . . and such a study would do greater honor to the memory of Maspero than Mercer has with his International Society of Gods."[123] There is a sting in that!

Almost twenty years later Mercer returned to the lists with another and a bigger book still on Egyptian religion, and again it fell to the lot of Kees to review it. He begins by taking Mercer to task for ignoring much recent archaeological work while making archaeology his defense.[124] Especially Dr. Kees "must express profound concern [*grundsätzliches Bedenken*]" with Mercer's failure to explain the *why* in all his glib syncretism. Kees is franker than ever: "Mercer should have omitted things which he did not understand, including annoyingly frequent references to 'confusion' in Egyptian thinking."[125] This has become an important factor in the study of Egyptian religion today: more and more the scholars are recognizing that the strangeness and obscurity in the Egyptian texts is probably less due to their ignorance and inability to think clearly than to our own. Kees notes that Mercer displays his usual diligence in the business of collecting and cataloging material, but whenever he digests it, his work is marked by "triviality and irrelevance that predominate over a real grasp of material." He comments on Mercer's weakness for making sweeping and pontifical statements, "which constantly run the risk of being easily refuted."[126] In concluding his study with a long list of some of Mercer's many mistakes, Kees says he is trying to avoid giving to "the well-intentioned reader a heightened dread of the labyrinth of Egyptian Religion and its incomprehensibility."[127]

But Kees was not the only one. Writing in another journal, Hans Bonnet, the author of the invaluable *Reallexikon der aegyptischen Religion,* reviewed the same work by Mercer, noting first of all that the author "misses the basic significance [*grundlegende Bedeutung*] of Egyptian religion" because he "collects a lot of unconnected data which are never brought into proper relationship," even while he continues to cling to his favorite but long outdated theories of Egyptian prehistory, "his entire study being controlled by a theory which is not only nonessential to the history of Egyptian religion" but also applies to a field "in which we can never count on achieving clarity."[128] In short, Dr. Mercer misses the point of everything. The assertion that we can *never achieve certainty* in some matter of Egyptian religion is an important one and was stated even more emphatically in a long review of Mercer's *The Religion of Ancient Egypt* by the eminent Eberhard Otto. This work, Otto writes, as "the fruit of a long and industrious scholarly career . . . shows us that a presentation of Egyptian religion which avoids a subjective attitude, but whose foundation lies outside the sphere of science is an impossibility . . . and it shows us the reason why it is now and perhaps always will be impossible to write [a] *history* of Egyptian religion."[129]

Instead of coming to grips with the problems he has raised, Mercer, according to Otto, leaves all the necessary explaining "to casual scattered remarks." The avoidance of a real method of coping with immensely hard problems "gives his description a rather disjointed and uncoordinated nature."[130] Since he can't escape facing certain problems of origins, Mercer, according to Otto, simply gets rid of them by thrusting them back into a dim prehistory where he posits a series of invasions or migrations, following Sethe's lead.[131] Instead of going to the basic sources, Otto observes, Mercer relies on "secondary sources," and even then fails to treat his sources critically. "He is often unclear, sometimes in matters of fundamental importance." "Many of his apodictic statements should not go unchallenged, . . . many of his interpretations of names cry for refutation by the philologist,"[132] his genealogies "contain many errors or theories no longer recognized today," and his work "belongs to an age of research whose scholarly goals are not in every point the same as those of the present generation of scholars."[133]

In his seventies Mercer, undaunted and undeterred, undertook a work that would intimidate the greatest Egyptologist—a translation and critical commentary on one of the oldest, largest, and most difficult books in the world—the Egyptian Pyramid Texts. Rudolf Anthes begins his review of this ambitious four-volume work by pointing out the dangers and hardships that attend any attempt at "translating a paragraph of these texts, in which each word is weighty."[134] Mercer is again charged with underestimating the intelligence of the Egyptians when he sees, for example, in the mysterious Enneads only a demonstration of their muddled thinking, and affects to detect in Pyramid Texts "a lack of common sense on the part of the Egyptians of the 3rd millennium."[135] Instead of accusing the Egyptians of ignorance, Anthes advises, "we should rather acknowledge the fact that *we* are not yet equal to the Pyramid Texts, although they represent excellent manuscripts."[136]

Mercer often attributes his own failure to come through to "corruptions in the text, mistakes in writing, errors in grammar and syntax, contradictions and confusions, expressions which seem ridiculous, and illogical expressions."[137] This is our old friend Reverend Mercer, taking the Egyptians to task, as he once did the Mormons, for being inexcusably ignorant of Egyptian. But Professor Anthes will not go for this; it is not the Egyptians but ourselves who are ignorant, and Mercer's introductory statement that "we have not yet a definitive text" of the Pyramid Texts "is evidently misleading and I feel compelled," writes Professor Anthes, "to contradict it."[138] There are imperfections enough in the translation—"imperfection[s] of this kind, I am sorry to say, [do] occur in the translation,"—but they are not due to any Egyptian incompetence. "Perhaps Professor Mercer was right in undertaking this task, for which—if I may say so frankly—hardly anyone is fully prepared," but instead of chiding the Egyptians, "the problematical situation of our understanding of the Pyramid Texts should have been indicated more often than it actually has been."[139]

Professor Anthes is one of a growing number of Egyptologists who suggest in all seriousness approaching Egyptian religious writings with the idea that after all they might make sense, since the Egyptians were not complete fools: "There exists some incongruity," he notes, "between the sober effectiveness of the Egyptians in the Old Kingdom, which is apparent mainly in politics, architecture and art, and what seems to be their inability for clear thinking in religious matters. This incompatibility is striking, the more so since government and religion did represent a unity which we may call governmental theology."[140] Professor Anthes objects to the illogic of saying (1) that everything the Egyptians did was part of their religion, (2) that their achievements were prodigious, and (3) that their religion was ridiculous. That simply won't go down with Anthes and others, though the old school of Egyptologists still clings to it. Even Gardiner, a brilliant representative of that school, showed some signs of weakening toward the end of his wonderful career, when he was willing to concede that Egyptian religion was "as alluring as a will-o'-the-wisp by reason of its mystery and even in spite of its absurdity";[141] and he suggested that while it was most dangerous to take seriously such seeming "unmitigated rubbish" as some of the Egyptian hymns, it was still also dangerous (though, of course, less dangerous) to take an "unsympathetic and even patronizing attitude towards the myths and religious practices of Pharaonic times."[142]

In reviewing Mercer's work *The Pyramid Texts,* T. George Allen, the foremost student of Egyptian funerary literature, did not mince words: "Would that the contents of these handsome volumes were fully in keeping with their appearance!"[143] The defects of those contents "spring from two main sources: faulty translation of German and violation of Egyptian grammatical principles." What a blow! It is bad enough for an Egyptologist to be criticized for ignorance of Egyptian in making translations from Egyptian, but when the reviewer recognizes his dependence on other sources and notes that it is in German that he is at fault, one wonders how this could have been received by the scholar who often lectured others on their ignorance of language. "Mistranslations of German are various," says Allen. "Egyptian grammar is often mistreated." Again Mercer is charged with superficiality: "Mercer himself states that analysis of the utterances [in the Pyramid Texts] has not 'been too

meticulous in unessential matters'; the truth is that his definition of 'unessential' has been far too liberal."[144]

In his pointed remarks about German, Professor Allen
was no doubt hinting at what the great French Egyptologist
Étienne Drioton said more openly in reviewing an earlier
book of Mercer's on the Pyramid Texts, that Mercer's words
on the Pyramid Texts simply follow Sethe, the great master
in that field, who had already translated them into German.
Because of this lack of originality, Drioton concludes, "This
investigation can bring no new light." Moreover, Drioton
observes that the method followed by Mercer cannot possibly lead to the conclusions he has adopted.[145] Mercer has
prefixed to his *History of Egyptian Religion* the remarkable
statement that Sethe had placed at the introduction of his
own history of the same subject: *Wer es nicht glauben will,
mag es nicht glauben* ("Whoever doesn't want to believe it
doesn't have to"). This had not been an attempt on Sethe's
part to disarm criticism, however, for he stated his position
with a characteristic frankness that Mercer does not follow,
when he said in a preceding sentence: "This is how for
thirty years the Egyptian religion has appeared to my eyes,
or, if you will, to my imagination [*Phantasie*]; the whole
thing is completely hypothetical."[146] This would place Sethe
today in the camp of Karl Popper, but one would hardly
expect such an admission from the confident Mercer—and
one does not get it.

In the same year that his vast work on the Pyramid
Texts appeared, this remarkable man published *Earliest
Intellectual Man's Idea of the Cosmos,* in which he brought his
Babylonian philological studies into conjunction with his
Egyptian to compare the earliest religious concepts of both
lands. Of this work the Sumerologist Salonen wrote to
Mercer, "Sumerian conditions may well be quite hazy.
Specifically as regards Sumer . . . the book contains annoy-
ingly many mistakes, incongruities and blunders. . . .

Sumerian and Babylonian names and words often appear in wrong forms."[147] Salonen then gives some examples of what he calls Mercer's "other outrageous mistakes!" He finds "the book is confusedly written and is full of tautology; . . . the part relating to Sumer could safely have been omitted."[148] In particular, "chronology does not seem to be one of Mercer's strong points, hence information which has been doomed several decades ago."[149] This recalls Mercer's own onslaught on a massively documented work on ancient chronology some years before: "Of course, no other self-respecting chronologist will for a moment agree. . . . One feels that with all that has been said, we shall still feel safer under the chronological guidance, in Egyptian matters, of Meyer and Breasted."[150] Here again, instead of giving the reasons, Mercer had simply appealed with his lofty "of course" to authority, though the chronologies of Meyer and Breasted were even then being seriously questioned.

Our purpose in this long digression about Dr. Mercer has not been primarily to discredit the authority of one whose authority has for years been used as a club to beat the Book of Abraham withal, but rather to provide us laymen with an instructive introduction to the limitations and pitfalls of Egyptology in general. What we have just beheld is the spectacle of some of the world's foremost Egyptologists laying down the law to one of their colleagues, who in turn was never backward in laying down the law to them. From this it should begin to appear that we are not here moving in a world of cold, indisputable scientific facts at all, but rather in an atmosphere of somewhat dazed and bemused speculation. And the puzzlement and bewilderment are if anything greater among the specialists today than they were in 1912.

Was Abraham Real? New Theories

To this day "scholarship has largely ignored exegetical analysis of these narratives," writes Thomas L. Thompson of the patriarchal stories, with Abraham's stories at their head.[151] Exclusively preoccupied with "theological and socio-logical trends," according to another specialist, they have avoided the "historical-descriptive task" of treating the patriarchs as real people, as a result of which "the current situation in Old Testament theology has been described as 'in crisis.'"[152] The trouble is that "archaeology has now thrust the world of the Old Testament into the historic past, and there can be no retreat from the study of parallels."[153] We have been accused of preoccupation with historic paral-lels where Abraham is concerned, but with Ebla nobody can escape it.

For along with a sudden resurgence of interest in the Old Testament in the 1970s comes an unparalleled concern for Abraham.[154] In the new studies, the whole problem of discovering Abraham is one of *fitting things together.* Given a body of data contained in an ancient document, what period of history, what geographical or cultural setting, what literary conventions fit it best? Students of the most advanced physical theory today confess that they cannot hope to describe or even imagine what the waves and par-ticles they deal with really are; what keeps them going and reassures their faith in the reality of those mysterious enti-ties is the principle of *consistency.* A hypothetical structure is worth working on if it is consistent within itself and agrees with whatever limited data are available; as long as the known data agree with each other and with experimen-tal predictions, we are on the right track. So it has always been with the study of the past. We never shall know what really happened or exactly what it was like back then, but consistency of sources keeps the game going. For example, we have seen that the Book of Abraham agrees remarkably well with the *Apocalypse of Abraham.* But will anyone main-tain for a moment that the *Apocalypse of Abraham* is actually the original version of his history? Of course not, but it in turn agrees remarkably well with other writings about Abraham that reach back into various times and regions. In our series in the *Improvement Era* we showed how the Abraham legends turn up in Egyptian, Babylonian, and even Greek traditions of great antiquity with a richness of detail that can hardly be accidental. "The Egyptian and Mesopotamian texts," writes Stan Rummel, "thrust Israel into a real world. Specific parallels, grounded on historical and cultural connections, replaced abstract speculation" of Wellhausen's day—"there can be no retreat from the study of parallels."[155]

But even before we consider the parallels, we have firm ground under our feet in the mere fact that the text of the Abraham story of 1835 has been placed in our hands. That someone has produced what purports to be an ancient document must in itself, as Friedrich Blass points out, command our respect and oblige us to give the benefit of the doubt to its claims until proven spurious.[156] *The Book of Abraham must have come from somewhere.* It is a document rich and clear in specific statements, inviting and never avoiding the closest attention of the critic. It is generally agreed that it could not have come from that papyrus called the Book of Breathings, nor can it possibly be the product of the clumsy and quickly abandoned gropings of the so-called Alphabet and Grammar. The Kirtland Egyptian Papers show us where it did *not* come from, and that is all. The existence of a very concrete text invites and deserves just the kind of examination to which both the Abraham literature and important Egyptian stories are being exposed at the present moment. If it is a fraud, that should become quickly apparent without any backdoor approaches seeking by a pointless preoccupation with method and intrigue to avoid a head-on confrontation with the text.

Abraham's emergence as a real person has been comparatively recent, following the fashionable trends of scholarship.

For example, only "within the last few decades" has "the basic historicity of the Sumerian epics . . . tacitly been taken for granted by most scholars who have dealt with them."[157] Before that it was, like Abraham, all myth, folklore, superstition, and poetic invention until a sudden *"bouleversement radical,"* as André Parrot called it, changed everything.[158] The weight of the evidence itself has been enough to bring this about, for the experts have come around reluctantly; indeed, "the general line in much modern scholarship," Bendt Alster observes, is "one that sets itself as a task to deprive the ancient literary sources of actual reality whenever possible, instead of asking what the texts intend to say." A serious research into any ancient texts, as he notes, requires examining *"similar texts from elsewhere."*[159] "It has become a commonplace," writes the Bible scholar Peter R. Ackroyd, "to acknowledge that the understanding of the Old Testament is deficient without a proper appreciation of its ancient *context*," meaning how it fits into a giant jigsaw along with "Egyptian, Mesopotamian, Hittite, Ugaritic, and North Semitic" sources.[160] Granted that "the fundamental truths of the Bible cannot be demonstrated by archaeology," an eminent Jesuit scholar notes, "still it becomes clearer and clearer that the Bible has its roots in the history of the Near East," so that "a new much deeper study is necessary" before we can get to the "true source of the faith of Israel." In particular the sensational discoveries at Ebla are forcing the world to consider more seriously than ever before the historical reality of the patriarchs, with Abraham at their head.[161]

Christian theologians who have hitherto disdained to debase their faith by digging for historical evidence now assure us that we cannot overlook what Maurice Wiles calls "the raw material in the light of which our faith judgments have to be made."[162] In the New Testament field, *"to the extent that Christians tend to overlook or forget the historical*

Jesus, they tend to structure Christian life more and more as a religion in the pejorative sense. . . . Access to the Christ of faith comes through our following of the historical *Jesus."*[163] A few years ago such statements as these by leaders of Christian thought would have been unthinkable. On all sides the discovery of new documents is forcing open the doors that have heretofore safely contained the ancient patriarchs, prophets, and saints in a vague and distant quarantine.

Further Abraham studies insist that something very significant was going on back there, which only increases our frustration at being unable to find out just what it was. The field of speculation is more wide open than ever; Herbert Werner reminds us that the Abraham question requires "investigations, experiments, and new approaches (*Angebote*)" as never before.[164] The big problem for him is how the stories got down to us: were they preserved out of a wealth of tales because they were peculiarly relevant as articles of faith, declarations of principle, and sermons? Granted they are edifying stories and would have been preserved for that if for no other reason, does it follow that they are fables? If they are, why do they lay such insistence on a particular time, a particular place, and particular historical conditions?[165] Werner confesses himself at a loss to explain why three different versions of intrigue between Abraham and a king involving his wife are given, and how they are related. He finds preposterous the supposed confrontations between those "mighty potentates and virtually disenfranchised aliens."[166] The reactions of the kings when they discover they have been duped are simply "astonishing," and make no sense at all. Along with such perplexing oddities, he notes certain overriding motifs that cannot be overlooked: the strange theme of the tribal mother (*Stammutter*) in danger, the recurrent motif of famine and the need for sacrifice to relieve it, and especially the dominance of drought in the picture. Werner's astonishing conclusion is that Abraham is really fleeing from "the absurdity of the world," after he has become convinced that Yahweh has let him down in Canaan, and moves to Egypt seeking a more rational existence. Actually, Werner decides, it is Abraham and not Pharaoh who should have been smitten in the palace.[167]

The Dutch scholar G. Hamming is led to equal, though different, extremes. He begins with the declaration that Abraham was before all else a writer of history who wrote down the story of the creation, as we have it in Genesis 2:4–12:4, under strong Egyptian influence.[168] Whereas Werner insists that the patriarchal narratives are full of such things as dreams and private conversations that no historian could possibly have known, Hamming corrects the proposition: Abraham *himself* could have known those things, making him alone the author of them: "Abraham himself is necessarily the author of whatever is true in his history." He reasons that "Abraham wrote a number of short accounts," setting forth "his view of history, his philosophy of culture and a number of personal reminiscences. Some of these accounts have been lost and some partly preserved."[169] Hamming lays emphasis on the technological sophistication of Abraham's world, rapidly moving toward economic and social collapse, in which only Egypt retained any virtue and integrity. Like Werner, Hamming cannot understand why the Egyptians took an outsider and an outcast like Abraham so seriously. Also, Abraham's concern with the priesthood makes him wonder.[170]

The New Dating Game

Discussions of Abraham today almost all center on problems of *dating*, with every scholar convinced that he can match conditions set forth in Abraham stories with a real historic setting so exactly that there can no longer be any doubt as to the time of Abraham.

The center of attention is John Van Seter's book *Abraham*

in History and Tradition, which places the patriarch squarely in the middle of the first millennium B.C.[171] This came out just before the discovery of the Ebla tablets, which have pushed the possibility of Abraham back to the middle of the third millennium B.C. So now we have a range of two thousand years in which the experts are seeking to find an exact date for Abraham!

We begin at one end with a theoretically possible date of 2400 or even 2500 B.C. suggested by the Ebla tablets, but this dating is too recent and surprising to have any serious champions yet.[172] Coming down half a millennium or more, with the greatest confidence André Parrot could announce that "all truly objective specialists are agreed: the way of life described in the accounts of Genesis . . . fits *perfectly* with what we know today, from other sources, of the beginning of the second millennium, but *imperfectly* with a more recent time."[173] How early in the second millennium? James L. Kelso puts his finger on the century between 2000 and 1900 B.C. and announces, "Here and only here in all of the Near East can Abraham be dated; but here in Middle Bronze I, he is as much at home as Abraham Lincoln in the Civil War period of the U.S.A."[174] More specifically, Hamming would have Abraham born very near to the year 1955 B.C.[175] On the other hand, we are assured that that time, "the Larsa period (2000–1800 B.C.), . . . most scholars believe to be slightly earlier than Abraham," although conditions would have been much the same "until well after Abraham's time."[176] William H. Stiebing now moves the date down from the Middle Bronze I favored by Nelson Glueck, William F. Albright, and others, to Middle Bronze II (1900 down to 1550 B.C.).[177] Still descending the scale, "Recently there has been a tendency to bring the patriarchs down into the Late Bronze Age (1600–1200 B.C.) or even into the Assyrian period nearly a thousand years later."[178] It was the ancient texts discovered at Mari and Nuzi that brought things down to the Middle

Bronze II dating and led Parrot to his dogmatic certitude; but now it is claimed that "the contracts of fifteenth century Nuzi are neither unique to their time and place, nor related to Genesis."[179] In fact, we are assured that those documents describe a world not so different from the Nimrod texts of the sixth century B.C., the time favored by Van Seters. Some have noted how the patriarchal narratives with their romantic and heroic allure suggest most strongly the traditions of the Amarna, Minoan, and Mycenaean worlds which flourished in the Eastern Mediterranean c. 1400–1100 B.C.[180] Indeed, the present writer finds abundant and striking parallels between the Abraham traditions and the myths and legends harking back to the bad old days of Greek and Levantine prehistory. The presence of Philistines in Abraham's history favors such dating, but of course is lightly dismissed as an obvious anachronism by those supporting other dates. But as Noel Weeks notes, "as long as the historian can dismiss inconvenient evidence as anachronistic it is hard to control his theses."[181]

Abraham's camels, long a subject of controversy, have been treated in the same high-handed manner. Albright insisted that the camel was not domesticated until about 1000 B.C., so naturally the camels of Isaac and Jacob had to go. James L. Kelso now brings them back by explaining that "the camel of Abraham's day was simply a luxury riding animal for the rich," which Abraham would not use in his caravans. Why not? The beast could cross the desert then as well as it does today.[182] To Van Seter's surprising and much-discussed dating of Abraham to the mid-sixth century B.C. (which, of course, puts him back into his old nineteenth-century category of a mythical being: only the Abraham *story* could be so late—no *real* Abraham could have been walking around long after Moses and the prophets!), telling objections are raised, for example, that the patriarchal narratives are full of accepted customs that would be an abomination to the exilic Jews—*they* certainly would never have invented the Abraham story, and twenty-seven of the thirty-eight names of patriarchal family members never turn up again in the Bible—they are unique to a much earlier time. In taking things back to the mythical Abraham of nineteenth-century scholarship, Van Seters uses the favorite argument of that school by conjuring up the all-sufficient *Sitz im Leben* of the exile: the story of Abraham would naturally appeal to people suffering the afflictions of the captivity, who accordingly must have invented it to give themselves comfort and encouragement. But Robert Martin- Achard points out, following Gerhard von Rad, "every generation . . . found itself faced anew with the same task . . . of understanding itself as Israel."[183] The sufferings of Abraham are relevant *whenever* Israel finds itself in straits.

The greatest windfall of nineteenth-century scholarship was the license to break down any ancient text into as many separate constituent parts as one chose; thanks to that, any scholar could spot the origin of any item of patriarchal tradition in the vagaries of scribes, the imaginations of storytellers by the campfire, the fervor of preachers, the *Tendenzschriften* (political agenda) of sectaries—in almost anything, in fact, but real history. In particular, oral tradition was the way out of any tight place: "Indeed the whole predominance of oral transmission in modern Biblical studies is a curious phenomenon," writes Noel Weeks. He asks, "Is the very lack of historical controls . . . the basis of its popularity?"[184]

So where do we stand? Ever since Albright's dating of Abraham collapsed "precipitately," according to Thomas L. Thompson, there has been a lack of any real consensus, so that today one can only conclude that the patriarchal narratives "appear to have taken shape in some still unsatisfactorily explained manner, over a period of time as yet undetermined." "Possibilities are infinite," he concludes, "and scholarly preferences are irrelevant. Alternative dates [i.e., to his own—favoring a late date, 'but this is only a guess'] have not and cannot be excluded."[185]

Notes

1. Louis C. Zucker, "Joseph Smith as a Student of Hebrew," *Dialogue* 3/2 (1968): 44.

2. Ibid., 43.

3. Ibid.

4. Ibid., 48.

5. Ibid., 47.

6. Ibid., 48.

7. Ibid.

8. Hugh W. Nibley, "Churches in the Wilderness," in *Nibley on the Timely and the Timeless* (Provo, UT: BYU Religious Studies Center, 1978), 156–61; reprinted in *The Prophetic Book of Mormon*, CWHN 8 (Salt Lake City: Deseret Book and FARMS, 1989), 289–95.

9. Hugh W. Nibley, *The Message of the Joseph Smith Papyri: An Egyptian Endowment* (Salt Lake City: Deseret Book, 1975), 133–35, esp. 133.

10. Zucker, "Joseph Smith as a Student of Hebrew," 49.

11. Nibley, "Churches in the Wilderness," 159; in *CWHN* 8:293.

12. Joseph A. Fitzmyer, *The Genesis Apocryphon of Qumran Cave I: A Commentary* (Rome: Biblical Institute, 1966), 50–59.

13. Hugh W. Nibley, "A New Look at the Pearl of Great Price," *IE* 71 (January 1968): 18–23; partially reprinted in this volume, pp. 86–91.

14. Ibid., *IE* 71 (February 1968): 15.

15. Ibid., *IE* 71 (March 1968): 20.

16. Ibid., *IE* 71 (September 1968): 70.

17. Ibid., 66.

18. Ibid., 78.

19. Ibid., *IE* 71 (October 1968): 81; (November 1968): 40–44.

20. Ibid., *IE* 71 (December 1968): 32–33.

21. Ibid., *IE* 72 (January 1969): 26–31.

22. Ibid., *IE* 72 (May 1969): 88.

23. Ibid., *IE* 72 (February 1969): 64–67.

24. Ibid., 66–67.

25. Ibid., *IE* 72 (May 1969): 87–91; (June 1969): 126–31; (July 1969): 97–100.

26. Ibid., *IE* 72 (May 1969): 88.

27. Ibid., *IE* 72 (June 1969): 126–31.

28. Ibid., *IE* 72 (November 1969): 116–20; reprinted in this volume, pp. 182–92.

29. Ibid., *IE* 73 (May 1970): 86–87.

30. Ibid., *IE* 73 (April 1970): 79–95; reprinted in this volume as chapter 8, "The Sacrifice of Sarah."

31. George W. E. Nickelsburg, ed., *Studies on the Testament of Abraham* (Missoula, MT: Scholars Press, 1976).

32. Nissim Wernick, "A Critical Analysis of the Book of Abraham in the Light of Extra-Canonical Jewish Writings" (Ph.D. diss., Brigham Young University, 1968).

33. Robert C. Webb [pseud.], *Joseph Smith as Translator* (Salt Lake City: Deseret Book, 1936), 106–17.

34. See Nibley, "A New Look at the Pearl of Great Price," *IE* 72 (January 1969): 31.

35. Adolph Jellinek, *Bet ha-Midrash*, 6 vols. (1853–77; reprint, Jerusalem: Wahrmann, 1967), 5:40–41.

36. *Bereshith Rabbah* 38:19.

37. Nibley, "A New Look at the Pearl of Great Price," *IE* 72 (November 1969): 120; in this volume, pp. 195–97.

38. Eusebius, *Praeparatio Evangelica (Preparation for the Gospel)* VII, 6–22, in *PG* 21:516–83; IX, 16, in *PG* 21:705–9.

39. Augustine, *Civitas Dei (The City of God)* XVI, 15.

40. *Clementine Recognitions* I, 32–33, in *PG* 1:1226–27.

41. Philo, *De Abrahamo*.

42. Editorial, "The Promise of Ebla," *BAR* 2 (December 1976): 41.

43. F. I. Anderson, "Ebla, the More We Find Out, the Less We Know," *Buried History* 13 (March 1977): 10–12.

44. David Noel Freedman, "The Real Story of the Ebla Tablets," *Biblical Archaeologist* 41 (December 1978): 148–64.

45. "Promise of Ebla," 42.

46. Nibley, "A New Look at the Pearl of Great Price," *IE* 72 (April 1969): 66–67.

47. Giovanni Pettinato, "The Royal Archives of Tell-Mardikh-Ebla," *Biblical Archaeologist* 39 (May 1976): 48.

48. "Promise of Ebla," 42.

49. Stan Rummel, "Using Ancient Near Eastern Parallels in Old Testament Studies," *BAR* 3 (September 1977): 7.

50. "The Appeal to Authority" originally appeared in the series, "A New Look at the Pearl of Great Price," *IE* 71 (January 1968): 20–22.

51. Samuel A. B. Mercer, "Joseph Smith as an Interpreter and Translator of Egyptian," *Utah Survey* 1 (September 1913): 30.

52. For example, see Janne M. Sjodahl, "The Book of Abraham,"

editorial in *Deseret Evening News*, 17 December 1912, 4; reprinted in *IE* 16 (February 1913): 326–33. The high critics erred egregiously especially where Egypt was concerned: "Dr. Von Bohlen, the honored co-laborer with Gesenius and De Wette, gave long chapters to the easy task of proving from overwhelming classical testimony that the Bible blundered almost every time it mentions an Egyptian custom. According to this great scholar, the statement that the Egyptians built with brick in ancient times, used asses, cultivated the vine, and used costly materials in constructions as the ark and the tabernacle, proved that the author of the Pentateuch was 'an absolute stranger to Egypt.'" Charles H. S. Davis, *Ancient Egypt in the Light of Modern Discoveries* (Meriden, CT: Biblia, 1892), 311.

53. Robert C. Webb, "Have Joseph Smith's Interpretations Been Discredited?" *IE* 17 (1914): 313, commenting on the first issue of the *Utah Survey* (September 1913). Robert C. Webb, "A Critical Examination of the Fac-Similes of the Book of Abraham," *IE* 16 (1913): 435, notes that after the great promises made before its publication, Spalding's book has turned out disappointingly thin and skimpy.

54. N. L. Nelson, "An Open Letter to Bishop Spalding," *IE* 16 (1913): 606–7, was more outspoken than the others: "A jury of Gentiles, prejudiced, ill-tempered and mad with the pride of human learning."

55. B. H. Roberts, "Remarks on 'Joseph Smith Jr., as a Translator': A Plea in Bar of Final Conclusions," *Deseret Evening News*, 19 December 1912, 11; reprinted in *IE* 16 (1913): 311. Cf. Junius F. Wells, "Scholars Disagree," *Deseret Evening News*, 19 December 1912, 4; reprinted under the same title in *IE* 16 (1913): 341–43. The editorial to which the *Times* referred appeared two days earlier in the *Deseret Evening News*, 17 December 1912, 4.

56. Editorial, "Museum Walls Proclaim Fraud of Mormon Prophet," *New York Times*, 29 December 1912, pt. 5:3. See fig. 28, p. 151.

57. Wells, "Scholars Disagree," 4; in *IE* 16 (1913): 343.

58. Sjodahl, "The Book of Abraham," 4; in *IE* 16 (1913): 333.

59. Attacks from Franklin S. Spalding, "Making New Friends in Utah," *The Spirit of Missions* 77/10 (October 1912): 114–18, are cited by Robert C. Webb, "The Galileo of Sociology," *IE* 17 (1914): 565–67; Mercer's long attack, "Joseph Smith as an Interpreter," 3–36, has been reprinted photomechanically along with Franklin S. Spalding, *Why Egyptologists Reject the Book of Abraham* (Salt Lake City: Modern Microfilm, 1965).

60. Roberts, "A Plea in Bar of Final Conclusions," *IE* 16 (1913): 310.

61. Mercer, "Joseph Smith as an Interpreter" 36.

62. Ibid., 17.

63. Ibid., 25.

64. Cf. Webb, "Have Joseph Smith's Interpretations Been Discredited?" 316: "In the Spalding literature the public has been thoroughly indoctrinated on the sufficiency of scholarly opinions, which, as we read, are 'always accepted *without question* unless there is grave reason to doubt'" (emphasis added).

65. Mercer, "Joseph Smith as an Interpreter," 12.

66. Charles R. Derchart, "Cybernetics and the Human Person," *International Philosophical Quarterly* 5 (1965): 32–33.

67. Webb, "Critical Examination of the Fac-Similes," 435.

68. Franklin S. Spalding, "Professor S. A. B. Mercer," *Utah Survey* 1 (September 1913): 3.

69. Mercer, "Joseph Smith as an Interpreter," 30.

70. Ibid.

71. Spalding, "Professor S. A. B. Mercer," 3.

72. Mercer, "Joseph Smith as an Interpreter," 7, 30.

73. Samuel A. B. Mercer, quoted in Franklin S. Spalding, "Rev. Spalding's Answer to Dr. Widtsoe," *IE* 16 (1913): 613.

74. "May We See Your Credentials?" originally appeared in the series, "A New Look at the Pearl of Great Price," *IE* 71 (May 1968): 54–57, and (June 1968): 18–22.

75. Franklin S. Spalding, *Joseph Smith, Jr., as a Translator* (Salt Lake City: Arrow, 1912), 19.

76. John A. Widtsoe, "Dr. Widtsoe's Reply to Rev. Spalding," *IE* 16 (1913): 617.

77. Emmanuel de Rougé, "Conference sur la religion des anciens Égyptiens," *BE* 26 (1918): 228.

78. Spalding, *Joseph Smith, Jr., as a Translator,* 29.

79. For vital statistics, see Spalding, "Professor S. A. B. Mercer," 3; *Who's Who 1967: An Annual Biographical Dictionary* (London: Adam and Charles Black, 1967), 2087.

80. Mercer quoted in Franklin S. Spalding, "Rev. Spalding's Answer to Dr. Widtsoe," *IE* 16 (1913): 611.

81. Mercer quoted in ibid., 615.

82. Ibid.

83. Ibid.

84. This letter, dated 19 February 1953, has been circulated by LaMar Petersen along with his own letter to Dr. Mercer, dated 16 December 1952 (BYU File M1268).

85. All from Mercer, "Joseph Smith as an Interpreter" 7–9.

86. Mercer quoted in Spalding, "Rev. Spalding's Answer to Dr. Widtsoe," 612.

87. Samuel A. B. Mercer, review of *The Dawn of Conscience*, by James H. Breasted, *Egyptian Religion* 2 (1934): 70.

88. Ibid., 71.

89. Ibid.

90. Samuel A. B. Mercer, review of *Myth and Ritual*, edited by S. H. Hooke, *Egyptian Religion* 1 (1933): 84.

91. Ibid., 85.

92. Samuel A. B. Mercer, review of *Der Kosmos von Sumer*, by Alfred Jeremias, *Egyptian Religion* 1 (1938): 38.

93. Samuel A. B. Mercer, "Arthur Edward Pearse Brome Weigall," *Egyptian Religion* 2 (1934): 75.

94. Samuel A. B. Mercer, review of *Die Völker der antiken Orients*, by Hermann Junker, *Egyptian Religion* 3 (1935): 64.

95. Ibid., 65.

96. Dr. Mercer has great confidence in his own capacity to see into the mind of the primitive: "And just as the imagination of children is less restrained than that of grown-ups, so the imagination of primitive men was vastly more active than is our imagination. So the men of Egypt saw heaven as an immense friendly cow standing over them." Samuel A. B. Mercer, *The Religion of Ancient Egypt* (London: Luzac, 1949), 21. In the margin of one of Jaroslav Černý's works on the religion of the Old and Middle Kingdoms, Dr. Mercer has written one eloquent word "Absurd!" In his own work, Mercer accepts without question the once fashionable but long-outmoded theory of animism as the key to the understanding of early Egyptian religion. Mercer, *The Religion of Ancient Egypt*, 299.

97. Samuel A. B. Mercer, review of *An Introduction to the Books of the Old Testament*, by W. O. E. Oesterley and T. H. Robinson, *Egyptian Religion* 3 (1935): 115.

98. Samuel A. B. Mercer, review of *Die Religion der Ägypter*, by Adolf Erman, *Egyptian Religion* 3 (1935): 160.

99. Samuel A. B. Mercer, review of *Semitic and Hamitic Origins*, by George A. Barton, *Egyptian Religion* 3 (1935): 160.

100. Ibid., 161.

101. Ibid., 162.

102. Ibid.

103. Samuel A. B. Mercer, "The Gorringe Collection of Egyptian Antiquities," *RT* 36 (1914): 176–78, with photograph.

104. Mercer, "Joseph Smith as an Interpreter," 11.

105. Ibid. (emphasis added).

106. Ibid., 13.

107. Samuel A. B. Mercer, trans. and ed., *Extra-Biblical Sources for Hebrew and Jewish History* (New York: Longmans, Green, 1913).

108. Samuel A. B. Mercer, *The Ethiopic Liturgy: Its Sources, Development, and Present Form* (Milwaukee: Churchman, 1915).

109. Samuel A. B. Mercer, *A Sumero-Babylonian Sign List* (New York: Columbia University Press, 1918).

110. Günther Roeder, *Short Egyptian Grammar*, trans. Samuel A. B. Mercer (New Haven: Yale University Press, 1920).

111. Samuel A. B. Mercer, *Ethiopic Grammar, with Chrestomathy and Glossary* (Oxford: Clarendon, 1920).

112. Samuel A. B. Mercer, *Assyrian Grammar with Chrestomathy and Glossary* (London: Luzac, 1921).

113. Samuel A. B. Mercer, *Religious and Moral Ideas in Babylonia and Assyria* (Milwaukee: Morehouse, 1919).

114. Samuel A. B. Mercer, *Growth of Religious and Moral Ideas in Egypt* (Milwaukee: Morehouse, 1919).

115. F. Praetorius, review of *The Ethiopic Liturgy, Its Sources, Development, and Present Form*, by Samuel A. B. Mercer, *ZDMG* 70 (1916): 263: "Völlig unzureichend sind aber zur Zeit noch des Verfassers Kenntnisse der äthiopischen Sprache. Die von ihm verübten zahlreichen Übersetzungsfehler wirken zuweilen wie erheiternde *Scherze*" (emphasis added). It would be hard to put it stronger than that.

116. Ibid.

117. Henry S. Gehmann, review of *The Ethiopic Text of the Book of Ecclesiastes*, by Samuel A. B. Mercer, *JAOS* 52 (1932): 260–61.

118. Hermann Kees, review of *Études sur les origines de la religion de l'Égypte*, by Samuel A. B. Mercer, *ZDMG* 84 (1930): 191.

119. Ibid.

120. Ibid., 192.

121. Ibid., 193.

122. Ibid., 192.

123. Ibid., 193.

124. Hermann Kees, review of *The Religion of Ancient Egypt*, by Samuel A. B. Mercer, *Orientalia* 20 (1951): 98.

125. Ibid., 99.

126. Ibid.

127. Ibid.: "Wir wollen doch bestimmt vermeiden, das dem gutwilligen Leser ein neues Grauen vor der Wirrnis ägyptischen Glaubens und seiner Unverständlichkeit ankommt."

128. Hans Bonnet, review of *The Religion of Ancient Egypt*, by Samuel A. B. Mercer, *Orientalische Literaturzeitung* 48 (1953): 355–56.

129. Eberhard Otto, review of *The Religion of Ancient Egypt*, by Samuel A. B. Mercer, *JNES* 12 (1953): 215; cf. Bonnet's review, 355: "The content and scope [*Anspruch*] of syncretism are a sealed book to Mercer, and so

he attains no insight whatever into the inner life of Egyptian religion and the forces and goals that move it. In spite of the abundance of material supplied therefore, his presentation offers the reader little of value."

130. Otto, review of *The Religion of Ancient Egypt*, 215.

131. Ibid., 215–16.

132. Ibid., 216.

133. Ibid., 217.

134. Rudolph Anthes, "Remarks on the Pyramid Texts and the Early Egyptian Dogma," *JAOS* 74 (1954): 35, reviewing Samuel A. B. Mercer, *The Pyramid Texts in Translation and Commentary*, 4 vols. (New York: Longmans, Green, 1952).

135. Anthes, "Remarks on the Pyramid Texts," 37.

136. Ibid., 35–36 (emphasis added).

137. Ibid., 35, citing Mercer, *Pyramid Texts in Translation and Commentary*, 8–9.

138. Ibid.

139. Ibid.

140. Ibid., 36.

141. Alan H. Gardiner, *Egypt of the Pharaohs* (Oxford: Clarendon, 1961), 427.

142. Alan H. Gardiner, "Hymns to Sobk in a Ramesseum Papyrus," *RE* 11 (1957): 55.

143. T. George Allen, review of *The Pyramid Texts in Translation and Commentary*, by Samuel A. B. Mercer, *JNES* 13 (1954): 119.

144. Ibid.

145. Étienne Drioton, review of *Literary Criticism of the Pyramid Texts*, by Samuel A. B. Mercer, *RE* 13 (1961): 148–49.

146. Kurt Sethe, *Urgeschichte und älteste Religion der Ägypter* (Leipzig: Brockhaus, 1930), 2–3.

147. A. Salonen, review of *Earliest Intellectual Man's Idea of the Cosmos*, by Samuel A. B. Mercer, *Orientalische Literaturzeitung* 54 (1959): 570–71.

148. Ibid., 571–72.

149. Ibid., 570.

150. Samuel A. B. Mercer, review of *A Scheme of Egyptian Chronology*, by Duncan Macnaughton, *Egyptian Religion* 1 (1933): 37–38.

151. Thomas L. Thompson, "A New Attempt to Date the Patriarchal Narratives," *JAOS* 98 (1978): 77.

152. Marvin E. Tate, "Old Testament Theology: The Current Situation," *Review and Expositor* 74 (1977): 279.

153. Rummel, "Using Ancient Near Eastern Parallels," 8.

154. Nickelsburg, ed., *Studies on the Testament of Abraham*, 12–22.

155. Rummel, "Using Ancient Near Eastern Parallels," 7–8.

156. Friedrich Blass, "Hermeneutik und Kritik," in *Einleitende und Hilfsdsziplinen,* ed. L. von Ulrichs et al. (Munich: Beck, 1892), 293–94.

157. Bendt Alster, "The Paradigmatic Character of Mesopotamian Heroes," *Revue d'Assyriologie* 68 (1974): 49.

158. André Parrot, *Abraham et son temps* (Neuchatel: Delachaux and Niestlé, 1962), 11–13.

159. Alster, "Paradigmatic Character of Mesopotamian Heroes," 50 (emphasis added).

160. Peter R. Ackroyd, "Foreign Theological Literature Survey: 1975–76: The Old Testament," *Expository Times* 88 (1976–77): 103 (emphasis added).

161. Jean-Louis Ska, "Les découvertes de Tell Mardikh-Ebla et la Bible," *Nouvelle Revue Théologique* 100 (1978): 398.

162. Maurice Wiles, "In What Sense Is Christianity a 'Historical Religion'?" *Theology* 81 (January 1978): 13.

163. Jon Sobrino, "The Historical Jesus and the Christ of Faith: The Tension between Faith and Religion," *Cross Currents* 27 (1978): 460.

164. Herbert Werner, *Abraham der Erstling und Repräsentant Israels* (Göttingen: Vandenhoeck and Ruprecht, 1965), 25.

165. Ibid., 28.

166. Ibid., 73–79.

167. Ibid., 87–95.

168. G. Hamming, *Abrahamisme* (Wageningen: Veenman and Zonen, 1967), 7, 13.

169. Ibid., 7.

170. Ibid., 60–63, 97–99.

171. John Van Seters, *Abraham in History and Tradition* (New Haven: Yale University Press, 1975).

172. "Promise of Ebla," 42.

173. Parrot, *Abraham et son temps,* 11.

174. James L. Kelso, "Abraham as Archaeology Knows Him," *Perspective* 13 (Winter 1972): 4–5

175. Hamming, *Abrahamisme,* 7.

176. C. Davey, "The Dwellings of Private Citizens," *Buried History* 13 (1977): 22.

177. William H. Stiebing, "When Was the Age of the Patriarchs?" *BAR* 1 (June 1975): 18.

178. Anderson, "Ebla, the More We Find Out, the Less We Know," 10.

179. Thompson, "New Attempt to Date the Patriarchal Narratives," 78.

180. Hugh W. Nibley, "A New Look at the Pearl of Great Price," *IE* 72 (November 1969): 125.

181. Noel Weeks, "Man, Nuzi and the Patriarchs," *Abr-Nahrain* 16 (1975–76): 80.

182. Kelso, "Abraham as Archaeology Knows Him," 9–11.

183. Robert Martin-Achard, *Actualité d'Abraham* (Neuchatel: Delachaux and Niestlé, 1969), 58.

184. Weeks, "Man, Nuzi and the Patriarchs," 79.

185. Thompson, "New Attempt to Date the Patriarchal Narratives," 76–77.

3

Joseph Smith and the Critics

Tucked away in a highly specialized corner of this highly specialized field are three highly specialized papyri applying with their highly specialized commentary illustrations to a highly specialized account of Abraham in Egypt. The peculiarities of the facsimiles and the explanations that go with them cry for careful specialized investigation. So the question we have to ask here of every member of the Spalding jury is not whether he knows a lot, but whether he is equipped to deal *with this particular problem.* The problem is complicated by emotional religious elements that make it necessary in screening the jury to ask two main questions of each: (1) whether he is equipped by training to give a thorough and definitive interpretation of the plates and texts in the Pearl of Great Price, and (2) whether he is temperamentally qualified to do so.

Five of the scholars consulted by Bishop Spalding for his 1912 publication were among the most learned men who ever lived. Each of them was a giant endowed far beyond the normal run of men with independence of mind, imagination, curiosity, insight, energy, and integrity. Yet as we look them over it appears that each is uniquely *un*qualified to pass judgment on Joseph Smith as a translator, at least on the basis of the information supplied by Spalding.

Figure 18. Archibald Henry Sayce
1845–1933

Let us take them in order of their seniority, labeling them
with the titles Dr. Spalding gives them.

Archibald Henry Sayce

"Dr. A. H. Sayce, Oxford, England," or, more fully, the
Reverend Archibald Henry Sayce (fig. 18), D. Litt., LL.D.,
D.D. (1845–1933). Sayce was born with a phenomenal I.Q.
and plenty of money, and "his attitude to life was that of a
fastidious ascetic," according to his fellow Welshman and
fellow genius F. L. Griffith.[1] Free to do pretty much as he
chose, he was constantly traveling about; he "knew about
every great personality in Europe of the last two generations";[2] and "in the course of his long life he seems to have
seen everything and everybody that was interesting."[3]

At the age of eighteen, according to Stephen H. Langdon, "he proved that he knew Hebrew, Egyptian, Persian

and Sanscrit [*sic*]," and that "he had a firm grasp of the state of cuneiform studies." In time he "had a good knowledge of every Semitic and Indo-European language, and could write good prose in at least twenty languages." And yet this paragon "never became a great specialist in any subject"; he was too volatile, "always moving from place to place. . . . Any subject lost its attraction for him as soon as the period of decipherment was passed."[4] He "left no lasting monument," writes Griffith; "one cannot but feel that his marvellous gifts were out of proportion to his accomplishment."[5] Or, as Langdon puts it, "his real greatness was never revealed in his work."[6] But how is one to measure gifts save by accomplishments or greatness apart from works?

In his younger years Sayce attacked the evolutionists hammer and tong, maintaining that "the whole application of a supposed law of evolution to the religious and secular history of the ancient Oriental world is founded on what we now know to have been a huge mistake."[7] But later in life he became even more vigorous in assailing fundamentalism: "When I was a boy," he recalled shortly before his death, "there were some old-fashioned people who still believed that . . . some of [the books of the Old Testament] were written by Moses himself . . . and we of the younger generation, trained in the critical methods of Germany, were unable to accept the dogma; it rested only on unproved assertions."[8] Of course there is no excuse for that sort of thing any more. "A new era has dawned upon us. The scientific method . . . has . . . furnished us with facts instead of theories."[9] And so he ticks off the well-worn and now discredited clichés of scientism with evangelistic fervor: "An inductive science . . . deals with objective facts and not with . . . tastes and predilections. . . . Like the geologist, the archaeologist has had to leave catastrophic theorizing to the literary amateur";[10] we must forget the idea that "similarities in technique [e.g., of pottery] . . . indicate relationship"—for diffusion is a myth.[11]

He has no patience with historians who want to measure civilization by the thousands of years, for he has proven that "civilized man can not be measured by millennia. . . . Civilized man in the fullest sense of the word is immeasurably old. . . . Archaeology is repeating the lesson of geology and physical science."[12] This is the sort of thing Griffith refers to when he writes, "His vivid imagination and insight framed pictures of events and of interpretation in which he too often mistook the sharp lines of the picture for fact,"[13] and of these "facts" he would brook no criticism for "he was impatient of the claims, the pride, and the reticence of exact scholarship."[14]

Sayce's Egyptological researches are typical of his methods. For a number of years his own Nile boat, the *Ishtar*, might be seen searching out unfrequented spots along the banks of the great river, where he would discover new ruins and inscriptions, only to leave them behind for others to study.[15] It is significant that of the many inscriptions he discovered and copied down, he is always careful to translate the Greek and Latin ones in full (though most of his readers could read Greek and Latin well enough for themselves), while he never attempts to translate any of the Egyptian inscriptions.[16] Why not? "His *métier* was that of a decipherer of any thing new," wrote Langdon, explaining that he lost interest as soon as the code was cracked.[17] But surely the deciphering of Egyptian was far newer and more challenging in the 1890s than the reading of Greek and Latin. In the same way, Sayce, though criticizing Joseph Smith more severely than any other member of the big five, is the only one of them to preserve complete silence regarding the facsimiles. Sayce's specialty was Assyriology, not Egyptology, and while in the former field, according to H. R.

Hall, "the Professor must be judged by his peers," his speculations in Egyptology "do not carry much conviction."[18]

There is another side to this remarkable man that we must not overlook, for though Dr. Sayce was greatly annoyed by people who took the Bible literally, he remained always a churchman and fiercely loyal to his church. "Attached by generations of his heritage to the ancient traditions of the Church of England," to follow Langdon, "Sayce regarded all learning which did not apply to the culture of his people and his Church as useless."[19] His native language was Welsh.

Now just how well does this man qualify to pass impartial judgment on Joseph Smith as a translator? By temperament he is the fastidious aristocrat moving in exalted circles, disdaining the vulgar; above all he is the austere, uncompromising churchman—how would he judge the efforts of an uneducated rustic from the American frontier? By training he is the spoiled dilettante to whom everything came easy, impatient of criticism, opinionated, and dogmatic in his own views. It is a toss-up as to which A. H. Sayce would be more intellectually hostile to Smith: the early clerical Sayce who "regarded as useless" all learning that did not support his church, or the scientific Sayce, invincibly opposed to supernaturalism. The two meet and mingle in the Sayce of 1912, who dismisses the Book of Abraham with eleven contemptuous lines. For all his great learning, I don't think Dr. Sayce rates a place on this particular jury.

W. M. Flinders Petrie

"Dr. W. M. Flinders Petrie, London University" (1853–1942). If it is possible to imagine a man more independent in his way and self-contained in his thinking than A. H. Sayce, that man must be Dr. Petrie (fig. 19). We can illustrate this by a story told by Professor Georg Steindorff to a small group

Figure 19. William Matthew Flinders Petrie
1853–1942

that met to celebrate Steindorff's eightieth birthday in 1942.
Petrie came down to meet the Nile boat one hot evening in
1894 as the young Steindorff disembarked at the scene of
Petrie's operations in upper Egypt. The great man conducted
his guests to his tent for dinner, which was to consist of an
enormous, heaping bowl of rice, completely covered with a
mantle of blue-bottle flies. Professor Petrie in his hearty
manner invited the party to fall to, but when some of them
hesitated he reached for a box of Keating's Insect Powder
and showered its contents liberally over both flies and rice,
saying as he did so, "I've found that it kills them—but it
doesn't kill me!" Such a man was not to be deterred from his
course by the opinions of others. Petrie's strength was his
weakness—his complete independence of mind made it possible for him to make real discoveries where the timid would
never have ventured, but at the same time it blinded him to

the valid objections that others might have to his theories and interpretations.

An only child, Petrie never went to school—he was from the first self-educated and self-directed; "he was incapable of teamwork," writes his biographer Guy Brunton—"Petrie seems to have felt no need of companionship; nor was he very sympathetic to the ideas of others."[20] With a somewhat limited "outlook on life in general," he boasted that he had never been to a theater.[21] Though he was the greatest practitioner of scientific archaeology in modern times, "even when visited by those having great experience in archaeology he preferred to talk rather than to listen";[22] and though archaeology was his life, "he never visited the excavations of others."[23] With his own work "there must be no interference or deviation," and "having once arrived at a conclusion, he was extremely averse to modifying it in any way."[24] So as time went on, "Petrie's views on all manner of subjects . . . crystallized into stated facts" from which he was not to be moved.[25]

This intransigence was abetted, if not actually caused, by the nature of Petrie's education, which in turn was determined by his complete inability to learn languages. At a tender age, he had a tutor to teach him "French, Latin, and Greek grammar, for which he had," according to Brunton, "no aptitude whatever. A breakdown resulted, and for two years he was left to his own devices." Then they tried again—"fresh attempts were made with the grammars, but it was found to be hopeless."[26] So he became his own teacher and did the things he was really good at: "Essentially a practical fieldworker of great ability, he made contributions of the highest value, but had no flair for research in epigraphy. He was prone to base his theories on inadequate premises."[27] He expressed his settled opinions on religion shortly before Spalding appealed to him, in a book in which he declares that any feeling of a need for repentance is the index of a "morbid mind,"[28] and that "the last branch of unbalanced Religious experience is that of Hallucinations," which "enter so much into the scope of mental disease that it is useless to begin upon the detail of so far-spreading a subject."[29]

So here we have another spoiled only child, a law unto himself (no need for *him* to repent!) reaping the rich rewards of independent thinking (and how we could use a little of that type of thinking in our own society!), but paying a high price for the luxury of always having his own way. Not a linguist by any means, he is hardly the man to call in for a study of all but illegible documents; and, utterly averse to any hint of the supernatural in religion, he is even less likely than Sayce to give Joseph Smith a fair hearing; then too, quite aside from his one-sided training and religious prejudice, would the man who had not the patience or courtesy to listen to the opinions of his most eminent colleagues or to visit their excavations take time off to give careful attention to the 80-year-old writings of a young farmer from New York? Indeed, while Petrie confirms statements of the Book of Abraham in a surprising number of instances, he would be the last man on earth to recognize the fact, and all Spalding got from him on the subject was a terse offhand opinion (fig. 20). What else could he expect? I think we should excuse Dr. Petrie from serving on this particular jury.

Eduard Meyer

"Dr. Edward Meyer, University of Berlin" (fig. 21). Eduard (Spalding misspelled the name) Meyer (1855–1930) knew more about the whole field of ancient history than any other man who ever lived. He was the greatest scholar since Scaliger, and it would be hard to think of some way in which his learning might have been more extensive than it was, or more productive—though he himself declared at the end of his life that his generation of scholarship has

Figure 20. Petrie had the rare good fortune to find these three unusual bronze hypocephali in situ in the Djed-hor family tomb at Abydos. He referred to them in his note to Spalding, but when he published them in 1902 he dismissed their inscriptions as "hopelessly confused," saying it would "be very undesirable to offer even a conditional translation." However, they are quite legible and assist us in understanding the texts found on other hypocephali of this type.

erred sorely in trying to be so everlastingly "scientific" about everything instead of trusting more to their intuition and instincts. Because of his whole-hearted and single-minded dedication to the documents of the past which from childhood he was determined to search thoroughly and

Figure 21. Eduard Meyer
1855–1930

systematically, Meyer's judgments often seemed to smack
of almost prophetic insight.[30] His mistakes, wrote Walter
Otto, were often more valuable than other men's facts;[31]
he laid the firm foundations of Egyptian chronology, vindicated the historicity of the Old Testament against Wellhausen and his school, was rivaled only by Breasted in his
contributions to Egyptian history, exploded the evolution-
ary theory of economic development, first showed the
importance of Iran in Jewish and Christian tradition, anticipated the Dead Sea Scrolls in discerning the important role
played by the desert sectaries in early Christian and Jewish
history, opened up the world of the Hittites, gave the world
the first real picture of ancient Greece, and was the last
human being to find himself in a position of being able to
write a general history of antiquity from the sources of his
own learning. Like the other members of the panel, he was

largely self-taught and always went his own way, a pioneer wherever he went; but unlike the others, he had a healthy sense of his own limitations and freely admitted his mistakes and changed his views when the evidence required it.[32]

Also, Meyer had his blind spots. He could not understand art, according to his biographer; he lacked any aesthetic sense; he was impatient and usually in a hurry, so that he often brushed aside or overlooked real problems, e.g., his history of the United States "is hasty, biased, superficial and inaccurate."[33] When the United States declared war on Germany in 1917, Meyer, it is said, ran down the street Unter den Linden with hair flying, declaiming wildly, and tearing his honorary Harvard diploma to shreds.

Still, if any scholar was competent to pass judgment on Joseph Smith, it should have been Meyer. An indication of his peculiar independence and deep insight is seen in the fact that he always regarded Mormonism as a phenomenon of enormous importance in the history of religions. Professor Werner Jaeger recalled that the only time Meyer was able to fill his lecture hall in Berlin was when he talked on the Mormons—then the place was packed, because then Meyer became alive as never before. Meyer, according to Walter Otto, "was the first secular historian ever to tackle the problem of the origin of Christianity—the central-problem of World History," and in Mormonism he saw the best guide.[34] He was convinced that "Mormonism . . . is not just another of countless sects, but a new revealed religion. What in the study of other revealed religions can only be surmised after painful research is here directly accessible in reliable witnesses. Hence the origin and history of Mormonism possesses great and unusual value for the student of religious history."[35]

He had visited Utah in 1904, and a year before Spalding's book appeared, he had published his *Ursprung und*

Geschichte der Mormonen. In that book Meyer had made it perfectly clear just what he thought about Joseph Smith, whom he regarded as a prophet in exactly the same sense in which Isaiah, Jeremiah, and (to a lesser degree) Mohammed were prophets. He was free to run the risk of paying such high tribute to the Mormon prophet because everyone knew that he did not for a moment believe that there ever was such a thing as a *true* prophet; in keeping with the lofty scholarship of his day, Meyer disdained to grant the smallest measure of probability to any proposition tainted with the supernatural. That, as Otto points out, is what spoiled what should have been his greatest work, that on the *Origins of Christianity,* in which "everything in the person of Christ must be explained on rationalistic grounds. He never allowed for the irrational element in the human character."[36] So it is no compliment to Joseph Smith for Meyer to place him among the real prophets, for Meyer begins from the premise that all prophets are self-deluded. Granted that premise, there is only one position, of course, that one can possibly take regarding Joseph Smith's claims to divine revelation and only one view that anyone can possibly take of his teachings in the Book of Abraham.

So Bishop Spalding was appealing to a judge who had already declared against any form of supernaturalism. Eduard Meyer, the great man that he was, was also a judge on whom Spalding could count with absolute trust to give only one answer to his question about the Book of Abraham. By stating with great emphasis and clarity his views on religion in general and Joseph Smith in particular, in effect he disqualifies himself for the jury.

James H. Breasted

"James H. Breasted, Ph.D., Haskell Oriental Museum, University of Chicago" (fig. 22). Professor Breasted (1865–1935) had his full share of those qualities which we have

Figure 22. James Henry Breasted
1865–1935

found to be most conspicuous in the three giants noticed so far: independence of action and judgment, boundless self-confidence, and equally boundless energy and exuberance. We have already seen how Professor Mercer chides his master for getting carried away too much. Breasted's training and temperament go together. He was trained in a school that knew all the answers—the Prussian school of the 1890s, which bolstered the individual's sublime confidence in himself as one who shared the corporate omniscience of the establishment. He was, a German reports, "most intimately tied to the German school of Egyptology from his first scientific beginnings,"[37] as "the dear, hearty comrade" of the German Egyptologists. His friend Eduard Meyer inspired him to take wide views, which in turn inclined him to make wide and sweeping pronouncements that disturbed some of his colleagues,[38] some of whom point out that he was

much too prone to generalize and "often interpreted evidence wrongly to suit his purposes."[39]

The French Egyptologists sometimes felt that Breasted
underestimated their work and so criticized him quite freely,
accusing him of being pro-German to the point of slighting
and even insulting French Egyptology, while putting forth
his own theories as settled facts and completely ignoring
any theories and even evidence that did not appeal to him.[40]
George Foucart comes right out and accuses Breasted of
being opinionated and unfair, noting that "in treating the
contradictions of his predecessors without charity [indul-
gence] Breasted makes himself vulnerable to the same treatment in the future."[41] In this Foucart was a true prophet, for
time has not been too kind to Professor Breasted's favorite
theories. As Professor Jéquier and Foucart see it, Dr. Breasted
with sublime self-confidence goes his way "bestowing his
criticism or approval freely on all sides," presenting his own
opinions as historical facts and his private reconstructions as
original texts,[42] and while his colleagues may find his affir-
mations most unconvincing, the general public is supposed
to accept them as official.[43]

We have ventured to quote such unpleasantries because
we have here exactly the high and authoritarian attitude
taken by Breasted in dealing with the Book of Abraham.
There is no doubt that he could have translated most of the
hieroglyphs if he had given himself the trouble, but, though
he professed himself most interested in the problem, he
never did. Why should he? He knew the answers already.
Like every other American professor in 1912, he belonged
to that school which firmly believed that evolution held all
the answers, as Jean Garnot observes, basing their boldest
speculations on implicit faith in the validity of analogies
with biological evolution, sublimely confident that the evo-
lutionary rule of thumb could give the perfect insight into
the mind of the "primitive."[44] Thus he can assure us that

"Set was doubtless some natural phenomenon, . . . and it is most probable that he was the darkness," though no Egyptologist would write that way today.[45] And he can tell us with convincing insight how copper was discovered when primitive man one morning noticed little beads of pure metal that had oozed from the rocks that banked his campfire somewhere in the Sinai Peninsula; it was not until 1945 that the Egyptologist Alfred Lucas called attention to the experiments of H. H. Coghlan, showing that it is quite impossible to smelt copper in any open fire.[46]

Breasted's main argument against the Book of Abraham is that the Hebrews were monotheists and the Egyptians polytheists: both points have always been disputed among Egyptologists, some of the greatest being ardent defenders of a standard Egyptian monotheism, yet for Breasted the question is settled once he has spoken. When the Mormons pointed out that Breasted had identified as the lady Isis in Facsimile 1 a figure that other Egyptologists had called Horus, Anubis, or a priest, Dr. Breasted impatiently remarked to Mercer: "One man says fifty cents, another man says half a dollar!" But it isn't the same at all; Isis and Horus are as different quantities as half a dollar and half a pound.

In our fatal year of 1912 Breasted completely misinterpreted many passages in the Egyptian wisdom literature, discovering among other things in them a "complaisant optimism" in a text that, Frankfort insists years later, "indicates no such thing, but represents, on the contrary, the deep religious conviction which inspired the 'teachings.'"[47] Errors due to the imperfect state of the evidence at one time are, of course, excusable—but they are nonetheless errors. Thus, of the great *Ancient Records* series, Alexander Scharff wrote in 1935, "Today we read many passages differently and more correctly."[48] "Unhappily," wrote Sir Alan Gardiner in 1961, "in Breasted's day our knowledge of Late-Egyptian syntax was not sufficiently advanced to enable him to

Figure 23. Friedrich Wilhelm Freiherr von Bissing
1873–1956

translate the damaged introduction of the Turin papyrus correctly."[49] So as knowledge increases, the verdict of yesterday must be reversed today, and in the long run the most positive authority is the least to be trusted. Few have been more positive than Breasted, and in nothing was he more positive than in his attitude toward Joseph Smith's pronouncements.

Friedrich Freiherr von Bissing

"Dr. Friedrich Freiherr von Bissing, Professor of Egyptology in the University of Munich" (fig. 23). Incredible as it may seem, there was one man in the world who actually surpassed Sayce, Petrie, Meyer, and Breasted in complete independence of thought and action, and that was von Bissing (1873–1956). Not yet forty years old in 1912, he was richer than all the rest of them put together; already hailed as "the generous Maecenas of Egyptology," von Bissing was rich enough not only to visit important excavations in Egypt when he chose, but also to finance them from his own pocket.[50] Even more than the others, he traveled and dug and collected everywhere,[51] "an archaeologist in the broadest sense of the word," recognized as "the last scholar who could see the Mediterranean as a unit, familiar with everything down to the most insignificant potsherd."[52] "For us today," wrote Hellmut Brunner, "it is simply inconceivable how one individual man could speak with equal authority on the etymology of the word 'Pavian,' the painting of el-Amarna, the fundamentals of Byzantine art, the structure of the personal pronouns in early Egyptian, or the exodus from Cnidus."[53]

Von Bissing was proud of being a dilettante, and his numerous writings on all subjects almost all take the form of short notes of a few sentences.[54] Most of them have to do with artistic history and criticism, which was his specialty, and allowed him to range as widely and speculate as freely as he chose.[55] Both rich and noble, "he was an original, stamped from a unique mold, willing to face all consequences without regard to praise or disapproving headshakes. . . . He went the way of his own convictions."[56]

Here, then, we have an incorruptible judge—but was he an unbiased one? Hardly. Whatever his scientific convictions or scholarly integrity, he was a member of the nobility: throne and church always had first and unquestioned claim on his loyalty, and nothing could budge him from his commitment to them.[57] In this he was much like the aristocratic Sayce, his scientific skepticism matched only by his uncompromising loyalty to a feudal society and a feudal religion—hardly the man to look with a kindly eye on the supernaturalism and humble simplicity of a Joseph Smith.[58]

As to von Bissing's technical knowledge, his specialty was ancient art, especially Egyptian art, but even in that,

Foucart maintains, "his conclusions go too far,"[59] and in his archaeological one-sidedness he often shows poor judgment.[60] Not surprisingly, he too often equated the old-fashioned or established view with the sound and safe one, insisting, for example, as late as the 1930s that there were no ties whatever between ancient Egypt and Mesopotamia,[61] and continuing to doubt the existence of the Hittites, whom he always puts in quotation marks. Even his approach to art was an old-fashioned, positivistic one, and he opened his *Systematic Handbook of Egyptian Art* with words that today seem hopelessly narrow: "A history of art must not be a history of culture."[62] For him, in fact, even the glories of Egyptian art were but a preparation for Greek art.[63] Hidebound and opinionated to the point of rudeness, aristocratic and aloof, fiercely loyal to the views and interests of one church, impatient of any disagreement or contradiction—is this the man to give a cool and patient hearing to Joseph Smith? He never offers to tell us what the facsimiles are but is completely satisfied that "every one figure is an absurdity," and that whatever the inscriptions say (though he does not read them), "they cannot say what Smith thought." His verdict is not surprising, but neither is it very convincing.

Second String

With the five giants accounted for, the other members of the team should not detain us long. But first, Théodule Devéria (1831–71, fig. 24) deserves a word of notice because he wrote the first, the longest, and the most carefully considered report on the facsimiles that has appeared to date.[64] Bishop Spalding gives short shrift to Devéria because, as he explains, "unquestionably, this matter is far too important to depend on the opinion of a youthful amateur. Such an important matter deserves the thoughtful consideration of mature scholars—of the world's ablest Orientalists."[65]

Figure 24. Théodule Devéria
1831–71

Youthful? When Devéria wrote his study of the facsimiles he was thirty-four—two years older than Mercer was when he did the same—fully matured and at the height of his powers.

Amateur? At seventeen, urged by the Egyptologist Jules Feuquières, Devéria had plunged into Egyptology while Charles Lenormand gave him Coptic lessons and August Harle, the best Hebraist of his time, pushed him in Hebrew. At nineteen he retranslated an important manuscript formerly rendered by Champollion; at twenty-three he was publishing in Egyptology and in the following year became attached to the Department of Antiquities of the Louvre, where he produced the first complete catalogue ever made of a major Egyptian collection. Still in his twenties, he succeeded the great Auguste Mariette as conservator of the Egyptian museum in the Louvre and, according to de Rougé, produced a work on the Turin Papyrus that "placed Devéria among the masters." It was only the jealousy of his superior at the museum, Mariette, that obscured his great contributions to Egyptology.[66]

Thoughtful consideration? Whereas Devéria wrote a long study, two of Spalding's experts dashed off notes of a hundred words only, and five of them wrote less than a page.

World's ablest Orientalists? Spalding deems four men besides Mercer superior to Devéria, but their combined output in Egyptology could not begin to approach that of the "youthful amateur." We have already considered Dr. Mercer; how about the others?

"Dr. John Peters, University of Pennsylvania. [In charge of expedition to Babylonia, 1888–95]." In 1912 Dr. Peters (1852–1921) was pastor of a church in New York and had not been at the University of Pennsylvania for twenty years (fig. 25). When Spalding's good friend, Professor Pack, discovered that Dr. Peters was not at the University of Pennsylvania as Spalding claimed, he was quite upset and wrote: "For an instant I was paralysed. . . . Could it be possible that Dr. Peters is not connected with the University of Pennsylvania, but is a rector in one of New York's fashionable churches? No. I could not believe it. . . . You had led the public to believe that Dr. Peters is at the University of Pennsylvania."[67] So while he was back East Dr. Pack made a number of visits and inquiries and summed up the results thus: "Now, Dr. Spalding, this looks like plain deceit. Am I mistaken? Why did you lead the public to believe that Dr. Peters is at the University of Pennsylvania when you knew he left there twenty years ago? . . . Why did you hide from the public the fact that Dr. Peters is a rector in your own church and has been for twenty years."[68]

To be sure, being the rector of anything need not prevent one from being also an Egyptologist, but Peters was

Figure 25. John Punnett Peters
1852–1921

never that. He had taught Hebrew at Pennsylvania for eight years, and he wrote popular books on the Bible and modern politics, but his name appears nowhere in connection with Egyptian studies. A career churchman, he had in 1912 just finished serving six years as canon-residentiary of the National Cathedral in Washington, D.C.[69] He is another of those devoted churchmen who, like Sayce and Mercer, combine with the dignity of the cloth an intellectual contempt for the supernatural and an ill-concealed impatience with those who would interpret the Bible too literally. Dr. Peters, in fact, wrote a book showing that the ancient patriarchs were nothing but myths, legendary figures "generously clothed with personal traits by successive generations of narrators" by whom "striking episodes have been introduced into their stories and even romances which have no inherent connection with the original legends."[70] Along with

Figure 26. Arthur Cruttenden Mace
1874–1928

"the racial and legendary elements," the history of Abraham combines "features of a purely romantic character, for which we are to seek no other meaning than the fancy of the story-teller."[71]

With such a view of Bible history, is Dr. Peters the man to give serious attention to the Book of Abraham as history? Peters's ideas reflect the consensus of scholarly opinion in his day, and that of the Spalding jury in particular. At that time the establishment was solidly against the whole concept of the Book of Abraham.

"Dr. Arthur C. Mace, Assistant Curator, Metropolitan Museum of Art, New York, Department of Egyptian Art" (fig. 26). Though he is not mentioned in any of the usual biographical sources nor in W. R. Dawson's *Who Was Who in Egyptology, 1910–1914,* Dr. Mace (1874–1928) had been a student of Petrie and had worked with the Hearst collection in Berkeley before going to the Metropolitan.[72] His chance for immortality came when Howard Carter, overwhelmed with work and expense on the tomb of Tutankhamun, asked for the assistance of a Metropolitan Museum crew who were working close by; Mace at the time was taking Dr. Lythgoe's place in charge of the work, and on instructions from the latter he joined the Carter enterprise and thus had a part in the most sensational archaeological discovery of the century.[73] Dr. Mace was an archaeologist and not a philologist. He assisted in the publication of discoveries by and for the museum, but when he came to inscriptions, even short and easy ones, he turned the work over to others.[74] His one serious attempt to deal with documentary sources, a study called "The Influence of Egyptian on Hebrew Literature" (1922), is described by Raymond Weill as nothing but an inferior rehash of Herrman Gunkel's work of 1909 on the same subject.[75]

"Dr. Albert M. Lythgoe, Head of the Department of Egyptian Art of the Metropolitan Museum" (fig. 27) should be added to the list, since Bishop Spalding intended to consult him instead of Arthur C. Mace, who was his understudy while he was abroad. Like Mace, Dr. Lythgoe (1868–1934) was a museum man and a collector who had been a pupil of Wiedemann at Bonn and assisted Reisner in the field. "His finest achievement," according to his obituary, "was the arrangement of the Egyptian Collection of the Metropolitan Museum of New York."[76] Arranging collections is not the same thing as interpreting abstruse texts, and the long interview with Lythgoe in the *New York Times* reads almost like a burlesque of pompous scholarship: "To make clear just how great a hoax the Mormon prophet perpetrated upon his people," Lythgoe explains to the reporters with magisterial ease exactly how Egyptian symbolism originated and just what Egyptian religion is all about, as he readily identifies solar hymns in the facsimiles

Figure 27. Albert Morten Lythgoe
1868–1934

and twice refers to Facsimile 1 as depicting the sacrifice of
Isaac by Abraham (fig. 28). The whole baffling complex presented "no puzzle to Dr. Lythgoe," though his strange theories of Egyptian religion and his guesses about the facsimiles found no echo even among the other members of the
Spalding panel.[77]

"Dr. George A. Barton." When he was challenged by the
Mormons, Bishop Spalding sought further support from
the learned and got it from Professor Barton (1859–1942),
acknowledged minister of the Society of Friends (orthodox)
1879–1922, deacon 1918, priest 1919, D.D. 1924.[78] In 1912 Dr.
Barton's book, *The Heart of the Christian Message*, had just
gone into its second printing. "Permit me first to say,"
Professor Barton began his contribution to the Spalding
cause, "that, while I have a smattering of Egyptology, I am
not an Egyptologist"[79]—and indeed we have already seen

Figure 28. Beware the wrong museum walls: The *New York Times* reporter in his caption for the hypocephalus at the left took the abbreviation for the British Museum (BM), to mean "Berlin Museum."

what Dr. Mercer thought of Barton as an authority on Egypt.[80] But he *was* a minister, thus bringing to five the number of *non*-Egyptologist ministers sitting in judgment as Egyptologists on Joseph Smith.

Barton believed that the "faker" Joseph Smith merely attempted to imitate Egyptian characters, the result being "untranslatable. . . . As they stand [they] do not faithfully represent any known writing."[81] As to the facsimiles, the experts disagree about them, Mr. Barton explained, because "these pictures were differently interpreted at times by the

Egyptians themselves," and some of the jury "have given the original interpretation of the symbolism, and some, the later Egyptian interpretations."[82] Odd, that that explanation should never have occurred to any of the experts themselves, who might have been very embarrassed had the Mormons chosen to exploit Professor Barton's foolish remarks.

In 1915 the University of Utah brought in Edgar J. Banks, "one of America's most distinguished archaeologists," to put the final seal of authority on the Spalding enterprise.[83] Banks (1866–1941) had already sounded off on the subject in the *Christian Herald* in 1913, and it was duly reported through the pages of the prestigious *Literary Digest* that Dr. Spalding's zeal had forever discredited Mormonism in the eyes of the more intelligent Mormons.[84] Mr. Banks pictured himself in *Who's Who* decidedly in the romantic tradition of Richard Haliburton. He had been U.S. consul in Baghdad in his youth, organized an expedition to excavate Ur, which, however, never got into the field, and claimed to have discovered in 1903 a "white statue of king David, a pre-Babylonian king of 4500 B.C. (oldest statue in the world)."[85] While Spalding was working on his grand design in 1912, the dashing Banks, as he tells us, was climbing Ararat (17,210 feet high—he put that in *Who's Who* too) and crossing the Arabian Desert on a camel (from where to where he does not say).[86]

It is amazing, unless one knows this type of glamor-mongering archaeologist, that Mr. Banks, after months in Salt Lake City as an expert on the subject, could come out with such howlers as that "Smith seems to have obtained the documents from a sea captain,"[87] that it was the Mormon officials themselves who "willingly supplied Bishop Spalding with copies of [the inscriptions]" with the request that he investigate their authenticity,[88] that hypocephali such as Facsimile 2 (of which fewer than fifty were known

Figure 29. Ernest Alfred Thompson Wallis Budge
1857–1934

at the time) existed by the millions: "It has been estimated that something like 20,000,000 of Egyptian mummies have been discovered. . . . Beneath each mummy's head, like a cushion, was a little disk of clay or papyrus, covered with mythological pictures. . . . The disks, found in great numbers, are nearly alike, varying only slightly with the period from which they come."[89] Banks also announced that Joseph Smith had never possessed any papyri at all but only such little plaster disks.[90] Apparently nothing Mr. Banks could say was too absurd to be swallowed by the open-mouthed scholars on the Bench as long as the magic words *science* and *progress* were evoked with ritual regularity.[91]

We should not leave our experts without a word about Sir E. A. Wallis Budge (1857–1934, fig. 29), who in 1903 had agreed with his colleague Woodward at the British Museum in declaring the Prophet's interpretation "bosh," "rubbish."[92] This was a demonstration of Budge's "ferocious bark, which could turn to biting if need be."[93] Others could bark back, however, and when Budge gave the Englishman Thomas Young priority over Champollion in the translation of Egyptian, an eminent French Egyptologist quoted Peter Renouf: "No person who knows anything of Egyptian philology can countenance so gross an error."[94] Jean Capart noted that the highest praise of Budge must also be his severest criticism—the phenomenal productivity for which he paid too high a price.[95] Animated by the laudable objective of providing as many texts as possible for students and as many translations as possible for the public, Budge dashed off the longest list of publications in the entire scope of *Who's Who*.[96] To do this he followed no plan, paid no attention to the work of others, never indicated his sources; according to Capart, his interpretation of figures is extremely defective, "and his translations are full of completely erroneous ideas."[97] "I can categorically declare," wrote the same critic, of Budge's *Gods of the Egyptians*, "that it is bad."[98] As R. Campbell Thompson observed, Professor Budge was always "in too great a hurry to finish."[99] Will anyone maintain that he was not in a hurry, his old impulsive blustering self, when he offhandedly condemned the interpretations of the facsimiles?

Consider for a moment the scope and complexity of the materials with which the student *must* cope if he would undertake a serious study of the Book of Abraham's authenticity. At the very least he must be thoroughly familiar with (1) the texts of the "Joseph Smith Papyri" identified as belonging to the Book of the Dead, (2) the content and nature of the mysterious "Sen-sen" fragment, (3) the so-called "Egyptian Alphabet and Grammar" attributed to Joseph Smith, (4) statements by and about Joseph Smith concerning the nature of the Book of Abraham and its origin, (5) the original document of Facsimile 1 with its accompanying hieroglyphic inscriptions, (6) the text of the Book of Abraham itself in its various editions, (7) the three facsimiles as reproduced in various editions of the Pearl of Great Price, (8) Joseph Smith's explanation of the facsimiles, (9) the large and growing literature of ancient traditions and legends about Abraham in Hebrew, Aramaic, Arabic, Greek, Slavonic, etc., and (10) the studies and opinions of modern scholars on all aspects of the Book of Abraham.

There are two propositions regarding the Book of Abraham that none can deny. The one is that Joseph Smith could not possibly have known Egyptian as it is understood today. The other is that the Prophet has put down some remarkable things in the pages of the Book of Abraham. Why should we waste time on proposition number 1? It is proposition 2 that provides us at last with firm ground to stand on—and none of the critics has ever given it a moment's thought!

What Joseph Smith tells us about Abraham in the book attributed to him can now be checked against a large corpus of ancient writings, unavailable to Joseph Smith, to which we shall often refer in the pages that follow. He has also given us, independent of any translated text, his interpretations of the three facsimiles. It is to these that we now address ourselves.

A hundred years ago Naville and Maspero agreed that "a philologically easily understood sentence, the words and grammar of which give us not the slightest difficulty," often conveys ideas that completely escape all the experts, these being also the ideas behind the pictures.[100] And today Professor Wilson and Anthes would concur in the same view. The latter calls attention to our "helplessness in the face of these mythological records," both "texts and pictures,"[101] while Dr. John A. Wilson suggests the amusing analogy of an Eskimo who had never heard of the Bible trying to make sense of the old hymn "Jerusalem the Golden."

The Mormons were not slow in calling attention to this fatal limitation to the understanding of the facsimiles: "I repeat," wrote Dr. John A. Widtsoe, "that something more must be done than to label a few of the figures Osiris, Isis or Anubis before Joseph Smith can be placed in 'the same class of fakers as Dr. Cook.'"[102] The mere names tell us nothing unless we can also tell "who and what were Isis and Horus and all the other gods of Egypt? Not by name and relationship, but as expressing the Egyptian's vision of the known and the unknown, the past, the present and the hereafter?"[103] Sjodahl and Webb asked similar questions, but the Mormons were ignored because they were not Egyptologists. Yet, shortly before, Georg Steindorff had written: "We know relatively little about Egyptian religion in spite of the abundance of pictures and religious texts of ancient Egypt which have come down to us. We know, it is true, the names and the appearances of a large number of divinities, we know in which sanctuaries they were honored, but until now we have but few notions about their nature, and the significance which the people and the priests gave to them and the legends attached to their persons."[104] And Jaroslav Černý can still write: "For the Old and Middle Kingdom there are hardly more than proper names to give us a glimpse into the beliefs of the common people and their relationship with the gods,"[105] while Jéquier points out that the "shocking contradictions" in the interpretation of religious imagery "show us that we have not yet found the truth."[106] There is nothing for it, says Jéquier, but for each scholar to continue on his way, "each interpreting in his own manner and according to his means . . . and so gradually penetrate the mystery of the Egyptian religions."[107] These were the very points that the Mormons were trying to make and that the opposition, determined at any price to give the impression of great and definitive knowledge, quietly ignored.

Notes

1. F. L. Griffith, "Archibald Henry Sayce," *JEA* 19 (1934): 66.

2. Thus Stephen H. Langdon, "Archibald Henry Sayce," *Archiv für Orientforschung* 8 (1932): 342.

3. Griffith, "Archibald Henry Sayce," 65.

4. Langdon, "Archibald Henry Sayce," 341.

5. Griffith, "Archibald Henry Sayce," 66, 65.

6. Langdon, "Archibald Henry Sayce," 341.

7. A. H. Sayce, *Monument Facts and Higher Critical Fancies* (New York: Revell, 1904), 118.

8. A. H. Sayce, "The Antiquity of Civilized Man," *Smithsonian Report* (1931): 518–19.

9. Ibid., 518.

10. Ibid., 529.

11. Ibid., 528.

12. Ibid., 517, 520.

13. Griffith, "Archibald Henry Sayce," 65.

14. Ibid., 66.

15. "Nécrologie," *CdE* 9 (1933): 283.

16. The one exception is an inscription from Aswan of only six characters, of which Sayce writes, "The inscription on the left reads, I think, 'Beloved of Khnum the Great, the Lord of the country of Râ-nefer.' . . . In the inscription on the right the island of Senem appears to be mentioned." The inscription on the right was much the longer one, yet no attempt is made to translate it. A. H. Sayce, "Gleanings from the Land of Egypt, § IV," *RT* 15 (1893): 147. See Greek inscription, "This I venture to translate," in ibid., 148. Cf. A. H. Sayce, "Gleanings from the Land of Egypt, § V" *RT* 16 (1894): 167–76; Sayce, "Gleanings from the Land of Egypt, § VI" *RT* 17 (1895): 160–64; Sayce, "Gleanings from the Land of Egypt, § X–XII," *RT* 20 (1898): 169–76; Sayce, "Gleanings from the Land of Egypt, § I and III," *RT* 13 (1890): 62–67, 187–91.

17. Langdon, "Archibald Henry Sayce," 341.

18. H. R. Hall, review of *The Religion of Ancient Egypt*, by A. H. Sayce, *JEA* 1 (1915): 77.

19. Langdon, "Archibald Henry Sayce," 341–42.

20. Guy Brunton, "William Matthew Flinders Petrie," *ASAE* 43 (1943): 4.

21. Ibid., 5.

22. Ibid., 4–5.

23. Ibid., 13.

24. Ibid., 5.

25. Ibid., 13.

26. Ibid., 4.

27. *Encyclopaedia Britannica*, 14th ed., s.v. "Petrie, Sir (William Matthew) Flinders."

28. W. M. Flinders Petrie, *Personal Religion in Egypt before Christianity* (New York: Harper, 1909), 22.

29. Ibid., 37.

30. His education is described by Walter Otto, "Eduard Meyer und sein Werk," *Zeitschrift der deutschen morgenländischen Gesellschaft* 85 (1931): 6; his unique aptitude and personality in ibid., 1–3.

31. Ibid., 8.

32. Some of Meyer's accomplishments are listed in ibid., 11–22.

33. Ibid., 5, 6 n. 2.

34. Otto, "Eduard Meyer und sein Werk," 20.

35. Eduard Meyer, *Ursprung und Geschichte der Mormonen* (Halle: Niemeyer, 1912), 1.

36. Otto, "Eduard Meyer und sein Werk," 21.

37. Editorial, *ZÄS* 72 (1936): flyleaf.

38. Ibid., (ii), and Gustave Jéquier, review of *Development of Religion and Thought in Ancient Egypt*, by James H. Breasted, *Sphinx* 17 (1913): 148–49.

39. Hans Bonnet compares Breasted to Kees, in review of *Totenglauben und Jenseitsvorstellungen der alten Ägypter*, by Hermann Kees, *Zeitschrift der deutschen morgenländischen Gesellschaft* 81 (1927): 179, 183; see also Jéquier, review of *Development of Religion and Thought*, 148–50.

40. See Jéquier, review of *Development of Religion and Thought*, 149; and George Foucart, review of *Ancient Records of Egypt*, by James H. Breasted, *Sphinx* 11 (1908): 40–42, who is particularly outspoken.

41. Foucart, review of *Ancient Records of Egypt*, 42.

42. Ibid.; Jéquier, review of *Development of Religion and Thought*, 148–49.

43. Foucart, review of *Ancient Records of Egypt*, 42; Jéquier, review of *Development of Religion and Thought*, 148–49.

44. Jean S. F. Garnot, *La vie religieuse dans l'ancienne Égypte* (Paris: Presses universitaires, 1948), 107–9.

45. James H. Breasted, *Development of Religion and Thought in Ancient Egypt* (London: Hodder & Stoughton, 1912), 40.

46. Alfred Lucas, "The Origin of Early Copper," *JEA* 31 (1945): 96–97.

47. Henri Frankfort, *Ancient Egyptian Religion* (New York: Columbia University Press, 1948), 64.

48. Alexander Scharff, "Nekrologe," *Jahrbuch der bayerischen Akademie der Wissenschaft* 6 (1935–36): 1–2.

49. Alan H. Gardiner, *Egypt of the Pharaohs* (Oxford: Clarendon, 1961), 291.

50. Thadée Smoleński, "O dzisiejszym stanie badań egiptologicznych (État actuel des recherches égyptologiques)," *Bulletin international de l'Académie des Sciences de Cracovie* 6–7 (1906): 77.

51. Hellmut Brunner, "Friedrich Wilhelm Freiherr von Bissing," *Archiv für Orientforschung* 17 (1955): 484.

52. Ibid., 485.

53. Ibid.

54. For a complete bibliography of his writings, see "Friedrich Wilhelm von Bissing: Verzeichnis seiner Schriften (1895–1956)," comp. Ingrid Wallert, in *ZÄS* 84 (1959): 1–16; and "Verzeichnis der Verfasser und ihrer Arbeiten: Bissing, F. W. V.," in a listing of authors and their contributions during the first one hundred years of the *Zeitschrift für Ägyptische Sprache und Altertumskunde*, in *ZÄS* 89 (1964): 3–4.

55. The vast range of his studies on art is discussed in "Grußwort an Friedrich Wilhelm Freiherrn von Bissing zum 22. April 1953," *ZÄS* 79 (1954): 1.

56. Brunner, "Friedrich Wilhelm Freiherr von Bissing," 485.

57. Ibid. In 1922 von Bissing became a voluntary exile for political reasons, in ibid., 484.

58. On his skepticism, see ibid., 485.

59. George Foucart, review of *Denkmäler ägyptischer Sculptur Lieferung 3*, by Fr. W. Freiherr von Bissing, *Sphinx* 11 (1908): 89.

60. Ibid., 93–94.

61. Friedrich W. von Bissing, "Probleme der ägyptischen Vorgeschichte," *Archiv für Orientforschung* 7 (1931–32): 24–30.

62. Herbert Senk, "Ägyptische Kunstgeschichte, zur Problematik ihrer Erforschung," *Orientalische Literaturzeitung* 58 (1963): 6.

63. Ibid., 7.

64. Théodule Devéria, "Fragments de manuscrits funéraires égyptiens considérés par les Mormons comme les mémoires autographes d'Abraham," *BE* 4 (1896): 195–202; see also Théodule Devéria, "Spécimen de l'interprétation des écritures de l'ancienne Égypte," *BE* 4 (1896): 165–93.

65. Franklin S. Spalding, *Joseph Smith, Jr., as a Translator* (1912; reprint, Salt Lake City: Modern Microfilm, 1965), 19.

66. All this from the biography by his brother, Gabriel Devéria, "Notice Biographique de Théodule Devéria (1831–1871)," *BE* 4 (1896): i–xlviii.

67. Franklin S. Spalding quoted in Frederick J. Pack, "An Open Question to Dr. Spalding," *IE* 16 (1913): 703–4.

68. Ibid., 704.

69. Albert N. Marquis, ed., *Who's Who in America* (Chicago: Marquis, 1912), 1648.

70. John P. Peters, *Early Hebrew Story: Its Historical Background* (New York: Putnam's Sons, 1904), 129.

71. Ibid.

72. Mace's work on mummy bandages while with the Hearst Egyptological expedition of the University of California is noted by G. Elliot Smith, "An Account of the Mummy of a Priestess of Amen Supposed to Be Ta-Usert-Em-Suten-Pa," *ASAE* 7 (1906): 157.

73. Howard Carter and Arthur C. Mace, *The Tomb of Tut-ankh-Amen*, 3 vols. (New York: Doran, 1923), 1:156–58.

74. Arthur C. Mace and Herbert E. Winlock, *The Tomb of Senebtisi at Lisht* (New York: Gilliss, 1916), 35 n. 1: "The greater part of these translations is due to the kindness of Dr. Alan H. Gardiner." Since the only inscriptions in the tomb were very short and easy ones, one wonders why Dr. Gardiner was needed to translate "the greater part" of them, and how much would be left to the genius of Dr. Mace. So also Carter and Mace, *Tomb of Tut-ankh-Amen*, 1:109: "Dr. Alan Gardiner kindly undertook to deal with any inscriptional material that might be found."

75. Raymond Weill, "Les transmissions littéraires d'Égypte à Israël," *Cahier complémentaire à la Revue d'Égyptologie* (1950): 48.

76. Obituary of Albert M. Lythgoe in *JEA* 20 (1934): 107.

77. Editorial, "Museum Walls Proclaim Fraud of Mormon Prophet," *New York Times*, 29 December 1912, pt. 5:1.

78. Albert N. Marquis, ed., *Who's Who in America (1924–25)* (Chicago: Marquis, 1924), 331.

79. George A. Barton, quoted in Franklin S. Spalding, "Rev. Spalding's Answer to Dr. Widtsoe," *IE* 16 (1913): 613.

80. Hugh W. Nibley, "A New Look at the Pearl of Great Price," *IE* 71 (May 1968): 57; reprinted in this volume, pp. 99–100.

81. Barton, quoted in Spalding, "Rev. Spalding's Answer to Dr. Widtsoe," 614.

82. Ibid.

83. Quotation is from a *Christian Herald* article citing Edgar J. Banks in "The Revolt of Young Mormonism," *Literary Digest* 51 (10 July 1915): 67, where Banks is also quoted: "Lately I have been delivering a series of lectures under the auspices of one of the departments of the University of Utah."

84. Ibid., 66: "The knowledge of such facts is working like a leaven.

... The Board of Regents of the University of Utah, avers Professor Banks, is 'predominantly Mormon' and 'making desperate efforts to check the growth of progress.'"

85. Marquis, ed., *Who's Who in America (1924–25)*, 303.

86. Ibid., 303–4.

87. Banks, cited in "The Revolt of Young Mormonism," 66.

88. Ibid.

89. Edgar J. Banks, cited in Sterling B. Talmage, "Letter and a 'Protest against Misrepresentation,'" *IE* 16 (1913): 774.

90. "The inscriptions are not upon papyrus, but upon small clay objects," in Banks, cited in "The Revolt of Young Mormonism," 66.

91. See his sanguine remarks quoted in Talmage, "A Letter and a 'Protest against Misrepresentation,'" 774–75. "At the close of one of the lectures a bright young Mormon student accompanied me to the club where I was stopping. He asked about Joseph Smith's translation of the Egyptian inscriptions, for he remembered the discussion of two years ago. He is now a Mormon only in name. A Mormon gentleman . . . showed me about the Temple grounds. He was ashamed of his religion . . . and he represents the younger generation of the Mormons." Banks, cited in "The Revolt of Young Mormonism," 67.

92. Reported in Junius F. Wells, "Scholars Disagree," *IE* 16 (1913): 342, reprinted from Junius F. Wells, "Letter to the Editor," *Deseret Evening News*, 19 December 1912, 4.

93. R. Campbell Thompson, "Ernest Alfred Wallis Budge" *JEA* 21 (1935): 69.

94. Ernst Andersson, review of *A Guide to the Egyptian Collections in the British Museum*, by E. A. Wallis Budge, *Sphinx* 12 (1909): 237.

95. Jean Capart, *Bulletin critique des religions de l'Égypte* (Leiden: Brill, 1939), 25.

96. Thompson, "Ernest Alfred Wallis Budge," 69.

97. Capart, *Bulletin critique des religions de l'Égypte*, 28.

98. Ibid., 25.

99. Thompson, "Ernest Alfred Wallis Budge," 68–69, noting that Budge "early relinquished" the writing of articles and turned out instead about 120 Oriental books. His work "undeniably does show this haste."

100. Édouard H. Naville, *Das aegyptische Todtenbuch der XVIII. bis XX. Dynastie, Einleitung* (Berlin: Asher, 1886), 2; Gaston Maspero, "Stèles funéraires de la XIIe Dynastie," *BE* 1 (1893): 22.

101. Rudolph Anthes, review of *The Shrines of Tut-Ankh-Amon*, by Alexandre Piankoff, *Artibus Asiae* 20 (1957): 92.

102. John A. Widtsoe, "Dr. Widtsoe's Reply to Rev. Spalding," *IE* 16 (1913): 618.

103. John A. Widtsoe, "Comments on the Spalding Pamphlet," *IE* 16 (1913): 457.

104. Georg Steindorff, "Religion of the Ancient Egyptians," in Karl Baedeker, *Egypt and the Sudan: Handbook for Travelers*, 6th ed. (Leipzig: Baedeker, 1908), cxii–cxxvi.

105. Jaroslav Černý, *Ancient Egyptian Religion* (London: Hutchinson's University Library, 1952), 54.

106. Gustave Jéquier, *Considérations sur les religions Égyptiennes* (Neuchatel: Baconniere, 1946), 7.

107. Ibid., 8.

4

Setting the Stage—
The World of Abraham

Hard Times Come Again

One of the main objections of the higher critics to the patriarchal stories as history was that they were altogether too idyllic in their peaceful pastoral setting, which belonged to the bucolic poets rather than to the stern realities of life. But as Professor Albright now reminds us, the calm pastoral life of the patriarchs has turned out to be a myth.[1] And the myth was invented by the scholars, for neither the Bible nor the Apocrypha gives it the least countenance: the world of Abraham that they describe was little short of an earthly hell. Furthermore, the peculiar nature of those terrible times as described in the written sources is in such close agreement with what is turning up in the excavations that it becomes possible to assign to Abraham a very real role and, possibly within a short time, a definite date, in history.

In reconstructing the world of Abraham, it is customary procedure first to determine an approximate date for the hero and then to look for things in the history of that period

"Setting the Stage—The World of Abraham" originally appeared in the series "A New Look at the Pearl of Great Price," IE 72 (October 1969): 89–95 and IE 72 (November 1969): 36–44.

which fit into his career. But since the world of Abraham has already been described for us in the traditional sources, we are going to reverse the process and withhold any attempt at dating until we have the clearest possible picture of what was going on; then, given enough details and particulars, the dating should pretty well take care of itself. What justifies such a course is the remarkable clarity and consistency of the accounts of the Bible and the ancient commentators when they describe the physical world of Abraham, the state of society, Abraham's reactions to the challenges that met him, and the wonderful body of covenants and ordinances that he handed on to us. Let us consider each of these briefly in order.

Each of the great dispensations of the gospel has come in a time of world upheaval, when the waywardness of the human race has been matched by a climactic restlessness of the elements. When Adam was cast out of the Garden of Eden, he found himself, we are told, in "a sultry land of darkness" where he was lost and confused,[2] where temporary survival was a matter of toil and sweat amidst the all-conquering dust—"for dust thou art, and unto dust shalt thou return" (cf. Genesis 3:17–19). Worse still, Satan was on hand to add to his burdens, deride his efforts, and make fearful inroads into the integrity of his progeny. Who but our first parents could have sustained the appalling "birth-shock" of sudden precipitation from one world to another, from the presence of God to thorns, thistles, and dust?[3]

If we fancy Noah riding the sunny seas high, dry, and snug in the ark, we have not read the record—the long, hopeless struggle against entrenched mass resistance to his preaching, the deepening gloom and desperation of the years leading up to the final debacle, then the unleashed forces of nature with the family absolutely terrified, weeping and praying "because they were at the gates of death," as the ark was thrown about with the greatest violence by

terrible winds and titanic seas.[4] Albright's suggestion that
the flood story goes back to "the tremendous floods which
must have accompanied successive retreats of the glaciers"[5]
is supported by the tradition that the family suffered terribly because of the cold, and that Noah on the waters
"coughed blood on account of the cold."[6] The Jaredites had
only to pass through the tail end of the vast storm cycle of
Noah's day, yet for 344 days they had to cope with "mountain waves" and a wind that "did never cease to blow"
(Ether 6:6, 8). Finally Noah went forth into a world of utter
desolation, as Adam did, to build his altar, call upon God,
and try to make a go of it all over again, only to see some of
his progeny on short order prefer Satan to God and lose all
the rewards that his toil and sufferings had put in their
reach.

All of Moses' life was toil and danger, the real, intimate,
ever-present danger such as only the Near East can sustain
at a high level for indefinite periods of time. No one would
ask to go through what Lehi did, or Jared and his brother,
or Joseph Smith in his dispensation. And the one who
suffered most of all was the Lord himself, "despised, . . .
rejected, . . . a man of sorrows, and acquainted with grief"
(Isaiah 53:3). In short, the leaders of the great dispensations
have truly earned their calling and their glory, paying a
price that the rest of the human race could not pay even if
they would. Preeminent among these was Abraham, whose
life, as the rabbis remind us, was an unbroken series of
supremely difficult tests.[7] As in some frightful nightmare,
the narrator ticks off the principal episodes: "But Sarai was
barren; she had no child" (Genesis 11:30). "Get thee out of
thy country, and from thy kindred, and from thy father's
house" (Genesis 12:1). " . . . going on still toward the south.
And there was a famine in the land" (Genesis 12:9–10). "The
Egyptians beheld the woman . . . and the woman was taken
into Pharaoh's house" (Genesis 12:14–15). "And Pharaoh . . .

said, What is this that thou has done unto me? . . . And they sent him away" (Genesis 12:18, 20). "And the land was not able to bear them, . . . and there was a strife" (Genesis 13:6–7). "[The kings came and made war.] And they took Lot . . . and his goods" (Genesis 14:12). "I go childless, and the steward of my house is this Eliezer of Damascus" (Genesis 15:2). "Lo, an horror of great darkness fell upon him" (Genesis 15:12). "My wrong be upon thee: I have given my maid into thy bosom; and . . . I was despised in her eyes: the Lord judge between me and thee" (Genesis 16:5). "Wilt thou also destroy the righteous with the wicked? . . . Oh let not the Lord be angry" (Genesis 18:23, 30). "Lo, the smoke of the country went up as the smoke of a furnace" (Genesis 19:28). "And Abimelech king of Gerar sent, and took Sarah" (Genesis 20:2). "They will slay me for my wife's sake" (Genesis 20:11). "And Abraham rose up early in the morning, and took bread, and a bottle of water, and gave it unto Hagar . . . and sent her away" (Genesis 21:14). "And Abraham reproved Abimelech because of a well of water, which Abimelech's servants had violently taken away" (Genesis 21:25). "Take now thy son, Thine only son Isaac, whom thou lovest, . . . and offer him there for a burnt offering" (Genesis 22:2). "I am a stranger and a sojourner with you: give me a possession of a burying place with you, that I may bury my dead" (Genesis 23:4).

Any one of these crises is enough to break any man's spirit. There are various standard lists of the classic "Ten Trials of Abraham," and while the later lists are confined to events mentioned in the Bible, the earlier ones significantly give a prominent place to Abraham's imprisonment in Mesopotamia and the attempt to sacrifice him.[8] But all are agreed that Abraham's career was an incredibly severe time of probation and that the problems he had to face were forced upon him largely by the evil times in which he lived.

Signs in the Heavens

On the night Abraham was born, his father had a party to celebrate the event. As the guests were leaving the house very late at night, they were astonished at the sight of a great fireball that came from the east at great speed and devoured four stars that converged from the four quarters of the heavenly firmament.[9] There have been times of intensified meteoric showers in history, and Abraham's time seems to have been one of them. Günter Lanczkowski has pointed out significant resemblances between the Genesis account of the destruction of Sodom and Gomorrah in Abraham's day and the famous Egyptian tale of the shipwrecked sailor, who was told by a great serpent how his whole race was wiped out by a huge flaming star that fell upon their island home.[10] Of this, Gerald A. Wainwright asks "whether the detail of the destruction of the serpents may not be the romanticized record of an actual event," in which the island, which he identifies with Zeberged or St. John, off Rās Benās, was blasted "by the fall of a meteorite" or "by an eruption . . . not later than the Twelfth Dynasty."[11] Even Jewish tradition tells of a time when "great dragon-like monsters had taken over the earth," until God cut them off suddenly,[12] and also of a "planet" that comes out of Scorpio and "spews gall and a drop of unhealthy blood that fouls the waters of the earth."[13] To a great comet that appeared periodically in the north "and destroyed crops and kings in East and West," the Greeks gave the name of Typhon,[14] identifying him with the Canaanite Reshef, the sky-god who came from Palestine to Egypt as a fiery meteorite rushing through the heavens[15] and whose sacred symbol was an iron meteorite in his shrine.[16] Now Reshef is closely bound up with Abraham, and we are told that "the stars fought for Abraham" the night he marched against the marauding kings, and slew his enemies "by the almighty power of God."[17] The Egyptians were, according to Wainwright, convinced that destructive falls of meteorites were an affliction particularly reserved for the wicked.[18]

It has been suggested that the remarkable interest in stargazing that meets us in the Abraham traditions and is so vividly brought home in the Book of Abraham may be the normal result of a period of unusual celestial displays. According to one tradition it was by observing the planets that Abraham was able to calculate that the earth itself was behaving erratically on its axis. This misbehavior had been apparent ever since the days of the flood and the tower, since the time when the world no longer stood firm, the order of the creation having been altered. The people of Abraham's day believed that "the heaven shifted once every 1656 years," and they devised a means to prevent this by building a series of towers, of which the great tower was the first; for their folly Abraham denounced them.[19] This is supposed to be the first time that the planets had been disturbed since the days of Adam: "Before the Fall the planets moved with greater speed and in shorter orbits than after."[20] In Abraham's day, Jupiter is said to have changed its orbit,[21] and even the fixed stars were troubled: "Because men had perverted the order of life, God altered the order of nature: Sirius became irregular and two stars were removed from their places."[22] Egyptian observers seem to say that Sirius was earlier a variable star, "ruling all the other stars," wrote Horapollo, "as it changes its brightness."[23] We have already seen that Abraham's contemporaries were singularly devoted to the star Shagreel-Sirius—which they associated with the sun, according to the Book of Abraham and other sources. The great mural discovered in 1929 at El-Ghassul, thought to be one of the "Cities of the Plain" of Abraham's day, is dominated by a huge and impressive star figure that has been identified with both the sun and Sirius and has been hailed as establishing "the meeting-point between the two

great empires of Egypt and Chaldea, where celestial phenomena played such an important role in the moral life
of men."[24] We can avoid the enticing twilight zone of science fiction by confining our conclusions to the minimal
speculation—which seems quite safe—that unusual displays in the heavens, whatever they were, belonged to the
general disturbances of Abraham's restless world.

Far more conspicuous in the reports are seismic and volcanic disturbances. When "the Lord broke down the altar of
Elkenah, and of the gods of the land, and utterly destroyed
them" (Abraham 1:20), it was no doubt in the same manner
in which he dealt with the proud and wicked Nephites:
"that great city of Moronihah have I covered with earth. . . .
I did send down fire and destroy them" (3 Nephi 9:5, 11).
Just so in the days of Abraham he dealt with Sodom and
Gomorrah, which like the American cities, lay along one of
the most active earthquake zones in the world. No minor
catastrophe or the death of a single haughty priest would
have caused "great mourning in Chaldea, and also in the
court of Pharaoh" (Abraham 1:20). The overthrow of the
altar and the wide destruction are confirmed by the legends.
Just as Abraham prayed on the altar, "there was a violent
upheaval of the heavens and the earth and the mountains
and all the creatures in them."[25] An older account, the
Pseudo-Philo, says that "God sent a great earthquake, and
the fire gushed forth out of the furnace and broke out into
flames and sparks of fire and consumed all them that stood
around about, . . . 83,500 of them. But upon Abraham there
was not the least injury from the burning of the fire."[26] The
attempted sacrifice is sometimes placed at the site of the
tower, in northern Mesopotamia, where the rites are interrupted as "the flame bursts with a roar from the furnace,"
which destroys many people and saves Abraham, but does
not bring the people to repentance.[27] The traditions consistently associate earthquakes with fires bursting from the

earth, as at Sodom and Gomorrah, which were overthrown while fire enveloped them from above and below (cf. Genesis 19:24–25): "the rivers of the region turned to bitumen, we are told, and the ground became sulphurous and burned, . . . while the five cities on their elevations toppled over."[28] Earthquakes, fumaroles, fissures, rumblings, sulphurous smells, etc., all go together in the story, as they do in nature.[29] "For fifty-two years," according to a well-known tradition, "God had warned the godless" by a series of preliminary rumblings and quakings; "he had made mountains to quake and tremble. But they hearkened not unto the voice of admonition."[30] The last twenty-five years were particularly ominous, with the earth subsiding and quaking almost continually.[31] All through the life of Abraham, even before the fall of the Cities of the Plain, we meet with earthquakes.

The Abraham cycle includes the tradition that one-third of the tower was swallowed up by the earth and one-third was burned by fire from heaven.[32] The Pearl of Great Price itself tells us that when Enoch led the people of God against their enemies, "the earth trembled, and the mountains fled, . . . and the rivers of water were turned out of their course; and the roar of the lions was heard out of the wilderness, and all nations feared" (Moses 7:13). The Jewish tradition is that in the days of "Enos," when men started to worship idols, the mountains on which men once farmed became broken up, rocky, and no longer arable.[33] The passage from the book of Moses reads like an accurate description of the great Assam earthquake of 1955—including even the "roar of lions . . . out of the wilderness." When Abraham's grandfather Nahor was seventy and his people had become confirmed idol worshipers, there was another great earthquake—but for all that they only increased in their wickedness.[34]

One of the best-known stories of the childhood of Abraham tells how the boy's father, out of patience with his son's lack of respect for the king's claim to divinity, took him to the palace for a personal interview with majesty, hoping the boy would be properly impressed. Just as the father and son entered the throne room, there was a short and violent earthquake, which shook the throne and threw all the courtiers off their feet. This shattered their dignity, and the king, impressed by the coincidence of the tremor with the appearance of Abraham, cried, "Truly thy God, Abraham, is a great and mighty god, and he is the King of all Kings."[35] In another version it is Pharaoh's palace that is shaken by an earthquake while Abraham is visiting there.[36] Carrying things to extremes, the *Apocalypse of Abraham* reports that when as a youth he was one day leaving his father's house, "there was a great clap of thunder, fire fell from heaven and burned up Terah, his house and all that was in it for 40 cubits around."[37] This seems to reflect the story of the death of Haran, who got involved with the idol worship of his father and suffered death as a substitute for Abraham while trying to extinguish supernatural fires.[38] One report has it that Nimrod sacrificed his victims in inextinguishable fires of petroleum, which Abraham, with the aid of God, nonetheless extinguished.[39] All in all, fire and earthquake go well together in the Abraham traditions: "and the fiery furnace fell down, and Abraham was saved."[40] "In Abraham's day," says the *Clementine Recognitions*, "the world was afflicted by fire, which, beginning at Sodom, threatened to destroy the entire world."[41] After the destruction of Sodom and Gomorrah, Abraham had to leave his beloved Mamre, because the entire region had been completely blighted by the catastrophe.[42] All plant life was destroyed, and seeds transplanted from Sodom would not grow anywhere.[43] No wonder Lot's daughters, hiding in a cave, thought they were the only surviving mortals.[44] "The entire landscape was desolation; there were almost no travellers; everything stopped."[45]

Archaeology confirms the general picture of disaster in Abraham's time. "Our archaeological discoveries in the Negeb," wrote Nelson Glueck, "are in harmony with the general historical background of the accounts in Genesis 12, 13, and 14."[46] Southern Canaan right to Sinai is marked by many sites of permanent settlements and caravan stopping places, reminding one that "all the plain of Jordan . . . was well watered every where, before the Lord destroyed Sodom and Gomorrah, even as the garden of the Lord, like the land of Egypt, as thou comest unto Zoar" (Genesis 13:10). Then suddenly all of these "sites were destroyed at the end of the Abra(ha)mitic period, and for the most part were not reoccupied ever again or not until at least a thousand years, and in most such instances not till about two thousand years had elapsed."[47] In Ghassul, the only City of the Plain that has been located so far, everything was ruined completely by an earthquake.[48] Otto Eissfeldt, one of the most sober and cautious of scholars, believes that the story of Sodom is "a very obscure and distorted memory of a real historical occurrence," noting that a great earthquake actually did take place at the southern end of the Dead Sea sometime in the second millennium B.C., and concluding that the best solution to the problems of the stories of Lot and Abraham in Genesis 19 is to regard them as real history.[49] While Robert Graves and Raphael Patai observe that "the shallower southern basin, beyond the Lisan peninsula [the tongue of land that protrudes into the Dead Sea from the east] may once have been a plain, encroached upon by the salt waters after severe earthquakes about 1900 B.C.," they would explain away the fire from heaven as a description of "the intense [summer] heat."[50] An easier explanation would be those fires which, according to seismologists, are always the main cause of destruction when cities suffer earthquake.

A century ago Bernhard Beer listed a number of ancient sources reporting the rather sudden formation of the Dead

Sea.[51] Yet until recently scholars have rejected the whole story as impossible. "Critical scholarship," writes Friedrich Cornelius, "insists emphatically that the inhabitants of Sodom and Gomorrah are purely fantasy"; yet it now appears that the Jordan Valley is a very active earthquake zone, and Cornelius calls attention to disturbances that afflicted the whole ancient world about the middle of the seventeenth century B.C., when "an enormous earthquake destroyed the Cretan palaces, Ugarit and Alalaḫ VII."[52] "It is quite possible," he notes, "that the southern end of the Dead Sea, a plain which is only 4 to 6 metres under the level of the sea, was formed by an earthquake." Though there is no lava in the area, "the ignition of earth gases among the tarpits (*Asphaltsee*) is virtually unavoidable in an earthquake," such as is described in Genesis 19.[53] André Parrot speculates that "Sodom was destroyed perhaps by an earthquake accompanied by a sinking of the ground-level, which caused a moderate extension of the Dead Sea which could have submerged the cities."[54] He suggests that we take seriously the notoriously persistent place names of the desert, which still designate features of the region as "Mt. Sodom" (Djebel Usdum), Zoar, etc., remembering that St. Jerome, who lived in Palestine, reported that the latter village was actually swallowed up by an earthquake in his day.[55] The fate of Sodom and Gomorrah reminds us of the account in the *Iliad* of how Hephaestus dried up the river Scamander and chased the Trojans out of the place with a mighty flame.[56] The fact that earthquakes of appalling violence have occurred in that very area within the last few years is a reminder that the disasters described, if not the mythical beings who personify their destructive wrath, could have been quite real. That such disturbances reached a peak in Abraham's lifetime is implied by the tradition that after him and because of him the state of nature has remained more stable.[57]

Great natural disasters do not come singly. Earthquakes and volcanoes are regularly accompanied by great storms. Typhon was not only the flaming meteorite; he was also the bringer of great storms and disastrous floods, according to the Egyptians, while Horus and Osiris held back the waters and cleared the skies.[58] The three great floods of water, wind, and fire were assigned by the old desert sectaries to the times of Noah, Abraham, and Lot, respectively; a tradition kept alive in the Old Syrian church has it that when the great wind destroyed the generation of the tower, only Abraham was saved.[59] It is interesting that Abraham should be made the central figure of some of the old stories of the great winds; even the story of Ram and Rud, the righteous brothers whose language was not confounded at the tower and who wandered back toward Eden, makes place for Abraham, for while Rud may be a Mandaean form of Jared, Ab-ram has been suggested for his brother.[60] What made it easy to confuse the two periods was the persistent report that Abraham did indeed have to cope with great winds and storms—but mostly hot winds. In the one hundredth year of his grandfather Nahor, "God opened the vessels of the Winds and the gate of the storms, and a great hurricane swept over the land, carrying away the idols and covering the settlements with sand-hills which remain to this day."[61] The poetic language is remarkably like that of Ether 2:24, "for the winds have gone forth out of my mouth," but the reality of the winds is attested in many old Egyptian and Babylonian sources, such as "The Lament for Ur" (Abraham's city?), in which we read of "the evil winds of Gibil and fire-god . . . the great heaven-storm with its floods, and the hot wind that darkens the sky," scatters the flocks, lays bare the fields, and depopulates the cities and the holy places "like a field desolate after the harvest."[62] The Egyptians have left us a whole literature of lamentation vividly describing the dire circumstances that attend the hot desert winds and the low Nile at times when even the ultra-stable government of Egypt was shaken to pieces.[63] Even the flood story of the Egyptians goes back to far distant climatic changing—not speculative, but a real experience of the human race. The best attested account of a superstorm, however, is found on the stele of the Pharaoh Amosis. In it, that monarch recounts in a dry, factual manner his tour of inspection of the disaster area: the face of the land was changed, a major valley was formed overnight, the land was in total darkness, so much so "that it was impossible to light a torch anywhere," and the most awesome aspect of the thing was the total silence that met the king wherever he went: "the population sat in total silence in the east and in the west, after God had shown his power."[64] Parallels to the Book of Mormon and Abraham 1:20 are no more striking than the genuinely religious interpretation that the pious Amosis puts on the event.

World Food Shortage

But far more conspicuous in the Abraham traditions than the raging storms and floods is the blasting heat and drought that bring famine to the scene. In the Book of Abraham, the prophet—even before the conflict with the people of Ur of the Chaldees—learns from the Lord that there is going to be a famine in the land; and after his escape from the altar the famine descends in earnest, blighting the whole land of Chaldea (Abraham 1:29–30). Leaving the country, Abraham, as his first act on crossing the border into Canaan, sacrifices to God, praying "that the famine might be turned away from my father's house, that they might not perish" (Abraham 2:17). But even in Canaan the famine only gets worse and worse, forcing the patriarch to go clear to Egypt for food, "for the famine became very grievous" (Abraham 2:21). Of the ten great famines to afflict the world, according to Jewish tradition, the greatest was that in Abraham's time, it being the first worldwide famine.[65] Needless to say, hunger (or famine) was one of the ten trials of Abraham.[66]

In the last days of Methuselah, when men began to apostatize and defile the earth and steal from one another, God purposely caused the harvests to fail.[67] This tradition is clearly recalled in the Pearl of Great Price (Moses 8:3–4). With the birth of Noah, things began to improve, and Noah himself sought to improve conditions by inventing plows, sickles, axes, and other agricultural machinery.[68] Next, when men reverted to evil during the time of the scattering from the tower, the time of God's wrath, it did not rain—the great winds were dry winds.[69] In the "Lament for Ur" we are told how "the good storm, Nannar, is driven out of the land, and the people . . . are scattered. . . . Everywhere corpses lie withering in the sun; . . . many die of hunger; the heat is unbearable; . . . all government collapses; . . . parents desert their children."[70] Kenan, the son of Enos, is said to have recorded the great famine that followed the preaching of his father.[71] Then in the days of Terah, just before the birth of Abraham, "Mastema [Satan] sent crows and birds" and by the starving birds the people were robbed of their grain and fruit and reduced to destitution.[72]

So we find Abraham at the age of four (some say fifteen) driving the birds from the fields, but politely explaining the situation to them and reaching an amicable understanding as he does so.[73] All his life he is escaping from heat, drought, and hunger, or helping others to escape from them. Everywhere he goes he digs wells and plants trees (most of which perish);[74] he invents important improvements in agricultural machinery and methods[75] and distributes food wherever he can. He undertakes search-and-rescue missions for wanderers in the desert when it was as hot as the day of judgment, God having released the fires of hell on the earth, and tangles with marauding bands amidst "dust" and "stubble."[76] But above all it is in a *ritual* capacity that Abraham is involved in the business of checking heat and drought. This may seem very strange until we realize that the running of the waters and the tempering of the blasting heat is the *Hauptmotiv* (main theme) of the great yearly ritual assemblies of Abraham's day from one end to the other of the inhabited world.[77] The Book of Abraham is aware of the strange system in which human sacrifice and famine are closely connected. The ancients, though they knew perfectly well that it was the sun that dried up the earth, nevertheless attributed the most deadly heat and drought to the Dog Star, or Sirius, who in Abraham's day was propitiated with "the thank-offering of a child," as "the god of Shagreel" (Abraham 1:10, 9). It was when famine prevailed in spite of everything that Abraham's father decided not to make such an offering of his own son: "a famine prevailed throughout all the land of Chaldea, and my father was sorely tormented, . . . and he repented of the evil which he had determined against me, to take away my life" (Abraham 1:30). But Abraham's brother, Haran, died in the famine (cf. Abraham 2:1). We are not told why this was permitted while the rest of the family survived, but numerous legendary accounts have it that Haran died as an offering in the fire in the place of Abraham.[78]

As we have seen, Abraham's delivery from the altar in the land of the Chaldees is often described as his escape from the fire of the furnace of Chaldea, and we are told how at the moment he was cast from the altar into the flames, the latter became a lush and lovely garden.[79] In the most mysterious episode in all his career, we find Abraham driving off birds of prey from a sacrifice while he is overcome with a *tardema*, which some scholars interpret as sunstroke.[80] The first altar Abraham built, according to Abraham 2:17, was for an offering and prayer "that the famine might be turned away from my father's house." What is most significant for our study is that the "Busiris" type of sacrifice, of which our Facsimile 1 is an illustration, has the specific object of propitiating the heavens in time of drought and famine.[81]

A World in Trouble

The great insecurity of life accompanying major natural upheavals, when men can no longer count on the stability of the earth itself, is not without marked psychological effect. A basic teaching of the Talmud is that there is a definite correlation between the behavior of man and the behavior of nature. The universe is so organized, according to this, that when man revolts against God's plan of operations, to which all other creatures conform, he finds himself in the position of one going the wrong way on a freeway during rush hour: the very stars in their course fight against him. The blight of nature follows the wickedness of man in every age. Thus, when Adam fell, an angel cut down all the trees of the garden but one; when Abel was murdered, all the vegetation in the world withered until Seth was born, at which time it bloomed again; but when men started worshiping idols in the time of Abraham's great-grandparents, the sea rose along the whole eastern Mediterranean seaboard, "flooding one-third of the land from Akko to Jaffa"; and when in the last days of Methuselah men again defiled the earth, God caused all the harvests to fail.[82] This same philosophy is strikingly expressed in the book of Moses in the Pearl of Great Price, especially in the seventh chapter, where we even hear the earth itself, personified as "the mother of men," weeping for the wickedness of her children that have defiled her (Moses 7:48). It was because of wickedness among the people that the birds came to destroy their crops when Abraham was a child. As it was in the days of Noah, so in the days of Abraham, a very old Christian writing explains, the world was ripe for destruction, according to the principle that whenever men fall away completely from God, destruction must follow.[83] Indeed, the people had sunk so low, says one very old source, that God caused their civilization to degenerate back to the stage of cave dwelling, and brought Abraham out of the land.[84]

After the flood, men were haunted by an understandable feeling of insecurity, to overcome which they undertook tremendous engineering projects; among these was the famous tower, which was to be the symbol of man's ultimate mastery of nature, being so ingeniously designed and solidly constructed as to be absolutely safe against flood, fire, and earthquake. Within the walls of the tower was to be stored the sum total of man's knowledge of the physical universe, enabling him to meet and master any situation that might arise—"and it was all done out of fear of another flood!"[85] A great economic boom and commercial expansion enabled them to undertake all kinds of engineering projects for controlling a dangerous nature, but the Lord fooled them by "altering the course of nature and creation."[86] That was in Abraham's day: the Nimrod legends are full of marvelous gadgets and structures—superbuildings, mechanical thrones and altars, flying machines, and whatnot. It was a time of great scientific and technological progress—the Abraham stories, including the Book of Abraham, are unique in their concern for a *scientific* understanding of the cosmos, as against a purely religious and moral teaching— but toppling on the edge of destruction: those hot winds were breathing down everybody's neck.

In desperation, men turned to worshiping idols. Why idols, of all things, in a scientific age? It was "because in the whole world the people were without a teacher or a lawgiver or any one who could show them the way of truth."[87] Of course, there was Abraham, but they didn't want him; and precisely therein lay the convenience of having idols. Even when the boy Abraham argued with his father that the idols were blind, dumb, and helpless, as anyone could see, and therefore could not possibly help others, Terah stuck to his idol business. The one salient, outstanding, universal, undeniable characteristic of all idols is their utterly passive helplessness; if men persist in worshiping them, it cannot be in spite of that quality, but *because* of it. The sophisticated people of Abraham's time wanted the sanction of holy beings which at the same time were one hundred percent compliant with their own interests and desires, just as people today search out those scriptures which support their interests and push the rest aside. As Brigham Young pointed out time and again, the enlisting of systematic piety in the interest of private greed and ambitions is the very essence of idolatry.[88] We can believe that the smart and cynical people of Abraham's day were sincere and devout in their idol worship—after all, Abraham's own father was willing to put him to death in support of the system.

Move On!

The Bible does not tell us why Abraham left Ur,[89] but the Book of Abraham (Abraham 1:1–2) clearly implies that he found the general atmosphere of Mesopotamia unbearable. There are indications that he was swept along to the west with many others under the pressure of world unrest and political crisis: "When you see the Powers fighting each other," says the Midrash, "look for the coming [lit. 'feet'] of the King Messiah. The proof is that in the days of Abraham, because these Powers fought against each other, greatness came to Abraham."[90] Recently E. MacLaurin has suggested that "the advancing armies of the great Semitic ruler Hammurabi were probably the cause of departure from his native city of Abraham."[91] Others emphasize religious reasons: he was escaping from the idolatrous rites and ceremonies of the fathers, according to Judith;[92] Terah left Ur because he hated Chaldea, on account of his mourning for

Haran, says Josephus;[93] and when the family moved, Abraham was in serious trouble with both Chaldeans and Mesopotamians and finally had to leave the country altogether.[94] He left for the west, according to the *Pseudo-Philo,* because his homeland had become completely degenerate and because he had become disgusted with the tower building and the whole business.[95]

The religious background of Abraham had been Babylonian, "Chaldean" rather than Egyptian, and that at a time, as Friedrich Cornelius puts it, "when Babylonian religious degeneracy was flooding the Syrian regions."[96] It was to escape this spreading miasma, some have maintained, that Abraham fled to the purer air of the west.[97] While on a return visit to Haran after fifteen years in Canaan, according to one story, Abraham was terribly shocked by the general immorality of the old home town and yearned for the simpler frontier life of Canaan.[98] A Roman soldier with a keen eye and a sound head has left us a description of the hot, sultry, mosquito- and lion-ridden district of Haran, with its voluptuous, rich, carefree, immoral inhabitants, and though his account is as far removed from Abraham's day as it is from our own, still this particular corner of the "unchanging east" has indeed remained unchanged even down to our times, as Parrot has strikingly demonstrated.[99] The ancient Ur to the south has been described by its excavators in much the same terms as are the great contemporary cities of the Indus Valley by their discoverers: they were depressing places to live—huge, ugly, monotonous, geometrical, rich, sultry, joyless metropolises.

But Abraham's Canaan did not offer escape for long. The fabulous prosperity of the Cities of the Plain turned them too into little Babylons.[100] The only "City of the Plain" yet discovered, El-Ghassul, displays astonishing luxury and sophistication, the style being Babylonian rather than

Egyptian, and apparently already in a state of decadence just before its destruction by an earthquake.

Some have explained Abraham's departure to the west simply as a test—he migrated because God told him to do so.[101] If it was a test, it was a severe one: Professor Albright has recently pointed out that the ancient pioneers, far from finding a golden west awaiting them, were "ethno-political intruders in the West,"[102] and as such "were not well received but were closely watched and were usually driven away [by the local inhabitants, who] bitterly resented any attempt on the part of outsiders to move in and take over their fields or pastures."[103] Even in Canaan, moreover, the Babylonian threat followed the patriarch, who was forced to leave Damascus, according to a very ancient source, because of military and political pressure from the east.[104] In Canaan, Abraham's nephew Lot, catching the spirit of the times, declared that he preferred suburban Sodom to the society of his uncle, saying, "I want neither Abraham nor his God!" and moved down into the crowded and prosperous plain.[105]

The Procrustes Cycle

A number of legends fit Abraham snugly into the peculiar category of victims of Procrustes (fig. 30). In the standard Procrustes-type story, of which there are many, a wandering hero and prince is entertained at the palace of a king who tries to subject him to a sacrificial death, but whose attempt fails when the hero at the last moment is miraculously freed and repays his host's inhospitality by putting either him or his priest to death. Among the most celebrated monsters of the Procrustes persuasion are Minos, Philomeleides, Amycus, Cycnus, Syleus, Antaeus, Phalarus, Cronus, Lityerses, Faunus, Cacus, Athamus, Proteus, Polyphemus, Eurytheus, Sciron, and many others, the most famous of all being Busiris of Egypt.

Among the heroes who met and bested them are

Figure 30. In the Theseus cycle of legends, our hero meets various challenges on his way to Athens. Procrustes, a nickname meaning "stretcher," lived by the road and invited travelers in for the night. His hospitality was only feigned since he would then stretch or chop them to fit his iron bed, giving rise to the expression *bed of Procrustes,* or *one-size-fits-all.* In this Athenian red-figure vase from 470 B.C., Theseus has turned the tables on the inhospitable Procrustes—shown clutching his bed—by using the villain's own ax to punish him.

Odysseus, Pollux, Menelaeus, Paris, Hermes, Jason, Bellerophon, Cytisorus, etc. The reader can look them all up in Pauly-Wissowa's *Real-Encyclopaedie der classischen Altertumswissenschaft* or a good classical dictionary, preferably Robert Graves's *The Greek Myths,*[106] which pays special attention to such sordid goings-on and shows us time and again that the terrible doings we hear about in the Abraham legends actually could have taken place.

The greatest hero of this cycle is Heracles, who serves us here as an example. Heracles was a wandering, suffering, conquering benefactor of mankind who, like Abraham, wandered through the world meeting and overcoming the enemies of the race and in the process becoming the father of many nations. After ridding Crete of bears, wolves, and serpents, he went to Libya, where the tyrant King Antaeus, the son of Mother Earth and Poseidon the water-god, would force all strangers to wrestle with him, murder them in the contest, and nail their skulls to the roof of the temple of his father.[107]

Heracles, accepting the challenge, killed Antaeus and turned his desolate kingdom into a blooming paradise. Then he moved on to Egypt where Antaeus's brother Busiris was king; every year, to combat the force of drought in his kingdom, he would sacrifice a noble stranger on the altar of Zeus.[108] Heracles, as we have seen, allowed himself to be led to the altar, and at the last moment burst his bonds and murdered the cruel king or, in some versions, his priest (fig. 31).[109] That labor performed, the hero went to Gaul, "where he abolished a barbarous native custom of killing strangers" and founded "a large city, to which he gave the name Alesia, or 'Wandering-town.'"[110] In Italy he accepted the challenge to duel with the wicked King Cacus, slew him on the Great Altar (the Ara Maxima), married the queen, Acca Larentia, and so became the father of the Romans. According to a later account, Cacus was an idol to whom the natives would offer up their infant children—exactly in the manner of the Phoenicians and the Chaldeans of Abraham's Ur![111] While he was at it, Heracles also killed Faunus, "whose custom was to sacrifice strangers at the altar of his father Hermes," marrying the royal widow to become the father of the Latin race.[112] He then reformed the Cronian

Figure 31. Busiris's custom of human sacrifice was ended by Heracles—this popular and often humorous subject was depicted on several Greek vases. This version, dating from 500 B.C., shows the giant black-figure Heracles throwing light- and dark-skinned Egyptians around like rag dolls. A priest pleads for mercy on the altar while Pharaoh, identified by his uraeus-shaped forelock, is facedown before his conqueror.

year-rites by supplanting the throwing of human victims into the river by the use of puppet substitutes.[113] At Celaenae, Lityerses, the son of Minos, would force his guests to compete with him in reaping his harvest, whip them if their strength flagged, behead them at sunset, and bind them up in a sheaf while singing a dirge for them; Heracles beat the king in the reaping game, cut off his head with his sickle, and threw him into the river.[114] The beheading, the dirge, the whipping, and the throwing into the river are all important in the Egyptian rites for Osiris, and remind us that Maneros, the son and successor of the first king of Egypt, also died in such a harvest rite. At Itonus, Heracles slew King Cycnus, who forced his guests to duel with him for a chariot and decorated his father's temple with their heads.[115] And he tore up the vineyards of the Lydian King Syleus, who used to make passing strangers toil amid the vines.[116] Here we should note that it was actually the custom in ancient Asia

Minor and Syria to seize and kill strangers in the vineyards during the vintage season.[117]

These few examples are enough to give one the idea. The noble Theseus got the best of Minos, the half-human monster who meant to murder his royal guest, and on his wanderings accepted King Sciron's routine challenge to wrestle—and threw him into the sea. And it was Theseus who finally settled the score with Procrustes himself; one can read all about that sort of thing in Marie Renault's *The King Must Die* and *The Bull from the Sea.*[118] Sciron's father was Cronus, the Cretan killer, who used to eat his guests; and his neighbor was the king of the Bebryces on the Black Sea, who also murdered his guests. King Philomeleides compelled all his guests to wrestle with him until the wandering Odysseus retired him, as did the wandering water-god Pollux to King Amycus, who forced every visitor to box with him and threw them all into the sea, where he finally ended up himself. Menelaus suffered the cruel hospitality of the old Man of the Sea, as Odysseus did of the Cyclops (another son of Poseidon), until each was able to turn the tables and force his host to help him on his way. And so on and on. Long ago Eugéne Lefébure noticed the kinship of these stories to the tale of the Egyptian Busiris, who was Heracles' most famous host.[119] Because he ties in directly with the Abraham legends, Busiris deserves a little more attention.

"Who does not know about the famous altars of Busiris?" which were proverbial among the ancients.[120] A whole string of classical writers from the fifth century B.C. to the sixth century A.D., a full thousand years, recount the lurid tale with the normal and expected variations. As Apollodorus tells it, Busiris was desperate when his kingdom was afflicted by a severe drought and famine, for the king, as everyone knows, was directly responsible for the prosperity of the land. The seer Prasius came from Cyprus and told the king that the dearth would end if a stranger were sacrificed annually, and Busiris obliged the visiting prophet by making him his first victim. Thereafter the sacrifice was repeated annually until Heracles put an end to it in the manner described, killing, according to Apollodorus, not only the king but his son as well and the priest or "herald" Chalbes—with a good Canaanitish name.[121] Names and details differ in various versions of the story, indicating that in the case of Apollodorus, who came along and tidied things up in the end, the name of Heracles was used as it often was as a convenient catchall to avoid serious and laborious historical research. Ovid, a much earlier writer, says that the seer who advised the king and suffered death at his hands was a Thracian, and Hyginus reports that he was the nephew of the king of the Phoenicians.[122] Pherecydes, a contemporary of Lehi, reports only that after Heracles had restored fertility to the land of Libya by slaying Antaeus, he went straight to Memphis "and there sacrificed [Antaeus's equally wicked brother] Busiris on the same altar on which he was accustomed to sacrifice strangers to Zeus."[123] What all sources agree on is the real essential, and that is that once long ago an illustrious stranger and seer visited the court of Pharaoh at his invitation and that the king tried to put him to death; in one case, at least, he succeeded, but in the most famous story of all, the stranger, whoever it was, got the best of the affair. We can neither accept nor reject the stories as they stand, for they are plainly conditioned by the memory of definite ritual practices, which were themselves very real and sometimes very important historic events. Abraham in the Book of Abraham emphatically tells us in the first chapter that the fate planned for him by the priest of Pharaoh was one that had been suffered by others before him—he was by no means the first, nor possibly the last, such victim. The picture is a complicated one.

In ancient times the name of Busiris was a byword for cruelty and inhospitality. The Emperor Maximin was so cruel, we are told, "that people called him Cyclops, Busiris, Sciron, Falaris, and Typhon."[124] It is interesting to see the name of Typhon, the slayer of Osiris, added to this list of authentic "Procrustean" heroes. Another emperor is accused of reviving the bloody altars of Busiris in rites more savage than sacred.[125] Busiris was remembered as one who sacrificed substitutes to pay for his sins: "It was he who would propitiate for his crimes by making the gods participants in the blood of innocent guests."[126] While some go so far as to accuse Busiris of cannibalism, Isocrates in the fifth century B.C. caused a sensation by an oration in praise of Busiris, in which he debunked the whole story.[127] Diodorus, more cautious, says that the story is probably Greek propaganda, spitefully circulated against Busiris when he closed Egyptian ports to Greek merchants in his desire to protect the cult of Osiris. He admits, however, that the tale does reflect the notorious hostility of the Egyptians to strangers unless they were scholars of world reputation, such as Orpheus, Homer, Pythagoras, and Solon.[128] At any rate, the cruel altar of Busiris remained proverbial.[129]

The oldest and best-informed Greek commentators were quite aware that Busiris was a place rather than a person, though it could be both. To Eratosthenes is attributed the observation that "hostility to strangers is a common barbarian trait, which is also found among the Egyptians: stories told in the Busirite nome about Busiris are a criticism of that inhospitality."[130] Herodotus reports that in his day the main temple of Isis in all the world stood in Busiris, which with Bubastis formed the nucleus of Egyptian cult life.[131] Indeed, since prehistoric times Osiris was known as "the Lord of Busiris," and it was from there that his rites spread to the other cult centers of Egypt, notably Abydos. I. E. S. Edwards even suggests that Osiris was probably a real king, "first the king and then the local god of the ninth Lower Egyptian *nome,* with its capital at Busiris";[132] while Henri Frankfort held that Busiris was the tomb of some forgotten king.[133] Every dead Egyptian needed to take a ritual journey to Busiris, to "appear there as the dead King Osiris," his presence in the place qualifying him as an Osiris.[134] The place was named, according to Sethe, after its local divinity, and was even older as a cult center than Heliopolis itself.[135] In the Pyramid Texts the king comes to Busiris for rites of human sacrifice,[136] and a Nineteenth-Dynasty monument has the same rites still celebrated in Busiris.[137] Edwards believes that the yearly passion play of Osiris was performed at Busiris as early as the First Dynasty.[138] "I am enduring in Busiris, conceived in Busiris, born in Busiris," boasts King Tutankhamun, reminding us that Busiris is preeminently the place of the lion couch.[139] When Heliopolis took over the ancient cult of Busiris under the guidance of the great Imhotep, it supplanted the human sacrifice by the use of substitutes, thus leaving Busiris the distinction, which is retained right down into the Middle Ages, of being the right and proper place for human sacrifices.[140]

Our Hospitality

When Abraham went forth into a starving world, he found the people understandably touchy and dangerous: "and they persecuted Abraham our father when he was a stranger, and they vexed his flocks" as well as his servants, "and thus they did to all strangers, taking away their wives by force, and they banished them. But the wrath of the Lord came upon them." This is the *Testament of Levi* speaking of Abraham in Shechem.[141] But he found the same hostility elsewhere, that worldwide cruelty and inhospitality which is best represented by the notorious Procrustes and especially by Abraham's own stomping grounds, Sodom and Gomorrah.

The Bible tells us that the Jordan depression was a

veritable paradise when Abraham first visited it, "before the
Lord destroyed Sodom and Gomorrah" (Genesis 13:10). It
is not surprising that "the men of Sodom were the wealthy
men of prosperity, on account of the good and fruitful land
whereon they dwelt. For every need which the world
requires, they obtained therefrom."[142] Nor is it very surprising that "they did not trust in the shadow of their Creator,
but . . . in the multitude of their wealth they trusted, for
wealth thrusts aside its owners from the fear of Heaven."[143]
Here Rabbi Eliezer seems to be quoting the same sources as
did Samuel the Lamanite (Helaman 13:18–39), both men
being diligent students of the old Jewish writings. He also
seems to be using the same source as King Benjamin
(Mosiah 4:16–26) as he continues: "The men of Sodom had
no consideration for the honour of their Owner [of their
wealth] by (not) distributing food to the wayfarer . . . but
they (even) fenced in all the trees on top above their fruit so
that they should not be seized; (not) even by the bird of
heaven."[144] This was in the authentic Babylonian tradition,
eyewitness accounts telling how the people of Babylon
"oppressed the weak, and gave him into the power of the
strong. Inside the city was tyranny, and receiving of bribes;
every day without fail they plundered each other's gods;
the son cursed his father in the street, the slave his master.
. . . They put an end to offerings and entered into conspira-
cies."[145] The people of Sodom and Gomorrah were not condemned for their ignorance of the God of Abraham but
rather for their meanness, their immorality, and their greed;
they were destroyed because they did not strengthen the
hand of the poor and heeded not the needy.[146] For them
everything existed for the sole purpose of being turned into
cash: they put a toll on all their bridges, with a *double* toll for
wading; they charged visitors for everything and had the
most ingenious tricks for getting money out of them.[147]

When Abraham's servant tried to help a poor man who

had been robbed and was being beaten up by a gang in Sodom, he was attacked by the mob, arrested, and dragged into court, where he was fined the price of bloodletting as a perfectly legitimate physician's fee.[148] For like the Nephites under the Gadianton administration, these people were careful to keep everything legal: thus they would pay a merchant good prices for his goods but refuse to sell him any food, and when he starved to death would piously confiscate all of his wares and his wealth.[149] Of course, "the richer a man, the more was he favored before the law," for it was wicked to encourage idleness by helping the poor.[150] Anyone helping the poor in Sodom got thrown into the river.[151] There are lurid tales of tender-hearted virgins, including Lot's daughter Pilatith, who suffered terrible punishment when they were caught secretly helping the poor.[152] It was one of these episodes, according to the Midrash, that finally caused God to decide to destroy the city.[153] Just south of Sodom was the great plain where the licentious yearly rites were held; in these all strangers were required by law to participate, and during the four-day celebration they were efficiently relieved of everything they owned[154]—the great pilgrimage centers of the Old World were understandably the worst places in the world for fleecing strangers, that being through the centuries the principal commercial activity of the natives.

It is not surprising that travelers and birds alike learned to avoid the rich cities of the plain, while all the poor emigrated to other parts.[155] Interestingly enough, the records of Ugarit, which some hold to be contemporary with Abraham, show that "the practice of killing merchants was . . . widespread" in that part of the world, even as the Amarna letters show us a world in which it is every man for himself.[156] Having no love for the stranger, the people of Abraham's homeland had even less to waste on each other, and finally there was so much crime and murder among them that everything came to a complete standstill.[157] Being grossly materialistic, they rated the hardware high above the software: "If a man fell and died [working on the tower] they paid no heed to him, but if a brick fell they sat down and wept." Seeing this, Abraham "cursed them in the name of his God."[158] One cannot help thinking of the church builders in Mormon 8:37 and 39, who adorn themselves "with that which hath no life" while calmly ignoring the needs of the living. "They were dwelling in security without care and at ease, without the fear of war, . . . sated with all the produce of the earth, but they did not strengthen . . . the hand of the needy or the poor, as it is said, 'Behold, *this* was the iniquity of thy sister Sodom.'"[159]

That this emphasis on wealth and status was the real wickedness of Sodom and Gomorrah is attested by both the Bible and the Pearl of Great Price, the latter holding up as a lesson in contrast to the world in which the patriarchs lived—"there were wars and bloodshed among them" (Moses 7:16). In the Old Testament, the one time in his life when Abraham refuses to deal with one who makes him an offer is when he coldly turns down the king of Sodom: It was after his victory over the marauding chiefs of the East that Abraham willingly accepted whatever the grateful king of Salem offered him as a reward, freely exchanging gifts and compliments with "the King of Righteousness"; but he absolutely refused to take anything whatever from the fawning king of Sodom, whose goods he had also rescued: "I have raised my hand to Jehovah El-Elyon," that he would not take so much as a shoestring from that king, "so that he can never say, 'I enriched Abraham.'"[160] He knew his Sodom and saw just what kind of a deal the king wanted to make for himself; and God applauded his wisdom and reassured him: "Fear not, Abram: I am thy shield" (Genesis 15:1). When Abraham and Lot started getting rich, their retainers took to quarreling, whereupon Abraham, determined to avoid involvement in that sort of thing, told Lot that he was welcome to Sodom while he, Abraham, withdrew to a less prosperous region: "Let there be no strife, . . . for we be brethren" (Genesis 13:8). The rich cities of the plain, where they failed to serve the Lord "by reason of the abundance of all things," were no place for Abraham.[161]

Bed or Altar?

The most famous thing about Procrustes, as everyone knows, was his bed, and it is this notorious item that ties his story very closely to the Abraham cycle. The story goes that when Abraham's servant Eliezer, being the exact image of his master and serving as his proxy in the most important negotiations, once visited Lot and Sodom on business for Abraham, he was entertained by an innkeeper whose unauthorized hospitality (which would, of course, encourage vagrancy!) got him banished from the town, while Eliezer himself was seized and taken to the marketplace to be thrown down on a very special kind of bed. All the cities of the plain, we are told, had such beds: the judges of the other cities—Shaqar of Gomorrah, Zabnak of Admah, and Manon of Zeboiim—had all taken counsel together and advised their people to "set up beds on their commons. When a stranger arrived, three men seized him by his head, and three by his feet, and they forced him upon one of those beds." There they stretched or contracted him violently to make him fit the exact length of the bed, saying as they did so, "Thus will be done to any man that comes to our land."[162] Beer, commenting on this, notes that Procrustes' epithet Damastes means "the Forcer," or "the Violator," that being, according to him, also the root meaning of the word Sodom![163]

So here is an authentic Procrustes story in which the victim on the bed is none other than Abraham's double. There is another Procrustes story of how the same Eliezer, again

looking exactly like Abraham, came to the house of King
Bethuel of Haran, where "they tried to kill him with cunning," the king arranging for poison dishes to be served
Eliezer at a banquet in his honor; but "it was ordained by
God that the dish intended for him should come to stand in
front of Bethuel, who ate it and died," the victim of his own
treachery.[164] What is behind these many stories of the
strangely inhospitable kings? The bed is an important clue.
Professor Lefébure noticed when he was studying the
Busiris tradition that the inhospitable kings specialized in
strange and ingenious contraptions for putting their noble
guests to death, such as bronze bulls or giant braziers.[165] The
altar of Busiris was held to be the fiendish invention of that
ingenious monarch, and no ordinary altar.[166] Graves compares the bed of Procrustes to the bed to which Sampson
was tied (another sun hero like Heracles) by his inhospitable Philistines.[167] In view of such things, somebody
should someday give serious consideration to Abraham's
strange insistence in the Book of Abraham that the altar on
which he was sacrificed required a special note and a special illustration, being "made after the form of a bedstead,
such as was had among the Chaldeans" (Abraham 1:13).
"And that you may have a knowledge of this altar, I will
refer you to the representation" (Abraham 1:12). For the
interesting fact is that all the Jewish legends of the attempted
sacrifice of Abraham make special mention of the peculiar
altar employed, each one describing and explaining it in a
different way.

Some of the oldest accounts mention the unusual altar
while not attempting to describe it beyond saying that it
was a *binyan* (Hebrew) or a *bunyan* (Arabic), i.e., a "structure" or "contraption."[168] But why not an ordinary altar? All
kinds of explanations are given. For one thing, nothing less
than a superholocaust will do for Abraham; so the king
sends a thousand camels for wood, and when "he had

[dug] a pit on a hill[?], and trees thrown upon it, and spread everything that the [thousand camels] carried, and set it on fire," the rites were underway.[169] Others explain that it was not the altar itself that was the "structure" but a wooden tower that the king had erected near his palace so that he could watch Abraham in the fire.[170] This might easily be a contamination of one of the well-known tower-building stories about Nimrod, such as the one in which he challenges Abraham to a duel as he comes out of the fire and builds a tower to give him an advantage against the god of heaven.[171] In the story of the sacrifice of Isaac, too, the piling up of the wood is an important detail; though the wood is never ignited and the instrument of sacrifice is really a knife, still the woodpile altar grows in the legends until it becomes a huge tower, "built straight up towards the heavenly throne of divine majesty."[172] It was after the attempted sacrifice had failed, we recall, that Abraham in the rites in the Plain of Shaveh near Sodom was invited to sit atop a high cedar tower or altar and be hailed as king.[173]

The superbonfire, "30 ells high and 30 ells broad," raised bothersome questions: How, for example, could you put Abraham into it without getting burned up yourself (fig. 32)? Since the victim had to have his blood shed by the knife before his remains could be committed to the flames, it would not do simply to light the wood and run; it was only when the sacrificial blade proved totally ineffectual that Satan appeared and suggested a solution to the problem, which was to throw the victim from the altar to the fire from a safe distance.[174] This explanation converted the altar into a sort of catapult or ballista.[175] Schützinger says that the first mention of the catapult is in Tha'labi,[176] but the account of that learned Persian has Jewish predecessors at least a thousand years older than his time, for in 4 *Maccabees*, we read of the heroic widow's sons being put to death by a Nimrod-type tyrant, two of them being tied to catapults[177] while a third is cast into a red-hot

Figure 32. In this Persian miniature from 1607, the artist portrays the
stark contrast between good and evil. Abraham sits in meditation on his
prayer rug surrounded by flames, after being thrown there by an awk-
wardly drawn catapult. Nimrod, with his feathered cap, stands astonished in his tower while the executioners look on in consternation. The
rhymed couplet reads:

> Since they gave themselves to evil,
> The fire of thirty-seven days died,
> From the midst of the fire and smoke,
> The Voice of Righteousness was heard.

brazier.[178] In another much older source than Tha'labi, the king
plans to hurl Abraham into an immense brazier.[179] This suggests certain Egyptian practices,[180] as well as the addressing of
the royal victim in Coffin Text 135 as "Thou who art raised
upon the scaffold!"[181]

According to the ʿAntar legend, Nimrod had an iron oven for his victims.[182] Just after Facsimile 1 was published, Joseph Smith wrote: "But if we believe in present revelation, as published in the 'Times and Seasons' last spring, Abraham, the prophet of the Lord, was laid upon the iron bedstead for slaughter."[183] Turning to that issue of the *Times and Seasons*, however, one finds no mention whatever of any *iron* bedstead, and so one naturally assumes that the word "bedstead" suggested to the Prophet the image of a standard iron bedstead.[184] Still, it is interesting that by far the fullest parallel to the story of Abraham on the altar is a very early account preserved in the East Syrian Christian church in the very place where the event was supposed to have taken place, in which the hero, by a familiar transposition, is changed into St. Elias, who is bound on a bed of iron that is heated for three hours.[185]

Abraham the Hospitable

The history of Abraham is a story of contrasts and extremes. If meanness and inhospitality reach an all-time high in Sodom and Gomorrah, Abraham holds the record for charity and compassion. The contrast is an intentional one and a mark of authentic Abrahamic literature.[186] The supreme example of such "coincidence of opposites" is found in the Pearl of Great Price, where, in contrast to the city of Enoch—the height of human perfection in this world—is set the most depraved society in all the universe: "and among all the workmanship of mine hands there has not been so great wickedness as among thy brethren" (Moses 7:36). In Abraham's day the world was in a desperate state, ripe for destruction.[187] And Abraham's own society was the wickedest: "When a man was cruel," says the Midrash Rabbah, "he was called an Amorite."[188] For the patriarchs, as Theodor Böhl notes, the future was grim—and none had better cause to know it than Abraham.[189] By very definition "Abraham the Hebrew" was a "refugee," a "displaced person."[190] The famous formula "Lekh lekha" (Genesis 12:1) is a double imperative, according to the rabbis, telling Abraham to get going and keep moving, from one land to another.[191] His whole career, as Martin Buber put it, was "an ever-new separation for him and his progeny" from the world and from his own people. "This entire history . . . is a consequence of choices and partings."[192]

If constant travel was one of the ten trials of Abraham, jeopardizing his family, fortune, and reputation,[193] travel in dangerous and hostile regions was a horror: such was the curse placed upon the wandering Jew for his meanness and want of hospitable feeling.[194] The Zohar has an interesting psychological note on the state of Abraham's world: It is when things are going badly that Satan loves to spread his accusations abroad: "For this is the way of . . . Satan, . . . to bring accusations against him on high, . . . reserv[ing] his indictment for the hour of danger, or for a time when the world is in distress"[195]—then hysteria adds fuel to the fires of destruction. In such times even the righteous have no guarantee of security, for while "the Holy One does not punish the guilty until the measure of their guilt is full,"[196] when that time comes, look out! "When punishment overtakes the world a man should not . . . let himself be found abroad, since the executioner does not distinguish between the innocent and the guilty."[197]

In the most inhospitable of worlds, Abraham was the most hospitable of men. It was said that charity was asleep in the world, and Abraham awakened it.[198] Even before he went to Canaan, he held continual open house near Haran, to try to counteract the evil practices of the time.[199] Then when he was forced to move, he dug wells and planted trees along his way, leaving blessings for those he would never see.[200] Arriving and settling in Beersheba, he built a garden and grove and put gates on each of the four sides of it as a welcome to strangers from all directions, "so that if a traveller came to Abraham he entered any gate which was in his road, and remained there and ate and drank . . . for the house of Abraham was always open to the sons of men that passed and repassed, who came daily to eat and drink in the house of Abraham."[201] He also operated a school at the place, that none might want for spiritual food: "Abraham's house thus became not only a lodging-place for the hungry and thirsty, but also a place of instruction where the knowledge of God and His Law were taught."[202] When his guests thanked him, he said, in the words of King Benjamin (an ardent student of early Jewish traditions; cf. Mosiah 4:19), "What, ye give thanks unto me! Rather return thanks ⅃ to your host, He who alone provides food and drink for all creatures."[203]

Inspired by the noble example and teaching of his uncle, Lot tried to operate the same kind of inn when he settled near Sodom, but he was soon reported to the authorities and had to operate secretly at night,[204] while his daughters practiced their charities with great stealth and suffered severe penalties when they were caught. Abraham's continued hospitality nearby was resented by the people of the plain as a standing rebuke to their own sensible practices.[205]

Not content to admit the weary wanderer at all hours to his pleasant grove and board, Abraham in those dangerous times used to undertake search-and-rescue missions in the desert. It was at noon of a phenomenally hot day when "the entire earth was being consumed with unbearable solar heat,"[206] as if God had "pierced one hole in the midst of Gehinnom, and . . . made the day hot, like the day of the wicked,"[207] or as if he had caused the sun to emerge from its protecting sheath, depriving the earth of its normal defense against deadly rays,[208] that Abraham, suffering terribly from illness, had his faithful Eliezer go out and search the byways for any lost wanderers. Eliezer couldn't find a soul,

which was no wonder on such a day; but Abraham still felt
uneasy—it was just possible that somebody might be out
there needing his help. So the old man went forth all alone
to search in that dusty inferno. For that supreme act of
involvement he received his supreme reward—the son he
had always prayed for. For as he was returning from his
mission of mercy, still alone, he was met by three men,
whom he at first, according to a very ancient tradition, took
to be Arabs.[209] Joyfully he led them to his tent, where he
soon discovered who they were: "Lord of the Universe!" he
cried, as he served them with food. "Is it the order of the
cosmos that I should sit while you stand?"[210] Then it was
that Abraham received the desire of his heart (Genesis
18:9–14) and the commendation of his good works: "Thou
hast done well to leave thy doors open for the wanderer
and the home-journeyer and the stranger," nay, were it not
for men like Abraham "I would not have bothered to create
the heaven, earth, sun, and moon."[211]

There is a story of how Abraham, to see what kind of a
wife Ishmael his son had got, visited his camp in the desert
as a simple wandering old man; Ishmael was away at the
time, and his wife turned the old tramp away. Abraham left
a message with her, however, by the cryptic wording of
which Ishmael knew who had been there—and advised
him to get another wife. Three years later Abraham visited
the camp under the same circumstances and was shown
kindness by the second wife, with whom he left another
message for Ishmael, commending her worth.[212] A more
famous story tells how when God sent Michael to fetch
Abraham back to his presence at the end of his life, the
patriarch was still his old hospitable self, kindly inviting
the dread stranger—representing Death itself—to be his
guest.[213] Ever since then, when the world is in an evil way,
the angels say to God: "The highways lie waste, the way-
faring man ceaseth, he hath broken the covenant. Where is

the reward of Abraham, he who took the wayfarers into his house?"[214]

Let It Begin with Me

Students of Abraham's life are impressed by the way in which he seems to start from scratch: with all the world going in one direction, he steadily pursues his course in the opposite. Granted that the tradition of the fathers, of which the Book of Abraham speaks so eloquently, was still known, yet his own father and grandfather had lost faith in it and departed from it. "Ten generations from Noah to Abraham . . . and there was not one of them that walked in the ways of the Holy One . . . until Abraham our father," says Rabbi Nathan, who asks where, then, did Abraham get the idea of starting things moving?[215] The common explanation that Abraham was self-taught—"God appointed the two reins of Abraham to act as two teachers"—still does not make him a privileged character, for all men have the same promptings of the Spirit if they will only listen to them: "for charity . . . was asleep, and he roused it."[216] The power was there, but it lay dormant from neglect: When all the inhabitants of the earth had been led astray in their own pride and self-sufficiency, Abraham still believed on the Lord, who then made a covenant with him.[217] Abraham received his covenant only after he had made the first move. Speaking of him, the Zohar says, "the prophetic spirit rests upon man only when he has first bestirred himself to receive it."[218] Again, "the stirring below is accompanied by a stirring above, for there is no stirring above till there is a stirring below."[219] But who was to start the stirring? It was Abraham's unique merit that he loved righteousness in a hard-hearted and wicked generation, without waiting for others to show him the way.[220] A wonderful illustration of this principle is set forth in the newly found 1831–32 account of Joseph Smith's first vision, in which he recounts how for three years he sought diligently for something that apparently interested nobody else, and finally, "I cried unto the Lord for mercy, for there was none else to whom I could go . . . and the Lord heard my cry in the wilderness."[221] This was exactly the case with the young Abraham, who at an early age angered his father by questioning all the values and beliefs of his society.[222]

For generations the world had moved ever farther and farther from God, until by Abraham's time it had become what the Pearl of Great Price describes as the worst of all worlds (Moses 7:36). Then Abraham single-handedly reversed the trend: "The Shechinah [spirit of God] came to earth at the Creation, but through human sin removed itself farther and farther from earth. Then Abraham . . . brought it down again."[223] He was, says the Midrash, like a man who saw a building all on fire and no one willing to put out a hand to save it: "He said, 'Is it conceivable that the world is without a guide?'"[224] So he did the only thing he could do and, exactly like Joseph Smith, appealed directly to God at an early age—it was he who made the first move, according to Abraham 2:12: "Thy servant has sought thee earnestly; now I have found thee."

This independence of mind got both prophets into trouble from the beginning. "The man Abram is singled out, and sent out. He is brought forth from out of the world of peoples and must go his own way."[225] The trials of both men begin immediately. What drives Abraham is set forth at the beginning of his story with great clarity and power: first of all, he is frankly seeking "greater happiness and peace and rest for me"; he wants to be more righteous, to possess greater knowledge than he has, to be a father of nations, a prince of peace, receiving and following divine instruction, to become "a rightful heir, a High Priest, holding the right belonging to the fathers" (Abraham 1:2). In short, he wants happiness, peace, rest, righteousness, knowledge, and light, and he wants to be able to hand them on to others—to his own progeny and to the world. The world is not interested in such things, but Abraham was willing to pay any price for them. The Midrash compares him to a son being soundly beaten by his loving father again and again, but never saying to his father, "I have had enough!" but only "Thine is the power."[226] "Abraham," says 1 Maccabees, "was accounted righteous only after he had been found true and faithful by passing through many testings."[227] He was chosen, says the Midrash, only after God saw that he would follow him through the greatest tribulations.[228] If Joseph Smith had based the Book of Abraham on his own experiences, one might account in part for the astonishing parallels between the situation in which the two prophets found themselves and their uncompromising and epoch-making behavior in that situation. But our parallels do not come from Joseph Smith's account; they come from the studies and commentaries of Jewish scholars: it is *their* Abraham who seems to be almost a carbon copy of Joseph Smith.

Doing the Right Thing

The wonderful thing about Abraham is that he always does the right thing, whether anybody else does or not. He had to get along with all sorts of people, most of them rascals, and he treats them all with equal courtesy—he never judges any man. After Pharaoh had tried to put him to death, and after he had taken his wife away from him, Abraham could still not refuse his old enemy in his need and laid his hand upon his head and healed him. He performed the same healing office for the king of the Philistines, who would also steal Sarah, and God recognized his great-heartedness and approved it: On the day that Abraham assured the increase of the house of Abimelech, the angels asked God that Abraham's own house might increase.[229] He was "the Friend of God" because he was the friend of man. "When Abraham went to the Holy One . . . with [a petition for] mercy," says the Midrash, "the Holy One . . . met him with mercy. When Abraham went to the Holy One . . . in singleness of heart, the Holy One . . . met him in singleness of heart; . . . with subtlety, the Holy One . . . met him with subtlety; and when Abraham asked to be guided in his doings, the Holy One . . . guided his doings for him."[230] Never, says Maimonides, did Abraham ever say to any man "God sent me to you and commanded me to do [or not do] so and so!"[231] for he knew that the priesthood operates "only by persuasion, by long-suffering, by gentleness and meekness" (D&C 121:41); it may command the elements and the spirits, "but never force the human mind." "Let there be no strife, I pray thee, between me and thee," he says to Lot; "if thou wilt take the left hand, then I will go to the right; or . . . the right hand, then I will go to the left" (Genesis 13:8–9). So Lot helped himself to the best land and as a result soon got all of his property carried away by raiders. Instead of saying "I told you so," Abraham got it back for him. He could have made a very good thing of this for himself when the king of Sodom, whose goods he had also rescued, came fawning to him ("wagging his tail," as the Midrash Rabbah puts it)[232] and trying to win him with flattery, but without denouncing the wicked king, he simply turned down his offer (Genesis 14:17–24).[233]

"If Abraham does not play fair, who will?" says the proverb. His passion for fair play breaks all the records in his pleading for the wicked cities of Sodom and Gomorrah, to whom he owed nothing but trouble. He knew all about their awful wickedness, but still, Josephus observes, "he felt sorry for them, because they were his friends and neighbors."[234] He appealed directly to the Lord's sense of fairness: "Wilt thou also destroy the righteous with the wicked?" (Genesis 18:23). The impressive thing is the way in which

Abraham is willing to abase himself to get the best possible terms for the wicked cities, risking sorely offending the Deity by questioning his justice: "far [be it] from thee . . . to slay the righteous with the wicked: . . . Shall not the Judge of all the earth do right?" (Genesis 18:25). "Behold now, I have taken upon me to speak unto the Lord, which am but dust and ashes" (Genesis 18:27). "Oh let not the Lord be angry, and I will speak" (Genesis 18:30). "Now, I have taken upon me to speak unto the Lord" (Genesis 18:31). "Oh let not the Lord be angry, and I will speak yet but this once" (Genesis 18:32). It was not an easy thing to do—especially for the most degenerate society on earth. It can be matched only by Mormon's great love for a people whom he describes as utterly and hopelessly corrupt, or by the charity of Enoch, Abraham's great predecessor: "Enoch . . . looked upon their wickedness, and their misery, and wept and stretched forth his arms, and his heart swelled wide as eternity," and declared "I will refuse to be comforted" until God promised to have compassion on the earth (Moses 7:41, 44; cf. 49–50).

Abraham learned compassion both by being an outcast himself and by special instruction, regarding which there are some interesting stories. When Melchizedek was instructing him in the mysteries of the priesthood, he told him that Noah and his people were permitted to survive ⊦ in the ark "because they practiced charity." On whom? Abraham asked, since they were alone in the ark. On the animals, was the answer, since they were constantly concerned with their comfort and welfare.[235] Again, Abraham once beheld a great vision (described also in the Book of Abraham) of all the doings of the human race to come; what he saw appalled him—he had never dreamed that men could be so bad, and in a passionate outburst he asked God why he did not destroy the wicked at once. The answer humbled him: "I . . . defer the death of the sinner, [who

might possibly] repent and live!"[236] When Abraham saw
with prophetic insight the crimes that Ishmael would commit against him and his house, he was about to turn the
youth out into the desert, but the voice of God rebuked him:
"Thou canst not punish Ishmael or any man for a crime he
has not yet committed!"[237] He learned by precept and experience that men are judged by God not as groups but as
individuals.[238]

ƴ   But Abraham's most famous lesson in tolerance was
a favorite story of Benjamin Franklin, a story which has
been traced back as far as a thirteenth-century Arabic writer
and may be much older.[239] The prologue to the story is the
visit of three angels to Abraham, who asked him what he
charged for meals; the price was only that the visitor
"invoke the name of God before beginning and praise it
when you finish."[240] But one day the patriarch entertained
an old man who would pray neither before eating nor after,
explaining to Abraham that he was a fire worshiper. His
indignant host thereupon denied him further hospitality,
and the old man went his way. But very soon the voice of
the Lord came to Abraham, saying: "I have suffered him
these hundred years, although he dishonored me; and thou
couldst not endure him one night, when he gave thee no
trouble?" Overwhelmed with remorse, Abraham rushed
out after his guest and brought him back in honor: "Go
thou and do likewise," ends the story, "and thy charity will
be rewarded by the God of Abraham."[241] In the oldest version of the story the Lord says, "Abraham! For a hundred
years the divine bounty has flowed out . . . to this man: is it
for thee to withhold thy hand from him because his worship is not thine?"[242] One is strongly reminded of the
Nephite law, which declared it "strictly contrary to the
commands of God" to penalize one's neighbor if he does
not choose to believe in God (Alma 30:7).

Once Abraham broke the ice, others began to follow.

Pharaoh returned his generosity by escorting him on his way.[243] Abimelech loaded him with gifts. The Hittites matched his fair dealings with their own.[244] "Again and again," writes Josef Bloch, "it is compassion and forgiveness alone that are the unfailing family trait of the true descendant of Abraham."[245] Luzzato discussed the polarity of the human race between "Abrahamism" and "Atticism," with "Abrahamism elaborating the poetry and practice of compassion and tenderness, while 'Atticism' articulated man's cold, calculating, self-centered approach to life."[246] A disciple of Abraham, according to a well-known tract of the Talmud, can be distinguished by "a good eye, a humble soul, and a lowly spirit," while the men of the world are marked by "an evil eye, a proud soul, and a haughty spirit."[247] "Man is only worthy of his name, he is only 'really a man' if he has fully acquired the virtues" of Abraham. "It is only then that he is worthy of being called 'lover of God,' or 'God-fearing,' like Abraham and David."[248] Like Brigham Young, Abraham sought to benefit his fellows in practical ways: as a young man back in Mesopotamia he invented a seeder that covered up the seeds as it sowed them, so the birds could not take them, and for this "his name became great in all the land of the Chaldees."[249] He apologized to the birds for driving them off, and came to an amicable understanding with them, for he was kind to all living things: "No one who is cruel to any creature," says an old formula, "can ever be a descendant of Abraham."[250]

Compassion is the keynote of Abraham's life and the teaching that makes the Pearl of Great Price supremely relevant to our own time. This is most unequivocally affirmed in what is the most remarkable passage of the book, where God himself weeps as he is about to bring the flood upon the earth. "Naught but peace, justice, and truth is the habitation of thy throne," cries Enoch; "and mercy shall go before thy face and have no end; how is it thou canst weep?

The Lord said, . . . in the Garden of Eden, gave I unto man
his agency; And unto thy brethren . . . have I given commandment, that they should love one another, . . . but
behold, they are without affection, and they hate their own
blood" (Moses 7:31–33).

Notes

1. W. F. Albright, *Yahweh and the Gods of Canaan* (Garden City, NY:
Doubleday, 1968), 64–65.

2. Micha J. bin Gorion, *Die Sagen der Juden*, 5 vols. (Frankfurt:
Rütten & Loening, 1913–27), 1:333.

3. We have discussed the reality of such a "fall" in Hugh W. Nibley,
"Tenting, Toll, and Taxing," *Western Political Quarterly* 19 (1966): 600–601,
628–29; reprinted in *The Ancient State*, CWHN 10 (Salt Lake City: Deseret
Book and FARMS, 1991), 34–35, 67–68. The specific mention of thistles,
thorns, and dust in Genesis 3:17–19 is a clear indication of drought conditions.

4. Bin Gorion, *Sagen der Juden*, 1:186.

5. Albright, *Yahweh and the Gods of Canaan*, 99.

6. *Genesis Rabbah* 32:11, in *Midrash Rabbah: Genesis*, trans. Harry
Freedman (London: Soncino 1939), 1:256.

7. Franz M. Th. Böhl, *Das Zeitalter Abrahams* (Leipzig: Hinrichs,
1930), 35–36.

8. Bernhard Beer, *Leben Abraham's nach Auffassung der jüdischen Sage*
(Leipzig: Leiner, 1859), 190–92 n. 819; Judah Goldin, trans., *The Fathers
according to Rabbi Nathan* (New York: Schocken, 1955), 132; Böhl, *Zeitalter
Abrahams*, 35–36; the older list is in Gerald Friedlander, *Pirkê de Rabbi
Eliezer* (New York: Hermon, 1965), 187–230.

9. *Sefer ha-Yashar*, VIII:1–2, 18a–20b (Salt Lake City: Parry, 1887), 17;
and bin Gorion, *Sagen der Juden*, 2:26–28.

10. Günter Lanczkowski, "Parallelmotive zu einer altägyptische
Erzählung," *Zeitschrift der deutschen morgenländischen Gesellschaft* 105
(1955): 258.

11. G. A. Wainwright, "Zeberged: The Shipwrecked Sailor's Island,"
JEA 32 (1946): 38.

12. Bin Gorion, *Sagen der Juden*, 1:12.

13. Ibid., 2:310.

14. Hephaestius of Thebes, *Astrologia* XXIV, in Theodor Hopfner,
Fontes Historiae Religionis Aegyptiacae (Bonn: Marcus and Weber, 1922),
562.

15. G. A. Wainwright, "Letopolis," *JEA* 18 (1932): 161.

16. Ibid., 160; G. A. Wainwright, "Amun's Meteorite and Omphaloi," *ZÄS* 71 (1935): 44.

17. Beer, *Leben Abraham's*, 30.

18. Wainwright, "Letopolis," 166.

19. Robert Eisler, *Iēsous Basileus ou basileusas*, 2 vols. (Heidelberg: Winter, 1930), 2:108.

20. Bin Gorion, *Sagen der Juden*, 1:104.

21. Ibid., 2:185: "shifting its position from west to east," whatever that means.

22. Ibid., 1:206.

23. Horapollo, *Hieroglyphica* I, 3, in Hopfner, *Fontes Historiae Religionis Aegyptiacae*, 577; Pseudo-Eratosthenes, *Astrothesiai Zodion*, 33, says Sirius gets its name from the fact that its brightness changes (*dia tēn phlogos kinēsin*), which can hardly refer to twinkling, since other stars twinkle just as much, in Hopfner, *Fontes Historiae Religionis Aegyptiacae*, 760.

24. Alexis Mallon, "Le disque étoilé en Canaan au troisième millènaire avant Jésus-Christ," *Mélanges Maspero* 1/1 (1935–58): 59.

25. Thaʿlabī, Kitāb Qiṣaṣ al-Anbiyāʾ (Cairo: Muṣṭafā al-Bābi al-Ḥalibī wa-Awlāduhu, A.H. 1340), 54.

26. *Pseudo-Philo* 6:17.

27. Leopold Cohn, "An Apocryphal Work Ascribed to Philo of Alexandria," *JQR* 10 (1897): 286.

28. Bin Gorion, *Sagen der Juden*, 2:238.

29. Cohn, "An Apocryphal Work Ascribed to Philo of Alexandria," 288–89.

30. Louis Ginzberg, *Legends of the Jews*, 7 vols. (Philadelphia: Jewish Publication Society, 1909–38), 1:253.

31. Beer, *Leben Abraham's*, 41.

32. Ibid., 9, 109 n. 84, for sources; also bin Gorion, *Sagen der Juden*, 2:58–59; *Sefer ha-Yashar*, 9:37–38.

33. Bin Gorion, *Sagen der Juden*, 1:154.

34. *Cave of Treasures* 25:17, trans. by E. A. Wallis Budge (London: Religious Tract Society, 1927), 138.

35. Bin Gorion, *Sagen der Juden*, 2:45. In some legends God shakes and even overthrows the throne of Nimrod as a warning, without any mention of Abraham; cf. Heinrich Schützinger, *Ursprung und Entwicklung der arabischen Abraham-Nimrod-Legende* (Bonn: Rheinische Friedrich-Wilhelms-Universität, 1961), 74.

36. Gustav Weil, *Biblische Legenden der Muselmänner* (Frankfurt: Rütten, 1845), 59.

37. *Apocalypse of Abraham* 8:6.

38. He was consumed by fire from heaven while Abraham was saved, Beer, *Leben Abraham's*, 16–17; a fragment of Josephus says that he was killed trying to put out the flames that were destroying his father's idols and house, Eisler, *Iēsous Basileus ou basileusas*, 1:523.

39. Schützinger, *Ursprung und Entwicklung der arabischen Abraham-Nimrod-Legende*, 100.

40. *Pseudo-Philo* 6:18. The two phenomena meet most dramatically in volcanic activity. The Egyptians have much to say about "the fire-island that emerged from the waters" at the time Egypt was first settled—perhaps a volcanic island emerging from the Mediterranean, Günther Roeder, "Die Kosmogonie von Hermopolis," *Egyptian Religion* 1 (1933): 10.

41. Clement, *Recognitiones (Clementine Recognitions)* I, 32, in *PG* 1:1226.

42. Beer, *Leben Abraham's*, 165 n. 464.

43. Bin Gorion, *Sagen der Juden*, 2:238.

44. Genesis 19:30–31; bin Gorion, *Sagen der Juden*, 2:239–40.

45. Beer, *Leben Abraham's*, 44. Also at the attempted sacrifice of Abraham, fire burned all the birds and made all the surrounding region desolate, Thaᶜlabī, *Kitāb Qiṣaṣ al-Anbiyāʾ*, 54.

46. Nelson Glueck, "Ancient Highways in the Wilderness of Zin," *Proceedings of the American Philosophical Society* 100/2 (1956): 154–55.

47. Ibid., 151.

48. Mallon, "Le disque étoilé en Canaan," 57–58.

49. Otto Eissfeldt, "Achronische, anachronische und synchronische Elemente in der Genesis," *JEOL* 17 (1963): 163–64.

50. Robert Graves and Raphael Patai, *Hebrew Myths: The Book of Genesis* (New York: McGraw-Hill, 1964), 169.

51. Beer, *Leben Abraham's*, 137 n. 260.

52. Friedrich Cornelius, "Genesis XIV," *Zeitschrift für die alttestamentliche Wissenschaft* 72 (1960): 5–6.

53. Ibid.

54. André Parrot, *Abraham et son temps* (Neuchatel: Delachaux & Niestlé, 1962), 105 n. 3.

55. Ibid., 105 nn. 3–4.

56. Homer, *Iliad* XXI, 211–382; Apollodorus, *Epitome* IV, 7.

57. *Lech Lecha* 86b, in *The Zohar*, trans. Harry Sperling and Maurice Simon, 5 vols. (London: Soncino, 1984), 1:288.

58. Plutarch, *De Iside et Osiride* 39–40.

59. Eisler, *Iēsous Basileus ou basileusas*, 2:109.

60. Ibid., n. 1. Interestingly enough, one of the most important

accounts of the wind-flood relates that there were no inhabitants in the Near East before the time of Noah, the world's population dwelling far to the eastward near the region of Eden, *Cave of Treasures* 26:15, 17, trans. Budge, 141–42. To this area, according to the Ram and Rud story of the Mandaeans, Jared and his brother returned.

61. *Cave of Treasures* 26:11, trans. Budge, 141.

62. Maurus Witzel, "Die Klage über Ur," *Orientalia* 14 (1945): 190, noting that this must be descriptive of a real historical event.

63. Hermann Kees, "Aus den Notjahren der Thebaïs," *Orientalia* 21 (1952): 86–97; E. A. W. Budge, *Egyptian Hieratic Papyri in the British Museum* (London: Trustees of the British Museum, 1923), 19.

64. Claude Vandersleyen, "Une tempête sous le règne d'Amosis," *RdE* 19 (1967): 133, 155–57; quotation is from 140.

65. Different lists (but both including famine) are found in August Wünsche, *Bibliotheca Rabbinica: Eine Sammlung alter Midraschim* (Hildesheim: Olm, 1967), 182, and Ginzberg, *Legends of the Jews*, 1:220–21.

66. Friedlander, *Pirkê de Rabbi Eliezer*, 189; bin Gorion, *Sagen der Juden*, 2:159.

67. Bin Gorion, *Sagen der Juden*, 1:174; cf. Helaman 11:4–6.

68. Bin Gorion, *Sagen der Juden*, 1:176.

69. Ibid., 2:83.

70. Witzel, "Die Klage über Ur," 190.

71. Bin Gorion, *Sagen der Juden*, 1:155. Among the oldest and most vivid products of Egyptian art are the famine reliefs from the Third Dynasty, showing the horribly emaciated condition of the people.

72. *Jubilees* 11:11–13.

73. Jan Bergman, *Legenden der Juden* (Berlin: Schwetschke & Sohn, 1919), 58. Bar Hebraeus, *Chronography*, trans. E. A. Wallis Budge, 2 vols. (London: Oxford University Press, 1932), 1:10, says he was fifteen when he drove off the *qarqāsê* (ravens? locusts?) who were eating all the crops of the Chaldeans.

74. *Jubilees* 24:18; bin Gorion, *Sagen der Juden*, 2:272.

75. *Jubilees* 11:22–24.

76. *Midrash on Psalms* 110:2, in William G. Braude, *Midrash on Psalms*, 2 vols. (New Haven: Yale University Press, 1959), 2:205.

77. Hugh W. Nibley, "The Hierocentric State," *Western Political Quarterly* 4 (1951): 226–30, 235–53; reprinted in *CWHN* 10:99–103, 110–34.

78. Eisler, *Iēsous Basileus ou basileusas*, 1:523.

79. E.g., *Maʿaseh Abraham Abinu*, in Adolph Jellinek, *Bet ha-Midrasch*, 6 vols. (1853–77; reprint, Jerusalem: Wahrmann, 1967), 1:34; cf. 32.

80. Genesis 15:9–12; cf. Josephus, *Antiquities* I, 10, 3.

81. This is well treated in Alexandre Moret, *La mise à mort du dieu en*

Égypte (Paris: Geuthner, 1927). Cf. Jean Bérard, "De la légende grecque à la Bible," *RHR* 151 (1957): 229.

82. These episodes are described, with the sources, in bin Gorion, *Sagen der Juden*, 1:317, 151, 153, 174.

83. *Clementine Recognitions* I, 29–33, in *PG* 1:1223–27.

84. *Pseudo-Philo* 7:1–4.

85. Bin Gorion, *Sagen der Juden*, 2:64, 48.

86. Ibid., 1:196–97.

87. *Cave of Treasures* 25:8–9, trans. Budge, 137.

88. E.g., *Journal of Discourses*, 5:353.

89. Cf. M. H. Segal, "The Religion of Israel before Sinai," *JQR* 52 (1961–62): 45.

90. *Genesis Rabbah* 42:4, in Freedman, *Midrash Rabbah: Genesis*, 1:346. The Lord "was chosen by our father Abraham when the nations were divided in the time of Phaleg," *Testament of Naphthali* 8:3, in *The Apocrypha and Pseudepigrapha of the Old Testament*, ed. Robert H. Charles, 2 vols. (Oxford: Clarendon, 1976), 2:363.

91. E. C. B. MacLaurin, "The Development of the Idea of God in Ancient Canaan," *Journal of Religious History* 2 (1963): 278.

92. Judith 5:6–8.

93. Josephus, *Antiquities* I, 6, 5.

94. Ibid., I, 7, 1.

95. *Pseudo-Philo* 7:1–4.

96. Cornelius, "Genesis XIV," 7.

97. Daniil A. Chwolsohn (Khvol'son), *Die Ssabier und der Ssabismus* (St. Petersburg: Buchdruckerei der Kaiserlichen Akademie der Wissenschaften, 1856), 1:620.

98. *Genesis Rabbah* 39:8, in Freedman, *Midrash Rabbah: Genesis*, 1:317; Beer, *Leben Abraham's*, 23.

99. See Parrot, *Abraham et son temps*, especially the illustrations.

100. Michael C. Astour, "Political and Cosmic Symbolism in Genesis 14 and in Its Babylonian Sources," in Alexander Altmann, *Biblical Motifs* (Cambridge: Harvard University Press, 1966), 74.

101. Ginzberg, *Legends of the Jews*, 1:218.

102. Albright, *Yahweh and the Gods of Canaan*, 107.

103. Ibid., 65. This applies whether Abraham was a caravaneer or shepherd: "The life of wandering shepherds was anything but pleasant."

104. Eusebius, *Praparatio Evangelica* (*Preparation for the Gospel*) IX, 16, in *PG* 21:705; cf. Josephus, *Antiquities*, I, 7, 2, who says that Abraham's house in Damascus was still being pointed out in his day.

105. *Genesis Rabbah* 41:7, in Freedman, *Midrash Rabbah: Genesis*, 1:337.

106. Robert Graves, *The Greek Myths*, 2 vols. (Baltimore: Penguin, 1955).

107. Ibid., 2:134, 146–47.

108. Apollodorus, *The Library* II, 5, 11.

109. Hyginus, *Fabulae* XXXI, 65, in Hopfner, *Fontes Historiae Religionis Aegyptiacae*, 349.

110. Graves, *Greek Myths*, 2:135.

111. *Descriptio plenaria totius Urbis* VIII, text in Hopfner, *Fontes Historiae Religionis Aegyptiacae*, 532–33.

112. Graves, *Greek Myths*, 2:137.

113. Ibid.

114. Ibid., 164.

115. Ibid., 197.

116. Ibid., 164.

117. Ibid., 167.

118. Marie Renault, *The King Must Die* (New York: Pantheon, 1962); and Marie Renault, *The Bull from the Sea* (New York: Pantheon, 1958).

119. Eugène Lefébure, "Le sacrifice humain d'après les rites de Busiris et d'Abydos," *BE* 36 (1915): 301–2.

120. Probus, Scholia on *Georgics* III, 4, in Hopfner, *Fontes Historiae Religionis Aegyptiacae*, 618.

121. Scholiast Apollonius of Rhodes, *Argon* IV, 1396.

122. Ovid is discussed by J. Gwyn Griffiths, "Human Sacrifices in Egypt: The Classical Evidence," *ASAE* 48 (1948): 411; Hyginus, *Fabulae* LVI, 59–60, in Hopfner, *Fontes Historiae Religionis Aegyptiacae*, 348, who also says that Heracles broke loose just as the sacrificial prayer was being uttered by the king, ibid., XXXI, 65, in Hopfner, *Fontes Historiae Religionis Aegyptiacae*, 349.

123. Quoted in Lactantius, *Divinae Institutiones* (*Divine Institutes*) I, 21, in *PL* 6:238–40; see Lefébure, "Le sacrifice humain d'après les rites de Busiris et d'Abydos," 273

124. Lampridius, in *Scriptores Historiae Augustae, Maximus Prior* VIII, 5, in Hopfner, *Fontes Historiae Religionis Aegyptiacae*, 557.

125. Claudian, in Rufinus, *Vitae Patrum (Life of the Fathers)* I, 254–56, in Hopfner, *Fontes Historiae Religionis Aegyptiacae*, 591.

126. Orosius, *Adversus Paganos Historiarum Libri Septem (Against the Heathens)* I, 11 (6–8), in Hopfner, *Fontes Historiae Religionis Aegyptiacae*, 636–37.

127. Isocrates, *Busiris 9–10*, in Hopfner, *Fontes Historiae Religionis Aegyptiacae*, 49, praises the high moral standards of Egypt, and points out that Busiris lived two hundred years before Perseus, while Heracles lived four generations after him (ibid., 15).

128. Diodorus, I, 67, discussed by Griffiths, "Human Sacrifices in Egypt" 410–11.

129. Griffiths, "Human Sacrifices in Egypt," 411–12; which Rufinus turns to sarcasm: "O kindly altars of Busiris!" Claudian, in Rufinus, *Vitae Patrum* I, 254–56, Hopfner, *Fontes Historiae Religionis Aegyptiacae*, 591.

130. Strabo, *Geography* XVII, 1, in Hopfner, *Fontes Historiae Religionis Aegyptiacae*, 76.

131. Herodotus, *Historiae* II, 59.

132. I. E. S. Edwards, *The Pyramids of Egypt*, rev. ed. (Harmondsworth, England: Penguin, 1961), 27.

133. Henri Frankfort, *Kingship and the Gods* (Chicago: University of Chicago Press, 1948), 200.

134. Jaroslav Černý, *Ancient Egyptian Religion* (London: Hutchinson's University Library, 1952), 106.

135. Kurt Sethe, *Übersetzung und Kommentar zu den altägyptischen Pyramidentexten*, 6 vols. (Gluckstadt: Augustin, 1934), 1:91, 80.

136. Pyramid Text 477 (§962, 964, 966).

137. The monument of Mentu-her-khepeshef; see Lefébure, "Le sacrifice humain d'après les rites de Busiris et d'Abydos," 285.

138. Edwards, *Pyramids of Egypt*, 30–31.

139. Alexandre Piankoff, *The Shrines of Tut-Ankh-Amon* (New York: Harper, 1955), 60.

140. E. A. W. Budge, *Osiris: The Egyptian Religion of Resurrection*, 2 vols. in 1 (New Hyde Park, NY: University Books, 1961), 1:212; Sethe, *Übersetzung und Kommentar zu den altägyptischen Pyramidentexten*, 1:80, 78–79; Coffin Text 37, in Adriaan de Buck, *the Egyptian Coffin Texts*, 7 vols. (Chicago: University of Chicago Press, 1935–61), 1:155. Even Min of Coptos survived as a sacrificial god at Busiris; see Henri Gauthier, *Les fêtes du dieu Min* (Cairo: BIFAO, 1931), 231–32, 234, 236–38.

141. *Testament of Levi* 6:9–11.

142. Friedlander, *Pirkê de Rabbi Eliezer*, 181, citing Rabbi Zeera.

143. Ibid.

144. Ibid., 181–82.

145. W. G. Lambert, *Babylonian Wisdom Literature* (Oxford: Clarendon, 1960), 5.

146. Ginzberg, *Legends of the Jews*, 1:248; Graves and Patai, *Hebrew Myths*, 167.

147. Bin Gorion, *Sagen der Juden*, 2:236. A visitor would often have an "accident" that put him at the mercy of the townsmen, ibid.

148. Cf. bin Gorion, *Sagen der Juden*, 2:236–37.

149. Ginzberg, *Legends of the Jews*, 1:247.

150. Ibid., 1:249.

151. *Vayera* 105b, in Sperling and Simon, *Zohar*, 1:339.

152. Ibid., 106b, in Sperling and Simon, *Zohar*, 1:342; bin Gorion, *Sagen der Juden*, 2:220–23.

153. Bin Gorion, *Sagen der Juden*, 2:227.

154. Ibid., 2:211–12, 228.

155. *Vayera* 105b–106a, in Sperling and Simon, *Zohar*, 1:340.

156. Anson F. Rainey, "Merchants at Ugarit and the Patriarchal Narratives," *Christian News from Israel* 14/2 (1963): 19.

157. TB *Sanhedrin* 109a–b.

158. Friedlander, *Pirkê de Rabbi Eliezer*, 176.

159. Ibid., 182 (emphasis added).

160. See Genesis 14:22–23; Josephus, *Antiquities* I, 10, 2.

161. *Vayera* 116a, in Sperling and Simon, *Zohar*, 1:362; cf. Deuteronomy 28:47.

162. Ginzberg, *Legends of the Jews*, 1:246–47; cf. Beer, *Leben Abraham's*, 41.

163. Beer, *Leben Abraham's*, 164 n. 441, noting that in Homer, *Iliad* XVI, 386–89, Procrustes suffers the same fate as Sodom.

164. Ginzberg, *Legends of the Jews*, 1:295.

165. Lefébure, "Le sacrifice humain d'après les rites de Busiris et d'Abydos," 274.

166. Claudian, in Eutropius, *Breviarium* I, 161–62, in Hopfner, *Fontes Historiae Religionis Aegyptiacae*, 591.

167. Graves, *Greek Myths*, 1:332.

168. Schützinger, *Ursprung und Entwicklung der arabischen Abraham-Nimrod-Legende*, 47.

169. Wolf Leslau, trans., *Falasha Anthology* (New Haven: Yale University Press, 1951), 27.

170. David Sidersky, *Les origines des légendes musulmanes dans le Coran et dans les vies des prophètes* (Paris: Geuthner, 1933), 33.

171. Max Seligsohn, "Nimrod and Abraham," in *The Jewish Encyclopedia*, 9:310.

172. Beer, *Leben Abraham's*, 66.

173. *Genesis Rabbah* 42:5; 43:5, in Freedman, *Midrash Rabbah: Genesis*, 1:347, 355.

174. Schützinger, *Ursprung und Entwicklung der arabischen Abraham-Nimrod-Legende*, 47, for sources on the problem.

175. *Ma'aseh Abraham Abinu*, in Jellinek, *Bet ha-Midrasch*, 1:32–34; Weil, *Biblische Legenden der Muselmänner*, 73.

176. Schützinger, *Ursprung und Entwicklung der arabischen Abraham-Nimrod-Legende*, 128.

177. *4 Maccabees* 9:26; 11:9–10.

178. Ibid., 11:17–20; 12:1.

179. Bernard Chapira, "Legendes bibliques attribuées à Ka‘b el-Ahbar," *REJ* 69 (1919): 99.

180. The Egyptians had "an altogether special type of furniture," by whose ministrations one possessed "a new means of spiritualizing the offerings—by literal combustion" in a metal brazier, Gustave Jéquier, "Notes et remarques," *RT* 33 (1911): 166–69. John Garstang, "Excavations at Hierakonpolis, at Esna, and in Nubia," *ASAE* 8 (1907): 148, has commented on the strange sacrificial structures in the necropolis at Esneh.

181. Coffin Text 135, in de Buck, *Egyptian Coffin Texts*, 2:160.

182. Schützinger, *Ursprung und Entwicklung der arabischen Abraham-Nimrod-Legende*, 106.

183. *Teachings of the Prophet Joseph Smith*, 260.

184. "The Book of Abraham 1:5," in *Times and Seasons* 3/9 (1 March 1842): 704.

185. George Foucart, *Bibliothèque d'Études Coptes*, 15 vols. (Cairo: Institut français d'archéologie orientale du Caire, 1919), 1: Fol. 11.

186. A contrast pointed out by Berend Gemser, "The Instructions of ‘Onchsheshonqy and Biblical Wisdom Literature," *Vetus Testamentum*, Supplement 7 (Leiden: Brill, 1959), 121–22.

187. *Clementine Recognitions* I, 32, in *PG* 1:1226.

188. *Genesis Rabbah* 41:7, in Freedman, *Midrash Rabbah: Genesis*, 1:338.

189. F. M. Th. de Liagre Böhl, "Babel und Bibel (II): The Patriarchenzeit," *JEOL* 17 (1963): 136.

190. J. C. L. Gibson, "Light from Mari on the Patriarchs," *Journal of Semitic Studies* 7 (1962): 61.

191. *Genesis Rabbah* 39:8, in Freedman, *Midrash Rabbah: Genesis*, 1:316.

192. Martin Buber, "Abraham the Seer" *Judaism* 5 (1956): 295–96.

193. *Genesis Rabbah* 39:11, in Freedman, *Midrash Rabbah: Genesis*, 1:319–20.

194. Michael Asin, "Logia et Agrapha Domini Jesu," 79-Ih., IV, 163, 9, in *PO* 13:407–8. The famous story of the hospitable Philemon and his wife Baucis has been tied to the age of Abraham through Lot by Joseph E. Fontenrose, "Philemon, Lot, and Lycaon," *Classical Philology* 13 (1944–50): 119, deriving both from "a subtype of the Babylonian flood myth."

195. *Vayera* 113b, in Sperling and Simon, *Zohar*, 1:357.

196. Ibid., in Sperling and Simon, *Zohar*, 1:356–57.

197. Ibid., 107b, in Sperling and Simon, *Zohar*, 1:345; so 113a, p. 357: "When the angel of destruction obtains authorisation to destroy, he does not discriminate between innocent and guilty."

198. *Midrash on Psalms* 110:1, in Braude, *Midrash on Psalms*, 2:205.

199. Friedlander, *Pirkê de Rabbi Eliezer*, 184–85.

200. *Jubilees* 24:18; bin Gorion, *Sagen der Juden*, 2:272.

201. *Sefer ha-Yashar* 22:11–12.

202. Ginzberg, *Legends of the Jews*, 1:271; cf. bin Gorion, *Sagen der Juden*, 2:231; Beer, *Leben Abraham's*, 56.

203. Ginzberg, *Legends of the Jews*, 1:271.

204. Friedlander, *Pirkê de Rabbi Eliezer*, 184–85; *Vayera* 105a, in Sperling and Simon, *Zohar*, 1:337.

205. Beer, *Leben Abraham's*, 206 n. 973.

206. Ibid., 37.

207. Friedlander, *Pirkê de Rabbi Eliezer*, 205.

208. Bin Gorion, *Sagen der Juden*, 2:201.

209. This tradition is discussed by J. Perlès, "Ahron ben Gerson Aboulrabi," *REJ* 21 (1890): 247.

210. The stories, based on Genesis 18, are told with the sources in bin Gorion, *Sagen der Juden*, 2:201–3, and Beer, *Leben Abraham's*, 37.

211. Bin Gorion, *Sagen der Juden*, 2:203.

212. Ibid., 2:258–63.

213. *Testament of Abraham* 1:1–5:2.

214. Ginzberg, *Legends of the Jews*, 1:281.

215. Goldin, *The Fathers according to Rabbi Nathan*, 131.

216. *Midrash on Psalms* 110:1, in Braude, *Midrash on Psalms*, 2:205.

217. Cf. *Pseudo-Philo* 7:1–4 and *Genesis Rabbah* 39:6, in Freedman, *Midrash Rabbah: Genesis*, 1:315.

218 *Lech Lecha* 77b, in Sperling and Simon, *Zohar*, 1:263.

219. Ibid., 88a, in Sperling and Simon, *Zohar*, 1:293.

220. Ibid., 76b, in Sperling and Simon, *Zohar*, 1:260.

221. Text reproduced and discussed by Dean C. Jessee, "The Early Accounts of Joseph Smith's First Vision," *BYU Studies* 9 (1969): 280–81.

222. Ginzberg, *Legends of the Jews*, 1:211.

223. Claude G. Montefiore, *A Rabbinic Anthology* (London: Macmillan, 1938), 84.

224. *Genesis Rabbah* 39:1, in Freedman, *Midrash Rabbah: Genesis*, 1:313.

225. Buber, "Abraham the Seer," 295.

226. *Midrash on Psalms* 26:2, in Braude, *Midrash on Psalms*, 1:357.

227. 1 Maccabees 2:52.

228. *Midrash on Psalms* 18:25, in Braude, *Midrash on Psalms*, 1:255.

229. Ginzberg, *Legends of the Jews*, 1:261.

230. *Midrash on Psalms* 18:22, in Braude, *Midrash on Psalms*, 1:250.

231. Maimonides, *Daalat* III, 302, in *The Guide for the Perplexed*, trans. Michael Friedländer, 2nd ed. (New York: Dover, 1956), 317.

232. *Genesis Rabbah* 43:5, in Freedman, *Midrash Rabbah: Genesis*, 1:355 n. 7.

233. Josephus, *Antiquities* I, 10, 2, contrasts the two kings who met Abraham at the same time, the king of Sodom being the opposite number to Melchizedek, "the righteous king."

234. Josephus, *Antiquities* I, 10, 1.

235. Bin Gorion, *Sagen der Juden*, 2:268–69.

236. K. Kohler, "The Pre-Talmudic Haggada," *JQR* 7 (1894–95): 584–85.

237. Beer, *Leben Abraham's*, 51.

238. *Vayera* 107a, in Sperling and Simon, *Zohar*, 1:343.

239. George A. Kohut, "Abraham's Lesson in Tolerance," *JQR* 15 (1905): 105, 110.

240. Ibid., 104; this story is independently attested by Tabari and early Jewish writers.

241. Ibid., 106.

242. Ibid., 110.

243. For which in turn Pharaoh enjoyed a special blessing, Z. H. Chajes, *Student's Guide through the Talmud* (London: East and West Library, 1952), 156.

244. For which they too received a special blessing, Beer, *Leben Abraham's*, 76.

245. Josef S. Bloch, *Israel und die Völker nach jüdischer Lehre* (Berlin: Harz, 1922), 513.

246. Jacob B. Agus, *The Vision and the Way: An Interpretation of Jewish Ethics* (New York: Ungar, 1966), 4.

247. *Aboth* v. 22, cited by Geza Vermes, *Scripture and Tradition in Judaism*, 2nd ed. (Leiden: Brill, 1973), 172.

248. *Seder Eliyahu*, cited by R. J. Zwi Werblowsky, "A Note on the Text of Seder Eliyahu," *Journal of Jewish Studies* 6 (1955): 217.

249. *Jubilees* 11:23, 21.

250. *Beẓah* 32b, cited by Beer, *Leben Abraham's*, 90; 204 n. 969.

5

The Rivals

Ritual as History

The very things that move the critics to treat the Abraham story as religious fiction or as hopelessly garbled tradition are what, in the opinion of the present writer, carry the greatest conviction of authenticity. In terms of *ritual* practices they all make sense. It is remarkable how completely the present Abraham literature avoids giving any countenance to the ritual explanation of things, even taking pains to warn the student, as does James L. Kelso, that there is not a trace of anything of a ritual or cultic nature in the Abraham tradition.[1] This is the more remarkable since scholars who deal with the parallel literature so important to understanding the patriarchal situation express a growing feeling of dependence upon the ritual elements of the tales they study. Two studies in the *Zeitschrift für ägyptische Sprache* not only illustrate this point very well, but are also of prime importance for the study of Abraham.

The first is by Jan Assmann, who has taken the famous Egyptian *Tale of the Two Brothers,* a very popular moralizing story suggesting the patriarchal narratives of Israel at many points, and shown the significance of some of its main episodes, first noting that it is only during the past fifteen

years or so that it has become the practice to subject
Egyptian literary pieces to such treatment.[2] Central to the
Two Brothers theme is a love triangle, much like those met
with in the patriarchal narratives, the most famous being
that of Abraham, Sarah, and Pharaoh, which we have
treated at some length.[3] This theme Assmann finds to be
combined with the perennial conflict between the farmer
and the herdsman, a confrontation that Werner finds most
prominent in the Abraham legends. Related to this in turn
is the departure of the hero from his home as an outcast—
as was Abraham.[4] As Assmann lays it out, the pattern of the
Two Brothers is remarkably like that of Joseph Smith's book
of Moses, chapter 1; when compared with the *Apocalypse of
Abraham* and the *Book of Adam*, Moses 1 tells essentially the
same story, all of which shows strong Egyptian influence.
Here is how Assmann puts it: (1) The hero is cast out of his
happy home, his original condition of life, against his will,
but for his own good as he realizes. (2) He must go forth to
undergo a series of trials and tests, (3) symbolic of overcoming death by resurrection, and so (4) return to his former home as a changed person, (5) being received back
when he identifies himself in a formal testing (*"Identifikation
in Form einer Prüfung"*). (6) Transfiguration and exaltation
go with coronation and marriage.[5]

All this, according to Assmann, is to be explained in
terms of a ritual background, an idea, he notes, that is at present enjoying a vigorous revival among scholars: "A wealth
of tales are now traced back to a type of *initiation*-ritual
which belongs to an earlier level of culture." This
"Initiationsthematik" has, moreover, "global connections,"
recurring all along the Fertile Crescent at the dawn of history. Whether it rests on oral or written transmission, its uni-
versality is assured, according to Assmann, because it deals
with the basic problems of human existence.[6] Though such
stories were preserved and transmitted for entertainment

and moral improvement, they always retained a perceptible "memory of their ritual origin." Assmann concludes by asking whether the Two Brothers really lends itself to the old ritual interpretation that at present is enjoying increasing favor among scholars and replies with a resounding affirmative—through the literary facade of the texts, the old Egyptian initiation ritual is still undeniable.[7]

The other article, by Strother Purdy, is even more enlightening and deals with the even more famous story of Sinuhe, which, as many scholars have noted, touches on the Abraham question at many points. Right at the outset we are confronted with the now-familiar Abraham enigmas, for Purdy assures us that we still "do not know whether it [the story of Sinuhe] is autobiographical or fiction, history or belles lettres—whether, in short, the events it relates ever happened or were an imaginary projection." To illustrate this point, he lists six totally different interpretations of its literary nature, each defended by eminent Egyptologists.[8] We need not leap to negative conclusions about Abraham when we learn "that Sinuhe has both fictional and historic identity [as] is now presumed by most scholars," and that the same holds true for the hero of the much later story of Wenamon.[9] How can you tell that there is any real history behind it? "Because the conditions he [the writer] describes are supported by purely historical sources." Purdy concludes, "Indeed, it is impossible to keep the literature of ancient Egypt out of an interlinked literary-historical nexus."[10] Though there is the widest disagreement among the specialists as to which part is history and which is fiction, with Abraham as with the Egyptians we are no longer justified in following the established school procedure of treating the whole thing as mythical.

The main issue raised by Egyptologists regarding the history of Sinuhe is the same one that confronts the reader of the Book of Abraham at the outset—just what is

Pharaoh's business and influence in *Canaan* at the time? On that there is no agreement. Many experts view Egypt's presence in Palestine and Syria in Sinuhe's day as pure literary invention. Purdy, on the other hand, points out that since so little documentation exists from the time, and since trade and intermarriage between Egypt, Palestine, and Syria continued over long periods of time, there is no justification for denying it in Sinuhe's day.[11] Indeed, so little is known about the period that the Sinuhe story itself has been called, along with the Khusobk stele, the *only* evidence that Egypt ever was in Palestine or Syria during the great Twelfth Dynasty.[12] Need we recall that the mingling of the cult of Pharaoh with that of the Canaanites was derided as one of the absurdities of the Book of Abraham? Purdy warns us against the pitfalls of reading Egyptian like English, noting that it may be Egyptian literary usage "to have Sinuhe talk so much about what he doesn't specify," things which could not escape an Egyptian audience but which leave us often in the dark.[13] In particular the court scenes (cf. our Facsimile 3) display discretion, where the hearer is "to imagine things tacitly occurring." All of which can be most instructive for the student of Abraham's account.

Though the story of Sinuhe furnishes a wealth of convincing details from which one may construct an account of Egypt in Canaan in those early days, Purdy finds the main thrust of the story, as Assmann does that of the Two Brothers, to be *ritual* in nature: Sinuhe's return to court is a kind of popular allegory of holy dying, with all its ritual accompaniments so near to the Egyptian heart.[14] The story mixes divine with human reference in the court of Pharaoh, which is a foretaste of heaven: Sinuhe, on his return to the court, is being initiated into the glory of the eternities and enters the other world; the king's letter inviting him to return to Egypt is "his passport to the West"[15]—his "Book of Breathings," as we have described it elsewhere.[16]

Likewise in the story of the Shipwrecked Sailor, that hero, laden with treasure got from a dragon in a lost world, and though a commoner, heads straight for the court of Pharaoh, where he is received in glory by the king and all the great and noble ones.[17] Such heavenly homecomings, reminiscent of the early Christian Pearl story, are routine in Egypt from the earliest times, e.g., in Utterance 422 of the Pyramid Texts.[18] It is also the subject of the *Testament of Abraham* and has a spiritual interpretation in the "Lebensmüde."[19]

Purdy points out one "proof" for the historicity of Sinuhe that keeps emerging unexpectedly but forcefully from time to time in the story. It is "the ring of truth" which "we intuit breaking through an artificial surface narrative with some convincing hint of actual experience."[20] Herbert Werner also notes how veristic touches and glimpses of a real world keep breaking through in Abraham stories.[21] As an example of this, Purdy notes how Sinuhe goes out of his way to explain the customs of Canaan to his Egyptian readers, e.g., "how an Egyptian funeral differed from an Asiatic one. . . . Clearly, the writer . . . wanted to give the reader enjoyment of things he would not otherwise know about; clearly he had a different kind of reader in mind."[22] Which is exactly what Abraham does when he explains Egyptian customs to the people back in Palestine (Abraham 1:12, 14): "Now, at this time it was the custom of the priest of Pharaoh . . ." (Abraham 1:8), " . . . after the manner of the Egyptians" (Abraham 1:11); describing for their benefit, e.g., just how an Egyptian altar looks (Abraham 1:12–13), and telling them where to turn for his drawing of one, exactly as the Egyptian funeral texts (e.g., the Amduat) tell the reader where to turn for a picture of a ship or monster.[23] The "ring of truth" strikes home again in Abraham's use of the first person in his narrative, the total absence of dialogue in it, the little shock that comes with being told that two royal ladies, Hathor and Maat, are "Pharaoh and the Prince of Pharaoh," respectively, though both are very obviously women. That is not the way one fakes old records.

What Alster says of Mesopotamia applies with double force to Egypt, that the latest studies should hopefully "teach us to hold the spiritual achievements of the early Mesopotamian world in greater respect" than we have. The real dimension of the thinking of both peoples is shown in what is "archetypal and paradigmatic" among them.[24] He quotes Eliade: "Reality is acquired solely through repetition or participation; everything which lacks an exemplary model is 'meaningless,' i.e., it lacks reality." Hence in ancient times "great monarchs considered themselves imitators of the primordial hero."[25]

To sum up, the latest studies of ancient tales long recognized by scholars as having significantly close points of resemblance to the biblical patriarchal narratives, with Abraham's story at their head, now assure us (1) that we cannot exclude the possibility of their containing historical elements because they also happen to have a mythical allure, for (2) myth and reality meet in *ritual,* a ritual that, while rehearsing something that is supposed to have happened far away and long ago, is nonetheless an overt act, an actual historical event in its own right. In a world in which every major occurrence in the life of the individual and the society was accommodated to ritual treatment and invested with cosmic significance, there is no point to distinguishing between ritual and history.[26] The stories of the Two Brothers and Sinuhe are now viewed as ritual inspiration specifically representing initiation rites. This, we have always maintained, goes also for the Abraham story as set forth in the Book of Abraham; the ritual features of these tales— Egyptian and Hebrew alike, especially with reference to initiation—we have demonstrated in a book on some of the Joseph Smith Papyri.[27] Everything in the Joseph Smith

Papyri suggests the possibility that Abraham's history is not to be separated from his involvement in certain royal rites of great significance, so that these particular episodes of his life could be truly represented in ritual texts which are at the same time historical. But this is not a discovery of the writer's. The revelations of the Prophet Joseph Smith made it clear from the beginning that we follow Abraham's example in ordinances as well as rules of life, for the archetype held up as the example for all Latter-day Saints to follow is certainly Abraham. As the very "seed of Abraham" (D&C 103:17), they are admonished to "go . . . and do the works of Abraham" (D&C 132:32). Regardless of the culture gap, as one scholar reminds us, we can still get a grasp on these ancient heroes because the "paradigmatic pattern" they provide is one that fits our own experience throughout life.[28] What is impossible about the reality, personality, or deeds of a man whose experiences we duplicate in our own lives?

Kings in Collision

All Abraham scholars begin by noting that the apocryphal material is no mere extension of the biblical, but deals with matters unmentioned in the Bible. The episodes on which they concentrate have to do with the infancy, boyhood, and young manhood of the patriarch, upon which the scriptures do not touch. "We must not lose sight of the fact," wrote Geo Widengren, "that the Old Testament, as it is handed down to us in the Jewish canon, is only one part— we do not even know if the greater part—of Israel's national literature."[29] Hence it is significant that the Abraham apocrypha, widely scattered in time and place, tell very much the same stories, suggesting their common origin in a lost portion of the record, for which "a number of scholars are beginning to recognize historical foundations to important parts of the tradition."[30] The central theme throughout is the machinations of a great cosmocrator, who fears, due to the findings of his astrologers, that the infant Abraham is a threat to his kingship and priesthood, a deadly rival. In a series of dramatic encounters he tries to prevent the birth of the child and then to destroy it, is duly confounded by the boy Abraham, and attempts to sacrifice the young man on an altar. To Abraham's challenge that his God is the giver of life, the would-be ruler of the world responds: "It is I who give life and I who take it!"[31] The supermonarch often goes by the name of Nimrod in the stories, but in the oldest versions he is plainly identified with Pharaoh.[32] In making the confrontation between Abraham and Pharaoh the pivotal theme of its history, with rival claims to priesthood and kingship the issue, the Book of Abraham has got off on the right foot and cleared a formidable hurdle.

The story of the sacrifice of Abraham (not Isaac!) we have treated elsewhere, and it will suffice here to quote our earlier summary of it.

> Briefly, this is the story. Abraham is bound on a specially constructed altar and raises his voice in prayer to God. As the priest brings the knife near to the victim's throat, God sends an angel who offers to rescue him from his dire predicament; but Abraham refuses the proffered help, saying that it is God and God alone who will deliver him. At that moment God speaks to Abraham, the earth trembles, fire bursts forth, the altar is overthrown, the officiating priest is killed, and a general catastrophe fills the land with mourning. . . . *Nimrod*, baffled in every attempt to dispatch his arch-rival, is convinced at last that Abraham possesses a power greater than his, and suddenly turns from cursing the prophet to honoring him, humbly soliciting the privilege of personally offering sacrifices to the God of Abraham. More surprises: Abraham refuses the astonishing offer, saying, "God will not accept from thee after the manner of thy religion." To this Nimrod replies, "O Abraham, I cannot lay down my kingship, but I will offer oxen," and after that time [he]

left Abraham, whom God had delivered from his power, in peace.[33]

Here we have the strange paradox of a king who was, as the Book of Abraham puts it, blessed in the kingship "with the blessings of the earth, and with the blessings of wisdom, but cursed . . . as pertaining to the Priesthood" (Abraham 1:26). This puts everybody in an embarrassing situation: the proud monarch has made an unheard-of concession to Abraham, but Abraham refuses to meet him halfway—he cannot give him what he wants. It was a painful and awkward impasse to which there was only one solution: Nimrod loaded Abraham with royal gifts and ordered his entire court to pay obeisance to him, after which "the king dismissed Abraham."[34] In the oldest version of the story, the *Genesis Apocryphon*, Pharaoh, after being rebuffed and offended by Abraham, whom he had "sought to slay," swears a royal oath to him, loads him with the highest honors, and orders him out of the country.[35]

What can Nimrod, the Asiatic terror, possibly have to do with Pharaoh? A good deal, to judge by the legends in which the two are constantly confused and interchanged. In the *Clementine Recognitions* the dispensations of the gospel, following an ancient Jewish formula, are given as ten, each being established by a prophet and revelator who finds himself opposed by a satanic rival and pretender;[36] when we get to Abraham (the third dispensation), we expect his opponent, in view of the rabbinic traditions, to be Nimrod, but it is not: it is Pharaoh. Why is that? In the legends, Bernard Chapira notes, "Nimrod has become the equivalent of Pharaoh," yet he is already Pharaoh in the oldest legends, including the one edited by Chapira himself.[37] Wacholder has noted that while Nimrod is indeed the archenemy in the rabbinical accounts, in the older "Hassidic" versions he is *Pharaoh*, a clear indication that the original stories go back to the time "when Egypt was a major power," when "the encounter between Pharaoh and the traveler from Ur of the Chaldees seemed a crucial event in the history of mankind"; only later, "from the rabbinic sources, Abram's journey into Egypt is relatively ignored,"[38] for the rabbis were strongly averse to having Abraham spending his time in Egypt.[39]

From the Egyptian side also come distinct echoes of the clash between the king and the holy man. In a story dating back at least to the Twenty-sixth Dynasty, Onchsheshonq, the priest of Re of Heliopolis (Moses and Joseph were both related by marriage to holders of that significant office), was falsely suspected by Pharaoh of plotting against his life. After the priest had spoken in his own defense, "Pharaoh had an earthen altar constructed at the gate of the palace." But instead of sacrificing Onchsheshonq, "he caused Horsiese the son of Ramose to be cast into the fire with all his (household) and all those who had conspired to overthrow Pharaoh."[40] Horsiesi was the bosom friend of Onchsheshonq—Pharaoh calls him his "brother." Onchsheshonq, saved from the flames and the altar by this "substitute" in the manner of Abraham's escape by the sacrifice of his brother Haran and the holocaust of all his house, was led off to prison by "the shepherd Pinehas"—another Jewish connection, suggesting Abraham's servant Eliezar, also a black man.[41] (Pinehas derives from the Egyptian *pa nehsi*, meaning a Nubian or black man. It is the Jewish *pinchom* or *Pincus*.)[42] Though in jail, he was daily fed with dishes sent from the palace, his go-between with Pharaoh being the courtier Thoth, who was his jailer. On the anniversary of his coronation Pharaoh freed all the prisoners but Onchsheshonq; expecting death, that hero asked for papyrus to make a book for the instruction of his progeny. The king allowed him pen and ink but no paper, so he wrote on potsherds his Book of Wisdom, to show forth to posterity how God had dealt with him. He begins with fervid admonition to trust in God no matter what happens and

closes with the ultimate wise counsel: "Be not weary in calling upon God, for in his own time he will hearken to the
scribe."[43] Ties between Egyptian and Hebrew wisdom literature are of great age, and this story is full of familiar over-
tones of Abraham and Joseph, the most striking being
the special altar erected for a rival threatening the throne
who is delivered from the flames and then goes to prison,
as Abraham is imprisoned by the king, who nonetheless
holds him in high esteem. Incidentally, the expression
"Grant that the *Ba* of the Osiris Sheshonq live (*ankh*)" in
figure 8 of Facsimile 2 contains the elements of the name
Onchsheshonq.

The legends make Hagar an Egyptian woman of the
Werner Foerster has observed that "the highlights of . . .
divine action" in the history of Israel are "firstly, the basic
event of Abraham's call, God's covenant, [and] secondly,
the deliverance from the 'furnace of Egypt.'"[44] The furnace
of *Egypt* is here the equivalent of the "furnace of the
Chaldees," the most venerable epithet of Abraham being
"he who was delivered from the furnace of the Chaldees."[45]
Of the moment of delivery a very old account says, "From
that day until today it is called Kaldawon, [signifying] what
God had said to the children of Israel: 'It is I who brought
you forth from *Egypt!*'" Which was it, Egypt or Chaldea
(Kaldawon)?[46]

The legends make Hagar an Egyptian woman of the
royal court and even a daughter of Pharaoh (Genesis 16:1,
3; 21:9, 21),[47] so that when the old Jerusalem Targum on
Jeremiah says that Hagar belonged to those very people
who threw Abraham into the furnace, we are obliged to
view his attempted sacrifice as an Egyptian show.[48] Even
more specific is the *Pseudo-Jonathan*, which reports that
Hagar was "the daughter of Pharaoh, the son of Nimrod,"
which makes Nimrod, if not a pharaoh, the father of one. In
one of the better-known stories, when Sarah lost her temper
with Hagar (and it is significant that we have here the same

sort of rivalry between Sarah the true "princess" and Hagar the Egyptian woman as we do between Abraham and Nimrod), she complained to Abraham, accusing her rival of being "the daughter of Pharaoh, of Nimrod's line, he who once cast thee into the furnace!"[49] Having Pharaoh as a son or descendant of Nimrod neatly bridges the gap between Asia and Egypt: one of the most famous foreign potentates to put a son on the throne of Egypt did in fact bear the name of Nimrod, and his son bore the family name of Shishak or Sheshonk, which turns up as the owner of Facsimile 2, a coincidence to be pursued hereafter.

The sort of thing that used to happen may be surmised from an account in the *Sefer ha-Yashar,* according to which "at the time Abraham went into Canaan there was a man in Sinear called Rakion [also Rikyan, Rakayan, suggesting the famous Hyksos ruler Khian]. . . . He went to King Asverus [cf. Osiris] in Egypt, the son of Enam. At that time the king of Egypt showed himself only once a year." In Egypt this Rakion by trickery raised a private army and so was able to impose a tax on all bodies brought for burial to the cemetery. This made him so rich that he went with a company of a thousand richly dressed youths and maidens to pay his respect to Asverus, who was so impressed that he changed the man's name to Pharaoh, after which Rakion judged the people of Egypt every day, while Asverus only judged one day in the year.[50] This would not be the first or the last time that a usurping Asiatic forced a place for himself on the throne, but the ritual aspects of the tale—the annual appearance of Osiris, the rule over the necropolis, the one thousand youths and maidens (as in the story of Solomon and Queen Bilqis)—are also conspicuous. We are also told that that wily Asiatic who came to the throne by violence and trickery was the very same pharaoh who would take Sarah to wife.[51]

The close resemblance between Nimrod's treatment of

Abraham and Pharaoh's treatment of Moses has often been noted.[52] And just as the careers of Abraham and Moses can be closely and significantly matched (which is not surprising, since the founders and makers of dispensations of the gospel necessarily have almost identical missions), so in the Koran, Nimrod and Pharaoh represent a single archetype—that of the supremely successful administrator who thinks he should rule everything. Likewise in the Qur'an it is not Nimrod who builds the tower to get to heaven, but Pharaoh—a significant substitution.[53] Even in the Jewish accounts, Pharaoh and Nimrod are like identical twins: both call themselves a Great Magician,[54] try to pass themselves off as God, order all the male children put to death, study the heavens, and pit the knowledge and skill of their wise men against the powers of the prophet.[55] The palace in which Nimrod shuts up the expectant mothers has conspicuous parallels in Egyptian literature (e.g., the Doomed Prince), and is designated in the Jewish traditions as the Palace of Assuerus—the Osiris or king of Egypt in the Rakion story above.[56] When the young Moses refuses to worship Pharaoh as the young Abraham refuses Nimrod, the idolatrous priests accuse both heroes of magic and trickery, the converts of both are put to death by the king, the subjects of both rulers offer up their children to idols, and Pharaoh, like Nimrod, finally declares war on God and builds a great tower, which falls.[57]

On the romantic side, Pharaoh sacrificed his own daughter because "she no longer honored him as a god"[58] and refused to lose her virginity in the fertility rites he sponsored, just as Ratha, the daughter of Nimrod, who fell in love with Abraham, also refused to participate in the licentious rites and sought even to join him in the sacrificial flames.[59] The situation is clearly indicated in the Joseph Smith Book of Abraham, where "three virgins at one time" were sacrificed, "the daughters of Onitah, one of the royal descent. . . . These virgins were offered because of their virtue; they would not bow down." In short, they refused to participate in the fertility rites and so "were killed upon this altar, and it was done after the manner of the Egyptians" (Abraham 1:11).[60]

One can appreciate the wisdom of the rabbinic distinction between Pharaoh and Nimrod, without which the wires would be hopelessly crossed between a Moses and an Abraham, who go through identical routines with the same antagonist-Pharaoh. Yet in the original version it was Pharaoh in both cases: the Nimrod who calls his magicians and wise men to counter the claims of Abraham, who loses the contest and ends up bestowing high honors on his guest, and who turns up as Pharaoh in the *Genesis Apocryphon,* the oldest known version of the story.[61]

Pharaoh's Misgivings

According to the Book of Abraham, the Egyptian pharaoh ruling "his people wisely and justly . . . would fain claim" the priesthood and went ahead and acted as if he really had it, "seeking earnestly to imitate that order established by the fathers in the first generations" (Abraham 1:26–27). The statement is exhaustively confirmed in Egyptian literature. While some intellectual and benevolent pharaohs like Psammetichus, Tefnakht, and Bocchoris were in the latter days of philosophical disillusionment amused by their own "divinity," they put on the best act they could for their subjects.[62] Other pharaohs, rough cynical conquerors or cunning politicians, adapted themselves to the traditional patterns and conducted the solemnities in their capacity as sacred monarch and high priest.[63] In either case it was an example of what Hermann Kees called the official state "Cant" of the Egyptians. The Egyptians "understood perfectly well how to twist and adjust things," wrote Hermann Kees, "so that the ideal concept of power matched the facts of history [tradition]," embracing "in the same high-sounding words both the highest human concept of ideal kingship and the most vicious self-interest."[64] Kings and high priests did not hesitate to manipulate divine oracles (usually statues) and forge documents.

All of which indicates that Pharaoh was always unsure of his authority over his own people. A newly discovered document that goes clear back to the Fifth Dynasty, the Inscription of Mtty, is an appeal for loyalty to Pharaoh that clearly shows how shaky his divine authority was at that early time,[65] teaching as later texts do that the king must set an example of loyalty.[66] Opinions still differ among scholars as to whether "the king thought of himself as a mere human being,"[67] being to his subjects just another Oriental potentate,[68] the Orientals being "able to see him as he was with clarity and detachment,"[69] or whether all detected a divine element, though not necessarily "total divinity" in the pharaoh.[70]

Of particular interest are those devout and sincere pharaohs who spent their days in the archives engaging in the constant search of Egyptian rulers for divine authority,[71] such men as King Neferhotep in the Thirteenth Dynasty,[72] the great Amenophis I, "a wise and inspired man," according to Manetho, who yearned to see the gods but feared to risk any force or trickery to get his wish,[73] or Ptolemy the son of Glaucias, "the recluse of the Serapeum," spending all his days in the library,[74] as does the hero of the Setne Khamuas story, searching in the House of Life for the book that bestows the knowledge of divine dominion and authority.[75]

The trouble was that they lacked revelation. In Egypt, Henri Frankfort observed, "The actions of individuals lacked divine guidance altogether."[76] The only hope was to cling to Pharaoh, so that when the throne shook, everybody was left "without certainty or direction,"[77] and though "living under the rule of a god incarnate, they were dependent on human wisdom alone for direction in their way of life."[78] Though Pharaoh is the "Great Intercessor," as François Daumas points out, "what he does is not miraculous . . . but only wonderful, . . . it is the normal power by which the course of the world continues."[79] Surprisingly, as Siegfried Morenz notes, the Egyptians claimed no inspired writings, and no Egyptian wise man ever claims to be commissioned from heaven.[80] Edwin R. Bevan noted long ago that the ancients have left us not a single instance in which men were supposed to have conversed with Zeus (in contrast with Adam, Enoch, Noah, Abraham, and Moses, who each conversed with God); all revelation came to the gentiles through voices, letters from heaven, natural objects, omens, inspired utterance (dreams, fits, etc.).[81] In the late times we hear of messages from the oracle of Ammon of both the Egyptians and the Greeks, but they were all delivered by *sortes* (lots, dice, books, moving statues, etc.).[82] It is important to bear this in mind, lest we fall into the error of supposing that the religion of Abraham and Israel was simply another tribal superstition or an offshoot from the archaic order. Between the gospel and the numerous spin-offs from the pristine faith taught by Adam to his children, there is all the difference between light and darkness—and the Egyptians felt the difference most keenly.

Abraham and Pharaoh in a Strange Setting

Now we come to the next hurdle—how to get Abraham and the pharaoh together in the days of Abraham's youth and long before his famous journey into Egypt. To do this, the Book of Abraham has "the idolatrous god of Pharaoh" go clear up into "Ur of the Chaldees"—where various other idolatrous gods representing local regions or rulers with exotic names gather to pay their respects and participate in solemn annual sacrificial rites.[83] One of the eminent critics of 1912 found the situation simply preposterous; it "displays an amusing ignorance," he declared loftily, since the "Chaldeans and Egyptians are hopelessly mixed together, although as dissimilar and remote in language, religion and locality as are today American and Chinese."[84] Actually, this is another one of those cases in which the Book of Abraham sets forth a situation well attested in Egyptian literature.

One of the striking things about the Abraham figure is the way in which the hero "is curiously involved in the pagan world,"[85] which is not surprising since, as one scholar puts it, "Abraham had no address," and was in danger wherever he went. The Book of Abraham brings the patriarch in his earlier years together with a priest of Pharaoh in "the land of Chaldea." Though until the late nineteenth century the consensus of scholarly opinion placed the Ur of Abraham in the Haran area of northern Mesopotamia, as Cyrus Gordon notes, "the excavations at Sumerian Ur [in the 1930s] threw us off the track," and for a while the great Sumerian Ur was favored as Abraham's city, but today "Ebla is putting us back on it."[86] When I discussed the matter in the April 1969 *Improvement Era*, the experts were about evenly divided between the northern and southern Ur,[87] but in 1976 Ebla definitely turned the scales in favor of the north. Robert Martin-Achard, observing that the ancient sources support both the Ur in Lower Mesopotamia and the home in Upper Mesopotamia, suggests that Abraham's parents perhaps lived in both places. After championing the southern Ur, he finally concludes, however, that "the true cradle of the patriarch's family is the country in the Haran region which the Bible calls Aram of the Two Rivers," a center of commerce and pilgrimage.[88] Cyrus Gordon would push into the extreme northwest, "the Urfa-Haran region of south central Turkey, near the Syrian border, rather than in southern Mesopotamia."[89] Noel Weeks finds that names like Nakhur (Nahor) and Banuyamina (Benjamin) in the Mari tablets "may confirm the northern Mesopotamian origin of the patriarchs,"[90] while James L. Kelso rests everything on the proposition that Abraham "was a caravaneer running a trade route from Haran to Damascus to Egypt."[91] In the Ebla tablets the key passage is "a reference to 'Ur *in* Haran.'" "Does this mean," asks the editor of the *Biblical Archaeology Review*, "that the Ur from which Abraham originally came was near Haran rather than 1,000 miles further away in southern Mesopotamia where 'Ur of the Chaldees' is supposedly located?"[92] This source is to be taken seriously in view of the fact that it mentions not only Abraham's Cities of the Plain in their correct geographical setting, but also Canaan, Haran, and "Ur in Haran."[93]

Granted that Abraham could be found in the Haran area, what about Pharaoh's priest? He, it would seem, held a double office, for "the priest of Elkenah was also the priest of Pharaoh" (Abraham 1:7). This was only a temporary state of affairs, however, for Abraham's "now at *this* time it *was* the custom" (Abraham 1:8) definitely implies that at the time of writing it was no longer so. Theodor Böhl's observation that when the curtain rises on the patriarchal dramas "Egypt no longer rules Canaan" suits well with the picture in the Book of Abraham where Pharaoh rules in Canaan only at the outset.[94] Also consistent with the modern reconstruction of the picture is the mixture of outlandish "strange gods," among whose number was counted "a god like unto that of Pharaoh." This is borne out by Abraham's careful specification that the sacrifices were made "even after the manner of the Egyptians," clearly implying that there was another tradition. One of the deities was "the god of Pharaoh" and the other "the god of Shagreel," who, we are flatly told, "was the sun." That deserves a brief notice.

The old desert tribes—whose beliefs and practices, as Albrecht Alt has demonstrated at length, are of primary importance in understanding the background of the Abraham traditions[95]—worshiped the star Sirius under the name of *Shighre* or *Shaghre,* and *Shagre-el* in their idiom means "Shagre is God." Sirius is interesting in ritual because of its unique association, amounting at times to identity with the sun. Shighre, according to Lane's *Dictionary,* designates *whatever* star is at the moment the brightest object in the heavens.[96] Raymond O. Faulkner has emphasized the identity of the king (the original *Roi Soleil*) with Sirius.[97] The king of Egypt in the rites of On is able, "with the Dog Star [Sirius] as a guide," to find the place of resurrection at "the Primeval Hill, an island . . . pre-eminently suitable for a resurrection from death."[98] The most important event in the history of the universe, according to the Egyptians, was the heliacal rising of Sirius, when Sirius, the sun, and the Nile all rose together in the morning of the New Year, the Day of Creation, as officially proclaimed from the great observatory of Heliopolis.[99] Without expanding on the theme, it will be enough here to note that the sun, the hill, and Sirius are inseparably connected in the rites, as they are in the Book of Abraham, where we find "the god of Pharaoh, and also . . . the god of Shagreel . . . the sun" receiving sacrifices side by side at Potiphar's Hill (Abraham 1:9).

Since the above paragraph was written, the name of Shigr (vowel unknown) "has turned up in a Ugaritic sacrificial list," i.e., as a local god receiving sacrifices in Canaan, and "though the data are quite scarce," according to Jacob Hoftijzer, even the gender of the name being uncertain, this deity, to whom "mighty acts" are attributed, may be "linked with Astar and . . . Ashtarte," to whom we refer presently.[100] Thus Shigr now moves beyond the realm of Arabic tradition into the very time, place, and situation most vividly suggested by the Book of Abraham Shagreel.

Incidentally, Potiphar meant "given of Re (the Sun)," and Abraham's native city, Aram Naharaim, was originally called Phathur or Petor, which may be a derivative.[101] It was an old cult place,[102] and of recent years attention has been drawn to the fact that all the main events of Abraham's life seem to take place at ancient cult centers.[103]

Pharaoh and Canaan—Visiting Celebrities

That "country in the Haran region which the Bible calls Aram of the Two Rivers" was that Naharina ("Two Rivers") which Martin Gemoll describes as "the classic land of the *Chaldeans* between Ararat and Mesopotamia,"[104] which contained that "Ur in Haran," which the Ebla tablets now identify as the most likely home of Abraham. It was a land that figures largely in the dynastic histories of the New Kingdom of Egypt, and important members of the royal family came from there. The annals of the great Eighteenth Dynasty have much to say of the heroic pharaohs and their daring campaigns in that part of the world. Their stories depict the conquerors in a formal ritualistic capacity consistent with their divine callings, but at the same time are full of romantic and human excitement. Thus Amenophis II, while telling how the Mitanni and Naharina brought tribute to him, takes special pride in his personal prowess with the bow (fig. 33), in which he excelled even the chiefs of the hill tribes of Retenu.[105] His son Amenophis III married the famous Queen Tiye, the daughter of a great prince who ruled from Karay in the south to Naharina in the north,[106] and later took to wife also the famous daughter of the Lord of the Mitanni. To his forefather, the great Thotmes III, the lands of Chaldea, Naharin, and Shinar (the biblical Shinar in northern Mesopotamia) all brought their tribute together.[107]

In dealing with these various lands, as William H. Stiebing points out, little is to be learned by attempting to make sharp distinctions of time and place, for we are concerned with "a *cultural* period" rather than a "chunk of time," during which "Palestine formed one cultural province with little diversity or local variation," in which "quite

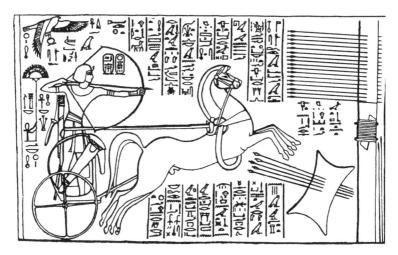

Figure 33. This red granite block from Karnak depicts Amenophis II (1439–1413 B.C.) showing off in front of his troops with a bow "no man could bend"; "he shoots at copper plates and pierces them as if they were papyrus. He cares little about wooden targets so great is his strength."

possibly, Amorites and Canaanites were ethnically and culturally identical."[108]

The most interesting ties between the court of Egypt and the Abraham country are a number of tales that might rightly be called missionary stories, all having to do with healing missions between the two lands, in all of which the leading character is a princess—like Sarah.

We begin with the famous Bentresh or Bakhtan stele (fig. 34).[109] It tells how it had been the custom of Pharaoh to make a trip every year to Naharina, where all the local rulers would hasten to pay him homage, rivaling each other in the richness of their gifts. On one occasion, the great idol, Khonsu of Thebes, as the special god of Pharaoh, was sent to that land to *heal the daughter of the king of Bakhtan.* Having miraculously fulfilled its mission, the image was retained in the land for over three years, during which time the gods of the surrounding regions (i.e., their idols) would come to

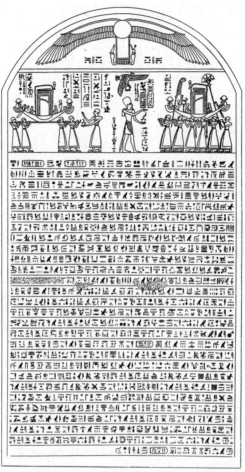

Figure 34. Discovered in the temple of Khonsu at Karnak, this Ptolemaic stele records an incident that supposedly occurred centuries before in the time of Ramses II. It tells how the king of Bakhtan implored Pharaoh to send a god to heal his daughter Bentresh, the Pharaoh's sister-in-law. The scene shows Pharaoh burning incense before Khonsu-of-Thebes-Beautiful-in-Rest carried on the shoulders of his priests on the right. This god indicated that his subordinate on the left, Khonsu-the-Plan-Maker, should go there as his deputy. After a seventeen-month journey he arrived amidst great rejoicing and cured her of the evil spirit that had possessed her.

Bakhtan to attend solemn annual rites in its honor. Finally, the god Khonsu appeared to the King of Bakhtan in a dream in the guise of the Horus-hawk, i.e., Pharaoh himself, in which form he flew back to Egypt. The king took the hint and returned the idol to Thebes with accumulated glory.

The Bentresh romance receives support from a better-attested historical event of the same type, namely the account of how the Lord of Mitanni (*also* in Naharina) sent his beautiful daughter (some believe it was none other than the gorgeous Nefertiti) to Egypt to become the wife of the aged and uxorious Amenophis III (fig. 35). She brought with her the *image of Ishtar of Nineveh,* the idolatrous deity of another great king, *to heal the ailing pharaoh* and to become a center of missionary activity. The ancient correspondence arranging the affair recalls that the same Ishtar of Nineveh had made such a courtesy call to Egypt years before under an earlier reign and had at that time been greatly honored in the land.[110]

An odd coincidence of the later journey deserves mention. For we learn from a scarab of Amenophis III that on her missionary junket from Naharina to Egypt the Princess Gilukhipa was accompanied by a train of 317 harem ladies, which with herself made a pious band of 318.[111] That number of 318 has always intrigued the doctors of the church and the rabbis alike, who have seen in it all manner of mystic symbolism, for that was the number of male converts that Abraham had made and joined to his household in Haran, and who also accompanied *him* out of the land of Naharina when he sallied forth on his fateful missionary calling into Canaan and Egypt.

In the stories of Bentresh, of Gilukhipa, of the earlier visit of Ishtar, and of Sarah in Egypt (in the *Genesis Apocryphon*), we see how royal missionaries circulated between Naharina and Egypt, making their conversions by healing members of the royal family on both sides of the line, a sort

Figure 35. Shown here full size, this clay letter tablet from Tushratta, Lord of Mitanni, to Amenophis III accompanied the image of Ishtar of Nineveh in c. 1354 B.C. It is written in cuneiform and has an Egyptian hieratic filing note in ink from the thirty-sixth year of the pharaoh's reign.

of stock theme that brings Sarah and Abraham into the picture. We also see how "the idolatrous god of Pharaoh" could visit "Ur of the Chaldees" to receive the homage of local idols, however strange the situation may have sounded to the critics of Facsimile 1. A surprising wealth of Egyptian and Asiatic lore revolves around the four particular idols depicted in Facsimile 1, but for the present the general situation suffices.

With a few bold, confident strokes, the Book of Abraham not only evokes the romantic and adventurous qualities of the Hebrew Abraham legends while recalling the details of those stories, but it also catches the spirit and sets the scene for an Egyptian idyll that is surprisingly akin to the ancient romances and annals celebrating the influence of Pharaoh in Canaan. The Princess of the Mitanni, with missionary zeal, brings the image of the Lady of Nineveh to help her restore the vitality of a failing pharaoh; another pharaoh is smitten with impotence and then healed when his relationship with Sarah, another princess, from "the classic land of the Chaldeans" is properly established. The same thing happens twice, with Sarah and Rebecca, to the king of Gerar. Wenamon, an Egyptian emissary and missionary of Amon to Palestine, was saved from death in Cyprus by the timely interposition of a queen during a religious ceremony. And the great Odysseus was saved when he clasped the knees of another queen in the palace of Phaeacia, another romantic island. These episodes seem to belong to the stock heroic repertory of the eastern Mediterranean just after the middle of the first millennium B.C., which also supplies us with an abundance of romances recalling in detail the story of Abraham on the altar, the most famous of such accounts being the Busiris stories of Egypt.[112]

And yet we can go back more than five hundred years earlier to the early Middle Kingdom, to the most famous of all Egyptian romances, and find yet another hero from Canaan and Naharina in mortal dread of an offended pharaoh, saved by the intercession of a gracious queen in the palace. This is our friend Sinuhe.[113]

Sinuhe's story begins, like Abraham's, with the hero under dire necessity of running away from home (cf. Abraham 1:1). After a harrowing journey in the desert, where he almost died of thirst, he was taken into the family of a great chief of the Retenu, who valued his knowledge of Egyptian—a clear indication of long-standing Egyptian influence in the area. The chief had heard about him from

Egyptian visitors to his country, for like Abraham, Sinuhe
had acquired something of a reputation for wisdom throughout the Near East, his fame having spread from the Egyptian
court. Like Abraham also, Sinuhe was an outcast by his own
choice, who through his prudence, courage, and courtesy
acquired great herds and riches, becoming a wise and hospitable leader and benefactor of the people of his adopted
tribes. He drove marauding bands from the pastures and
wells of his friends, as did Abraham; and, like Abraham,
he was forgiven for an unwilling offense to Pharaoh and
loaded with royal gifts—courtly garments and ointments—
for he was a prince in his own right. While Sinuhe was still
in Naharina, Pharaoh summoned the princes of the *four*
principal surrounding regions to testify as character witnesses for the hero, reminding us of the four canopic figures
invited to Abraham's reception, which, we are told in the
Book of Abraham, represented the four regions and were
identified with local kingdoms, coming to offer homage to
the idolatrous god of Pharaoh in Abraham's Ur of the
Chaldees. As we have seen, the latest study of Sinuhe treats
it as a ritual, specifically an initiation text.

Along with Sinuhe's story, the *Tale of the Two Brothers*[114]
also qualifies as a ritual and initiation text. Here again
familiar "patriarchal" motifs have attracted the notice of
scholars from the beginning, in particular the striking parallel to the story of Joseph and Potiphar's wife with which
the account begins. As a result of such a domestic triangle,
Bata, the exploited and overworked younger brother, is
forced to flee his homeland (Abraham and Joseph again),
settling down in the Valley of the Cedar, which can only be
Canaan, the land where the conifers (ash) grow on the
mountains. There Bata builds himself a magnificently furnished palace to which the local gods of all the surrounding
lands gather to pay him homage: "Hail Bata," they greet
him. "Have you abandoned your city because of your

brother's wife? Behold, he has slain her, and until you return there is great mourning in the land." At once numerous rites and legends spring to mind: the romantic triangles of the Heroic Age. Here the story culminates in the sacrificial death of Bata at the great year-rite ordered by Pharaoh at the persuasion of a wanton queen—exactly matching an important Abraham legend.[115] The main thing to note here is that in this tale of some antiquity we again find an Egyptian prince being royally received at an assembly of local gods in the land of the Chaldees. When the Lady has been brought to Egypt from the Valley of Cedar, she instigates the sacrifice of Bata in the form of a bull at a great festival held by Pharaoh, which takes us back to Abraham on the altar where, in the Jewish legends, he is placed in jeopardy by the machinations of the wicked hierodules.

Yet another tale, the *Tale of the Doomed Prince*,[116] starts out on an Abraham theme with a childless king praying for a son, as Abraham did for Isaac. His prayer is answered, but the babe is put under a curse, to keep him safe from the effects of which he is shut up in a high tower. This recalls the like precautions taken to save the babe Abraham when a jealous king of Babylon sought his life. The prince, grown older, escapes from the tower, goes forth into the desert, and comes to *Naharina*. Upon his arrival there, all the local princes come to greet him and pay their respects "to the prince of Egypt." They tell him how the great overlord of Naharina has shut his daughter up in a high tower with seventy windows seventy cubits above the ground; all the princes of the land have tried to win her hand by climbing up to her but all have failed. Again we are reminded how Nimrod shut all the young women of the land in a high tower to prevent the conception of Abraham. Naturally the prince of Egypt succeeds in getting the damsel, but the lord of Naharina absolutely refuses to let his daughter marry an Egyptian. This is the ethnic complication that enlivens the

famous story of Joseph and Asenath, with elements of the
Abraham and Sarah vicissitudes added—it was Pharaoh
who kept them apart. In the Doomed Prince version the fair
princess threatens to sacrifice herself if she is not allowed to
marry her beloved, even as Pharaoh's daughter Ratha
insisted on being sacrificed on the altar rather than be separated from Abraham. Finally the king relents and the lovers
are united in the manner of Abraham and Sarah in Egypt
and in Gerar. In this story, rivalry between the Egyptian and
the princess of Canaan again comes to the fore, with the
"Chaldean" princes again paying reluctant homage to the
representative and heir of Pharaoh.

The story of Astarte is a tale equally at home in Egypt
and Canaan. It is assumed that it was brought to Egypt
from the north and became adapted to a Memphite audience.[117] While a "romantic interest attached to the Syrian
goddess Astarte," and "her worship spread over almost the
entire Near Eastern area," according to Alan H. Gardiner,[118]
the story turns up at a very early time among the Hittites
and Hurrians far to the north.[119] In Egypt it was thoroughly
naturalized at Memphis, the ceremonial heart of the land,
where Astarte appears as the daughter of Ptah, no less, in
whom Theodor H. Gaster sees "simply an Egyptianization"
of Baal of Canaan.[120] His office in the story is to bestow victory and "kingship eternal" on a monarch-Pharaoh, in this
case; it is the old coronation drama.

The central theme of the tale is how the Lady made a
journey to Egypt, bringing a payment of tribute as well as a
healing influence to the land to appease the troubled forces
of nature. Both versions of the myth, Egyptian and Ugaritic
(Canaanite), contain important details binding it to the
Book of Abraham, which we shall note below; here it will
suffice to point out some particulars that bring it into the
Egyptian-Canaanite circuit. Thus the overlord of Canaan,
Baal, objects to the placing of windows in a palace or tower

under construction lest certain virgins, "his daughters (or brides!) . . . abscond or be abducted through them."[121] This is not only an old Egyptian motif, as we have just seen, but is an important theme in the Abraham legends;[122] it was in Canaan that Abimelech looked out of the window at Rebecca (Genesis 26:8; cf. 2 Samuel 11:2). Again, a message is carried to Astarte by a messenger bird, who sings the telegram under her window, thus identifying the story firmly with the Solomon-Sheba cycle, in which Solomon's hoopoe carries his message to the queen, flying with it through the window. Scholars have also noted the undeniable ties with the old Egyptian story of the Two Brothers—the tower motif among them.[123]

Right on the border between Egypt and Canaan was discovered the so-called al-Arish shrine, a *naos* cut from a single block of granite (fig. 36) and covered with inscriptions telling an epic tale to which we shall refer below. Here it suffices to recall that the happy ending of the story calls for a great celebration in Memphis to which Pharaoh invites or rather summons all the Asiatics to be present before the throne of the universe where stand the *four* idols of Pharaoh.[124] So again we find "the [*four*] idolatrous gods of Pharaoh" meeting together with Canaanites and Egyptians in a great common year-rite.

From all this it would appear that the situation depicted and explained in the Book of Abraham—with the idolatrous gods of a country (for which the designation "Ur of the Chaldees" can now be fully justified) participating in yearly sacrificial rites involving both Egypt and Canaan—far from being a wild fantasy of Joseph Smith, was really the correct routine situation.

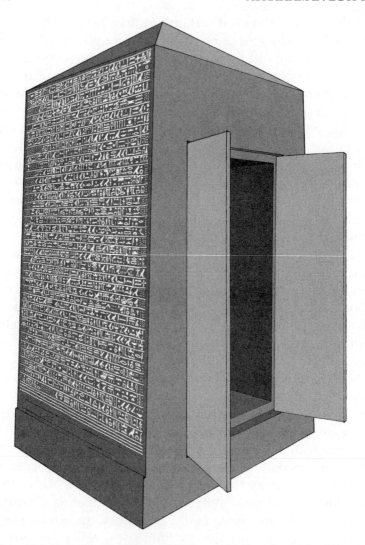

Figure 36. Carved from a block of black granite four feet high, this *naos* is covered with a lengthy inscription honoring the god Shu. Its pyramid-shaped top suggests the original mound of earth at the creation. A golden image of the god would have been kept within the doors and brought out for festivals. The shrine was found at al-Arish on the eastern coast of the Delta (see map pp. 666–67).

Notes

1. James L. Kelso, "Abraham as Archaeology Knows Him," *Perspective* 13 (Winter 1972): 21.

2. Jan Assmann, "Das ägyptische Zweibrüdermärchen (Papyrus d'Orbiney)," *ZÄS* 104 (1977): 5.

3. Hugh W. Nibley, "A New Look at the Pearl of Great Price," *IE* 73 (April 1970): 79–82; reprinted in this volume, pp. 343–81.

4. Assmann, "Ägyptische Zweibrüdermärchen," 19–20.

5. Ibid., 23–24.

6. Ibid.

7. Ibid.

8. Strother Purdy, "Sinuhe and the Question of Literary Types," *ZÄS* 104 (1977): 112.

9. Ibid., 113.

10. Ibid.

11. Ibid., 119.

12. Ibid., 114.

13. Ibid., 117.

14. Ibid., 123–25.

15. Ibid., 127.

16. Hugh W. Nibley, *The Message of the Joseph Smith Papyri: An Egyptian Endowment* (Salt Lake City: Deseret Book, 1975), 75–76.

17. Adriaan de Buck, *Egyptian Readingbook* (Leiden: Nederlands Instituut voor het Nabije Oosten, 1963), 100–106.

18. Pyramid Text 422 (§752–64).

19. See Eugene D. Welch, "The Lebensmüde and Its Relationship to the Harpers' Songs of the Middle-New Kingdoms" (Ph.D. diss., Brandeis University, 1978).

20. Purdy, "Sinuhe and the Question of Literary Types," 120.

21. Herbert Werner, *Abraham der Erstling und Repräsentant Israels* (Göttingen: Vandenhoeck and Ruprecht, 1965), 70.

22. Purdy, "Sinuhe and the Question of Literary Types," 124.

23. Erik Hornung, *Das Amduat: Die Schrift des verborgenen Raumes*, 3 vols. (Wiesbaden: Harrassowitz, 1963–67), 1:62–74.

24. Bendt Alster, "The Paradigmatic Character of Mesopotamian Heroes," *Revue d'Assyriologie* 68 (1974): 51, 60.

25. Mircea Eliade, *The Myth of the Eternal Return* (London: Routledge and Kegan Paul, 1955), 34, 37, as quoted in Alster, "Paradigmatic Character of Mesopotamian Heroes," 51.

26. Nikolaus Schneider, "Götterthrone in Ur III und ihr Kult," *Orientalia* 16 (1947): 59.

27. Nibley, *Message of the Joseph Smith Papyri*.

28. Alster, "Paradigmatic Character of Mesopotamian Heroes," 51–54.

29. Geo Widengren, "Early Hebrew Myths and Their Interpretation," in *Myth, Ritual and Kingship*, ed. Samuel H. Hooke (Oxford: Oxford University Press, 1958), 158.

30. Marcel Mauss, "Critique interne de la 'Legende d'Abraham,'" *REJ* 82 (1926): 35.

31. Nibley, "A New Look at the Pearl of Great Price," *IE* 72 (January 1969): 28–31.

32. Ibid., *IE* 72 (April 1969): 69–72.

33. Ibid., *IE* 72 (May 1969): 88.

34. Ibid., *IE* 72 (March 1969): 76–84.

35. Nahman Avigad and Yigael Yadin, eds., *A Genesis Apocryphon* (Jerusalem: Hebrew University Press, 1956), col. 20:9, 26–34.

36. *Clementine Recognitions* III, 61, in *PG* 1:1308–9.

37. Bernard Chapira, "Légendes bibliques attribuées à Ka'b el-Ahbar," *REJ* 69 (1919): 101.

38. Ben Zion Wacholder, "How Long Did Abraham Stay in Egypt?" *Hebrew Union College Annual* 35 (1964): 43–45.

39. Ibid., 45.

40. Bruno H. Stricker, "De Wijsheid van Anchsjesjonq," *JEOL* 15 (1958): 14.

41. Bernhard Beer, *Leben Abraham's nach Auffassung der jüdischen Sage* (Leipzig: Leiner, 1859), 194 n. 853.

42. Ephraim Stern, "Phineas," in *Encyclopaedia Judaica*, 13:465–66.

43. Stricker, "Wijsheid van Anchsjesjonq," 15–33.

44. Werner Foerster, *From the Exile to Christ* (Philadelphia: Fortress, 1964), 141.

45. Werner G. Kümmel, "Christian Dietzfelbinger Pseudo-Philo: Antiquitates Biblicae (Liber Antiquitatum Biblicarum)," in *Jüdische Schriften aus hellenistisch-römischer Zeit*, 6 vols. (Gütersloh: Mohr, 1975), 1:117 n. 18b.

46. Wolf Leslau, trans., "Teũ'eũzaēza Sanbat," in *Falasha Anthology* (New Haven: Yale University Press, 1951), 28 n. 195.

47. Micha J. bin Gorion, *Die Sagen der Juden*, 5 vols. (Frankfurt: Rütten & Loening, 1913–27), 2:188.

48. Beer, *Leben Abraham's*, 148.

49. Ibid., 35.

50. Bin Gorion, *Sagen der Juden*, 2:148–53.

51. Beer, *Leben Abraham's*, 128.

52. Israel Lévi, "Le lait de la mère et le coffre flottant," *REJ* 59 (1910): 9–10.

53. Qur'an 40:37.

54. Chapira, "Légendes bibliques attribués à Ka'b el-Ahbar," 94.

55. Ibid.; Isidore Loeb, review of *Le Mistére du Viel Testament*, by James de Rothschild, *REJ* 4 (1882): 304.

56. Chapira, "Légendes bibliques attribués à Ka'b el-Ahbar," 94.

57. Ginzberg, *Legends of the Jews*, 1:177–81.

58. Gustav Weil, *The Bible, the Koran, and the Talmud* (New York: Harper, 1846), 145.

59. Beer, *Leben Abraham's*, 16, 112.

60. Nibley, "A New Look at the Pearl of Great Price," *IE* 72 (February 1969): 64–67; (March 1969): 76–84.

61. Ibid., *IE* 73 (April 1970): 79–95; reprinted in this volume as chapter 8, "The Sacrifice of Sarah."

62. Alexandre Moret, *Histoire de l'Orient* (Paris: Presses universitaires, 1929), 726.

63. Cf. Ibrahim Harari, "Nature de la stèle de donation de fonction du roi Ahmôsis à la reine Ahmès-Nefertari," *ASAE* 56 (1959): 139–201.

64. Hermann Kees, *Aegypten* (Munich: Beck, 1933), 172.

65. Peter Kaplony, "Eine neue Weisheitslehre aus dem alten Reich," *Orientalia* 37 (1968): 1–62, 339–45.

66. Peter Kaplony, "Das Vorbild des Königs unter Sesostris III," *Orientalia* 35 (1966): 405.

67. Rudolf Anthes, "Egyptian Theology in the Third Millennium B.C.," *JNES* 18 (July 1959): 181.

68. Hermann Kees, review of *La divinité du pharaon*, by Georges Posener, *Orientalistische Literaturzeitung* 64 (1962): 476–77.

69. François Daumas, "Le sens de la royauté égyptienne à propos d'un livre récent," *RHR* 160 (1961): 136, quoting Georges Posener, *De la divinité du pharaon* (Paris: Societé Asiatique, 1961), 103.

70. Kees, review of *Divinité du pharaon*, 476–77.

71. Siegfried Morenz, *Ägyptische Religion* (Stuttgart: Kohlhammer, 1960), 260.

72. Max Pieper, *Die grosse Inschrift des Königs Neferhotep in Abydos* (Leipzig: Hinrichs 1929), 13–14.

73. Josephus, *Against Apion* I, 232–36.

74. Euguene Revillout, "Le reclus du Sérapéum, sa bibliothèque et ses occupations mystiques," *Revue Égyptologique* 1–2 (1880–82): 160–63; 143–45.

75. Francis L. Griffith, *Stories of the High Priests of Memphis* (Oxford: Clarendon, 1900), 20.

76. Henri Frankfort, *Ancient Egyptian Religion* (New York: Harper, 1961), 81.

77. Ibid., 85.

78. Ibid., 81.

79. Daumas, "Sens de la royauté égyptienne," 147.

80. Siegfried Morenz, *Gott und Mensch im alten Ägypten* (Leipzig: Koehler and Amelang, 1984), 24.

81. Edwyn R. Bevan, *Sibyls and Seers* (Cambridge: Harvard University Press, 1929), 99–100.

82. *Itinerarium Alexandri* 50–52, in *Fontes Historiae Religionis Aegyptiacae,* comp. Theodor Hopfner (Bonn: Marcus and Weber, 1924), 512.

83. Nibley, "A New Look at the Pearl of Great Price," *IE* 72 (February 1969): 67; (March 1969): 76–85; (April 1969): 66–72.

84. Franklin S. Spalding, *Joseph Smith Jr. as a Translator* (Salt Lake City: Arrow, 1912), 28.

85. Robert Martin-Achard, *Actualité d'Abraham* (Neuchatel: Delachaux and Niestlé, 1969), 130–37.

86. Cyrus Gordon, "Where Is Abraham's Ur?" *BAR* 2 (June 1977): 52.

87. Nibley, "A New Look at the Pearl of Great Price," *IE* 72 (April 1969): 66–72.

88. Martin-Achard, *Actualité d'Abraham*, 14.

89. Gordon, "Where Is Abraham's Ur?" 20.

90. Noel Weeks, "Man, Nuzi and the Patriarchs," *Abr-Nahrain* 16 (1975–76): 74.

91. Kelso, "Abraham as Archaeology Knows Him," 7.

92. Editorial, "The Promise of Ebla," *BAR* 2 (December 1976): 42.

93. Ibid.; David N. Freedman, "The Real Story of the Ebla Tablets," *Biblical Archaeologist* 41 (December 1978): 148–64.

94. F. M. Theodor de Liagre Böhl, "Babel und Bibel (Pt. II)," *JEOL* 17 (1964): 138–39.

95. Albrecht Alt, *Essays on Old Testament History and Religion*, trans. R. A. Wilson (Oxford: Blackwell, 1966), 30–45.

96. Edward W. Lane, *An Arabic-English Lexicon*, 8 vols. (London: Williams and Norgate, 1863), s.v. "shigre."

97. Raymond O. Faulkner, "The King and the Star-Religion in the Pyramid Texts," *JNES* 25 (1966): 158–59.

98. Henri Frankfort, *Kingship and the Gods* (Chicago: University of Chicago Press, 1948), 120.

99. Faulkner, "King and the Star-Religion in the Pyramid Texts," 159–60.

100. Jacob Hoftijzer, "The Prophet Balaam in a 6th Century Aramaic Inscription," *Biblical Archaeologist* 39 (March 1976): 15–16.

101. Nibley, "A New Look at the Pearl of Great Price," *IE* 72 (March 1969): 80–81.

102. Louis Ginzberg, *The Legends of the Jews*, 7 vols. (Philadelphia: Jewish Publication Society, 1909–13), 1:298–99; Nibley, "A New Look at the Pearl of Great Price," *IE* 72 (March 1969): 82.

103. Alt, *Essays on Old Testament History and Religion*, 3–77.

104. Martin Gemoll, *Israeliten und Hyksos* (Leipzig: Hinrichs, 1913), 36–37.

105. James H. Breasted, *Ancient Records of Egypt*, 4 vols. (Chicago: University of Chicago Press, 1906–7), 2:310.

106. Ibid., 2:345.

107. Ibid., 2:204 n. b.

108. William H. Stiebing, "When Was the Age of the Patriarchs?—Of Amorites, Canaanites, and Archaeology," *BAR* 1 (June 1975): 17, 21.

109. De Buck, *Egyptian Readingbook*, 106–9; Paul Tresson, "Un curieux cas d'exorcisme dans l'antiquité: La stèle égyptienne de Bakhtan," *Revue biblique* 42 (1933): 57–78; Adolf Erman, "Die Bentreschstele," *ZÄS* 21 (1883): 54–60.

110. Moret, *Histoire de l'Orient*, 504–7.

111. De Buck, *Egyptian Readingbook*, 67.

112. Nibley, "A New Look at the Pearl of Great Price," *IE* 72 (November 1969): 116–17; reprinted in this volume, pp. 182–89; ibid., *IE* 73 (April 1970): 84–95; in this volume, pp. 356–76.

113. Aylward M. Blackman, *Middle-Egyptian Stories* (Brussels: Fondation égyptologique reine Elisabeth, 1932), 1–41.

114. "The Tale of the Two Brothers," in Alan H. Gardiner, *Late-Egyptian Stories* (Brussels: Fondation Égyptologique Reine Élisabeth, 1932), 9–30; cf. n. 2 above.

115. Nibley, "A New Look at the Pearl of Great Price," *IE* 72 (February 1969): 65–67.

116. "The Tale of the Doomed Prince," in Gardiner, *Late-Egyptian Stories*, 1–9.

117. Theodor H. Gaster, "The Egyptian 'Story of Astarte' and the Ugaritic Poem of Baal," *BiOr* 9 (1952): 84.

118. Alan H. Gardiner, "The Astarte Papyrus," in *Studies Presented to F. L. Griffith* (London: Oxford University Press, 1932), 74.

119. Gaster, "Egyptian 'Story of Astarte' and the Ugaritic Poem of Baal," 84.

120. Ibid., 83.

121. Ibid.

122. Beer, *Leben Abraham's*, 2.

123. Gardiner, "Astarte Papyrus," 77.

124. M. Georges Goyon, "Les Travaux de Chou et les tribulations de Geb, d'après le Naos 2248 d'Ismaîlia," *Kêmi* 6 (1936): 18, 37–38.

6

Pharaoh and Abraham:
Where Is Thy Glory?

The Common Quest: Kings and Priests

The Book of Abraham brings out the main points of rivalry between the patriarch and the pharaoh in high relief: Each claims to possess the only true priesthood and with it the only true kingship. The earliest legends of Egypt and Mesopotamia introduce us to a scene repeated over and over again in the apocalypses and testaments of the patriarchs, prophets, and apostles, of a great and terrible monarch who feels his divinity threatened and his dominion challenged by an emissary of the true God. He summons his wise men to appear before him and solve the problem, but invariably their wisdom proves dismally inadequate for the task, as the servant of God wins the upper hand and the great king suffers and concedes defeat. Often the showdown takes the form of a battle of the magicians. The theme is central to the Abraham legends,[1] as we have shown elsewhere, but it is nowhere more at home than in Egypt, where, as a number of recent studies have shown, the divinity of pharaoh was perpetually in question. This surprising state of things is abundantly attested in the declarations of the kings themselves and is so clearly set forth

254

in the Book of Abraham that we need only set the statements of that book side by side with the royal inscriptions to see how the two confirm and support each other.

Such an exercise will be enormously facilitated by the labors of Professors Sethe and Breasted, who have brought together in the compass of the *Urkunden* and the *Ancient Records* enough material to satisfy the market for parallels without the necessity of more than occasionally quoting from other sources.

Right at the outset we are met with a striking phenomenon, when the Book of Abraham, after a short introductory sentence in which the author identifies himself, instead of going on with the story, pauses to present an imposing list of his aspirations and attainments in the long second verse in which the editors are unable to make a pause for breath. This is typically Egyptian,[2] and these are the same blessings as the Egyptian king (or commoner, following his example) wishes or claims for himself in the typical Egyptian autobiography.

Abraham wants in the first instance what all pharaohs ask for—a happy, peaceful, untroubled life.

Abr. 1:2. And, finding there was greater *happiness* and *peace* and *rest* for me,

[The standard formula for the living pharaoh is usually interpreted as an *optative* (a wish or desire).][3]

Urk. 4:234.[4] [May the king receive] all life (*ꜥnḥ*), stability (security, *ḏd*), dominion (*wꜣs*, Glück = felicity, so Sethe), health, happiness (expansion of heart), all peace (*ḥtp*, with the basic meaning of *rest*).

Urk. 4:154. The greatest
gifts of the gods are: "life,
stability (security), felicity
(dominion, *wȝs*), happi-
ness, in everlastingness
(*ḏ.t*)."

I sought for the blessings
of the fathers,

Urk. 4:194. A solicitous
(*nḏty*) son does what is
pleasing (advantageous,
ȝḥ.wt) to his fathers who
begot him, endowing rites
(festivals), for the gods
who created his perfection
(*nfrw*).

Urk. 1:147. [The king
prays that he] may be
together in the same place
[with his father and
grandfather forever].

Urk. 1:76. [Henku] was
one who loved his fathers.
Urk 1:79. And was glori-
fied in them.

and the right whereunto I
should be ordained to
administer the same
[blessings];

AR 2:31. Thutmosis I:
Amon-Re, king of the gods
is his father . . . [he] is
given life, stability, satisfaction, health, joy of his
heart upon the throne of
Horus, leading all the living like Re, forever.

I became a rightful heir,	Urk. 4:197. The Son of Amon upon his throne[s], and his heir whom he has placed upon the earth. . . . I magnify him (*dí shm=f*) even as he magnifies me.
having been myself a follower of righteousness,	[A typical Egyptian expression, here in place of the usual "I was a follower of his Majesty."[5] A "follower (*šms*) of righteousness (*Mꜣꜥ.t*)"; Maat being "the truth as personification of truth and the right . . . with its own cult and priestly offices"[6] and a "(*šms*)" being one who follows the standard of a divinity,[7] i.e., is dedicated to the principles represented by the same.]
desiring also . . . to be a greater follower of righteousness,	AR 2:365–66. [The king] is one who taketh thought, . . . [who is constantly] searching . . . [in the] desire . . . to make Egypt flourish as in the beginning, by the plans of Truth [Maat, Righteousness].
desiring also to be one who possessed great knowledge and . . . to possess a greater knowledge,	Urk. 4:19–20. The king alone is taught by Sothis, praised by Seshat [the Book-Lady, patroness of

learning]; the reputation (attainment, *šfy.t*) of Thoth himself [the god of learning] goes with him, it is he who causes him to know so much. He is superior to [leading] the scribes in exact knowledge. He is the Great Master [of great power—Thoth].

PT 250 (§267). This is the king, . . . so says he who is in charge of wisdom, being great, and who bears the god's book, (even) Sia. [Note: The personification of intelligence and understanding who is at the right hand of Re.][8]

Westcar Papyrus.[9] King Cheops spent his days in searching the archives (files, *íp.wt*) of the sanctuary of Thoth, that he might construct another like it [cf. the House of Life].[10]

AR 2:365–66. [Karnak Pylon depicts the king as a deep student:] He is one who taketh thought, who maketh wise with knowledge, . . . loving examples of truth, rejoicing in plans, . . . searching bodies

(hearts), knowing what is
in the heart (mind). . . . He
rejoices in remembering.

AR 2:317. [Atum]
appointed him to be king
of the living, . . . creative
(progressive) in knowl-
edge, wise in execution.

[desiring to be] a prince of
peace,

AR 2:424.[11] The chiefs of
Retenu (*Rtnw*) [Canaan]
the Upper, who knew not
Egypt since the time of the
god, are craving peace
from his majesty. . . . There
shall be no revolters in thy
time; but every land shall
be in peace.

AR 2:143.[12] [Ineni:] I continued powerful in peace, I
met no misfortune, my
years were [passed] in
gladness of heart.

Urk. 4:280. I have united
for thee the Two Lands in
Peace; . . . thy fame (might)
is great in all lands, like
Re-Atum in the years of
his glory (the Golden
Age). . . . I give to thee all
lands, all of mankind
(*pȝ.wt*) which my eye
encompasses (encircles,

šnn.t; cf. Shinehah,
Abr. 3:13).

and to be a father of many
nations,

Urk. 1:168–69. [To Sahure:]
I give to thee all these
nations; . . . you shall be
head of all the living Kas,
seated in glory on the
throne of Horus forever. All
hearts shall be captive to
you, all the common people
will be yours. I give to thee
all foreign lands and islands
of the sea.

AR 2:366. I am his first born,
. . . under his authority; I
was endowed with his
might, I was endued with
his power.

AR 2:62–63. He caused that
[the princes of] all
[coun]tries [should come],
doing obeisance. . . . I am his
son, beloved of his majesty.

AR 2:101. Thou hast given to
me the kingdom of every
land . . . while I was a youth;
. . . they are made my subjects; . . . all countries.

and desiring to receive
instructions, and to keep
the commandments of God,

Urk. 4:272. [Father Amon]
I have carried out all thy
instructions (*sbꝫ.yt=k*); yea,

thy heart delights in what I have done.

AR 2:389.[13] Thou [the king] art the Only One of [Aton], in possession of his designs (or instructions, $s\underline{h}rw$).

I became a rightful heir,

PT 260 (§316–23). Righteousness ($M_3{}^\varsigma.ty$) has judged . . . and ordered that the throne of Geb shall revert to me. . . . I put a stop to the affair in Heliopolis [the perennial dispute between Horus and Seth over the kingship], . . . for I am the alter-ego of my father.

PT 606 (§1688–89). Sit on this throne of Re; . . . take possession of the heritage of your father Geb in the presence of the great company of the Ennead in On [which proclaim his legality.]

Urk. 4:198. A son, acting out of love in his heart for his father [am I]. . . . For he has put it into my divine heart to make his monument, that I might establish *his* authority (power

to act, *sḥm*), even as he has
established *my*
authority, that I might
make firm his house
forever.

Urk. 4:65–66. This is the
plain truth, and I say it for
the benefit of all men, . . .
ye [who follow instruc-
tions] will hand on your
offices to your children.

a High Priest,

[In Egypt] it is not possible
for a king to rule without
the priesthood.[14] [The king
officiates at Heliopolis in
the capacity of a priest.][15]

The privileged situation of
the king derives from his
role as priest, . . . not as
one distinguished . . . by
birth. . . . Thus reverence is
not directed to the person
of the officiant, but to the
priesthood with which he
is invested.[16]

[E. Blumenthal writes on
the triple office of prophet,
priest, and king, as] the
Egyptian ideology of kingship [adopted by the
Maccabees].[17]

[That the king should be a
High Priest seems almost

incomprehensible to us, but it was the combining of these royal and priestly powers that was the Key to everything.][18]

[The main purpose of the great festivals was to establish the king's divine authority by his appearing in public] as the true High Priest.[19]

Libanius to the Emperor Julian: The Emperor rejoices in the title of priest no less than in that of king, and the name matches the function, for he surpasses kings in matters of state as much as he does priests in holy ordinances, . . . as we learn from the wise Egyptians.[20]

holding the right belonging to the fathers.

Urk. 1:85. Verily their offices (assignments, spheres of authority, *iȝ.wt*) are like those of their fathers.

Abr. 1:3. It was conferred upon me from the fathers; it came down from the fathers,

Urk. 4:284–85. [I give to thee the throne of Geb (the primal earth-father), and the office of A]tum (cf. Adam). [I (Amon the

father of the gods) give to
thee my seat of inheri-
tance] under me. . . . I am
[thy] beloved father who
establishes thy authority
(*sꜣḥ*), . . . who confirms thy
titles. [In the Pyramid
Texts the right to rule is
established by formal
demonstration of patriar-
chal descent from Geb.][21]

Setne: [The secret of priesthood and kingship:] The
father of my father told it
to my father [who] told
it unto the father of my
father, saying . . . [the resting place of Ahure and
Merabher son] is by the
south corner of the
house.[22]

from the beginning of
time; yea, even from the
beginning,

[The Egyptians always
trace their royal authority
to the *pꜣw.t*, "primeval
time, the beginning of
time," for them "a man of
ancient family" is a
pꜣw.ty.][23]

Urk. 4:95. How pleasing to
the hearts of men . . . that
you glorify the *Ḫnty-
imntyw,* the great god of
the beginning of time (*sp
tpy*), whose place Atum

preferred, which he magnified before his created ones [?] for whose sake [the land was settled, so Sethe], whom the kings of Egypt served since the land was first settled.

Urk. 4:180. The king is foreordained (sr) to the throne of Geb [the primal ancestor, the principle of patriarchal succession], and the office of Ḫprí [the principle of ongoing creation], at the side of my Father [Amon].

[It was the principle of sp tpy, basing everything on the types and models set forth "at the beginning of time," that allowed Egypt to enjoy "2500 years virtually undisturbed by revolution." When this tie with the "beginning" was broken in the late period, the whole thing collapsed.][24]

or before the foundation of the earth, down to the present time,

Urk. 4:96. Geb [the primal earth-god] has opened to thee what is in him; Tenen [the first settler of the earth] has given to thee his possessions; the inhabitants of the desert and the sown are all under thy administration (plans).

Shabako Stone [thought to be the oldest Egyptian document] describes the Council of the gods at the Creation, when Ptah [the Creator] grants his power (*sḥm*) to his heirs, the gods and the spirits.[25]

even the right of the first-born, or the first man, who is Adam, or first father,

Thus were all gods created, Atum and his lineage. . . . Thus the spirit-creation of the gods took place, and the preexistent (*ḥms.wt*) spirits.[26]

So it was said: He who begot Atum and the other gods is Ptah [the Opener, Father]; all things come forth from him. . . . And after all things were created by his word, Ptah was well pleased with everything.[27] [Sethe sees a direct connection between this and Genesis 1:25.][28]

Urk. 4:180. [The king is] foreordained (*sr*) to rule over the Two Lands, to the thrones of Geb and the Office of *Ḫprí* [Geb the primal ancestor, *Ḫprí* the principle of ongoing creation], at the side of my father.

[Thutmosis III claims Atum, Re, Amun, Hathor, Osiris, Dwdn, Ptah, Horus, Seth, Thoth, each of whom figures as the primal parent and creator.][29]

through the fathers unto me.

"The right of the king to his kingdom" was established only by "the divine genealogy of Heliopolis" in which the misnamed Ennead is really the line of ancestors.[30] The great council at On would proclaim him king by acclamation upon establishing "the pedigree of the gods or the lineage of Horus," going back to Atum (Adam), being the primeval deity.[31]

Urk. 4:284. I [Amon] give thee my seat, my authority (s₃ḥ) and mine inheritance which I inherited. . . . I am thy father.

Abr. 1:4. I sought for mine appointment unto the Priesthood according to the appointment of God

The king got his authority by *appointment:* The "Great Corporation" of Heliopolis acknowledged the divine rightness of the king on earth, with the acknowledgment of his divine descent; this was pronounced in the course of a court procedure.[32]

Urk. 4:284. I [Amon] give thee the throne of Geb and the Office of Atum.

[The king must "justify" his title by proving legitimate descent from "the Fatherhood of *Geb*."][33]

unto the fathers concerning the seed.

Urk. 4:249. The two lands are filled with the children of thy children; multitudinous is the number of thy seed; thy *Ba* is created in the hearts of thy people (*pꜥ.t*); she [Hatshepsut] is the daughter of K₃-mwt.f [the coronation priest doubling for the king].

Urk. 4:198. A son does what he does for his father out of the love in his heart. . . . For he has put it into my divine heart to make his monument, that I might establish his authority [power, *sekhem*] even as he has established my authority, that I might make firm his house forever.

Abr. 1:26. [The theme is resumed:] Established by the fathers in the first generations, in the days of the first patriarchal reign, even in the reign of Adam, and also of Noah, his father . . . [Here Noah is called the *father* of Pharaoh.]

Shabako. So all the gods and all the spirits came together to hail God upon his throne. . . . They rejoiced before him in his temple, the source of all good things.[34]

[Following this pattern, the king] passes through the secret doors in the glory of the Lord of Eternity, following the footsteps . . . in the ways of the Great Throne. Then the heavenly court enters and mingles with the gods, with Ptah the Ancient of Days (lit. Lord of Years),[35] [being received into the company] of the gods who were before and after him, [with the gods of Ta-tenen (the first settlement of the earth)].[36]

O Happy Breed!

Most of the above citations have been from the Old and Middle Kingdoms of Egypt. For the *later* period, after the Eighteenth Dynasty, the important autobiographies have been collected and compared by Eberhard Otto, who provides the student with translations of seventy-five of them. He has also shown how in form and content these later biographies conform closely to the patterns followed from the beginning, making them relevant to the study of Abraham's account, no matter when he lived.[37]

The subjects of the Egyptian autobiographies from every period display the same trait of character as those inculcated in the "Teachings" (*sboyet*) of Ptahotep, of the king who taught his son Merikare, of Amenemhet I in a message to his son, of Amenophis IV addressing his officials from the throne, of the wise Amenemope, even of the Eloquent Peasant. Some of the gems of this literature are, as Otto duly notes, contemporary and spiritually akin to the Wisdom Literature of the Jews, Aramaeans, and Nabataeans—the people of Canaan.[38] The autobiographies of the New Kingdom are, like Abraham's, frankly ego-centered (the *Testament of Abraham* and the *Apocalypse of Abraham* surprised scholars by being written in the first person, a convention quite alien to normal apocalyptic), and the authors leave us in no doubt as to where their desires, ambitions, and values lie: mainly to have a happy life, a large posterity, and a blessed memory.[39] The model upheld is the patriarchal figure—"I was a god to my family"[40]—who at the same time feels his own dependence on God's (in the singular!) guidance and mercy.[41] Our hero—like those before him a pillar of strength to others in time of crisis,[42] the "Wall" and support of all in time of need,[43] bold and independent in thought and action,[44] with quick intelligence to "solve difficult problems"[45]—is concerned before all for the care of the poor and the weak.[46] Self-disciplined and good-natured,[47] utterly devoid of any trace of meanness, arrogance, or covetousness,[48] kind-hearted and fair to everyone, with special concern for the helpless,[49] he is ever aware that the secret of survival in bad times is working together.[50] Of course his hospitality is boundless.[51]

The same humane and enlightened spirit that made Abraham a legend in the East is strikingly displayed in the famous El-Bersheh tomb (fig. 37), on whose walls a great nobleman of the mid-eighteenth century B.C. (the time usually assigned to Abraham) depicts in magnificent relief how large and well-organized bodies of happy workmen under good-natured overseers and wise officials carried out monumental building operations in a spirit of high enthusiasm, genuine religious fervor, and merry competitive camaraderie amidst cheery songs and quips—the great man wanted everybody to be happy in serving God.[52] Of course it is idealized, but it does show where the Egyptian's values lay, and they were the same as Abraham's.

The ultimate model of this patriarchal perfection was, of course, the king, whose rule is an expression of God's rule on earth,[53] and without whom the world could not survive.[54] Naturally the autobiographies regularly stress the subjects' personal proximity to the pharaoh,[55] whether in holding office or receiving special honors.[56] Yet it is interesting to note that it is not the king's person but his sacred *office* of kingship and priesthood that are the real source of power and authority in the land.[57] It is from that fact that the inevitable rivalry between Pharaoh and Abraham arises, each claiming to hold a unique dispensation from the God of heaven.[58]

It is in Egypt that Abraham is most at home. In his own country he was an outcast, pushed from place to place in Canaan; it is only in Egypt that he comes to his own.[59] He was, in fact, almost as thoroughly Egyptianized as his noble descendant Joseph, whose own father and brothers settled permanently on Pharaoh's lands and adopted the customs (Genesis 50:2–14, 26).

Otto raises the question regarding the autobiographies that we have discussed above—the subjects are supposed to have written them personally, but who, Otto asks, really wrote them? Usually, he finds, it was the old man's son who was responsible for getting his story written on stone. He would consult with the overseer of the temple workshop, who would in turn go to the priests of the temple for a properly composed text, which they would supply by consulting

Figure 37. The most famous depiction of the Egyptian ability to move heavy objects is found in the tomb of Djehutihotep. The white alabaster statue from the quarries of Hatnub is about 20 feet high and weighs 60 tons. Some liquid is poured in front of the sledge while the foreman standing on the statue claps his hands to set the beat. A priest walks backward burning incense before the marvel. The 172 movers, "troops of goodly youths," were divided into four teams. The top and bottom rows

the temple library of handbooks on correct forms and phrases. Yet after all it was the man's own story, and he always got credit for writing it.[60] With such formality, it is no wonder that the biographies all emphasize the same things, and this very regularity is a valuable check on the authenticity of our picture of Abraham in the Book of Abraham.

Uniquely intimate ties between the spirit of Abraham and the ways of the Egyptians have come to the fore in the

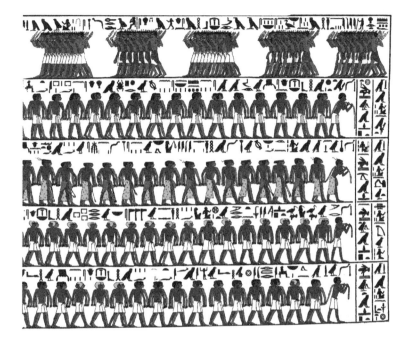

are comprised of men from the western and eastern halves of the province, while the two middle rows consist of young soldiers and priests, all competing with each other in this productive tug-of-war. On top, seven groups of soldiers waving green branches and carrying sickle swords come out from the temple compound to greet the statue's arrival, "the townsmen all rejoicing."

study of Egyptian jurisprudence by Schafik Allam, who maintains that the Egyptians were the first, and long the only, people in the world to recognize "the full legal independence of the individual (*a pleine capacité juridique de l'individu*)" applying equally to male and female.[61] Along with that we find in Egyptian law "apparently the first recognition of the system of the family structure" as the foundation for society, this being based on a "patrilinear, patrilocal, patriarchal, and monogamous" tradition and organization.[62]

Records of the Fathers

A significant point of resemblance and rivalry is the claim of both the king and the patriarch to exclusive possession of and access to certain *written records* which went back to the beginning of time and confirmed his particular claim to legitimacy of priesthood and kingship. Both seem to be speaking of the same records.

Abr. 1:28. But I shall endeavor, hereafter, to delineate the chronology running back from myself to the beginning of the creation, for the records have come into *my* hands, which I hold unto this present time.

PT 250 (§267). I [the king] became Sia who bears the god's book at the right hand of Re.

[Neferhotep (Thirteenth Dynasty)]. My heart desires to see the books of the primeval times of Atum, spread out before me for careful research, to discover if possible the god in his true nature, and the gods of the Ennead (great council) as they naturally are, and the service due them . . . that I might be united with them; that I may know God in his true form, that I may represent him [in an image] as he was in the beginning, that I might officiate as their proxy and improve their memorials on earth, that they might confirm to me mine inheritance . . . over all that the

Sun embraces in its round
(*šnn*).[63]

[Ramses IV spent his days
investigating (the annals)
of Thoth who is in the
House of Life (the archives
of the royal genealogy—
Gardiner); he says:] I have
not left unseen . . . any of
them all, in order to search
out both great and small
among the gods and god-
desses, and I have found
. . . the entire Ennead [the
king's ancestral line—
Anthes]. He understood
things like Thoth, and has
penetrated into the annals
like the maker thereof,
having examined the
annals of the House of
Life.[64]

[Setne, Pharaoh's librar-
ian, is told in a dream in
the temple of Chons the
Creator to copy a book in
the temple library which
was written by Thoth him-
self,[65] a book of all knowledge which vindicates the
Pharaoh's claim to the
throne.[66] The son of
Pharaoh seeks for the
book in vain, and the rule
of the king is challenged

and his throne forfeit until the young son of the librarian produces the necessary documents.[67]]

AR 2:374. [Amenemhet:] I was introduced into the divine book; I beheld the excellent things of Thoth; I was equipped with their secrets; I opened all their passages. [I myself kept the lists (census and genealogical records) and records of everything.][68]

Abr. 1:31. *The records* of the fathers, even the patriarchs, concerning the *right of Priesthood,* the Lord my God preserved in mine own hands;

[The *gnwt*] clearly indicated ancient historical records . . . and is habitually translated by scholars as "annals." But nothing of the kind had been recognized by Egyptologists until . . . H. Schaefer, . . . L. Borchardt, and K. Sethe . . . diagnosed the true nature [of the *gnwt* as royal genealogies going back to prehistoric times.][69]

AR 2:31. [Lands are now in fealty to Thutmosis I, which have been forgotten, since] they were not seen in the archives of the ancestors since the

Worshipers of Horus [the first mortal king of Egypt].

AR 2:281. [The king governs by virtue of the forty rolls of the law set out before his vizier as he sits in formal court to handle all the business of the kingdom (see fig. 42, pp. 308–9).]

therefore a *knowledge* of the beginning of the *creation,* and also of the *planets,* and of the *stars,* as they were made known unto the fathers, have I kept even unto this day,

[The king's] authority was founded not in the social, but in the *cosmic order,* [in which] the story of the *creation* held the clue to the understanding of the present.[70]

[The preexistent Corporation at Heliopolis (the great observatory)] apparently was the court which performed the nomination of the king by acclamation. . . . I prefer to call it either the pedigree of the gods or the lineage of Horus, and *not* the Ennead. . . . The pedigree was looked upon by the Egyptians as a *cosmogonic concept* with Atum as the primeval deity.[71]

AR 2:149. I [the Vizier Senmut] had access to all the writings of the prophets; there was nothing which I did not know of that which had happened since the beginning.

AR 2:385. [The Vizier Ramose enters] into the secret things of heaven, of earth; . . . master of secret things of the palace; attached to Nekhen, prophet of Maat, chief justice.[72]

PT 257 (§304). The king is older than the Great One, to whom belongs the power on his throne; the king assumes authority, eternity is brought to him and understanding. . . . The king takes possession of the sky. . . . We see something new, say the primeval gods.

and I shall endeavor to write some of these things upon this record, for the benefit of my posterity that shall come after me.

Urk. 4:61. [Inni:] I speak unto you, O ye people, hearken that ye may do good as I have done, that you may receive like good in return, that you may follow my example.

AR 2:193. [Thutmosis III:] My majesty hath done [made] this [autobiography] from desire to put them before my father Amon, in this great temple of Amon, (as) a memorial forever and ever. [An inscription on the temple walls for public edification.]

AR 2:297. [Intef:] If ye would bequeath your offices to your children; whether (ye be) one that readeth these words upon this stela. [Give a thought to the subject and speak a word in his memory.]

Jubilees 39:6. [Joseph in Egypt] remembered the words which Jacob his father used to read from amongst the words of Abraham.

Jubilees 45:16. Israel . . . gave all his books and the books of his fathers to Levi his son that he might preserve them and renew them for his children unto this day.

Would Abraham Dare?

Some of the latest studies cast doubt on the reliability of the tradition that brings Abraham and Pharaoh together. The mere idea of an ordinary alien standing in the presence of the divine monarch, they argue, is quite far-fetched, and that anyone else on earth should lay claim to the same virtues and blessings as the pharaoh may at first sight seem utterly presumptuous to us.[73] And yet the Egyptians did not think so. Hundreds of inscriptions preserve the memories and laud the merits of ordinary Egyptian subjects who seem to lay claim to the merits of Pharaoh himself, sharing the resounding boasts and pious formulas with each other and with the king. Indeed, they tell us sometimes that Pharaoh took an active interest in their tombs and memorials and helped them to plan and erect them. The list of important men who left such monuments is an impressive and ever-growing one. Over a period of three thousand years they all claim much the same things for themselves—the very things for which the monarchs wished to be remembered and revered through the ages. These qualities are named with almost equal frequency, no one predominating over the others, so that it is impossible to list them in order of importance. They are (1) proximity to the seat and source of power and glory; for any Egyptian this means nearness to the king and his family. (2) Administrative competence: The subject is reliable, alert, prompt, tireless, efficient, resourceful, devoted in service to the king. (3) This required certain qualities of mind—wisdom, understanding, knowledge, in short, intelligence. (4) Dedication to public interest, kindness, and humanity; this is perhaps that trait most consistently proclaimed: The subject is devoid of any trace of partiality, snobbishness, rudeness, impatience, cruelty; he treats all men and women as equals and does all things with even-handed impartiality. (5) As a result he enjoys recognition by the king but also by the common people; he is concerned to please them both, (6) for he is aware of a judgment hereafter (the inscriptions often reminded the reader not to lose sight of that either!) and hopes to spend eternity in a state of blessed happiness. (7) Often there is an insistence on the honest bona fides of the statements put forth that might suggest a "smooth, shallow rhetoric" with which the Egyptians have been charged. But to whatever degree the parties actually realized the perfections thus set forth, the persistence of the same formulas over thousands of years in tombs that, far from depicting a rigid formality, show the greatest freedom and variety in the reliefs, inscriptions, and architecture, shows us those qualities which the Egyptians prized above all others. Literary compositions such as the Wisdom Literature with its sage admonitions, the Eloquent Peasant pleading the cause of the underdog, or the Negative Confessions in the Book of the Dead all confirm the same set of values. It is a thing that puts our own civilization to shame with its depressing union of "covetousness, and . . . feigned words" (D&C 104:4)—greed and hypocrisy; and it explains the astounding stability of the Egyptian civilization—they were good people who took the long view, and their biographical reports may well be summed up as mirrors of faith, hope, and charity. Only a few kings and their captains celebrating extraordinary displays of daring and valor boast of military exploits, and even they usually emphasize the blessings of peace and humanity that they are bringing to the conquered. A few now classical examples of the ideal types described are worth noting both as edifying models of civic virtue and in particular as men cast in the very mold of Abraham, whose great-grandson Joseph was the model of official Egyptian virtues.[74]

A Noble Race

Urk. 1:1–7. The restless and beneficent public activities of the earliest records recall the life of Abraham, as officials dig canals (the oldest calling), measure fields, distribute land, direct the hunt, settle people in new towns and villages, plant trees and vineyards, build, cultivate, plan, making the most of water, land and desert, collect taxes and use them wisely. Government is the foundation of civilization, not its enemy.

Urk. 1:38–40. A physician follows Sahure on his expeditions, and has the right to sit in a chair. His closing line: "I never harmed any man or woman."

Devoid of any trace of the cruelty or barbarism that we so often associate with the ancients, these men seek to exemplify the same moral principles as those taught in the Old and New Testaments.

Urk. 1:69–71. The pious Inti loved good and eschewed evil and, doing what was pleasing to God, became acceptable (*ım3ḥ*) to the Great God, acceptable to the king, and popular with the common laborers, for he never harmed anyone.

Urk. 1:72. "Recognized by the king (a common title), . . . I never infringed on the rights of others," for whoever offends must answer the offended at the judgment in the presence of the Great God.

Urk. 1:76–79. Henku wishes well to all who pass by. He was loved by [his?] fathers, praised by his mothers, gave bread to all the hungry, clothed the naked, caused the herds of large and small beasts to multiply, even fed the wolves of the mountain and the birds of the heaven. He brought poor peasants into the region, settled them down, and promoted them to positions of dignity and self-respect. "I never went after the property of anyone; . . . the weak never complained of the strong under my supervision; I was never haughty." He worked with his brother, a revered priest, for the public good, bringing in settlers and increasing the herds. Loved by his father, honored by his mother, a pillar of strength to his brother, charming to his sister, he is now glorified [*špss*] before the god, the king, his father, mother and children . . . and their fathers.

Urk. 1:98–110. The famous Uni [Weni] enjoyed the king's complete confidence. Though of low origin outranked by many, he held the highest military command because of his competence. Where he commanded, no traveler lost his sandals, no bread was taken from any village, no man lost a goat; his eye was on everything, and though his soldiers respected the people, he took good care of them, seeing to it that the army returned vastly enriched with a minimum of casualties. The people he conquered, however, not only submitted to him—they actually liked him.

Urk. 1:120–31. Herkhuf, also famous. He leaves this world loved by his father, praised by his mother, beloved of all his family. He fed and clothed the poor, ferried the boatless who needed a lift. "Let no one judge or despise his brother! . . . His offices pass to his posterity from son to son forever."

Urk. 1:143. An ascending scale of recognition: Loved by his father, praised by his mother, honored (*ım₃ḫ*) in the presence of the king, honored by the god of his city, he is Ibi the beloved.

Urk. 1:194–96. Memi's efficiency was noted, he was summoned to the palace, trusted with a position of leadership, for the king knows how to recognize real ability and merit, and appreciated both his good humor and his integrity.

Urk. 1:198–201. Sheshi the priest: Always truthful, giving satisfaction, speaking and doing only what is true [a common formula], loved by all; open and free with his brothers; firm and decisive in action. He feeds the hungry, clothes the naked, buries the man who has no son to bury

him, ferries the man without a boat. Respectful to his father,
delightful to his mother, taking care of [šdı] their children.

Urk. 1:203–4. Idu always did and said what was right,
true, and pleasing to God and man; feeding the hungry,
etc., respectful to father, etc., never speaking evil of anyone. God and the common people alike blessed him.

Urk. 1:215–21. Chief Architect Nekhbu: called to the
palace; immensely versatile, he held many offices; was
put in charge of everything and never bungled. He was a
peacemaker, always calm and even-tempered, univer-
sally popular. Never said an unkind thing or spoke disre-
spectfully of anyone. For his draining of the marshes he
got a special award from the king.

Urk. 1:221–24. Nefer-ka, a high priest at Cusae: Honored by
the king, the Great God, *and* the people. Beloved by his
father and mother, brothers and sisters. Always busy, cheerful of conversation, discreet in dealing with higher-ups, etc.
"This is spoken in truth and not by way of boasting."

AR 2:299.[75] Intef is wise, learned, and perceptive; void of
deceit, gentle, encouraging the timid, perceiving their
thoughts, reading minds, checking mere rhetoric with
truth, not favoring his friends above others, willing to
hear petitions and to judge fairly; protector of the weak,
father of the fatherless and the orphan, at the service of
the poor, advocate of those who are at the mercy of the
powerful, shelter of the orphan. Praised for his character;
the worthy thank God for him; everybody prays for his
health, etc. Such "were my qualities of which I have testi-
fied; there is no deceit therein; these were my excellencies
in very truth [without qualification]." I did not play with
words but showed myself as I was. I did not violate the
injunctions of conscience, but followed its promptings.
The people regarded him as inspired.

> AR 2:385. Ramose: "A doer of truth, a hater of deceit, . . .
> approaching his lord, whom the Lord of the Two Lands
> loved because of his remarkable traits, who enters the
> palace, and comes forth with favor, . . . the mouth that
> makes content in the whole land, . . . master of all
> wardrobes, entering into the secrets of heaven, of earth
> [and of the nether world]; master of secret things of the
> palace, . . . prophet of Maat."[76]

Sentiments expressed in the famous tomb of Petosiris
(which we have discussed elsewhere)[77] might have been
taken right out of the Hebrew Psalms or Wisdom Literature.

> It is good to walk in the way of God; . . . who keeps
> to the Way of God passes all his life in joy; . . . he remains
> ever young; his children increase. . . . Walk in the Way of
> the Lord Thoth, who will give you even such great favors
> after death as he gave you in life.[78]

Naturally the Egyptologists of 1912 (the same who took
Joseph Smith to task) dismissed such statements as naive
and empty boasts, foolish routine, primitive incantations.[79]
But as Hermann Kees has pointed out, the dignified for-
malism of the utterances contains great freedom and variety
of expression, showing them to be personal messages reflect-
ing the real values of the speakers, and no mere "Hallmark"
greetings.[80] Does the above passage ring less true than the
first Psalm, which it so much resembles?

Others Who Dared: Glory Unlimited

All this prepares us to draw a step nearer to Abraham
in viewing the careers of two especially remarkable men
whose fame actually surpassed that of the pharaohs under
whom they served. One of them is the subject of a special
study by Sethe,[81] and the two are brought together and compared in a recent and significant book, *Egyptian Saints:
Deification in Pharaonic Egypt*, by Dietrich Wildung.[82] Sethe
entitles his work *Imhotep, der Asklepios der Aegypter, ein*

vergötteter Mensch. These titles suggest to one contemplating the picture of Abraham enthroned with the insignia of divinity and royalty in Facsimile 3 of the Book of Abraham that he too may have attained to such heights. Who gets the royal treatment at Pharaoh's court? "As long as he lived," writes Wildung, "and no matter what he did, no king of Egypt was able to ascend to the realm of the gods. Two mortals did."[83]

The two commoners, benefactors of the race and permanent models for others to follow, were Imhotep and Amenhotep Son-of-Hapu (figs. 38 and 39). They lived twelve hundred years apart, the one under Djoser of the Third Dynasty, the other born about 1450 B.C., in the Eighteenth Dynasty. The veneration bestowed on these men by their own and all succeeding generations closely resembles the esteem in which the great patriarchs from Adam to Moses were held by Israel. But the man they most resemble in every particular is Abraham. And they were real men, historical figures beyond a doubt, whose existence is attested in many monuments and documents, including highly personal portrait statues. Though in time they were hailed as gods and worshiped in their own temples (fig. 40), they were still, before everything else, examples of great-hearted human beings, whose beneficent labors like "the works of Abraham" were held up as examples to be equaled and, if possible, surpassed by others of their fellow mortals.

Why just two of them? Because only these two were great enough to deserve such honors. There were indeed others who were venerated for having the very same qualities but in a lesser degree; and some of those, revered in the "Admonition" literature, *nearly* made the grade. Their glory is purely a matter of real achievement, and it was recognized by all, from Pharaoh down, without jealousy or resentment. Joseph Smith teaches us that it was specifically

Figure 38. Imhotep was the architect of the world's first cut-stone build-ing, the Step Pyramid of Djoser. For centuries he was honored by the people, especially scribes. This small Ptolemaic statue shows him hold-ing an open scroll on his lap with the inscription "water from every scribe," the usual oblation poured on the ground by scribes before they mixed their ink.

Figure 39. Amenhotep, son of Hapu, is shown in this gray granite statue at age 80 (c. 1360 B.C.). The wrinkled face of this sage counselor is probably a portrait from life. The inscription says he will intercede with the gods for supplicants who visit the temple of Karnak.

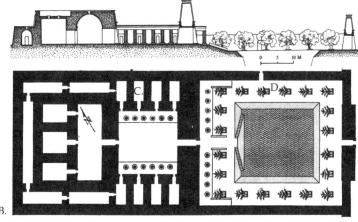

Figure 40. The funerary temple of Amenhotep, son of Hapu, was planted with ornamental trees and bushes around a sunken pool to create a garden paradise in the midst of the desert. This restful atmosphere helped the sick in their recovery. From within the courtyard one looks over the sacred pool to the second pylon (A) from point D. The ground plan (B) shows the symmetrical arrangement of the complex with numerous side chapels. The third chapel on the right (C) contained a mural (see fig. 78, pp. 454–55).

in Egypt that the greatness of Abraham was fully recognized, to the point of having him sit on Pharaoh's throne. He also tells us why Abraham was so esteemed. Let us compare his qualities and deeds with the fully certified achievements of the ancient Egyptian "saints" whose portraits Professor Wildung has placed before us so conveniently in numerous texts and photographs.

I.   First, *Abraham:* the man of intellect, "more intelligent than they all," ever seeking "to possess a greater knowledge," keeper of records (Abraham 1:2), writing textbooks for his people to explain the Egyptian learning to them (cf. Abraham 1:12–14).[84]

Compare him with *Imhotep:* the patron of intellectuals and scribes, often portrayed in the act of reading a book;[85] he was the keeper and transmitter of the ancient records, many of which he alone could understand and interpret. He was the Chief Scribe, improving the writing system, searching out and restoring the holy books of the past, the explainer of hidden books, seeking to grasp the wholeness of man's existence through pure science, the great book man.[86] An author in his own right, "he restores and explains the hardest texts." The restless inquiring mind, "the great solver of difficult problems," he was Chief Scribe, Minister of Education, Science, and Religious Ordinances, whose wisdom was passed down to future ages. He was the great teacher, ever encouraging study in others.

The same kudos for *Amenhotep,* "a really excellent scribe," a top mathematician, "the first in calculating everything," a master of language and eloquence; a man of ideas "promoted for the quality of his plans"; like Imhotep an original and inventive mind, who solves impossible problems by his strokes of genius.[87] Just as able administrators in Egypt held many offices, so such men of genius as these would not think of confining themselves to narrow specialties, and sought ever to cast light on one science by the study of others reaching deep into the past. Amenhotep was called one "who guides the ignorant through the events since the primeval times," etc.[88]

II. *Abraham:* the great High Priest (Abraham 1:2; D&C 84:14; Facsimile 2, figures 2, 3, and 7).[89]

Imhotep: "The Book of the order of the temple . . . was made by the chief lector-priest [directing ordinances] Imhotep-the-Great, Son-of-Ptah." Prophet, giver of oracles, greeter in the temple, supervisor and researcher of genealogies; temple guide and instructor, mediator for those who come to the temple. Repairer and restorer of temples and rites. Keeper of the temple books as chief ritualist.[90]

III. *Abraham:* a man of practical ingenuity and technical skills, ever planning, planting, building, inventing, designing. His lectures on astronomy (Facsimile 2, discussed below) were both practical and inspirational. He wrote about such subjects as magnetism and the wheels of nature, according to Jewish tradition.[91]

Imhotep: Minister of Mines and Building; Minister of Science. Invented new techniques of employing stone in building, Master Architect, supervisor and initiator; skilled with his own hands. He founded the schools of science at Memphis that endured for ages.[92] Inspired thinker of penetrating insight, master calculator of unfailing accuracy, especially noted for his astronomical interests and achievements,[93] which made him "much later" the patron saint of astrology.

IV. *Abraham:* the friend of man desiring to be "a prince of peace" (Abraham 1:2), the digger of wells, the planter of trees, the ever hospitable, ever tolerant, ever courteous public benefactor.[94]

Both Egyptian heroes were commoners like Abraham.
Amenhotep was a humble villager until he was summoned to court when he was over fifty years old. They
are both unassuming, pleasant, mild, and engaging in
manner, "friends to all men," advocates for the common
people with Pharaoh; mediators for everyone in the temple and palace; teachers and leaders whose counsel was
available to all, whose wisdom became the folk wisdom
of the land.[95] Relievers of famine, givers of life to the people (Imhotep by searching in the books was able to end a
seven-year famine). Chief administrators to smooth the
workings of government and human relations. Great
physicians and healers to whom all could come,[96] at
whose shrines thereafter humble pilgrims were healed
and rejuvenated and, above all, blessed with offspring,
for, like Abraham, they were family men, Imhotep being
the great patron of family life, whose blessings gave children to the childless.[97]

There is an ideal type of person to which the Egyptian
aspires, and it is not the pharaoh, but the exalted mortals,
who show really impressive resemblance to such figures as
Enoch and Abraham. So much are they a type that "one of
the great hopes of the Egyptians was to be united with
Amenhotep and Imhotep in the after life, . . . safe in their
companionship"[98]—for us the plain equivalent of going to
"the bosom of Abraham." Moreover, Imhotep and Amenhotep became wholly identified with *each other* in cult, their
very bodies becoming "completely united" in one. At the
same time both are identified with Ptah, the Creator and
first parent of the race, and are usually depicted in his form
but with their *own* faces. Moreover, both are freely fused
with other heroes: The large Greek population of Egypt in
later days readily identified Imhotep with their own Aescu-
lapius, the god of healing, giving him both his Egyptian and
Greek names. Also, as a builder and technician he was
given the name Daedalus, and as a scribe he is both named

and depicted as the Egyptian Thoth, while as a patron of learning he is Hermes.[99]

Our two superheroes provide us with some very helpful hints in investigating Abraham's doings at court. Their own candid camera shows us how we should view such pictures as Facsimile 3. Thus, in one scene from Amenemhet's tomb, which is "even larger than some of the royal mortuary temples in the area," we see the great man as "high steward of Memphis," seated among dinner guests at a banquet in his honor. "It is difficult," writes Wildung, "to decide if Amenhotep . . . is assisting at the dinner as a living person, or if he is an important person from the immediate past who participates in the dinner magically."[100] Is this a dinner party in the past, the present, or the happy future? All three are found in Egyptian tombs; in any case the illustrious guest is present in spirit, and if the meal is a sacramental one, as seems likely, the time can be any time. If Imhotep and Amenhotep, living twelve hundred years apart, can fuse together into a single personality by virtue of their common traits, we need not be too surprised to find Abraham being repeatedly put in the same situations as Adam, Noah, Enoch, and others, and actually being *identified* with them in a hundred monuments of apocryphal literature. Even now, to be exalted means for Latter-day Saints to "do the works of Abraham; enter ye into my law and ye shall be saved. But if ye enter not into my law ye cannot receive the promise . . . made unto Abraham" (D&C 132:32–33).

From the monuments we learn that these men's disciples made up regular *schools* that survived for centuries, and again we are reminded of Abraham, Enoch, and some of the prophets in the light of new researches. Their "communities" resembled those of the desert sectaries, and indeed, the Essene societies are in a number of cases to be traced in their origins to Egypt. At any rate there was a school of Imhotep in operation at Memphis, and he was

venerated right into the nineteenth century at nearby
Saqqara, where he had begun his career more than forty-
five hundred years before! Significantly his shrine at that
place is a ruin called "the prison of *Joseph.*" This puzzles
Wildung, who writes: "We cannot describe the reason why
the temple was referred to as the prison of the Biblical Joseph."[101] For a clue we may consider Wildung's own
observation that the worship of the two heroes began at
their tombs, which as the objects of pilgrimage became
shrines and temples. But Moslems and Christians would
not repair to the tomb of an unknown pagan (Imhotep). If
the age-old worship were to continue (and such folkways
are virtually indestructible), it would have to be under different auspices: It was established practice to transfer the
shrines of ancient gods and heroes to Christian and Moslem
saints simply by a change of names. There was Joseph, a
great favorite with humble Christians, Jews, and Moslems
alike; was not he too like Imhotep and Amenhotep the
grand vizier of Egypt, the highest officer in the land, riding
forth with Pharaoh to the wild cheers of the populace
whom he had saved from a seven-year famine just as
Imhotep had done? Does not the great canal, a triumph of
ancient engineering that watered the land for hundreds
of miles parallel to the Nile, to this day bear the name of
Joseph's Canal? Was not his own great-grandfather the same
type of popular hero as Imhotep and Amenhotep? To that
great-grandfather Abraham, the humble people of Egypt,
who were neither Christians nor Moslems in the late period,
addressed their prayers on Coptic ostraca.[102] But Joseph,
alas, had no tomb in Egypt; he was buried in Canaan
(Exodus 13:19). Not to worry. He had something almost as
good if not better, the prison where he was entombed for
years.[103] Right into the present century the pilgrims continued to come to the old tomb shrine of *Imhotep* as they had

always done, to pray for health and children—and they called it the Prison of *Joseph*.

This keeps our patriarch well within the Egyptian cultural orbit. Wildung mentions one detail that surprisingly and vigorously associates his divine Pharaoh with Abraham. He notes that part of Pharaoh's propaganda to "sell" the idea of his divinity to the public was the diligent propagation of the story that as an infant he was nursed by the Lady Hathor, the horned Cow-goddess herself, in a cave.[104] Now the same story was told about Abraham, only in this case it was his mother, Amitla, who did the nursing.[105] At an early time scholars noted that Amitla was Amalthea, who nursed the infant Zeus himself in the Dictaean Cave;[106] but instead of the horned cow-mother, she was the goat-mother whose milk was equally nourishing and whose horn was the original cornucopia, or Horn of Plenty. Pharaoh, Horus, Zeus, and Abraham—there is a type and a shadow in all things! Well, all this leads to an alarming expansion of parallels and associations that cannot be handled here, but that shows us that Abraham has to be considered in an ancient cultural context almost as broad as that which now discovers his seed among all the inhabitants of the earth.

Where to Go for a Sabbatical: "The Learning of the Egyptians"

The wisest of the Greeks had enormous admiration for the intellectual powers of the Egyptians, inseparable in their view from their high moral discipline. It was the boast of the greatest Greeks, or of their disciples, that they had studied in Egypt. Strabo as a tourist on the spot describes the big barracklike buildings at Heliopolis where the priests still lived in his day. Formerly they were full of philosophers and astronomers, he says, but all that is given up now, and everything is given over to the business of the religious (*hieropoioi*) and the explaining of texts to foreigners.[107] Strabo also tells how the guides would take the tourists to see the very rooms where Plato and Eudoxos lived during their years of study at Heliopolis. German scholarship at the turn of the century routinely rejected any such possibility, yet no one doubts that Plato was the teacher of Aristotle, and Aristotle the teacher of the man who founded Alexandria, where Greeks and Egyptians taught and learned together for centuries in an exchange that conditioned the thinking of the Western world ever after. Alexandre Moret noted that Plato uses expressions that are to be found "word for word" in the Pyramid Texts and the later Theban theological writings.[108] These texts, he explains, "were discussed in the college of Heliopolis, where Plato heard them from the lips of those who initiated him."[109] The great Origen, a native Egyptian, as his name shows, who grew up practically on the campus of the University of Alexandria, where his father was a professor, is proud to record that Moses got his religion as well as his education from the Egyptians.[110] In Origen's day the Egyptian scholars were still endlessly philosophizing about their ancient native mysteries and scriptures, while the common people listened without understanding a thing.[111] Origen had more to do with the forming of Christian theology, as the world has known it to the present time, than any other man. The romantic Heliodorus was convinced that Homer himself "received a religious education in Egypt," which induces him to express in symbolic words things that really have a deeper and very secret meaning.[112] Egypt, wrote Chaeremon, is the goal of all students of philosophy and religion, which is studied there at all levels. There one finds the most rigid asceticism, the most ancient teachings and monuments that go back to the beginning of mankind. He tells how some pious groups would go out into the desert to follow a communal life of religious asceticism, exactly like the Coptic monks of a later day and the Essenes, who first turn up in Egypt.[113]

The great attraction of Egypt was at all times the exciting combination of religious *and* scientific thinking, mantic and sophic, intuitive and intellectual, the ancient and the progressive; the solid and visible achievements of the ancient Egyptians bade the observer take their message seriously, as it does today. The Egyptians, Theophrastus observed, are, on the one hand, the most rationally minded of all people, and yet they live in an ambience submerged in ancient and recondite religious lore: This tradition is deeply religious and at the same time persistently intellectual—the perfect example, one would say today, of the "bicameral" blend.[114] The Egyptians were convinced, writes Philippe Derchain, that the universe was organized and must be sustained by an effort of thought, and that if men ever forgot their responsibility and gave up intense mental concentration, ritually actualized by words and gestures, their world would collapse.[115] Magic and superstition that gain the upper hand at the end were not the whole story in the great days. "The place taken elsewhere by meditation and a philosophic bent," Gardiner noted, "seems with the Egyptians to have been occupied by exceptional powers of observation and keenness of vision. . . . The most striking feature of Egyptian [language] in all its stages is its concrete *realism*."[116] Herodotus describes the Egyptian doctors as ever striving for exact knowledge, "always cataloging and carefully marking off the years."[117] Diodorus describes how they worked everything into a single system: They discovered the motions of the stars and the laws of harmony and the cosmos, all of which are connected; they invented writing and the ritual services of the temples; they even first cultivated the olive; and all the basic knowledge of the Greeks comes from them—it all goes back to the sacred "Hermetic" books, for Hermes (Thoth) as the scribe of Osiris was privy to all his knowledge and secrets.[118] They believed, according to Manetho, that the force which moves the universe in all its expanse is the *same* force that draws the iron to the lodestone "by a good and saving principle."[119] The most wise Egyptians, having measured the earth, tamed the waves of the sea, measured the Nile, calculated the distribution of the stars in the heavens, have given the world the severest mental disciplines; and *Nectanebos*, the last pharaoh, was one who mastered the cosmic elements by study.[120] Hippolytus insisted that the Egyptians were strictly scientific in their study even of God, determined to reduce everything to numbers as if for a computer, and coming up with the standard god of the philosophers.[121]

Egypt was the goal of all students of philosophy and religion.[122] According to Herodotus, all real scholars make an effort to visit Egypt.[123] Chaeremon reports that they do not find it easy, for the Egyptian sages are very secretive, contemplative, withdrawn, and alarmingly intelligent,[124] also austere and upright in their morals. They had a genuine passion for learning, especially study of the stars.[125] This was the sort of thing that had an irresistible appeal to men like Pythagoras; of course, there were also such men in other lands, however rare, and from the earliest times contact was established between them by traveling students or by the wise men themselves who would visit one shrine after another.[126] Hippolytus tells how the great Democritus, inventor of the atom, studied "with the gymnosophists in India, the priests and astrologers in Egypt and with the Magi in Babylonia."[127] Apollonius of Tyana also made it a point to visit the gymnosophists of both India and Egypt as well as the Magi of Persia, all of whom taught a common doctrine.[128]

Two illustrious visitors to Egypt are almost always mentioned together—Solon and Pythagoras.[129] They were contemporaries of Lehi. Solon's teaching, in fact, as even Tertullian observes, sounds exactly like the prophets of Israel. The Egyptians were greatly impressed by the wisdom of

Solon and received him warmly,[130] though one wise man said to him with a despairing (or admiring?) shake of the head: "O Solon! Solon! You Greeks never grow up. No Greek is ever old!"[131] Pharaoh Amasis was delighted when Pythagoras visited him and gave him letters of introduction to the priestly schools up the Nile. But though the great man was more than welcome at court, the holy men of the schools were aloof, cool, and withdrawn, complying only reluctantly and partially to the king's express wishes, until it became clear to them that their visitor was a superbrain after all— then they took him to their bosom.[132] As a result, when Plato and others came many years later, they did not have so hard a time being received. But it all suggests Abraham.

Seeing Egypt through the eyes of Greek visitors gives us a distorted view, not only because they were outsiders, but because they were latecomers, arriving after Egypt had long been in decline. Strabo vividly describes the situation; Chaeremon could only shake his head and smile.[133] Thebes claimed the first and oldest astronomical observatory—the Upper Egyptian Heliopolis, they called it—but when Heliodorus visited it, he found that the renowned learning of the Egyptians had degenerated to raising up fantasies and deceiving men's hopes, mingling everything together, "living in the gutter and in the stars," the two tendencies meeting in the study of astrology.[134] Strabo found the system and the discipline still in force at Heliopolis, though he notes that the philosophers and astronomers were producing nothing of significance—after the lights go out the administration carries on undisturbed. There are still scholars who would deny the Egyptians any real science, especially astronomy. Santillana explains the situation convincingly: Some scholars do not recognize the true dimensions of Egyptian science, he says, because they are merely philologists and diggers who cannot recognize advanced scientific language when they see it.[135] On the other hand there are scientists and mathematicians like Otto Neugebauer who recognize *only* modern scientific notation and so miss the Egyptian signals.[136]

All this is peculiarly relevant to the case of Abraham. The intellectualism of the Egyptians has always struck a strongly sympathetic note in the intellectualism of the Jews; both express the same attitudes and put forth the same ideas in the same terms.[137] If Abraham and Sarah would carry out their missionary labors, the Zohar assures us, it was essential for them to visit Egypt, for by going there Abraham "distinguished himself and he raised himself there to a higher eminence."[138] It was the prophets and the sages who informed Pharaoh of the high station of Sarah as a princess, according to Eumolpus, and this is borne out by the *Genesis Apocryphon,* wherein Pharaoh's messengers praise her intellect even above her fabulous beauty.[139] Abraham, like Pythagoras, had to face the well-known jealousy of the Egyptian wise men (as when they failed to heal the king, and he succeeded), and a stock theme of ancient literature, especially taken to heart in apocalyptic writings, is that of the contest between the pompous wisdom of the king's regular counselors and the pious stranger from afar, whether Daniel, Moses, Thomas the Apostle, Abraham, etc. "According to tradition, Balaam was one of Pharaoh's three counsellors, and his sons Yanes and Yimbres were the chief magicians of the king," Geza Vermes has observed.[140] This Balaam advised Jethro the Kenite to flee *to* the court of Pharaoh to escape a murder charge in Midian, thus reversing the adventure of Moses.[141] Mambres was the most famous of Pharaoh's magicians competing in the court with Moses.[142] If we go back to the Pyramid Texts, we even find Pharaoh's serpent, in the manner of Moses' staff, swallowing up seven other serpents in a battle of the magicians.[143] But in spite of the importance of magicians at court, it was the truly wise man who was most welcome.[144]

Among illustrious travelers who left their mark in Egypt, Abraham must be taken seriously. In the first century B.C. Artapanus wrote that Abraham stayed twenty years in Egypt, and "according to Pseudo-Eumolpus, Abram lived in Heliopolis, where he instructed the Egyptians in the discoveries made by *Enoch* and by himself."[145] Whether Abraham really made the visit or not, there is, according to Wacholder, "no reason to doubt that the ancients, having converted a minor episode into a major theme, infused into it great significance."[146] Who are "the ancients" here? Wacholder points out that "to judge from the rabbinical sources, Abram's journey into Egypt is relatively ignored." But in an earlier age, "to the ancients . . . the encounter between Pharaoh and the traveler from Ur of the Chaldees" was "a crucial event in the history of mankind."[147] Wherever would they get the idea unless something really happened? Certainly the rabbis, strongly averse to sympathetic ties between Abraham and the Egyptians, would not have invented such things. The Emperor Julian, a strong anti-Christian and champion of the old paganism, noted that Abraham must have been a very great man because of the real impact he had on the Egyptians."[148] And Origen, a native of Egypt, says that it was common in his day for Egyptian soothsayers to command the demons by the God of Abraham without having the least idea who Abraham might be.[149] The vivid memory of Imhotep that survived down to Christian times in Egypt, though that hero lived possibly one thousand years before Abraham, as well as that of Abraham's own great-grandson and other benefactors of the race, leaves no doubt that the veneration of Abraham in the land could well go back to his actual sojourn there.

The Big Red and White Schoolhouse

Imhotep, as we have seen, was the teacher of Egypt; and yet he represents himself in his autobiography as the student

of a greater one: "I was the real *pupil of the King,* a favorite in
the palace. . . . I restored everything that was lost in the
words of the gods; I made clear what was hidden in the holy
books." One of the earliest kings announces, "I have come
to my throne; . . . I have become Sia [intelligence, under-
standing] who bears the god's book, at the right hand of
Re."[150] The picture of the king having the books spread out
before him meets us as much in the Jewish and Christian
apocryphal writings as it does in the Egyptian, and in both
cases the king is the source of knowledge and wisdom on
the throne of glory. "The king assumes authority," says
another Pyramid Text; "eternity is brought to him and
understanding is established at his feet for him."[151] He rules
not by virtue of birth alone, but by virtue of his knowledge
and wisdom, making the fullest use of the written records,
the sacred books.[152]

The palace school flourished as early as the Old Kingdom,
where cherished knowledge was transmitted as a sacred trust
from teacher to pupil as if from father to son.[153] These court
schools were copied in the provincial courts as well, according to M. Korostovstev, with the same patriarchal rapport
between master and pupil.[154] Every court strived to be an
intellectual center, with its library and its staff of copyists
and scholars,[155] and to attract to its "chamber of learning"
($ˤ.t$-$sbꜣ$) "the great intellectuals and their best students."[156]
What more is to be expected than that Abraham be remembered far and wide in Egypt for "reasoning upon the
principles of Astronomy, in the king's court" (Facsimile 3)?

The king not only appreciates knowledge and skill, but
also accepts the possessors of such as his *intimate friends.*
Such phrases as "never was such a thing ever done (for anyone by the king) before on earth," or "never was such an
honor ever shown to another human being," show us that
the sure way to proximity to the seat of majesty, which was
the ultimate bliss for any Egyptian, was to possess real

talent and ability. Thus, Ptah-wash, a chief architect, judge, and vizier, holding the usual multiplicity of assignments, also *tutored* the king's children—that was his greatest calling; and when he was sick, the king had his personal physician attend him while he, the pharaoh, prayed for his health and later mourned his passing.[157] The king does not hesitate to enter actively into the routine work of these men: "His Majesty wrote with his own fingers to praise me for everything being done exactly as he wanted it." This from another man of many callings, who on his tomb inscription reproduces some of the royal correspondence—a letter written *by the king's own hand* in reply to a letter about a new building. He also includes a speech by the king on the same subject and tells how personally concerned the king was for the welfare of those who worked with him; such a one was a *smr-wˁtꜣ ımı ıb n nb=f*, "a chosen companion near to the heart of his lord."[158] The king was always thinking of others and personally made arrangements for the funeral of this Senjemib to whom in return he turns for valuable advice.[159] How far removed this is from the well-known stereotype, only too well-deserved in most lands, of the typical Oriental despot, to say nothing of a ruler of heaven and earth! A high priest of Memphis tells how he was educated at the court of Menkaure, a great intellectual center, participating in countless important ceremonies at the side of Pharaoh, "pleasing the heart of his master every day," and even marrying the king's daughter. Yet the king never forgot his unique and lofty office and responsibilities; undue intimacy would have broken the spell: "His majesty allowed me to kiss his foot instead of the ground before him."[160] Was that groveling? No more than the bowing down of Joseph's brothers to him, first in dreams and then as an Egyptian reality, when he still protests that he is only a mortal like them: "Am I in the place of God?" (Genesis 50:19). We have a letter of the king to another vizier summoning him to the palace in the most

gracious terms—no "sneer of cold command" so familiar to
the observer of executive operations, civil and military, in
other societies: "If N. would come to the palace today the
king would be most delighted, pleased beyond expression
to see the excellent scribe and his dear friend; it would
indeed be to their mutual pleasure," etc.[161]

It was because the king's position was absolute that he
could afford to *relax and be natural* without the slightest risk
of losing face. Sinuhe, in a popular tale that nonetheless
in form and content is meant to be a typical funerary autobiography, mingles with the royal family on terms of the
most intimate nursery fun, with the queen and the children
shrieking with delight when they recognize him after his
travels; and yet so overpowered is he at first on being admitted to the royal presence that he faints dead away. It was
the paradoxical congruity of divinity with warm humanity
that made this Middle Kingdom tale so enormously
popular—that is the way the people liked to think of their
lord and king. This coincidence of opposites reaches its
height with Ikhanten, who never lets us forget his sublimely
exalted divinity while he plays parlor games with his wife
and kids—more of this below.

The *pharaoh* fancied himself not merely as an exalted
one, but specifically as a *teacher in the strictest sense of the
word,* summoning the court together for *lessons.* "I have
informed the priests of their duties," says Thutmosis I; "I
have led the ignorant to that which he did not know"; the
long address of the king to the assembled priests is reproduced on the monument.[162] Sesostris III has left for us what
the king said in instructing his son and seal-bearer in his
duties in the presence of all the court.[163] A scene from the
famous Punt reliefs of Hatshepsut (fig. 41)—*not* a funerary
or judgment scene!—is described and labeled: "Sitting in
the audience-hall, the king's appearance with the atef-
crown [the crown worn in Facsimile 3 figure 1] upon the

great throne of electrum, . . . the grandees, the companions of the court, came to hear . . . a royal edict to his dignitaries, . . . companions of the king."[164] They have come to listen to the teaching of the one on the throne. Most famous is Thutmosis III's address to the assembled court on the occasion of the installation of the Vizier Rekhmire (fig. 42): It is not just instructions for the new official, but a discourse on government and law in general, such a speech as Solon or Plato or their Sophist imitators would have given. He tells everyone exactly how business should be conducted, even to details—the forty rolls of the law spread out before the vizier as he officiates, the exact position in the court where everyone sits and stands, the keeping and sealing of reports and letters, etc.[165] But the strongest emphasis is laid on the moral qualities necessary in whatever one does: Judging justly, not showing partiality, sending two men forth both satisfied, judging the weak and the powerful alike, pleasing the people as well as the king; going forth over the land every morning to bestow favors, to hear appeals of the people, not preferring the great above the humble, rewarding the oppressed, punishing whoever deserves it.[166] The Egyptians, writes Hellmut Brunner, "sought not for prosperity but for the salvation of men,"[167] and that is the secret of their preeminence.

Amenophis IV describes himself as a superintellectual, endowed not only with the ultimate right and authority to rule, but also with the necessary ability and concern. As a tutor of others, "He trains the youth, . . . the good ruler!"[168] As the great teacher propounding his own particular views on theology, he is very appreciative of those who receive, believe, and follow what he teaches and takes special delight in those who really take his teachings to heart. "I am appointing thee," he says to one Merire, "to be 'great seer' of the Aton in the temple of Aton. . . . O my hearer of the call, who hears the teaching. . . . Put gold at his throat and at

Figure 41. In this throne-room scene Queen Hatshepsut is dressed as a man and wears the traditional clothing of a pharaoh, a symbol of the authority she claimed. She wears the Atef crown of Osiris and the horns of Amun. Her throne is of electrum, a natural alloy of gold and silver,

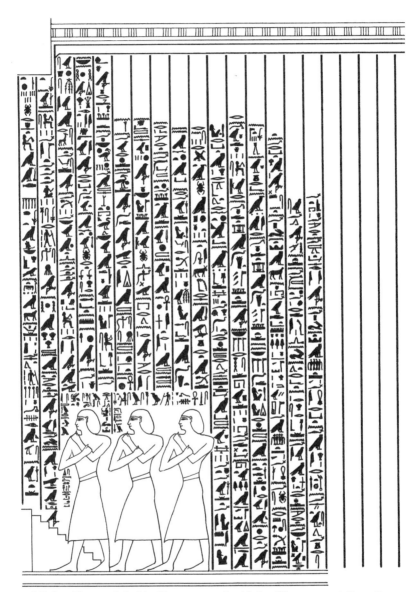

while her Ka stands behind her crowned with her Horus name. Guardian lions wearing colorful bands are shown flanking her throne platform. Three courtiers listen intently, holding their arms in a gesture of respect.

Figure 42. Rekhmire became vizier to Hatshepsut's successor, Thutmosis III. In his tomb, after the scene in which the king instructs him in his duties, Rekhmire had himself depicted delivering justice to the people in the hall of judgment, its pillars inscribed with the king's names. Outside on the central axis, flanked by soldiers and bureaucrats, supplicants

prostrate themselves to "smell the earth." The forty scrolls of the law are carefully arranged on floor mats before Rekhmire. In the midst of all this judicial dignity, an unexpected and possibly symbolic goose is under his chair. It could be a reference to the earth-god Geb, the "Great Cackler," or just a family pet.

his back, and gold on his legs, because of his hearing the teaching of Pharaoh."[169] Merire is "favored of his lord every day, . . . because of the exceeding greatness of my excellence, . . . because of my hearing his teaching."[170] The king's uncle, Ay, who later became king himself, reports, "I have carried out his teaching. . . . How prosperous is he who hears thy teaching of life."[171] And the official Mai: "My Lord has advanced me, (because) I have carried out his teaching, and I hear his word without ceasing. . . . O my lord, wise like Aton, satisfied with truth. How prosperous is he who hears thy teaching of life!"[172] In the Westcar Papyrus, the great Khufu, hearing of a wise man aged 110 years, sends his son to the village to fetch him in all reverence, and upon meeting him says, "How does it happen that I have never met you?"[173]

The king who teaches is, in all honesty, *eager to be taught as well.* An important type of statue found in the tombs is the stock figure of the "Prinzenerzieher" or educator of princes, a commoner who is depicted bearing a small image of a king or god in his hands to show that in his capacity of instructor and protector of kings he possesses greater power and authority than royalty itself. Strabo says that the Egyptian priestly philosophers were accepted as intimate associates of the king, especially in the study of astronomy (fig. 43).[174] Thus a high priest of Amon records in his autobiography that he was among the divine fathers of the priestly college who engaged in teaching the Divine Prince about the secrets of one who "enters into the sky and sees what is in it."[175] We have already mentioned the daughter of Psammetichus II calling upon certain *khabasu* in Heliopolis to witness the birth of one who will "take the helm" of government and "reason (*wadj*) with you, ye star-reckoners, concerning the secret teachings of the great court (*ws.t*) of the gods," and who will also receive Osiris into his "ship of a Thousand."[176]

Figure 43. This almost life-size granodiorite statue represents Anen, second prophet of Amun and brother of Queen Tiye (fig. 62, pp. 406–7). Instead of the usual spotted panther skin, the priest's robe of authority, his robe is covered with five-pointed stars. This emphasizes his claim to special astronomical knowledge as written on the back pillar: "The lector priest who knows the procession of the sky, chief of sightings in the great house."

The same sources that identify Abraham's Pharaoh with Nimrod tell how that monarch, after unsuccessfully trying to sacrifice Abraham on an altar, had a throne erected for him, and commanded all his court of 365 nobles (the year-rite, of course) "to bow down at the soles of the feet of Abraham our father! . . . And they brought their sons and submitted them to his law and said, 'Teach us thy ways in certainty.'"[177] When "they brought their children for him to teach from the throne,"[178] according to another source, "Abraham looked into the heavens and said: 'Praise God whom sun, moon, stars and planets all serve!' And the kings departed, recognizing Abraham's God."[179] The throne (*bema*) was made of the same cedar wood that the same people had gathered to make an altar and a bonfire for the sacrifice of Abraham. And so we get the logical sequence of Facsimiles 1 and 3, with the hero passing from the altar to the throne, where he sits and teaches astronomy to the court. His formal introduction, "Praise be to God whom sun, moon, stars," etc., is a clear declaration that the subject of his discourse is to be astronomy.

Notes

1. Bernhard Beer, *Leben Abraham's nach Auffassung der jüdischen Sage* (Leipzig: Leiner, 1859), passim.

2. James B. Pritchard, *Ancient Near Eastern Texts*, 2nd ed. with supplement (Princeton: Princeton University Press, 1969), 231.

3. Alan H. Gardiner, *Egyptian Grammar* (Oxford: Oxford University Press, 1957), 50, 239.

4. Kurt H. Sethe, *Urkunden der 18. Dynastie* , 4 vols. (Leipzig: Hinrichs, 1932), 1:234.

5. *Wb*, 4:486.

6. Ibid., 2:20.

7. Ibid., 4:485.

8. Adolph Erman, *The Ancient Egyptians* (New York: Harper Torchbooks, 1966), 41.

9. Kurt H. Sethe, *Aegyptische Lesestücke* (Leipzig: Hinrichs, 1924), 29.

10. Hugh W. Nibley, *The Message of the Joseph Smith Papyri: An Egyptian Endowment* (Salt Lake City: Deseret Book, 1975), 78.

11. James H. Breasted, *Ancient Records of Egypt: Historical Documents from the Earliest Times to the Persian Conquest* (Chicago: University of Chicago Press, 1906–7), 2:424.

12. Urbain Bouriant, "Une stèle du Tombeau d'Anna," *RT* 12 (1892): 106–7.

13. Karl Piehl, "Varia," *ZÄS* 21 (1883): 127–28; cf. Karl Piehl, "Varia V," *ZÄS* 25 (1887): 37–38.

14. Plato, *Statesman* 290 D–E.

15. Plutarch, *De Iside et Osiride* 6.

16. Alexandre Moret, *Du caractère religieux de la royauté pharaonique* (Paris: Leroux, 1902), 230.

17. Elke Blumenthal and Siegfried Morenz, "Spuren ägyptischer Königsideologie in einem Hymnus auf den Makkabäerfürsten Simon," *ZÄS* 93 (1966): 21–22.

18. Wilhelm Czermak, "Vom grossen Gedanken Aegyptens," *Archiv für ägyptische Archäologie* 1/10 (1938): 210.

19. Claas J. Bleeker, *Egyptian Festivals: Enactments of Religious Renewal* (Leiden: Brill, 1967), 121–22.

20. Libanius, *Orationes* XII, 80.

21. Joachim Spiegel, "Das Auferstehungsritual des Unaspyramide," *ASAE* 53 (1955): 378.

22. Francis L. Griffith, *Stories of the High Priests of Memphis* (Oxford: Clarendon, 1900), 39–40.

23. Raymond O. Faulkner, *A Concise Dictionary of Middle Egyptian* (Oxford: Griffith Institute, 1964), 87.

24. Hellmut Brunner, "Zum Verständnis der archaisierenden Tendenzen in der ägyptischen Spätzeit," *Saeculum* 21 (1970): 161.

25. Kurt H. Sethe, *Dramatische Texte zu altägyptischen Mysterienspielen* (Leipzig: Hinrichs, 1928), line 53.

26. Ibid., lines 56–57.

27. Ibid., line 58.

28. Ibid., line 58, f.

29. Hugo Müller, *Die formale Entwicklung der Titulatur der ägyptischen Könige* (Glückstadt: Augustin, 1938), 65.

30. Rudolf Anthes, "Zum Ursprung des Nefertem," *ZÄS* 80 (1955): 88.

31. Rudolf Anthes, "Egyptian Theology in the Third Millennium B.C.," *JNES* 18 (July 1959): 173.

32. Ibid.

33. Spiegel, "Auferstehungsritual des Unaspyramide," 378.

34. Sethe, *Dramatische Texte*, line 61.

35. Ibid., line 63.

36. Ibid., line 64.

37. Eberhard Otto, *Die biographischen Inschriften der ägyptischen Spätzeit, ihre geistesgeschichtliche und literarische Bedeutung* (Leiden: Brill, 1954), 1, 18, 87, 122–25.

38. Ibid., 42.

39. Ibid., 28–29.

40. Ibid., 40.

41. Ibid., 20–21, 32.

42. Ibid., 91–93, 123.

43. Ibid., 98–99.

44. Ibid., 7, 79, 124.

45. Ibid., 75.

46. Ibid., 97.

47. Ibid., 75.

48. Ibid., 68, 76.

49. Ibid., 98–99.

50. Ibid., 78–79.

51. Ibid., 98–99.

52. Percy E. Newberry, *El Bersheh*, 2 vols. (London: Egyptian Exploration Fund, 1893), 1:19–22; plates xii, xv.

53. Otto, *Biographischen Inschriften*, 102.

54. Ibid., 115.

55. Ibid., 106–7.

56. Ibid., 108, 111–12.

57. Ibid., 102, 110.

58. Hugh W. Nibley, "A New Look at the Pearl of Great Price," *IE* 72 (January 1969): 30–31.

59. Herbert Werner, *Abraham der Erstling und Repräsentant Israels* (Göttingen: Vandenhoeck and Ruprecht, 1965), 87–91.

60. Otto, *Biographischen Inschriften*, 123–24.

61. Schafik Allam, "Le droit égyptien ancien," *ZÄS* 105 (1978): 5–6.

62. Ibid., 5.

63. Max Pieper, *Die grosse Inschrift des Königs Neferhotep in Abydos* (Leipzig: Hinrichs, 1929), lines 2–4.

64. Alan H. Gardiner, "The House of Life," *JEA* 24 (1938): 162.

65. Griffith, *Stories of the High Priests of Memphis*, 58.

66. Ibid., 30.

67. Ibid., 51–59.

68. Heinrich Brugsch, *Thesaurus Inscriptionum Aegyptiacarum* (Leipzig: Hinrichs, 1883–91), 1292–98.

69. Alan H. Gardiner, *Egypt of the Pharaohs* (Oxford: Clarendon, 1961), 62.

70. Henri Frankfort, *Ancient Egyptian Religion* (New York: Harper, 1961), 50–51.

71. Anthes, "Egyptian Theology in the Third Millennium B.C.," 173.

72. Piehl, "Varia," 127–35; Piehl, "Varia V," 37–45.

73. Werner, *Abraham der Erstling und Repräsentant Israels*, 79.

74. *Jubilees* 40:8, in *The Apocrypha and Pseudepigrapha of the Old Testament*, ed. R. H. Charles, 2 vols. (Oxford: Clarendon, 1976), 2:71.

75. Brugsch, *Thesaurus Inscriptionum Aegyptiacarum*, 1479–84.

76. Piehl, "Varia," 127–28; Piehl, "Varia V," 37.

77. Nibley, *Message of the Joseph Smith Papyri*, 66–67.

78. Gustave Lefébvre, *Le Tombeau de Petosiris*, 3 vols. (Cairo: IFAO, 1923–24), 1:88–89; Nibley, *Message of the Joseph Smith Papyri*, 66–69.

79. Friederick W. von Bissing, "Ägyptische Weisheit und griechische Wissenshaft," *Neue Jahrbücher* 39 (1912): 90–93.

80. Hermann Kees, *Totenglauben und Jenseitsvorstellungen der alten Ägypter* (Leipzig: Hinrichs, 1926), 29–31.

81. Kurt H. Sethe, *Imhotep, der Asklepios der Aegypter, ein vergötteter Mensch* (Leipzig: Hinrichs, 1902).

82. Dietrich Wildung, *Egyptian Saints: Deification in Pharaonic Egypt* (New York: University Press, 1977).

83. Ibid., 28.

84. Nibley, "A New Look at the Pearl of Great Price," *IE* 73 (January 1970): 58; cf. Nibley, *Enoch the Prophet*, *CWHN* 2 (Salt Lake City: Deseret Book and FARMS, 1986), 30–31, 143–44, 217.

85. Wildung, *Egyptian Saints*, 43.

86. Ibid., 43–47.

87. Ibid., 84.

88. Ibid., 87.

89. Nibley, "A New Look at the Pearl of Great Price," *IE* 73 (January 1970): 59–64.

90. Wildung, *Egyptian Saints*, 67.

91. Kaufmann Kohler, "Abraham," in *Jewish Encyclopedia*, 12 vols. (New York: Funk and Wagnalls, 1901), 1:85.

92. Wildung, *Egyptian Saints*, 76.

93. Ibid., 55.

94. Nibley, "A New Look at the Pearl of Great Price," *IE* 72 (November 1969): 118–19.

95. Wildung, *Egyptian Saints*, 35.

96. Ibid., 46, 56.

97. Ibid., 50–55.

98. Ibid., 105.

99. Ibid., 64, 74–75; Hans Bonnet, *Reallexikon der ägyptischen Religions-geschichte* (Berlin: de Gruyter, 1952), 323.

100. Wildung, *Egyptian Saints*, 89.

101. Ibid., 78.

102. Origen, *Contra Celsum (Against Celsus)* I, 22, in *PG* 11:697–700.

103. Wildung, *Egyptian Saints*, 78.

104. Ibid., 20.

105. Nibley, "A New Look at the Pearl of Great Price," *IE* 72 (January 1969): 30–31.

106. Bernard Chapira, "Légendes bibliques attribuées à Ka'b el-Ahbar," *REJ* 69 (1919): 95.

107. Strabo, *Geography* XVII, 1, 29.

108. Alexandre Moret, "La doctrine de Maât," *RdE* 4 (1940): 12–13.

109. Ibid.

110. Origen, *Against Celsus* IV, 93, in *PG* 11:1172.

111. Ibid., I, 12, in *PG* 11:677.

112. Heliodorus, *Aethiopica* III, 14, in Theodor Hopfner, *Fontes Historiae Religionis Aegypticae* (Bonn: Marcus and Weber, 1922–25), 456.

113. Chaeremon, in Hopfner, *Fontes Historiae Religionis Aegypticae*, 179–82.

114. Theophrastus, in ibid., 56; cf. R. A. Schwaller de Lubicz, *Le temple dans l'homme* (Cairo: Schindler, 1949), 30–36.

115. Philippe Derchain, *Le Papyrus Salt 825 (British Museum 10051), rituel pour la conservation de la vie en Égypte* (Brussels: Academy Royale, 1965), 4, 10–12.

116. Gardiner, *Egyptian Grammar*, 3.

117. Herodotus, *Historiae* II, 145.

118. Diodorus Siculus, *The Library of History* I, 16, in Hopfner, *Fontes Historiae Religionis Aegypticae*, 97.

119. Manetho in Hopfner, *Fontes Historiae Religionis Aegypticae*, 72.

120. Diogenes Laertius, in ibid., 431–32.

121. Hippolytus, *Refutario Omnium Haeresium*, IV, 43–44, in ibid., 433.

122. Diogenes Laertius, in ibid., 431.

123. Herodotus, *Historiae* I, 30; II, 177; II, 123. Cf. Alan B. Lloyd, *Herodotus, Book II* (Leiden: Brill, 1975), 49–60.

124. Porphyry, *De Abstinentia* IV, 6–8, in *Chaeremon, Egyptian Priest and Stoic Philosopher*, ed. Pieter W. van der Horst (Leiden: Brill, 1984), 16–23.

125. Chaeremon, in Hopfner, *Fontes Historiae Religionis Aegypticae*, 179–80; Diodorus Siculus, I, 81, in ibid., 123.

126. Philostratus major, *Life of Apollonius of Tyana*, in ibid., 442–43.

127. Hippolytus, *Refutario Omnium Haeresium* I, 13, in ibid. 432.

128. Philostratus major, *Life of Apollonius of Tyana* VI, 6, in ibid., 445.

129. For examples, see ibid., 119, 137, 224, 431, 545, 553, 655, 668.

130. Ibid., 267–68, 668.

131. Scholia on Plato, *Timaeus* 22B, in ibid., 707.

132. Antiphon Sophista, in ibid., 769–70.

133. Strabo, *Geography* XVII, 1, 29.

134. Heliodorus, *Aethiopica* III, 13–14, 16, in Hopfner, *Fontes Historiae Religionis Aegypticae*, 455–56.

135. Giorgio de Santillana, *The Origins of Scientific Thought* (Chicago: University of Chicago Press, 1961), 11–12.

136. Schwaller de Lubicz, *Temple dans l'homme*, 1–5.

137. Eugene Revillout, *L'ancienne Égypte d'après les papyrus et les monuments*, 4 vols. in 2 (Paris: Leroux, 1907), 1:129–64.

138. *Lech Lecha* 82a, in *The Zohar*, trans. Harry Sperling and Maurice Simon, 5 vols. (London: Soncino, 1984), 1:271–74.

139. Nahman Avigad and Yigael Yadin, eds., *A Genesis Apocryphon* (Jerusalem: Hebrew University Press, 1956), col. 20:2–8.

140. Geza Vermes, *Scripture and Tradition in Judaism* (Leiden: Brill, 1961), 137.

141. Ibid., 167.

142. William Groff, "Moïse et les magiciens à la cour du Pharaon," *RT* 21 (1899): 219.

143. Pyramid Text 318 (§511).

144. Alan H. Gardiner, "Professional Magicians in Ancient Egypt," *Transactions of the Society of Biblical Archaeology* (1917): 31–34.

145. Ben Zion Wacholder, "How Long Did Abraham Stay in Egypt?" *Hebrew Union College Annual* 35 (1964): 54; Flavius Josephus, *Antiquities* I, 166–70; Philo, *De Abrahamo* 69–80.

146. Wacholder, "How Long Did Abraham Stay in Egypt?" 44.

147. Ibid., 43.

148. Julian the Apostate, *Orationes* 354B, in Hopfner, *Fontes Historiae Religionis Aegypticae*, 541–42.

149. Origen, *Against Celsus* I, 22, in *PG* 11:697–700.

150. Pyramid Text 250 (§268).

151. Ibid., 257 (§307).

152. Ibid., 250 (§267–68).

153. Dimitri Meeks, review of *Pisty Drevnevo Egipta (Les scribes de l'ancienne Égypte)*, by M. Korostovstev, *RdE* 19 (1967): 189.

154. Ibid., 190.

155. Ibid., 191.

156. Ibid., 189–90.

157. Sethe, *Urkunden der 18. Dynastie*, 1:40–43.

158. Ibid., 68.

159. Ibid., 65–66.

160. Ibid., 51–53.

161. Ibid., 179–80.

162. Breasted, *Ancient Records of Egypt*, 2:40.

163. Ibid., 70.

164. Ibid., 120.

165. Ibid., 267–94.

166. Ibid., 298–300.

167. Hellmut Brunner, "Zum Verständnis der archaisierenden Tendenzen in der ägyptischen Spätzeit," *Saeculum* 21 (1970): 160.

168. Breasted, *Ancient Records of Egypt*, 2:405.

169. Ibid., 406–7.

170. Ibid., 408.

171. Ibid., 410.

172. Ibid., 413.

173. Sethe, *Aegyptische Lesestücke*, 29–30.

174. Strabo, *Geography* XVII, 1, 5.

175. Alan H. Gardiner, "The Tomb of Amenemhat, High-Priest of Amon," *ZÄS* 47 (1910): 92.

176. Constantin E. Sander-Hansen, *Die religiösen Texte auf dem Sarg der Anchnesneferibre* (Copenhagen: Levin and Munksgaard, 1937), 36–37.

177. Adolph Jellinek, *Bet ha-Midrasch*, 6 vols. (1853–77; reprint, Jerusalem: Wahrmann, 1967), 5:41.

178. Ibid.

179. Cf. Facsimile 3, end.

7

The Sacrifice of Isaac

Types and Shadows

While it is the unique and different that most engages the modern fancy, the Egyptian, as we have seen, was intrigued by the repeated and characteristic events of life. The most important of these events were ritualized, just as we ritualize the inauguration of a president or the Rose Bowl game, repeating the same plot year after year with different actors. Hence, if Abraham and Sarah went through the same routine with King Abimelech as with Pharaoh, it is not because either or both stories are fabrications, as scholars have so readily assumed, but because both kings were observing an accepted pattern of behavior in dealing with eminent strangers. Likewise, if Abraham was put on an altar bed like dozens of others, it was because such treatment of important guests had become standard procedure for combating the drought prevailing in the world at that time.

Repeating patterns of history suggest ritual as a means of dramatizing and controlling events, but they exist in their own right—they are not invented by men. In the exodus of

"The Sacrifice of Isaac" originally appeared in the series "A New Look at the Pearl of Great Price," IE 73 (March 1970): 84–94.

the Saints from Nauvoo, thousands of people suddenly found themselves moving west in the dead of winter amid scenes of some confusion. But within three days the entire host was organized into twelve main groups—one under each of the apostles—and companies of fifty and one hundred. Instantly and quite unintentionally the order of Israel in the wilderness and the Sons of Light in the Judean desert was faithfully duplicated. A student of history three thousand years from now might well reject the whole account as mythical, since it so obviously reduplicated an established pattern.

To one who is aware of the interplay of pattern and accident in history, the stories of the sacrifice of Isaac (fig. 44) and of Sarah are perfect companion pieces to the drama of Abraham on the altar. Take first the case of Isaac, who is just another Abraham: a well-known tradition has it that he was in the exact image of his father,[1] so exact, in fact, that until Abraham's hair turned white, there was absolutely no way of distinguishing between the two men in spite of their age difference.[2] "Abraham and Isaac are bound to each other with extraordinary intimacy," writes a recent commentator; "the traditions regarding the one are not to be distinguished from those concerning the other," e.g., both men leave home to wander, both go to Egypt, both are promised endless posterity and certain lands as an inheritance.[3] What has been overlooked is the truly remarkable resemblance between Isaac on the altar and Abraham on the altar.

First, in both stories there is much made of the preparatory gathering of wood for a "holocaust" that never takes place. Abraham is commanded, "Take now thy son . . . and offer him . . . for a *burnt* offering" (Genesis 22:2, emphasis added). "Behold, I offer thee now as a holocaust," he cries in the *Pseudo-Philo*.[4] Accordingly, he "bound Isaac his son, and laid him upon the altar on the wood,"[5] sometimes described as a veritable tower, just like the structure that

Figure 44. This is the painted arch over the Torah shrine from the Dura-Europos synagogue in Syria (c. A.D. 300). The artist shows us the facade of Herod's Temple with the menorah on the left. On the right is one of the earliest depictions of the sacrifice of Isaac. The images, starting from the foreground, are the substitute ram, Abraham holding the knife, and Isaac balancing precariously on a pointed altar as Sarah stands in the door of her tent. Of the dozens of figures on the synagogue's four walls, only these are painted with their backs toward the viewer. When the congregation stood facing the shrine, they faced the vanished temple in Jerusalem, over 350 miles away, and beheld the hand of God reaching out to save them, as it had saved Abraham, Isaac, and Sarah before them.

Nimrod had built for Abraham.[6] And while the Midrash has Isaac carrying the wood of the sacrifice "as one carries a cross on his shoulder,"[7] so Abraham before him "took the wood for the burnt offering and carried it, just as a man carries his cross on his shoulder."[8] According to one tradition, the sacrifice was actually completed and Isaac turned to ashes.[9] On the other hand, when the princes announced their intention of putting Abraham in a fiery furnace, he is said to have submitted willingly: "If there is any sin of mine so that I be burned, the will of God be done."[10] Indeed, the Hasidic version has it that "Abraham our father offered up his life for the sanctification of the Name of God and threw himself into the fiery furnace."[11] The famous play on the words "Ur of the Chaldees" and "Fire [ʾūr] of the Chaldees" was probably suggested by these traditions—not the other way around—since Isaac escapes from the flames in the same way that Abraham does; i.e., the original motif requires a fire, not a city called Ur.

For all the emphasis on sacrificial fire, it is the knife that is the instrument of execution in the attempted offerings of Abraham and Isaac: "And Abraham stretched forth his hand, and took the knife to slay his son" (Genesis 22:10). It was always the custom to slaughter (zābaḥ) the victim and then burn the remains to ashes; the blood must be shed and the offering never struggles in the flames. Many stories tell how the knife was miraculously turned aside as it touched the neck of the victim, whether Abraham or Isaac: suddenly the throat is protected by a collar of copper, as it turns to marble, or the knife becomes soft lead.[12] But in the usual account it is dashed from the hand of the officiant by an angel who is visible to the victim on the altar but not to the priest.[13] If the wood under Abraham and Isaac was never ignited, neither did the knife ever cut.

Being bound on the altar, Abraham, as the Book of Abraham and the legends report, prayed fervently for deliverance. Exactly such a prayer was offered as Isaac lay on the altar, but though in this case it was Isaac who was in mortal peril, it was again Abraham who uttered the prayer for deliverance: "May He who answered *Abraham* on Mt. Moriah, answer you, and may He listen to the voice of your cry this day!"[14] And just as the angels appealed to God when they saw Abraham on the altar, so later when they saw Isaac in the same situation they cried out in alarm: "What will happen to the covenant with Abraham—'My covenant will I establish . . . with Isaac'—for the slaughtering knife is set upon his throat. The tears of the angels fell upon the knife, so that it could not cut Isaac's throat."[15] It is still *Abraham* for whom the angels are concerned, even though it is the life of Isaac that is in intimate danger. Everything seems to hark back to the original sacrifice—that of Abraham. Thus, at the moment that Isaac was freed from the altar, God renewed his promises to *Abraham,*[16] the very promises that had been given at the moment of Abraham's own deliverance (Abraham 1:16, 19); while he in turn prayed to God that "when the children of Isaac commit trespasses and because of them fall upon evil times, be mindful of the offering of their father Isaac, and forgive their sins, and deliver them from their suffering."[17] Thus Abraham's prayer for deliverance is handed down to all his progeny.

In both sacrifice stories an angel comes to the rescue in immediate response to the prayer, while at the same time the voice of God is heard from heaven. This goes back to Genesis 22:11–12, 15–18, where "the angel of the Lord" conveys to Abraham the words of God speaking in the first person: "And the angel of the Lord . . . said, By myself have I sworn, saith the Lord." As the rabbis explained it, "God makes a sign to the Metatron, who in turn calls out to Abraham" or "the Almighty hastened to send his voice from above, saying: Do not slay thy son."[18] That this complication is ancient and not invented by the doctors, whom it puzzled, is indicated in the lion-couch situation in which, as we have seen, the appearance of the heavenly messenger is accompanied by the voice of the Lord of all, which is heard descending from above. It is Abraham who establishes the standard situation: how many times in his career did he find himself in mortal danger only to pray and be delivered by an angel? An angel came to rescue the infant in the cave

when his mother had given him up for dead; the same angel
came to rescue the child Abraham from the soldiers, saying,
"Do not fear, for the Mighty One will deliver thee from the
hand of thine enemies!"[19] The same angel delivered him first
from starvation in prison and then from death in the flames.
So it is not surprising that the angel who comes to rescue
Isaac puts a stop to the proceedings by calling out "Abraham, Abraham" (Genesis 22:11–12), while Isaac remains
passive throughout.[20]

One of the strangest turns of the Abraham story was
surely Abraham's refusal to be helped by the angel, with its
striking Egyptian parallel.[21] Surprisingly enough, the same
motif occurs in the sacrifice of Isaac. For according to
the Midrash, God ordered Michael, "Delay not, hasten to
Abraham and tell him not to do the deed!" And Michael
obeyed: "Abraham! Abraham! What art thou doing?" To
this the patriarch replied, "Who tells me to stop?" "A messenger sent from the Lord!" says Michael. But Abraham
answers, "The Almighty Himself commanded me to offer
my son to Him—only He can countermand the order: I will
not hearken to any messenger!" So God must personally
intervene to save Isaac.[22] Such a very peculiar twist to the
story—the refusal of angelic assistance in the moment of
supreme danger—is introduced by way of explaining that
it is God and not the angel who delivers; so in the Book of
Abraham: "And the angel of his presence stood by me, and
immediately unloosed my bands; And his voice was unto
me: Abraham, Abraham, behold, my name is Jehovah, and I
have heard thee, and have come down to deliver thee"
(Abraham 1:15–16). Everything indicates that this is the old
authentic version.

In both sacrifices the role of Satan is the same, as he
does his best at every step to frustrate the whole business.
As the man in black silk pleaded with Abraham on the altar
to be sensible, yield to the king, and so save his own life,

even so he addresses him at the second sacrifice: "Are you crazy—killing your own son!" To which Abraham replied, "For that purpose he was born." Satan then addressed Isaac: "Are you going to allow this?" And the young man answered, "I know what is going on, and I submit to it."[23] First Satan had done everything in his power to block their progress on the road to the mountain,[24] and then as a venerable and kindly old man he had walked along with them, piously and reasonably pointing out that a *just* God would not demand the sacrifice of a son.[25] It was even Satan, according to some, who dashed the knife from Abraham's hand in the last moment.[26] In both stories it is Satan who suggests the sacrifice in the first place[27] and then does everything in his power to keep it from being carried out. Why is that? The explanation is given both times: Mastema suggests the supreme sacrifice in order to discredit Abraham with the angels, for he is sure that the prophet will back out in the end. As soon as it becomes perfectly clear, therefore, that Abraham is *not* backing out, Satan becomes alarmed, and to keep from losing his bet he wants to call the whole thing off.

In an important study, Roy Rosenberg has pointed out that the sacrifice of Isaac has its background in the Canaanitish rite of the substitute king, which rite was "celebrated in both Persia and Babylonia in connection with the acronical rising of Sirius . . . [as] Saturn, the god who demanded human sacrifices."[28] We have already noted that the worship of Sirius played a conspicuous part, according to Abraham 1:9, in the rites involving the sacrifice of Abraham. In connection with the offering of Isaac, Rosenberg lays great emphasis on a passage from the book of *Enoch:* "the Righteous One shall arise from sleep and walk in the paths of righteousness," the figure on the altar being the Righteous One.[29] At once we think of the weary one or the sleeping one who arises from the lion couch. What confirms the association is the report that as Isaac was about to be sacrificed, the *Arelim* began to roar in heaven. For the Arelim are the divine lions, whose role in Egyptian sacrificial rites we have already explained. Thus, even the lion motif is not missing from our two sacrifice stories.

The close resemblance between the sacrifices of Abraham and Isaac, far from impugning the authenticity of either story, may well be viewed as a confirmation of both. Joshua Finkel points out that there are many close parallels to the story of the sacrifice of Isaac in ancient literature and that "their atmosphere is ritualistic,"[30] that is, they belong to a category of events that follow a set pattern and yet *really do happen.* "In the mountain of the Temple of the Lord, Abraham offered Isaac his son," according to a Targum, "and in this mountain—of the Temple—the glory of the Shekhinah of the Lord was revealed to him."[31] What happened there was the type and shadow of the temple ordinances to come, which were in turn the type and shadow of a greater sacrifice. The one sacrifice prefigures the other, being, in the words of St. Ambrose, "less perfect, but still of the same order."[32] Isaac is a type: "Any man," says the Midrash, "who acknowledges that there exist two worlds . . . is like Isaac," and further explains, "Not *Isaac* but *In Isaac*—that is, a portion, of the seed of Isaac, not all of it."[33] In exactly the same sense Abraham too is a type: "and *in* thee (that is, in thy Priesthood) and *in* thy seed . . . shall all the families of the earth be blessed" (Abraham 2:11). Far from being disturbed by resemblances, we should find them most reassuring. Is it surprising that the sacrifice of Isaac looked both forward and back, as "Isaac thought of himself as the type of offerings to come, while Abraham thought of himself as atoning for the guilt of Adam," or that "as Isaac was being bound on the altar, the spirit of Adam, the first man, was being bound with him"?[34] It was natural for Christians to view the sacrifice of Isaac as a type of the crucifixion, yet it is the Jewish sources that comment most impressively on the sacrifice of the Son. When at the creation of the world angels asked, "What is man that You should remember him?" God replied: "You shall see a father slay his son, and the son consenting to be slain, to sanctify My Name."[35]

But if Isaac is a type of the Messiah as "the Suffering Servant," Abraham is no less so. Even while he labors to minimize any spiritual resemblance between Christ and Abraham, J. Alberto Soggin reluctantly confesses that the historical and literary parallels between the two are most conspicuous.[36] An important point of resemblance between the two sacrifices is the complete freedom of will with which the victim submits. "I know what is going on," says Isaac on the altar, "and I submit to it!" In time the main significance of the Akedah, the binding, was on the free-will offering of the victim for the atonement of Israel; we are even told that Isaac at the age of thirty-seven actually "asked to be bound on the Day of Atonement and Abraham functioned as the High Priest at the altar."[37] In the same way, a great deal is made of Abraham's willingness: "I was with thee," says God in the Midrash, "when thou didst willingly offer for My name's sake to enter the fiery furnace."[38] When Abraham refused to escape, though, Prince Joktan opened the way for him; the prince told him, "Your blood will be upon your own head," to which the hero cheerfully agreed.[39] The Hasidic teaching was that "Abraham our father offered up his life . . . and threw himself into the fiery furnace."[40] There need be no sense of competition between the merits of father and son here—others too have made the supreme sacrifice—but the significance of Abraham's test on the altar, as Raphael Loewe points out, is that Abraham in Nimrod's furnace is the *first* of those who willingly gave "up his life for the sake of the sanctification of the divine Name."[41] This assigns a very important place in the history ⌐

of the atonement to the drama depicted in the Book of Abraham and strongly attests its authenticity.

The Resurrection Motif

In the Egyptian versions of the lion-couch drama, the resurrection motif was paramount. The sacrifices of Isaac and Abraham, apart from typifying the atonement, were also foreshadowings of the resurrection. There are persistent traditions in each case that the victim actually was put to death, only to be resurrected on the spot. We have seen in the Abraham stories how, when no knife could cut his throat, he was catapulted into the fire, which thereupon was instantly transformed into a blooming bower of delicious flowers and fruits amid which Abraham sat enjoying himself in angelic company (fig. 45).[42] This at once calls to mind the image found in numerous (and very early) Oriental seals and murals of the revived or resurrected king sitting beneath an arbor amid the delights of the feast at the New Year.[43] St. Jerome cites a Jewish belief that Abraham's rescue from the altar was the equivalent of a rebirth or resurrection.[44] It is Abraham who leads out in the resurrection: "After these things," says the *Testament of Judah*, "shall Abraham and Isaac and Jacob arise unto life, and I (Judah) and my brethren shall be chiefs of the tribes of Israel."[45]

The stories of the resurrection of Isaac are quite explicit. As Rabbi Eliezer puts it, "When the blade touched his neck the soul of Isaac fled and departed, but when he heard his voice saying 'Lay not thy hand upon the lad, . . . ' his soul returned to his body, and . . . Isaac stood upon his feet. And Isaac knew that in this manner the dead in the future will be quickened. He opened his mouth and said: Blessed art thou, O Lord, who quickeneth the dead."[46] Another tradition is that "the tears of the angels fell upon the knife, so that it could not cut Isaac's throat, but from terror his soul escaped from him"—he died on the altar.[47] Another has it that as the knife touched his throat "his life's spirit departed—his body became like ashes," i.e., he actually became a burnt offering;[48] or, as Geza Vermes puts it, "though he did not die, scripture credits Isaac with having died and his ashes having lain upon the altar."[49] But he only dies in order to prefigure the resurrection, for immediately God sent the dew of life "and Isaac received his spirit again, while the angels joined in a chorus of praise: Praised be the Eternal, thou who hast given life to the dead!"[50] In another account God orders Michael to rush to the rescue: "'Why standest thou here? Let him not be slaughtered!' Without delay, Michael, anguish in his voice, cried out: 'Abraham! Abraham! Lay not thine hand upon the lad. . . . ' At once Abraham left off from Isaac, who returned to life, revived by the heavenly voice."[51] Isaac is a symbol of revival and renewal—"is any thing too hard for the Lord?" (Genesis 18:14). At his birth, we are told, both Abraham and Sarah retained their youth.[52] And "just as God gave a child to Abraham and Sarah when they had lost all hope, so he can restore Jerusalem."[53] When Robert Graves surmises that "Abraham according to the custom would renew his youth by the sacrifice of his first-born son," he is referring to a custom which Abraham fervidly denounced, but which was nonetheless observed in his own family, according to the Book of Abraham, which reports that his own father "had determined against me, to take away my life" (Abraham 1:30). The famous Strasbourg Bestiary includes a vivid scene of the sacrifice of Isaac preceeded by the drama of the sacrificial death and resurrection of the fabulous phoenix bird, the Egyptian and early Christian symbol of the resurrection (fig. 46).

Why the insistence on the death and resurrection of Israel? Because a perfect sacrifice must be a *complete* sacrifice, and the rabbinical tradition, especially when it was directed against the claims of the Christians, insisted that

Figure 45. A bas-relief from the northern palace of Ashurbanipal at
Nineveh (c. 645 B.C.) shows the royal couple taking their ease in a garden
of pine and palm trees under a grapevine bower; the king is reclining on
a high bed supported on the backs of two lions, while the queen sits on a

the sacrifice of Isaac was the perfect sacrifice, thus obviating
the need for the atoning death of Christ. "Though the idea
of the death and resurrection of Isaac was generally rejected
by rabbinic Judaism," writes Rosenberg, still the proposition was accepted "that Isaac was 'the perfect sacrifice,' the
atonement offering that brings forgiveness of sins through
the ages."[54] Accordingly, the blood of the Paschal Lamb is
considered to be the blood of *Isaac*,[55] and according to some
Jewish sectaries the real purpose of the Passover is to celebrate the offering of Isaac rather than the deliverance from
Egypt.[56] It wasn't only the sectaries, however: "Rabbinic
writings show clearly that sacrifices, and perhaps the offering of all sacrifice, were intended as a memorial of Isaac's
self-oblation."[57]

throne with a footstool and drinks from her cup. Musicians perform on the left while their personal fan bearers gently waft the perfumed air from the two incense burners on the ground.

The Uncompleted Sacrifice

But the stories of Isaac's "resurrection" are scattered, conflicting, and poorly attested, however persistent, and this leads to serious difficulty: "The main problem was, of course," writes Vermes, "the obvious fact that Isaac did not actually die on the altar."[58] The whole biblical account, in fact, focuses on the dramatic *arrest* of the action at its climax—"Lay *not* thine hand upon the lad" (Genesis 22:12, emphasis added). It has been claimed, in fact, that the story of Isaac's sacrifice really records the abolition of human sacrifice, when Abraham decides it will not be necessary.[59] But the validity of the sacrifice, according to the rabbis, lay in Isaac's complete *willingness* to be offered. Abraham may have known that Isaac was in no real danger when he said,

A.

Figure 46. In a long panel on the exterior of the Strasbourg Cathedral (c.
A.D. 1300), Christ appears in majesty in the center (A), flanked by various
prophets and animals who typify his mission. The phoenix (B), consumed by flames, symbolizes his death and resurrection as does
Abraham's sacrifice of Isaac (C). The ram caught in the thicket awaits the
role of substitute sacrifice.

with perfect confidence, "My son, God will provide himself
a lamb for a burnt offering" (Genesis 22:8), and when, without equivocation, he told the two young men who escorted
them to the mountain: "I and the lad will go yonder and
worship, and come again to you" (Genesis 22:5); Isaac did
not know it—it was he who was being tested. But Abraham
had already been tested in the same way; if "Isaac . . .
offered himself at the Binding," so before his day the youthful "Abraham . . . threw himself into the fiery furnace. . . . If
we follow in their footsteps, . . . they will stand and intercede for us on the holy and awesome day."[60] Isaac was
being tested even as other saints are tested, since the testing
of the righteous here below is essential to the *plan* of the
universe. The Midrash, in fact, strongly emphasized the
parallelism between the sacrifice of Isaac and the willing
martyrdom of *other* heroes and heroines, including many
who suffered terribly painful deaths.[61] Isaac, in short,
belongs to the honorable category of those who were willing to be "Partakers of Christ's sufferings," as all the saints
and martyrs have been (for example, 1 Peter 4:13).

The second problem raised by the claim that Isaac's
sacrifice was the ultimate atonement is that the shedding of
blood did *not* cease with it: "If Isaac's self-offering on
Mount Moriah atoned for the sins of Israel," asks Vermes,
"why should animal victims be offered daily for the same
purpose in the sanctuary on Mount Zion?"[62] Circumcision

no less than the Akedah "remains a never-ceasing atonement for Israel," being performed by Abraham himself and
on "the Date of Atonement, and upon the spot on which the
altar was later to be erected in the Temple,"[63] but for all that,
no one claims that all the law is fulfilled in it. "Students of
Christian origins have come increasingly to realize," writes
Rosenberg, a Jew, "that the sacrifice of Isaac was to be reen-
acted by the 'new Isaac,' who, like the old, was a 'son of
God.'"[64] The early Christian teaching was that, as he was
about to sacrifice his son on the mountain, Abraham "saw
Christ's day and yearned for it. There he saw the Redemption of Adam and rejoiced, and it was revealed to him, that
the Messiah would suffer in the place of Adam."[65] But the
old Isaac, called in the Targum "the Lamb of Abraham,"[66]
neither suffered sacrificial death nor put an end to the shedding of blood. His act was an earnest of things to come, and
that puts it on the same level as the sacrifice of Abraham.

This explains, we believe, the absence of the story of
Abraham on the altar from the pages of the Old Testament.
Vermes points out that whereas in the biblical version of
the sacrifice of Abraham "the principal actors . . . are Abraham and God," other versions, even in very early times,

"somewhat surprisingly shift the emphasis and focus their interest on the person of Isaac."[67] Whatever the reason for this shift, it was a very emphatic one: "The Binding of Isaac was thought to have played a unique role in the whole economy of the salvation of Israel, and to have a permanent redemptive effect on behalf of its people."[68] It completely supplanted the earlier episode of the sacrifice of Abraham on the ancient principle that the later repetition of an event causes the earlier occurrence to be forgotten.[69] The principle is nowhere better illustrated than in the story of Abraham himself: the names Abram and Sarai are unknown to most Christians, because of the explicit command, "Do *not* call Sarah Sarai" anymore; "do *not* call Abraham Abram"—those were once their names but no more![70] When Israel finally returns to God and goes to Abraham for instruction, we are told that instead of teaching them himself, he will refer them to Isaac, who will in turn pass them on to Jacob and so on down to Moses—it is from the *latest* prophet of the latest dispensation that the people receive instruction.[71] On this principle the only words of the Father in the New Testament are those which introduce his Son and turn all the offices of the dispensation over to him (Matthew 3:17; 17:5).

It was necessary to overshadow and even supplant the story of Abraham's sacrifice by that of Isaac if Isaac were to have any stature at all with posterity. Scholars long declared both Isaac and Jacob, imitating Abraham in everything, to be mere shadow figures, mythical creatures without any real personalities of their own. Jacob, to be sure, has some interesting if not altogether creditable experiences, but what is left for Isaac? The three stand before us as a trio: "Abraham instituted the morning prayer, . . . Isaac instituted the noon prayer, . . . [and] Jacob . . . the evening prayer," i.e., they all share in establishing a single body of rites and ordinances.[72] One does not steal the glory of the other. Great emphasis is laid by the rabbis on the necessary equality of merit and glory between Abraham and Isaac, while each emphasizes some special aspect of the divine economy. Abraham was the Great One, Jacob the Little One, and Isaac who came in between was "the servant of the Lord who was delivered from bonds by his Master."[73] The special emphasis on Isaac is as the sacrificial victim. If his sacrifice was "an imperfect type," it was still more perfect than the earlier sacrifice of Abraham on a pagan altar, and in every way it qualified to supersede it. Though it was an equal test for both men, "purged and idealized by the *trial* motivation,"[74] the second sacrifice was the true type of the atonement. In the long and detailed history of Abraham the story of the sacrifice in Canaan could safely be omitted in deference to the nobler repetition, which, while it added no less to the glory of Abraham, preserves a sense of proportion among the patriarchs.

Abraham gets as much credit out of the sacrifice of Isaac as he does from his own adventure on the altar—he had already risked his own life countless times; how much dearer to him in his old age was the life of his only son and heir! And since the two sacrifices typify the same thing, nothing is lost to Abraham and much is gained for Isaac by omitting the earlier episode from the Bible. But that episode left an indelible mark in the record. The learned Egyptologist who in 1912 charged Joseph Smith with reading the sacrifice of Isaac into Facsimile 1 and the story of Abraham was apparently quite unaware that ancient Jewish writers of whom Joseph Smith knew nothing told the same story that he did about Abraham on the altar. The important thing for the student of the Book of Abraham is that the sacrifice of Abraham was remembered—and vividly recalled in nonbiblical sources—as a historical event. This makes it almost certain that it *was* a real event, for nothing to the supreme glory of Abraham would do definite damage to Isaac's one claim to fame. If the binding on the altar—the Akedah—was to be the "unique glory of Isaac," it was entirely in order to quietly drop the earlier episode of Abraham that anticipates and overshadows it, just as it is right and proper to forget that the hero was once called Abram.

Back to the Lion Couch

Studies of the sacrifice of Isaac emphasize as its most important aspect the principle of substitution, which is also basic in the sacrifice of Abraham. As Finkel expressed it, "evidently the primary aim of the story (of Isaac) was to give divine sanction to the law of substitution."[75] Isaac was not only saved by a substitute, but he himself was substituting for another. A ram by the name of Isaac went at the head of Abraham's herd. Gabriel took him and brought him to Abraham, and he sacrificed him instead of his son. As he did so, Abraham said, "Since I brought my son to you as a sacrificial animal be in thine eye as if it were my son lying on the altar." Accordingly, "whatsoever Abraham did by the altar, he exclaimed, and said, 'This is instead of my son, and may it be considered before the Lord in place of my son.' And God accepted the sacrifice of the ram, and it was accounted as though it had been Isaac."[76] Himself noble, Isaac was saved by the substitution of a "noble victim."[77]

But more important, Isaac himself was a substitute. "In Jewish tradition," writes Rosenberg, "Isaac is the prototype of the 'Suffering Servant,' bound upon the altar as a sacrifice."[78] Rosenberg has shown that the title of Suffering Servant was used in the ancient East to designate "the substitute *king*"—the noble victim. Accordingly, the "new Isaac" mentioned in 4 *Maccabees* must be "a 'substitute king' who dies that the people might live."[79] The starting point in Rosenberg's investigation is Isaiah 52:13 to 53:12, which "seems to constitute a portion of a ritual drama centering about a similar humiliation, culminating in death, of a 'substitute' for the figure of the king of the Jews." If we examine these passages, we find that they fit the story of Abraham's sacrifice even better than that of Isaac.

Thus, beginning with Isaiah 52:13, we see the Suffering Servant raised up on high, reminding us of the scene from the Midrash: they "felled cedars, erected a large dais for him, and set him on top, while uttering praises before him [in mockery], saying: 'Hear us, my Lord!' [and the like]. They said to him, 'Thou art king over us; thou art a god to us!' But he replied, 'The world does not lack its king, and the world does not lack its God!'"[80] Here Abraham both rejects the office and denounces the rites. The Midrash also indicates that the rites of Isaac were matched by heathen practices, his Akedah resembling the binding of the princes of the heathen, since every nation possesses at its own level "a 'prince' [as its] guardian angel and patron."[81]

In the next verse (Isaiah 52:14), the picture of the Suffering Servant with "visage . . . marred" recalls Abraham led out to sacrifice after his long suffering in prison while the princes and the wise men mock. Verse 15, telling of the kings who shut their mouths in amazement, recalls the 365 kings who were astounded to behold Abraham's delivery from the altar. In Isaiah 53:1 the arm of the Lord is revealed, as it is unbeknownst to the others in the delivery of Abraham (cf. Abraham 1:17). Isaiah 53:2 emphasizes the drought motif, which, as we have seen, is never missing from the rites of the substitute king. In verses 3 to 7 the Suffering Servant is beaten that *we* may be healed—a substitute for all of us. In verse 8 he is "taken from prison and from judgment" to be "cut off out of the land of the living," exactly as Abraham was according to the traditions. Verse 9 reminds us of Abraham in wicked Canaan, and verse 10—"it pleased the Lord to bruise him"—recalls the description of Abraham as a son being mercilessly beaten by a loving father but never complaining. Finally the reward: Because his soul was placed as an offering, he shall see his progeny, his days shall be lengthened, and he shall prosper greatly (see verses 10–12)—all "because he hath poured out his soul unto death" (Isaiah 53:12). Such was the reward of Abraham, with the assurance also that by the knowledge gained he would be able to sanctify others (see verse 11). In the end the Suffering Servant becomes the great intercessor: "He bare the sin of many, and made intercession for the transgressors" (Isaiah 53:12), just as Abraham does, as the great advocate for sinners living and dead. Thus Isaiah 52:13–53:12, while vividly recalling the suffering of Isaac, is an even better description of Abraham on the altar.

The sacrifice of the substitute king is found all over the ancient world. According to Rosenberg, the rite was "celebrated in both Persia and Babylonia in connection with the acronical rising of Sirius," sometimes identified in this connection with Saturn, "the god who demanded human sacrifice."[82] The Book of Abraham has already apprised us of the importance of Sirius (Shagreel) in the sacrificial rites of the Plain of Olishem, and it even labors the point that human sacrifice was the normal order of things in Canaan in Abraham's day. We have taken the position from the first that Abraham was put on the altar as a substitute for the king, an idea first suggested by the intense rivalry between the two, as indicated both in the legends and in the Book of Abraham. Since the series in the *Improvement Era* began, Rosenberg's study of the sacrifice of Isaac has appeared, with the final conclusion that in the earliest accounts of that event "both the Jewish and Christian traditions stem ultimately from the ancient Canaanite cult of Jerusalem, in which periodically the king, or a substitute for the king, had to be offered as a sacrifice."[83] It was to just such a cult—in Canaan—that we traced the sacrifice of Abraham, and that is why we have been at such pains to point out the close and thorough-going resemblances between the two: they are essentially the same rite and have the same background.

If the one reflects "the ancient Canaanite cult" in which a substitute for the king had to be offered, so does the other. Rosenberg says the sacrifice of Isaac most certainly goes back to that cult, and the Book of Abraham tells us flatly that the sacrifice of Abraham does. Certainly the Abraham story in its pagan setting is much nearer to the original substitute-king rite in all its details than is the Isaac story, which is a sizable step removed from it. The substitute sacrifice is a red thread that runs through the early career of the prophet: The life of the infant Abraham was saved when his brother Haran substituted a slave child to be killed in his place;[84] then Haran himself dies for Abraham in the flames;[85] and then Abraham was saved from the lion couch when the priest was smitten in his stead (Abraham 1:17, 29); finally his life was saved by his wife Sarah, who was willing to face death to rescue him again from the lion couch. This last much-misunderstood episode deserves closer attention.

Notes

1. Bernhard Beer, *Leben Abraham's nach Auffassung der jüdischen Sage* (Leipzig: Leiner, 1859), 47; Louis Ginzberg, *Legends of the Jews,* 7 vols. (Philadelphia: Jewish Publication Society, 1909–38), 1:262; for Rashi's explanation, see Gerald Abrahams, *The Jewish Mind* (London: Constable, 1961), 51 n. 1.

2. Micha J. bin Gorion, *Die Sagen der Juden,* 5 vols. (Frankfurt: Rütten & Loening, 1913–27), 2:325.

3. Horst Seebass, *Der Erzvater Israel und die Einführung der Jahweverehrung in Kanaan* (Berlin: Töpelmann 1966), 105.

4. Geza Vermes, *Scripture and Tradition in Judaism,* 2nd ed. (Leiden: Brill, 1973), 199–200, for text.

5. Ibid., 209.

6. Beer, *Leben Abraham's,* 66, 182 n. 717.

7. Israël Levi, "Le sacrifice d'Isaac et la mort de Jésus," *REJ* 64 (1912): 169.

8. Bin Gorion, *Sagen der Juden,* 2:300.

9. Beer, *Leben Abraham's,* 67.

10. *Pseudo-Philo* 6:11; cf. Isaac's speeches in Beer, *Leben Abraham's,* 65.

11. Nahum N. Glatzer, *Faith and Knowledge: The Jew in the Medieval World* (Boston: Beacon, 1963), 178.

12. Bin Gorion, *Sagen der Juden*, 2:303.

13. Cf. Beer, *Leben Abraham's*, 67—sometimes Abraham lets the knife fall, and sometimes it is not the angel but Satan who dashes it from his hand; cf. bin Gorion, *Sagen der Juden*, 2:287.

14. Vermes, *Scripture and Tradition in Judaism*, 195 (emphasis added).

15. Ginzberg, *Legends of the Jews*, 1:281.

16. *Pseudo-Philo* 32:2–4; complete Latin text in Vermes, *Scripture and Tradition in Judaism*, 199–200 (emphasis added).

17. Ginzberg, *Legends of the Jews*, 1:284.

18. *Pseudo-Philo* 32:4.

19. *Ma'aseh Abraham Abinu*, in Adolph Jellinek, *Bet ha-Midrasch*, 6 vols. (1853–77; reprint, Jerusalem: Wahrmann, 1967), 1:28.

20. Bin Gorion, *Sagen der Juden*, 2:287.

21. Discussed in Hugh W. Nibley, "A New Look at the Pearl of Great Price," *IE* 72 (August 1969): 76. In all the apocryphal accounts of Abraham on the altar he refuses the assistance proffered by the angel, saying that God alone will deliver him. *Ma'aseh Abraham Abinu*, in Jellinek, *Bet ha-Midrasch*, 1:34, and *Midrash de Abraham Abinu*, in Jellinek, *Bet ha-Midrasch*, 5:41; Ka'b al-Ahbar, text in Bernard Chapira, "Légendes bibliques attribuées à Ka'b el Ahbar," *REJ* 70 (1920): 37.

22. Beer, *Leben Abraham's*, 68.

23. Levi, "Le sacrifice d'Isaac et la mort de Jésus," 169.

24. Ginzberg, *Legends of the Jews*, 1:276–77.

25. *Sefer ha-Yashar* 23:25–28.

26. Bin Gorion, *Sagen der Juden*, 2:287.

27. Levi, "Le sacrifice d'Isaac et la mort de Jésus," 166–67.

28. Roy A. Rosenberg, "Jesus, Isaac, and the 'Suffering Servant,'" *Journal of Biblical Literature* 84 (1965): 382.

29. Ibid. 385, quoting the book of *Enoch* 92:3, which Rosenberg calls "the most important text yet discovered of the Jewish apocalyptic literature."

30. Joshua Finkel, "Old Israelitish Traditions in the Koran," *Proceedings of the American Academy for Jewish Research* (1931): 15.

31. Vermes, *Scripture and Tradition in Judaism*, 195.

32. Jean Daniélou, "La typologie d'Isaac dans le christianisme primitive," *Biblica* 28 (1947): 392.

33. *Midrash on Psalms* 105:1, in William G. Braude, *The Midrash on Psalms*, 2 vols. (New Haven: Yale University Press, 1959), 2:180.

34. Bin Gorion, *Sagen der Juden*, 2:307–8.

35. Vermes, *Scripture and Tradition in Judaism*, 201; cf. Beer, *Leben Abraham's*, 68.

36. J. Alberto Soggin, "Geschichte, Historie und Heilsgeschichte im Alten Testament," *Theologische Literaturzeitung* 89 (1964): 732–33.

37. Gerald Friedlander, *Pirkê de Rabbi Eliezer* (New York: Hermon, 1965), 227.

38. *Genesis Rabbah* 39:8, in *Midrash Rabbah: Genesis,* trans. Harry Freedman, 10 vols. (London: Soncino 1939), 1:316; *Midrash on Psalms* 119:3, in Braude, *Midrash on Psalms*, 2:248.

39. *Pseudo-Philo* 6:11; bin Gorion, *Sagen der Juden*, 2:81.

40. Glatzer, *Faith and Knowledge*, 178.

41. Raphael Loewe, "Apologetic Motifs in the Targum to the Song of Songs," in *Biblical Motifs*, ed. Alexander Altmann (Cambridge: Harvard University Press, 1966), 166, with Tanḥuma text supplied in his note 35.

42. So in the *Maʿaseh Abraham Abinu*, in Jellinek, *Bet ha-Midrasch,* 1:34. According to the *Sefer ha-Yashar* 8, "Abram walked in the midst of the fire for three days and three nights," cited in Vermes, *Scripture and Tradition in Judaism*, 73. Kaʿb al-Ahbar, Qiṣṣat Ibrahim Abinu, text in Chapira, "Légendes bibliques attribuées à Kaʿb el Ahbar," 42; cf. *Midrash de Abraham Abinu*, in Jellinek, *Bet ha-Midrasch*, 5:40–41. According to Thaʿlabī, Kitāb Qiṣaṣ al-Anbiyāʾ (Cairo: Muṣṭafā al-Bābi al-Ḥalibī wa-Awlāduhu, A.H. 1340), 55, it was the "Angel of the Shadow" who sat with Abraham in the fire, i.e., he was sacrificed.

43. Anton Moortgat, *Tammuz* (Berlin: de Gruyter, 1949), 63, 114, 139–42.

44. Beer, *Leben Abraham's*, 113 n. 136.

45. *Testament of Judah* 25:1.

46. Friedlander, *Pirkê de Rabbi Eliezer*, 228.

47. Ginzberg, *Legends of the Jews*, 1:281.

48. Beer, *Leben Abraham's*, 67.

49. Vermes, *Scripture and Tradition in Judaism*, 205.

50. Beer, *Leben Abraham's*, 69.

51. Ginzberg, *Legends of the Jews*, 1:281–82.

52. Ibid., 1:206, 287.

53. Sofia Cavalletti, "Abrahamo come messia e 'ricapitolatore' del suo popolo," *Studie Materiali* 35 (1964): 263.

54. Rosenberg, "Jesus, Isaac, and the 'Suffering Servant,'" 388.

55. Ibid.

56. Ibid., 386, citing *Jubilees* 18:18.

57. Vermes, *Scripture and Tradition in Judaism*, 209.

58. Ibid., 205.

59. So Zacharie Mayani, *Les Hyksos et le monde de la Bible* (Paris: Payot, 1956), 21.

60. Glatzer, *Faith and Knowledge*, 178.

61. Vermes, *Scripture and Tradition in Judaism*, 202–3.

62. Ibid., 208.

63. Ginzberg, *Legends of the Jews*, 1:240.

64. Rosenberg, "Jesus, Isaac, and the 'Suffering Servant,'" 388.

65. Nibley's translation of *Cave of Treasures* 29:13–14, trans. E. A. Wallis Budge (London: Religious Tract Society, 1927), 149–50 (Fol. 25b col. a).

66. Rosenberg, "Jesus, Isaac, and the 'Suffering Servant,'" 388, citing the fragmentary Targum to Leviticus 22:27.

67. Vermes, *Scripture and Tradition in Judaism*, 193.

68. Ibid., 208.

69. Oscar Holtzmann, *Der Tosephtatraktat Berakhot,* supplement to *Zeitschrift für die alttestamentliche Wissenschaft* 23 (Töpelmann: Gießen, 1912): 12–13.

70. Ibid.

71. Beer, *Leben Abraham's*, 206 n. 974.

72. *Midrash on Psalms* 55:2, in Braude, *Midrash on Psalms*, 1:493.

73. Vermes, *Scripture and Tradition in Judaism*, 203, citing Targum to Job 3:18.

74. Finkel, "Old Israelitish Traditions in the Koran," 14.

75. Ibid., 12.

76. Ginzberg, *Legends of the Jews*, 1:283.

77. Finkel, "Old Israelitish Traditions in the Koran," 12.

78. Rosenberg, "Jesus, Isaac, and the 'Suffering Servant,'" 385.

79. Ibid., 383, 385.

80. *Genesis Rabbah* 42:5, in Freedman, *Midrash Rabbah: Genesis,* 1:347.

81. *Genesis Rabbah* 56:5, in ibid., 1:495 n. 1.

82. Rosenberg, "Jesus, Isaac, and the 'Suffering Servant,'" 382.

83. Ibid., 388.

84. Beer, *Leben Abraham's,* 15. That Haran died as a substitute for Abraham is clearly indicated in *Midrash de Abraham Abinu,* in Jellinek, *Bet ha-Midrasch,* 5:40; Vermes, *Scripture and Tradition in Judaism,* 73; Ginzberg, *Legends of the Jews,* 1:216; bin Gorion, *Sagen der Juden,* 2:96–97; Beer, *Leben Abraham's,* 15–17; *Genesis Rabbah* 38:13, in Freedman, *Midrash Rabbah: Genesis,* 1:310–11.

85. Beer, *Leben Abraham's,* 16–17.

8

The Sacrifice of Sarah

A Fateful Journey

The history of Palestine has been to a remarkable degree a story of "boom and bust," from prehistoric times down to the present; and that happy and unhappy land has never had a greater boom or a more spectacular bust than occurred in the days of Abraham. Hebron was a brand new city, bustling with activity, when Abraham and his family settled there.[1] Just to the east were the even more thriving cities of the valley, to which Lot migrated to improve his fortune. Preliminary rumblings and prophetic warnings of things to come went unheeded by a populace enjoying unprecedented prosperity (today this is called "nuclear incredulity"), but nonetheless, the area was hit hard by a famine that forced Abraham to move out of Hebron after he had lived there only two years. Everybody was moving to Egypt and settling in the area nearest to Canaan and most closely resembling the geography and economy of the Jordan depression, namely, "the land of Egypt, as thou comest to Zoan," in the eastern Delta, where there had always been camps and villages of Canaanites sojourning

---

"The Sacrifice of Sarah" originally appeared in the series "A New Look at the Pearl of Great Price," IE 73 (April 1970): 79–95.

343

in the land. Abraham settled in Zoan, the local capital, a city of Asiatic immigrants that was even newer, by seven years, than Hebron—practically a tent city. There the family lived for five years before they attracted the dangerous interest of Pharaoh.[2]

The story of how Sarah ended up in the royal palace is now available in the recently discovered *Genesis Apocryphon,* and the account is a thoroughly plausible one. Pharaoh's regular title in this document, "Pharaoh Zoan, King of Egypt," shows him to be one of those many Asiatics who ruled in the Delta from time to time while claiming, and sometimes holding, the legitimate crown of all Egypt. The short journey from Canaan into his Egyptian domain is described in significant terms: "now we crossed (the border of) our land and entered the land of the sons of Ham, the land of Egypt," as if the family was definitely moving from one spiritual and cultural domain to another.[3] This is interesting because the Book of Abraham lays peculiar emphasis on the Hamitic blood of this particular pharaoh as well as his anxious concern to establish his authority—always a touchy point with the Delta pharaohs, whose right to rule was often challenged by the priests and the people of Upper Egypt. In his new home, Abraham, an international figure in the caravan business, entertained local officials both as a matter of policy and from his own celebrated love of hospitality and of people.

One day he was entertaining three men, courtiers of Pharaoh Zoan, at dinner.[4] Abraham would host such special delegations again, in Canaan: there would be the three heavenly visitors whom he would feast "in the plains of Mamre" (Genesis 18:1–8), and the "three Amorite brothers" whom he would have as guests.[5] The names of these last three were Mamre, Armen, and Eshkol. Mamre and Eshkol are well-known place names, and if we look for Armen, it is a place name, too, for in the Ugaritic ritual-epic tale of

Aqhat, it is the "man of Hrnmy" who hosts "the Lords of Hkpt [Ḥw.t-k₃-Ptḥ = Egypt, i.e., Memphis]" who come from afar.[6] If this seems to put Abraham's party in a ritual setting, its historicity is vindicated by the name of the leader of the palace delegation, who is called "ḤRQNWŠ. B. Z. Wacholder explains this as "an early transliteration of *archōnēs*," designating its bearer as "the archon, the head of the household," and obviously indicating Hellenistic influence.[7] But *archōnēs* is neither a name nor a title, and the "early transliteration" leaves much to be desired. On the other hand, we find in pharaonic times, in the employ of *Sshmt.t*, the divine lady of the eastern Delta, the very district where our little drama is taking place, a busy official and agent bearing the title of Hr-hknw, "the Lord of Protection," whose business was to police the area and keep an eye on foreigners, with whom he was Pharaoh's contact man; he is, in fact, according to Hermann Kees, none other than our old friend Nefertem,[8] the immemorial frontier guard of the northeastern boundary, the official host, border inspector, and watchdog (or rather watch lion) of the foreigners coming to Egypt—especially from Canaan. Nothing could be more natural than to have this conscientious border official checking up on Abraham from time to time and enjoying his hospitality. And since it was his duty to report to Pharaoh whatever he considered of interest or significance on his beat, it is not surprising that a report of "ḤRQNWŠ and his aides to the king contained a glowing account of Abraham's dazzling wife. Her beauty had already caused a sensation at the custom house, according to a famous legend.[9] If nothing else, her blondness would have attracted attention among the dark Egyptians: the Midrash reports, in fact, that Abraham had warned her against this very thing: "We are now about to enter a country whose inhabitants are dark-complexioned—say that you are my sister wherever we go!"[10] This admonition was given as the family passed from

Abraham's homeland in northern Mesopotamia (Aram Naharaim and Aram Nahor) into Canaan—clearly indicating that the people of Abraham's own country were light-complexioned.[11]

In reporting to Pharaoh, his three agents, while singing the praises of Sarah's beauty in the set terms of the most sensuous Oriental love poetry,[12] make a special point of mentioning that "with all her beauty there is much wisdom in her,"[13] lauding her "kindness, wisdom, and truth" even above her other qualities.[14] They went all out in their description not only because the subject was worthy of their best efforts, but because they hoped to put themselves in good stead with the king by both whetting and satisfying his desire.[15] The royal reaction was immediate. Asiatic pharaohs were polygamous and aggressive: "Sarah was taken from me by force";[16] without further ado the king "took her to him to wife and sought to slay me."[17] Josephus says that this pharaoh deserved the punishment he got because of his high-handed manner towards the wife of a stranger.[18] But as we all know, Abraham was saved when Pharaoh was assured by Sarah herself that he was her brother and would thus not stand in the way of their marriage; instead of being liquidated, he was, therefore, as the brother of the favorite wife, "entreated . . . well for her sake" (Genesis 12:16).

Sarah on the Lion Couch

Abraham was saved and Pharaoh was pleased and everything was all right except for poor Sarah. It was now her turn to face the test of the lion couch! As we have seen, not only the royal altar but also the royal bed was a lion couch. And this was to be more than a test of Sarah's virtue, for should she refuse, the king would be mortally offended—with predictable results for the lady. His unhesitating move to put Abraham out of the way had made it clear enough that His Majesty was playing for keeps. After all, three princesses of the royal line had already been put to death on the lion altar for refusing to compromise their virtue (Abraham 1:11), and there was no indication that Sarah would be an exception.

The story of Sarah's delivery from her plight follows the same order as the stories of Abraham and Isaac. First of all, being brought to the royal bed "by force," she weeps and calls upon the Lord to save her, at which time Abraham also "prayed and entreated and begged . . . as my tears fell."[19] As he had prayed for himself, so the patriarch "prayed the Lord to save her from the hands of Pharaoh."[20]

And though experience may have rendered *him* perfectly confident in the results, it was the less-experienced Sarah who was being tested. The prayer for deliverance closely matches that on the first lion couch: "Blessed art thou, Most High God, Lord of all the worlds, because Thou art Lord and master of all and ruler of all the kings of the earth, and of whom thou judgest. Behold now I cry before Thee, my Lord, against Pharaoh Zoan, king of Egypt, because my wife has been taken from me by force. Judge him for me and let me behold Thy mighty hand descend upon him."[21] Even so Abraham had prayed for deliverance from the altar of "Nimrod": "O God, Thou seest what this wicked man is doing to me," with the whole emphasis on the king's blasphemous claims to possess the ultimate power in the world: in both cases Abraham is helpless against the authority and might of Pharaoh, but still he will recognize only one king, and he calls for a showdown: "that night I prayed and begged and said in sorrow . . . let thy mighty hand descend upon him . . . and men shall know, my Lord, that *Thou* art the Lord of all the kings of the earth!"[22] This is exactly the point of Abraham's prayer in the *Ma'aseh Abraham Abinu*[23] and Abraham 1:17, where God says, "I have come down . . . to destroy him who hath lifted up his hand against thee, Abraham, my son."

So while all "that night Sarah lay upon her face," calling upon God, Abraham "without the prison" also prayed[24] "that he may not this night defile my wife."[25] It was, as one might by now expect, just at the moment that Pharaoh assayed to seize Sarah that an angel came to the rescue, whip in hand: "As Pharaoh was about to possess Sarah, she turned to the angel who stood at her side (visible only to her) and immediately Pharaoh fell to the ground; all his house was then smitten with plague, with leprosy on the walls, the pillars, and furniture."[26] Whenever Pharaoh would make a move toward Sarah, the invisible angel would strike him down.[27] To justify such rough treatment of the poor unsuspecting Pharaoh, the Midrash explains that he was not unsuspecting at all: "an angel stood with a whip" to defend her, because she told Pharaoh that she was a married woman, and he still would not leave her alone.[28] According to all other accounts, however, that is exactly what she did not tell him, having her husband's safety in mind. The almost comical humiliation of the mighty king in the very moment of his triumph is an exact counterpart of the crushing overthrow of "Nimrod" at the instant of his supreme triumph over Abraham. "His illicit lust was checked," says Josephus, "by disease and *stasis*—revolution,"[29] suggesting that his kingly authority was overthrown along with his royal dignity and prowess.

What saved Sarah, according to the Aramaic *Genesis Apocryphon*,[30] was the sending by El Elyon, the Most High God, of a *rwḥ mkdš* or *rwḥ bʾyšʾ* which Avigad and Yadin render "a pestilential wind" and "a wind that was evil," respectively. Other scholars however, prefer "spirit" (of plague) to "wind,"[31] and while *mkdš* is not found in the dictionary, *miqdāsh* which sounds exactly the same, is a very common word indicating the dwelling place of God, so that *rwḥ mkdš* suggests to the ear "the angel of the presence," such as came to rescue both Abraham and Isaac on the altar.

Rwḥ bʾyšʾ in turn suggests to the ear "the spirit of fire," reminding us of a number of accounts of a mysterious being who stood with Abraham in the flames when he rescued him from the altar. The confusion of the rescuing angel with the wind is readily explained if our Aramaic text was written from dictation, as many ancient documents were.

The smiting of all of Pharaoh's house simultaneously with his own affliction is insisted on by all sources and recalls the "great mourning in Chaldea, and also in the court of Pharaoh" in Abraham 1:20. And just as the king in the Abraham story, when he is faced with the undeniable evidence of a power greater than his own, admits the superiority of Abraham's God and even offers to worship him, so he tells the woman Hagar when Sarah is saved, "It is better to be a maid in Sarah's house than to be Queen in my house!"[32] The showdown between the two religions is staged in both stories by the king himself when he pits his own priests and diviners against the wisdom of the stranger and his God, the test being which of the two is able to cure him and his house. An early writer quoted by Eusebius says, "Abraham went to Egypt with all his household and lived there, his wife being married to the king of Egypt who, however, could not approach her. . . . And when it came about that his people and his house were being destroyed he called for the diviners (Greek *manteis*), who told him that Sarah was not a widow, and so he knew that she was Abraham's wife and gave her back to him."[33] The first part of the statement is supported by the *Genesis Apocryphon*, which says that Sarah lived two years in Pharaoh's house, during which time he was unable to approach her. During that time she was in no danger of his wrath, however, since as far as Pharaoh was concerned it was not her reluctance but only his illness that kept them apart.[34]

Though Pharaoh's doctors and soothsayers gave him

useful advice, as they do "Nimrod" in his dealings with
Abraham, it is the healing that is the real test: "And he sent
and called of all the wise men of Egypt and all the wizards
and all the physicians of Egypt, if perchance they might
heal him from that pestilence, him and his house. And all
the physicians and wizards and wise men could not heal
⊹ him, for the wind [spirit, angel] smote them all and they
fled"[35]—just as the host of wise men summoned by Nimrod
to advise him on how to get rid of Abraham were forced to
flee ignominiously in all directions by the miraculous fire
which left Abraham unscathed. All the wisdom and divinity
of Egypt having failed, Pharaoh's agent "ḤRQNWŠ went
straight to Abraham "and besought [him] to come and to
pray for the king and to lay [his] hands upon him that he
might live."[36] To this request Abraham magnanimously
complied after Sarah was returned to him: "I laid my hand
upon his head and the plague departed from him and the
⊹ evil [wind spirit] was gone and he was cured [lived]."[37]
When the healing power of Abraham's God, in contrast
to the weakness of his own, became apparent, Pharaoh
forthwith recognized Abraham by the bestowal of royal
honors—even as "Nimrod" had done when Abraham
stepped before him unscathed.[38]

That these stories are more than belated inventions of
the rabbinic imagination is apparent from the significant
parallels with which Egyptian literature fairly swarms. A
veritable library of familiar motifs is contained in the late
Ptolemaic Tales of Khamuas. They begin with "Ahure's
Story," telling how an aging pharaoh, in order to assure the
royal succession, wanted to force the princess Ahure to
renounce marriage with her beloved brother Neneferkaptah
and wed the son of a general, contrary to "the law of Egypt"
but consistent with the practice of the Asiatic pharaohs.[39]
The damsel goes weeping to her wedding,[40] but at the last
moment the old king changes his mind, the princess mar-

ries her true love, and the couple is showered with royal gifts and honors.[41] They have a child, but Neneferkaptah in his zeal for knowledge steals a heavenly book from Thoth and, as a result, first the child, then the mother, and finally the father pay for the guilt of Neneferkaptah by falling into the Nile, all duly ending up "in the necropolis—hill of Coptos."[42]

In these episodes one can hardly fail to recognize the legends of Abraham in Egypt: the true lovers separated by Pharaoh only to be reunited; father, mother, and son as sacrificial victims; the king paying for the blight on the land until a foreign substitute can be found; the humiliation of Pharaoh, etc. Most significant, perhaps, is that these are consciously recurring motifs, with the same characters turning up in a succession of episodes centuries apart. And the fictitious situations are not without historical parallels. Here we have a well-attested historical account of a pharaoh who married a fabulously beautiful princess from the north who thought of herself as a missionary, and to whose religion the king was converted by a miraculous healing, showing us at the very least the sort of thing that *could* have happened in Sarah's time. The healing of Pharaoh by the laying on of hands described in the *Genesis Apocryphon* is a thing which appears absolutely nowhere else in any of the known records dealing with Abraham and should be studied with great care. Without the evidence of the New Testament, we should never suspect that there was any ancient and established tradition behind it: "The healing of the sick by expelling, with the laying on of hands, the evil spirits," writes Vermes, "is unknown in the Old Testament but a familiar rite in the Gospels. . . . The nearest Old Testament parallel is 2 Kings, V. 11."[43]

That we are dealing here with ritually conditioned events rather than unique historical occurrences is apparent from the complete repetition of Sarah's Egyptian experience with *another* king many years later. Abimelech, the king of Gerar, a small state lying between Canaan and Egypt, also took Sarah to wife and would have put Abraham to death had she not again announced that he was her brother.[44] Again Sarah prayed and again an angel appeared, this time with a sword, to save her.[45] At the same time, according to one tradition, "the voice of a great crying was heard in the whole land of the Philistines, for they saw the figure of a man walking about, with a sword in his hand, slaying all that came in his way."[46] This was "on the fatal night of the Paschal feast," i.e., at the time of the drama of the Suffering Servant, and the king became so ill that the doctors despaired of his life.[47] Just as Pharaoh had done, the king summoned all his wise counselors and again they were helpless and abashed (Genesis 20:8); again Abraham's wife was restored to him (Genesis 20:14); and again "Abraham prayed unto God: and God healed Abimelech" (Genesis 20:17).

What is behind all this is indicated in the nature of the illness that afflicted the houses of both Abimelech and Pharaoh. As to the first, "the Lord had fast closed up all the wombs of the house of Abimelech, because of Sarah Abraham's wife" (Genesis 20:18). The legends elaborate on this: "in men and beast alike all the apertures of the body closed up, and the land was seized with indescribable excitement."[48] In short, every creature was rendered sterile until Abraham administered to Abimelech, whereupon "all his house were healed, and the women could bear children with no pain, and they could have male children"; at the same moment, Sarah, barren until then, became fruitful, "the blind, deaf, lame, etc., were healed, and the sun shone out 48 times brighter than usual, even as on the first day of creation."[49] To celebrate the birth of Isaac, all the kings of the earth were invited to Abraham's house, and during the festivities Sarah gave milk to all the gentile babies whose mothers had none, and "all proselytes and pious heathen are the descendants of these infants."[50] As for Pharaoh, the common tradition is that the plague which smote his house, whether leprosy or some other disease, rendered all the people impotent and sterile.[51]

That this was the nature of the complaint is implied in the tradition that Abraham's powers of healing the sick by prayer were especially devoted to the healing of barren women.[52] By emerging victorious from the contests with Pharaoh and Abimelech, both Sarah and Abraham by their mutual faithfulness reversed the blows of death, so that they became new again and had children in their old age.[53] As the Zohar puts it, Abraham received a new grade of knowledge and henceforth "begat children [on a] higher plane."[54]

Here Sarah appears as the central figure in that ritual complex that marks the New Year all over the ancient world and has been noticed in these studies in its form of the Egyptian *Sed* festival. The theme of Sarah's royal marriages is not lust but the desire of Pharaoh and Abimelech to establish a kingly line. Sarah was at least sixty-one when she left the house of Pharaoh and eighty-nine when she visited Abimelech. Pharaoh's only interest in Sarah, Josephus insists, was to establish a royal line; or, as Bernhard Beer puts it, "his object was rather to become related to Abraham by marriage," i.e., he wanted Abraham's glory, and that was the only way he could get it.[55] Abimelech's interest is completely dominated by the fertility motif, for he contests with Abraham over "a well of water, which Abimelech's servants had violently taken away" (Genesis 21:25), even as Sarah had been violently taken away; and just as Abimelech surrendered and pleaded his innocence in the case of Sarah (Genesis 20:9), so he pleads ignorance also in the case of the well and even chides Abraham again for not enlightening him: "I wot not who hath done this thing: neither didst thou tell me, neither yet heard I of it, but to day" (Genesis 21:26). To complete the scene, Abraham concludes the episode by planting one of his groves in the land of the Philistines (Genesis 21:33). If Sarah is the bounteous and child-giving mother, Abraham no less presides over the life-giving waters.

That this is the ritual setting of the Abimelech episode is confirmed by documents probably as old as Abraham that describe the goings-on among the Canaanites on the coast to the north of Gerar. These are the famous Ugaritic texts from Ras Shamra, and the best known of them is the story of Krt. The latest critical study of the Krt drama maintains that it is both a ritual and a historical document, "the subject of the first tablet" being "the rehabilitation of the royal house after disaster, with the wooing of Krt," while the second tablet describes the royal wedding and in the third we have "the illness and threatened eclipse of Krt" (the ritual king), when his "oldest son Yṣb takes advantage to seek to supplant him."[56] The drama has a definite moral and social object, according to John Gray, "such as the securing of a legitimate queen and the establishment of the royal line."[57] In the Krt story the powers of the old king are failing, and he is told by his youthful would-be successor: "In the sepulchral cave thou wilt abide. . . . Sickness is as (thy) bedfellow, Disease (thy) concubine."[58] Just so Abimelech is told that if he takes Sarah to wife, "thou art a dead man!" (Genesis 20:3). After three months of sickness, "Krt is passing away, . . . [in the] sepulchral chamber, like a treasury with a gate"—it is so much like the lion-couch scene in the *Sed* festival that we are not surprised to learn that Krt is first frantically mourned and then revived by two ladies.[59] The cure is effected by the lady Qudshu, whom we have already learned to know as the common heirodule of Egypt and Canaan (fig. 47).[60] First she arrives weeping at the house of Krt. "Shrieking, she enters the inmost chambers";

Figure 47. On the lower register of this stele, the chief royal craftsman Qeh and his family are worshiping Anat, a popular Asiatic goddess of love and war who wears the familiar Atef crown. On the upper portion, Anat, as the lady "Qudshu, Mistress of Heaven," is standing on her lioness. She offers flowers to Min on the left and Reshef on the right. The latter is another Asiatic deity as shown by his non-Egyptian beard and the gazelle-head crown.

but then she starts to revive the king, who is not completely dead yet,[61] and finally "she returns, she washes him. She has given him a new appetite for meat, she opens his desire for food."[62] The king rises from his bier, victorious: "As for Death, he is confounded; as for Šᶜtqt, she has prevailed!" So of course there is a great feast as the king "takes his seat on his royal throne, even on the dais, the seat of his government."[63] It is the lion-couch drama all over again, but the Abimelech elements are prominent too, as when the king's wise men and counselors all are summoned and asked, "Who among the gods will abolish the disease, driving out all the sickness?" Seven times the challenge is put, but "there is none among the gods who answers him"—the doctors are abashed. They must yield to the true god, El the Merciful, who says, "I myself . . . shall provide that which will abolish the disease"—and he does.[64] Of course, it rains and everything grows at last (Mot, the name of the adversary, means both death and drought); Krt on his bier is even called "Sprouts"—a vivid reminder of the Egyptian "Osiris beds" (fig. 48).[65]

The Ugaritic Krt Text gives strong indication that the adventures of Sarah with Egyptian and Palestinian kings follow the common ritual pattern of Palestine and Egypt; indeed, the point of both stories is that Sarah and Abraham resist and overcome powerful and insidious attempts to involve them in the very practices of the idolatrous nations which Abraham had been denouncing since his youth. It would be impossible to avoid coming face to face with such practices in any comprehensive account of either Abraham or Sarah, and one of the best and most vivid descriptions of the rites is contained in the Book of Abraham. We are dealing here with a worldwide ritual complex of whose existence no one dreamed in 1912 and which is still largely ignored by Egyptologists.[66] It is not only the idea of romantic love that is one of the special marks of the patriarchal narratives, as

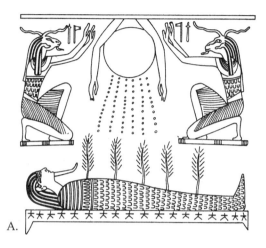

Figure 48. The ram-headed Khnum, "the Great God," worships the life-giving rays of the sun, which generate the five seedlings sprouting from the mummified body of Osiris (A). His body rests on the star-filled *pt* or symbol of heaven, showing the cosmic significance of this event. The ancient Egyptians shaped Nile mud in the form of Osiris. On this cloth-covered wooden bed (B) found in a tomb, they had planted seeds that germinated in the mud.

Cyrus Gordon points out; even more conspicuous is the repeated recurrence of a ritual love triangle in which a third party threatens to break up a devoted couple. Such is the story of Hagar, who sought to supplant Sarah in Abraham's household and was turned out into the desert to perish of thirst—always the water motif! Being in imminent danger of death, Hagar prays, "Look upon my misery"—which happens to be the opening line of Abraham's prayer on the altar[67]—whereupon an angel appears and tells her, "God has heard your prayer," promising her a son (Genesis 16:11). So here, to cut it short, we have Hagar praying for deliverance from a heat death, visited by an angel, and promised the same blessing in her hour of crisis as was given to Sarah and Abraham in theirs. There is a difference, of course: by "despising" and taunting her afflicted mistress and then by deserting her, Hagar had *not* been true and faithful, and the angel sternly ordered her back to the path of duty, while the promises given to her offspring are heavy with qualifications and limitations. The issue is as ever one of authority, for, as Josephus puts it, Hagar sought precedence over Sarah, and the angel told her to return to her "rulers" (*despotas*) or else she would perish, but if she obeyed she would bear a son who would rule in that desert land.[68] She too founded a royal line.

In maintaining that "Abraham's marriage with Keturah (Genesis 25:1–6) can have no historical foundation,"[69] scholars have overlooked the *ritual* foundation of the story, clearly indicated by the name of Keturah, which enjoys a prominent place in the Adonis ritual cycles of Phoenicia and Syria.[70] As Gray points out in his study of Krt, these ritual events could very well become history as well when the sacrifices and marriages were repeated at "the accession of each new king" and "at royal weddings."[71] The ritual content of the thing, far from discrediting it as history, is the best possible evidence for some sort of historical reality behind it. The ritual triangle is repeated when Bethuel the king of Haran tries to take the beautiful Rebekah away from Isaac's agent, Eliezer (who, we are told was the exact image of Abraham); the wicked king was slain by his own treachery and the noble couple departed laden with royal gifts.

The Humiliation of the King

In this last story the real hero is Eliezer, while the bridegroom-to-be, Isaac, lurks ignobly in the background.

Abraham likewise in the affairs with Pharaoh and Abimelech not only takes a back seat but appears in a rather uncomplimentary, if not actually degrading, position. This is an indispensable element of the year-drama everywhere: the temporary humiliation of the true king while a rival and substitute displaces him on the throne and in the queen's favor. We have seen both Abraham and Isaac in the roles of substitute kings or "Suffering Servants," and now we must make room for Sarah on the stage, for the play cannot take place without her. The Suffering Servant is the true king during the period of his ritual humiliation, representing his death; at that time his place is taken by a pretender, an inter-rex, tanist, Lord of Misrule, etc., who turns out to be the *real* substitute when the time for his death arrives. Both are substitutes but in different capacities: the one king sits on a real throne but suffers a make-believe burial; the other sits on a make-believe throne but suffers a real burial. As we saw in the *Sed* festival, the main purpose of all this shuffling is to spare the real king the discomfort of a premature demise: the true king is always vindicated in the end. If Abraham was rudely thrust aside by his royal rivals in Egypt and Palestine, and if Sarah was made the unwilling victim of their kingly arrogance, it was only to show who the real king was—*they*, as it turned out, were for all their pride and power the pretenders, claiming the divine honors that really belonged to Abraham. Abraham is the rival of Pharaoh and Abimelech, both of whom are ready to put him to death in order to raise up a royal line by Sarah.[77] That he is the real king, restored to his rightful queen in the end, is made perfectly clear in the almost comical complaints of the two kings that they, who had contemptuously thrust the helpless Abraham aside, were actually the victims of his power: "And Pharaoh called Abram, and said, What is this that *thou* hast done unto me?" (Genesis 12:18, emphasis added), while Abimelech echoes his words: "Then Abimelech called

Abraham, and said unto him, What hast thou done unto us?
. . . thou has done deeds unto me that ought not to be done"
(Genesis 20:9). The roles of victim and victor are almost
ludicrously reversed. And just as Pharaoh-Nimrod complained that Abraham had escaped the altar by a trick, so
does Pharaoh-Zoan complain that Sarah has escaped his
couch by a ruse: "why didst thou not tell me that she was
thy wife? . . . Now therefore behold thy wife, take her, and
go thy way" (Genesis 12:18–19).

The Sarah story starts out with Abraham and Sarah alike
at the mercy of the triumphant and irresistible king, and it
ends up with the king humiliated by pain and impotence,
humbly suing Abraham for succor and then acknowledging
that superior power and priesthood of his rival. There is no
injustice here: Abraham does not invade their kingdoms or
seek their thrones, but the other way around—they coveted
his rightful domain and were properly rebuked.

While the humiliation of the rightful king before his
return to the throne is a central episode of the great year-
rites throughout the ancient east,[73] the queen plays quite a
different role: she is ageless and immortal, the Mother Earth
itself, taking a new spouse at each cycle of renewal and
disposing of the old one.[74] This makes her the dominant
figure of the rites, which have a distinctly matriarchal
background—as is clearly indicated in the Book of Abraham, where, moreover, the tension between the old matriarchal and rival patriarchal orders is vividly set forth: While
Abraham is completely devoted to the authority of "the
fathers, . . . even the right of the first-born" (Abraham 1:3),
Pharaoh was put on the throne by his mother (Abraham
1:23–25), so that though he "would fain claim" patriarchal
authority (Abraham 1:27), "seeking earnestly to imitate that
order established by the fathers" (Abraham 1:26), the
importance of the female line still outweighed that of the
fathers, as it always did in Egypt. The conflict between

Pharaoh's would-be patriarchal role and the claims of the matriarchy is further reflected in the putting to death of three princesses of royal blood who refused to play the game Pharaoh's way and compromise their virtue (Abraham 1:11–12). Abraham opposes the royal claims that his father ardently supported, in secure possession of "the records of thy fathers, even the patriarchs, concerning the right of Priesthood," which records "God preserved in mine own hands" (Abraham 1:31). And in return Terah volunteered his own son as a victim in the sacrificial rites (Abraham 1:30). This should be enough to explain how Sarah and Abraham get involved in all these very pagan goings-on.

Recently Gordon has demonstrated the singularly close parallelism between the stories of Sarah and Helen of Troy, the main theme of both being the winning back of the captive queen by her rightful husband: In turn each of the rival husbands is made to look rather ridiculous as the lady leaves first one and then the other.[75] In the earliest Babylonian depictions of the year-motif we see the "imprisoned or buried" bridegroom, whom the bride must rescue and revive,[76] even as Isis rescues and revives her husband and brother Osiris in the Egyptian versions. And so we have Abraham in an oddly unheroic role, gratefully accepting the presents and favors that Pharaoh bestows upon him as the *brother* of Sarah the king's favorite wife![77]

Brother and Sister

Still less heroic is the supposed subterfuge by which Abraham got himself into that undignified position. The best biblical scholars in Joseph Smith's day as well as our own have found nothing to condone in what is generally considered an unedifying maneuver on the part of Abraham to save his skin at the expense of both Sarah and Pharaoh. "Abram appears to have laboured under a temporary suspension of faith," wrote the most learned commentator of

Joseph Smith's time, "and to have stooped to the mean and foolish prevarication of denying his wife. . . . And had not the Lord miraculously interposed, . . . Abraham must have sunk under his timidity, and forfeited his title to the covenant."[78] How they all missed the point! Far from denoting a suspension of faith, the turning over of his wife to another required the greatest faith yet, and that is where the Book of Abraham puts the whole story on a meaningful and edifying footing. For it was God who commanded Abraham: "See that ye do on this wise: Let her say unto the Egyptians, she is thy sister, and thy soul shall live" (Abraham 2:23–24). As to the "lie" about the family relationship of Abraham and Sarah, a number of factors must be considered. Technically, the Bible explains, Sarah was indeed Abraham's half-sister on his father's side (Genesis 20:12). To this physical relationship, the Zohar adds a spiritual, reporting that "Abraham always called her 'sister' because he was attached to her inseparably. . . . For the marital bond can be dissolved, but not that between brother and sister"—so by an eternal marriage that the world did not understand they were brother and sister.[79] More to the point, in Syria, Canaan, and Egypt at the time it was the common custom to refer to one's wife as one's "sister," and Abraham's life reflects both the Semitic and the Hurrian cultural and legal patterns,[80] so that "Sarah was . . . a 'sister-wife,' an official Hurrian term signifying the highest social rating."[81] On the other hand, everyone knows that it was custom for pharaohs of Egypt to marry their sisters, and in the Egyptian love songs the nonroyal lovers regularly address each other as "my sister" and "my brother." The same custom appears in Canaan and even in the *Genesis Apocryphon,* the opening fragments of which show us the mother of Noah berating her husband Lamech for suspecting her virtue, but addressing him throughout the scene as "my Brother and my Lord."[82] Indeed, in Abraham's day "both in Egypt and

Canaan," according to Albright, "the notion of incest scarcely existed. In fact, Phoenicia and Egypt shared a general tendency to use 'sister' and 'wife' simultaneously."[83]

But whatever the *reservation mentale* behind the statement that Abraham and Sarah were brother and sister, the point of the story is that it was meant to convey to the kings that the two were *not* married—the sophistry of the thing would only render it more unsavory did we not have the real explanation in the Pearl of Great Price.

Sarah on Her Own

By telling Pharaoh and Abimelech that Abraham really was her brother, Sarah put the two kings in the clear. From then on *they*, at least, were acting in good faith. The Bible makes this very clear: the moment Pharaoh learns the truth, he lets Sarah go, saying to Abraham, "why didst thou not tell me that she was thy wife? Why saidst thou, She is my sister? so I might have taken her to me to wife" (Genesis 12:18–19). "I did what I did," says Abimelech, "with perfect heart and pure hand," to which the Lord replies in a dream, "I knew that, and I forgave thee" (cf. Genesis 20:5–6). So it is made perfectly explicit that it is not the kings who are being tested—God honors and rewards them both for their behavior, which is strictly correct according to the customs of the times.

It must be Abraham and Sarah who are being tested then. But Abraham too is out of it, for, as we have seen, the Lord *commands* him to ask Sarah to say he is her brother, and he obeys. But no one commands Sarah—the whole thing is left up to her as a matter of free choice. It is she and she alone who is being tested on the lion couch this time. It is incorrect to say with Robert Graves that "Abraham gave Sarah to Pharaoh,"[84] for he was in no position to do so: he was completely in Pharaoh's power—he had already taken

Sarah by force—and Pharaoh was listening only to Sarah! The rabbis who knew the ancient law say that only unmarried women were taken into the harem of Pharaoh, and that these could not be approached by the king without their own consent.[85] It might mean death to her if she refused, but still to refuse was within her power, while Abraham was helpless to save her and Pharaoh was acting in good faith—throughout the story every crucial decision rests with Sarah and Sarah alone.

Why do we say that no one commands Sarah? God commanded Abraham to propose a course of action to Sarah, but Abraham did not command Sarah—he asked her humbly for a personal favor: "Therefore say unto them, *I pray thee*, thou art my sister, that it may be well with *me* for *thy* sake, and *my* soul shall live because of thee" (Abraham 2:25; Genesis 12:13, emphasis added). He explained the situation to her—"I, Abraham, told Sarai, my wife, all that the Lord had said unto me"—but the decision was entirely up to her. According to the Midrash, on this occasion Abraham "made himself of secondary importance, . . . whereupon he really became subordinate to Sarah."[86] Everything was done for her sake: "the Lord plagued Pharaoh and his house with great plagues because of [Sarah]" (Genesis 12:17).[87] Abraham was given both life and property "for Sarah's sake," and the king "entreated Abram well for her sake" (Genesis 12:16). Sarah was legally and lawfully married to both kings and was thus the legitimate recipient of their bounty. Pharaoh, according to Rabbi Eliezer, "wrote for Sarah a marriage document, (giving her) all his wealth, . . . [including] the land of Goshen."[88] He "took her to him to wife and sought to slay me," says Abraham in the *Genesis Apocryphon*,[89] "and I, Abraham, was saved because of her and was not slain."[90] From this Vermes concludes that Abraham was indebted to Sarah for his life but not for his prosperity, having received riches in return for healing Pharaoh.[91] But the verses on which he bases this view may be more easily interpreted as meaning that it was to Sarah rather than Abraham that Pharaoh gave the treasures, the badly damaged lines reading:

> 31. . . . And the King gave him a large . . . the gift (?) much and much raiment of fine linen and purple [several words missing].
> 32. . . . before her, and also Hagar [several words obscured] . . . and appointed men for me who would escort out [several words missing].[92]

Now the Jewish traditions are quite explicit that it was to Sarah that Pharaoh gave the royal raiment and the maid Hagar. Since Abraham is writing in the first person, it is not absolutely certain who the "him" is in line 31, but the "her" in the next line is certainly Sarah, and there is no indication that the gifts and Hagar were not for her. The Bible clearly states that Abraham came into possession of Hagar only later when Sarah "gave her to her husband Abram to be his wife" (Genesis 16:3), i.e., Sarah gave more than permission to marry—she actually handed over her property to him, for Hagar was her personal maid (Genesis 16:1). And when Hagar behaved badly, Abraham, to keep peace, gave her back to Sarah again: "Behold, thy maid is in thine hand; do to her as it pleaseth thee" (Genesis 16:6). When Sarah sent Isaac forth to school (as she thought) or to the rites on Mount Moriah, "she dressed him in the royal garments and crown that Abimelech had given her."[93] Everything indicates that she was a princess in her own right—the gifts of her royal husbands did not so much bestow as recognize her royalty, for which they eagerly sought her hand in the first place, hoping to raise up kingly lines by her. Before her name was changed to Sarah, "Princess of all people," it had already been Sarai, "Princess of her own people," according to the Midrash; and before she ever married Abraham she was well known by the name of Jiska, "the Seeress," either ⚹

because she had the gift of prophecy or because of her shining beauty, or both.[94]

The rabbis have resented the superior rating of Sarah with its matriarchal implications and attempted to cover it up. Granted that everything that Pharaoh gave to Abraham was for Sarah's sake, the doctors must conclude that Pharaoh acted unwisely, and they hold up as a proper example the case of Abimelech, who, according to them, gave his gifts to Abraham rather than Sarah. Yet these same authorities report that this same Abimelech gave to Sarah "a costly robe that covered her whole person, . . . a reproach to Abraham, that he had not fitted Sarah out with the splendor due his wife"—it would seem that Sarah has her royal claims after all.[95]

Actually the idea of rivalry between Abraham and Sarah is as baseless as that between Abraham and Isaac when we understand the true situation, in which neither party can fulfill his or her proper function without the other. Having been commanded of the Lord, Abraham explained his situation to his wife and asked her whether she would be willing to go along (Abraham 2:25). According to the *Genesis Apocryphon*, he did not like the idea at all—it was a terrible sacrifice for him: "And I wept, I Abram, with grievous weeping."[96] Would he have wept so for his own life, which he had so often been willing to risk? Why, then, did he ask Sarah to risk her person to save him: "Say unto them, I pray thee, thou art my sister . . . and my soul shall live because of thee"? Plainly because nothing else would move Sarah to take such a step. There was nothing in the world to keep her from exchanging her hard life with Abraham for a life of unlimited ease and influence as Pharaoh's favorite except her loyalty to her husband. By a special order from heaven Abraham had stepped out of the picture and Pharaoh had been placed in a legally and ethically flawless position, and Sarah knew it: "I Abraham, told Sarai, my wife, all that the Lord had said to me." Why is the brilliant prospect of being Queen of Egypt never mentioned as an inducement or even a lightening of Sarah's burden? Sarah apparently never thinks of that, for she was as upset as Abraham: "Sarai wept at my words that night."[97] Still, the proposition was never put to her as a command, but only as a personal request from Abraham: "Please say you are my sister for the sake of my well being, so that through your ministration I shall be saved, and owe my life to you!" (cf. Genesis 12:13); and so with Abimelech: "This will be a special favor which I am asking of you in my behalf" (cf. Genesis 20:13). Abraham is abiding by the law of God; the whole question now is, *Will Sarah abide by the law of her husband?* And she proved that she would, even if necessary at the risk of her life. It was as great a sacrifice as Abraham's and Isaac's, and of the same type.

The Cedar and the Palm: A Romantic Interlude

Some famous episodes are associated with the crossing of the border into Egypt, such as Abraham's beholding Sarah's beauty for the first time as they wade the stream— "In comparison with her, all other beauties were like apes compared with men."[98] It was under like circumstances that King Solomon is said to have first beheld the beauty of the Queen of Sheba.[99] Again, Abraham concealed his wife's beauty by trying to smuggle her across the border in a trunk, on which he was willing to pay any amount of duty provided the officials would not open it; of course, they could not resist the temptation and were quite overpowered by this Pandora's box in reverse.[100]

But the story of the cedar and the palm has the most interesting parallels of all: "And I, Abram, dreamed a dream in the night of our going up into the land of Egypt, and what I beheld in my dream was a cedar tree and a palm-tree . . . [words missing] and men came and tried to cut down and uproot the cedar while leaving the palm standing alone. And the palm tree called out and said, 'Do not cut the cedar! Cursed and shamed whoever [words missing].' So the cedar was spared in the shelter of the palm."[101] We have seen that Abraham was often compared with a cedar, and that the palm could be either Sarah or the hospitable Pharaoh.[102] But when we read in the *Genesis Apocryphon* that "for the sake of the palm the cedar was saved,"[103] we recall the unforgettable image of the mighty Odysseus, clad only in evergreen branches, facing the lovely princess Nausicaa, as in an exquisitely diplomatic speech he compares her with the tall sacred palm standing in the courtyard of the temple at Delos. In return for the compliment, the princess dresses the hero in royal garments and conducts him to the palace. Later, when the two meet for the last time, the damsel makes good-natured fun of the way she had saved the mightiest man alive, but in return Odysseus solemnly tells her that it was no joke: "For you really did save my life, lady, and I shall never forget it!"[104] Here, then, the palm again saved the cedar. If scholars are now inclined to compare Sarah with Helen of Troy, it is pleasanter and even more appropriate to compare her with the chaste and clever Nausicaa, the most delightful of ancient heroines.

The humiliation of Odysseus, who appears first supplicating the princess while covered with dirt and leaves and then trails after her wagon publicly dressed in women's clothes, is a moment of matriarchal victory, as is the humiliation of Abraham. The meeting ground of the two stories is appropriately Egypt, for in the *Tale of the Two Brothers*, in which scholars have discerned the background of a wealth of biblical motifs, especially those of the patriarchal stories, we meet the same strange combination of elements: the hero as a cedar tree threatened with destruction, the royal laundry ladies by the river, the trip to the palace, the humiliation of the king and his ultimate restoration, and all the rest.[105] The felling of the cedar is also the fall of Adonis in the Attis-Adonis cult, related in turn to the Osiris mysteries and the cult of Sirius. Already in the Pyramid Texts Osiris is the king "who takes men's wives from them"— why should not Pharaoh be an Osiris in this as in other dramatic situations?[106] When Sarah died "hospitality ceased; but when Rebekah came the gates were again opened."[107] In all these operations Rebekah, we are assured, "was the counterpart of Sarah in person and spirit," the living image of Sarah.[108] Sarah is thus the ageless mother and perennial bride: the whole point of the birth of Isaac is that she becomes young again—"Is any thing too hard for the Lord?" (Genesis 18:14). Firmicus Maternus informs us that the early Christians saw in the Egyptian cult of Serapis, the last stage of the Osiris mysteries, the celebration of the Sarras-pais, "the son of Sarah," with Sarah as the mother of the new king.[109] Which may not be so farfetched, since that was exactly Pharaoh's intention in taking her to wife, according to Josephus.

Here it is in order to note that the legends of Abraham's birth and childhood are dominated by the conflict between matriarchy and patriarchy, with Abraham's mortal foe and rival, Nimrod, as the archdefender of the matriarchy. To forestall the birth of Abraham, foretold by the stars, he first attempts to bar all contact between men and women; then he orders all expectant mothers shut up in a great castle: when a girl baby is born, she and her mother are sent far from the castle showered with gifts and crowned like queens, while all boy babies are immediately put to death.[110] And while Abraham's father supports Nimrod and tries to destroy the infant, his mother saves him by hiding him in a cave. Her name, Emtelai, is a reminder that this is the age-old Amalthea motif.

Breaking the Mold

Facsimile 1 and the explanation thereof admonish the student not to be too surprised to find father Abraham deeply involved in the abominable rites of the heathen. This, admittedly, is not a healthy situation, but then the point of the whole thing is that Abraham is fighting the system, and his is a lifelong struggle. In the process of meeting the foe on his own ground, he finds himself in one unpleasant situation after another—unpleasant and strangely familiar. The familiarity of the setting, as we have insisted all along, vouches for the authenticity of the tradition. The Abraham stories are poured into an ancient mold—but Abraham cracks the mold. One of the most striking examples of the shattered mold is the famous romance of Joseph and Asenath, a reediting of the story of Abraham and Sarah in an authentic Egyptian setting.

Everything in this romantic tale reverses the order of the conventional Near Eastern romance. True, it begins with the maiden locked up in her tower, the proud heiress of the matriarchy disdaining all men and rejecting all lovers, according to the standard fairy-tale formula going back as far as the Egyptian romances of the Doomed Prince and the Two Brothers. But presently she falls desperately in love with Joseph, of whose love she feels abjectly unworthy. Gerhard von Rad insists that the Joseph stories are the purest fiction, *"durch und durch novellistisch,"* and have no place in the patriarchal histories.[111] But he overlooks the all-important ritual element that places Joseph and Asenath in the long line of holy couples: Adam and Eve, Abraham and Sarah, Isaac and Rebekah, Jacob and Rachel, Moses and Zippora, Aaron and Elisheba, etc.[112] The undeniable link between the Abraham and the Joseph romances is the key name of Potiphar; for just as the testing of Abraham takes place at Potiphar's Hill, so the triumph of Joseph over the practices of the heathen and the wicked prince of Egypt takes place at Potiphar's castle, Potiphar being none other than the father of Asenath. In the rites of the sacred marriage (the *hieros gamos*), an angel instructed Asenath to change her black garment of death to a pure white wedding dress, the most ancient, primal wedding garment, whereupon she kisses the feet of the heavenly visitor (who, incidentally, is in the exact image of Joseph!), who takes her by the hand and leads her out of the darkness into the light.[113] The two then sit upon her undefiled bed to partake of bread and wine supplied by the bride while the angel miraculously produces a honeycomb for a true love feast in the manner of the primitive Christians.[114]

If one compares this with the *"Setne"* romance or the tales of the Two Brothers or the Doomed Prince, or with the stories of Aqhat or Krt, or numerous Greek myths, one will recognize at every turn the same elements in the same combination—but what a difference! The heathen versions are full of violence and bestiality, with one brother murdering another and the lady deceiving and destroying her lovers: there is no better example of both the ritual and historical situation than the account in the eighth chapter of Ether where the throne is transmitted after the manner of "them of old" by a series of ritual murders supervised by the queen. In the *Sed* festival, Moret points out, the king's wife represented the unfailing fecundity of the earth, while the pharaoh was one whose failing powers were arrested by a sacrificial death, effected since the middle of the fourth millennium B.C., by the use of a substitute.[115] This is the sort of thing in which Abraham and Sarah become unwillingly involved—a desperate perversion of the true order of things. The first pharaoh, being a good man who "judged his people wisely and justly all his days," had tried hard to do things right, would "fain claim" the right of the priesthood, and was always "seeking . . . to imitate that order established by the fathers" (Abraham 1:26–27). But the best

he could come up with was an *imitation,* being "cursed . . .
as pertaining to the Priesthood." Abraham, possessed of the
authentic records (Abraham 1:28), knew Pharaoh's secret—
that his authority was stolen and his glory simulated—and
refused to cooperate, turning to God instead for the knowledge and the permission necessary to restore the ancient
order (Abraham 1:2). For this he was rewarded and received the desire of his heart, but only after being put to the
severest possible tests. Forced against his will to participate
in the false ordinances, he resisted them at every step, even
to the point of death. What breaks the mold is the sudden,
unexpected, and violent intervention of a destroying angel,
which puts an end to sacrificial rites and in their place
restores an ordinance of token sacrifice only, looking forward to the great atonement. Neither Abraham, Isaac, nor
Sarah had to pay the supreme price, though each confi-
dently expected to, and was accordingly given full credit
and forgiveness of sins through the atoning sacrifice of the
Lord. In them the proper order and purpose of sacrifice was
restored after the world had departed as far from the ancient plan as it was possible to get.

    In their three sacrifices the classic rivalry and tension
between father and son and between patriarchy and matriarchy are resolved in a perfect equality. On Mount Moriah,
Isaac showed that he was willing to suffer on the altar as
Abraham had been; in Egypt it was made perfectly clear
that Sarah was Abraham's equal and that he was as dependent on her for his eternal progress as she was on him.
The two kings knew that without Sarah they could not
attain to the glory of Abraham, but she knew that without
Abraham her glory would be nothing, and she refused all
substitutes. "Do this," says Abraham to his wife at the
beginning of the story, "for the sake of benefitting me, [and]
for your own advantage"—[*lə-maʿan yîṭaḇ lî ba-ʿaḇûrek̲*] (cf.
Genesis 12:13). According to the *Midrash,* Abraham and

Sarah kept the whole law from ʾalef to taw, "not under compulsion, but with delight."[116] They kept the law fully and they kept it together. Why is it, asks the archaeologist André Parrot, that we never read of the God of Sarah, Rebekah, and Rachel, but only of the God of Abraham, Isaac, and Jacob? The answer is given in Abraham 2:22–25, where Abraham obeys a direct command from God, though he is free to reject it if he will, while Sarah receives it as the law of her husband, being likewise under no compulsion. It is indeed the God of Sarah, Rebekah, and Rachel to whom they pray directly, but they covenant with him through their husbands. "If . . . he guards [the holy imprint]," says the Zohar, speaking of the ordinances of Abraham, "then the Shekhinah does not depart from him"—but how can he be sure he has guarded it? "He cannot be sure of it until he is married. . . . When the man and wife are joined together and are called by one name, then the celestial favor rests upon them . . . and is embraced in the male, so that the female also is firmly established."[117] It was by their usual faithfulness, according to rabbinic teaching, that Abraham and Sarah reversed the blows of death, so that they became new again and had children in their old age.[118] Just so, when Asenath was anointed with the oil of incorruptibility and then became the bride of Joseph, she was told, "from this time on art thou created anew, formed anew, given a new life."[119] When Sarah had passed through the valley of the shadow in order to save her husband's life, Abraham received a new grade of knowledge, after which he "begat children [on a] higher plane."[120] This is that measure of exaltation promised in Abraham 2:10–11: "for as many as receive this Gospel shall be called after thy name, and shall be accounted thy seed. . . . And in thy seed after thee (that is to say, the literal seed, or the seed of the body) shall all the families of the earth be blessed, even with the blessings of the Gospel . . . even of life eternal." It was this doctrine that

led to the discussions among the Jewish doctors on whether
Abraham and Sarah were actually given the power to create
souls.[121] "Abraham obtained the possession of both worlds,"
says an ancient formula, "for his sake this world and the
world to come were created."[122] Abraham's covenant, as
André Caquot observes with wonder, "appears to be outside of time and space."[123] Or as the Prophet Joseph Smith
put it, "Let us seek for the glory of Abraham, Noah, Adam,
the Apostles," naming Abraham first of all.[124]

And Abraham earned his glory: "The sacrifice required
of Abraham in the offering up of Isaac, shows that if a man
would attain to the keys of the kingdom of an endless life,
he must sacrifice all things."[125] But Isaac was in on it too—
the stories of Isaac and Sarah teach us that salvation is a
family affair, in which, however, each member acts as an
individual and makes his own choice, for each must decide
for himself when it is a matter of giving up all things, including life itself, if necessary. But "when the Lord has thoroughly proved him, and finds that the man is determined to
serve Him at all hazards," only then "the visions of the heavens will be opened unto him," as they were to Abraham,
"and the Lord will teach him face to face, and he may have
a perfect knowledge of the mysteries of the Kingdom of
God."[126] If Abraham knew that "God would provide a sacrifice," Isaac did not; if he was perfectly sure of his wife, she
was not and prayed desperately for help—husband, wife,
and son each had to undergo the terrible test alone.

But every test is only a sampling: as a few drops of
blood are enough for a blood test, so, as Julian Morgenstern
points out, the rite of circumcision demanded of Abraham
expressed the idea that a token shedding of blood "redeems
the remainder."[127] Circumcision, then, is an arrested sacrifice.
When one reaches a critical point in an act of obedience at
which it becomes apparent that one is willing to go all the
way, it is not necessary to go any farther and make the

costly sacrifice. Abraham called the spot where he sacrificed Isaac "Jehovahjireh," signifying that God was perfectly aware all the time of what was going on and knew exactly where Abraham stood: "For now I know that thou fearest God, seeing thou hast not withheld thy son."[128] He knew that Abraham would certainly carry out the sacrifice, and he let him go as far as possible for the sake of his instruction, and then he had him complete the ordinance with a token sacrifice, which was to be repeated by his progeny in the temple.[129] Cyril, the last "primitive" Christian bishop of Jerusalem, has left us a report on how the early Christians thought of this *token* sacrifice. The first step in becoming a Christian, he says, is to renounce all the idols (as Abraham did); next, one must escape the power of Satan, described as a ravening lion; then come baptism, anointing, and the receiving of a garment;[130] the candidate is then buried again three times in water, to signify Christ's three days in the tomb. "We do not really die," Cyril explains, "nor are we really buried, nor do we actually rise again after being crucified. It is a token following of instructions (*en eiponi hē mimēsis*), though the salvation is real. Christ was really crucified and buried and literally rose again. And all these things are for our benefit, and we can share in his sufferings by imitating them while enjoying the rewards in reality. O how everflowing is God's love for man! Christ received the nails in blameless hands and feet, . . . while I may share in the suffering and reward of salvation without the pain or suffering!"[131] He goes on to note that one then becomes "a Christ," an adopted, but nonetheless a real, son of God, "receiving the very form of the Son of God."[132]

Cyril describes the priesthood standing in a circle around the altar ("leave the altar if thy brother hath aught against thee"), the mutual embracing "which signifies a complete fusion of spirits," and then "that thrilling hour when one must enter spiritually into the presence of

God."[133] Throughout this ancient and forgotten discourse the emphasis is on the token or mimetic nature of the ordinances, along with the quite real and necessary part they play in achieving salvation. Julius Maternus, describing the same rites, says that they match the Osirian mysteries very closely, and he accuses the Egyptians of stealing their ordinances from Israel back in the days of Moses.[134]

The important thing in the early Christian rites is that every individual *must* imitate the suffering and burial of Christ; this is the great essential of the ordinances, as it is the fundamental principle of all Jewish sacrifice as well. This we learn from the sacrifices of Abraham, Isaac, and Sarah; each was interrupted and by the providing of a substitute became a token sacrifice, acceptable to God because of the demonstrated intention of each of the three to offer his or her life if necessary. The perfect consistency of the three sacrifices is a powerful confirmation of the authenticity of the Book of Abraham.

Notes

1. *Jubilees* 13:10; *Genesis Apocryphon* 19:9–10.
2. *Genesis Apocryphon* 19:23.
3. Ibid., 19:13.
4. Ibid., 19:24, 27.
5. Ibid., 21:19–22.
6. Cyrus H. Gordon, *The Common Background of Greek and Hebrew Civilization* (New York: Norton, 1965), 159–60.
7. Ben Zion Wacholder, "Pseudo-Eupolemus' Two Greek Fragments on the Life of Abraham," *Hebrew Union College Annual* 34 (1963): 110–11.
8. Hermann Kees, "Bubastis," *Orientalische Literaturzeitung* 53 (1958): 311; see also Hermann Kees, "Ein alter Götterhymnus als Begleittext zur Opfertafel," *ZÄS* 57 (1922): 117–19.
9. The story of Sarah in the trunk, *Genesis Rabbah* 40:5, in *Midrash Rabbah: Genesis,* trans. Harry Freedman, 10 vols. (London: Soncino 1939), 1:328–29.
10. Cf. Nibley's translation here with *Genesis Rabbah* 40:4, in Freedman, *Midrash Rabbah: Genesis,* 1:328.

11. Ibid.

12. *Genesis Apocryphon* 20:2–8.

13. Ibid., 20:7.

14. Ibid., 19:25.

15. They held an auction, each trying to buy her in order to make a gift of her to Pharaoh, *Genesis Rabbah* 40:5, in Freedman, *Midrash Rabbah: Genesis,* 1:329–30.

16. *Genesis Apocryphon* 20:11.

17. Ibid., 20:9.

18. Josephus, *Antiquities* I, 8, 1.

19. *Genesis Apocryphon* 20:12.

20. *Sefer ha-Yashar,* cited in Geza Vermes, *Scripture and Tradition in Judaism,* 2nd ed. (Leiden: Brill, 1973), 113.

21. *Genesis Apocryphon* 20:12–15.

22. Ibid., 20:12–16.

23. *Maʿaseh Abraham Abinu,* in Adolph Jellinek, *Bet ha-Midrasch,* 6 vols. (1853–77; reprint, Jerusalem: Wahrmann, 1967), 1:34.

24. *Genesis Rabbah* 41:2, in Freedman, *Midrash Rabbah: Genesis,* 1:333.

25. *Genesis Apocryphon* 20:15.

26. Bernhard Beer, *Leben Abraham's nach Auffassung der jüdischen Sage* (Leipzig: Leiner, 1859), 25, discussing sources on 128 n. 219.

27. Robert Graves and Raphael Patai, *Hebrew Myths: The Book of Genesis* (New York: McGraw-Hill, 1964), 144.

28. *Genesis Rabbah* 41:2, in Freedman, *Midrash Rabbah: Genesis,* 1:333–34.

29. Josephus, *Antiquities* I, 8, 1.

30. *Genesis Apocryphon* 20:16.

31. So Eva Osswald, "Beobachtungen zur Erzählung von Abrahams Aufenthalt in Ägypten im 'Genesis Apokryphon,'" *Zeitschrift für die alttestamentliche Wissenschaft* 72 (1960): 15, 19.

32. Micha J. bin Gorion, *Die Sagen der Juden,* 5 vols. (Frankfurt: Rütten & Loening, 1913–27), 2:158.

33. Eusebius, *Praeparatio Evangelica (Preparation for the Gospel)* IX, 17, in *PG* 21:708.

34. *Genesis Apocryphon* 20:17–18.

35. Ibid., 20:18–27.

36. Ibid., 20:21–22.

37. Ibid., 20:29.

38. Ibid., 20:30–34, cf. Louis Ginzberg, *Legends of the Jews,* 7 vols. (Philadelphia: Jewish Publication Society, 1909–1938), 1:203; cf. bin Gorion, *Sagen der Juden,* 2:97; *Maʿaseh Abraham Abinu,* in Jellinek, *Bet-ha-Midrasch,* 1:35, 41; Thaʿlabī, *Kitāb Qiṣaṣ al-Anbiyāʾ* (Cairo: Muṣṭafā al-Bābi

al-Ḥalibī wa-Awlāduhu, A.H. 1340), 55; Vermes, *Scripture and Tradition in Judaism,* 73; Beer, *Leben Abraham's,* 18; 113 n. 136.

39. F. L. Griffith, *Stories of the High Priests of Memphis* (Oxford: Clarendon, 1900), 16–19.

40. First Tale of Khamuas 3:3, in ibid., 18.

41. First Tale of Khamuas 3:5–6, in ibid.

42. Griffith, *Stories of the High Priests of Memphis,* 27.

43. Vermes, *Scripture and Tradition in Judaism,* 115 n. 2.

44. Nahman Avigad and Yigael Yadin, *A Genesis Apocryphon* [Hebrew and English] (Jerusalem: Hebrew University, 1956), 26, note that the *Genesis Apocryphon* version of the affliction and healing of Pharaoh "is actually much closer to Genesis xx, dealing with Sarah and Abimelech."

45. Bin Gorion, *Sagen der Juden,* 2:250.

46. Ginzberg, *Legends of the Jews,* 1:258.

47. Beer, *Leben Abraham's,* 45.

48. Ginzberg, *Legends of the Jews,* 1:258.

49. Beer, *Leben Abraham's,* 46–47.

50. Ginzberg, *Legends of the Jews,* 1:263.

51. Beer, *Leben Abraham's,* 128 n. 219; Ginzberg, *Legends of the Jews,* 1:224.

52. *Genesis Rabbah* 39:11, in Freedman, *Midrash Rabbah: Genesis,* 1:321.

53. Ferdinand W. Weber, *System der altsynagogalen palästinischen Theologie aus Targum, Midrasch und Talmud* (Leipzig: Dörffling & Franke, 1880), 256.

54. *Vayera* 103b, in *The Zohar,* trans. Harry Sperling and Maurice Simon, 5 vols. (London: Soncino, 1984), 1:333.

55. Josephus, *Antiquities* I, 8, 1. Sarah was ten years younger than Abraham; cf. Beer, *Leben Abraham's,* 25.

56. John Gray, *The Krt Text in the Literature of Ras Shamra,* 2nd ed. (Leiden: Brill, 1964), 2.

57. Ibid., 4.

58. Ibid., 28, lines 31, 35–36.

59. Ibid., 24, lines 86, 88–89.

60. See Hugh W. Nibley, "A New Look at the Pearl of Great Price," *IE* 72 (September 1969): 92; see John Gray, *The Legacy of Canaan* (Leiden: Brill, 1965), 25 n. 5.

61. Gray, *Krt Text,* 28, line 5.

62. Ibid., 28, lines 10–12.

63. Ibid., 28, lines 13–14, 23–24.

64. Ibid., 27, lines 26–27. The word for "do" is here *ʾeḥtrš,* meaning to perform an ordinance.

65. Ibid., 26, lines 4–12.

66. See Claas J. Bleeker, *Egyptian Festivals: Enactments of Religious Renewal* (Leiden: Brill, 1967), 37–43.

67. Ginzberg, *Legends of the Jews*, 5 n. 308; *Ma*ʿ*aseh Abraham Abinu*, in Jellinek, *Bet ha-Midrasch*, 1:32.

68. Josephus, *Antiquities* I, 10, 4.

69. So Frederick J. Foakes-Jackson, *The Biblical History of the Hebrews* (Cambridge, England: Heffer & Sons, 1917), 25, noting at the same time that Isaac is "no more than a tribe-name."

70. W. F. Albright, *Yahweh and the Gods of Canaan* (Garden City, NY: Doubleday, 1968), 147–48.

71. Gray, *Krt Text*, 10.

72. Josephus, *Antiquities* I, 8, 1; bin Gorion, *Sagen der Juden*, 2:250.

73. Gray, *Krt Text*, 5.

74. Cf. James G. Frazer, *The New Golden Bough*, ed. Theodor H. Gaster (New York: Anchor, 1961), 172–73; Claas J. Bleeker, "The Position of Queen in Ancient Egypt," in *The Sacral Kingship* (Leiden: Brill, 1959), 261–68.

75. Cyrus H. Gordon, *Before the Bible* (New York: Harper and Row, 1962), 143, 147; cf. Herbert Haag, "Der gegenwärtige Stand der Erforschung der Beziehungen zwischen Homer und dem alten Testament," *JEOL* 19 (1965–66): 517; Cyrus H. Gordon, *Ugarit and Minoan Crete* (New York: Norton, 1966), 151.

76. E. Douglas Van Buren, "The Sacred Marriage in Early Times in Mesopotamia," *Orientalia* 13 (1944): 15.

77. Beer, *Leben Abraham's*, 25.

78. William Hales, *A New Analysis of Chronology and Geography, History and Prophecy*, 4 vols. (London: Rivington, 1830), 2:111.

79. *Vayera* 112a, in Sperling and Simon, *Zohar*, 1:353.

80. Ephraim A. Speiser, "The Wife-Sister Motif in the Patriarchal Narratives," in *Biblical and Other Studies*, ed. Alexander Altmann (Cambridge: Harvard University Press, 1963), 18.

81. James L. Kelso, "Life in the Patriarchal Age," *Christianity Today* 12 (21 June 1968): 918.

82. *Genesis Apocryphon* 2:9.

83. Albright, *Yahweh and the Gods of Canaan*, 128.

84. Robert Graves, *King Jesus* (London: Cassell, 1950), 59.

85. Discussed by Beer, *Leben Abraham's*, 126–27 n. 206.

86. *Genesis Rabbah* 40:4, in Freedman, *Midrash Rabbah: Genesis*, 1:329.

87. Cf. *Genesis Apocryphon* 20:24–25.

88. Gerald Friedlander, *Pirkê de Rabbi Eliezer* (New York: Hermon, 1965), 190.

89. *Genesis Apocryphon* 20:9.

90. Ibid., 20:10.

91. Vermes, *Scripture and Tradition in Judaism*, 116.

92. *Genesis Apocryphon* 20:31–32.

93. Beer, *Leben Abraham's*, 61.

94. Ibid., 18. "Indeed, in prophetical power she ranked higher than her husband," Ginzberg, *Legends of the Jews*, 1:203.

95. Ginzberg, *Legends of the Jews*, 1:260.

96. *Genesis Apocryphon* 20:10–11.

97. Ibid., 19:21.

98. Ginzberg, *Legends of the Jews*, 1:222.

99. Thaʿlabī, *Qiṣaṣ al-Anbiyāʾ*, 223.

100. Beer, *Leben Abraham's*, 24, 127 n. 214.

101. *Genesis Apocryphon* 19:14–16.

102. See Nibley, "A New Look at the Pearl of Great Price," *IE* 72 (September 1969): 94 n. 162: In a number of cases the hospitable lotus is identified with the royal palm, suggesting the palm branch as a symbol of honorable reception.

103. *Genesis Apocryphon* 19:16.

104. Homer, *Odyssey* VIII, 461–68.

105. The story has recently been made available in paperback by Adolf Erman, *The Ancient Egyptians*, trans. Aylward M. Blackman (New York: Harper Torchbooks, 1966), 150–61.

106. Alexandre Moret, *La mise à mort du dieu en Égypte* (Paris: Geuthner, 1927), 13.

107. Bin Gorion, *Sagen der Juden*, 2:330.

108. Ginzberg, *Legends of the Jews*, 1:297.

109. Firmicus Maternus, *De Errore Profanarum Religionum (The Error of the Pagan Religions)* XIII, 1–2, in Theodor Hopfner, *Fontes Historiae Religionis Aegyptiacae* (Bonn: Marcus and Weber, 1922), 520.

110. Beer, *Leben Abraham's*, 2–3; 101 n. 18.

111. Gerhard von Rad, "Josephsgeschichte und ältere Chokma," *Vetus Testamentum*, Supplement 1 (Leiden: Brill, 1953): 120.

112. Leon Nemoy, *Karaite Anthology: Excerpts from the Early Literature* (New Haven: Yale University Press, 1952), 300.

113. *Joseph and Asenath* 15:10–11.

114. Ibid., 15:14; 16:1–11.

115. Moret, *Mise à mort du dieu en Égypte*, 51–52.

116. *Midrash on Psalms* 112:1, in *The Midrash on Psalms*, ed. William G. Braude, 2 vols. (New Haven: Yale University Press, 1959), 2:210.

117. *Lech Lecha* 94a, in Sperling and Simon, *Zohar*, 1:310.

118. Weber, *System der altsynagogalen palästinischen Theologie*, 256.

119. *Joseph and Asenath* 15:4–6.

120. *Vayera* 103b, in Sperling and Simon, *Zohar*, 1:333.

121. Gershom G. Scholem, *On the Kabbalah and Its Symbolism* (New York: Schocken, 1965), 170–72, with sources.

122. George F. Moore, *Judaism in the First Centuries of the Christian Era: The Age of the Tannaim*, 3 vols. (Cambridge: Harvard University Press, 1927), 1:538.

123. André Caquot, "L'alliance avec Abram," *Semitica* 12 (1962): 62.

124. *Teachings of the Prophet Joseph Smith*, 162.

125. Ibid., 322.

126. Ibid., 150–51.

127. Julian Morgenstern, "The 'Bloody Husband' (?) (Exod. 4:24–26) Once Again," *Hebrew Union College Annual* 34 (1963): 39.

128. Genesis 22:14; Beer, *Leben Abraham's*, 71, on the meaning of the name.

129. Vermes, *Scripture and Tradition in Judaism*, 194–95; bin Gorion, *Sagen der Juden*, 2:308.

130. Cyril of Jerusalem, *Catechesis* XIX [I], 1–11, in *PG* 33:1065–76.

131. Ibid., XX [II], 5, in *PG* 33:1081.

132. Ibid., XXI [III], 1, in *PG* 33:1088.

133. Ibid., XXIII [V], 3–4, in *PG* 33:1112.

134. Firmicus Maternus, *The Error of the Pagan Religions* 14, in *PL* 12:1012.

9

All the Court's a Stage:
Facsimile 3, a Royal Mumming

What Is Going On in Facsimile 3?

ν   The first step in identifying an ancient object is to recall and collect every known example of the document or artifact for meaningful comparison. For Facsimile 3 (fig. 49) this is a large order indeed; there are literally hundreds of Egyptian pictures resembling this one.[1] But after we have assembled the first hundred, it becomes apparent that none of them is exactly like any other. The same figures appear over and over again and in much the same attitudes, but that does not mean that they all tell the same story.

It was in regard to such compositions as our Facsimile 3 that Alan H. Gardiner observed that "somewhat similar representations" can belong "to a wholly different set of ceremonies," discernible only by the accompanying inscriptions.[2] The figures are used in various combinations to depict varying situations, and each representation must be interpreted, as one Egyptologist puts it, in the light of an accepted Egyptian "syntax" of symbols. Compositions most closely resembling Facsimile 3 are classified as (1) presentation scenes, (2) offering scenes, and (3) judgment scenes, or combinations of the same. But before taking a closer look, it is

382

Figure 49. In his woodcut of Facsimile 3, Reuben Hedlock tried to capture the complex patterns on the robes of figures 1 and 4 and the fringed and pleated garments on figures 5 and 6. The incense cone and lotus on the head of figure 5 are less distinct. The star-filled heaven above them seems appropriate to illustrate Abraham's teachings on astronomy.

important to emphasize what many Egyptologists are insisting on today as never before, namely, the folly of giving just *one* interpretation and one only to any Egyptian representation. This is the pit into which Joseph Smith's critics have always fallen: "This cannot possibly represent 'A' because it represents 'B'!" "The value of an Egyptian presentation," Eberhard Otto reminds us, "depended on seeing the *greatest possible* number of meanings in the briefest possible formulation."[3] Heretofore, critics of the Joseph Smith explanations have insisted on the *least* possible number of meanings, namely one, to every item, and as a result have not only disagreed widely among themselves, but also exposed their efforts to drastic future revision. The Egyptians "considered it a particular nicety that symbols should possess multiple significance," wrote Henri Frankfort, "that one single interpretation should not be the only possible one."[4]

We are most fortunate in possessing the doctoral thesis
of a native Egyptian Egyptologist, Ali Radwan, who has
brought together for comparison about one hundred scenes
belonging to our Facsimile 3 category. Why only a hundred?
Because he is confining himself to one dynasty, the Eighteenth, and to scenes depicting royal audiences but found
only in private, not royal, tombs. The title of the thesis is
"Representations of the Ruling King and Members of His
Family in the Private Tombs of the Eighteenth Dynasty."[5]
Though the royal audience scene (and all the scenes are
"audiences" like our Facsimile 3)[6] is presented with characteristic variations in each period of Egyptian history, the
situation depicted is a timeless one, recognizable from
pre-dynastic monuments on down to the latest times—a
welcome consistency, since we do not know Abraham's
dates.[7] The audience scenes collected by Radwan are not
funerary; all take place during the lifetime of the pharaoh
and the tomb owner,[8] and the owner of the tomb who com-
missions the mural or relief is always personally involved
in the event.[9] Though the pictures are found in tombs and
are sometimes thought of as projected into the reaches of
eternity,[10] they all record a very real and happy party at the
palace, to which the tomb owner is invited; it is the high
point in his life, and the picture is like a photograph taken
to immortalize the moment of his closest proximity to
Pharaoh:[11] "Zealous scribes make a permanent record of the
events of the celebration" even as they happen.[12] The writings are transcribed to imperishable stone, inscriptions that
accompany the pictures describing the event and recording
memorable speeches and conversations on the occasion, for
the edification of posterity.

The purpose of the audience is to honor the tomb owner
in recognition of services of a wide variety. Thus when we
see Pharaoh in the presence of the court honoring an official
whose efficiency has brought in a bumper grain harvest to

Figure 50. Tomb of Khaemhet. Starting in the upper right register, an incense cone is placed on Khaemhet's head, and he is invested with the "gold of honor" necklace before appearing in the presence of his pharaoh (cf. Gen. 41:42). Finally Amenophis III, protected by the sun (which holds an ankh to his nose; see fig. 62, pp. 406–07) and enthroned in majesty under the royal canopy, congratulates him on his agricultural success to general rejoicing by the court. Depicted the same size as the king, Khaemhet bows his head in acknowledgment—but not to the same degree as the courtiers behind him.

the royal storehouses, we inevitably think of Joseph in Egypt (cf. fig. 50).[13] Surprisingly, the atmosphere is not one of overpowering majesty, but of cheerful intimacy. "Intimate contact with the king was an essential to a proper biography," Radwan assures us.[14] Intimacy is the keynote. Even the constant reminders of coronation motifs, the *Sed* festival, and the New Year's celebration only heighten the atmosphere of warmth and friendliness, for that was the time for the family open house with the exchanging of gifts among people of every class and connection.[15] With personal contact at a premium, immediate servants of the palace enjoyed a special, we might say, and unfair advantage (*le Roi m'a vu!*), and though high officials are not to be denied their claims on the king, by far the great majority of the tomb owners who enjoy the attention of the royal family are servants of the palace, especially butlers—"principal waiters." It is therefore completely in order to find the main subject in our Facsimile 3 to be one "Shulem, one of the king's principal waiters," without whom we never would have gotten this particular story.

A conspicuous, almost unfailing, element in the picture is the festive but formal bouquet, usually of lotus or papyrus, either carried or placed on a stand as in our Facsimile 3—a symbol of acceptance and welcome ("Abraham in Egypt"), whose significance we treat below.

From the beginning, the main problem of the exultant tomb owner was how to indicate the real presence of Pharaoh mingling in the man's private affairs without being guilty of *lèse majesté*—the king is never directly pictured in scenes from the Old and Middle Kingdoms.[16] At first the famous *ḥtp dj nsw* formula, "a boon from the King," alone served to indicate the royal presence.[17] Next, as tomb owners risked "growing intimacy," the king's name appeared in the inscriptions reporting his presence on the scene.[18] After that, his royal cartouches in all their formal splendor indicated that he was really there.[19] Finally the king himself is portrayed, seated on a throne under a kiosk.[20] This is a standard scene in which the seated figure is being honored by a number of standing figures, usually three or four, though it may include, besides the tomb owner and the king, members of the owner's family as well as the king's family, the owner's friends, and the king's friends, besides which "there are always spectators,"[21] including officials, servants, guards, grooms, fanbearers, etc., in a surprising variety of combinations, no two exactly alike. Naturally the king sits while the others stand, but there are exceptions, almost exclusively in the case of *teachers*,[22] always shown in the act of teaching, which permit the revered mentor to sit while his youthful charge, in full royal regalia, stands before him.[23] The edifying scene goes clear back to the Old Kingdom.[24] Occasionally foreigners, especially Asiatics, are summoned to appear both to give obeisance and to receive "the breath of life" from the presence of Pharaoh.[25] When such are present, the tomb owner appears as one employed in the foreign service (fig. 51), since no matter how exotic the scene, the tomb owner had to have a reason for being in personal attendance.[26]

In the little dramas presented by the small and limited number of stock figures, props, and gestures used, we see "King and commoner standing together in the presence of Osiris, or the owner of the stele standing before two queens, or the King standing as an intercessor between the praying tomb owner and a divinity."[27] "As a rule the King is seated in his Kiosk," or later, standing at the Window of Appearances alone or accompanied by others, either human or divine. It may be significant that figure 1 in our Facsimile 3 has no kiosk or window; a brief sampling will suffice to indicate the range of possible interpretations to such a drawing (see figs. 52–63).

If we were to insert Facsimile 3 into the hundreds of scenes just like it available from the whole reach of Egyptian archaeology and ask an expert to interpret it along with the rest, he would, as we now realize, have to take quite a number of things into consideration. Let us look at some of them.

Take figure 1 in Facsimile 3, for example: This is obviously Osiris in royal attire, but a recent study of that familiar personage admonishes us that "one must never forget" that "there is such a variety of representations of Osiris with the crook, flail, and $w3s$-scepter . . . that no certain identification

Figure 51. Tomb of Nebamun, 90. The scribe Nebamun sits on his lion-
footed chair, his pen case and papyrus carrying-tube under it, receiving
flowers and food offerings. As a representative of Pharaoh, he deals with
the foreigners who come to trade in Egypt. A bearded Asiatic sheikh is

is possible," unless the picture is accompanied by a written
text.[28] It is only by the aid of specific *written labels*, another
commentator asserts, that they can *tell* which god is which,
what the context of the drama is, and just what activity is
being indicated.[29] "In all of these books," writes Natacha
Rambova, "the process is always the same, but it is

seated in his presence, an honor accorded him in deference to his rank. The colorful dress of the sheikh's wife is carefully reproduced. Servants and children in Canaanite clothing bring their trade goods to be recorded and shipped upriver on the Nile as shown in the top and bottom registers.

described or portrayed variously as seen from different angles of significance," while accompanying texts convey "a picture of many analogies and intricate patterns of relationship."[30] Which episode of which story does a particular picture present? It all depends—let no scholar attempt to tell us once and for all what Facsimile 3 really

Figure 52. Tomb of Amunuser. Thutmosis III, wearing the Osiris insignia, including the Atef crown, is enthroned in a high kiosk. In addition to its usual form, the crown is flanked by protective uraei wearing the cow horns and sun of the goddess Hathor. The same kind of horns entwine with a pair of horizontal ram's horns as well as a pair of unusual downward-curving ram's horns. All three pairs of horns emerge from the sacred *nemes* headcloth, another unusual feature. Before the king stands the owner's father (with his son and three courtiers, not shown). A lively discussion is going on, which ends with the king's permitting the old vizier—shown wearing the archaic robes of his office—to resign and be replaced by his son, a scribe.

Figure 53. Tomb of Rekhmire. Amunuser's nephew Rekhmire eventually became vizier to Thutmosis III as well. The pharaoh sits in his kiosk dressed in an elaborate feather-patterned robe (cf. Fac. 3, fig. 1; see fig. 49, p. 383) with the Atef crown, this time with an unusual Horus falcon spreading its wings protectively around the crown from the back. The pharaoh's Ka or double stands behind him crowned with his Horus name and holding the royal standard in one hand and the Maat feather in the other, in a pose very similar to that in his uncle's tomb. The pharaoh gives the assembled court a lecture on government, which is recorded in this representation, celebrating the installation of the famous vizier.

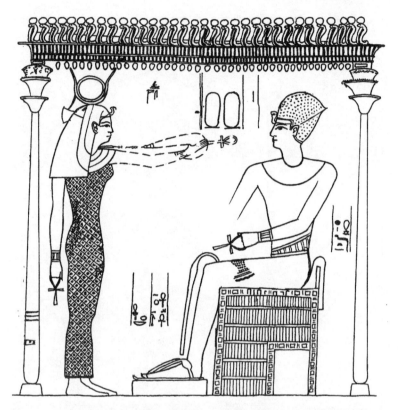

Figure 54. Tomb of Thanuro. King Amenophis II is enthroned under a kiosk, his name on the wall and his *wife* standing in the kiosk as the goddess *Hathor*. Radwan is at a loss to explain "in what connection and performing what function she appears in the kiosk before the King." Though simply painted and not as elaborate as other examples, this scene shows the flexibility possible in these compositions. She may be offering a menat necklace to her husband as in figure 55, opposite.

represents. Even the exact date and location of a document give no sure clue to its identity, for the things were often handed around, like the Ramesseum Papyrus, which, though belonging originally to a great pharaoh, comes to us from the library of a private citizen who lived two hundred

Figure 55. Tomb of . . . , overseer of horses. King Thutmosis IV is in his kiosk; a woman dressed as Hathor offers him a menat necklace and ankh, the symbol of life. Behind her the tomb owner holds two large bouquets of papyrus in full bloom. In two lower registers Asiatics bring tribute to the foot of the throne steps "from the Lords of Naharina"—Abraham's neighbors on the scene.

years later, while the actual content of the thing belongs clear back in the First Dynasty. Such considerations are important where Abraham is concerned. And since Facsimiles 1 and 3 are ritual scenes, we must bear in mind what Gardiner wrote about the Ramesseum scenario: "To me, above all things, it seems salutary to be reminded of the one-sidedness and incompleteness of our sources. . . . How tantalizingly the dramatic text edited by Sethe introduced

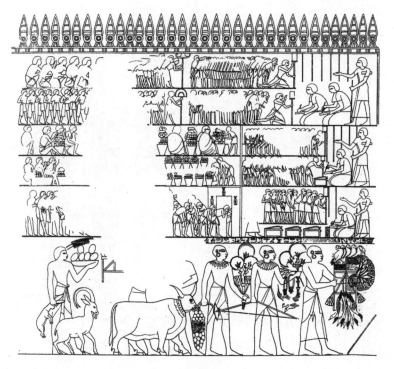

Figure 56. Tomb of Haremheb, royal scribe. The living King Thutmosis IV is in the kiosk with Maat standing behind him like Hathor, as in other scenes (cf. Fac. 3, fig. 2; see fig. 49, p. 383). The tomb owner brings flowers;

us to coronation rites of which the conventional sources betrayed not a single glimpse."[31] So we must be prepared for unconventional as well as conventional sources. To understand what an Egyptian document is trying to convey, nay, "to grasp even the simplest situations," according to Philippe Derchain, requires comparison of all possible parallel texts, rigorous analysis of every detail, and an intimate dictionary knowledge of each word.[32]

It becomes apparent with the first glance at Facsimile 3 that we have here nothing like a *portrait* of Abraham or

in a lower register six men, three of them his brothers, bring flowers and sacrificial animals "for the Ka of the King," the figure standing behind the king in figures 52 and 53. This is unique; such sacrifice is not found elsewhere.

anybody else. Well, don't expect such: of countless portraits of individuals on funeral stelae, "out of most of the stelae we can only guess the sex, sometimes at the approximate age of the individual";[33] even the magnificent royal portraits are not portraits, according to a recent study: The Egyptians at all times avoid trying to depict personalities and at all times prefer static representation in which only the sketchiest indication is enough to evoke the ideal behind the appearance,[34] yet another study affirms that it is only "by an

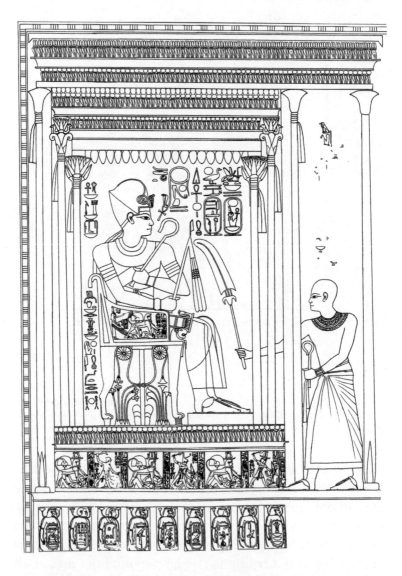

Figure 57. Tomb of Surer, chief steward. In this tomb the king is shown three times with Surer standing behind him. In this particular scene the king is receiving him; Surer stands on the steps flanked by lions and

hawk-headed sphinxes (cf. Solomon's throne in 1 Kings 10:20) offering symbolic but real gifts: a divine staff and a pectoral necklace with the king's name on it.

Figure 58. Tomb of Kheruef, steward to Queen Tiye. The king and queen sit in the kiosk; Kheruef brings gifts of elaborate jewelry. In the register behind him are nine figures representing the "Friends of Pharaoh" and his entourage. At the top right the king makes offerings to an Osiris

statue, whose head is the Djed pillar. In the bottom register boatmen pull their skiffs piled high with food through papyrus thickets next to a scene of butchering an ox in which the first cut or "Royal Haunch" is removed (see fig. 85, pp. 500–501).

Figure 59. Tomb of the vizier Ramose. Amenophis IV, wearing the blue
Khepresh crown, sits in the kiosk with Maat (cf. Fac. 3, fig. 4; see fig. 49,
p. 383), "the Daughter of Re, at home in the palace, Mistress of Heaven,
Mistress of the Gods, may she give millions of years," symbolized by the
notched palm rib she is holding. Before them the owner appears *four*

effort of imagination on our part," deliberately blocking out
our aesthetic reactions, that we can achieve "the most
authentic contact with the document."[35] Instead of being
upset by this, the critics now see the wisdom of it; as
Samuel G. F. Brandon puts it, speaking of a typical ritual
scene like Facsimile 3: "Despite the bizarre iconography . . .

times, dressed in archaic robes (see fig. 52, p. 390). Three of the four depictions hold ram- and hawk-headed staffs of the gods. Four texts explain that he is offering bouquets from Amun, meaning that the flowers offered were first obtained from the Temple Amun.

the great spiritual significance of the idea which inspired it must be patent to all who contemplate it."[36]

Turning to the basic composition of our Facsimile 3, we find a standard situation in which a man or woman is being introduced by another person to an august personage who is seated. This is the minimum cast for an offering scene, a judgment, or a presentation. It is familiar from hundreds of

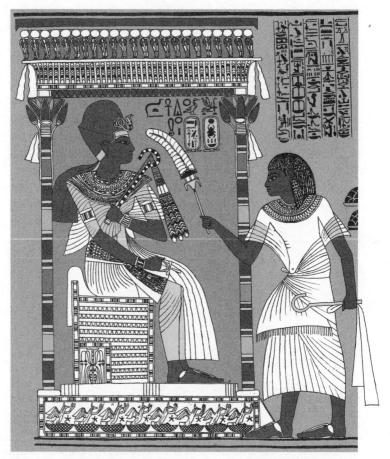

Figure 60. Tomb of Huy. Tutankhamun sits in the kiosk; before him
stands Huy in Osiris regalia. On the bottom right, Canaanite princes in
brilliantly colored robes kneel with tribute to Huy, the "King's Son of
Cush." Huy the Blessed says to the king: "Thou art Re, thy image is his

funerary stelae where the usual theme is the bringing of a
food offering to the person on the chair. But among these
are many in which both the food and the offering formula
are missing, emphasis being placed on the presentation of
the individual to royalty as a mark of special honor.

image [a religious pun on the royal name]. Thou art the sky on its four supports. . . . The Lord of Retenu come to thee . . . asking for the bread of life." It is Huy, not the king, who wears the royal white robes of Osiris.

Sometimes the person on the throne is a god, sometimes a king, sometimes the owner of the stele himself, receiving members of his own household. Sometimes the same scene is repeated at two or three different levels, the same reception being dramatized in heaven, on earth, and in the underworld, all at the same time! It is usual for various

F.   E.

Figure 61. Tomb of Neferhotep. Horemheb the king (A), standing in regalia and accompanied by two attendants (B), gives an address while leaning on a large cushion. May, the royal treasurer (C), stands before him with two men dressed as viziers (D) bowing behind him. Neferhotep, with upraised arms (E), is being adorned and anointed by two

members of the family still living on earth to be shown as present on these occasions, which take on the festive air of a cheerful family celebration, with various sons and daughters, etc., crowned with cones of party scent, bearing huge festive lotuses or bouquets for the happy event.

Who's Who?

In Facsimile 3 the person on the throne is indeed Osiris, and yet he is here supposed to be a normal human being. As everyone knows, the deceased in Egyptian funerary

D. C.   A.   B.

servants. He is called "the Father-in-Law of Amun," that is, the king's father-in-law. He leaves with another king's father-in-law, to be received by his *own* father (F). The strange scene is described in the inscription. This unusual composition implies that it was a specific event Neferhotep wanted to preserve for eternity.

texts is regularly designated as "the Osiris So-and-So," but how far does this identity go, and how literal was it supposed to be? It once puzzled scholars greatly: If this constant exchange, mixing, shifting of identification of persons happens on every page of the written text, so as to make our heads whirl, why should we expect perfectly logical unilinear consistency in the drawing?[37] But Derchain finds in that very freedom of exchange "an admirable logic," deserving the serious study it has not yet received.[38] At the center of Egyptian religion, Rudolf Anthes observes, was

Figure 62. Tomb of Huya, Amarna 1. Ankhenaton and Nefertiti are greeted by their daughters as they receive blessings from the hands of the sun; on the right, Amenophis III sits facing Queen Tiye with her daughter

not a dogmatic certitude (such as Joseph Smith's critics insist on); instead we find what he describes as a sort of marvelously interwoven and ever-shifting arabesque.[39] Ulrich Luft finds even the oddest drawings "always moving" because of the pure idealization that lies behind them.[40] What we have in these free but conventional drawings is "unbridled chains of associations and conclusions," according to Frankfort,[41] to deal with which "we must attempt to hear the resonance of this polyphony of meaning."[42] And more recently Otto insists that "we must be prepared to recognize a mysterious plurality of meaning (*geheimnissvolle Vieldeutigkeit*)" in these things, which is found "in its purest and most secret form" in the temple, but even there in rites of an "undogmatic universal religious sense."[43] We may see in our Facsimile 3 what Robert Hari perceives in a composition much like it (fig. 64), "one more example of the Egyptian taste for playing with analogies."[44] Rigid interpretation becomes even less satisfactory when we consider, with Wolfgang Helck, that through the centuries "old designations (*Bezeichnungen*), formulas, and rites, while

and three of her ladies-in-waiting. The presence of the king, who has long been dead, is puzzling to Radwan. It shows the eternity of family ties and the eternal nature of the things done here.

retaining their verbal form (*Wortlaut*) intact, change their inner meaning."[45]

Over a century ago Edouard Naville observed "that there is nothing harder than to recognize the distinctive marks of each individual deity" in an Egyptian picture, for while "every divinity has specific emblems which are like ideograms of his particular qualities,"[46] these are swapped around with a total indifference toward the individual gods, the distinctions between them having become almost expunged by the process of equating, equalizing, interpenetrating, as names, forms, powers all become confused in a common basic nature which is the mark of the Egyptian gods. Jan Bergman defines the process as one of proximity, association, fusion, and finally complete identification.[47] Within the past year Naville's view has been confirmed in a study of that anonymous God who reveals the proper way of life (*Lebenslehren*), and who has no other name but "God" (*Ntr*) and can be designated indiscriminately as singular or plural; he is almighty, omniscient, hidden, and righteous; he is Creator, Ruler, Judge, and Sustainer; he

Figure 63. Tomb of Hekerneheh, nurse of the king's son. This scene shows a teacher, the owner's father, seated in a high-backed chair holding little Thutmosis IV, in his full regalia, on his lap, "the eldest beloved son of the king, who became the Lord of the Two Lands." The teacher is called "the attendant of the king in every place, praised by the people of the palace, the Father of the God, Guardian of the God, Beloved of the Ruler, Educator of the King's Oldest, Dearest Son." In the upper register the prince wears on his breast a tablet with the name of his father, thus showing that in him the teacher is dealing with the king himself.

requires man's worship, obedience, and trust.[48] Yet everything about him is "unspecific," so that he is freely identified with the king, the sun-god, or any other god, and at every local shrine was identified with the local divinity and "looked upon as the all-embracing divine power, . . . the embodiment of divinity per se"; in short, he is "any god one pleases."[49]

With things so wide open, it is not surprising that

C.   B.   A.   D.   E.   F.

Figure 64. An elegantly carved stele of Pharaoh Horemheb found at
Karnak depicts Amun-Ra "King of the Gods" (A) with Mut "Mistress of
Heaven" (B) gently touching his shoulder. Their son, Khonsu of Thebes
(C), holds the composite staff of *ankh, djed,* and *wes* scepter with the crook
and flail. Horemheb (D) offers flowers to the gods with a lioness-headed
goddess (E) supporting him. She is "Great of Magic"; she may be Isis as
well as Sekhmet since it is not specified in the inscription. The Nile god
Hapy (F), shown with female breasts and a large male paunch, brings the
abundance of the river as an offering.

mortals also get into the act. The absorption of the individual into the essence and image of a god in the funerary context was noted from the very beginning.[50] But more specifically, in representations such as Facsimile 3 we are often reminded of the possibility of finding ourselves on any one or all of *three levels* of existence by what might be called "the rule of three." "The logicality of the Egyptian mind is one of its most striking aspects," wrote Gardiner, "and nothing is more remarkable than the impartiality with which the living, the dead, and the gods were regarded. *Men, gods, dead . . .* indicate a hierarchical classification of human and superhuman beings. . . . All three classes had the same needs and were treated in the same manner. . . . In actual fact temple, tomb, and house of the living all bore strong resemblance to one another."[51] In two important books Alexandre Moret demonstrated at length the fundamental principle (1) that the rites of palace, temple, and tomb are essentially the same; (2) that the same ordinances are performed in heaven, earth, and underworld, and (3) by the living, the dead, and the immortals; and (4) that god, king, and commoner are all engaged in the same ritual activities at different levels.[52] The power of the gods was "short circuited," as Georges Posener puts it, and "became a faculty of the King; he became their substitute and so identified himself with them."[53] In the other direction, as "Horus the heir of Geb, possessed by his father,"[54] the pharaoh was also the type and model for *all* men,[55] so an *ordinary Egyptian* can pray "that he be permitted to enter eternity . . . and behold the One Lord of All seated upon his Great Throne," and "to receive the crown which the god condescends to hand down to him," which glory in turn he shall hand on to his own children, who "shall be established" upon his throne in his "offices of eternity."[56] "On every page they confound the human Osiris-N [i.e., the deceased] with the god Osiris," wrote Louis Speleers with annoyance; "this confusion was deliberate and should not disturb the reader who is prepared for it. . . . Useless to seek for an explanation, . . . [it lies] in the derangement of their brains."[57] This is the cheapest of all explanations; there must be something better.

Who Is Sitting on My Throne?

The formula "You shall do what Osiris did, for you are he who is upon his throne,"[58] implies that "the throne 'makes' the king."[59] "The throne made manifest a divine power which changed one of several princes into a king fit to rule."[60] When the king or his substitute rises from the lion couch, having overcome the powers of death (Facsimile 1) at the *Sed* festival, it is the throne rather than the man that is acclaimed as he seats himself upon it.[61] *Which* throne one sits on makes no difference, for there is only one, the archetypal throne of heaven, earth, and underworld.[62] But who would sit on Pharaoh's own throne while he was alive and standing by? "No Pharaoh of Egypt," cried one of Joseph Smith's learned critics, "would have resigned his throne, even temporarily, to Abraham or any other person—hence . . . this would be an 'impossible occurrence.' "[63] But it has since been shown that there was ample precedent in Egypt for just such an event.

It goes back to the very ancient title of "*Rpꜥt* on the Throne of Geb," Geb the earth-god representing the principle of royal *patriarchal* succession here below. As Helck has unraveled it, we may begin with the *Sed* festival, marking the end of one reign and the beginning of another in a single rite: The old king is dead on the scene—it is his funeral—but his successor has not yet ascended the throne, which is therefore still his. Because of his condition, however, somebody must act for the late king until the new one takes over, and that one is the *Rpꜥt*—originally the son himself "in his expectation of the throne," in his role of Horus and therefore "like his father a descendant of Geb."[64]

Following the example of the *Sed* rites, the prince could represent his father on various missions, bearing the title "for specific assignments as substitute (*Stellvertreter*) for the king, authorized to give commands" in his name, and called the Son of Geb to proclaim his legitimate station.[65] With the growing business of the empire the king would need more substitutes than one, and at a very early time important court officials not of royal blood were detailed to represent royalty on various missions and given the title in a "truly patriarchal" spirit to show they were acting for the king and as the king.[66] The great Imhotep, a man of genius but for all that a commoner, held the title of *Rpˁt* on the Throne of Geb in the Third Dynasty;[67] that other wise man, Amenophis son of Hapu, boasts that he played "*rpˁt* in the drama of the Sed festival,"[68] even as the official Ikhernofret had the honor of being the king's understudy in playing the role of Horus.[69]

"By Politeness of the King" (Facsimile 3, Figure 1)

The title of *Rpˁt* placed its bearer on the king's own throne, and the royal insignia went with it. Pharaoh would bestow his very personal *shen*-ring, which proclaimed his supreme rule over all upon which the sun looked down, on trusted officials going forth to speak for him in distant parts.[70] There was an element of risk in trusting others so far, and cases are known of men who seized the crown by exploiting the office of *Rpˁt*.[71] Hence it was a mark of supreme honor to receive such a token of royal confidence, and its bestowal at all times depended on one thing alone— the good pleasure of the gracious king. In his divine calling all things belonged to him and were held by others only as his stewards.[72] As Ibrahim Harari points out, "the conception of legality" rested on "the principle of extension of the personal control of the king. The law was personal and centralized in essence."[73] There was no limit to what could be given and no questioning of the right to bestow whatsoever gifts and honors it pleased "the politeness of the King" to distribute to whom he would.[74] Moreover, Pharaoh not only could but did endow commoners with holy office and power, as when the Vizier Rekhmire claims "a participation in the divine privileges of the King,"[75] or when the royal Intendant Rensi in the story of the Eloquent Peasant, "by participating in the King," as François Daumas puts it, "participates in Re himself. He *is* by participation, Re himself."[76] It was as a chosen representative of Pharaoh that the officiating priest in every temple "*is* the king in person, . . . as son and successor of the gods," not as a mere substitute, but by Egyptian thinking, he is "the Pharaoh himself."[77] And foreigners from Abraham's country were not excluded from such glory, as the story of Abraham's own great-grandson makes clear, so that according to the legends, it was hard to tell when the king rode forth with his vizier whether the people were cheering him or his minister.[78]

Is the man on the throne in the Osiris regalia king or commoner, living or dead, human or divine? In the Ramesseum drama the king's robe "is at one and the same time the mourning cloak of the living king and the personification of the dead king."[79] Siegfried Schott found it virtually impossible to tell whether the characters in tomb reliefs are supposed to be alive or dead, whether the scenes are in this world or below;[80] it is equally difficult to distinguish a festival from a funeral, or a public from a private rite.[81] The transmission of royal authority combines terrestrial and celestial glory, Osirian and solar, in a single figure.[82] The deep pits that interrupt the passages to royal tombs of the Old Kingdom are now viewed as places of mourning *and* rejoicing, of burial and rebirth, where the king is enclosed in the womb, and waters of the underworld, even as he emerges as the rising sun from the waters of life.[83] A recent reexamination of the tomb of Pepi I finds "mournful yet joyous rites in progress," as the king seats himself on the throne to achieve heights of "stellar immortality" at the moment he touches the *depths* of the abyss.[84] "Such tensions," the investigator remarks, "deserve to be investigated,"[85] though it is next to impossible for the modern student to avoid, in Bergman's words, "undermining this doctrine of the Double Nature by our modern logic."[86]

Inasmuch as we are asked to view Facsimile 3 as an illustration of an episode in the life of Abraham, let us see where testing it as such will get us. First of all, we note that this is the stock way of representing anybody in a position of power and glory. That is how the king appears at the *Sed* festival, how he appears in glory either living or dead, how he is shown at his coronation and while being crowned as Osiris at his funeral, for "it is plain that the cult of the dead is closely associated with the other cults."[87] In lively parties (no funeral cult!) when Cleopatra appeared as the New Isis (cf. Facsimile 3, figure 2), her companion Marc Anthony "in Egyptian eyes had to be Osiris" (our figure 1).[88] With "a steady thinning out of the barrier between the defunct as Osiris and the actual god Osiris," even the ordinary person came to be shown as Osiris in funerary documents.[89] It began, of course, with the king as Osiris in heaven, earth, and underworld, "sitting on his very throne . . . doing what Osiris is wont to do among the . . . Imperishable Stars."[90] His son assumes the identical aspect while serving his father enthroned on earth, in heaven, and in the underworld—the last of these being the situation with which figure 1 types are normally identified.[91] But the *ordinary* Egyptian assumes the same garb of royalty and divinity as at an early time "royal crowns and scepters began to appear among the objects depicted in the coffins of commoners," in what Frankfort calls "a wholesale usurpation by common men" of "the immense prestige of the royal prerogatives."[92] Ordinary individuals would borrow, "apparently without a

qualm, many of the Pyramid Texts, including their implications of royalty."[93] It was a game anybody could play—one
gathers the impression that the compilers of the Book of the
Dead included any religious material suitable for recitation
as a spell regardless of its contents.[94] So let no one exclude
the man Abraham from the majestic seat of figure 1 on the
grounds of his being but an ordinary mortal.

One Big Family

The three worlds are kept in mind in every situation, in
what Gertrud Thausing calls "a constant repetition of the
same drama" in a series of "concentric circles."[95] Each level
reflects the others: "the king is a revelation of the godhead
which he incorporates," and "through everything that happens, behind the human performance . . . the divine must
clearly shine through."[96] This prepares us for what we find
in the memorial stelae on which scenes resembling our
Facsimile 3 are commonest. Take the stele of Apeni (fig. 65),
"pharaoh's chief boatman": "In the upper register," writes
Harry R. H. Hall, "Apeni, followed by *his* father . . . and his
mother, Taye, offers to Osiris," an Osiris who exactly resembles our figure 1, behind whom is seated our figure 2,
"Isis with the headdress of Hathor."[97] In the middle register
Apeni is offering food and drink to two august couples at a
party, and in the lower register Apeni himself is seated with
his sister (wife) to receive an offering from a servant. But at
every level it is a family affair; the basic pattern of ritual in
Egypt, Moret demonstrated, was the *culte familial,* the doctrine of the family being but the echo of the royal and divine
pattern (doctrine).[98] The carefully kept genealogies, from
Pharaoh to day laborer,[99] and the enigmatic ordinances of
sealing one's family to be joyfully reunited in the next
world, simply underscore the obvious fact that the Egyptian
loves nothing so much as scenes and reminders of the
happy family circle. A striking feature of the palace art of

Figure 65. This stele of Apeni, chief boatman, shows the variety of gatherings, divine and domestic, enjoyed by the Egyptians.

the Amarna period and the tomb of Tutankhamun is the seemingly incongruous combination of divine majesty with the cozy intimacy of family fun. The royal family charades were carried down to the courts of the Ptolemies, with their mingling of intimate play, theatrical splendor, and the allure of the Egyptian mysteries.[100] On the question of whether the playing of games can be reconciled with solemn ordinances, some recent studies have yielded interesting results. †

In 1973 Kate Bosse-Griffiths pointed out that domestic scenes from the household of Tutankhamun are beyond any doubt intimate, playful, informal, quite charming. "All these objects show the young king and his queen in a variety of actions which apparently have nothing to do with funerary themes. . . . On the whole, the inclination has been to interpret the scenes in a domestic sense."[101] But while nearly all students have noted their charming informality, Bosse-Griffiths's study shows conclusively that they are also ritual scenes, all, in fact, suggesting a *coronation*; indeed, she concludes, "it seems likely that all 'intimate' scenes of the King and Queen are representations of happenings during the coronation"(fig. 66).[102] The persistent recurrence of the coronation motif in the rites of temple, palace, and tomb is fully illustrated in Moret's collection of materials, but the study of Hari surprises us with interesting confirmation of Bosse-Griffiths's findings, when he affirms that the exalted rites of the coronation were actually the subject of regular family-night fun in the palace, as "scenes of the intimate domestic life of the royal family" show them renewing the coronation rites in private, with the queen functioning as the high priest.[103] We are reminded of Hatshepsut's account of how her father made love to her mother in the disguise of the god Amon, with "attendant priests . . . masked to represent his fellow-deities."[104] In the New Kingdom coronation game, "inside the shrine" the king consorts with *Wr.t-Ḥkꜣw* the goddess (the Coronation Lady), while "on the outside"

A.   A.

it is the queen whom he embraces.[105] Such masking and mumming in the manner of Hellenistic, Oriental, and medieval courts (down to the nineteenth century) meets us in the hoary Egyptian Pyramid Texts full-blown in scenes very reminiscent of our Facsimile 3.[106]

Should the popular image of the Egyptian rulers as the last word in lofty, mysterious, morose, and inaccessible majesty cast doubt on the new picture, we have only to remember Sinuhe's story of how the royal children and even the queen let out happy shrieks of amazement and surprise and had the time of their lives when they recognized their old friend Sinuhe in rugged desert Asiatic garb entering the palace. Because many years had elapsed since his departure, and the children who knew him would have grown up, the story stretches the imagination; but that is permitted since this is the sort of palace life the Egyptians loved. The treasures of Tutankhamun alone make that clear. The common boast of great ones in their autobiographies is not the recognition and office they achieve so much as the measure of love and affection they enjoy in the royal family and in their own. Strother Purdy calls our attention to the picture on an Egyptian offering table "showing a parallel to the scene of intercession at the court in Sinuhe," attesting the reality of such celebrations and giving "evidence of popular participation in an association of the being of the king with a hope for the afterlife."[107] In the Sinuhe picture we see "the queen as goddess . . . as Nofru . . . and as

Figure 66. This is the rear of a small golden shrine found in Tutankhamun's tomb. On each of its twelve panels, Queen Ankhsenamun ministers to her husband in a wide variety of activities, frequently as a priestess. In the upper register the "Great Heiress" anoints his arm from the incense cone on the tray she holds in her left hand. In the lower register she advances to her enthroned husband, carrying two palm ribs from which hang symbols of kingly rejuvenation. Ankhsenamun's title, Beloved of "Great of Magic," an epithet of Isis (A), indicates her great authority.

Hathor-Nut, protectress in the afterlife," though very much alive, while "the royal children, enacting the role of Hathor priestesses, intercede for him by invoking the goddess."[108] Everybody is in the act, taking the part of some divinity or other, and everybody has fun: "in language that mixes divine with human reference," the scene at court is for Sinuhe a return to an order of eternal joy and youth. The court is a foretaste of heaven.[109] For the Egyptian the family circle is the nearest thing to heaven on earth—and it takes everybody in.

Mystique of the Mask

The common binding element between god, king, and ordinary mortal was priesthood and ordinance. At the coronation the officiating priest "was absolutely thought of as the embodiment of the god himself,"[110] and on other ritual occasions the priest embodied the king as a substitute king to whom all power is delegated—he is "the Pharaoh himself."[111] Substitution and dramatization—mumming and *masking*—make it possible to accept quite readily the shifting of roles and identities that is so Egyptian (fig. 67); there was a distinct understanding that while the ultimate reality of things was to be found in a higher world, men prepared for it by going through the motions.[112] Who is to say to what degree an actor or a Hopi Kachina-dancer identifies himself here below with the mask he wears? As early as the First

Figure 67. This sacred procession from the temple of Denderah depicts a priest wearing an Anubis head mask being guided by his fellow priest behind him (A). In a drawing from six centuries later in Rome (B), a shaven Egyptian priest stands before a pedestal displaying an Anubis mask, the neck of which has a little door for visibility. The only surviving example of a real Anubis mask is this one in pottery (C), so heavy that it rested on the shoulders. The wearer would have had difficulty seeing out of its small eye holes. Whether mask or puppet, this seven-inch-high wooden jackal's head (D) had the added feature of a moving jaw closed by pulling a string.

A.

B.

C.

D.

Dynasty the rites were dramatized with "an astoundingly
variegated" cast of gods played by disguised humans,[113]
while "the number of masked priests and priestesses in
the late New Kingdom is bewildering, and that number
increases in the Ptolemaic and Roman times."[114] Just as
Pharaoh "while wearing the insignia was regarded as the
actual deity,"[115] so important men boast in their autobiographical inscriptions of having dressed up for various
ritual parts. One boasts that he took various parts in the *Sed*
festival, that he "took the part of the 'Beloved Son' . . . in the
mysteries of the Lord of Abydos."[116] Another man is depicted
curiously dressed up in a semi-royal costume, without the
uraeus and holding the royal Osiride insignia (fig. 68; cf.
Facsimile 3, figure 1).[117] The fact "that a person or cult-object
during the changing phases of the rite can play a number of
different roles" offers, as Bergman notes, "no difficulty to
the 'logical' religious thinking of the Egyptians."[118] Figure 1
in Facsimile 3 can be either god, king, or human, since
everything is "saturated with the religious cult of the
Osirian mysteries," at every level,[119] and there is "a general
resemblance of costume and insignia" between the king and
Osiris even when taken independently.[120]

Contemporary research is laying increasing emphasis
on the coronation as the primal nucleus of all the ritual
dramatization. It was carried out by masked priests representing gods;[121] the play could be taken on tour throughout
the land[122] or repeated daily in the temples in a "small, con-
densed version of the coronation ceremony."[123] Kurt Sethe
describes the Ramesseum drama as "a festival play of ceremonial character . . . a mimetic presentation with the king
in the principal roles, an authentic mystery play," with the
enthronement (the bestowal of power—and glory) as its
theme.[124] We still do not know the plot of the play, according to Frankfort, because "the Mystery Play of the Succession presents us with an undifferentiated sequence of

Figure 68. The stele of Khabekhnet shows Horakhty in the boat of the sun traveling through the heavens. The goddess Hathor, "Mistress of Heaven and All Lands," emerges as a cow from the mountains of the west. Before her stands her priest with the title "He who knoweth how to see." Surprisingly, he is depicted as a young figure dressed in royal Osiris regalia with the side lock of braided hair of a royal prince or *sem*-priest.

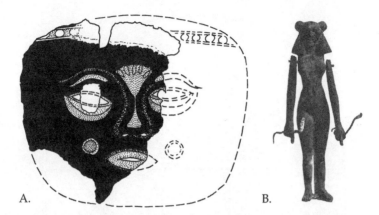

Figure 69. Though fragmentary and highly stylized, this is one of the few
surviving cartonnage masks (A) used in religious ceremonies. This small
wooden statue (B) with articulated arms shows a woman wearing the
mask of the goddess Beset. When the statue was carried, the arms would
have moved as if she were dancing.

scenes concerned with 'divine things,'" in which we are still
in the dark as to the plan and the aim of the action.[125]

Another study by Bosse-Griffiths suggests games of
masking the royal family when it calls attention both to cartonnage Bes-mask(s) worn by impersonators of male or
female Bes, a comic dancing deity, and a number of Beset
amulets. "I should like to suggest," writes Bosse-Griffiths,
"that the Beset-figures of Amarna with their girlish faces are
impersonations of the king's daughters."[126] To us that might
seem disrespectful, but Bosse-Griffiths concludes her essay
by showing how the Egyptians could bring together seemingly incongruous figures and exchange them for each other
in free-wheeling impersonations in which she finds that
"there is no discord whatsoever between them" (fig. 69).[127]
We are now a step nearer to recognizing in Facsimile 3 a
court scene of the nature described in Joseph Smith's
"Explanation," but the hardest thing to accept should be
what follows next.

Facsimile 3, Figures 2 and 4: Questions of Gender

Anyone wishing to demolish Joseph Smith's interpretation of Facsimile 3 with the greatest economy of effort need look no further than his designating as "King Pharaoh" and "Prince of Pharaoh" two figures so obviously female that a three-year-old child will not hesitate to identify them as such. Why then have Egyptologists not simply pointed to this ultimate absurdity and dismissed the case? Can it be that there is something peculiarly Egyptian about this strange waywardness that represents human beings as gods and men as women? We have already hinted at such a possibility in the case of Imhotep in which, to carry things further, we see both his wife and mother dressed up as goddesses, the latter as Hathor herself (fig. 70).[128] Even more surprising, Dietrich Wildung notes an instance in which "we can identify Anat [the Canaanites' version of Hathor] as ꜣAnat of Ramses [the king] *himself in the shape of a goddess*" (fig. 71).[129] There you have it—the Lady Hathor, who is figure 2 in Facsimile 3, may be none other than Pharaoh himself. The two ladies in the facsimile, figures 2 and 4, will be readily identified by any novice as the goddesses Hathor and Maat. They seem indispensable to scenes having to do with the transmission of power and authority. The spectacle of men, kings, and princes at that, dressed as women, calls for a brief notice on the fundamental issue peculiar to the Egyptians and the Book of Abraham, namely, the tension between the claims of *patriarchal vs. matriarchal succession.*

In the Book of Abraham, as in many ancient versions of the Abraham story, the hero in his youth challenges a king's assertion of divine authority (Abraham 1:5–6), claiming to have the true authority himself (Abraham 1:2–3). The king takes up the challenge and tries to make a ritual offering of Abraham as the well-known substitute king (Abraham 1:18 and Facsimile 1). Abraham's miraculous delivery converts

Figure 70. In this roll-out drawing of a pillar from a temple of Imhotep at Deir el-Bahri, Imhotep is enthroned holding the *w3s* scepter and ankh. His mother, Khereduankh, stands behind him dressed as Hathor. She is followed by his wife Renpetnefret, also dressed as a goddess and crowned with the *rnpt*, the notched palm-rib symbol of endless years, a sacred wordplay on her name.

the king, who petitions Abraham for his priesthood and offers his own honors in exchange—such is the burden of many legends and of Facsimile 3; he also covets Abraham's wife in hopes of establishing a priestly line in the true succession.[130] Why was Pharaoh, "a righteous man, . . . blessed . . . with the blessings of wisdom" (Abraham 1:26), denied

Figure 71. In this bas-relief from the temple of Anath built by Ramses II at Tanis, the Pharaoh precedes the goddess, but their titles are in a curious arrangement. The inscription reads, "Anath, Mistress of Heaven, of Ramses," with the king's name written above her head, an unexpected place to find his royal title.

that priesthood, which he "would fain claim it from Noah, through Ham" (Abraham 1:27)? Certainly not because of Ham, "a just man [who] walked with God" (Moses 8:27), but rather because he claimed it through the wrong line, "that *lineage* by which he *could not* have the right of Priesthood" (Abraham 1:27). What was wrong with it? Simply this: It was not the patriarchal but the *matriarchal* line he was following. Even while "seeking earnestly to

imitate that order established by the *fathers* in the first generations [what the Egyptians called the *pȝwt*], in the days of
the first *patriarchal* reign" (Abraham 1:26), he nonetheless
traced his descent and his throne to "a woman, who was the
daughter of Ham, the daughter of Egyptus" (Abraham
1:23); this woman "discovered the land" and "settled her
sons in it" (Abraham 1:24). Her eldest son became the first
pharaoh, ruling "after the manner" of the patriarchal order
(Abraham 1:25), which the king sought earnestly to "imitate." Thus the government of Egypt was carried on under
the fiction of being patriarchal while the actual line was
matriarchal, the queen being "the wife of the God and
bearer of the royal lineage."[131] But however noble it may be,
a matriarchal line cannot claim patriarchal authority, even
though all the parties concerned are sympathetically portrayed. In all of which there is no mention of race, though
enemies of the church have declared with shock and out-
rage that these passages are proof of Mormon discrimina-
tion against blacks.

The tension between patriarchal and matriarchal authority (to be discussed below) meets us at every step in the
royal inscriptions as one of the dominant notes in Egyptian
civilization. The old matriarchal tradition is clearly
announced in Facsimile 3 by the presence of Hathor (figure
2) in her usual position immediately behind the throne. She
is *Ḥw.t-Ḥr*, the "house" (womb) from which Horus, the legitimate heir to the throne, must emerge; she is "both the
King's mother, his wife [as such called his sister] . . . par
excellence the goddess of the Kingship."[132] Her horned headdress with the sun's disk—the new king appearing between
the horns of the mother cow—appears all the way from prehistoric glyphs on canyon walls down to paintings on the
walls of Christian Coptic monasteries.[133] The same crown
may be worn by any goddess functioning in her capacity, for
as the old Mediterranean Mother-goddess, to whom kings

were merely consorts, she has countless ways of appearing. "It was quite impossible," wrote E. A. Wallis Budge, "for any worshipper of Hathor, however devout, to enumerate all the forms of the goddess which existed."[134] She is the heavenly cow, the mother of the sun-god himself, and also his daughter; she is Nut the Sky-goddess and also the daughter of Nut.[135] She has things both ways: She is the ruler and the ruled, with alternating assertions of patriarchal and matriarchal priority. Acting in her capacity of Queen Mother as the oldest daughter of Geb, she is the regent with full right to the title of *Rpᶜt*.[136] Indeed, it is *her* throne upon which the king sits by her favor as Lady of the Mysteries;[137] no one enters the pharaoh's presence without her approval; it is she "according to whose plans the royal office is passed on," and "he is chosen whom *her* heart desireth to sit upon the throne!"[138]

In her special capacity as the one closest and dearest to the king, Hathor is identified with Isis, who is "the divine mother and princess, . . . the female Sun."[139] Like Hathor, Isis commands the throne, for in the words of Siegfried Morenz, "She is the embodiment of the Throne, . . . is the Egyptian Kingship itself, which *is embodied in the living King Horus*, at whose death it enters into Osiris."[140] With the idea of the Great Lady actually "embodying" the king, the incongruity of figure 2 as "King Pharaoh" begins to dissolve. "The throne 'makes' the king," wrote Frankfort; "the term occurs in Egyptian texts—and so the throne, Isis, is the 'mother' of the king. This expression might be viewed as a metaphor, but the evidence shows that it was not."[141] To the king she says: "I reward thee with *my* throne as king of all the lands. . . . I give to thee the office of Atum on the throne of Shu."[142] True, the son must succeed his father, but who knows who his father really is? It is the mother alone who holds the sure keys to that all-important legitimacy on which patriarchal succession depends; it is Isis "the Lady of Life" who represents and guarantees the continuity of the line;[143] only when Mother Hathor greets the new king as Horus at the coronation is "the king acknowledged as legitimate and is free to receive the crown."[144] As the king rows his mother in a boat at the feast of Opet (cf. Abraham 1:24), she reminds him that she is his mother, and that all the power and authority he possesses come from her.[145] If only because it is the mother who has the last word in matters of legitimacy, divine authority is transferred by women rather than men in Egypt.

Yet remarkably enough the Egyptian record never conveys any sense of dominant and submissive between male and female; even in the stiff formality of the Old Kingdom, as Gardiner notes, "A loveable trait is the evident equality of the sexes: both in the reliefs and in the statues."[146] "There are very few Middle Kingdom stelae," writes Purdy, "that do not include wife and children, most often on the same scale as the dead man";[147] and Otto has shown how this equality of man and wife persists right down to Roman times.[148] Though there are plenty of ambitious and scheming women in the land, the power and glory of father and mother seem to maintain an even balance, and the fabled rivalry between Hathor and Re is dissolved in a perfect love match. On the Old Kingdom monuments husband and wife are represented as absolute equals, according to Jacques Pirenne; not until the Fourth Dynasty do a few cases of female subordination appear.[149]

Since Hathor installs the king "as guarantor of the world order," it is not surprising that she is also identified with Maat (our figure 4 in Facsimile 3) at the coronation, hailed as "Hathor the Great, the Lady of Heaven, the Queen of the Gods and Goddesses, Maat herself, the *female son* [sic] . . . Maat who brings order to the world at the head of the Sun-bark, even 'Isis the Great,' the Mother of the Gods."[150] In the prehistoric shrine of Cusae "Maat was like the double [Ka] of Hathor";[151] the two always operate together at coronations: "Maat is before him and is not far from his majesty. . . . Hathor the Great One is with him in his chapel."[152] To signify his own wholeness of heart, the king presents the Maat-image to Hathor.[153] Maat (the female son) is the younger of the two—indeed, who is not younger than the primordial mother? While "Isis the divine *mother*" says at the coronation, "I place my *son* on the throne," the younger goddess standing by as Nephthys "the Divine *Sister*" says, "I protect thy body my *brother* Osiris."[154] Here the two ladies as Isis the venerable and Nephthys the maiden appear as mother and daughter,[155] standing in the same relationship to each other as "Pharaoh" and "Prince of Pharaoh," whom they embody in Facsimile 3 (figures 2 and 4 respectively).

The presence of Maat is as essential to the rites of transmitting legitimate rule as that of Hathor-Isis herself: they are the two indispensables.[156] Maat is "the very essence of Re," his daughter, his Ka who fills him with life, his mother; she never leaves him, for she is his royalty.[157] The two Maat feathers on his crown assert his legitimacy and are identified with the uraeus, which paralyzes all who would challenge his authority.[158] She appears in the very form of Horus, the son, at the transmission of the kingship,[159] her establishing of royal authority overshadowing all her other offices.[160] The king at his coronation as son and successor is filled with Maat, identified with her in every respect, the complete "possessor of Maat." Moreover, the figure and meaning of Maat was well-known to the ancient Canaanites of Abraham's day and later adopted by the Jews in Egypt to become the classic Wisdom figure of their own Wisdom Literature;[161] a carving found in the palace of Ahab depicts a hawk-headed Horus presenting a statuette of Maat to the sun-god (fig. 72). Indeed, it is in Abraham's time and country, according to André Parrot, that an infinite number of these presentation scenes (surprisingly like Facsimile 3) are found on Mesopotamian seals, in which "the mediatrice is

Figure 72. This small ivory plaque was intended to ornament palace furniture. It depicts the god Horus crowned with a sun offering a tiny seated
Maat figure to the infant Harpocrates, also crowned with a sun. He is
seated on a lotus with a finger to his mouth. Egyptian images like this
were popular with Phoenician craftsmen, who sold them to royal courts
throughout the Near East. This one was found in Samaria, the capital of
Israel.

. . . almost always a woman," which he finds puzzling, since
the prerogative of administering the rites of religion was
reserved to males.[162]

Mixing It Up

All this switching of sexes is understandable, if unset-
tling, in a symbolic sense—after all, Job says of the righteous man, "his breasts are full of milk" (Job 21:24). But
Facsimile 3 is supposed to be an actual scene in the palace;
would the family-night charades go so far? Granted that a
bisexual nature was the rule for Egyptian divinities, who
could freely change their outward appearance to match

special functions,[163] still in a purportedly historical scene in which men are represented as women we need something more specific. To begin with, Hathor and Maat were always known for the *masks* that represent them, these masks being regularly worn by men. The horned Hathor mask, originally life-sized, was carried hanging around the neck of the officials and was gradually reduced in size for convenience, though even in the later period it is still quite large—plainly meant to be worn originally *as* a mask (fig. 73).[164] In the Old Kingdom, the son of Cheops wore the Hathor mask in his office of Intendant of the Palace, and other high officials wore it too; in the Middle Kingdom it was still the mark of men serving the king's most intimate needs as his personal attendants.[165] The Egyptian chief judge, as he mounted the bench to represent the king, would suspend a large Hathor mask from his neck to signify that the court was formally in session, just as lawyers and judges in England submerge their personal identities in wigs and robes.[166] This Hathor mask seems to have been at all times interchangeable with the Maat-symbol, usually a huge greenstone feather that is sometimes shown in ritual scenes taking the place of the Lady's face and head. The symbols are so freely applied that Budge identified the "cow-headed goddess" in the presentation scene of the Kerasher Papyrus, which is very closely related to our Facsimile 3, as "either Isis-Hathor *or* Maat" (fig. 74).[167]

The wearing of these two amulets or masks means complete identification: "Maat places herself as an amulet at thy neck [fig. 75A]; . . . thy right eye is Maat, thy left eye is Maat, thy flesh is Maat, . . . and thy members; . . . thy bandelette is Maat, thy garment . . . is Maat."[168] The reference here is specifically to clothing; plainly the new king, the young one, is all dressed up as Maat—she embodies him in her person in spite of sex."[169] So let no one be shocked by figure 4. She is "the female Horus, the youthful, . . . Isis, the great, the

Figure 73. In this bas-relief from an Old Kingdom tomb, a dignitary of the court carries the *sekhem* scepter in his left hand and the Hathor mask on the staff in his right.

mother of God, born in Dendera on the eve of the child in its cradle (the New Year)."[170] That is, she is not Pharaoh, but the "Prince of Pharaoh," the new king. On the other hand, from a Pyramid Text it is clear that the king wore not only the horned headdress of the royal mother Hathor, but her complete outfit as well—combined with the Maat feathers: "His royal robe is upon him as Hathor, while his feather is a falcon's feather,"[171] signifying both Horus (the falcon) and Maat as his "double."[172] Even older is the appearance of King Narmer in predynastic times, decked out with "heads ⨍ of Hathor on his waistcloth," showing him to be clothed in her power (fig. 75B).[173] Though the Maat-image came to take precedence over the Hathor, both continued side by side until the end with the same meaning; the chief judge of Sheshonq III, though designated as "Prophet of Maat," wears not the Maat but the Hathor emblem (fig. 75C).[174] On the other hand, in a family scene from El Amarna, the queen and her children *all* appear decked out with Maat feathers in their hair, which Norman Davies suggests are actual "*impersonations* of Maat."[175] And the two ladies share the affection of the king when in a cozy family-circle scene Mother Isis-Hathor says to him, "Kiss thy daughter Maat, place her on thy breast like a flower to enliven thy heart"— referring to the Maat and Isis-symbol suspended from the neck, representing the intimate embrace of wife or child.[176]

The supreme assertion of feminine authority at the coronation is the pervasive and aggressive presence of the feminine mystique itself in the person of the commanding Madame *Wr.t-Ḥkꜣw*, "The Great Enchantress," "The Lady Great of Magic" or "of Miracles," who is on hand "specifically as the Goddess of the Coronation," to perform the necessary wonders and transformations.[177] She appears in coronation scenes usurping Hathor's place directly behind the throne as well as her title of "the Lady of Heaven," in which capacity she is closely "syncretized"

F.   E.   D.

Figure 74. This psychostasy scene is usually found in the Book of the
Dead, but here it is in the Book of Breathings, just as in Joseph Smith
Papyrus I, X, and XI. Kerasher's version shows him (A) being led by
Anubis (B) while Thoth (C) introduces him to Osiris (E) and Isis (F).
Before them appear the four sons of Horus on a lotus and a table piled

with Mut and Mother, who is Isis, performing all the offices
of Hathor and Maat while all the time preserving her own
identity, announcing that it is she who places the crown on
the king's brow.[178] For as Isis is the throne, *Wr.t-Ḥkȝw* is the
crown by virtue of "her assimilation to the crown . . . by a
sort of projection"—the latest interpretation.[179] At the
moment of crowning, Thoth says to the king, "*Wr.t-Ḥkȝw* in

C.   B.   A.   G.

high with food offerings (D). All are obligingly labeled above their heads, but unfortunately the label above the cow-headed figure (G) appears damaged, hence Budge's apparent confusion. Kerasher is depicted as a curly-haired Nubian (cf. Fac. 3, fig. 6: "Shulem, one of the king's principal waiters"; see fig. 49, p. 383).

the form of the Uraeus joins herself to thee upon thy head," the uraeus, as is well-known, being either or both of the two motherly serpent goddesses W3dj.t and Buto, who protected and reared the infant king Horus in their nest in the marshes of Khemmis.[180] Even as the uraeus, *Wr.t-Ḥk3w* remains herself, however: "*Wr.t-Ḥk3w* as a real divinity (no mere epithet) assimilates herself to the crown and the

A.

B.

C.

king."[181] Sex is no obstacle; after all, the king cannot be separated from his crown, and even in the palace charades the queen takes the part of the high priest.

Magic indeed! Here is the familiar good fairy, one of "the Seven Hathors" of the nursery tales, who presides at christenings and anniversaries and who can transform anything to anything else; and to make her act complete, she can enter into the living queen, as in the coronation scene from the chapel of Hathor at Deir el-Bahri, where the living queen, Ankhesenamon, "plays the same role and thus identifies herself with *Wr.t-Ḥkꝫw*.[182]

To summarize, during family night at the palace we behold the family renewing coronation rites in private, with the queen functioning as the high priest, "anointing the king, putting the flower wreath around his neck and shaking the sistrum before him," the sistrum being the exclusive scepter of Hathor.[183] At the same time *Wr.t-Ḥkꝫw* is on hand, "specifically the goddess of the coronation . . . holding in her hand the symbol of life . . . while she conducts the king to Hathor who makes the *nyny* gesture,"[184] a good description of our Facsimile 3—what Joseph Smith's critics mistakenly took for a star in Hathor's hand is an *ankh*-symbol of life. Our figure 4 is, of course, *Wr.t-Ḥkꝫw*, or can be, for there are other such scenes in which *Wr.t-Ḥkꝫw* appears "playing the role usually assigned to Maat."[185]

Figure 75. This finely made bronze amulet (A) was suspended around the neck of a judge, reminding everyone of the need for the presence of Maat, the goddess of truth. On the famous palette of Narmer, two large (3.5 in.) Hathor heads flanking his name protect him from above, while four tiny (3/16 in.) ones appear at the top of the pendants over his waistcloth (B). The chief judge of Sheshonq III is shown crouched in the typical form of votive statues placed in the temples (C). The Hathor pendant is carved on his knees to show it was hanging from his (concealed) neck.

Too Many Women?

But would "King Pharaoh" and the "Prince of Pharaoh" *actually dress up* as the goddesses who embodied their majesty at the moment of transition? If the son of Cheops wore the Hathor mask with his royal robe upon him as Hathor and the Maat feather on his head or breast,[186] the high priest of Heliopolis could appear at the *Sed* festival wearing "a peculiar garment, suggesting a woman's apparel,"[187] and the king could identify himself with the Great Mother "by enveloping himself with her bande-lette."[188] It was no doubt the worldwide "primitive" practice of masking and miming, as natural and as spontaneous as dancing, of which it was a part, that suggested such things. "Because there was no *real* identification or fusion," Erik Hornung explains, "the god could with impunity take any form or sex he pleased without disturbing anyone."[189] Isis as
‣ Neith was "two-thirds man and one-third woman," making it possible for her to fuse with Chnum, the Creator, both male and female elements being indispensable to any act of creation.[190] This woman comes forth wearing the familiar white crown but adding a beard to her costume, thus "show-ing her androgenous character."[191] In the same spirit the king appears in the coronation rites as Hapy the Nile, the feeder of the land, heavily bearded but with all the attri-butes of a pregnant woman, whereby, according to Hari, he is identified with the Lady *Wr.t-Ḥkꜣw.*[192]

Is it the principle of the couvade, practiced by some of our grandparents in the Old Country, when the father pre-tended to give birth to the child so as to lay full claim to its legitimacy? The queen laid claim to patriarchal rites in the same way: "I played the role of the husband," says Isis to the king, "even though I am a woman, in order to cause thy name to live on earth."[193] Maat appears in the male form of Horus to show that she is the bearer of the kingship, and at the real coronation the queen in her office of *Rpꜥt* would be

"at great pains to conceal her sex."[194] Everybody knows that
the ambitious Queen Hatshepsut wore a false beard and
preempted the masculine gender in her inscriptions, but at
the same time her great architect Senmut "had himself represented with a female head," as did the High Priest
Horsiesi of the Twenty-second Dynasty; Capart sees in this
a continuation of the Old Kingdom custom of wearing
female masks.[195] Let us recall that Hall was puzzled to find a
figure of Hathor-behind-the-throne labeled not with her
own name, but with the coronation-cartouche of Amenophis
III, as if for the occasion the goddess (our figure 2) actually
was that great pharaoh in person.[196] Certainly his son, the
famous Akhenaton, Amenophis IV, was fond of proclaiming to the world his total identification with Maat, and to
prove that he was "both 'Mother' and 'Father' . . . the King
assumed the latter's hermaphrodite form and had himself
depicted in the strangest bodily shapes,"[197] which have
caused a great deal of speculation but have, according to the
latest studies, never been fully explained.[198] Most striking is
the way his wife, the celebrated Nefertiti, shares equal
billing with him, their figures being "equated in size, in
symbolism of stance and gesture, and in their relationship
to the sun disc."[199] In one scene we even find "the Queen . . .
sitting on the seat with the royal emblems and the king on
an undecorated one."[200] She "drives her own chariot," and
in the coronation scenes she wears the king's crown and in
victory scenes plays a masculine and kingly role.[201] Though
some have viewed Ikhnaton's behavior as a personal whim,
its ritual nature is now generally recognized; Ikhnaton
thought of himself "as an extension of Maat,"[202] "it being
characteristic that at this time . . . Ikhnaten was represented
in female forms. . . . The Prophet, by his feminine body of
many forms honors his god, the womb of the universe."[203]

Though Egyptian family relationships were, as Gardiner
puts it, "calculated to make the brain reel,"[204] we cannot

escape them. Neither could the Libyans, Ethiopians, Persians, Macedonians, and Romans, who could claim to satisfy the people of Egypt as their rulers. Ptolemy Philadelphus and his sister Arsinoe not only enacted the roles, but also presented themselves as the actual incarnations of Osiris and Isis, in a "purely Egyptian" dramatization of their royalty. And the Romans were scandalized when the great Antony played Dionysius = Osiris to Cleopatra's Isis, while Roman nobles played shockingly undignified roles in the same cast. Yet the time came when a warrior emperor, converted to the mysteries of Egypt, could proclaim his world rule on special memorial gold coins issued in Egypt depicting him in the guise of the mother goddess Demeter [Hathor] with the inscription Galliena Augusta—"a combination that strikes the modern mind as ridiculous," writes the historian, but "is not so alien from ancient sentiment."[205]

Crown and Scepter

In most compositions resembling Facsimile 3, the seated majesty wears the same crown as is worn by figure 1. Sometimes the person on the throne and the one being presented to him both wear it.[206] Both the whiteness and the feathers are symbolic of the heavenly light that burst upon the world at the coronation,[207] the "luminous" quality of the one who mounts the throne.[208] The two feathers are both the well-known Maat feathers, "feathers of truth," and Shu feathers, symbolic of the light that passes between the worlds.[209] Osiris "causes brilliance to stream forth through the two feathers," says the famous Amon-Mose hymn, "like the Sun's disk every morning. His White Crown parted the heavens and joined the sisterhood of the stars. He is the leader of the gods . . . *who commands the Great Council* [in heaven], and whom the Lesser Council loves."[210] What clearer description could one ask than Joseph Smith's designation of the crown "as emblematical of the grand Presidency in heaven"? He tells us also that this crown is "representing the priesthood." The "most conspicuous attribute" of the godhead, according to Jaroslav Černý, was power;[211] the Egyptians, wrote Posener, "did not worship a man" in the Pharaoh, "but 'the power clothed in human form.' "[212] One shared in the power, Morenz explains, by achieving "the maximal approach of the individual to the 'divine nature,' symbolized by his wearing an *atef* crown."[213] The *atef* is the crown in our Facsimile 3, and anyone in a state of sanctification could wear it, but it emphasized, according to Morenz, a sacral rather than a kingly capacity, i.e., it "represented the priesthood" of the wearer.[214]

With the crown go the *crook and flail*, the receiving of which was a necessary part of the transmission of divine authority. Percy Newberry, in a special study, concluded that both crook and flail are "connected with the shepherd," the former "the outward and visible sign of . . . authority," marking the one who bore it as "chief shepherd"; by it "he rules and guides . . . and defends" his flock.[215] The flail was a contraption shepherds used to gather laudanum, according to Newberry's explanation (which, however, has met with no enthusiastic acceptance by other scholars). Ancient sources tell us what it signified, as when the official who bears it at the archaic festival of Sokar is described as "drawing the people of Tameri [the Beloved Land, Egypt] to your lord under the flail," suggesting the cattle driver, as does the prodding and protecting crook of the shepherd.[216] And like the crook, the whip also serves to protect the flocks: "Men and *animals* and gods praise thy power that created them," says Anchnesneferibre addressing Osiris, "there is made for thee a flail [*nkhakha*], placed in thy hands as protection."[217] As symbolic of the power that created, it is held aloft by the prehistoric Min of Coptos, being the whip of light or of power, bestirring all things to life and action.[218]

In their administrative and disciplinary capacities both

crook and scourge are indeed symbolic of Pharaoh's "justice
ℽ and judgment." But in the hands of a commoner? Wolfhart
Westendorf calls attention to "claims to royal prerogatives"
found in the "tombs of the monarchs and dignitaries, who
took over the whip, crook, scepter, and other elements of the
king's garb, in order to be completely equipped in death
with all the attributes of Osiris."[219] Gardiner claimed that
those who appear in the trappings of our figure 1 were imitating *not* Osiris but the living king.[220] But it is all the same:
The man on the throne holding "the sceptre of justice and
judgment in his hand" is not necessarily either the king or
Osiris, though he aspires to both priesthood and kingship.
A scene from the Temple of Karnak shows Amon on the
throne handing his crook and whip to the living king, who
kneels before him; but the king already holds his own crook
and flail (fig. 76), while Khonsu standing behind the throne
in the garb of Osiris *also* holds the crook and flail.[221] The
freedom with which the sacred symbols could be thus
handed around shows that Abraham would not have to
grasp Pharaoh's *own personal* badges of office, but like many
another merely be represented with the universal emblems
to indicate the king recognized his supreme priesthood, as
the Abraham legends recount.[222]

The All-Purpose Lotus

Of all Joseph Smith's interpretations of the figures in
Facsimile 3, that of figure 3 is certainly the least realistic. He
correctly identifies it with figure 10 in Facsimile 1 and tells
us that in both cases it is not a picture of anything, but a
symbol, which does not depict or even represent but "*signifies* Abraham in Egypt."[223] The lotus, perhaps the richest of
all Egyptian symbols, can stand for the purest abstraction,
as when it indicates nothing but a *date* in one tomb or a *place*
in another.[224] In Facsimile 3 we are told that it points to two
things, a man and a country, indicating the special guest-to-

Figure 76. The great hypostyle hall at Karnak built by Seti I and his son Ramses II was the largest covered space in the world for centuries. The walls were carved with huge representations of the mysteries of kingship. Here Ramses II kneels before Amun-Ra and holds out his hand to receive two *heb-sed* canopied thrones, the symbol of renewed kingship. Khonsu stands at the far right holding the composite scepter.

host relationship between them. Most of the time the lotus announces a party situation, adding brightness to the occasion; etiquette required guests to a formal party to bring a lotus offering to the host—hence the flower served as a token both of invitation and admission.[225] Budge observed how in the *Kerasher Manuscript*, in which the person being presented wears exactly the same peculiar lotus headdress as our Shulem (figure 5), "instead of the bullock-skin dripping with blood, which is generally seen suspended near the throne of the god, masses of lotus flowers are represented," giving a totally different aspect to the scene.[226] Yet, while the lotuses "seem to have figured prominently" in formal occasions, according to Aylward Blackman, we still do not understand the flower offerings, any more than we do the combination of lotus stands and small libation vessels such as our figure 3.[227] It would now seem that these tall and narrow Egyptian ritual stands originated in Canaan.[228]

Quite as conspicuous as its aesthetic appeal is the appearance of the lotus as the heraldic flower of Lower Egypt, specifically the Delta. As such it is never missing from court and coronation scenes;[229] it is specifically the emblem of the fierce lion-god Nefertem who guards the eastern Delta against invaders and supervises the movements of strangers, like Abraham, at the border.[230] In coronation situations the interlaced stems of lotus and papyrus plants that form the conventional support of the throne represent the binding together of the Two Lands on that joyful occasion, as well as the reawakening, the new year, the phoenix, i.e., the young Horus on the throne, along with the outpouring of light and knowledge over the reborn world.[231] Two studies still pursue the illusive lotus, repeating much of Jean Capart's conclusions of twenty years ago. Capart noted that the lotus belongs to "the genuine abstractions" of Egyptian art, becoming ever more abstract through the years;[232] Derchain begins his study of the lotus with the reminder that it is almost impossible to understand what the Egyptians are trying to convey in depicting even the simplest situation and the admonition not to be led astray by the obvious aesthetic appeal of the thing.[233] He finds that the lotus appears "everywhere . . . as a symbol of rebirth . . . and creation; it represents a new world, a new day, a new dispensation," while at the same time it denotes the loving relationship of married couples and sweethearts, including royal ones (fig. 77),[234] the significant thing being that all the coronation motifs are combined in it.

Figure 77. This beautiful ivory cabinet lid shows Tutankhamun and his wife strolling in the royal garden among cornflowers, mandrakes, pomegranates, and poppies. Ankhsenamun offers her husband bouquets of lotus, papyrus, and mandrake fruit. He leans comfortably on his walking stick, a pose not seen before this period in royal art. She wears an unusual crown consisting of an incense cone flanked by uraei serpents.

A study by Waltraud Guglielmi begins by pointing out
the great complexity of the lotus symbol and the difficulty
of understanding it; its most obvious and important connections are with the ideas of regeneration and rebirth.[235] He
notes next that the lotus stands for the bounty of the land of
Egypt.[236] It is a gift that the king brings to the god in the
temple and is connected with the arrival of migratory birds
from afar, the birds representing not only welcome guests,
but alien and hostile invaders.[237] Sometimes, also, they were
thought of as weary wanderers returning to Egypt from
afar.[238] The lotus is definitely a welcome to Egypt given by
the king to human and divine visitors; the divinity who
received the token reciprocated by responding to the king:
"I give thee all the lands of thy majesty, the foreign lands to
become thy slaves. I give thee the birds, symbols of thine
enemy."[239] In receiving a lotus, the king in return ritually
receives the land itself, while the god in accepting a lotus
from the king promises him in return the reverent obedience of his subjects.[240] "The flowers are mostly heraldic
plants . . . associated with the crowns of Upper and Lower
Egypt," for in some the main purpose of lotus rites is "to
uphold the dominion of the King" as nourisher of the
land.[241] Moreover, its significance is valid at every level of
society, the lotus being a preeminent example of how
mythological themes and religious symbolism were famil-
iarly integrated into the everyday life of the Egyptians.[242] In
some reception scenes the lotus before the throne (our figure
3) is supporting the four canopic figures, correctly designated by Joseph Smith in Facsimile 2, figure 6, as representing "this earth in its four quarters," proclaiming the rule of
the man on the throne over all the earth.[243]

The numerous studies of the Egyptian lotus design are
remarkably devoid of conflict, since this is one case in
which nobody insists on a single definitive interpretation.
The points emphasized are (1) the abstract nature of the

symbol, containing meanings that are far from obvious at
first glance; (2) the lotus as denoting high society, especially
royal receptions, at which the presentation of a lotus to the
host was obligatory and showed that the bearer had been
invited; to be remiss in lotus courtesy was an unpardonable
blunder, for anyone who refuses the lotus is under a curse;[244]
(3) the lotus as the symbol of Lower Egypt, the Delta with
all its patriotic and sentimental attachments; (4) the lotus as
Nefertem, the defender of the border; (5) the lotus as the
king, or ruler, defender, and nourisher of the land; (6) the
lotus as the support of the throne at the coronation. It is
a token of welcome and invitation to the royal court and the
land, proffered by the king himself as guardian of the border.

In Radwan's large collection of royal audience scenes
from the Eighteenth Dynasty, those coming as guests to the
palace bear bouquets of lotuses or (more rarely) papyrus to
their host and sometimes receive the same in return from
him. The exchange of the two commonest "backyard weeds"
of the land can only be symbolic; when, for example, "the
Lords of Naharina," bringing gifts to the king, are led into
his presence by the tomb owner bearing two big papyrus
bouquets, no one could be impressed by the rarity or value
of the gift.[245] The lotus accompanies a wish for a gift of life
and protection, Radwan notes, quoting Hans Bonnet: "The
Gods themselves are present in the bouquets."[246] The important thing, Radwan concludes, "is the fact that the meeting
of a person with Pharaoh or his reception by him took place
with flowers."[247] It goes farther than that, however; at the
above-mentioned *Sed* festival of the valley the guest both
receives the bouquet of Amon while his entourage bears
lotuses from the royal lake into the palace,[248] and he actually
is "Nefertem at the nose of Re," i.e., he is the lotus.[249] In the
famous chapter 17 of the Book of the Dead, Nefertem's
business is to keep undesirable characters out of Egypt.[250]

Nowhere was the welcoming lotus more in evidence

than during the great festival of the valley, celebrating the arrival in Egypt and the inaugural river cruise of "the Lady of Intoxication," who, as we shall presently see, discovered and settled the land. Everywhere she is greeted in her new domain with the lotus presentation.[251] What, then, could better "signify Abraham in Egypt" than the formal lotus that adorns Facsimiles 1 and 3, just as the lotus in Facsimile 2, with the four figures commonly shown standing upon it, signifies "the earth in its four quarters"—all the world within the sway of Pharaoh.

Why Shulem?

But where does Abraham come in? What gives a "family-night" aspect to our Facsimile 3 is figure 5, who commands the center of the stage. Instead of his being Abraham or Pharaoh, as we might expect, he is simply "Shulem, one of the king's principal waiters." To the eye of common sense, all of Joseph Smith's interpretations are enigmatic; to illustrate his story best, the man on the throne *should* be Pharaoh, of course, and the man standing before him with upraised hand would obviously be Abraham teaching him about the stars, while figure 6 would necessarily be Abraham's servant (Eliezer was, according to tradition, a black man).[252] But if we consult the Egyptian parallels to this scene instead of our own wit and experience, we learn that the person normally standing in the position of 5 is the owner of the stele and is almost always some important servant in the palace, boasting in the biographical inscription of his glorious proximity to the king. Hall's collection of biographical stelae includes a Chief of Bowmen, Singer of Amon, Chief Builder, Scribe of the Temple, Chief Workman of Amon, Fan Bearer, King's Messenger, Guardian of the Treasury, Director of Works, King's Chief Charioteer, Standard Bearer, Pharaoh's Chief Boatman, Intendant of Pharaoh's Boat-crew, Warden of the Harim, the

Queen's Chief Cook, Chief of Palace Security, etc.[253] All these men, by no means of royal blood, but familiars of the palace, have the honor of serving the king in intimate family situations and are seen coming before him to pay their respects at family gatherings. Some of them, like the King's Chief Charioteer, have good Syrian and Canaanite names, like our "Shulem"—how naturally he fits into the picture as "one of the King's principal waiters!" The fact that high serving posts that brought one into close personal contact with Pharaoh—the greatest blessing that life had to offer to an Egyptian—were held by men of alien (Canaanite) blood shows that the doors of opportunity at the court were open even to foreigners like Abraham and his descendants.

But why "Shulem"? He plays no part in the story. His name never appears elsewhere; he simply pops up and then disappears. And yet he is the center of attention in Facsimile 3! That is just the point: These palace servants would in their biographical stelae glorify the moment of their greatest splendor for the edification of their posterity forever after. This would be one sure means of guaranteeing a preservation of Abraham's story in Egypt. We are told in the book of *Jubilees* that Joseph in Egypt remembered how his father Jacob used to read the words of Abraham to the family circle.[254] We also know that the Egyptians in their histories made fullest use of all sources available—especially the material on the autobiographical stelae served to enlighten and instruct posterity.[255] Facsimile 3 may well be a copy on papyrus of the funeral stele of one Shulem who memorialized an occasion when he was introduced to an illustrious fellow Canaanite in the palace. A "principal waiter" (*wdpw*) could be a very high official indeed, something like an Intendant of the Palace. Shulem is the useful transmitter and timely witness who confirms for us the story of Abraham at court.

Taking Facsimile 3 and one of those family-night

coronation games in the palace in which the various parts of
the play were freely exchanged among the household, we
are reminded that all the world was summoned to coronation ceremonies to give the new king their recognition and
submission,[256] true to which rule each of the five figures in
our Facsimile 3 represents a different social stratum, from divinity to slave, though (and this is important) all belong to
the same universe of discourse—it is all the same family. In
all of Pharaoh's doing, "the subordinates, to the degree to
which they approach the king, are participants in his condition, receiving thereby a parcel of divinity."[257] There is no
limit to individual glory, for by virtue of "participating in the
king" an individual, "since the King is Re, . . . participates on
the next level with Re himself. He is by participation, Re
himself."[258] "For every participant, taking part in sacred
rites" entails "a certain sanctification of the individual." All
the world got into the act, for when small-scale dramatiza-
tions of the coronation were celebrated at local festivals in
the provinces, the local "great ones" of the land were summoned to do honor, like the four local idols in Facsimile 1,
while all the common people joined in the feast.[259]

At the most exalted level, it was "through the 'democratization' of the king's initiation plainly made possible
through the 'democratization' of the priesthood, that the
individual initiate (miste) was included in the kingly ideology and becomes even as the king answerable to Maat."[260]
After all, that is Maat (figure 4) who holds the center-stage
position in the little drama of Facsimile 3, and there is no
reason why the principle should not apply in this case,
though, of course, nothing is proven one way or the other,
save that the story that Joseph Smith tells is by no means
that "impossible event" that his critics have declared it to
be. After all, three generations later the man on the throne
was Abraham's own great-grandson. Of Rekhmire, that
vizier of Thotmes III who sat in state while his majesty dis-

coursed in the best academic fashion to the attentive court, James Breasted wrote, "He is a veritable Joseph, and it must be his office which the Hebrew writer had in mind in the story of Joseph."[261] Rekhmire's successor under Amenophis III was Amenhotep, the son of Hapu (see fig. 39, p. 288), who had himself portrayed in a frescoe "seated on a throne, wearing the Hathor pectoral at his neck," while an inscription proclaims that he "received the insignia (ḫkr.w) worked in gold and all manner of precious stones, the emblem of Hathor being placed at his neck in electrum and all precious stones, he being seated on a throne of gold before the royal dais, his limbs clothed in fine linen" (fig. 78).[262] What more could a commoner ask in the way of royal splendor? And it was all made possible and acceptable "by politeness of the king" (Facsimile 3, figure 1), to use the felicitous phrase of the Book of Abraham.

Let us recall the tradition of how the king ordered a throne erected for Abraham after his miraculous deliverance from the altar and commanded all his nobles and their children to do obeisance to the man on the throne and hear his discourse on astronomy.[263]

Figure 78. Reconstructed from many fragments, this painting originally covered the rear wall of the third chapel in the funerary temple of Amenhotep, son of Hapu (see fig. 40, p. 289). He is shown receiving floral offerings from his mortuary priests who wear the white shoulder band of their office over their left shoulders. On the left he holds the *sekhem*

scepter, while on the right he holds a white ostrich-feathered fan. He wears the "Gold of Honor" necklace and the Hathor pendant, symbol of his authority. The text describing this scene (A) is duplicated on the other side, as if to ensure its survival over the centuries. This is the only painting to have survived from the entire temple complex.

Notes

1. James Breasted, ed., *Medinet Habu*, 8 vols. (Chicago: University of Chicago Press, 1930), 1: plates 1, 26, 43–44; 2: plates 78, 107–8, 119; 3: plates 144, 176, 178–79, 291, 295, 310–13, 317, 322, 324, 327, 337, 339–40, 342–43, etc.; Gustave Lefébvre, *Le Tombeau de Petosiris*, 3 vols. (Cairo: IFAO, 1923–34), 3: plates xvi, xli, lii.

2. Alan H. Gardiner, "The Baptism of Pharaoh," *JEA* 36 (1950): 6.

3. Eberhard Otto, "Zur Bedeutung der ägyptischen Tempelstatue seit dem Neuen Reich," *Orientalia* 17 (1948): 454 (emphasis added).

4. Henri Frankfort, *The Cenotaph of Seti I at Abydos*, 2 vols. (London: Egypt Exploration Society, 1933), 1:29.

5. Ali Radwan, *Die Darstellungen des regierenden Königs und seiner Familienangehörigen in den Privatgräbern der 18. Dynastie* (Berlin: Hessling, 1969).

6. Ibid., 3.

7. Ibid., 23–40, 49, 75–77, 96–97, 106.

8. Ibid., 23, 73, 84.

9. Ibid., 84, 98.

10. Ibid., 104.

11. Ibid., 23, 39–40.

12. Ibid., 27.

13. Ibid., 24.

14. Ibid., 1.

15. Ibid., 10–13, 77–78, 90, 97.

16. Ibid., 41.

17. Ibid.

18. Ibid., 43–44.

19. Ibid., 41.

20. Ibid., 3.

21. Ibid., 35.

22. Ibid., 86–92.

23. Ibid., 91–92.

24. Ibid., 86.

25. Ibid., 65–73.

26. Ibid., 72–73.

27. Ibid., 2.

28. Bengt J. Peterson, "Der Gott Osiris-Ptah, der Herr des Lebens," *ZÄS* 95 (1968): 138.

29. Eberhard Otto, *Gott und Mensch nach den ägyptischen Tempelinschriften der griechisch-römischen Zeit* (Heidelberg: Winter, 1964), 8–9.

30. Natacha Rambova and Alexandre Piankoff, *The Tomb of Ramesses VI*, 2 vols. (New York: Pantheon, 1954), 1:36.

31. Alan H. Gardiner, "A Unique Funerary Liturgy," *JEA* 41 (1955): 16.

32. Philippe Derchain, "Le lotus, la mandragore et le perséa," *CdE* 50 (1976): 65.

33. Ludmila Matiegka, "Individual Characteristics of Figures on the Egyptian Stelae," *Archiv Orientalni* 20 (1952): 27.

34. Ulrich Luft, "Kunst und Ideologie in den Bilderwerken der Pharaohnen," *Altertum* 21 (1975): 173–74.

35. Derchain, "Lotus, la mandragore et le perséa," 66.

36. Samuel G. F. Brandon, "A Problem of the Osirian Judgment of the Dead," *Numen* 5 (1958): 112.

37. Cf. Louis Speleers, *Textes des cerceuils du Moyen Empire égyptien* (Brussels: n.p., 1946), lxxxv.

38. Philippe Derchain, "Sur le nom de Chou et sa fonction," *RdE* 15 (1975): 116.

39. Rudolf Anthes, "Remarks on the Pyramid Texts of the Early Egyptian Dogma," *JAOS* 74 (1954): 38–39.

40. Luft, "Kunst und Ideologie," 174.

41. Henri Frankfort, *Kingship and the Gods* (Chicago: University of Chicago Press, 1948), 128.

42. Ibid., 131.

43. Otto, *Gott und Mensch*, 83, 85.

44. Robert Hari, "La grande-en-magie et la stèle du temple de Ptah à Karnak," *JEA* 62 (1976): 104.

45. Wolfgang Helck, "*Rpˤt auf dem Thron des Gb*," *Orientalia* 19 (1950): 433.

46. Édouard Naville, *Das ägyptische Todtenbuch der XVIII. bis XX. Dynastie*, 3 vols. (1886; reprint, Graz, Austria: Akademische Druck- und Verlagsanstalt, 1971), 1:20.

47. Jan Bergman, *Ich bin Isis* (Stockholm: Almquist and Wiksell, 1968), 272.

48. Winfried Barta, "Der anonyme Gott der Lebenslehren," *ZÄS* 103 (1976): 79–81.

49. Ibid., 85–88.

50. Richard Lepsius, *Älteste Texte des Todtenbuches* (Berlin: Hertz, 1867), 46.

51. Alan H. Gardiner, *The Attitude of the Ancient Egyptians to Death and the Dead* (Cambridge: Cambridge University Press, 1935), 10 (emphasis added).

52. Alexandre Moret, *Le rituel du culte divin journalier en Égypte*

(Paris: Leroux, 1902); and Alexandre Moret, *Du caractère religieux de la royauté pharaonique* (Paris: Leroux, 1902), 218.

53. Georges Posener, *De la divinité du pharaon* (Paris: Imprimerie Nationale, 1960), 44.

54. Helck, "*Rpʿt* auf dem Thron des Gb," 426.

55. Peter Kaplony, "Das Vorbild des Königs unter Sesostris III," *Orientalia* 35 (1966): 404–5.

56. Alan H. Gardiner, *Egyptian Grammar* (Oxford: Oxford University Press, 1957), 168–69.

57. Speleers, *Textes des Cerceuils*, lxi, lxxiii.

58. Pyramid Text 365 (§625), in Raymond O. Faulkner, *Ancient Egyptian Pyramid Texts* (Oxford: Clarendon, 1969), 120.

59. Henri Frankfort, *Ancient Egyptian Religion* (New York: Harper, 1961), 6; Philippe Derchain, *Rites Égyptiens* (Brussels: Fondation Égyptologique Reine Elisabeth, 1962–64), 46; Hermann Junker, *Die Onurislegende* (Wien: Hoelder, 1917), 45.

60. Frankfort, *Ancient Egyptian Religion*, 6–7.

61. Eric Uphill, "The Egyptian Sed-Festival Rites," *JNES* 24 (1965): 381.

62. Frankfort, *Ancient Egyptian Religion*, 6–7; Moret, *Rituel du culte divin journalier en Égypte*, 91; *Wb*, 2:61; N. Schneider, "Götterthrone in Ur III und ihr Kult," *Orientalia* 16 (1947): 59, 63–65.

63. Robert C. Webb, pseud., *Joseph Smith as Translator* (Salt Lake City: Deseret Book, 1936), 113.

64. Helck, "*Rpʿt* auf dem Thron des Gb," 430–31.

65. Ibid., 432–33.

66. Ibid., 418–21; David Lorton, review of *Recherche sur les messagers (wpwtyw) dans les sources égyptiennes profanes*, by Michel Valloggia, *Bibliotheca Orientalis* 34 (1977): 49.

67. Helck, "*Rpʿt* auf dem Thron des Gb," 416; Lorton, review of *Recherche sur les messagers (wpwtyw)*, 49.

68. Helck, "*Rpʿt* auf dem Thron des Gb," 434.

69. Hermann Kees, *Totenglauben und Jenseitsvorstellungen der alten Ägypter* (Leipzig: Hinrichs, 1926), 349.

70. Winfried Barta, "Der Königsring als Symbol zyklischer Wiederkehr," *ZÄS* 98(1972): 12–16.

71. Helck, "*Rpʿt* auf dem Thron des Gb," 417, 433.

72. Hermann Kees, *Aegypten* (Munich: Beck, 1933), 42–44, 194–97.

73. Ibrahim Harari, "Nature de la stèle de donation de fonction du roi Ahmôsis à la reine Ahmès-Nefertari," *ASAE* 56 (1959): 201.

74. Helck, "*Rpʿt* auf dem Thron des Gb," 417; Otto, "Zur Bedeutung der ägyptischen Tempelstatue," 463; Kees, *Aegypten*, 42–44, 194–97.

75. François Daumas, "Le sens de la royauté égyptienne à propos d'un livre récent," *RHR* 160 (1961): 145–46.

76. Ibid., 146.

77. Moret, *Rituel du culte divin journalier en Égypte*, 4–5.

78. Alexander Altmann, "The Gnostic Background of the Rabbinic Adam Legends," *JQR* 35 (1944–45): 380, 388, 390–91.

79. Kurt H. Sethe, *Der dramatische Ramesseumspapyrus* (Leipzig: Hinrichs, 1928), 213.

80. Siegfried Schott, *Das schöne Fest vom Wüstentale* (Wiesbaden: Akademie der Wissenschaft und Literatur, 1952), 87–88.

81. Ibid., 90.

82. Paul Barguet, "Le livre des portes et la transmission du pouvoir royale," *RdE* 27 (1975): 35.

83. Claude Vandersleyen, "Le sens symbolique des puits funéraires dans l'Égypte ancienne," *CdE* 50 (1975): 152–54.

84. Jean Leclant, "À la Pyramide de Pépi I," *RdE* 27 (1975): 148.

85. Ibid., 148 n. 6.

86. Bergman, *Ich bin Isis*, 68 n. 1.

87. Ibid., 222.

88. Ilse Becher, "Augustus und Dionysus—ein Feindverhältnis," *ZÄS* 103 (1976): 92.

89. Siegfried Morenz, "Das Problem des Werdens zu Osiris in der griechisch-römischen Zeit Ägyptens," in *Religions en Égypte hellénistique et romaine* (Paris: Presses universitaires, 1969), 82–83.

90. Pyramid Texts 365–66 (§622–33).

91. Ibid., 426 (§776).

92. Frankfort, *Ancient Egyptian Religion*, 104–5.

93. T. George Allen, "Additions to the Egyptian Book of the Dead," *JNES* 11 (1952): 177.

94. Hugh W. Nibley, "A New Look at the Pearl of Great Price," *IE* 72 (August 1969): 75–76.

95. Gertrud Thausing,"Das 'Aufhacken der Erde,'" *Archiv für ägyptische Archaeologie* 1 (1938): 12.

96. Hans Bonnet, *Reallexikon der ägyptischen Religionsgeschichte* (Berlin: de Gruyter, 1952), 396.

97. Henry R. H. Hall, *Hieroglyphic Texts from Egyptian Stelae in the British Museum* (London: British Museum, 1925), 13, plate XLVI (emphasis added).

98. Alexandre Moret, "La Doctrine de Maât," *RdE* 4 (1940): 2; Moret, *Caractère religieux de la royauté pharaonique*, 63.

99. Günther Vittmann, "Die Familie der saitischen Könige," *Orientalia*

44 (1975): 378–87; Bernadette Letellier, "Autour de la stèle de Qadech: une famille de Deir-el-Médineh," *RdE* 27 (1975): 162–63.

100. Becher, "Augustus und Dionysus—ein Feindverhältnis," 94–95.

101. Kate Bosse-Griffiths, "The Great Enchantress in the Little Golden Shrine of Tut'ankhamen," *JEA* 59 (1973): 100.

102. Ibid., 108.

103. Hari, "Grande-en-magie," 106.

104. M. Murray, "Ritual Masking," *Mélanges Maspero 66* (1935–38): 253.

105. Bosse-Griffiths, "Great Enchantress," 101.

106. Pyramid Text 422 (§752–64).

107. Strother Purdy, "Sinuhe and the Question of Literary Types," *ZÄS* 104 (1977): 126.

108. Ibid., 125.

109. Ibid., 125–26.

110. Bonnet, *Reallexikon der ägyptischen Religionsgeschichte*, 325.

111. Moret, *Rituel du culte divin journalier en Égypte*, 4–5.

112. Erik Hornung, *Der Eine und die Vielen* (Darmstadt: Wissenschaftliche Buchgesellschaft, 1973), 87–90.

113. Ibid., 96, 102.

114. Murray, "Ritual Masking," 253–54.

115. Ibid., 253; Bonnet, *Reallexikon der ägyptischen Religionsgeschichte*, 325.

116. Heinrich Schäfer, *Die Mysterien des Osiris in Abydos unter König Sesostris III*, vol. 4 in Untersuchungen zur Geschichte und Altertumskunde Aegyptens (Leipzig: Hinrichs, 1905), 15.

117. Hall, *Hieroglyphic Texts from Egyptian Stelae*, 11, plate XXXI.

118. Bergman, *Ich bin Isis*, 83 n. 2.

119. Sethe, *Dramatische Ramesseumspapyrus*, 99.

120. Alan H. Gardiner, review of *The Golden Bough*, by James G. Frazer, *JEA* 2 (1915): 124.

121. Moret, *Caractère religieux de la royauté pharaonique*, 87.

122. Sethe, *Dramatische Ramesseumspapyrus*, 96.

123. Bergman, *Ich bin Isis*, 89.

124. Sethe, *Dramatische Ramesseumspapyrus*, 95–96.

125. Frankfort, *Kingship and the Gods*, 125.

126. Kate Bosse-Griffiths, "A Beset Amulet from the Amarna Period," *JEA* 63 (1977): 105.

127. Ibid., 106.

128. Dietrich Wildung, *Egyptian Saints: Deification in Pharaonic Egypt* (New York: University Press, 1977), 63.

129. Ibid., 27 (emphasis added).

130. Nibley, "A New Look at the Pearl of Great Price," *IE* 73 (April 1970): 79–95; reprinted in this volume as chapter 8, "The Sacrifice of Sarah."

131. Constantin E. Sander-Hansen, *Das Gottesweib des Amun* (Copenhagen: Munksgaard, 1940), 47.

132. Bergman, *Ich bin Isis,* 122.

133. Friedrich W. von Bissing, "Die Kirche von Abd el Gadir bei Wadi Halfa und ihre Wandmalereien," *Mitteilungen des deutschen archäologischen Instituts zu Kairo* 7 (1937): 155–57.

134. E. A. Wallis Budge, *The Gods of the Egyptians or Studies in Egyptian Mythology,* 2 vols. (London: Methuen, 1904), 1:433.

135. Bonnet, *Reallexikon der ägyptischen Religionsgeschichte,* 280–81.

136. Bergman, *Ich bin Isis,* 145; Helck, "*Rpˤt* auf dem Thron des Gb," 421.

137. Günther Roeder, "Der Isistempel von Behbêt," *ZÄS* 46 (1909): 65.

138. Bergman, *Ich bin Isis,* 169.

139. Philippe Derchain, "La Couronne de la justification," *CdE* 30 (1955): 256–57.

140. Siegfried Morenz, "Ägyptische Nationalreligion und sogenannte Isismission," *Zeitschrift der deutschen morgenländischen Gesellschaft* 111 (1961): 434.

141. Frankfort, *Ancient Egyptian Religion,* 6.

142. Roeder, "Isistempel von Behbêt," 65, 67.

143. Bergman, *Ich bin Isis,* 147.

144. Bonnet, *Reallexikon der ägyptischen Religionsgeschichte,* 397.

145. Walther Wolf, *Das schöne Fest von Opet* (Leipzig: Hinrichs, 1931), 63.

146. Alan H. Gardiner, *Egypt of the Pharaohs* (Oxford: Clarendon, 1961), 91; Jacques Pirenne, *Histoire des institutions et du droit privé de l'ancienne Égypte,* 3 vols. (Brussels: Fondation Égyptologie Reine Elisabeth, 1932–35), 2:5, 381.

147. Purdy, "Sinuhe and the Question of Literary Types," 120; cf. Pirenne, *Histoire des institutions et du droit privé,* 2:382.

148. Otto, "Zur Bedeutung der ägyptischen Tempelstatue," 457–58.

149. Pirenne, *Histoire des institutions et du droit privé,* 2:381.

150. Gertrud Thausing, "Der ägyptische Schicksalsbegriff," *Mitteilungen des deutschen archäologischen Instituts zu Kairo* 8(1939): 53; Bergman, *Ich bin Isis,* 170, 177.

151. Bernhard Grdseloff, "L'insigne du grand juge égyptien," *ASAE* 40 (1940): 197.

152. Constant de Wit, "Inscriptions dédicatoires du temple d'Edfou," *CdE* 36 (1961): 65.

153. Jacques Vandier, "Iousâas et (Hathor) Nébet-Hétépet," *RdE* 16 (1964): 143.

154. Cf. de Wit, "Inscriptions dédicatoires du temple d'Edfou," 277.

155. Ibid., 278.

156. Hellmut Brunner, "Zum Verständnis des Spruches 312 der Sargtexte," *Zeitschrift der deutschen morgenländischen Gesellschaft* 111 (1961): 445.

157. Bonnet, *Reallexikon der ägyptischen Religionsgeschichte,* 432–33.

158. E. A. Wallis Budge, *The Book of the Dead (Papyrus of Ani),* 3 vols. (New York: Putnam, 1913), 2:380, plate 7, lines 30–35.

159. Brunner, "Zum Verständnis des Spruches 312 der Sargtexte," 445.

160. Moret, *Rituel du culte divin journalier en Égypte,* 143.

161. Siegfried Morenz, *Ägyptische Religion* (Stuttgart: Kohlhammer, 1960), 133.

162. André Parrot, *Abraham et son temps* (Neuchatel: Delachaux and Niestlé, 1962), 27–28.

163. Bergman, *Ich bin Isis,* 275–79.

164. Grdseloff, "L'insigne du grand juge égyptien," 185–202.

165. Ibid., 199–200.

166. Ibid., 194.

167. E. A. Wallis Budge, *The Book of the Dead (Papyrus of Hunefer)* (London: Paul, Trench, Trubner, 1899), 34.

168. Moret, *Rituel du culte divin journalier en Égypte,* 141–42.

169. Bergman, *Ich bin Isis,* 216.

170. Thausing,"Ägyptische Schicksalsbegriff," 60.

171. Pyramid Text 335 (§546).

172. Grdseloff, "L'insigne du grand juge égyptien," 197; cf. 187–98.

173. W. M. Flinders Petrie, "The Geography of the Gods," *Ancient Egypt* (1917): 114.

174. Grdseloff, "L'insigne du grand juge égyptien," 194–95.

175. Norman de G. Davies, *The Rock Tombs of El Amarna,* 6 vols. (London: Egypt Exploration Fund, 1906), 4:19 n. 2.

176. Bergman, *Ich bin Isis,* 192–93.

177. Hari, "Grande-en-magie," 103–4.

178. Ibid., 102–3.

179. Ibid., 107.

180. Hugh W. Nibley, *The Message of the Joseph Smith Papyri: An Egyptian Endowment* (Salt Lake City: Deseret Book, 1975), 26–27, 58, 104–5.

181. Hari, "Grande-en-magie," 103.

182. Ibid., 105.

183. Ibid., 106.

184. Ibid., 104.

185. Ibid., 102, 107.

186. Pyramid Text 335 (§546); Grdseloff, "L'insigne du grand juge égyptien," 199.

187. Siegfried Schott, *Mythe und Mythenbildung im alten Ägypten* (Leipzig: Hinrichs, 1945), 14.

188. Moret, *Rituel du culte divin journalier en Égypte*, 189.

189. Hornung, *Die Eine und die Vielen*, 88.

190. Bergman, *Ich bin Isis*, 277.

191. Erik Hornung, *Das Amduat: Die Schrift des verborgenen Raumes*, 3 vols. (Wiesbaden: Harrassowitz, 1963–67), 2:27; Bonnet, *Reallexikon der ägyptischen Religionsgeschichte*, 515.

192. Hari, "Grande-en-magie," 101.

193. Wilhelm Spiegelberg, "Varia," *ZÄS* 53 (1917): 95–96.

194. Alexandre Moret, *Kings and Gods of Egypt* (New York: Putnam, 1912), 28.

195. Jean C. Capart, "Sur un Texte d'Hérodote," *CdE* 20 (1944): 223.

196. Hall, *Hieroglyphic Texts from Egyptian Stelae*, 13, plate XLVI.

197. Wolfhart Westendorf, *Painting, Sculpture, and Architecture of Ancient Egypt* (New York: Abrams, 1969), 138–39; Alexandre Moret, *Histoire de l'Orient* (Paris: Presses universitaires, 1929), 528.

198. Roland Tefnin, review of *Akhenaten and Nefertiti*, by Cyril Aldred, *CdE* 52 (1977): 83–85.

199. Julia Samson, "Nefertiti's Regality," *JEA* 63 (1977): 91.

200. Ibid., 96.

201. Ibid., 88.

202. Rudolf Anthes, "Die Maat der Echnaton von Amarna," *JAOS* 72/14 (1953): 31.

203. Moret, *Histoire de l'Orient*, 528.

204. Gardiner, "Adoption Extraordinary," 26.

205. Andras Alföldi, "The Crisis of the Empire (A.D. 249–270)," in *Cambridge Ancient History*, ed. Stanley A. Cook, 12 vols. (Cambridge: Cambridge University Press, 1981), 12:189.

206. Cf. László Kákosy, "Selige und Verdammte in der spätägyptischen Religion," *ZÄS* 97 (1971): 100.

207. S. Mayassis, *Mystères et intiations dans la préhistoire et protohistoire de l'anté-Diluvien à Sumer-Babylone* (Athens: BAOA, 1961), 299–304.

208. Ibid., 301; cf. Pyramid Text 437 (§800); 459 (§865); 513 (§1172).

209. Theodor Hopfner, *Plutarch über Isis und Osiris*, 2 vols. (Prague: Orientalisches Institut, 1941), 1:70.

210. Günther Roeder, *Urkunden zur Religion des alten Aegypten* (Jena, Germany: Diederichs, 1915), 24.

211. Jaroslav Černý, *Ancient Egyptian Religion* (New York: Hutchinson's University Library, 1952), 59.

212. Posener, *Divinité du pharaon*, 102.

213. Morenz, "Problem des Werdens," 81.

214. Ibid.

215. Percy E. Newberry, "The Shepherd's Crook and the So-called 'Flail' or 'Scourge' of Osiris," *JEA* 15 (1929): 85–87.

216. Ricardo A. Caminos, *Late-Egyptian Miscellanies* (London: Oxford University Press, 1954), 420.

217. Constantin Sander-Hansen, *Die religiösen Texte auf dem Sarg der Anchnesneferibre* (Copenhagen: Levin and Munksgaard, 1937), 105–6.

218. Cf. Eugène Lefébure, "Le Cham et l'Adam Égyptiens," *BE* 35 (1912): 7.

219. Westendorf, *Painting, Sculpture, and Architecture*, 84.

220. Gardiner, review of *The Golden Bough*, 124.

221. Georges A. Legrain, *Les temples de Karnak* (Brussels: Vromant, 1929), 217, fig. 129.

222. Nibley, "A New Look at the Pearl of Great Price," *IE* 72 (May 1969): 88.

223. Ibid., *IE* 72 (September 1969): 89.

224. Kurt H. Sethe, *Urkunden des alten Reichs*, 4 vols. (Leipzig: Hinrichs, 1932), 1:111.

225. Nibley, "A New Look at the Pearl of Great Price," *IE* 72 (September 1969): 89–93.

226. Budge, *Book of the Dead (Papyrus of Hunefer)*, 34.

227. Aylward M. Blackman, "A Study of the Liturgy Celebrated in the Temple of Aton at El-Amarna," in *Recueil d'études Égyptologiques dediées à la mémoire de Jean François Champollion* (Paris: Champion, 1922), 517, 521.

228. Shmuel Yeivin, "Canaanite Ritual Vessels in Egyptian Cultic Practices," *JEA* 62 (1976): 114.

229. Nibley, "A New Look at the Pearl of Great Price," *IE* 72 (September 1969): 91.

230. Ibid.

231. Schott, *Schöne Fest vom Wüstentale*, 48–54.

232. Jean Capart, "Au pays du symbolisme," *CdE* 32 (1957): 232–33, 236.

233. Derchain, "Lotus, la mandragore et le perséa," 65–66.

234. Ibid., 71.

235. Waltraud Guglielmi, "Zur Symbolik des 'Darbringens des Straußes der sḥ.t,'" *ZÄS* 103 (1976): 103.

236. Ibid., 103.

237. Ibid., 104–6.

238. Ibid., 108.

239. Ibid.

240. Ibid., 110–11.

241. Ibid., 111–12.

242. Ibid.

243. Nibley, *Message of the Joseph Smith Papyri*, 82.

244. Siegfried Schott, *Urkunden mythologischen Inhalts,* vol. 6 in Urkunden des ägyptischen Altertums (Leipzig: Hinrichs, 1929), 139.

245. Radwan, *Darstellungen des regierenden Königs,* 57.

246. Ibid., 3.

247. Ibid.

248. Schott, *Schöne Fest vom Wüstentale,* 56, 60.

249. Ibid., 111.

250. Hermann Grapow, "Totenbuch 17," in *Religiöse Urkunden: Ausgewählte Texte des Totenbuchs* (Leipzig: Hinrichs, 1915–17), 57–59.

251. Schott, *Schöne Fest vom Wüstentale,* 48–51.

252. Bernhard Beer, *Leben Abraham's nach Auffassung der jüdischen Sage* (Leipzig: Leiner, 1859), 194 n. 853.

253. Hall, *Hieroglyphic Texts from Egyptian Stelae,* 3.

254. *Jubilees* 39:6.

255. Kaplony, "Vorbild des Königs unter Sesostris III," 405–6.

256. Bonnet, *Reallexikon der ägyptischen Religionsgeschichte,* 400.

257. Daumas, "Sens de la royauté égyptienne," 146; cf. Max Guilmot, "Le titre Imj-Khent dans l'Égypte ancienne," *CdE* 39 (1964): 39–40.

258. Daumas, "Sens de la royauté égyptienne," 146.

259. Frankfort, *Kingship and the Gods,* 128–30.

260. Bergman, *Ich bin Isis,* 300.

261. James H. Breasted, *Ancient Records of Egypt,* 4 vols. (Chicago: University of Chicago Press, 1906–7), 2:271.

262. Grdseloff, "L'insigne du grand juge égyptien," 201–2.

263. Adolf Jellinek, *Bet ha-Midrasch,* 6 vols. (1853–77; reprint, Jerusalem: Wahrmann, 1967), 5:41, 50.

10

A Pioneer Mother

A Grim Beginning

Matriarchal primacy in Egypt was traced by the Egyptians to a certain great Lady who came to the Nile Valley immediately after the flood and established herself and her sons as rulers in the land. Since this is the same story that is told in Abraham 1:21–27, it is fortunate that the Egyptian sources are both abundant and specific. It was Hermann Junker who first called attention to them in the early 1900s; in short order the eminent Egyptologists Kurt Sethe and Wilhelm Spiegelberg joined in the hunt, and by 1917 the most important sources had been brought together and published. More recently, however, even more impressive texts have come to light, in particular the great Leiden Book of Breathings, Leiden Papyrus T32.[1]

Question: What is the nature of the original documents?

Answer: They are mythological and ritual papyri and include numerous temple inscriptions; some of the accounts are quite long and detailed. The record stretches from the Palermo Stone and the Pyramid Texts at the beginning of Egyptian history to pronouncements of Roman emperors and scholars at the end of it, and it is safe to say that any major mythological or ritual text in Egyptian is almost bound to refer somewhere to the circumstances under which the woman came to Egypt and established her son on the throne. Though that may seem like a sweeping statement, it is here made with confidence, though it must necessarily be the subject of a somewhat ambitious special study hereafter. Sethe wanted to discount some of the later texts purely because of their lateness, but since they were found to tell the same story as the very oldest writings, the early and late documents impressively support each other.[2]

Question: How old is the story?

Answer: All are agreed that it goes back to prehistoric times; Sethe would place it one thousand years before Menes, the founder of the First Dynasty.[3] Naturally, German scholarship began by designating the whole thing as "a wild exotic growth of popular religious fantasy."[4] Yet all soon recognized two clear-cut episodes as the archaic nucleus of the epic profusion: (1) the story of the "Sun's Eye" and (2) the story of the Great Trek across the desert to Egypt. Both tales climax in the arrival of the Lady in Egypt, and both stories are inseparably joined as early as the Pyramid Texts, which confirm their great antiquity.[5]

Question: Do you think these accounts have any value as history?

Answer: Yes. For one thing, from the beginning to the end of their history the Egyptians dramatized the events of the story in uncomplicated and unchanging "Founder's Day" ceremonies that appear singularly detached from the great cults of Re and Osiris and were regarded as strictly historical.[6] The claim of one particular spot to be the original place of arrival was never challenged; though Egyptian temples are notoriously competitive in their claims to precedence, no one ever questioned the traditional spot where the Lady landed, and Junker is puzzled by the "unearned celebrity" of a shrine that was celebrated for no other reason than its being the Egyptian Plymouth Rock, to which

nonetheless, as the holiest spot in the land, all the gods and
the faithful of Egypt were required to make an annual pilgrimage.[7] The literary texts confirm "what stands independently in a thousand different places on the same theme,"
and the investigators are agreed that what all the texts boil
down to is a single straightforward story, singularly devoid
of abstract, symbolic, or mystical content, of how once long
ago a great Lady came from far away and settled in Egypt.[8]
But we must not oversimplify; though the scattered sources
agree on a remarkably consistent story, it is nonetheless
quite a detailed one.

Question: How does it begin?

Answer: The story opens with Re in heaven commis-
sioning his daughter, regularly designated as his "Eye," to
go down and finish up the liquidation of the human race in
the flood.[9] As in the book of Enoch, we hear a good deal of
comings and goings between heaven and earth in preparation for the flood; we see Shu, the inspired contact man
between the two worlds, depart from earth in disgust.[10] So
does Re himself, who up until then had consorted with men
on earth; now he withdraws his presence from them and
calls a council in heaven to decide what is to be done with
the unruly human race.[11] He tells the assembly that he is
about to send a flood and that all things are to return to the
primal *ḥuḥu* of the great waters of Nun, even as it was
before the creation, in the beginning.[12] *Ḥuḥu* is the primordial chaos, the *tōhû-wā-bōhû* of Genesis 1:2. So even as in
Abraham 1:24, the Egyptian story of earthly dominion begins
with the flood. And there can be little doubt that it was *the*
flood, and not the seasonal inundation, that even so was
regarded as but a repetition of the original.[13]

As the curtain rises we see all nature in upheaval as the
skies darken and the waters descend.[14] The turmoil of
nature is ritually represented as the work of Seth, who
throws all things into confusion.[15] The personification of

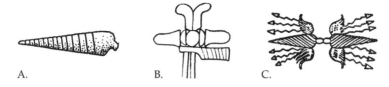

Figure 79. The belemnite (from the Greek *belemnon* or dart, cf. Ephesians 6:16) is the fossilized internal shell of an extinct genus of cephalopod, related to the squid and octopus; it takes several forms including the spiral (A). It was thought to be a thunderbolt from heaven that had turned to stone on striking the earth. Letopolis, the city of Min, is the only source of these fossils in Egypt. Not surprisingly, the symbol of the city, the thunderbolt of Min, is made up of two belemnites (B; see fig. 104, p. 636). The thunderbolt motif continued into Roman times as shown by this detail from a coin (C).

violent atmospheric disturbances and world disorder, his thunderbolt emblem, the *belemnite* (fig. 79), which is found at prehistoric shrines throughout the land and in many other parts of the world, attests the reality of those early catastrophes.[16] But human depravity contributes its full share to the vast calamity, for mankind had turned against its loving creator (Moses 5:28–34). It sounds very much like the Enoch literature, and Shu, in order to accomplish his mission between heaven and earth, must move through the same cosmic storms as those faced by Enoch and the other holy messengers.[17]

The end of the age in the utter dissolution of all things is signified in the fatal illness of its ruling deity (reminding us of Aeschylus's *Prometheus*). Re, no longer the supreme god but called "the son of a greater one," declares: "My limbs are sick, weak, shaking, just like the other time; but this time I will not return again—everything is changed; I will leave my son Shu in charge."[18] In the famous Turin Papyrus, the lamentable condition of Re, combining extreme senility with a deadly serpent's sting, sets all the gods to weeping, until his daughter Isis heals him in return for his transmitting to

her the secret of his name, and handing over his Eye to her
son Horus; since she is his Eye, this guarantees that the
authority of the rulers of Egypt in the new age will be kept
in the matriarchal line.[19] It is interesting also that almost
every Egyptian king, as Ferdinand Wüstenfeld observed, is
remembered in tradition as "the first after the flood," indicating that the end of the flood is indeed the legendary
beginning of the dynastic history of Egypt.[20]

Question: What was Shu's mission?

Answer: To repeople the earth after the flood, taking Re's
place among men. To perform that office, his companion is
Tefnut, the Daughter of Re, the Sun's Eye.[21] "The individual
character of Tefnut," according to Rudolf Anthes, remains a
mystery. Though they have a "relation with moisture,"
Tefnut and Shu "apparently refer to human society and not
to a myth."[22] In most tales dealing with the repopulation of
the earth, the primal pair are Shu and Tefnut, the parents of
Atum, whose mating marks the separation of earth and
heaven in a new creation.[23] Let there be a garden, a field of
rest, says Re as he plants a new Eden. The story is told in
the *Book of the Cow* (fig. 80), the Cow being the Flood-Lady
herself, who first took the ailing Re from earth up to heaven
on her back and then brought the flood; for she was both
Hathor the Cow and Mut the Mother in her capacity of a
cosmic personification of the primal waters of the Helio-
politan Nun. "The Great Flood *and* the first living thing to
emerge from it are represented as a cow, called Methyer,

Figure 80. In Tutankhamun's tomb, as in that of his predecessor
Thutmosis III (see fig. 13, p. 67), the first hour of the Amduat was painted
on the western wall as a symbol for the other eleven hours not shown.
As another level of protection, the *Book of the Cow* was carved in elegant
low relief on the inner rear wall of the outermost golden shrine. The
image shows the goddess Nut as a cow whose belly is lined with stars.
Eight Heh gods steady her legs as she rises to heaven with Ra. The god
Shu holds up her belly, allowing the two solar boats to pass below.

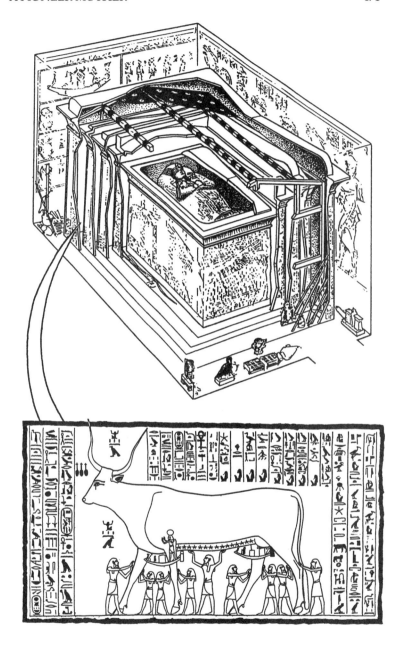

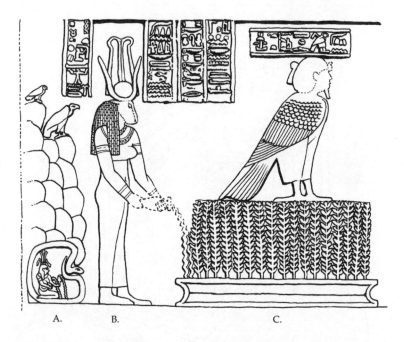

Figure 81. A bas-relief in Hadrian's gate at Philae shows the rocky cliffs of
Bigge with a Horus falcon and a vulture goddess on top. At the bottom a
great serpent encircles Hapy, who kneels within, pouring out water from
a vase. This represents the source of the Nile emerging from the caves of
Elephantine (A). The cow-headed figure is labeled Isis (B)—not Hathor—
as she pours milk over the sacred grove on the island of Bigge (C), where
the Ba of Osiris, the human-headed falcon rests.

'the Great Flooding.'"[24] In the very ancient Salt Papyrus,
Shu and Tefnut in establishing a new race on earth also set
up their primal shrine at the caves of Elephantine (fig. 81),
the source of the waters of the flood. Their doings are presented not as the first creation, but the end of one dispensation and the founding of another.

　　Question: But why Re's daughter?

　　Answer: She cannot very well be the founder and ruler
of a kingdom on earth and still remain by his side in the sky.

She is his comfort and counsel, his aide and nurse; it is to her that he reveals the weariness of his heart, the failing of his strength.[25] As she wept with him and for him, "her eye poured forth like a cloudburst, like the sky dark with storm," a familiar "Enoch" motif (cf. Moses 7:28).[26] "At the time when the Daughter of Re entered heaven, he called her the Eye of Re (the apple of his eye), the diadem on his brow, . . . because he loved her."[27] As the diadem as well as the Eye, she is his defender and protectress, the uraeus serpent on his brow who terrifies all who stand in his way.[28] And yet the main theme of the prologue in heaven is how the girl cooperated with a deceitful serpent to force Re to divulge to her his true name, the ultimate secret of his power and authority.

Question: And that is a loving daughter?

Answer: That shows us what it is all about: By getting her father mortally ill of a serpent bite that only she can cure, she forces him to give her the key to the supreme patriarchal authority, so that she will be able to hand it on to *her* earthly son.[29] Thus in Egypt is "preserved the curse in the land" (Abraham 1:24), that equation and confusion of patriarchal and matriarchal authority that forever plagued the pharaohs, never able to be sure of their lineage. We shall discuss this matter further on.

The Daughter of Re is not all sweetness and light—there is a sinister side to her nature, for she is terrible in her wrath, all the more terrifying for its being righteous wrath.[30]

Question: Couldn't Re have found someone else to do the dirty work?

Answer: The council of gods advised him: "Send down your Eye to deal with them!" So "down went Hathor (the Cow) and smote the human race upon the desert places; then she returned and reported to Re, who said, 'It is well.'"[31] Though "her majesty came as the excellent Wḏjat eye," to establish a glorious order of life on the emergent land, she arrived first "in her form of Sekhmet," the terrible lioness of the desert.[32] Re explained to her that this was the only course open to him because of the horrible depravity and rebellion of the human race; violent intervention is an act of kindness, since "my purpose is to reduce them to some semblance of reason!" So her mission is a double one, both tragic and joyful. As the prehistoric Seth and Min were "gods of the blessed yet dangerous storm,"[33] so Hathor, their inseparable female companion, appears in a First Dynasty ivory carving "flanked by a pair of thunderbolts,"[34] while her counterpart "Neith the sky- and warrior-goddess," with her own thunderbolt, brings her red crown to Min's capital in predynastic times.[35]

Question: But deserts at the time of the flood?

Answer: Not as paradoxical as it seems. In ancient flood literature, as in present-day experience, the alarming occurrence—side-by-side and rapid alteration between the wildest extremes of weather, hot and cold, wet and dry—is a commonplace. The perceptive E. A. Wallis Budge saw in the pair Shu and Tefnut the personification of alternative drought and flood respectively,[36] and as Isis, the Lady brings forth both deadly drought and deadly flood.[37] Thus the weeping Eye of Re extinguishes the Flaming Eye and "cools the ways."[38] The same Eye of Re goes forth as a flame, driving away the flood serpent and taking possession of heaven and earth amid mighty thunderstorms and deluges of rain.[39] Chaos still prevails on earth,[40] as it does in all the earliest accounts of the "separation" of the people (the Tower of Babel story) after the flood.[41] The coming forth of the Sun's Eye represents the passing (overcoming) of the great cloud serpent who had darkened the sky and swallowed the sun.[42] Fire and water mix in the flood traditions, and the tears of the Lady came from a blazing Eye to overcome the wicked.[43] As mistress of both fire and water she has ambivalent functions: As the Eye of Re, the life-giving Sun, she causes the waters to subside.[44]

A Coming-Out Party

Question: Why both tragic and joyful?

Answer: Because she is coming to put an end to one race and establish another.[45] She arrives to find the land still under water, the slaughter of mankind in its final stages, and proceeds to finish them off in a ceremonial orgy of blood.[46] For the ritual she orders red ochre to be mixed with beer, "looking like the blood of humans," and seven thousand jars of it to be poured out to cover the earth to a depth of three spans.[47] Assisted by her handmaidens, she treats the red beer mash and brews a "victory-drink of beer and blood" by order of the high priest of Heliopolis, or makes red pomegranate wine to celebrate the completion of her task. Beer mixed with ochre concludes the great debacle *y* of the flood: "It was the blood of mankind."[48]

Plutarch, commenting on these Egyptian rites, says that "wine makes men wild because the vine was fertilized in soil rich with the blood of the wicked victims of the flood," for which reason, he observes, Egyptian priests may not touch wine, and Pharaoh himself may drink it only on this particular day.[49] For drunkenness renews the guilt of the ancestors. Seth, the ever-violent and abominable storm-god, is also the prehistoric god of drunkenness.[50] Five hundred years earlier, Pindar gives us the Greek version. The festival of Deucalion (Noah) was celebrated in wine with songs about the great storms and the destruction of the world by the force of the black waters, and about how Zeus suddenly dried up the waters and the race of Japetus (Japheth) came forth to repeople the earth.[51] Recall that Noah right after the flood "planted a vineyard" and also "drank of the wine and was drunken," not without a hint of scandal (Genesis 9:21–24), which resulted in the cursing of Canaan. And it

was Canaan's line "which preserved the curse" in Egypt
(Abraham 1:24). Just what that curse was can only be
explained after we have looked into the role of the woman.
So much for the grim side of her mission.

Question: And the bright side?

Answer: The wine not only whets her orgiastic rage—it
also puts an end to it. It brings release; Hathor of the wine
jar soon finds her wrath appeased.[52] Indeed, the wine was
drugged to make all forget the terrible things they had just
been through—it was a blessed cup of Lethe,[53] a cheering
cup, to celebrate the New Year and forget the past, looking
forward to a happy future. Re also gives his weeping son
Horus the red pomegranate wine for consolation. Shu, like
Deucalion, "caused the heavens to shine after darkness, it
was the hue of the sky the hue of wine" when the sky was
black "amidst storms and gloom."[54] But when the sky
brightens, "you see Hathor bringing the mother of her
mother on the day of the Feast of Intoxication; . . . you hear
the castanets at the Illumination of the ꜣIw.t, (with) the dancing of the sweet-voiced singing girls . . . at the Floodhouse
when his Majesty goes to the Shrine of the Waters."[55] The
mixing of water and wine, which was the destruction of the
race by the flood, becomes the bringing of life and happiness: "On the day of Everlasting Time, water is brought to
your Ba . . . on the Day of Intoxication, . . . on the day when
the flood-waters were everywhere."[56] "You praised the
Great Lady at the primal Hill of Jars." She is again beautiful to mankind as she joins with the Ennead in holding back
the waters at the end of the period. On the night before the
New Year she hears the cry of the slain before the dawn, but
with the new day comes joy.[57] *The changing nature of the wine*
definitely relates our Egyptian story to the biblical flood. In
the very old Christian *Apocalypse of Baruch,* we are told that
Noah after the flood hesitated to plant the vine, "for Adam
was destroyed by it"—the grape being the forbidden fruit

in many old Adam accounts; so he prayed for forty days with tears streaming down (an Enoch motif), until an angel appeared to reassure him: "Arise Noah, plant the vine; its bitterness shall be *changed to sweetness,* and its curse shall be changed to a blessing. What it yields shall be *the blood of God.*"[58]

Question: You referred to her as Hathor. How is she related to Pharaoh?

Answer: She is designated by countless names to indicate her various functions. Before all else she is the Great Mother; she was also the consort, hierodule, Lady of Carousing and Intoxication, even before she was called the Sun's Eye, according to some.[59] But all these roles go together naturally in the flood story, and in that situation her special name is Tefnut. At the beginning of the flood story Re summons "my Eye, Shu, Tefnut, Geb, . . . Nut and all the preexistent parents who were together in the Nun, and all those who preside over the primeval waters."[60] These are divine primal parent couples, with Shu and Tefnut leading the parade,[61] while the Eye is Tefnut herself in her capacity of special emissary of Re. Since she had two offices to perform, one of destruction and one of inauguration, and since she found the land inhabited though she was its discoverer, there has been some doubt as to whether she made one trip to earth or two. Spiegelberg always inserts an "again" in passages telling of her coming to the valley overland, and the Egyptians explained that she had been in the land formerly but had forgotten all about it when she finally crossed the desert to settle the land for good.[62] She had already played Eve to Shu's Adam.

The Itinerary

Question: Where did she come from on the journey?

Answer: The first thing to notice is that she comes from a far-off mysterious place, "from the land of the gods,"[63] a place far removed.[64] She is, in fact, most commonly referred to as "the Lady from Afar," and, as such, is a stranger to the land.[65] Her escort is Onuris, that being the Graecized form of *In.ḥr.t*, "Bringer of the Distant One," or "He who brought the Lady from Afar," sometimes shown in the hieroglyphic as a walking man bearing the "far" (*Ḥr*), or sky-symbol, in his right hand.[66] The distant place in the sky is here deliberately vague, but all are agreed that her mysterious homeland lay to the east.[67]

While Junker, who always insisted on an African origin, put her homeland in the far southeast, the African Punt, the consensus of opinion favors the northeast. The trouble is that certain key names may be found in either Asia or Africa. Punt itself would seem to be not in Africa but in Canaan, and when "her majesty came . . . to see the Nile of Egypt and all its wonders, turning her back on St.t," St.t may be Nubia but is more properly Asia.[68] The women of Thebes venerated their patroness, Hathor the Sun's Eye, as the carousing hierodule of Canaan.[69] But if she came from the east, it was by a roundabout way, for all are agreed that she entered the Nile Valley by the Wadi Hammamat, far to the south.[70] Some sources tell of her long detour through Arabia, and all hark back to her trip through the desert.[71] "She comes through eastern desert by El Kab as an authentic desert woman," writes Junker, "plodding along with her crooked staff."[72] As Hathor, she comes smelling the earth, "advancing along the ways," as cattle do on a long hot drive.[73] Her companion is shown as Horus bearing a plainsman's spear and lasso.[74] The situation is vividly depicted in two ritual texts edited by Siegfried Schott. The *Victory over Seth* begins with the depravity of the human race and the council in heaven (almost identical with the Shabako and Pyramid Text versions),[75] after which we follow the Lady as she meets the challenge of the journey in her various forms, terrible and benign, overcoming the evil opposition in the desert and on the waters.[76] The other text, the *Secret Ritual for Overcoming Evil,* tells the same story. At the sight of human wickedness the Great God hides his face in anger on that day and drinks blood,[77] for the human race has rebelled against him.[78] Thoth "appeases the Eye after its rage, he who fetched the Great Lady from afar, who embraced the Eye of Re on the day on which it was exalted,"[79] who pacified the combatants after the battle and put an end to conflict.[80] The rebels would defile the Great Mother's settlement at Khemmis as she comes as Hathor to Egypt[81] to end the abominations of the ancients.[82] "The Mistress of Life in the head of her Creator (as his Eye) afflicts those who would do evil. . . . O Lord of Brawling at the waters of the Valley-mouth (*ꜥndty*), he who is above the Floodwaters of the Sea . . . come and protect me from the death and destruction of this day and the terror of one who comes and seizes!"[83] "Woman, yield not before the storm!"[84]

As Sekhmet, the lioness of the desert, she arrives with her nomad company to overwhelm and bind the evil ones; the Eye becomes established at the holy mound or complex, prevailing against the evil powers that had tried to establish themselves there, who "tried to trick the Mother, . . . who have rebelled against the breasts,"[85] who have rejected the lotus.[86] In the story of Astarte, in which we have already seen Egypt and Canaan sharing a tradition with the Abraham legends, what we deliberately passed over was that in the Egyptian version, when "the daughter of Ptah" who is Astarte "is fetched from the land of the '*Asiatics*' . . . we find the goddess in tears," writes Alan Gardiner, and "it seems legitimate to conclude that she did not find her task an agreeable one."[87] Yet just three lines later we find her singing and laughing![88] What is going on? In this document she was viewed as a wrathful and furious goddess—why in this particular context is not clear. However, it is clear that the sea is demanding tribute and is ready in a damaged

passage *"to cover the earth and the mountains"*; "to what can
the allusion be," asks Gardiner, "except to a threatened
submergence of the world by the sea?" What follows is
almost entirely unreadable, but "perhaps the *dénouement* of
the story consisted in a description how an end was finally
put to the sea's interminable exactions."[89] The main motifs
of the text itself as they emerge are a scene in heaven, a general embracing, great upheavals of earth, sky, and especially
sea; Astarte is summoned, she weeps about something, then
suddenly she "sang and laughed at him . . . as she sat on the
shore (?) of the sea," after having passed through a terrible
journey. "Then he said to her: Whence comest thou, O
daughter of Ptah, thou angry and furious goddess? Hast
thou ruined thy sandals which were (beneath) thy feet, and
hast thou rent the clothes which were upon thee, through
this going and coming which thou hast made in the sky and
the earth?" She goes back and reports to the Council in
Heaven, which does her obeisance. Thus the Canaanite version confirms the picture. "The general situation in this
Egyptian tale," writes Theodor Gaster, "accords perfectly
with that implied in the Ugaritic poem."[90] In the latter, the
sea Yamm is in complete domination "as lord and master of
the gods and perhaps also of the earth."[91] "Baal, [in heaven]
however, inspired by 'Anat' [the Lady]" fights and finally
overcomes the waters.[92] Gaster concludes that both these
stories "simply mythologize seasonal conditions at the time
when the rivers became swollen and the sea is beset with
autumnal squalls. Not until the waters abate or are confined
is the earth released from their oppressive domination."[93]
Certainly such seasonal events were dramatized, but always
in terms of a much greater world catastrophe.

There is much more material that would trace the
Lady's journey to Egypt by the short route from, or at least
through, Canaan.[94] "Let us frankly admit our ignorance,"
wrote Gardiner, warning against any attempt to "adjudicate

between those who advocate the line of approach from the Red Sea through the Wâdi Hammâmât and the town of Coptos, and those who favor the northerly route from Palestine."[95] In either case the immigrants, whether led by Horus or Hathor-Nebet-Hetepet, come from the same far and mysterious place.

For the Canaanites to lay claim to the Egyptian mysteries, it was necessary to reverse the direction of her journey. In a famous story told by Plutarch, Isis, coming from Egypt, arrives at Byblos, exhausted after the long journey, and sits sorrowing by a spring.[96] She pays no attention to anyone but the young girls who come from the court of the queen, and she celebrates with them, braiding their tresses and endowing them with divine fragrance. She then becomes the nurse to the young prince, feeding the child, as the infant Abraham was fed, by letting it suck her finger. But when the queen interrupts the ordinances of the mysteries that would make the babe immortal, the offended Isis departs from the land, sailing back to Egypt and taking with her the oldest son of the king, who became Maneros, the first heir to the throne of Egypt and patron of bibulous festivities.[97] There are many variations on the theme, but the shifting directions of the journey between Egypt and Canaan are not without historical foundation. There is, for example, much evidence to identify Qadschu, Ksh.t, Kn.t, the great hierodule goddess of Canaan, with Hathor; for she not only became extremely popular with the women of Thebes, who identified her with Hathor Mistress of Punt and Mafkat,[98] but also enjoyed among them special esteem as the Sun's Eye. As early as the Coffin Texts,[99] Hathor is designated as the Mistress of Byblos, and inscriptions found in Palestine equate Isis with Hathor and with the local Baalat Gebal as well as the Lady Astarte, in which role she is shown holding the child Horus.[100] The inevitable mix-up of Horus with Osiris as Isis's companion in Canaan is explained by

Aristides, a contemporary of Plutarch, who says that Isis took to wandering after the death of her husband Osiris, fleeing with her son Horus and first settling in Byblos; but when Horus slew Typhon (Apepi, the serpent occupant of the land) in Egypt, she found it safe to settle there permanently.[101]

These unmistakable variants of the Sun's Eye story—the demise of the divine parent, the long journey, the exhausted Lady by the water, cheered and comforted by a celebration of local damsels, the overcoming of the serpent, the establishing of the youthful companion as king of the land—are confirmed by the Greek version of the same tale, acquired from Egypt by way of Canaan; it is this particular story, according to Siegfried Hermann, that shows us how "on Syrian soil Egyptian tradition meets the Greek mind with which it enters into a happy symbiosis."[102] It is no less than the foundation of the great Eleusinian Mysteries. The story is told in the *Homeric Hymn* to Demeter, in which the goddess comes as a stranger from afar, wandering in desperation at a time when the earth is blasted with drought. Arriving at Eleusis, she sat down by a stream, exhausted and sorrowing; there she was met by the crone Iambe, who was able to cheer her up with her lively dancing. In gratitude she founded her temple there and established her mysteries and then proceeded to set up other such shrines and mysteries in various places throughout the land to celebrate the victory and rule of her daughter Kore.[103]

The mystery cult is not the main point of the thing, Hermann finds, being a secondary element, while the ladies themselves were in the earliest times not great goddesses, but rather pitiful suffering figures.[104] The three leading motifs of both the Canaanite and Greek myths, according to him, are (1) the blight of nature, (2) the settling of the woman in the land, and (3) the establishment of the mysteries. In reference to the last named, in Byblos, Osiris is to

Isis as the maiden Kore is to Demeter, the lost child who sits enthroned in the dark underworld from which he or she must be liberated by the mysteries.[105] The confusion of Osiris—both husband and child of Isis[106]—with Horus is inevitable and has led to many suggestions by way of explanation, but it does not change the story. The predominance of the female element may well be responsible for Kore supplanting Horus in the role of the child; indeed, the *Homeric Hymn* opens by announcing that Adonis, i.e., the Syrian Osiris = Horus, has stolen the honors of Kore.[107] The tension between male and female is apparent in Plutarch's account of how Horus became so resentful of his mother's tolerance of his rival and brother Typhon that he snatched the crown from her head only to have Thoth (Hermes) replace it with a Hathor mask—she was still number one.[108]

These myths became a plaything for all sorts of irresponsible poets, priests, and quacks to kick around, but behind them, Plutarch assures us, lies the core of historic events that really took place if we could only get back to them.[109] Recall that when the waters of the flood subsided, Noah was in a desert world—*kharbu* (Genesis 8:13)—and soon came the terrible winds that dried everything out, nature quickly reverting from one extreme to another even as mankind just as quickly reverted to their old wicked ways.[110]

It is a depressing picture; during the crossing to Egypt things could not have been worse. The long Demotic account of the Sun's Eye tells all about it. In order to survive the ordeal, the traveler must turn herself into a *raging lioness;* her mane smokes with fire; her back has the color of blood; her face becomes a blazing solar disk, withering and searing all before it like the noonday sun; "the desert was enveloped in a vast cloud of dust by the beating of her tail; tornadoes spun out over the desert when she snapped her teeth; fire shot out of the ground when she whetted her claws. The forests withered and clouds of gnats rode on the smoke of her breath, . . . then the desert opened its mouth, stone spoke to sand, and the hills shook for two hours."[111] The woman's form of Hathor-Tefnut the Lion-Lady simply reflects, Bonnet observes, the terrible times in which she was living.[112] While they are crossing the desert, her guide, who has taken the form of an ape for survival, tries to maintain her sanity and his own by telling her animal fables, all of which deal with the utter treachery and depravity of the human race so richly deserving of what has befallen it.[113]

Question: Then the flood had no beneficial moral effect?

Answer: On the contrary, even in her fiercest form the Lady brings good as well as bad news. Her face and her word are a consuming fire to the wicked, but a blessing to the righteous,[114] even as the flame of Tefnut is a cooling north wind to her beloved.[115] If the lion-headed Hathor-Tefnut is death, the lion-headed Hathor-Isis is birth and life.[116] To the rebellious, she is the Lady of Slaughter, pleased with blood, the Queen of Fire who burns up Apophis the serpent enemy of Re.[117] But to her followers, she is the rising sun that leads the way, Sothis the guiding star, who brings joy wherever she passes.[118] Her grim mission accomplished, the Sun's Eye again takes up her proper position in the heavens, where something had plainly gone wrong.[119]

As she nears Egypt, she chooses a milder form for survival in a less savage desert; her welcoming hymn says, "Come to me [Mother], we desire to see thee in Egypt, thou gazelle of the desert!"[120] The dwellers of the wadis along the Nile bring her presents of gazelles and greetings: "Be happy! Do not be angry with us when you come!"[121] Here a word more about the *wine* is in order. As Hellmut Brunner explains it, Re sent out his Eye as Sekhmet, the lioness of the desert, to destroy everything, but presently it is no longer blood but beer that delights her; the *Blutrausch* is turned into a *Bierrausch*, as the healing waters of the Nile cool and

appease her rage.[122] The wine not only was an escape valve
to release the tension and wrath, but wiped out any feelings
of guilt and remorse for the excesses of her anger. "Her
daily requirement of intoxication with music and dancing"
is no longer orgiastic, as she changes from the flaming
lioness Sekhmet to the good-natured cat Bast.[123] While her
companion "cools her glow" in an affectionate embrace,[124]
she is crowned as the "Mistress of Intoxication."[125] Everywhere along the river the women let down their hair in
unrestrained fun and games to greet the Lady to her
domains.[126] "At the time her Majesty came from Bwgm, when
she was permitted to look upon the Nile of Egypt . . .
Dendera was drenched with liquors, with choice wines."[127]
The motives are all intermingled in the Leiden Papyrus T32:
Here comes Hathor the Mother "on the Day of the Feast of
Intoxication, . . . the Night of the Coming of the Cow."[128] She
"enters into the presence of Re . . . on the day when his children carry him; . . . on the Day of Everlasting Time, water is
brought to you when you take possession" of the land,[129]
"setting out for your estate . . . on the Day of Intoxication."[130]
"Hathor brings the cake to the party on the Wag Festival
(the New Year's Day) . . . on the Day of bringing in the
liquors."[131]

Question: Isn't this simply the old familiar vegetation
rite of the year?

Answer: In Egypt it is doubtful if anything is simply
one thing. Plutarch says Osiris is not only the god of wine
on the occasion, but also represents all life-giving liquids
(e.g., the water and the milk that are also so prominent), his
trees and springs being equally sacrosanct.[132] The unmistakable elements of the bizarre wine story appear in almost all
of the many ritual combat texts from every period.

In the "Fending Off of Evil" we read: "The Mistress of
Life on the head of her Creator [i.e., as the Eye of Re] does
damage to those of evil mind. . . . O Lord of the Slaughter

beside the ʿnḏty-water, who is above the Flood of the Sea,
. . . come and protect me from dying on this day, and from
the terror of one who comes and seizes!"[133] In this the
dreaded evil is the evil of the flood, sent by an angry god:
the Great God hides his face in anger on that day and
drinks blood as a consuming fire whose hand holds life
while death is in his footsteps.[134] For the human race has
rebelled against him.[135] But after her wrath, the Eye of Re,
the Lady who was brought from afar, is pacified with the
destruction of the rebels.[136] In the piece called *Victory over
Seth*, Seth is the primordial storm-god, and the story begins
with Isis complaining, sending her voice to Re in heaven:
"Turn thy face to me, Lord of the Gods! Behold thy commandments are held in contempt. I am Isis the daughter of
thy daughter! I have been turned from laughter: the Evil
One has returned to his ways, running rampant in the
world." So the gods were in consternation, and in the Great
Council Thoth pronounced a curse on Seth, forbidding him
to enter Egypt.[137] So the Lady goes down and wades in the
blood of Seth and his beheaded followers, in which capacity
she is the Mistress of Slaughter, wielding her deadly knives,
Sekhmet the raging lioness coming across the desert, as the
Flaming one, the Fire-serpent![138] In the prehistoric rite of sacrificing the oryx, she is "Nekhbet, the White Lady, the Eye
of Re, . . . whose countenance is terrible to the enemies of
her father, until she has satisfied herself and is appeased
with drinking their blood. It is the Eye of Re, the great
Flame . . . Sekhmet, mighty against her enemies," etc.[139]

The drama of Edfu is a later text but a very ancient rite:
"Rejoice O ye women of Busiris, . . . behold Horus (her
champion) . . . drunken with the blood of the enemy which
his lance has shed! . . . He has poured forth a river the color
of blood, like Sekhmet in the midst of carnage. . . . Come, let
us celebrate with a dance (ballet) on this theme. . . . Drink
the blood of the enemy and also that of their women-folk!

... Take your places for the dance with him!" A description of a woman's antiphonal chorus in the manner of the "Maiden choruses" of Alcaeus or Alcman follows.[140] Perhaps the oldest of all is the drama contained in the Ramesseum Papyrus, Scene 22: The king's children bring in a *shpn.t* jar of wine, which is designated as the Eye, represented soon after by a string of red carnelian beads.[141]

The New Home

Abraham 1:24: "This woman discovered the land."

Question: Then the whole tradition may be of ritual origin?

Answer: The reverse is more likely true. Her story is a remarkably human one, singularly free of theological complications. Led by the "hearing-bird" and the "seeing bird"—the two scouting birds of omen that fly before the leaders of all great migrations to spy out the country when they move into unknown territory, she discovers a new land: "I found no god; . . . no goddess was there," she announces; it was she alone who "opened the land."[142] Her toilsome journey across the desert was, moreover, anything but the effortless progress of a goddess, and her arrival in the valley is depicted in the most convincingly human terms. As the troupe approach their goal, becoming ever more exhausted, the ape encourages the Lady to one last effort, surpassing himself in describing the beauties of the land that lies ahead; "after many days," he says, "only four days more!"—and all are greatly heartened.[143] As he promised, the first trees soon begin to appear—palms with delicious dates and oil for anointing, then the papyrus and the fruits of the kuki palm, mulberry, and sycamore as the delighted ape leads on.[144] The whole company urge her on: "Come down into Egypt, O Gazelle of the Desert, mighty one of *Bwgm*. . . . when you arrive in *Bwgm*, at the Abaton, in Philae, all Egypt will rejoice!"[145] The desert finally behind her, she rests in the shade of trees by the water, enjoying their fruit while a paean is sung to the glorious greenness of the valley.[146]

Question: Where is Bwgm?

Answer: It has been variously located at El Kab, Ombos, and Bigge, but whatever its exact location, one thing is certain, as Sethe points out: "Bwgm is plainly designated as the place of arrival, where the goddess coming from afar first settled down."[147] It is very near the mouth of the wadi, arroyo, or ravine down which the company descended into the valley of the Nile.

Question: Couldn't they see the river long before they reached it?

Answer: No. The view opened out to them suddenly when they reached the *pga*, which Sethe renders, "*Öffnung, Engpass, Eingangsschlucht, Mündung*," i.e., the abrupt opening out of the canyon,[148] down which the Lady's approach, "taxing on the heart" (*šms ib=s*), is described as a beating through the brush (a *Pürschgang*), written with a jackal making its way through the underbrush.[149] Nothing is more exhausting and exasperating than fighting one's way through the gnats, thickets, and heat at the bottom of a desert canyon.[150] The woman is officially welcomed to Egypt as "Hathor Mistress of the Mouth of the Desert Canyon," and as "Mafd.t the Lady of the Turquoise route at the head of the Canyon of Bwgm,"[151] while her companion is "Lord of the Land of the Gods, Ruler of Punt, who passes through the gorge and goes by Bwgm." She is "the virgin whose heart relaxes in the Valley of the Myrrh-road, on the trek with Punt behind her."[152] In the dramatic rites, she is first received by a priest who represents Ptah the Creator himself, and who finds her sitting at the mouth of a ravine while the apes who live in the cliffs sing and dance to amuse her and the desert-dwellers bring her baby gazelles as presents.[153] A recent geological study of Egypt at the beginning of its civilization contrasts the vast river filling the floodplain with the immediate proximity of "the entire high desert of Egypt, . . . exceptionally arid and almost certainly drier than today,"[154] and notes the "frequency of gazelle at the floodplain sites."[155]

Abraham 1:24: "When this woman discovered the land it was under water."

Question: Wasn't the Nile more than a river at that time?

Answer: Geological studies by William Arkell and others of the high benches bordering the river show that it was then a moving lake like the Amazon, filling the valley.[156] Quite apart from the annual inundation, large parts of Egypt would have remained permanently under water were it not for the elaborate system of dikes and canals maintained since the days of the first pharaoh, Menes.[157] The inundation itself, however, was regarded by the Egyptians as a repetition of the great flood, the waters of Nun; and they believed that it issued forth from the very spot, the Abaton, where the Lady settled in Egypt, i.e., she is the Flood-Lady and arrives during the flood, but as it is subsiding:[158] "You land as a Ba, you fly as a Ba . . . above the rushes, above the primal sea."[159] That was "on the day when the Flood waters were everywhere."[160] Recall also the belief that the waters of the flood dried up everywhere in the world *except* at her new home, the caves of the Abaton, where they still remained.

Question: What did Tefnut do when she got to the river?

Answer: Exactly what you would expect. She took a bath. Hot and dusty, after the briefest salutation and a breather, she wasted no time in jumping in: "You kiss the ground beneath the glorious Ished-tree . . . and sit in the shade."[161] "You leap ashore at the Lotus Bank of Nejt. . . . You wash yourself at the Valley-mouth of Andjet; you wash off your limbs in the pool of "Ḥqȝ.t (the frog-goddess)."[162] Here the name of the valley Andjet is written with the symbol of a Bedouin on the march. The bathing rite is a

very important one, and Junker sees in it the normal procedure of bathing the goddess in the Nile as she emerged
from the hot and dusty desert.[163] But the rites always belong
to the Abaton, her final destination on the *island*.

Question: Why the island?

Answer: The muddy, marshy, brush-entangled, varmint-
infested, ill-defined margin of an inundated floodplain is no
place to set up housekeeping.[164] It was the natural habitat,
as we read in the Harris Magical Papyrus, for lions, crocodiles, and snakes, who posed a real threat to the pioneer
Mother and her company.[165] But there out on the broad
bosom of the flood—high, dry, and inviting—lay the rocky
islands of Philae and Bigge (figs. 82–83), side by side, offering security and rest. Forthwith a "lotus bark decked all
over with greenery" was put together for the crossing.[166] In
just this part of Egypt are found those prehistoric pictures
of leaf-bedecked ceremonial ships in which "what is
remarkable," according to Westendorf, "is the predominance of feminine figures," in the dancing position; a
damsel of heroic size stands in the midst of the bark while
gazelles and ostriches of the desert line the shore.[167] To
match this, we read: "Sekhmet (the traverser of the desert)
arrives and settles down at the Abaton, the Landing place,
bathing herself on the island, which is therefore called the
Pure Island, the holiest spot in all Egypt."[168] It was Hathor
the Great who came from Kns.t and Bigge as the Great Wps,
and "washed her limbs at the Abaton."[169] An inscription on
Bigge identifies that island as "the place where Wps
stopped when she came out of Kns.t with the flame all
about her; . . . the Goddess came and her heart was
glowing—but at this locale (it includes the neighboring
island of Philae), her flame was cooled; Thoth washed the
goddess. Therefore the district is called Abaton to this
day."[170] "Abaton," meaning that the place is off-limits to

mortals, recalls familiar classical legends of dire punishment suffered by human intruders on the bathing of a goddess. At all times any priest or scribe who would rehearse
the story was required to be first washed off with a washing of floodwaters in a washing of nine days—no ordinary
inundation.[171] Incidentally, the Lady's son also inaugurated
his career in Egypt with a bath, the subject of a special ritual
in the temple of Memphis. The bath, supervised by his
mother, was in preparation for his royal progress to take
over the rule of the land, and took place at the immemorial
starting place for such ceremonial cruises, Coptos,[172] or in its
rival shrine to the north, the Field of Rushes or the hidden
"Bee-marsh of Chemmis."[173]

Question: And what did she do after the bath?

Answer: What she needed most, having already eaten
on the other shore, was a complete rest; on the island she
slept—blacked out in the arms of her beloved companion.
Philae is called "the place where Shu and Tefnut came to
rest as they sailed down the river from Bwgm."[174] After a
formal welcoming to the island by a full chorus and orches-
tra, total silence was enjoined on all.[175] The public was
strictly barred from the island; a ritual hush was enforced
as long as the Lady was in the temple, and the priests performed their offices in whispers.[176] "No drum, harp or flute
could be heard there, and no mere human could set foot on
the spot at any time."[177] Since the island was a little Eden
with a tree of life, serpent, and the rest (for repeating the
beginning of the race), "no bird or fish might be hunted or
caught" near the island.[178]

On the great ceremonial cruise about to be discussed, the
queen repeated her island routine wherever she landed.
Thus at Denderah, stepping from her boat, "she enters the
great hall rejoicing and rests there on the holy *sh*-bed,
especially prepared for her."[179] "When the Lady of Heaven

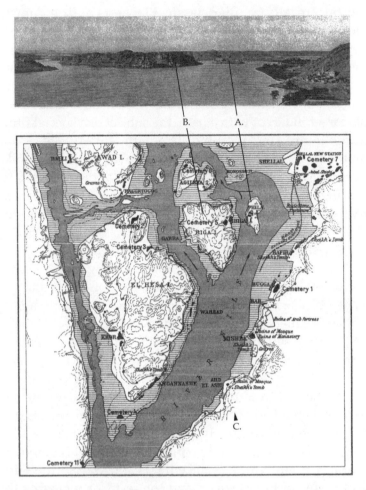

Figure 82. This 1913 photograph shows the sacred islands of Philae (A) and Bigge (B) from the south (C). The region is full of evidence of Egyptian occupation going back to predynastic times. Its strategic location just north of the first cataract of the Nile insured that trade and military control of the area was vital. Though most of the surviving monuments are of later periods, it is certain that they are built on the sites of previous temples. The island of Philae in particular showed evidence of continual rebuilding. Note the presence of a temple to Imhotep (see fig. 38, p. 287) before the first pylon.

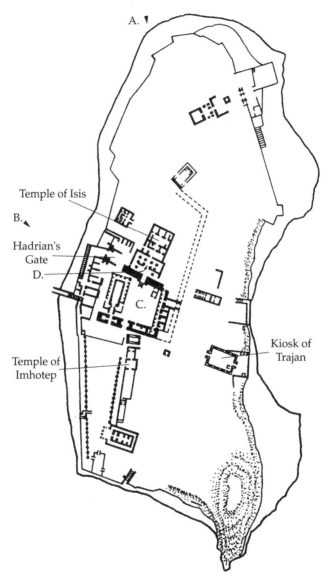

The letters here refer to the following views of the island of Philae in figure 83.

Figure 83. These 1839 engravings show what the island of Philae and its temples may have looked like. Pictured upriver looking to the south (A) are the huge columned Kiosk of Trajan on the left and the rear of the Temple of Isis. The small obelisk (22 ft. high) on the right of the largest pylon was taken to England as a lawn ornament where Young and Champollion made use of its inscriptions to decipher hieroglyphics. The island of Bigge is in the foreground on the right. Looking east across Bigge (B), we can see the extent of the Temple of Isis with the innermost sacred rooms hidden behind thick walls on the left and the pylon gate-

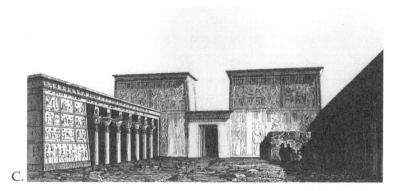

C.

D.

ways opening to the south on the right. On the enormous stone roof are chapels dedicated to Osiris with numerous lion-couch scenes within. Standing in the courtyard before the second pylon looking north (C), we get a sense of the massive quality of architecture in these Ptolemaic structures (c. 50 B.C.). Within the hypostyle hall behind the second pylon looking north (D), the columns evoked the papyrus, lotus, and palm trees of the primeval marsh at the dawn of creation. The images of the gods in their boats—as seen on the lintel over the central axis of the temple— were carried by the priests through these halls (cf. fig. 34, p. 240), reenacting the mystery of creation from the waters of chaos beneath their feet.

comes to her house . . . you lie down to rest and spend the
night in the Temple of Mut; . . . you awake by night in the
Temple of Rest."[180] In the hour when she rests you see "the
Great Lady when she sets foot on the river-bank on the night
on which she rested her domain."[181] As she sleeps, the faithful ape sits guard at her head and sings her aubade when
she awakens on her first day in Egypt.[182]

The Holy Regatta

A predynastic ivory tablet from Naqada shows the
guardian goddess of the South making her triumphal entry
into the land by ship (fig. 84).[183] She comes from the far
south and floats down the stream; the southernmost festival, which was at Esneh, where she is called both Sekhmet
and Tefnut, was repeated at Edfu, celebrating in "festival
cruises on the river Re's eternal memory of the arrival of
his daughter."[184] All down the river a line of local festivals
"commemorate the great river journey which the goddess
once undertook when she first . . . came to Egypt."[185]

The situation is recalled in the famous Westcar Papyrus.
Behold King Snofru being rowed over the waters of the
temple lake by the fair virgins of the court, each dressed in
the accoutrements of the cruising Hathor. Some scholars see
in each of them a representation of one of Hathor's handmaidens.[186] The experts are also in disagreement as to
whether the king in the boat is supposed to be Re in his
solar bark or simply the king himself.[187] Elisabeth Staehelin
lays the greatest emphasis on the extreme antiquity of the
tale: The "palace lake has an atmosphere of the primitive
marshes, the swampy domain of Hathor," the "Hathor-
Atmosphaere," which recalls the Lady in her double capacity of Mistress of Heaven and Lady of the Two Lands—
"Mistress of Women." Essential to the picture is the idea
of the rebirth or regeneration of the land with Hathor

Figure 84. Shown here full size, this small ivory label is one of the oldest known examples (c. 3100 B.C.) of hieroglyphic writing and demonstrates an already highly developed system. This jar label was discovered in the tomb of Neith-hotep, one of King Aha's wives. In the upper register on the right, symbols of the Two Ladies of the North and South are within a palace with a pointed roof. The *serekh* palace facade is next with the Horus falcon above the king's name. The largest image on the label is the high-prowed boat with the ox head at the top. In later centuries this was known as the Henu boat of Sokar. The second register shows the king, holding a staff, emerging from a palace building to oversee the cooking of food in the center. A type of oil is mentioned on the right, but the bottom register remains obscure. Though small and simply carved, this label displays images that were used throughout the next three millennia.

preeminently the "Patroness of Love, of Joy, of Fertility, of birth and rebirth"—it is Hathor bringing life to the land. Need we say that the lotus figures prominently in the picture?[188] Here, then, going back to the earliest times, we find in a firmly founded mythological account, preserved in popular tales as well as public ceremonies, the figure of the Lady sailing on the flood with the king himself to establish a rebirth of life in the land amid rites of joyful and amorous celebration among the women.[189]

Some splendid though damaged bas-reliefs from the tomb of one Kheruef at Thebes (fig. 85), a steward of the famous Queen Tiye (*iimi-r pr n ḥm.t wr.t* or *nyswt* = "Overseer of the House of the Great Wife of the King"), contains scenes showing the establishing of the order of the land at the *Sed* festival, with the setting up of the Djed-pillar (A) and the dancing of Oasis women (B). "It is impossible to say with certainty," writes A. Fakhry, "why these dancers were brought from the Oases and not from other parts of Egypt as well."[190] Need we recall that it was the Oasis people who danced for the Lady when she had crossed the desert as Sekhmet?

Most important is the southern side of the wall. The king sits enthroned as the archaic Horus-Hawk in his *Sed* robe (C), the abstract symbols of life and power acting as his fan bearers, givers of the breath of life (D). Hathor (not Tiye) is enthroned beside him (E), her right arm around his shoulder, the arm wearing a large and conspicuous image of *Ḥeḥ* while her left hand holds a palm-rib scepter resting on an identical *Ḥeḥ* figure (F).[191] Queen Tiye stands behind the couple wearing a Hathor crown combined with Min feathers (G). Beneath the throne, instead of the usual bound foreign captive, as on the opposite side to the north (H), we see fourteen Rekhyt birds, symbolic of the native people of Egypt, crouching over archaic palace-facades (*serekh*) housing symbolic lotus and papyrus plants (I)—it is the settlement of Egypt that is being celebrated rather than foreign conquest.[192] Before the throne, Kheruef, the tomb owner, is being awarded the "gold of honor" (J). Likewise lively festivities are in progress—a throng of singers and dancers, *all women*, are putting on a show.[193] Eight crowned princesses hold up as many open jars, while more jars of the same two types await sealed in stands before them (K). Behind them "we find 15 girls performing different dances," one mournful and downcast, others with upward looks as if in glad surprise (L).[194] The dance dramatizes events explained in an inscription above the dancer's heads.

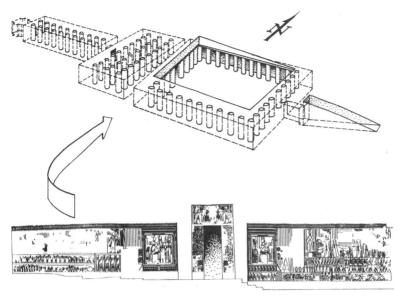

Figure 85. The tomb of Kheruef is one of the most elegant in the Theban necropolis. Though unfinished and later defaced, the elegant bas-reliefs continue to impress the visitor. The western portico of the sunken court-yard (above) is divided by the central doorway into two halves showing the main events of Kheruef's career in service at the court (see the enlargements on the following pages as well as fig. 58, p. 398–99).

Next we see the king and queen passing through the palace gates to initiate the royal progress (M): "He wears the crown of Upper Egypt and instead of the Uraeus at his forehead he has a falcon standing with a Uraeus on its head" (N).[195] It is Horus going forth to claim his own. The couple are preceded by the standards, first in the upper register of Wep-wawet (O), the faithful dog of the hunt and the migration, opening the ways, then of the king's double (P), then the archaic boomerang of the primitive nomads of the desert (Q). In the lower register Thoth (R) and the Horus-hawk (S) march ahead, exactly as in our story. The king is seen striding forth under the protection of his Mother,

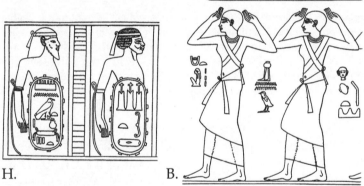

H.   B.

the Great Vulture-Goddess, who spreads her sheltering
wings over his head (T) while the uraeus serpent holds the
life-sign before his face.[196] Next the company take to the
water: "The King wears the jubilee robe and is together with
the queen standing inside a booth in a boat (U) at whose
prow sits the child Horus; the boat is drawn by twenty persons who . . . are the high officials of the palace." Kheruef

himself is at the front of the boat followed by three busy functionaries—as the tomb owner he belongs in this ceremonial celebration of the Great Regatta.[197] "The last scene of these ceremonies shows three male figures whose bodies resemble the Nile god, the first of them has a lion's head and holds a wand in the shape of a hand" (V); the heads of the others are destroyed, but the first figure certainly

L.

V.   U.

suggests the taming (by the restraining hand) of the wild (lion-headed) waters, which was the occasion of the original celebration.[198]

Question: In those passages in which "you" do so-and-so at each stage of the ceremony, who is the "you"?

Answer: The initiated, ritually identified with the victorious, divine king in his funeral text. Thus, "you travel over the earth; . . . you alight upon the earth at the temple of the

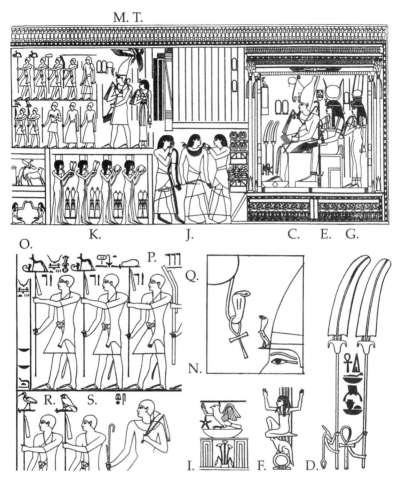

god: You receive the deed of your inheritance. . . . O, Osiris, do not keep away from your temples; come to every shrine which is thine, . . . Great Bull, Lord of Love."[199] The primal *acclamatio* is the *hnw*-rite,[200] the welcoming of a king or god to a community, the happiest and holiest of occasions. "Its sense," writes Adolphe Gutbub, "is always equivalent to that of the apparition of a god"[201]—a parousia, a "joyful meeting" with divinity.[202] And it is always a *navigation* rite, requiring the carrying of an oar to mark the arrival.[203] It was an all-out festivity, with much shaking of the Hathor-sistrum and general drunkenness.[204] At Edfu, Hathor arrives to such a greeting "not in the usual processional bark . . . but in a Flood-boat . . . rowed by the Ennead."[205]

Frequently the migration drama meets us in a funerary context: "The earth trembles, . . . countries and regions weep for thee. . . . Come to thy temple; be not afraid. Thy son Horus avenges thee. . . . Life is given to thee by the most excellent wife. . . . Thou drivest off rain in storms, thou grantest that the earth may be lighted by the radiance of light. . . . O thou that proceedest from the body of the Uraeus which is upon thy head [i.e., *Wrt* as the mother of the king]."[206] Here the funeral procession of Osiris becomes the dark journey through the calamity of the deluge with only Osiris added to the usual characters in the ship, which ends up in victorious light.[207] As early as the Pyramid Texts the phraseology of the Eye of Re story was being trans-ferred to the sufferings of Osiris. When Osiris appears in the role of the new king, claiming the land for himself under the aegis of his mother,[208] he is really a latecomer upstaging Horus-Min with his funerary fixtures.[209] The same applies to Sokar, who in turn, with his great ceremonial cruise, shares Osiris's act. Anthes has suggested that because of Sokar's very early association (possible identity?) with Horus in the Ship of Maat, which was a celestial as well as an earthly vessel, "the idea that Sokar was originally a god of the dead may have to be basically changed."[210] It is the ship of the fearful passage of the Amduat, the royal ceremonial bark, the processional bark of Sokar, the funeral vessel that takes people to heaven, the ship that sails down the river on the royal progress, the Neshmet bark that must battle the mon-ster Apepi on the water; it is all one. If there is resting by the way, it can be rest in the palace, drifting on the sacred lake of palace or temple, dalliance in the Golden Room at the shrine of the Lady, rest beneath a shady festive bower at harvest time, rest in the tomb, rest in the womb anticipating birth. And birth is at one and the same time the rising of the sun daily, seasonally, or yearly, the emergence of the king at his birth or his coronation or his funeral "when he flies to heaven" (eliciting another burst of parallels), of the lotus, of the light, of the corn, of the god, etc.

Inevitably Osiris appears in the context of the royal cruise, since cruising was part of a funeral, but his epithets on the occasion betray the nonfunerary origin of the event. The hero in the boat is the Lord of Love, the Lady's consort; the Great Bull is Ka-mut.f, "Bull of his Mother," and *Ka-nakht*, the Victorious Bull—titles the new king takes at his coronation. Note how male and female cooperate in every operation. The new king is the darling of the people, the cynosure of all eyes, "the youthful Adored One, the Opener of the Roads," yet it is the powerful presence of the goddess that dominates throughout—"Hathor has overpowered the rebel against Re in her name of Sekhmet; Hathor the embodiment of every queen."[211] It is significant that the title of queen does not exist in Egypt—it is always as the mother, the sister, the wife, or the daughter of the god that the woman exercises her power, which is for that reason all the more pervasive: The king can never escape her; she is always right at his side, as his closest relative, bound by perfect ties of love; the matriarchy is there to stay. On her original tour, "the Lady speaking from the river" brings life to Egypt; "what joy is with her coming!"[212] From El Kab, where she is received as Nekhbet the Mother, she proceeds to Thebes as Mother Mut for her seven-day festival; thereafter in her human form of Tefnut she goes the length of the land, ending up at Heliopolis in the north, where Re receives her as his daughter. Then the whole company goes to Memphis for the grand winding-up of the journey, where the faithful ape is given his discharge and resumes his proper form of Thoth the Great.[213]

The best account of the whole operation is found in our ever-informative Leiden Papyrus T32: After rest and refreshment she goes forth with her companion Sokar, visits the House of Life and flies to the temples of Busiris and Abydos, thence to the temple of Horus and Seth, where she eats in the House of the Victor (contest for the throne between Horus and Seth—pacification and victory). Then she visits all the shrines and temples in the land, and the Caves of the Nile, where the king embraces her in her own Temple of the Cow. Both then go to the West Bank on the Day of Crossing the Waters; the crew lift up the bark with joyous shouts and set it down carefully in the water—and so they are off to assert their dominion: "The White Crown is the pilot and the Red Crown is the helmsman!" We are here referred back to the two cooling themselves in the breeze at the Mouth of the Canyon, slaking their thirst with water, then crossing the water to the Hill of Djeme, where they join with all of Egypt in a great picnic on the Day of the Feast of the Rowing; they visit the Benben Temple of Heliopolis for the New Year's rites, and see the King of the Gods rowing the sacred bark of Sektet (the Lady), going to the city of the Two Sisters in the holy place; Hathor bringing the mother of her mother on the Day of Drunkenness on the Night of the Arrival of the Cow (Hathor) to receive water at the altar of the Sun-goddess (Re's Eye). On the Day of Everlasting Time water is brought to your Ba when you take possession of the land, taking your place in the ship, setting out for your domain on the Day of Intoxication.[214]

There is much more to the same effect. One of the purposes of the Sun's Eye is to establish the worship of Re in the land, centering in Heliopolis: "The Eye of the Sun has come to his city, refreshing herself on the Day of Sailing to Edfu, to Msn, to Denderah," and many other places.[215] At each place she is greeted with joyful hymns of welcome, as "Shu dances and Thoth waves his arms."[216] As she, all in gold, enters the great hall for her refreshment and rest, her arrival is like fulness after famine, light after darkness, life after death.[217] As all the gods must make their ritual pilgrimage cruises to her shrine every year,[218] so all mortals must celebrate her coming in ceremonial regattas at their local shrines.[219] There were lighted barges with songs and revelry on the waters by night and sham battles by day.[220] It was before all else a gay time for the women—it was their festival. It was called "The Festival of the Water-Journey of the Goddess," established by order of her father Re when she came from *Bwgm* to see the Nile of Egypt.[221] At Denderah it was dramatized on a sacred lake where she rested "in the hall upon the lake," which represented the floodwaters.[222] Her flood bark rides on the subsiding flood: The sea is quiet (one can sail upon it); all its enemies are annihilated. Even their corpses exist no more, they will be no more upon this earth.

Question: One quotation said her companion was Sokar?

Answer: Since Sokar also cruises in a solar ship, the fusion was inevitable. He sails through the Underworld, you will recall, but it is the same sort of royal progress: "Thebes rejoices when Sokar appears in his holy ship. . . . Welcome! Welcome! say the crew when you sit in glory; . . . your footsteps will not be turned away from his secret places, you visit them in procession."[223] "You enter the cave beneath the Ished tree [both found on the Lady's island!]; you ascend to the god " Htp [the Resting One] in the arms of his pyramid [the embracing mother of heaven]; . . . you cross over in the bark of the Lady Shabty; . . . you leap ashore at the Lotus-bank of Ndjty;[224] . . . you follow the Great Lady wherever she sets her foot on the riverbank on the night she rests in her domain; you have escorted her when she went to the landing-place on the night of illumination of the gods through the Way of Darkness."[225]

There the whole thing is adapted to the funeral situation to which, as Junker notes, it does not originally belong: This is *not* a typical funeral text.

Question: You think it commemorated a real cruise?

Answer: After all is said and done, the experts agree that it boils down to the real coming of a real princess from a distant land to Egypt long, long ago. A king of the Thirteenth Dynasty recalls in his autobiography how "the Majesty of this god entered the Neshmet-ship to make his cruise. . . . The banks were overflowing. . . . The king himself appeared on the Lake to unite himself with the god."[226] And we have an account of how the famous Pharaoh Tirhaqa, a thousand years later, made the great ritual cruise the whole length of the Nile from Nubia and back again to announce to the Egyptians his assumption of royal power; significantly, it was his *mother* who was especially honored in the ceremony as the New Hathor, installing her son on the throne.[227] Especially enlightening is the very ancient routine in the Dramatic Papyrus from the Ramesseum, which rehearsed the coronation play at points along the river, the king himself taking roles in every scene as "the new ruler after his coronation progressed through his dominions," repeating the drama of his coronation in many places: "Everywhere the King appears in the play standing upright in a ship."[228] This is supported by an ivory comb from the First Dynasty, which shows the king as the Horus-falcon as "he stands in a boat beneath which two wings representing the sky are spread" (fig. 86).[229] Here it is only fair to note that Joseph Smith explains Facsimile 2, figure 4, the outspread wings over the boat, as "signifying expanse, or firmament of the heavens." As Horus-falcon he is the victorious new king. Victorious against whom? Against Seth, the storm-god who brought the flood.[230] The four canopic figures restrain

Figure 86. Shown here full size, the ivory comb of King Djet shows his serpent name-glyph in the center within the *serekh* palace facade flanked by two *wȝs* scepters and an ankh. A high-prowed boat with the Horus-falcon within (cf. fig. 84, p. 497) rests on outstretched wings, a symbol of heaven, protecting the king below.

Typhon in the north, Typhon being Seth, and guide the ship safely by its rope or chain.[231] "Rejoice Ladies of Buto and river-people of the lagoons!" says the Edfu dramatic text. "Horus appears at the head of his ship" as the new king in the glory of his coronation, with "Sekhmet (the Lady) stand-ing before him," as he comes "in his capacity of the victori-ous king taking possession of the throne of his father." His mother, Isis, is the real leader of the expedition, even direct-ing the fighting, while all the great shrines along the river rejoice together in celebration, especially the women, hailing the youthful hero as their darling.[232]

The same romantic excitement breathes in the famous Festival Songs of Isis and Nephthys, where the Ladies hail the young king with endearing terms on his royal progress, which is also a triumphal march of conquest through the land: "Thou art proclaimed mighty in thy circuit."[233] The Evil One (Seth) floods the earth, but Nut (the mother) drives him away, under darkened skies.[234] All the great hymns in the Bremner-Rhind Papyrus touch upon the themes of the great migration and the royal progress: "Come to thy temple and be not afraid, . . . O ye gods in the watery deep, ye gods amidst the followers of the deep. We follow after the Lord of love. . . . Messenger from heaven to earth, hail! . . . Re is avenged, disasters are no more," etc.[235] The familiar elements appear in proper order: the flood,[236] the combat,[237] the pacification of the land,[238] the mother taking charge of the operation,[239] the royal progress[240] with its marriages at the shrines along the river,[241] and the epithalamiums (wedding songs) on the way.[242] The Ritual of Bringing in Sokar is an archaic boat procession in which we see Hathor, "the Traverser of the Ways," on her journey, overcoming as Sekhmet the last opposition in the land, coming in peace, and duly resting.[243] The prominence of the heavenly ship throughout reminds one of the Ark and the Babylonian "Magur-boat," suspended between the waters from above and the waters from below (as earth) and heaven mingled in one catastrophic deluge.[244] The situation is a familiar one, but is it historical? Is it only, as Santillana avers, the transfer of observations of the starry heavens to a mythical earthly setting? Egyptologists have always asked whether the old rites and stories are descended from historic or cosmic nature myths.[245]

Three Is a Crowd

Question: Just what is the relationship of the king to the Lady in all this?

Answer: She has two males escorting her—one her guide, the other her intimate. The guide was Thoth, the god of wisdom himself, serving for the occasion in the form of an ape, which he often takes in his lunar capacity; here the moon-god as the faithful satellite of the Sun's Eye, vicar and lieutenant of the Re himself, is able to represent the Sun in nocturnal regions where the Sun does not go.[246] As the ape, he is also most fit to survive in the desert and to watch by night. But while Thoth is her *escort*, her *consort* is Shu: Thoth only "prepares a place for her on the island beside her brother."[247] During the journey Shu keeps a very low profile;[248] her son follows and fears her, while it is Thoth, the Lord of Knowledge, who pacifies her and keeps up her spirits.[249] Even in Egypt he still takes charge until they reach their final destination in the presence of Re.[250] But *never* does Thoth appear as the Goddess's consort or relative.[251]

Question: Shu is her brother?

Answer: Yes, the Lady "came from Kns.tt with her brother, . . . stopped in Snm.t with her brother, [and] . . . came out of Bwgm with her brother."[252] To Shu is said: "You came to Egypt with your sister Tefnut and rejoiced the heart of your father Re."[253] He is Haroeris, "who came with his sister and did not go far from his father; who made his children mighty against his enemies."[254]

Question: But you have said that Shu and Tefnut were the couple who repeopled the world after the flood?

Answer: As Zandee has noted, flood and creation motifs are mingled in Shu and Tefnut's "Ship of a Million," and their work is to establish (*smn*) the world order both in the beginning and after the cataclysm.[255] "They rejoiced in the Nu (the flood), and became the parents of this earth," opposing the flood dragon Apophis.[256] They were husband

and wife: It is common for the royal couple in Egypt to address each other as brother and sister, and often they actually were. When Tefnut rests in the Abaton, it is in the arms of Shu, whose loving embrace cools her anger,[257] as he clasps "the Good Sister" to his bosom. Then "came Tefnut," says an inscription, "with her brother Shu to this place, the Abaton. . . . Re was with her and Thoth behind her to bless her *union* with her brother."[258] "Her Majesty came out of Bwgm while Shu went ahead as the image of Re, overcoming the opposition of the waters with the aid of the Wdjat-Eye."[259] The picture is painted on a vast celestial canvas in the Pyramid Texts, as rendered by Raymond Faulkner:

> O Re, recognize me. . . . She who excludes whomsoever she should exclude opens the doors of the horizon at the ascent of the Day-bark. I know the Hall . . . from which you go forth when you go aboard the Night-bark; . . . commend me—*four times repeated*—to the four blustering winds . . . who contend with fierce roaring. . . . May they not make opposition . . . when I come to you and tell you this name of yours of "Great Flood which came forth from the Great One." . . . Take me with you, . . . who away storms for you, who dispel the clouds for you, and who break up the hail for you. . . . Set me over the Vulture-goddess [Mut, the Mother].[260]

Shu sails over to the island with her, and there he never leaves her side.[261] While she stays in Bigge as "the center of radiance," he goes forth to subdue the land for her[262] and returns to report his successes.[263] But almost always they conquer as a team:

> Rejoice women of Busiris, Horus has overcome his enemies! Exult ye dwellers in the Edfu nome, Horus has overcome the enemy of his father! . . . How good it is to appear in your bark, Horus of Edfu, . . . wearing the Double Crown of Horus! Sekhmet prevails against

your enemy [Seth], and Thoth the Great assures your protection![264]

Sekhmet, as we have noted, is the Lady coming as a lioness out of the desert to occupy the valley and subdue all opposition to her rule. It is *her* flame that goes ahead of them over the waters,[265] driving the prowling lions from the riverbank, forcing the crocodiles to stay in the water and the snakes to keep in their holes so that the land may be safe for people.[266] It also clears the land in all directions and subdues the rebellious and unconverted.[267] After her first night's rest she goes forth to inspect the land, beginning with a tour of the fields and a bounty to the poor,[268] after which she graciously receives ambassadors from the western lands and listens to their eulogies, and then "goes forth rejoicing."[269]

But the real fighting is left up to her *son* in his capacity of Horus the Hawk, the youthful hero who proves his powers by overcoming the opposition in combat before he mounts the throne under his mother's auspices. Even when he fights, it is under her aegis as she advances "with red face against the enemies of her *son*, destroying his opponents," so that he can rule.[270] They plan their campaign against the rebels together on the first night in their palace. He goes forth to suppress all opposition "on the day of inspection and [takes] possession with a feather on his head and Maat in his heart,"[271] Maat being at one and the same time the Lady who "unites with her lord with cries of Joy," the ship that bears him, and the embodiment of law and order which he brings to the land.[272]

Question: If they found the land empty, why did they have to fight, and whom?

Answer: For one thing, the hero had to conquer an evil opposition in order to rule, since a contest for the inheritance was a virtually indispensable condition of oriental kingship. Geologists and archaeologists are agreed that when the real authors of Egyptian civilization arrived, no one was living in the valley, but there were prior occupants in the deserts immediately adjoining on either side, and Horus's perennial opponent is Seth, the god of the desert and desolation. It is interesting, however, that the unfailing opponent of the Lady and her son is the amphibious monster snake Apophis, who does all he can to arrest the progress of their cruise; it is not at all surprising that those who disputed the occupancy of the land should be identified with other troublesome beasts as well.[273]

Question: As you tell it, sometimes the hero is Shu and sometimes he is Horus; sometimes he is Tefnut's brother and sometimes he is her son.

Answer: Yes, and he is also the husband of Tefnut and her twin, though as the husband of Tefnut the royal person of the father is utterly negligible. And we must not forget Thoth, for already in the Pyramid Texts "Horus and Thoth appear to supplement each other."[274] This should not surprise us by now. In the same spirit Ikhnaten and his wife, the celebrated Nefertiti, cruise together on their solar barks where "the manner in which they are paired suggests indeed, that *they* are assimilated to Shu and Tefenet."[275] Schafik Allam has found that "the Hathor-bark and the Solar-bark stand in close relationship to each other," in fact, "*Sie gehen in einander über* (They go over one another)."[276] So when the Lady in her heavenly capacity of "Sothis of Heaven gives the kingship to her Son," it is when the land is flooded and the Temple of Denderah is decked and prepared for the great wedding ceremony when Sirius (Sothis) and the Sun (Re) unite in their rising.[277] Thus, we see how motifs and properties of the play can be mixed, as heavenly things reflect the earthly, at least in the case of the boats,[278] while the familiar outlines of the drama remain unmistakably recognizable.

A section of Brugsch's thesaurus is devoted to the *periplus* or ritual cruise,[279] which begins at the New Year,[280] the king coming in the royal ship and laying him down to rest,[281] hence funerary motif, on his wedding day, the Lady cruising with him.[282] The *periplus* of Hathor is later the *navigium* of Isis when she came from Phoenicia following the conquest of the land;[283] yet it is our old friend the Daughter of Re, for she arrives at Bwgm[284] and is received by "a very great festival . . . when the women dance";[285] trying to match this with local festivals leads to conflicting dates as attempts are made to match the event with the calendar.[286] Yet in the end the Lady stands forth as none other than the Daughter of Re, the Sun's Eye.[287] As heir to the throne, Horus is ex officio the *son*, making him also her son, "her warlike Son Horus," who conquers the challenger at Bigge and thereby earns the throne.[288] Her son takes over the rule of his father at the New Year, as Horus of the Strong Arm; he is hailed as he returns to his dwelling on the day of Apportioning the Fields.[289] The Mother's first stop on her grand cruise is the Temple of Horus and Seth, the combatants, where she comes to feast in the House of the Victor, the new king.[290]

However confused the family relationships seem to us, the main object seems always to preserve a perfect balance between the claims and the importance of the male and female. As a mother, she does it all for him—and seems quite patronizing (or rather matronizing) about it: "Words of Hathor, Lady of the Valley, Eye of Re, companion at Edfu, Isis the Great, Divine Mother: I give thee (Horus) the power to smite thine adversaries. . . . I make all mankind love thee and submit to thee." Thus we see her in the Sokar chapel at Denderah as she "installs her *son* [the son of Osiris] on his eternal throne."[291] "Come in peace, O hero of the mighty arm," she tells him. "I have made all thine enemies submit, I have caused the antelopes of the desert to obey thine orders. Thou art the master of Egypt and of the desert!"[292] It is she who summons all the world to bow the knee to her

son,[293] she who protects him in the palace,[294] as she did in the
tent during the migration. He is hailed at his coronation as
"the god beloved of his mother," and it is she who brings to
him the "*patriarchal* Crown . . . of the Father of the gods,"[295]
taking matriarchal charge of the patriarchal offices. It is she,
"the Mother of the God; the Mistress of Philae, by whose
command every king mounts the throne."[296] The conqueror
occupies the land for his mother; in the Pyramid Texts he
invites her to come and take over after he has put everything in readiness for her.[297] Recognizing him as her favorite,
she makes him king; through her he becomes the protector
of Egypt,[298] and upon his coronation after putting the wealth
of the land at her disposal, he is conducted immediately
into the Temple of Neith, his mother.[299] The story of Re and
the Sun's Eye, which begins with the Daughter cleverly cap-
turing the supreme secret and key to her father's power,
ends when Nun commands Re himself to share his throne
equally with his Eye—that is what the whole thing has been
getting at, equality of authority between male and female.[300]

As the first settler, the Lady was designated throughout
Egypt as (Hathor)—Nebet-Hetepet, "the Lady who rests,"
or "settles down," or "is appeased."[301] This title has been the
subject of a long and exhaustive study by Jacques Vandier,
which agreeably confirms the story we have been trying to
tell. It deserves a brief summary here.

Our heroine is "(Hathor)—Nebet-Hetepet," also called
Iousaas. Her name Nebet-Hetepet means at first sight
"Mistress of Peace,"[302] both making it and receiving it:
"Thoth has appeased her in this her name of Hetepet";[303]
"Thoth appeases the Eye in his [!] name of Hetepet."[304] Pun-
ning on her name, she says to the king, "I give thee the Two
Lands in Peace."[305] It also signifies peace in the sense of
satisfaction;[306] the root meaning includes to rest, occupy (the
throne), settle down.

Originally one lady only,[307] she was in Egyptian fashion

with the greatest freedom identified with a number of roles,[308] being assimilated to no less than twelve other goddesses,[309] mostly with Hathor,[310] hence with the cow Mehet-Quret, the Great Flood,[311] taking also her form from Hathor.[312] By far her commonest epithet is *Eye of Re:* She is "Hathor the Great, . . . Eye of Re, . . . daughter of Re as his Left Eye, . . . Eye of Tum, . . . Living Eye, Pupil of the Wdjat-Eye."[313] She is "Hathor . . . the Eye of Re, who gives the King the lifetime of Re in the sky."[314]

Her second most common epithet is Mother of Shu and Tefnut,[315] her name being invented by Egyptian theologians to give Atum a mate in the conception of that pair.[316] She is often identified with Tefnut herself,[317] thanks to her participation in the Onuris cycle. She comes with the ceasing of the tempest, as the Powerful One who protects Re; she is Iousaas the Eye of Re on her arrival, hence the uraeus serpent.[318] Her name, Iousaas, "emphasizes the mysterious character of the place from which she comes" under circumstances closely associated with the (re)creation of the world.[319] Hermann Kees renders her name Iousaas as meaning "When she arrived she was already great."[320]

The name Hetepet denotes a place as well as a woman—the place where she rested, or settled down, or both.[321] Kees suggests that Iousaas was the tamarisk tree of Hathor that bowed to the new arrivals in Egypt, or was the tree or thicket under which the king was born.[322] Nebet-Hetepet was a willow tree, growing at the water's edge; willows and flowers (lotuses?) grew at her temple.[323]

Ritually,[324] Hetepet is the place where the initiate bathes and rests, along with the crew of the Sun-ship.[325] Horus is nourished in Hetepet, loved by the golden Hetepet-Hathor.[326] She arrives by water, takes the king in her arms, establishes the fear of him in the land, protects him, exalts him in her House of Nebet-Hetepet, and makes his name known.[327] She brings the produce of the earth, the gifts of the higher ground in the region of the New Lands.[328]

In her capacity of Mut (mother) she is Sekhmet, the lioness of the desert.[329] She comes from afar as the lioness, but after being appeased is transformed into the genial cat Bast.[330] Hence in her lion-headed form she is Sekhmet-Bastet-Nebet-Hetepet,[331] and is called "the Mother of the Two Lions (Shu and Tefnut)."[332] Her great celebration is the Pioneer Day, 19th of Thoth, the Festival of Shu and Tefnut, the day "when the Sister arrived."[333] At that time Nebet-Hetepet and Iousaas are commingled and identified with Hathor, who says to the king: "I make you drunken; I renew the intoxication and the happiness."[334] She is praised as the Eye of Re, illuminating the land on her arrival.[335] The king offers wine to Hathor-Nebet-Hetepet, Lady of Intoxication, "who makes rejoicing."[336] Presenting the wine to her and Re-Harakhti-Atum, he hails her as "Wife of Re-Harakhti, Lady of Hetepet, Eye of Re whom his heart loves." Upon receiving the wine, she says: "I sanctify thy Majesty in the capacity of Horus, Lord of Rejoicing, that you might overcome your enemies." As the king gives her the Wdjat-Eye, she speaks as "Hathor the Great, Mistress of Denderah, Eye of Re, . . . Sekhmet the Great, Mistress of all the Sekhmets, the Great Neseret (fire-breath of Sekhmet) who burns the enemy, Hetepet the Mistress of Hetepet."[337] It is Hetepet who made the beer when she ordered the Nile to flow.[338] Her great festival is the wine celebration of the south;[339] she is Mistress of Intoxication and of the Lotus.[340]

As Hathor, she bestows kingship at the *Sed* festival;[341] she is *Wr.t-Ḥkꜣw* and Wsrt, the Power of the Crown, supreme authority.[342] Her main insignia are the Hathor crown and sistrum,[343] though she wears all the Mother crowns,[344] mostly the Hathor crown (cf. Facsimile 3, figure 4) and the Hathor-Maat crown.[345] At Medinet Habu the king calls Nebet-Hetepet "his Mother,"[346] and on his statue-inscription Pharaoh Nimrod implores her protection.[347]

As Hathor = Iousaas-Nebet-Hetepet, the ceremonial bark is made for her.[348] At Philae, wearing a full-sized Hathor mask, she is "at the head of Bigeh . . . at the head of Philae."[349] She is "Ruler of Gods and Goddesses, . . . the Eye of Re, the Mistress of Heaven," who dwells at *Philae.*[350] There her name Hetepet is found curiously written with a house-sign signifying settlement.[351] It is she who commands at Bigge, who founded Thebes.[352] At Philae she is the sustainer of the universal order, head of Bigge; listed officially between Tefnut and Maat as "The Eye of Re," "Mistress of Heaven, Queen of all Gods,"[353] intimate of the famous God of the Abaton.[354] She is "at the same time mother and daughter";[355] identified with both Hathor and Tefnut, she appears "sometimes as the mother and sometimes as the daughter of Re."[356] In Ptolemaic times she appears in the Onuris cycle as Mehet and Flood-Cow,[357] and at the same time as Tefnut and Bastet.[358] Significantly, though she is related to Shu on every level of family ties, *never* is she linked with her traveling companion Thoth as a divine family couple.[359] Her annual cruise was the most popular of Egyptian national celebrations.[360]

Vandier has considerable difficulty placing her origin in On, since the legends concentrate heavily in the south: She makes her cruise either to bring the cult of the north to the south or, what is far more likely from the evidence, to import the cult of the south to the north.

Unintentionally Vandier has brought together the main themes of our story all in proper context. One may find the various episodes turning up in ritual dress in countless texts; but more significant are the many substantial sources in which the same motifs are set forth in the same sequence, from cataclysm to coronation, with the great river procession as the central theme.[361]

Abraham 1:25: "Pharaoh, the eldest son of Egyptus . . ."

Question: What is the relative authority of mother and son here?

Answer: There is a mingling of identities, male and female. "Atum says, 'This is my living daughter Tefnut, who is ever with her brother Shw. His name is Ankh [life, oath, covenant]; her name is Maat [truth, legitimacy]. . . . Behold, I stand between them and they are joined after the manner of the [lit. my] flesh. . . . As I stand their arms embrace me. As for my son, he lives begotten in my name. . . . The human race came forth from my Eye whom I sent forth when I was alone and exhausted with Nun. . . . Atum, exalted in his glory, begot [lit. made] Shw and Tefnut . . . before the first mortal was born.'"[362] Or take this passage: "The Good Sister Tefnut Lady of Ombos . . . Eye of Re, the Good Wife to Her Brother Shu . . . I take thee into my arms [says Re?], O Mistress of all wives, my Daughter."[363] During her great cruise, "Hathor, originally Horus's mother, must, as the mother also of Re, so *distribute* herself," as Junker puts it, "that she is also the *daughter* of the Sungod, the *wife* of the older Horus, and the *mother* of the younger Horus."[364] Hence, the cruise is variously interpreted as (1) the cruise of the Sun's Eye to join the Sun, (2) a daughter visiting her father, and (3) a bride visiting her fiancé for the nuptials.[365] In every case she formally hails the other as king. Gustave Jéquier suggests that the purpose of these various relationships was to mingle the male and female lines so inextricably as to forestall any questions of priority.[366]

Inevitably, this sort of thing leads to serious complications and shocking family scandals[367] that figure in the earliest legends of other ancient people as well (Moses 5:53). That is the curse behind the mingling of patriarchal and matriarchal succession in the Book of Abraham. Note the queen's exuberant behavior in the Leiden Papyrus T32: She circumambulates the flood house of Thebes with His

Majesty; comes to her house when the children rejoice to call him their father; spends the night with him in the Temple of Mut on her festival; as Mut in the Temple of Rest, she gives birth to the child Shu, the reborn Sun amidst great rejoicing; she shows the babe to His Majesty, who comes hurrying to behold his new offspring, is joined by Ka-mut.f, the new heir to the throne at the Feast of all the Gods; then receives a present on the Day of Biting the Fruit in the temple of Iat Wr.t; as Mut, she bears the child every year, thus renewing youth; and goes forth as Sothis the (time-measuring) Mistress of the Beginning of the Year; receives a formal address from the king and the praises of all the gods at the End of the Year. As the Eye of Re, she is also the Eye of Horus, the daughter and yet the mother of both of them.[368] The ritual silence of the Abaton is to allow the Lady to rest from her labors both of travel *and* travail, for she has just given birth to Harpocrates, "resurrected and reborn at every New Moon, the revived and reborn Osiris,"[369] to whom she says: "O, Osiris, take water from my hands; I am thy *Sister*, thy Great *Wife*," and, of course, his Mother![370] It is the rebirth of nature with the year, her tears in labor refreshing and reviving all animal and vegetable life.[371] Shu and Tefnut repair to the Caves of the Nile, the life-giving waters of the great flood, to inaugurate a new age, rebuild the shrine, and bring forth the god again. It is the day of conception, birth, and coronation all at once,[372] on which "you see the *Old One* coming forth from the womb [!] of his mother . . . on the Day he appears in glory, . . . the Day of the Festival of the Eternities."[373] In the same day's ritual at Edfu she debarks, enters the chamber to rest "on the Day of Embracing," celebrates her wedding, mounts the throne, and gives nourishment to the reborn Osiris.[374]

Question: Why all the emphasis on family?

Answer: Because family ties are stronger than any legal declaration. The title of queen, as we have noted, does not exist in Egypt, the one royal title being that of king's mother, spouse, or daughter;[375] in all three roles the woman may be designated as royal sister. This was no mere legal fiction either; at all times one of the most striking features of the palace portraits, as we have seen, is the loving intimacy between royal parents and children, for all their majestic aloofness from ordinary mortals.

This was later expressed in the Isis cult with its double obsession with both mother love and romantic fervor. When Tirhaqa's mother sailed from the far south to the north and back again to establish her son on the throne, she identified herself with Isis sailing with her son Horus: Every land "paid homage to this king's Mother; . . . even as Horus liveth for his mother Isis, thou art elevated on the throne of Horus."[376] Here Mama gets top billing, and if we go back to the beginning it is still the same, as in the earliest Pyramid Text, where Nut the Mother declares, "The King is my beloved son, my first-born upon the throne of Geb, with whom he is well-pleased, and he has given to him his heritage in the presence of the Great Ennead."[377]

Even earlier, an inscription of King Khasakhemhui of the Second Dynasty unites Horus and Seth in his own royal person, while the real uniter of the lands is the Lady in her travels through the country.[378] Aha, whom some equate with Menes, the first king of a united Egypt, has left us a picture of himself making a triumphal progress through the land on a ship with Mother Mut, the protecting goddess of the South, beside him.[379] How persistent the matriarchal priority was appears in Augustine's report that Isis of the South was the bringer of Egyptian civilization, "ruling a great empire with justice, so that today it is a capital crime for any one to say that the first ruler of Egypt was a man."[380] "I am called the Mistress of the Land," says the Sun's Eye, "the daughter who is in the land. . . . After Re made me mistress over the Two lands he also made me queen over the whole earth."[381]

Thus the Lady keeps hitting back right to the end, finally triumphant in the worldwide cult of Isis, the White Goddess.[382] If the king was to inherit from Hathor, she had to be *"en quelque sort comme sa mère,"* as Jéquier puts it, "somehow to be his mother."[383]

Question: Can't the Tefnut epic have belonged to the Osiris cult, that is, the funeral rites, from the beginning?

Answer: Of course, it got involved in the religion, as everything else in Egypt eventually did. Osiris and the Lady were brought together at the Abaton in two capacities—as mother and child, and as husband and wife. Osiris sleeps in the Abaton preparatory to his glad awakening, and, as at other shrines in Egypt, the Lady, as Isis, watches over her sleeping spouse, but as the Abaton she watches with Tefnut, showing how the two motifs are brought together.[384] Both Osiris and Tefnut slept in anticipation of a glad awakening at the same spot,[385] and upon awakening, both set forth on a joyful, triumphal progress through the land.[386] How the two celebrations are fused and confused is apparent from an inscription telling how Sokar, who is Osiris in his most underworld aspect, is received with rejoicing in Thebes as he arrives in his holy ship after traversing the desert *with Her Majesty,* who then rows the soul of *Re*(!) across the water to Thebes.[387]

As to the mother and child, the caves from which the Nile is born at Philae are also the caves where Osiris sleeps to be reborn as the new pharaoh;[388] the milk jars of the Lady make him a child again at the Abaton festivities, thus giving the king an eternity of lives.[389] Resurrection is rebirth, and though the relics of the dead Osiris were distributed among many shrines of Egypt, the most important one, the thigh, ⊬ which held the key to the resurrection, was kept at Bigge, the Egyptian "Plymouth Rock," and to it all the gods made their yearly pilgrimages.[390] But just before their arrival at the place, Isis would have to make the ritual crossing to keep the soul of Osiris alive.[391] Even the mysteries cannot efface the stubborn memory of that historical event.

The cosmic connections of the Abaton as the place of creation, the first land, to which Chnum the Creator would come down every year to visit the garden and revive both Osiris and the life of the land by causing the Nile to flow,[392] are properly proclaimed by its famous appointments. On the island was a ring of 365 altar stones, covered with vegetation and ritually drenched with water, tended to by priests in monthly shifts, three times each day.[393] There also the original nilometer regulated the flow of the Nile to the life of the land and correlated it with the times and seasons on a scientific basis.[394] The whole complex belongs to the cycle of creation and rebirth, with special reference to the flood: "You renew your youth every year at the child-bearing of Nut, receiving millions of years . . . on the Day of the Going-forth of Sothis the Mistress of the Beginning of the Year."[395] "You establish yourself in the land at the feast of the Fixing of Times, on the Day of the Great Coming Forth [*tr.t*, the first day of winter, the solstice]."[396] "You go down to the Holy Land when the trees are planted on the Day of the Queen's Visit."[397]

In a study of the earliest recorded ceremonial ships of the Egyptians, Anthes has brought together various elements of our story and offered explanations of their inter-relationships. His conclusions are these: (1) The Lady's ship is the "Maat-boat," since very possibly "the name of the ship was originally Maati, '[the ship] belonging to Maat,' which was at an early time reinterpreted as a dual," as it is usually read today. "The boat represented in prehistoric times the embodiment of Maat throughout the entire land, as the source [*Sitz*] of kingly authority and tribute."[398] (2) Yet it is called the *king's* Maat-boat, which Anthes finds puzzling, "since it belongs to Re and not to Horus-the-King." He decides that this refers perhaps to an archaic rite in which the king brought Maat to Re in a boat ceremony taking place on the last day of the year, in which "the King was either Re in the Maat-boat" himself, or else while functioning as leader of the Maat-boat brings Re with him."[399] (3) In these rites the trio Re, Maat, and Horus is everything, and Horus was to begin with simply "the form of the living king of the prehistoric period";[400] also the ship was at first a real boat belonging to the king, but by the Old Kingdom "existed only in rituals as representing the heavenly bark."[401] (4) Is the sacred *wjȝ*-bark, which persists throughout Egyptian history, the same as the old Maat-ship? Anthes thinks it was, the "parallel forms of boat" matching the parallel appearance of the king as either Re on the last day of the year[402] or Horus on the first day of the year.[403]

(5) The longest Pyramid Text on the subject is most enlightening: "N [the king] mounts up with the rain-cloud [*ygp* = cumulonimbus] [then] he descends. . . . Maat is in the presence of Re on this day of the Festival of the Beginning of the Year. The heavens are calmed [*htpw*], and the earth rejoices, for they have heard that N [the king] has deposed Maat [Anthes reads *wdd*, instead of *isft* = repelled] . . . by virtue of the true pronouncement [*ts mȝ*] which has come from his mouth by which he has petitioned [*dbḥ.nN*] to be confirmed in the rule."[404] (6) This surprising downgrading of Maat refers, Anthes suggests, to "the aspiration of the king to speak as ruler with the authority of a king" [*das Bestreben des Königs, als Herrscher königlich Recht zu sprechen*.][405] Whatever the reason, it points to the unmistakable prehistoric rivalry between the two, and the fact that it is mentioned at all in the Pyramid Texts is clear indication that the woman had the prior right to rule.

Though "no clear picture has emerged" from all this, in Anthes's opinion, the generous sampling of prehistoric Egyptian ritual boat pictures that he supplies with his article leads to further speculation.[406] For they show a type of vessel that was early recognized, e.g., from the famous Gebel al-Arak knife handle (fig. 87), as being not Egyptian riverboats, but Mesopotamian seagoing vessels, the "Magur-boats" described as the archetype of the ark of the Babylonian and Sumerian flood stories.[407]

Egypt . . . Egyptus: Who's in Charge Here?

Question: What about the name Egyptus?

Answer: Verses 21 through 25 in Abraham 1 must be read carefully to get straight a number of specific propositions:

1. Egypt is the "Chaldean" name for the land: "Egyptus, which in the *Chaldean* signifies Egypt" (Abraham 1:23). Here the Book of Abraham is right: Egypt is not the Egyptian name for the land,[408] but was first applied to it by the Canaanites ("in the Chaldean"), making its first known appearance in Ugaritic as *"Ḥkpt,* that being an adaptation of the old Egyptian name for Memphis, *"Ḥw.t-kз-ptḥ* which the Egyptians did *not* apply to the land as a whole, but only to the city.[409] It was the "Chaldeans" who gave it to the land. Such is the prevailing, but by no means only, explanation of the name among scholars.

2. The Egyptians, like Pharaoh himself, were of mixed stock, being partakers "of the blood of the Canaanites" (Abraham 1:21–22). Unhindered by natural boundaries, the Canaanites at all times filtered into Egypt by the oldest road in the world, presenting a recurrent menace throughout all her [Egypt's] history, according to Gardiner.[410] The Delta that attracted them was like the garden of the Lord, offering tempting grazing and farming lands from the earliest times. Examination of skulls from Canaan shows "an array of cranial characteristics surprisingly similar to those of ancient Egypt."[411]

Question: Who were the Canaanites?

Answer: "The title 'Canaanites,' if it be used at all, must

Figure 87. The carved ivory handle (shown here full size) of a flint knife discovered at Gebel al-Arak is a tantalizing glimpse of a lost world. The bearded figure holding two lions by the throat is recognized as the ancient Near Eastern motif of the Master of Animals. Two hunting dogs wearing collars rest their paws on the central pierced boss that was perhaps used to fasten the knife with a thong to a belt. The carefully rendered animals, wild and domestic, display a lifelike animation. On the other side we see more struggles, this time among men fighting with weapons while high-prowed boats pick their way past floating corpses.

be reserved for the third-millennium Semitic inhabitants of Syria-Palestine and their second-millennium descendants."[412]

3. There has been a great deal of hair-splitting on the subject of Egypt and Canaan, but one sure thing is that Canaanite blood was shared one way or another by almost every pharaoh whose line can be traced:[413] *"Pharaoh, the eldest son of Egyptus, the daughter of Ham"* (Abraham 1:25) *"and Egyptus"* (Abraham 1:23). The name Egypt is a title, as was Pharaoh (*"which . . . signifies king by royal blood"*— Abraham 1:20), and was given to the land, just as the title of Pharaoh (like that of Caesar) was given to all who ruled after him. As in the Old Testament, "father" can mean ancestor, or "son" or "daughter" can mean "descendant";[414] this is clear from Abraham 1:26, where *Noah* is called Pharaoh's *father*.

4. Pharaoh's claim to the priesthood was invalid because he insisted with great force that it was the patriarchal priesthood of Noah, received through the line of Ham (Abraham 1:25–27). His earthly rule was blessed (Abraham 1:26), but he could not, of course, claim patriarchal *lineage* through his mother. There is an interesting parallel here with the case of Job, who, according to a newly found *Testament of Job*, though the most righteous of men and a direct descendant of Jacob or Israel, cannot claim a place among the patriarchs of the line because it is through his mother that he relates to Jacob, while his father's line, through Esau, was invalid because Esau had forfeited the priesthood.[415] Pharoah finds himself in exactly that situation: The male line of Ham had become rebellious, while the female line was not patriarchal.

Question: But Ham was a righteous man and, like his father Noah, even "walked with God" (Moses 8:27).

Answer: The tradition was widespread and persistent among the ancient Jews that the royal and priestly succession of Ham was made void through the transgression of his male descendants, Cainan, Cush, Nimrod, all of whom broke the covenant and forfeited the priesthood by laying unworthy claims to it. Some accounts say it was Ham himself who sinned (the story of the stolen garment); some say it was Cush, some Ham's younger son Canaan, some Nimrod (this is the most common); but all agreed that something went wrong that broke the line.[416]

Question: But why the curse on the *land?* (Abraham 1:24).

Answer: It means, exactly as in the Book of Mormon, that those who dwell in the land will be cursed if they do not follow God's counsels and *blessed* if they do.[417] As Noah was apportioning out the *lands,* according to the book of *Jubilees,* he pronounced a curse on *any* of his descendants who should defile the land given him by God through iniquity;[418] most explicitly he warned Canaan—a bull's-eye for Abraham (Abraham 1:21–24). This is the standard curse on *any* promised land (Alma 37:28, etc). There is one element of the Old World curse, however, that we should mention. In the traditions of Ham, Canaan, and Cain, which are connected in various ways, there is constant reference to sexual promiscuity, which definitely has something to do with the curse. Thus we are told that Nimrod slew his father Canaan and married his mother Sachlas, thus launching his rule on a matriarchal footing and introducing that fatal triangle, which is the abomination of the ancients. "The seed of Noah," says a recently found source, "followed after the sons of Sachlas, going against the will of Noah in their pride, and so perverted the whole population."[419] Another recent discovery tells us that Satan himself rested his claim ⌐ on a matriarchal line, as do his followers, "Canaan and Cain, who is also Re (the Sun)."[420] This surprising equating of the Hebrew Cain to the Egyptian Re in a writing attributed to John points to some very old traditions. Whether or not the story of "Re and the Sun's Eye" is of Canaanite origin, as Cyrus Gordon maintains,[421] the Egyptian story of

Astarte establishes definite connections and seems to go back even to distant Hurrian and Hittite flood legends.[422] In Abraham 1:21–27 we certainly see something of that confusion that results from the mingling of patriarchal and matriarchal claims that left the pharaohs forever in doubt as to just where they stood on authority.

> Pharaoh, being a righteous man, established his kingdom and judged his people wisely and justly all his days, *seeking earnestly to imitate* that order established by *the fathers* in the first generations [the *pawt*], in the days of the first *patriarchal* reign, even in the reign of Adam, and also of Noah, his *father,* who blessed him with the blessings of the earth, and with the blessings of wisdom, but *cursed* him as pertaining to the Priesthood. Now, Pharaoh being of that *lineage* by which he *could not* have the right of Priesthood, notwithstanding the Pharaohs *would fain claim it* from Noah, through Ham. (Abraham 1:26–27)

Question: Why could they not have it?

Answer: Because, as noted, it came through a matriarchal succession, the first pharaoh being "the eldest son of Egyptus, the *daughter* of Ham, and it was after the manner of the government of Ham, which was *patriarchal*" (Abraham 1:25). Pharaoh was of a more righteous line than the sons of Ham, but daughters do not transmit patriarchal succession. In all of this, please note, there is no word of race or color, though that has been the main point of attack on the Book of Abraham by the enemies of the Prophet.

More of Pharaoh's Misgivings

Question: You mean the pharaohs really were in doubt about their glory?

Answer: Desperately. We have touched on this touchy theme already. As Kees points out, these inscriptions, hymns, prayers, and rites are only outer form—actually Pharaoh was always unsure of his authority.[423] Recently

Georges Posener noted that Pharaoh's claims to divinity are pure metaphor, without content, never taken literally. The royalty is divine, but the king? Nobody was fooled, according to Posener; the people viewed the king "with lucidity and detachment" as an ordinary human being.[424] The frequent reassurances in Egyptian autographies from the king on down, that the subject is not merely boasting, indicated to François Daumas that he is doing just that, "that the writers of the official texts were conscious of their boasting [for-fanterie]." Pharaoh searched in the archives personally for confirmation of his divinity; he was not a god but the servant of the gods; he could not heal the sick; and even in popular tales he performs no miracles. And yet he was conceded a sort of theoretical divinity.[425] No wonder he was impressed when, according to the *Genesis Apocryphon*, Abraham laid hands upon him and healed him! Here was a man he could truly honor. Hear how a great pharaoh of the glorious Eighteenth Dynasty betrays his misgivings by protesting much too much: "I am his son; he commanded that I be upon his throne while I was still in the nest. He begot me right willingly. This is no fiction, there is no deception in it—ever since my majesty was a small child, while I was still a nursling in his temple, before my invitation [*bs*] as a priest, . . . I was raised up to the exalted place of the Lord. . . . [This is no] fiction."[426] Then follows a heavenly journey and theophany very much in the manner of the theophanies in the testaments and the apocalypses of the Hebrew patriarchs and prophets: "The gates of heaven he opened to me, the doors of the horizon. I flew to heaven as a divine hawk to behold his majesty. I saw the forms of transition [*ḥprw*] of the glorious one of the horizons upon the secret ways of heaven. Re himself confirmed [*smn*] me; I was enobled with the glory [*ḥꜣw*] that was upon his head. . . . I was fitted out with all his brightness [*ꜣḥwt*]; I received a fulness [*s.saa*] of the perfection of the gods, even as Horus received his enlightenment [*ip d̲.t*] in the Temple of my father Amon-Re. I was [endowed] with the authority [*sȝḫw*] of a god."[427] The formula "this is no lie or trick" (*nn grg nn iw-ms*) lives on in the claim of the Hellenistic pharaohs that the king of Egypt is uniquely incapable of lying and emerges in a moving tale of Alexander the Great and Darius, who were both pharaohs, Darius by conquest and inheritance, and Alexander, according to our source, by birth.

Question: Alexander the Great?

Answer: The same. His mother, so the story goes, consorted with an Egyptian soothsayer visiting the land of Macedon, who was really the refugee Pharaoh Nectanebo in disguise.[428] The source of that tale provides us with the other. Darius, it tells us, through the proper rites had been recognized as legitimate king of Egypt; his rival Alexander had been declared the legitimate Son of Amon—he too was Pharaoh.[429] Alexander found the defeated Darius on the point of death in his tent, and with characteristic nobility laid his hands upon his head to heal him, commanding him to arise and resume his kingly power, and concluded his blessing: "I swear unto thee, Darius, by all the gods that I do these things truly and without faking [*periplasmenos*]." To which the great king replied with a gentle rebuke: "Alexander my boy [*teknon mou*], . . . do you think you can touch heaven with those hands of yours?" Whereupon he died.[430] Here Alexander used the Egyptian formula, "truly and without deception," but it still did not work; Abraham hits it on the head when he says: "Pharaoh, being a righteous man, established his kingdom, . . . seeking *earnestly* to *imitate* that order" (Abraham 1:26). Listen to this from another great pharaoh: "Hear ye Fathers-of-the-god of this temple, ye priests, etc. [these are priestly titles], make libations at my pyramid and sacrifice at my altar. Reverence [*smnkh*] the monuments of my majesty; pronounce my name, recall [recite] my titles, give praise to my image [statue], honor the likeness [*hnty*] of my majesty; cause my name to be in the mouth of your servants and my memory to be before your children. Because I was a one deserving [*mnkh*] to be king because of what he did to make his name worthy of remembrance even for his singular courage, and what I did in this land, whereof ye all know. This is not fiction—it is before you; it is no mere boasting."[431]

Question: What is he worried about?

Answer: Legitimacy. "The Pharaohs, who insisted on divine nativity, were all suspected of not having the purest solar blood in their veins," wrote Alexandre Moret, who makes much of the Canaanite contamination of that blood.[432] Professor Gerhard Fecht has shown that it was the ruling class of Egypt that supported the sacred person of Pharaoh, while the common people took a fatalistic and pessimistic view of things—it was not popular superstition that established and maintained the divine monarchy, but the political and economic interests of the aristocracy.[433]

Question: Then the pharaoh was not so all-important after all?

Answer: As a king there was no better. Recall the text: "Pharaoh, being a righteous man, . . . judged his people wisely and justly. . . . [He sought to imitate the priesthood order of] *Noah, his father*, who blessed him with the blessings of the earth, and with the blessings of wisdom, but cursed him as pertaining to the Priesthood" (Abraham 1:26). What a number of studies point out is that it was specifically his claim to *divinity* that was denied him. Peter Kaplony's long study demonstrates the legal and moral insecurity of the pharaoh, citing a newly discovered text showing that the Egyptians of the Fifth Dynasty had serious doubts about the *divinity* of Pharaoh.[434] Kees shows that a state "cant" was necessary to defend Pharaoh's pretensions to sanctity, which were always doubted.[435] We learn of great kings spending their days in the archives "trying to learn about

God in his true form," to be sure of their own divine callings.[436] What is perhaps the oldest of all Egyptian ritual
texts, used at the installation of Menes, the first king of the
First Dynasty, tells how Horus was blessed with the blessings
of the earth by Geb the earth-god, the wise first parent, to
be his heir and successor, "born on the day of the Opening
of the Ways,"[437] the beginning of history. But the claim was
challenged by Seth, to whom originally Geb had assigned
an equal portion of the earth with Horus.[438] The Beatty
Papyrus 1 recounts that when all the Council in Heaven
approved Horus as king, the Most High God was silent and
angry with the assembly for slighting Seth. The issue was
never settled, and we shall return to it again.[439]

Abraham 1:23: "which in the Chaldean signifies Egypt."

Question: Is there any evidence that the land got its
name from such a person?

Answer: There are plenty of ancient legends dealing
with the subject. One of the oldest, certainly unknown to
Joseph Smith, was reported by Herakleides: "It was first a
woman named Aegyptia who established her son and introduced weaving. Because of her, the Egyptians set up an
image of Athena, as Ephorus says in his work on Europa."[440]
Athena is none other than Neith, by which name the Lady
is often designated in the north of Egypt. In classic times
when the Greeks and Egyptians rivaled each other in
learned philological and historical speculations about the
origin of Egypt, a great many conflicting stories circulated.
"They say," Diodorus writes, "that the people with Osiris
(when he came to Egypt) built a city in the Egyptian
Thebaid . . . which they named after the Mother, but which
later generations changed to Diospolis (city of Zeus-Re),
and which some call Thebes. . . . But there is much disagreement about this, both among the historians and the
priests."[441] From Isocrates, a diligent researcher of the fourth
century B.C., we learn that a granddaughter of Zeus, being

the mother of both Busiris of Egypt and his brother, the terrible Antaeus, who ruled the desert immediately west of the Nile, "was, they say, the first woman to rule, after whom the country was named."[442]

A commentator to Plato explains how the Lady could come from Canaan but still arrive through the Wadi Hammamat far in the south by a detour: "Egypt was named after Egyptus the son of Belus [the Canaanite Baal] and Anchirhoea, the daughter of Nile, who was king of Egypt [there is your mixed blood again!]. This Egyptus was sent by his father to settle in Arabia, but returned and named the land of Blackfeet 'Egypt' after himself."[443] "Some say that Osiris was a cultivator in Arabia, and that the city [Thebes] was not built by Osiris but by a much later king. And some say that Osiris was a cultivator in Arabia Felix, and is the same as Dionysus, the father of the vine and of civilized living."[444] There is the wine motif again, going with the founding of Egyptian civilization. According to others it was not Osiris but Isis who first brought agriculture and letters to the valley, "for which reason the land was named after her," while "the Egyptian people were named after a former king of Egypt called Egyptus, they having been formerly called Aerii [Re-people?]."[445] More juggling with the name is found in the Pseudo-Plutarch account: when the Nile refused to rise, a king of Egypt found himself forced to sacrifice his daughter. Grieving, the king, whose name was Egyptus, cast himself into the river Melana (Black), whose name was accordingly changed to Aegyptus river.[446] Diodorus tells us that the Nile "was known as Aegyptus after a former king of the land."[447] Josephus bestows the name on the founder of the great Nineteenth Dynasty: "Sethos was another name for Aegyptus," who was also called Rameses.[448]

Question: And where does all this get us?

Answer: All this is only the beginning. We have just scouted a few offhand possibilities—merely scratched the surface. By all means let us keep the door open. For example, the entering of the Lady from the north is certainly a possibility that must be considered; if ever there was a flood figure it was Ptah of Memphis, that one whose name, most scholars think today, gave the name to Egypt through Canaanite editing. His good Semitic name makes him Ptah the Opener—of what?—of TaTenen, the newly emergent land. Before the learned began to favor the Ptah name for Egypt, the universal consensus was that the name was derived from the Egyptian word *Kemi,* meaning the Black Land. *Kem* means black and is easily interchanged with *khm,* meaning hot and dry, that being also the name of Khem-Min, as Eugène Lefébure argues.[449] Certainly the ancients called Egypt, as in the *Genesis Apocryphon,* "The Land of the Children of Ham." In the oldest manuscript copy of the Book of Abraham, the name Egyptus appears in Abraham 1:23 as Zeptah. Isidore says that the pharaoh of Joseph was called Zaphanath, which the Egyptians interpreted as "salvator mundi," since he saved the land from famine; but its original meaning, says Isidore, was *absconditorum repertorem*—he who searches what is hidden or forbidden.[450] This comes near enough to Abraham 1:23, rendering "Zeptah" as "that which is forbidden." During the throne controversies of the Nineteenth Dynasty, a successful aspirant through the lineage of his wife, the "Great Daughter of the King" and "Wife of the God," Ta-wsrt, took the name of Siptah. It was in 1912 that George Daressy discovered "a hitherto unknown king" by the name of Si-Ptah, and pointed to a relief at Sehel showing Seti I standing "worshipping the names of Si-Ptah" who was a pharaoh at the time.[451] Maspero identified Ramses-si-Ptah with Merenptah-si-Ptah, whom others identified with Seti I himself.[452] The point is that the Ramessides, who were half Canaanite, adopted the name of Si-Ptah to "placate" the

Egyptians by resting their alien dynasty on the oldest and most respected title to the land, the name of Si-Ptah.[453]

A more serious candidate is presented in the name of Koptos or Coptos. Coptos was the oldest settlement of Egypt, marking the spot where the main route from the East comes upon the Nile Valley right where the great bend in the river makes a broad plain—the ideal place for a settlement. "We do not know where Nakada II people (the bringers of classic Egyptian civilization) came from," wrote Elise Baumgartel, but "we find their earliest remains in that part of Egypt where the Wadi Hammamat joins the Nile Valley. Koptos is situated at this junction, and at no great distance across the river are *Nubet, the Capitol, and Diospolis Parva*."[454] "It is via Koptos that the Asiatic conquerors entered the Nile Valley in prehistoric times and founded historic Egypt," Raymond Weill asserts.[455] "From the earliest times Koptos was a very important entrepôt; it could not be otherwise with its location. All the roads converge on Koptos, including the great trade and mining roads."[456] Egyptian civilization really began with the arrival of the "Second Civilization," according to Moret, coming "from Elam by way of the Persian Gulf, the Red Sea, and the route that goes from Qoseir to Koptos = Wadi Hammamat."[457] Pliny finds it significant that Philae, "the island sacred to Isis," the second Eden, was *juxta oppidum Copton*, "right next to Coptos town."[458]

Now some have maintained that this place, Coptos, with the oldest temple and the oldest settlement in Egypt, gave its name to the country. "There existed in Egypt from prehistoric times a nome which bore the still obscure name of Kebti (Koptos). . . . [The name was] derived from [the] . . . pre-Misraim inhabitants who called their capital Kebti and the land and even their river probably by the same name."[459] Where the early inhabitants got the name, W. J. Phythian-Adams does not say, but since it could be applied to river, land, nome, town, and temple, there is no reason why a person couldn't bear it, and good reason for supposing that a person did. It is interesting that there are many Coptos legends having to do with the beginnings of the Egyptian kingdom, whereas the name of Memphis, *Ḥw.t-kꜣ-Ptḥ*, which most scholars favor as the original, is never mentioned anywhere in that connection and is only applied to Egypt as a whole, as we have seen, by the Canaanites.[460] The Egyptians always remembered what happened at Coptos: "At Coptos," says Aelian, writing at the very end, "they worship Isis . . . and the same Coptites [note the name!] reverence female oryxes while sacrificing male oryxes, in the belief that the female oryxes are Isis' pets."[461] Which reminds us how the desert dwellers brought baby oryxes to the Lady as she sat in view of the plain of Coptos, and of the oryxes that regularly accompany the dancing goddess on the ceremonial bark. Derchain has shown us that the very oldest sacrifice in Egypt was the slaying of a male gazelle by the goddess in honor of her son Pharaoh, usually at Philae and always near there.[462] The key to the whole history is the venerable figure of the god Min of Coptos, to which we shall return.

Abraham 1:23: "Egyptus, which in the Chaldean signifies Egypt, which signifies that which is forbidden."

One thinks also of Egypt as the land forbidden to the saints in early Christian and Jewish literature, cursed for its fleshpots and its stews. But this passage definitely has a philological thrust. It tells us that the "Canaanite" or common old Semitic root *GPT (the vowels change constantly, but the root meaning of the consonant combination always remains the same) designates something forbidden. Well, if you take that combination of a guttural, a labial, and a dental in that order in any Semitic language, what do you get? In Arabic, the commonest meaning is to conceal, cover over, tuck, crouch, usually with the basic idea of concealing with the hand; thus *kafata*, conceal, forbid; *kabata*, conceal out of shame; *qabada*, cover, shrink from; *qabut*, our word *capuchin*, all-enveloping cloak, modesty, shame; *khabith*, impure, taboo; *khafata*, to maintain a holy silence, keep a secret; *khafada*, lower the voice, abash, humble; *hafitha*, to keep secret, and so on for over one hundred examples. Or Hebrew and Aramaic: *kabah*, cover or hide; *qafdah*, shrinking, horror; *qafats*, draw together, close; *khaba*, wrap or hide, etc. In Babylonian and Assyrian *khpt* means hidden and forbidden; in the Book of the Dead the *khebt*-chamber is the forbidden place where all is hidden.[463] For that matter, the suggested name *Ḥw.t-kȝ-Ptḥ*, the *secret* name of Memphis, can mean the hiding place of Ptah. The island of the Abaton is, as its name shows, forbidden to all mortals, and the Lady of Bigge, that "very hidden, very secret one," was in her caves of the Nile, in her hiding place, which were at once the secret source of the Nile and the dark mountain of the Duat.

Before all, however, came *Kh.b.t*, the hidden marsh where Isis, according to some accounts, bore, and, according to all accounts, nursed the infant Horus—the most secret place in the world and the only place where Seth could not find him; the nest hidden in the bullrushes was the most forbidden place on earth. So we have no shortage of candidates for the original form of "Egypt, which signifies that which is forbidden" (Abraham 1:23).

Notes

1. Editor's note: Although we cite the pages for the translation of T32 used by Nibley, a newer, more accurate translation is to be found in François R. Herbin, *Le livre de parcour l'éternité* (Leuven: Peeters, 1994).

2. Hermann Junker, *Die Onurislegende* (Vienna: Hoelder, 1917), v.

3. Kurt H. Sethe, "Zur altägyptischen Sage vom Sonnenauge das in der Fremde war," vol. 5, part 3, in Untersuchungen zur Geschichte und Altertumskunde Aegyptens, 15 vols. (1912; reprint, Hildesheim: Olms, 1964), 5.

4. Wilhelm Spiegelberg, "Der ägyptische Mythos vom Sonnenauge

in einem demotischen Papyrus der römischen Kaiserzeit," *Sitzungs-berichte der königlichen preussischen Akademie der Wissenschaften. Philosophisch-historische Klasse* 15 (1915): 888.

5. Junker, *Onurislegende*, iv.

6. Ibid., v–vii.

7. Hermann Junker, *Das Götterdekret über das Abaton* (Vienna: Hoelder, 1913), 87–88; Wilhelm Spiegelberg, *Der ägyptische Mythos vom Sonnenauge* (Strassburg: Schultz, 1917), 53.

8. Junker, *Onurislegende*, vii, 11–12, 115.

9. Adriaan de Buck, *The Egyptian Readingbook* (Leiden: Nederlands Instituut voor het Nabije Oosten, 1963), 123–26.

10. Georges Goyon, "Les travaux de Chou et les tribulations de Geb, d'après le Naos 2248 d'Ismaïla," *Kemi* 6 (1936): 14, 31–32.

11. *Book of the Cow,* col. 16, in Charles Maystre, "Le livre de la vache du ciel dans les tombeaux de la Vallée des Rois," *BIFAO* 40 (1941): 68 (text from the tomb of Seti I); cf. Alexandre Piankoff, *The Shrines of Tut-Ankh-Amon* (New York: Pantheon, 1955), 27; de Buck, *Egyptian Readingbook,* 123–24.

12. Book of the Dead 175, in E. A. Wallis Budge, *The Egyptian Book of the Dead (The Papyrus of Ani),* 3 vols. (New York: Putnam, 1913), 2:563–64, 3: plate 29, lines 17–18; Coffin Text 79–80, in *The Egyptian Coffin Texts,* ed. Adriaan de Buck, 7 vols. (Chicago: University of Chicago Press, 1935–61), 2:24–25, 34–35.

13. Günter Lanczkowski, "Ägyptische Prophetismus im Lichte des alttestamentlichen," *Zeitschrift für die alttestamentliche Wissenschaft* 70 (1958): 35.

14. Philippe Derchain, *Le Papyrus Salt 825 (British Museum 10051), rituel pour la conservation de la vie en Égypte,* 2 vols. (Brussels: Palais des Academies, 1965), 1:1–7; Goyon, "Travaux de Chou," 13–17, 32; Jan Zandee, "Sargtexte, Spruch 75," *ZÄS* 99 (1972): 48, 50; Bremner-Rhind Papyrus 16:4–14, in *The Papyrus Bremner-Rhind (British Museum no. 10188),* ed. Raymond O. Faulkner, vol. 3 of *Bibliotheca Aegyptiaca* (Brussels: Fondation Égyptologique Reine Elisabeth, 1933), 29–30.

15. Hermann te Velde, *Seth, God of Confusion* (Leiden: Brill, 1967), 25; Siegfried Schott, ed., "Das Buch vom Sieg über Seth," in *Urkunden mythologischen Inhalts,* vol. 6, part 5, in Urkunden des ägyptischen Altertums, ed. Kurt Sethe and Heinrich Schäfer (Leipzig: Hinrichs, 1929).

16. Te Velde, *Seth, God of Confusion,* 25; Gerald A. Wainwright, "The Origin of the Storm-Gods of Egypt," *JEA* 49 (1963): 13–17; Hugh W. Nibley, "The Arrow, the Hunter, and the State," *Western Political Quarterly* 2 (1949): 341; reprinted in *The Ancient State,* CWHN 10:16; Hugh W.

Nibley, "Tenting, Toll, and Taxing," *Western Political Quarterly* 19 (1966): 599–603; reprinted in *The Ancient State, CWHN* 10: 33–35, 41.

17. Coffin Text 80, in de Buck, *Egyptian Coffin Texts*, 2:28–31.

18. Cf. Piankoff, *Shrines of Tut-Ankh-Amon*, 29; E. A. Wallis Budge, *Legends of the Gods* (London: Paul, Trench, Trübner, 1912), 14–41.

19. Eugène Lefébure, "Un chapitre de la chronique solaire," *ZÄS* 21 (1883): 27–31.

20. Ferdinand Wüstenfeld, "Die älteste aegyptische Geschichte nach den Zauber- und Wundererzählungen der Araber," *Orient und Occident* 1 (1862): 332–33.

21. Coffin Text 80, in de Buck, *Egyptian Coffin Texts*, 2:32–34; Rudolf Anthes, "Egyptian Theology in the Third Millennium B.C.," *JNES* 18 (July 1959): 198.

22. Anthes, "Egyptian Theology," 198–99.

23. *Book of the Cow*, cols. 37–38, 42–43, in Maystre, "Livre de la vache du ciel," 79–82; cf. Piankoff, *Shrines of Tut-Ankh-Amon*, 29–30, 35.

24. Papyrus Salt 825 3/6–7, in Derchain, *Papyrus Salt 825*, 2:3–4; Hermann Kees, *Der Götterglaube im alten Aegypten* (Leipzig: Hinrichs, 1941), 75.

25. *Book of the Cow*, cols. 26–27, in Maystre, "Livre de la vache du ciel," 74–75; cf. Piankoff, *Shrines of Tut-Ankh-Amon*, 29–31, 35.

26. Spiegelberg, "Der ägyptische Mythos vom Sonnenauge," 883.

27. Hermann Junker, *Der Auszug der Hathor-Tefnut aus Nubien* (Berlin: Akademie der Wissenschaft, 1911), 21.

28. Spiegelberg, "Der ägyptische Mythos vom Sonnenauge," 877; Spiegelberg, *Der ägyptische Mythus vom Sonnenauge*, 27.

29. Lefébure, "Chapitre de la chronique Solaire," 28–31.

30. Sethe, "Zur altägyptischen Sage," 17.

31. *Book of the Cow*, cols. 12–14, in Maystre, "Livre de la vache du ciel," 65–67; cf. Piankoff, *Shrines of Tut-Ankh-Amon*, 30.

32. Alan H. Gardiner, "Hymns to Amon from a Leiden Papyrus," *ZÄS* 42 (1905): 20–21.

33. Wainwright, "Origin of the Storm-gods of Egypt," 19.

34. Ibid., 15.

35. Ibid., 17.

36. E. A. Wallis Budge, *The Gods of the Egyptians or Studies in Egyptian Mythology*, 2 vols. (London: Methuen, 1904), 2:87.

37. Bremner-Rhind Papyrus 7:1–8:27, in E. A. Wallis Budge, *Egyptian Hieratic Papyri in the British Museum* (London: Trustees of the British Museum, 1910), 3, plates 2–3.

38. Zandee, "Sargtexte, Spruch 75," 52–53.

39. Siegfried Schott, "Das Buch von der Abwehr des Bösen," in *Urkunden mythologischen Inhalts*, 63, 69.

40. Schott, "Buch vom Sieg über Seth," 38–39, 55–57.

41. Spiegelberg, *Der ägyptische Mythos vom Sonnenauge*, 55; Coffin Text 79, in de Buck, *Egyptian Coffin Texts*, 2:23–27.

42. Junker, *Onurislegende*, 2; Sethe, "Zur altägyptischen Sage," 18, 38.

43. Bremner-Rhind Papyrus 3:1–10, in Faulkner, *Papyrus Bremner-Rhind*, 5–6.

44. Cf. Pyramid Text 439 (§812), in Raymond O. Faulkner, *The Ancient Egyptian Pyramid Texts* (Oxford: Clarendon, 1969), 146; Sethe, "Zur altägyptischen Sage," 9.

45. *Book of the Cow*, cols. 25–26, in Maystre, "Livre de la vache du ciel," 73–75; cf. Piankoff, *Shrines of Tut-Ankh-Amon*, 30–31.

46. Schott, "Buch von der Abwehr des Bösen," 67, 69.

47. *Book of the Cow*, cols. 18–19, 22, in Maystre, "Livre de la vache du ciel," 69–72; cf. Piankoff, *Shrines of Tut-Ankh-Amon*, 28; de Buck, *Egyptian Readingbook*, 125.

48. *Book of the Cow*, cols. 15–19, in Maystre, "Livre de la vache du ciel," 67–70; cf. Piankoff, *Shrines of Tut-Ankh-Amon*, 28; Schott, "Buch vom Sieg über Seth," 49.

49. Plutarch, *De Iside et Osiride* VI, 8.

50. Te Velde, *Seth, God of Confusion*, 5–7.

51. Pindar, *Olympian Odes* IX, 43–55.

52. Junker, *Auszug der Hathor-Tefnut aus Nubien*, 83.

53. *Book of the Cow*, cols. 22–23, 25–26, in Maystre, "Livre de la vache du ciel," 72–75; cf. Piankoff, *Shrines of Tut-Ankh-Amon*, 28–29.

54. Coffin Text 80, in de Buck, *Egyptian Coffin Texts*, 2:30; Zandee, "Sargtexte, Spruch 75," 52–53; Spiegelberg, *Der ägyptische Mythos vom Sonnenauge*, 35.

55. Leiden Papyrus T32, 3/10–20, in Bruno H. Stricker, ed., "De Egyptische Mysteriën: Pap. Leiden T32 (Vervolg)," *OMRO* 34 (1953): 18–19, 26 (Nibley's translation adapted from Stricker's).

56. Leiden Papyrus T32, 5/1, 29; 6/11, in Stricker, "Egyptische Mysteriën (Vervolg)," 22, 24; and "De Egyptische Mysteriën: Pap. Leiden T32 (Slot)," *OMRO* 37 (1956): 56.

57. Leiden Papyrus T32, 4/22–28, in Stricker, "Egyptische Mysteriën (Vervolg)," 21–22.

58. *Baruch* (Slavonic) 4:13–15 (emphasis added).

59. Hans Bonnet, *Reallexikon der ägyptischen Religionsgeschichte* (Berlin: de Gruyter, 1952), 282.

60. Piankoff, *Shrines of Tut-Ankh-Amon*, 27.

61. Ali Radwan, *Die Darstellungen des regierenden Königs und seiner*

Familienangehörigen in den Privatgräbern der 18. Dynastie (Berlin: Hessling, 1969), 16, 55a; Heinrich K. Brugsch, *Thesaurus Inscriptionem Aegyptiacarum* (Leipzig: Hinrichs, 1883–91), 9, 38; Anthes, "Egyptian Theology," 198, 210.

62. Junker, *Onurislegende,* 115; Spiegelberg, "Der ägyptische Mythos vom Sonnenauge," 876.

63. Junker, *Onurislegende,* 119; Sethe, "Zur altägyptischen Sage," 31.

64. *Book of the Cow,* cols. 37–38, in Maystre, "Livre de la vache du ciel," 79–80; cf. Piankoff, *Shrines of Tut-Ankh-Amon,* 29; Bonnet, *Reallexikon der ägyptischen Religionsgeschichte,* 281.

65. Junker, *Onurislegende,* 114, 163–64.

66. *Wb,* 1:91.

67. Junker, *Onurislegende,* 73, 78, 119; Junker, *Auszug der Hathor-Tefnut aus Nubien,* 12.

68. Junker, *Auszug der Hathor-Tefnut aus Nubien,* 31, 77; *Wb,* 4:327–28, 348; 3:488.

69. Rainer Stadelmann, *Syrisch-Palästinische Gottheiten in Aegypten* (Leiden: Brill, 1967), 119, 122; Pierre Montet, *Le drame d'Avaris* (Paris: Geuthner, 1941), 27, 35.

70. W. M. Flinders Petrie, "The Geography of the Gods," *Ancient Egypt* 4 (1917): 110.

71. Sethe, "Zur altägyptischen Sage," 34.

72. Junker, *Onurislegende,* 163–64.

73. E. A. Wallis Budge, "On the Hieratic Papyrus of Nesi-Amsu, a Scribe in the Temple of Amen-Rā at Thebes, about B.C. 305," *Archaeologia* 52 (1890): 147–48.

74. Junker, *Onurislegende,* 49.

75. Schott, "Buch vom Sieg über Seth," 7–9.

76. Ibid., 1–2, 31–33.

77. Schott, "Buch von der Abwehr des Bösen," 69, 117.

78. Ibid., 73.

79. Ibid., 101.

80. Ibid., 103.

81. Ibid., 113.

82. Ibid., 117.

83. Ibid., 67.

84. Ibid., 63.

85. Ibid., 133–35.

86. Ibid., 139.

87. Alan H. Gardiner, "The Astarte Papyrus," in *Studies Presented to F. Ll. Griffith* , ed. Stephen R. K. Glanville (Oxford: Milford, 1932), 79.

88. Ibid., 82.

89. Ibid., 80.

90. Theodor Gaster, "The Egyptian 'Story of Astarte' and the Ugaritic Poem of Baal," *BiOr* 9 (1952): 82.

91. Ibid.

92. Ibid.

93. Ibid., 85.

94. Stadelmann, *Syrisch-Palästinische Gottheiten in Aegypten,* 110–23; Coffin Text 61, in de Buck, *Egyptian Coffin Texts,* 1:261.

95. Alan H. Gardiner, *Egypt of the Pharaohs* (Oxford: Clarendon, 1961), 397–98.

96. Plutarch, *De Iside et Osiride* 15.

97. Ibid., 15–17.

98. Montet, *Drame d'Avaris,* 35.

99. Coffin Text 61, in de Buck, *Egyptian Coffin Texts,* 1:261.

100. Siegfried Hermann, "Isis in Byblos," *ZÄS* 82 (1957): 54.

101. Ibid., 53–54.

102. Ibid., 55.

103. Ibid., 52.

104. Ibid., 51.

105. Ibid., 52.

106. Ibid.

107. Hesiod, *Homeric Hymn* 2 (to Demeter), 1–3.

108. Plutarch, *De Iside et Osiride* 19.

109. Ibid., 20.

110. Nibley, "Tenting, Toll, and Taxing," 599–600; in *CWHN* 10: 33–34.

111. Spiegelberg, "Der ägyptische Mythos vom Sonnenauge," 884; Spiegelberg, *Der ägyptische Mythos vom Sonnenauge,* 35.

112. Bonnet, *Reallexikon der ägyptischen Religionsgeschichte,* 281.

113. Spiegelberg, "Der ägyptische Mythos vom Sonnenauge," 880–81.

114. Spiegelberg, *Der ägyptische Mythos vom Sonnenauge,* 33.

115. Ibid.

116. Gustave Jéquier, *Considérations sur les religions Égyptiénnes* (Neuchatel: Baçonnière, 1946), 241, 243.

117. Bremner-Rhind Papyrus 23:17–24:8, in Faulkner, *Papyrus Bremner-Rhind,* 47–49.

118. Spiegelberg, *Der ägyptische Mythos vom Sonnenauge,* 31–32.

119. Junker, *Onurislegende,* 133, 143, 146.

120. Spiegelberg, *Der ägyptische Mythos vom Sonnenauge,* 53.

121. Junker, *Auszug der Hathor-Tefnut aus Nubien,* 11–12.

122. Hellmut Brunner, "Die theologische Bedeutung der Trunkenhert," *ZÄS* 79 (1954): 82.

123. Junker, *Auszug der Hathor-Tefnut aus Nubien,* 31–32.

124. Ibid., 38–40.
125. Ibid., 46, 60.
126. Ibid., 75; Schafik Allam, *Beiträge zum Hathorkult* (Berlin: Hessling, 1963), 123.
127. Junker, *Onurislegende,* 113.
128. Leiden Papyrus T32, 3/10–12, in Stricker, "Egyptische Mysteriën (Vervolg)," 18.
129. Leiden Papyrus T32, 4/26–5/1, in ibid., 22.
130. Leiden Papyrus T32, 5/5, in ibid.
131. Leiden Papyrus T32, 5/29–30, in ibid., 24.
132. Plutarch, *De Iside et Osiride* 36.
133. Schott, "Buch von der Abwehr des Bösen," 65–67.
134. Ibid., 69.
135. Ibid., 73.
136. Ibid., 101–3.
137. Schott, "Buch vom Sieg über Seth," 25–27.
138. Ibid., 49–53.
139. Philippe Derchain, *Rites égyptiens* (Brussels: Fondation Égyptologique Reine Elisabeth, 1962), 53.
140. Étienne Drioton, *Le texte dramatique d'Edfou* (Cairo: BIFAO, 1984), 40–43.
141. Kurt H. Sethe, *Der dramatische Ramesseumspapyrus,* Untersuchungen zur Geschichte und Altertumskunde Aegyptens, 10, vol. part 2, 177, 180.
142. Spiegelberg, *Der ägyptische Mythos vom Sonnenauge,* 37.
143. Spiegelberg, "Der ägyptische Mythos vom Sonnenauge," 886; Spiegelberg, *Der ägyptische Mythos vom Sonnenauge,* 41, 43.
144. Ibid., 49.
145. Junker, *Auszug der Hathor-Tefnut aus Nubien,* 46.
146. Spiegelberg, *Der ägyptische Mythos vom Sonnenauge,* 23, 49.
147. Sethe, "Zur altägyptischen Sage," 22.
148. Ibid., 34.
149. Ibid., 23.
150. Drioton, *Le texte dramatique d'Edfou,* 58–59, gives specific pages.
151. Junker, *Auszug der Hathor-Tefnut aus Nubien,* 34.
152. Sethe, "Zur altägyptischen Sage," 23–24.
153. Ibid., 34.
154. Fred Wendorf et al., "The Use of Barley in the Egyptian Late Paleolithic," *Science* 205 (28 September 1979): 1342.
155. Ibid., 1343.
156. Ibid., 1342.
157. Herodotus, *History* II, 99; Kurt H. Sethe, "Menes und die

Gründung von Memphis," in *Beiträge zur ältesten Geschichte Ägyptens* (Leipzig: Hinrichs, 1905), 123–24.

158. Spiegelberg, *Der ägyptische Mythos vom Sonnenauge*, 37; Bonnet, *Reallexikon der ägyptischen Religionsgeschichte*, 513–14.

159. Leiden Papyrus T32, 4/17, in Stricker, "Egyptische Mysteriën (Vervolg)," 21.

160. Leiden Papyrus T32, 6/11–12, in Stricker, "Egyptische Mysteriën (Slot)," 56.

161. Leiden Papyrus T32, 3/13, in Stricker, "Egyptische Mysteriën (Vervolg)," 19.

162. Leiden Papyrus T32, 4/13–15, in ibid., 21.

163. Junker, *Onurislegende*, 127.

164. See Drioton, *Texte dramatique d'Edfou*, 53–62; Wendorf, "Use of Barley," 1341.

165. Harris Papyrus 6:1–7:12, in Budge, *Egyptian Hieratic Papyri in the British Museum*, plates 25–26.

166. Spiegelberg, *Der ägyptische Mythos vom Sonnenauge*, p. 35, col. XIII.

167. Wolfhart Westendorf, *Painting, Sculpture, and Architecture of Ancient Egypt* (New York: Abrams, 1969), 13.

168. Junker, *Götterdekret über das Abaton*, 45.

169. Ibid.

170. Source not found; see preface.

171. *Book of the Cow*, cols. 78–80, in Maystre, "Livre de la vache du ciel," 98–99; cf. Piankoff, *Shrines of Tut-Ankh-Amon*, 32–33.

172. Siegfried Schott, "Die Reinigung Pharaos in einem memphitischen Tempel (Berlin Papyrus 13242)," *Nachrichten der Akademie der Wissenschaften in Göttingen. Philologisch-historische Klasse* 3 (1957): 45–52.

173. Ibid.

174. Junker, *Onurislegende*, 96.

175. Junker, *Götterdekret über das Abaton*, 23.

176. Ibid., 23, 31, 45–47.

177. Ibid., 45–47.

178. Ibid., 31.

179. Junker, *Auszug der Hathor-Tefnut aus Nubien*, 76–77.

180. Leiden Papyrus T32, 3/21–23, in Stricker, "Egyptische Mysteriën (Vervolg)," 19.

181. Leiden Papyrus T32, 5/14–15, in ibid., 23.

182. Spiegelberg, *Der ägyptische Mythos vom Sonnenauge*, 51, 53.

183. Vladimir Vikentiev, "Les monuments archäiques: la tablette en ivoire de Naqada," *ASAE* 33 (1933): 208–34.

184. Junker, *Auszug der Hathor-Tefnut aus Nubien*, 74.

185. Ibid., 72–73.

186. Elisabeth Staehelin, "Zur Hathorsymbolik in der ägyptischen Kleinkunst," *ZÄS* 105 (1978): 76–77.

187. Ibid., 77.

188. Ibid., 77–78, 81.

189. Ibid., 80–81.

190. Ahmed Fakhry, "A Note on the Tomb of Kheruef at Thebes," *ASAE* 42 (1943): 483.

191. Ibid., 489.

192. Ibid., 490.

193. Ibid., 496–99.

194. Ibid., 496, plate xl.

195. Ibid., 492.

196. Ibid., 493.

197. Ibid., 494.

198. Ibid., 500.

199. Bremner-Rhind Papyrus 5:12–24, in Budge, *Egyptian Hieratic Papyri in the British Museum,* plate II (author's translation).

200. Hugh W. Nibley, *The Message of the Joseph Smith Papyri: An Egyptian Endowment* (Salt Lake City: Deseret Book, 1975), 202.

201. Adolphe Gutbub, *Textes fondamentaux de la théologie de Kom Ombo* 2 vols. (Cairo: BIFAO, 1973), 1:62–63.

202. Ibid., 64.

203. Ibid., 65.

204. Ibid., 67.

205. Junker, *Onurislegende,* 116.

206. Bremner-Rhind Papyrus 14:1–16:15, in Faulkner, *Papyrus Bremner-Rhind,* 25–30.

207. Schott, "Buch von der Abwehr des Bösen," 67.

208. Joachim Spiegel, *Die Götter von Abydos* (Wiesbaden: Harrassowitz, 1973), 67, 69, 71.

209. Ibid., 66.

210. Rudolf Anthes, "Die Sonnenboote den Pyramidtexten," *ZÄS* 82 (1958): 89.

211. Schott, "Buch von der Abwehr des Bösen," 133–44; Raymond O. Faulkner, "The Bremner-Rhind Papyrus II," *JEA* 23 (1937): 13; Bremner-Rhind Papyrus 2:1–23; 3:9–14; 19:29–30, in Faulkner, *Papyrus Bremner-Rhind,* 3–6, 39.

212. Bremner-Rhind Papyrus 19:13–15; in Faulkner, *Papyrus Bremner-Rhind,* 38; cf. Faulkner, "Bremner-Rhind Papyrus II," 12–13.

213. Spiegelberg, "Der ägyptische Mythos vom Sonnenauge," 887.

214. Leiden Papyrus T32, 2/2–7, 18–21, 2/30–3/2, 5, 9–12, 5/1–3,

11–15, in Bruno H. Stricker, "De Egyptische Mysteriën: Pap. Leiden T32," *OMRO* 31 (1950): 56–58; Stricker "Egyptische Mysteriën (Vervolg)," 18, 22–23.

215. Sethe, "Zur altägyptischen Sage," 4–5.

216. Junker, *Auszug der Hathor-Tefnut aus Nubien,* 44–46.

217. Ibid., 76.

218. Junker, *Götterdekret über das Abaton,* 39.

219. Junker, *Auszug der Hathor-Tefnut aus Nubien,* 72–73.

220. Diodorus Siculus, *The Library of History* I, 22, 2.

221. Junker, *Auszug der Hathor-Tefnut aus Nubien,* 74–76.

222. Ibid., 77–79.

223. Leiden Papyrus T32, 3/15, 4/8–9, in Stricker, "Egyptische Mysteriën (Vervolg)," 19–20.

224. Leiden Papyrus T32, 4/12–14, in ibid., 21.

225. Leiden Papyrus T32, 5/14–16, in ibid., 23.

226. Pieper, *Grosse Inschrift des Königs Neferhotep in Abydos* (Leipzig: Hinrichs, 1929), lines 15–16.

227. Cf. Francis L. Griffith, "A Stele of Tirhaqa from Kawa, Dongola Province, Sudan," *Mémoires de l'Institut Français d'Archéologie Orientale* 66 (1935–38): 426–27; Montet, *Drame d'Avaris,* 203.

228. Sethe, *Der dramatische Ramesseumspapyrus,* 96.

229. Anthes, "Egyptian Theology," 171.

230. Te Velde, *Seth, God of Confusion,* 74, 146–48.

231. Brugsch, *Thesaurus Inscriptionem Aegyptiacarum,* 121–23.

232. Drioton, *Texte dramatique d'Edfou,* 40–41, 77–78.

233. Bremner-Rhind Papyrus 14:13, in Faulkner, *Papyrus Bremner-Rhind,* 26.

234. Bremner-Rhind Papyrus 5:5–10, in ibid., 9.

235. Bremner-Rhind Papyrus 12:1–13:30, in ibid., 22–25.

236. Bremner-Rhind Papyrus 5:6, in ibid., 9.

237. Bremner-Rhind Papyrus 9, in ibid., 16–18.

238. Bremner-Rhind Papyrus 17, in ibid., 31–32.

239. Bremner-Rhind Papyrus 19, in ibid., 37–39.

240. Bremner-Rhind Papyrus 23, in ibid., 45–48.

241. Bremner-Rhind Papyrus 27, in ibid.,60–65.

242. Bremner-Rhind Papyrus 6:1–2, in ibid., 10–11.

243. Bremner-Rhind Papyrus 32:1–54, in ibid., 86–92.

244. Hugh W. Nibley, "There Were Jaredites," *IE* 59 (August 1956): 566–67; reprinted in *CWHN* 5:350–64.

245. Siegfried Schott, *Mythe und Mythenbildung im alten Ägypten* (Leipzig: Hinrichs, 1945), 28.

246. Bonnet, *Reallexikon der ägyptischen Religionsgeschichte,* 806.

247. Junker, *Auszug der Hathor-Tefnut aus Nubien*, 66.

248. Spiegelberg, "Der ägyptische Mythos vom Sonnenauge," 879–80.

249. Junker, *Auszug der Hathor-Tefnut aus Nubien*, 30.

250. Spiegelberg, "Der ägyptische Mythos vom Sonnenauge," 887.

251. Jacques Vandier, "Iousâas et (Hathor) Nebet-Hetepet," *RdE* 18 (1966): 87.

252. Junker, *Auszug der Hathor-Tefnut aus Nubien*, 33.

253. Ibid., 29.

254. Junker, *Onurislegende*, 133.

255. Zandee, "Sargtexte, Spruch 75," 57.

256. Bremner-Rhind Papyrus 28:26, in Faulkner, *Papyrus Bremner-Rhind*, 70.

257. Junker, *Auszug der Hathor-Tefnut aus Nubien*, 38–39, 58–60.

258. Ibid., 55–58.

259. Source not found; see preface.

260. Pyramid Text 311 (§495–500), in Faulkner, *Ancient Egyptian Pyramid Texts*, 97A.

261. Junker, *Götterdekret über das Abaton*, 24.

262. Junker, *Onurislegende*, 96.

263. Leiden Papyrus T32, 6/27–28, in Stricker, "Egyptische Mysteriën (Slot)," 57.

264. Drioton, *Texte dramatique d'Edfou*, 116–17.

265. Junker, *Auszug der Hathor-Tefnut aus Nubien*, 81; Harris Papyrus, cols. 1–7, in Budge, *Egyptian Hieratic Papyri*, 23–26.

266. Harris Papyrus, col. 6, in Budge, *Egyptian Hieratic Papyri*, 25.

267. Papyrus Salt 825 10/1–11/7, in Derchain, *Papyrus Salt 825*, 1:141.

268. Leiden Papyrus T32, 1/28–2/1, in Stricker, "Egyptische Mysteriën," 56.

269. Leiden Papyrus T32, 3/17–18, in Stricker, "Egyptische Mysteriën (Vervolg)," 19.

270. Junker, *Auszug der Hathor-Tefnut aus Nubien*, 32.

271. Coffin Text 8, in de Buck, *Egyptian Coffin Texts*, 1:24–27.

272. Bremner-Rhind Papyrus 32:10–11, in Faulkner, *Papyrus Bremner-Rhind*, 88.

273. Nibley, "There Were Jaredites," 390–91, 460–61; in *CWHN* 5:343–49.

274. Anthes, "Egyptian Theology," 187.

275. Julia Samson, "Nefertiti's Regality," *JEA* 63 (1977): 91 (emphasis added).

276. Allam, *Beiträge zum Hathorkult*, 120.

277. Brugsch, *Thesaurus Inscriptionem Aegyptiacarum*, 9–10, 110.

278. Anthes, "Egyptian Theology," 193.

279. Brugsch, *Thesaurus Inscriptionem Aegyptiacarum*, 492–94.
280. Ibid., 492.
281. Ibid., 493.
282. Ibid., 494.
283. Ibid., 500–501.
284. Ibid., 502.
285. Ibid., 503.
286. Ibid., 504.
287. Ibid., 505.
288. Junker, *Götterdekret über das Abaton*, 29.
289. Leiden Papyrus T32, 6/27–28, in Stricker, "Egyptische Mysteriën (Slot)," 57.
290. Leiden Papyrus T32, 2/1–4, in Stricker, "Egyptische Mysteriën," 56.
291. Philippe Derchain, "La pêche de l'oeil," *RdE* 15 (1963): 18.
292. Derchain, *Rites égyptiens*, 44.
293. Alan H. Gardiner, *The Library of A. Chester Beatty* (Oxford: Oxford University Press, 1931), 15, 17, 26, plate XXI, line 27.
294. Junker, *Onurislegende*, 44.
295. Philippe Derchain, "La couronne de la justification," *CdE* 30 (1955): 256.
296. Junker, *Götterdekret über das Abaton*, 59.
297. Pyramid Text 356 (§581), in Faulkner, *Ancient Egyptian Pyramid Texts*, 114.
298. Adolf Erman, "Die Naukratisstele," *ZÄS* 38 (1900): 127–28.
299. Ibid., 129–30.
300. *Book of the Cow*, cols. 11–12, in Maystre, "Livre de la vache du ciel," 64–65; cf. Piankoff, *Shrines of Tut-Ankh-Amon*, 27.
301. Vandier, "Iousâas," *RdE* 17 (1965): 120.
302. Ibid., *RdE* 16 (1964): 83.
303. Ibid., 85.
304. Ibid., *RdE* 18 (1966): 104.
305. Ibid., *RdE* 16 (1964): 92.
306. Ibid., *RdE* 17 (1965): 109.
307. Ibid.
308. Ibid., 112.
309. Ibid., 115–17.
310. Ibid., 119–20.
311. Ibid., *RdE* 16 (1964): 86.
312. Ibid., 129; ibid., *RdE* 17 (1965): 117.
313. Ibid., *RdE* 16 (1964): 143; cf. George Daressy, "Ramsès-Si-Ptah," *RT* 34 (1912): 39–52.

314. Vandier, "Iousâas," *RdE* 16 (1964): 93.
315. Ibid., *RdE* 17 (1965): 124.
316. Ibid., *RdE* 16 (1964): 60.
317. Ibid., *RdE* 18 (1966): 125–29.
318. Ibid., *RdE* 16 (1964): 70.
319. Ibid., 57.
320. Ibid.
321. Ibid., 56.
322. Ibid., 58.
323. Ibid., 68–69, 72–73.
324. Book of the Dead 125.
325. Vandier, "Iousâas," *RdE* 16 (1964): 62–63.
326. Ibid., 63.
327. Ibid., 66.
328. Ibid., 65.
329. Ibid., 98.
330. Ibid., *RdE* 18 (1966): 81.
331. Ibid., *RdE* 17 (1965): 103.
332. Ibid., *RdE* 16 (1964): 139.
333. Ibid., 131.
334. Ibid., 132.
335. Ibid., 133.
336. Ibid., 138.
337. Ibid., 134–35.
338. Ibid., 136.
339. Ibid., *RdE* 17 (1965): 158.
340. Ibid., *RdE* 18 (1966): 107.
341. Ibid., *RdE* 16 (1964): 96.
342. Ibid., *RdE* 17 (1965): 127.
343. Ibid., 135–36; ibid., *RdE* 18 (1966): 76.
344. Ibid., *RdE* 16 (1964): 88.
345. Ibid., 91, fig. 5.
346. Ibid., 95.
347. Ibid., 107.
348. Ibid., 74.
349. Ibid., 140.
350. Ibid., 143–44.
351. Ibid., 144.
352. Ibid., *RdE* 18 (1966): 129.
353. Ibid., 115.
354. Ibid., 117.
355. Ibid., 104.

356. Ibid., *RdE* 16 (1964): 142.
357. Ibid., 86.
358. Ibid., *RdE* 18 (1966): 79.
359. Ibid., 87.
360. Ibid., 99.
361. Pyramid Text 217 (§152–60); 248–49 (§262–66); 254–59 (§276–315) (cf. el-Arish inscription); 263–66 (§337–63); 271 (§388–91) (the Flood Cow); 311 (§495–500); 338–39 (§551–53) (crossing the desert); 412 (§721–33); 470 (§910–19); 473 (§926–38); 483 (§1011–19); 496 (§1065–66); 504 (§1082–83); 508 (§1107–19); 510–11 (§1128–61); 548 (§1343–48); 554 (§1370–72); 577 (§1520–30); 581 (§1551–57); 610 (§1710–23); 627 (§1771–85); 676 (§2007–17); 685 (§2063–70); 690 (§2092–119); 697 (§2169–75). The events are described as seen through the eyes of the new king. Joachim Spiegel, "Das Auferstehungsritual der Unaspyramide," *ASAE* 53 (1955): 339–439, describes the funeral rites of the Pyramid Texts in terms of a cruise. Derchain, *Papyrus Salt 825*, is the primal Shu and Tefnut story. Coffin Texts 1, 3, 14, 40, 50, 75–76, 80, 83–84, 91, 96, 126–27, 129–30, in de Buck, *Egyptian Coffin Texts*, 1:7, 10, 44, 173, 227, 317, 325–26, 328, 331–32, 334–35; 2:3, 36, 48, 50, 62, 75–76, 80, 148, 150, etc., esp. no. 77. Stricker, "Egyptische Mysteriën," tells the story in detail with the deceased participating in every episode. Book of the Dead 125, 175: the flood story. Sethe, *Der dramatische Ramesseumpapyrus*, passim: performed during an actual cruise, everything in terms of a ritual feast. The flood and migration themes are found in Raymond O. Faulkner, "The Bremner-Rhind Papyrus-I," *JEA* 22 (1936): 121–40, and Raymond O. Faulkner, "The Bremner-Rhind Papyrus-III," *JEA* 23 (1937): 166–85. The romantic side of the story is found in Faulkner, "Bremner-Rhind Papyrus-II," 10–16. Jan Zandee, "Book of Gates," *Liber Amicorum* (Leiden: Brill, 1969), 282–324: migration, cruise, conquest, and reception from shrine to shrine. Constantin E. Sander-Hansen, *Die Texte der Metternichstele* (Copenhagen: Munksgaard, 1956): Osirification of the cruise. Étienne Drioton, *L'Écriture énigmatique du livre du jour et de la nuit* (Cairo: BIFAO, 1942): the cruise in earthly terms. Jean-Claude Goyon, *Le Papyrus du Louvre N. 3279* (Cairo: BIFAO, 1966), 8, 34, 48: full cast of flood and migrations figures. Constantin E. Sander-Hansen, *Die religiösen Texte auf dem Sarg der Anchnesneferibre* (Copenhagen: Levin and Munksgaard, 1937), 139–40, 148–50: the festive progress. Gustave Lefébvre, *Le Tombeau de Petosiris*, 3 vols. (Cairo: IFAO, 1923–24), 1:88–102: the cruise and progress; 104: cruise is given a "spiritual" interpretation by his son. Walter Wreszinski, "Das Buch von Durchwandeln der Ewigkeit nach einer Stele im Vatikan," *ZÄS* 45 (1908): 111–22: the cruise is the subject of the whole story. Hermann Junker, *Die Stundenwachen in den Osirismysteriën nach den*

Inschriften von Dendera, Edfu, und Philae (Vienna: Hölder, 1910), passim: an interesting variation. G. Nagel, "Un papyrus funéraire de la fin du Nouvel Empire," *BIFAO 29* (1927): 1–27, also an interesting variation.

362. Coffin Text 80, in de Buck, *Egyptian Coffin Texts,* 2:32–33, 39.

363. Junker, *Auszug der Hathor-Tefnut aus Nubien,* 65–66.

364. Junker, *Onurislegende,* 118.

365. Ibid., 118, 121–22.

366. Jéquier, *Considérations sur les religions Égyptiénnes,* 198.

367. Gardiner, *Library of A. Chester Beatty,* 13–26.

368. Leiden Papyrus T32, 3/20–4/4, in Stricker, "Egyptische Mysteriën (Vervolg)," 19–20.

369. Junker, *Götterdekret über das Abaton,* 44–45.

370. Ibid., 59 (emphasis added).

371. Source not found; see preface.

372. Leiden Papyrus T32, 6/1–4, in Stricker, "Egyptische Mysteriën (Slot)," 56.

373. Leiden Papyrus T32, 4/25–5/1, in Stricker, "Egyptische Mysteriën (Vervolg)," 22.

374. Junker, *Onurislegende,* 116.

375. Montet, *Drame d'Avaris,* 198.

376. Griffith, "Stele of Tirhaqa from Kawa," 426–27.

377. Pyramid Text 3 (§2–3).

378. Siegfried Schott, *Hieroglyphen* (Wiesbaden: Steiner, 1950), 34–35.

379. Vikentiev, "Monuments archäiques," 208–34.

380. Augustine, *De Civitate (The City of God)* XVIII, 3, in *PL* 41:563.

381. Spiegelberg, *Der ägyptische Mythos vom Sonnenauge,* 29.

382. Robert Graves, *The White Goddess* (London: Faber and Faber, 1959), 64–67, 247–48.

383. Jéquier, *Considérations sur les religions Égyptiénnes,* 198.

384. Junker, *Götterdekret über das Abaton,* 34–35, 39.

385. Ibid., 28.

386. Leiden Papyrus T32, 6/16–20, in Stricker, "Egyptische Mysteriën (Slot)," 57.

387. Leiden Papyrus T32, 3/15–16, in Stricker, "Egyptische Mysteriën (Vervolg)," 19.

388. Junker, *Götterdekret über das Abaton,* 46.

389. Ibid., 11.

390. Ibid., 45.

391. Ibid., 55.

392. Ibid., 40.

393. Ibid., 18–20.

394. Ibid., 44.

395. Leiden Papyrus T32, 4/2–3, in Stricker, "Egyptische Mysteriën (Vervolg)," 20.

396. Leiden Papyrus T32, 4/22, in ibid., 21.

397. Leiden Papyrus T32, 5/31, in ibid., 24.

398. Anthes, "Sonnenboote den Pyramidtexten," 86.

399. Ibid., 87.

400. Ibid.

401. Ibid., 89.

402. Pyramid Text 627 (§1785).

403. Ibid. (§1774).

404. Ibid. (§1774–76).

405. Anthes, "Sonnenboote den Pyramidtexten," 87; cf. Pyramid Text 627 (§1774–76).

406. Pyramid Text 627 (§1774–76).

407. Nibley, "There Were Jaredites," 566–67, 602, 630–32, 672–75; in CWHN 5:350–80.

408. E. A. Wallis Budge, The Nile: Notes for Travellers in Egypt (London: Cook, 1890), 27.

409. William F. Albright, Yahweh and the Gods of Canaan (London: Athlone, 1968), 137 n. 69.

410. Gardiner, Egypt of the Pharaohs, 36.

411. Arthur Keith, "The Men of Lachish," Palestine Exploration Fund Quarterly 72 (1940): 9.

412. J. C. L. Gibson, "Light from Mari on the Patriarchs," Journal of Semitic Studies 7 (1962): 51.

413. Alexandre Moret, Histoire de l'orient (Paris: Presses universitaires, 1929), 269–70, 503.

414. Anthes, "Egyptian Theology," 194–95.

415. Frederick C. Conybeare, "Testaments of Job and of the XII Patriarchs," JQR 13 (1901): 111–13.

416. Louis Ginzberg, Legends of the Jews, 7 vols. (Philadelphia: Jewish Publication Society, 1909–13), 1:177–78, 318–19; Bernhard Beer, Leben Abraham's nach Auffassung der jüdischen Sage (Leipzig: Leiner, 1859), 7, 105; Micha J. bin Gorion, Die Sagen der Juden, 5 vols. (Frankfurt: Rütten & Loening, 1913–27), 2:20, 33, 40–41, 52.

417. Wolfgang Richter, "Urgeschichte und Hoftheologie," Biblische Zeitschrift 10 (1966): 99.

418. Jubilees 8:11–15, 22, 28; 9:14.

419. Apocalypse of Adam 74:1–75:30, in Nag Hammadi Library in English, ed. James Robinson (San Francisco: Harper and Row, 1981), 259.

420. Apocryphon of John, texts in Martin Krause and Pahor Labib, Die drei Versionen des Apokryphon von Johannes (Wiesbaden: Harrassowitz,

1962); Walter C. Till, *Die gnostischen Schriften des koptischen Papyrus Berolinensis 8502,* Texte und Untersuchungen, vol. 60 (Berlin: Akademie Verlag, 1955), 43.

421. Cyrus H. Gordon, *Before the Bible: The Common Background of Greek and Hebrew Civilizations* (New York: Harper and Row, 1962), 127.

422. Albrecht Götze, "Kleinasien," in *Kulturgeschichte des alten Orients* (Munich: Beck, 1933), 3:1:3:82–85.

423. Hermann Kees, "Kulttopographische und mythologische Beiträge," *ZÄS* 64 (1929): 100.

424. Georges Posener, *De la divinité du pharaon,* Cahiers de la société asiatique, vol. 15 (Paris: Imprimerie Nationale, 1960), 103.

425. François Daumas, "Le sens de la royauté égyptienne à propos d'un livre récent," *RHR* 160 (1961): 131–43.

426. Kurt H. Sethe, *Urkunden der 18. Dynastie,* vol. 4 of Urkunden des ägyptischen Altertums, 1:157.

427. Ibid., 159–60.

428. Pseudo-Callisthenes, *Historia Alexandri Magni* II, 21; Anthony J. Spalinger, "The Reign of King Chabbash: An Interpretation," *ZÄS* 105 (1978): 145–47.

429. Ilse Becher, "Augustus und Dionysus—ein Feindverhältnis," *ZÄS* 103 (1976): 94.

430. Pseudo-Callisthenes, *Historia Alexandri Magni* II, 21.

431. Sethe, *Urkunden der 18. Dynastie,* 1:100–101.

432. Alexandre Moret, *Du caractère religieux de la royauté pharaonique* (Paris: Leroux, 1902), 61–62.

433. Gerhard Fecht, "Schicksalsgöttinnen und König in der 'Lehre eines Mannes für seinen Sohn,'" *ZÄS* 105 (1978): 14–42.

434. Peter Kaplony, "Eine neue Weisheitslehre aus dem alten Reich," *Orientalia* 37 (1968): 343.

435. Kees, *Aegypten,* 172.

436. Pieper, *Grosse Inschrift des Königs Neferhotep in Abydos,* 12–13, lines 4–6.

437. Kurt H. Sethe, *Die dramatische Texte zu altägyptischen Mysterienspielen,* in Untersuchungen zur Geschichte und Altertumskunde, vol. 10, 28.

438. Ibid., 23, 27.

439. Gardiner, *Library of A. Chester Beatty,* 14.

440. Etymologicum Magnum 352, 50 s.v. "epoichomenen" in Theodor Hopfner, *Fontes Historiae Religionis Aegyptiacae* (Bonn: Weber, 1922–25), 51.

441. Diodorus Siculus, *Library of History* I, 15, in Hopfner, *Fontes Historiae Religionis Aegyptiacae,* 96.

442. Isocrates, *Busiris* 10, in Hopfner, *Fontes Historiae Religionis Aegyptiacae*, 48.

443. Scholiast to Plato, *Republic,* in Friedrich Dübner, *Platonis Opéra* (Paris: Firmin-Didot, 1873), 3:25b.

444. Pseudo-Plutarch, *De Fluviis,* in Hopfner, *Fontes Historiae Religionis Aegyptiacae*, 99.

445. Isidore, *Etymologiae* VIII, 84–85; IX, 2, in Hopfner, *Fontes Historiae Religionis Aegyptiacae*, 724–25.

446. Pseudo-Plutarch, *De Fluviis* XVI, 1, in Hopfner, *Fontes Historiae Religionis Aegyptiacae*, 397.

447. Diodorus Siculus, *Library of History* I, 19, in Hopfner, *Fontes Historiae Religionis Aegyptiacae*, 99.

448. Josephus, *Against Apion* I, 102; cf. I, 231.

449. Eugène Lefébure, "Le Cham et l'Adam égyptiens," *BE* 35 (1912): 9–10.

450. Isidore, *Etymologiae* VII, 7, in Hopfner, *Fontes Historiae Religionis Aegyptiacae*, 724.

451. Daressy, "Ramses-Si-Ptah," 49–50.

452. Gardiner, *Egypt of the Pharaohs,* 249.

453. Ibid., 250–51.

454. Elise J. Baumgartel, *The Cultures of Prehistoric Egypt* (Oxford: Oxford University Press, 1947), 44 (emphasis added).

455. M. Raymond Weill, "Koptos," *ASAE* 11 (1911): 103.

456. Ibid., 99–100.

457. Moret, *Histoire de l'orient,* 62.

458. Pliny, *Natural History* X, 49, 94.

459. W. J. Phythian-Adams, "Aiguptos: A Derivation and Some Suggestions," *Journal of the Palestine Oriental Society* 2 (January 1922): 95–99.

460. Albright, *Yahweh and the Gods of Canaan,* 137 n. 69; cf. 94–100.

461. Aelian, *De Natura Animalium* X, 23, in Hopfner, *Fontes Historiae Religionis Aegyptiacae*, 420.

462. Derchain, *Rites égyptiens,* 38–62.

463. Book of the Dead 125, line 21.

11

The Trouble with Ham

It Starts with Min

Egyptus may point to Coptos as the Lady's first settlement, but there is no doubt who was the first *man* who lived there. It was Min, formerly known as Khem, the woman's consort, first king and royal ancestor of all the pharaohs. Kurt Sethe suggested reversing the titles, with Min the name of the land and Coptos the name of the king.

The most impressive thing about Min of Coptos is the manifest antiquity of everything about him, and the immense age and conservatism of his cult.[1] All down through history Min insists on showing up at the national celebrations like some fossil intrusion from the beginning of time.[2] For behind his familiar cult figure, Min is a historic person. He is the first comer in the land, manifestly a stranger in Egypt, coming as the *ḥry-wḏb*, Lord of the Migration, to settle in Coptos after a long journey "from the Land of the Gods."[3] He is always Lord of the Desert, Opener of Roads, Patron of Caravans and Bedouins, who comes leading his hosts from the East, specifically, Henri Gauthier maintains, from Canaan.[4] The true Mother of Min is the queen of the East, "the venerated 'Beduin Woman' of legendary times," whose role could be played in the rites only by the wife of the

pharaoh in person.[5] Min's name was written heraldically
exactly like the Lady's, with two crossed arrows or the
⨉double-headed arrow, the classic thunderstone or lightning
symbol, which marks Min as the great storm-god,[6] identified with Amon-Zeus [the name Ammon is derived from
Min]; as "opener of the rain-cloud," "the god above the
clouds,"[7] Min comes with the "red band of Sekhmet [the
Storm-Lady], the Eye of Horus, . . . as the god of storm and
flood."[8] "I am Min of Coptos," he says, as he confronts the
dangers of the wild river and the lions, crocodiles, and
snakes on its banks. "I am the god Shu in the image of Re,
seated with the Eye of my Father protecting against all evils
on the waters."[9]

As the original settler of the land, Min is a true Adam-
figure: "Min the Coptite, great god in the midst of the
delightful [*im3*] trees, . . . having dominion in the garden
[*skht.w*], . . . who created the Tree of Life, who came forth
from [or created] vegetation; who caused the flocks and
herds to live."[10] All living things proceed not from him but
from his Eye—the woman. "Hail to thee holy garden, where
the divine members are formed [lit. brought together, or
organized]; Min Lord of the animals provides them with
sustenance, assuring them of perpetual food [bread]. . . .
Min supplier of provender for the mouth."[11] One always
entered the shrine of Min through his garden, where his
activity, according to Paul Guiyesse and Eugène Lefébure,
"recalls in many respects the history of Adam."[12] Though it
is not his original office and calling, Min seems to have
acquired the attributes of a god of fertility and agriculture
as soon as he settled in the broad and fertile plain of
Coptos.[13] In fact, his association with the famous "Night of
the Drop" (he being among other things the "Lord of the
Dews") takes his agricultural role right back to the migration of the Lady. For the Night of the Drop, i.e., the night on
which the Nile begins to rise, is, according to the Pyramid

Texts, "the night of the great deluge." The rising of the river coincides with the shedding of the woman's tears; hence, it is called "the great river of tears of the great goddess."[14] A Phoenician informant told Pausanius that once at the time of the feast of Isis, when, thanks to the tears of the Lady (so the people believed), the Nile begins to rise and bring life to the fields, "the Roman governor of Egypt bribed a man to go down into the shrine of Isis in Coptus." The man returned and reported the mysteries but died immediately.[15] We have already heard about the great weeping of the time when the Lady discovered the land under water; here it is specifically connected with the rites of Coptos and with the fertilizing virtues of Min.

His first and highest calling, however, is that of archetype and parent of all the kings of Egypt. All the former kings of the land line up on the right hand and on the left hand of Pharaoh as he offers sacrifices and sings hymns of praise to his father Min.[16] The two rites centering around Min, the coronation and the cutting of the first sheaf (fig. 88), always go together, but the coronation has clear priority in age and importance.[17] Together the rites celebrate the beginning of a new life cycle, the begetting of the race and founding of the nation, as the king goes to the dwelling of his father Min to celebrate a million jubilees and hundreds of thousands of years on his throne: "Min comes to his temple of Millions of Years to guarantee the integrity of the King's crown."[18] Every king at his coronation takes the place of Min as the vanquisher of his enemies who silences all opposition as "he *unites* the power of Horus with that of Seth," and then "rests in Thebes and Coptos" after his labors.[19]

His temple is modestly designated as his dwelling, "the House of Min in the town of Coptos of the Nome of the Two Falcons,"[20] and always had the form of the primitive beehive-shaped hut with a conical roof of the first settlers and nomads (fig. 89).[21] It is the conical hut of leaves or grass

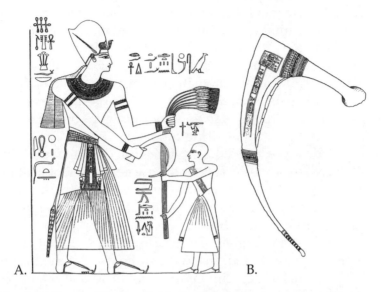

Figure 88. Ramses III cuts a sheaf of grain in a ritual scene from his mortuary temple at Medinet Habu (A). Its symbolic nature is shown by the priest who holds the already severed sheaf in his hands for the king to cut. An actual wooden sickle covered with sheet gold and electrum and set with serrated flint blades was discovered in the tomb of Tutankhamun (B). The inlaid inscription of colored glass describes the king as "beloved of Hu," the personification of food.

common to the African rain forests and the veldt.[22] Min's role is clearly defined: "Come, come Horus, Mighty Bull, great in kingship, to the dwelling of Min-Amon where his son [the king] is! Build a monument, thy house, establish a *smn* [shelter] within this land, a gathering point for life, stabilizing the years [calendar], establishing the North and South firmly, even as Re does, forever!"[23]

In the usual Egyptian shuffling of divine names, Min is more often identified with Horus than with any other deity.[24] Yet his name definitely establishes him as an early Ammon: Min, Men, Menu, and Amun are all forms of the same name.[25] Throughout his important study of the hero,

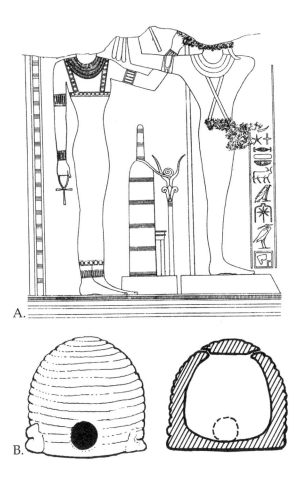

Figure 89. This carving on a temple wall shows Min standing on the Maat 𝑝 stone, with a representation of his own temple behind him (A). The form of this temple, tall and circular, is uniquely his. It features a wooden mast set before it, topped with bull horns on a flower capital. A coil of rope between the horns is somehow tied to the apex of the temple. The goddess is unidentified since we have neither her crown nor an inscription. The recently discovered alabaster honey pot (B), 2 1/4 inches high, demonstrates the use of coiled rope beehives in Egypt, c. 1550–1000 B.C. Two small bees flank the circular doorway, originally closed with a stopper.

however, Eugène Lefébure in 1915 insisted on referring to him by no other name than *Khem,* which he identified with the biblical *Ham.*[26] Though his philological speculations may have gone far afield, still, the basic ties between Min-Amon and Khem-Horus are far too close and extensive to be ignored, as they have been by all save a few French scholars, while the characters and deeds of Ham and Min, by whatever name you choose to call the latter, present the most convincing parallels. If Min's name was long read incorrectly as Khem, there was a reason for it, since the Egyptians themselves were wont to write the name phonetically as *Khm* beside the belemnite-symbol as well as the name *Mn*—apparently there was a choice.[27] The Khem-connections meet us everywhere. Lefébure observes that the letters of the Hebrew Ham "correspond exactly" with the word written by the *Greeks* to designate the Egyptian name of Panopolis, Khemmis, Min's headquarters.[28] Gauthier, following Herodotus,[29] notes that Min's land is par excellence the country of the Hamites.[30] Min had the peculiar archaic epithet of the Bald One, applied also to Horus[31] and to that Nimrod of Ham's line who would claim the priesthood of Abraham. The persistent tradition surviving among the modern natives of Egypt that Ham was the founder of Coptos[32] shows that folk memory is an enduring depository of lost history.

Min's Royal Progress

Before searching for him abroad, however, we should consider that great national celebration of the Egyptians, which was distinctively and properly Min's show—the *pr.t Mnw*—the great Expedition, *Sortie, Auszug,* or "The Coming Forth of Min" from Coptos. It was celebrated as early as the Old Kingdom, and all Egypt participated.[33] The purpose of the ritual march from Coptos was, of course, to establish the rule of Min in all the valley and to receive the joyous welcoming acclamation of the inhabitants or to silence those disinclined to accept the new rule. Immediately upon receiving the crown, the king goes forth, as elsewhere in the ancient world, on his great royal progress,[34] "taking possession of the river-banks and fields," inspecting the lands over which he now rules as *ḥry-wḏb*, Lord of the Terrain.[35] Min is Horus the Avenger, going forth on his birthday.[36] And since that was the New Year, the day of creation, the renewal of life, his procession inevitably becomes identified with those of Sokar and Sothis, who *also* go forth in ships at the New Year. Joachim Spiegel suggests that the fusion took place in the Fourth Dynasty.[37]

Question: If the new king entered the land as his mother's companion and champion, how could he be born or suckled as an infant by Nephthys the wet nurse in the secret nest in the *Kh.b.t*, marshes of Khemmis, the ultimate hiding place from Apophis, who sought his destruction?[38]

Answer: In one tradition Khemmis is the final goal of Min's coronation progress;[39] in another it is his cradle. That is a typical example of the absorption of one historical or mythological episode into the celebration of another, facilitated by deliberate geographical vagueness favoring a freely invented mythical locale.[40] Khemmis is where the youthful king escapes the chaotic powers of the Deep and of Darkness at the beginning of the world, which time can be either at the creation or after the flood, since the latter event was but a repetition of the world's beginning. In each case the emergence of the lotus, the Cow, and the newborn rising Sun represent the same things, while the place of beginning itself can be the Primal Hill of Hermopolis, the Field of Reeds or Paradise, or the Field of Offerings of Heliopolis, or the Lakes of Shu, the Island of Fire, the Lake of the Two Swords, the Necropolis, the Hall of Judgment, Land of the Dead, Place of Rebirth, Place of Beginning, Place of Renewal, the Holy Land, the West (Coffin Texts),

the East (Book of the Dead). In one tradition Khemmis is in
the marshes of the Delta; in another it is near Coptos. When
great centers like Hierakonopolis, Hermopolis, and Heliopolis
vied for priority as the point of origin of the human drama,
each naturally took into its ritual repertoire whatever sce-
narios were most widely acceptable, consciously avoiding
being too specific. The Metternich Stele in which both
Khemmis and Hotep (the place of settlement) are moved
from Upper Egypt to the vicinity of "the meadow of
Heliopolis,"[41] where Tefnut breaks into the security of the
Delta by a ruse and harms the child Horus,[42] may reflect the
resentment of the northern priests to the southern claims to
priority. It is this confusion that has obscured the real picture of the coming of the Lady and her son to Egypt.

As the Strong Horus, Min naturally figured as the son
of Osiris when the Abydos rites were introduced; but his
original calling was not funerary, and the way in which the
various figures became identified remains obscure, according to Spiegel.[43] Min came forth from his house after resting
there—a detail that Gauthier finds puzzling, but which the
reader at this point has surely been expecting.[44] The sortie
of Min became an episode in the life of the king, his coronation or the anniversary of it.[45] The first act of the king on
going forth is to shoot an arrow into each of the four cardi-
nal points of the compass, signifying his taking possession
of all the world within range (the four directional arrows
being both his emblem and that of the Lady);[46] at the same
time he released four birds, called "the Four Messengers of
Min," to the four directions (fig. 90), with instructions to
"announce that the great lord of Heaven has seized the
White and the Red Crown."[47] As early as the Pyramid Texts,
we read of the king riding the four birds in the manner of
Abraham's Nimrod, who also shot the four arrows and
claimed the rule of the world—which is another story, but
not quite.[48] In another rite three birds go forth, a falcon, a

Figure 90. Ramses III recorded the ceremonies of his *Sed* festivals on his mortuary temple at Medinet Habu. Here priests release birds to the four quarters of the world to demonstrate Ramses' dominion over the whole earth.

vulture, and an ibis, representing Shu or Horus, Mut the Lady, and Thoth, our migrating trio.[49] Through all this, Min is viewed *as a historic figure*, founding the kingdom at Coptos[50] and establishing his rule in the land as Amon of Thebes[51] and at Pe = Apu = Akhmim = Panopolis = Khemmis, Ham's town (directly across the river from Coptos), which always remained his other residence.[52]

After almost half a century of research, Gauthier's portrait of Min still stands essentially unaltered in Spiegel's recent study. Min is Wep-wawet, "The Opener of the Ways," "in the function of the new king" at his coronation, which always marks the ascension of a *new* king, his office of harvest-god being secondary.[53] He is Min-Horus the Son, the strong Horus taking over the land, the living monarch as Min vindicating his claim to the throne, except at Coptos, where he always appears as the visiting king in person. His expedition was not a regular event, but took place only when a new king came visiting to announce his succession to the throne. A famous stele in the Louvre sums up his authority: "I praise Min and exalt Horus of the upraised arm. Hail to thee! Min comes forth with the tall feathers, son of Osiris, born of the goddess Isis, great in the *sn-wt*-shrine, great in Akhmim, he of Coptos, Horus of the smiting arm, Lord of Majesty who silences the arrogant, Prince of all the Gods, great of incense when he comes down from *Mdʒ*-land, esteemed in Nubia."[54]

If Horus is one from afar, so is Min, a lord of foreign lands[55] and the patron of strangers in Egypt,[56] himself an alien. His festival at Denderah was reserved for strangers— not just for any strangers, however, but strangers from particular lands: from Keneset, Punt, the lands of Madjaiu, east and west,[57] which Min-Khem in the role of Ammon-Re brings into subjection and hands over to the rule of Horus.[58] Those were the regions over which Ammon ruled in the mythical beginning: "The vast Hamitic zone corresponds to that of Khem," the pure primal ethnic stock of the Egyptians,[59] the early African and Asiatic heritage. The whole stretch of lands to the west of Egypt, from the Libyans and Berbers in the north down through the Madjaw and Tehennu, and the eastern and western Msh'i—all were supposedly descendants of Min-Khem.[60] This marks also the empire of the biblical Ham, and though none of the nations mentioned were black, large parts of the vast domain were both originally black country and later occupied or reoccupied by them. With his roots deep in central Africa, "it is natural," wrote Lefébure, "that Khem-Horus should pass as the father of the black races."[61] Moreover, the Egyptian as well as the Israelite record puts the land of Canaan under Ham = Khem's dominion—the "land of the Gods" being Asiatic as well as African.[62]

Black and White

As ruler of great nations which were neither black nor Egyptian,[63] as well as ruler of the blacks themselves, our hero has definitely a dual personality, representing that civilizing mixture from which pharaonic civilization emerged in time. Thus Lefébure observes that Khem has two types of primitive dwelling: (1) the rectangular Egyptian building with its trees at the entrance and (2) the beehive-shaped shrine with the bull's skull mounted on a pole before the entrance, that being the typical village hut of the African rain forests converted to a shrine by the bucranium (ox skull).[64] Hence he is the bringer and father of two cultures. As Ammon he was peculiarly suited to become the god of the empire at the beginning of the New Kingdom. He was both Khem (as the Moon and Bull-god), and "everything that does *not* belong to Khem" (as Ammon-Re the sun— and ram-god).[65] In keeping with this, the Pharaoh himself as Ammon is the Ram, symbol of begetting the race, performing the same function as a bull, Ka-mut-ef and spouse of his mother.[66] Hermann te Velde has recently shed light on the dual nature of the hero when he points out that Horus and Seth (whom he equates with Min in the earliest times) *necessarily* share the kingdom at all times, even though only Horus rules; according to the Egyptians the principle of opposition is necessary in all things. Horus's rule would not be complete unless it had its counterside, the dark side to counterbalance the light. Dominion must always be a dual concept in Egypt.[67] The great showdown between Horus and Seth ends in reconciliation.[68]

Other-world texts engraved in royal tombs show the subject people who stand before Horus in order of proximity

as, first, Egyptians and the dwellers of adjacent deserts,
then the Amu or Asiatics, the Tamehu of the Sahara regions
to the west, then the eastern and western Nehesi, the
Ethiopians on both sides of the Red Sea, and then the
blacks.[69] In these ethnic texts it is explained that the Amu
and Tehemu are the children of the Sun's Eye (the Lady herself) and are descendants of Horus as are the blacks, the latter deriving from the common ancestor "in his role of
Khem."[70] For aside from Khem-Min himself, Horus is the
only other deity represented as a Negro,[71] described in an
inscription from the temple of Edfu as "the son of Isis and
Osiris, who is a black of Ethiopia, who overcame Set."[72] A
black person here appears as the true heir to the throne and
the victor over the adversary.

It is not only Lefébure who is impressed by Min's special relationship to the black people; Gauthier and Spiegel
no less strongly emphasize it. What has especially attracted
the attention of students of Min-Khem is the role of a *black
priest* in his rites. He leads the hymn at the harvest rites,
which, according to Lefébure, reads: "O ebony Khem, black
as pitch, . . . a bull coming from the lands of the strangers!"[73]
In what might be called a minimal statement of Min's relationship to the blacks, Gauthier explains that "the Negro of
Punt . . . is a priest [or perhaps a cantor] of black color. One
may assume that . . . the ceremony of the 'Coming Forth of
Min' included a number of black participants or at least one
black individual. Min's relationship to the Negroes has not
yet been clearly defined, but it seems to have been quite real
and intimate."[74] Actually the black priest was a figure of
central importance in the elaborate rites of Min. It is he, "the
Black Man [Nehesi] of Punt," who leads the chorus of greeting as Min comes into the land of the South: "Words spoken
by the Negro of Punt before the face of this god. Recite as
follows: Thou art beloved, O Min. Hail to thee, Min Lord of
Sn.wt [a stopping place on the Lady's migration], Lord of

Paa [Khemmis], . . . mighty is thy countenance, in the form of a bull, coming over the foreign mountains, rejoicing to be promoted to the rank of King of the Gods!"[75] As Lefébure puts it, "the Negroes passed for the sons and worshippers of Khem," with a black priest administering his rites coming from the same land as the god.[76] The dark color of the chief singer of Min relates him, Gauthier points out, to the black or dusty color of Min himself, shown in rites of a clearly Negro background.[77]

Following the well-known pattern by which conquerors become the accepted rulers of the conquered,[78] Min is both the conqueror and the leader of the blacks: "Horus the Mighty One who overthrows the Blacks is the first of the Nubians. The ithyphallic god was even represented at times with a black face. . . . It is precisely in this capacity of god of the blacks that he is equated to Min; Amon is painted blue, a color often confused with black."[79] "Hail to thee," he is greeted, "Min Lord of Ipw and Snw, the true lapis lazuli of the house of Sekhmet"—reminding us that in this capacity he is still the companion of Sekhmet, the woman who crossed the desert to Egypt.[80] His rule is challenged, and "Min is justified before his enemies in heaven, by the judges of every god and goddess," i.e., the same tribunal that settles the dispute between Horus and Seth,[81] which also goes back to rivals at the time of the invasion. Herodotus reports that though the Egyptians shun foreign customs, an exception is the festival near Khemmis, in the vicinity of Thebes, where the hero who dwells in his shrine brings prosperity to the land; what is foreign about him is his ready identification with the wandering hero *Perseus,* and the close resemblance of his celebration to that of the Greek ritual games. The locals claimed that Perseus came to Khemmis when he learned about it from his mother and later he returned to the place "and recognized all his kinsmen there."[82] But Perseus is also king of the Ethiopians, ancestor of the Cephenes or

Phoenicians—he is one of those fruitful heroes like Abraham and Herakles, who really get around.[83] No less important than his African connections are Min's Canaanite connections, which correspond closely with those of the biblical Ham.[84]

Here we may refer to one important detail in the Abraham text, namely, that the Lady who came to Egypt "settled her *sons* in it" (Abraham 1:24); we are told that "the eldest son of Egyptus, the daughter of Ham" established the "first government of Egypt," (Abraham 1:25), but who were the sons? One thinks at once of the inseparable pair Horus and Seth, who in the beginning enjoy equal billing and equal honor, ruling the land in turns, consistent with the "deeply rooted Egyptian tendency to understand the world in dualistic terms," requiring that two brothers rule at once "in polar antagonism," while only one received the homage of the race.[85] The Lady could have survived more than one son on the throne (cf. the story of the Two Brothers), and her sons could have ruled in succession. In some legends she outrages Horus by recognizing Seth as well as him.[86] Abraham 1:24 says she "afterward settled her sons in it"— not that they all became kings.

Lefébure maintained that the Egyptians were somewhat embarrassed and confused by the genealogy of Min—how could they, the only real people, share the honors of the divine ancestor with all those other nations and races? While they were the children of Horus and Sekhmet, the Mother of the Eye, she who "created them and she who protects their souls," they conceded that the blacks were the children of Horus also, but it had to be in another capacity and by virtue of another type of marriage.[87] The fundamental problem is the same for the ethnic as for the closely related matriarchal question; there was nothing wrong with the matriarchal line as such, but in competition with the patriarchal claims it leads to all manner of trouble and confusion. There is also no debate as to whether black or white is preferable; the question is, when they are mingled, which shall predominate? The Egyptians would neither claim Min as their own nor deny him. He is both the leader of the blacks and their conqueror—a perfectly natural combination, for the Egyptians are plainly of mixed race, including black elements, "a fusion of the conquered and the conquerors," as their language, a mingling of Hamitic and Semitic, shows.[88] Min, like Horus, must clear his title to the throne from time to time, but the claim is always in doubt.

The perennial showdown to determine the right to the throne takes place in terms of black versus white as well as patriarchy versus matriarchy in the exciting and romantic Setne romances. There is a wonder child Si-Osiris brought to the court of Pharaoh as a boy by his father to display his precocity in settling the dispute between rival claimants to the throne, the white Horus and the black Horus. Here one cannot resist recalling the legend of how the boy Abraham was brought to the court of Nimrod by his father and there displayed his precocity by discrediting that monarch's claim to the throne.

The prologue to the Setne story centers entirely around Coptos and the attempt by a son and heir of Pharaoh to obtain the book of all knowledge hidden in the Abaton there beneath the waters, guarded by the endless serpent, and jealously withheld by its author, an earlier prince of Egypt who sleeps there with his wife and child—beneath the temple of Isis of Coptos and Harpocrates *her* child.[89] In the second story ("Manifestation in Thebes"),[90] Setne Khamuas takes his young son, the boy Si-Osiris, to the court where Pharaoh is troubled by a letter from the *Nehes* (the black Man) of Ethiopia challenging his kingly and priestly competence by a missive that he is supposed to read without opening the seal. The boy is a wonder child and superscribe at the age of twelve and easily reads the letter, which

tells how, many centuries before, Hor the son of the Sow,
thereafter called the son of Negress, planned to humiliate
Pharaoh and blast the land with drought, taking the Pharaoh
Si-Amon to Ethiopia by night and there afflicting him with
five hundred lashes.[91] (When the priests of Heliopolis, competing with the great shrine of the South, claimed Min of
Coptos for their own, they hailed him as the son of the
White Sow.)[92] The beating went on for three nights, and the
pharaoh's wise men were helpless. But at last, the knowledge of the boy Si-Osiris turned the tables, and the viceroy
of Ethiopia received the identical treatment that had been
administered to Pharaoh.[93] Then "said Hor the son of the
Negress, . . . let me be sent to Egypt . . . that I may strive
against him." Before going, he set up a sign with his mother
the Negress so that she could come to his aid when he was
hard pressed; the sign was the upheavals of nature and the
blood-red sky that went before the Negress in the manner
of Sekhmet of the desert. The black and the white Horus
contend with the identical claims and identical methods,
until the Negress must come to the rescue of her son, but
both are turned into sacrificial *sem*-geese. To save their lives
they swear: the Negress never to return to Egypt, her son
not to return for fifteen hundred years. For every fifteen
hundred years the same drama is repeated, since the black
Hor did not repent; he returned to Egypt after fifteen hundred years to find his opponent awaiting to meet him in the
shape of the boy Si-Osiris: "I prayed before Osiris in Amenti
to let me come forth to the world again," for the showdown.[94] And so it goes on, mixing "Egyptus" motifs—
matriarchy, upheavals of nature, the journey from afar,
etc.—with familiar themes from the Abraham legends, the
wonder boy at court challenging the arrogant monarch, the
humiliation of the king, etc., this time matching black versus white, with neither winning in the end.

Though Francis Griffith found this to be "one of the

finest works of imagination that Egypt has bequeathed to us,"[95] the elements it contains are all familiar. Even the odd detail that the usurper was taken in shame back home in an aerial boat matches Nimrod's flying chariot, which let him down with an undignified landing. The things to note, however, are the never-settled rivalry between a black and a white Horus and the tension between the races, as also between the matriarchal and patriarchal orders; in the story the black prince never goes anywhere without his mother or does anything without her instructions.

The first Setne story (Si-Osiris is the second) tells how the seat of wisdom and mystic power was transferred in a series of ceremonial water processions from the Abaton of Isis at Coptos to the court of Pharaoh at Memphis, after the sinister matriarchal power of Tabubue (a Shulamite figure) was broken,[96] another indication of the prior claims of the south in the founding legends.

If one sees in this story the repetition of motifs of hoary antiquity (lunar cycles), its persistence in Egyptian folklore is attested in the *Life of Shenute,* the greatest of the Coptic fathers, which tells how the saint drove the devil out of a great bronze statue in the center of the marketplace of Akhmim (Panopolis), to which the people would repair for oracles and healings. He pierced the heel of the statue, and as the devil fled from it and dissolved in the air like smoke, he cried: "I come out of this statue, O Shenute, because of the awful torments you have made me suffer." Then he took the form of a black man of Abyssinia of enormous size and frightening countenance, and so departed.[97] Thus the black Horus survives in Coptos right down to Christian times.

Min = Khem and the Lady

As he mounts the steps of the throne, "Isis the Mistress of Authority (*skhm*)" awaits the new Min at the top—she is the throne itself.[98] "He kisses the earth before Hathor the

Mistress of the High House," and she "beholds the beauty of Min as he marches forth."[99] The two tall feathers on his head "very pointedly recall *Shu and Tefnut*," according to Spiegel.[100] Min is never without his mother, who is his wife; in the lists of primal deities Min's name is always coupled with that of Heket-Hathor,[101] while his defunct predecessor on the throne goes to heaven to be reenthroned there as Min, "mindful of his beloved Eye."[102] The final goal of his expedition is Khemmis, the marsh where Isis bore the new king[103] and hid him in the bulrushes.[104] In the famous seventeenth chapter of the Book of the Dead, Min and Horus meet and fuse in the heroic son and companion of Isis, the victorious invader of the land.[105] In the foundation inscription of the temple of Denderah Min is "the son of Isis the Great at Apu (Panopolis), she who protects her son Horus."[106] There was a tradition that Min begot Horus to take the place of Osiris, who was drowned.[107] In the Middle Ages Makrizi reports that the temple of Coptos "had for its center a young black girl holding in her arms an infant of the same color"—Isis and the black Horus.[108] Indeed, the spreading of the cult of Isis in the West, including Europe, coincides with the introduction of black virgins all over the Christian world. Defending northern priority, the Metternich Stele insists that the healing Min of Coptos is really the son of the White Sow of Heliopolis.[109]

As the supreme sex symbol of gods and men, Min behaves with shocking promiscuity, which is hardly relieved by its ritual nature. A surviving prehistoric statue of Min, "for us the earliest example not only of a free standing image of a god but of monumental statuary in general," stood in the conical hut at Coptos; it became the stock figure of the fruitful Ammon with upraised arm, found on temple walls all over Egypt, to proclaim the king's reproductive office.[110] His title of Min "who embraced the Wd3.t Eye" makes him both husband and son of the Lady.[111] But his promiscuity went far beyond that. "The Egyptians," wrote Plutarch, "are accustomed to call Horus 'Min' meaning visible," referring to the symbol of reproduction publicly paraded at his festival.[112] The Greeks identified him with the lustful Pan and gave the name of Panopolis to his city of Apu = Akhmim = Khemmis.[113] His sacred plants were aphrodisiacal,[114] and he is everywhere represented as indulging in incestuous relationships with those of his immediate family. He had the most numerous and varied religious entourage of all the gods, consisting mostly of his huge harem.[115] The hymns, or rather chanting, of his worshipers were accompanied with lewd dancing and carousing—rock and roll—to the exciting stimulus of a band of sistrum-shaking damsels.[116]

But for all its licentiousness, the cult of Min was of venerable antiquity and strictly high class—only ladies of the highest birth, the hierodules of Ammon-Zeus, could belong to the harem,[117] the king himself being officially the "Guardian of the Virginity of the *Harim*."[118] "The Egyptians honor Ammon [Zeus]," wrote Strabo, "by consecrating to him a young virgin which the Greeks call Pallades [hierodule], of the greatest beauty and highest birth."[119] So Abraham: "Now, this priest had offered upon this altar three virgins . . . of the royal descent directly from the loins of Ham [Khem = Min = Amon]. These virgins were offered up because of their virtue; they would not bow down [cooperate as hierodules], . . . and it was done after the manner of the Egyptians" (Abraham 1:11). The rites of Min were secret, and the chief priest was "the overseer of the Mysteries of the God Menti in his character of *Kamutef*," literally the "Bull of his Mother."[120] The chief of women was, of course, the Lady herself, "who watches over Min,"[121] who "goes forth in procession from his shrine (*naos*) to permit Isis his Mother to look upon his charms."[122] His special bull titles always denote his too-intimate relationships with his

mother.[123] For he is the divine beast, the irrepressible rampant bull ready for anything. In this regard he is the double
of Seth, the two occupying prehistoric shrines directly
opposite each other on the two sides of the Nile below
Thebes. Their outstanding characteristic, as te Velde describes it, is their insistence on going beyond the bounds of
discretion and morality, completely unrestrained in their
appetites and passions.[124]

    The whip that the Min images hold with upraised arm
⁊ is always viewed as a fertility symbol (cf. the Lupercalia);
some Egyptologists have maintained that it signifies that
Min took advantage of his mother by brute force, seizing
the matriarchal rule of the land by violence and incest—a
tradition also associated with Ham and Nimrod on counts
of both brutality and gross immorality.[125] What suggested
that was Min's commonest epithet, Ka-mut-ef, "Bull of his
Mother," the title that the youthful successor to the throne
went by at the coronation, by virtue of which he mounts the
throne with his mother's approval and as her champion.[126]

    As the king cuts the sacred sheaf at the coronation, his
Lady walks around him seven times in a circle uttering
appropriate incantations; then he buries his face in the sheaf
and presents it before the nose of Min, saying: "Hail to Min
on the sheaf! The king (at his coronation) beholds the crown
on thy brow, he brings it to thee. Hail to thee, Min who
makes his mother conceive! How mysterious and hidden is
that which thou doest in the dark!"[127] "Thy heart unites
[*dmi*] with the heart of the king," says a hymn to Min, "as
the heart of Horus is united with his mother Isis when he
consorts with her and gives his heart to her as they lie side
by side inseparably."[128] Of the four children of Ham, Lefébure
notes, only Egypt [Heb. *Miṣraim*] refused to acknowledge his
descent from the line of Ham, cursed as it was by Noah in
the person of Canaan. Why? Because they regarded that
line as the "product of obscene nocturnal rites."[129] In the

matriarchal order where the queen can take any number of consorts, the male line of descent can never be guaranteed as pure.

Question: Were these "the abominations of the ancients?"

Answer: They were plainly related to that perversion of rites of which ancient legends (e.g., the Enoch stories) have so much to say. In the Abraham traditions the great per-verter Nimrod marries his mother, Sachlas, and claims to possess the priesthood through his inheritance of the gar-ment of Noah that was stolen by Ham and passed down as an illegal heritage to his descendants.[130]

Question: Why must we dwell on this disturbing theme?

Answer: To make clear that the taboo placed upon the matriarchal succession was more than a mere legal techni-cality. Throughout the ancient world the matriarchal rites tend to be orgiastic and obscene, which should disqualify them for higher things. Any looseness or license in a sacral society puts the patriarchal order out of business; without strict moral controls, paternity is always in doubt. On the other hand, no amount of domestic disorder can ever jeop-ardize the claims of motherhood. Hence religions centered in the mother cult tend to be morally permissive and volup-tuous, easily degenerating into "the abominations of the ancients." Consider what happened to this abominable cult, which the Book of Abraham, please note, makes no efforts to gloss over as it was practiced by Abraham's own father in the Canaanitish version of the cult that was at the time closely knit to Egypt. The Ammon connection takes us to the oracle of Zeus-Ammon in the Sahara, from which Alexander the Great spread the imperative of its authority throughout the known world,[131] hence on to the Baal-Hammon of Carthage with its well-known abominations of child-sacrifice and ritual prostitution,[132] imported directly from Abraham's Canaan—since Carthage was a Phoenician city. We can follow it directly from the oracle of Ammon

into Greece in the *Pseudo Callisthenes* and into Italy and the
Roman world with their Janus cult,[133] which takes us in turn
to Facsimile 2 of the Book of Abraham, where for the present we must call a halt.

Question: Did Min make the cruise with his mother?

Answer: The sortie from Coptos was expressly by boat:
"Come, *sail* to thy fields," the people sing, "toward thy glorious *ksb.t*-plants, green as turquoise and lapis-lazuli." The
great temple at Karnak was "a resting-place during the procession of the sacred ships bearing the statue of the ithyphallic Amon Bull-of-His Mother."[134]

The Curse of Ham

Scripture and tradition tie Pharaoh's genealogy inseparably to Ham, and hence to the famous curse that "belongs
to the red thread of history," as Wolfgang Richter puts it.[135] Or,
to follow the Book of Abraham, "Thus, from Ham, sprang
that race which preserved the curse in the land" (Abraham
1:24). Which was cursed, the land or the people? "It can only
be the land that it meant," Richter concludes,[136] for as F. M.
Theodor Böhl maintains, classification of people by race is
"a concept utterly foreign to the ancient Orient"—the curse
of Ham belongs to *whoever* oppresses Israel, whether Babylonians, Assyrians, Philistines, Phoenicians, or Canaanites,
each of which in their time has been assigned by ancient
and modern writers to the line of Ham.[137]

When Noah divided up the lands among his sons,
according to the book of *Jubilees,* he pronounced "a curse on
every one that sought to seize the portion which had not
fallen [to him] by his lot."[138] So when Canaan, the son of
Ham, coveted and occupied "the land of Lebanon to the
river of Egypt," refusing to move out even when his father
and his brothers fervidly urged him to do so, they reminded
him that he would surely come under "the curse by which
we bound ourselves by an oath in the presence of the holy

judge, and in the presence of Noah our father."[139] From ancient times the wise men have speculated and argued about why Canaan was cursed for Ham's offense in Genesis 10:24–27. Some say that the editors of Genesis made a mistake and "put Ham in the place of Canaan,"[140] and *Jubilees* itself says that Ham was outraged at the injustice to Canaan;[141] yet, as we have seen, Canaan did deserve cursing, only for another crime. "Why, since the whole of the folly was Ham's, was Canaan cursed?" one early writer asks, and answers, he was not; no one is ever cursed or blessed without deserving it. "When the youth [Canaan] grew up, and attained the full measure of his understanding, Satan entered into him, and became to him a teacher of sin." Accordingly, "he renewed the work of the house of Cain."[142]

This follows closely the traditions found in the Book of Mormon (Mosiah 5:13–15; Helaman 6:27; Ether 8:15) and the book of Moses (5:49). Epiphanius, an early and well-informed writer, reports that "Canaan, the violent one," invaded Palestine, but even though he was out of order, "God suffered him to remain *if he would repent;* . . . but he did not repent," so after many years came "'the fulness of the iniquity of the Amorrians.'"[143] We find reference to this tradition in the Book of Mormon: "Cursed be the land forever and ever unto those workers of darkness and secret combinations, even unto destruction, except they repent before they are fully ripe" (Alma 37:28, 31). Nephi was referring to the children of Canaan when he warned his brothers against feeling superior to them: "Do ye suppose that the children of this land, . . . who were driven out by our fathers . . . were righteous? . . . Do ye suppose that our fathers would have been more choice than they if they had been righteous? Behold I say unto you, Nay. Behold, the Lord esteemeth all flesh in one; he that is righteous is favored of God." Then he makes the significant statement that "the Lord did *curse* the land against them, and *bless* it

unto our fathers" (1 Nephi 17:33–35). The *same* land is both
blessed and cursed, and the inhabitants likewise are blessed
or cursed not by virtue of their family connection, but
according to their behavior: "It is a holy land; and I curse it
not save it be for the cause of iniquity" (Enos 1:10). The old
Hasidic curse on the land of Canaan is virtually identical
with that which is pronounced on this promised land in the
Book of Mormon:[144]

> The Lord gave Canaan to Abraham on the condition
> that his heirs should follow in his footsteps. When
> Ishmael did not adhere fully to his father's teachings,
> Isaac received the inheritance. When Esau did not com-
> ply with the true tradition, Israel was given the heritage.
> When Israel became habitually delinquent, his heirloom
> reverted to Esau [i.e., Romans, Christians, Gentiles].
> When Esau's followers degenerated they were compelled
> to surrender Canaan to Ishmael [the Moslems]. . . . The
> land was lost by Ishmael to Edom [Esau] ["the Gentiles"
> = "Idumea or the world," D&C 1:36] and will shortly be
> given up by Edom to its rightful owner—Israel.[145]

The point of the legends is that Canaan acted willfully
and wrongly; for that reason the land was cursed *for him*. As
might be expected, both Jews and Canaanites, avoiding
such moral responsibility, have preferred through the centuries to argue their respective rights to the land on legal
grounds alone. Thus the Talmud reports a formal debate
between a Jewish and a Canaanite lawyer in the presence of
Alexander the Great as to who had the better right to the
land that Alexander had taken by violence and was now
presuming to reassign with no better right than that of
Canaan of old.[146] It was believed by the Jews that Abraham's
Hebron was actually built by Ham for his son Canaan;[147]
even the Jewish doctors were divided about equally on the
relative merits of the two claims,[148] a clear indication that the
Canaanites were there from the beginning. On the other

hand, Israel and her neighbors were never in any doubt that
Yahweh had given the land to the Jews, and thought of it as
theirs.[149] That this issue should be very much alive at the
present day admonishes us not to treat even these ancient
traditions too lightly.

The principle that righteousness and wickedness are their
own blessing and cursing was very much alive in the wisdom of the Egyptians. The genealogy of Pharaoh, according
to Rudolf Anthes, who made special studies of the subject,
was not concerned with purity of blood, but with purity of
life and religion.[150] The royal line begins when "Atum, the
very old one [cf. Adam the Ancient of Days] was assimilated to Horus as the ruler of Egypt and the heavenly
god."[151] In their constant effort to assure the purity of the
Egyptian blood, culture, and religion,[152] ritual played an
important part, in particular the right of the patriarchal
blessing. The infant heir to the throne received such a blessing when "Thoth and Ammon, in the place of Horus and
Seth, purify the child, lay their hands on it, and give it a
blessing and good wishes."[153] Those pharaohs who were not
born to the royal line but married into it also received the
proper blood and family ties by such a blessing.[154] Indeed,
it will be recalled that the seed of Abraham consists mostly
of adopted children (Galatians 3:29).

The episode in the *Genesis Apocryphon* in which Abraham heals the ailing Pharaoh by laying his hands on his
head and blessing him has caused much head scratching
among scholars and clergy;[155] that ordinance marks both the
end of the king's attempt to raise up a royal line by Sarah
and the acknowledgment of Abraham's true relationship to
Sarah the queen.[156] At many points this relates to the classic
story of the marriage of Joseph and Asenath,[157] which
explains the mingling and reconciling of the blood of Ham
with the blood of Israel. For Asenath, it will be recalled, was
the daughter of the high priest of Heliopolis (Genesis 41:45;

46:20), and hence of the pure line of Ham; she was also the wife of Joseph and the mother of our own vaunted ancestor Ephraim (Genesis 41:50–52; 46:20). The purpose of the story is to tell how she became an Israelite and he became the heir of Pharaoh.

It was the blessings that did it. The first step was for Joseph to lay his right hand upon the head of his future bride and say: "Lord God, Father of Israel . . . who leadeth from dark to light, from error to truth, and death to life [well-known Egyptian formulas], Oh bless this maiden; give her life; renew her through thy Holy Ghost."[158] In rites that follow, she renounces the luxury, splendor, and rank of an Egyptian princess, but not her parentage, and is disowned by the mass of the Egyptians.[159] Then she is washed and clothed in white by an angel,[160] who registers her name in the Book of Life,[161] with the declaration, "From this day forward thou art newly created and formed and given a new life, eating the bread of life and receiving the anointing with the oil of immortality"—more familiar Egyptian and Hebrew ordinances. Then she is given a new name.[162] Next comes a surprise: having been adopted into the covenant as all of Abraham's converts were, becoming the seed of Abraham by adoption, the maiden has yet to be married. And that ordinance is performed by Pharaoh himself, who, after giving the couple his blessing,[163] crowns them with golden crowns.[164] Laying his hands on their heads, he then pronounces the operative blessing: "May the Lord, the Most High God, bless you, and multiply and exalt and glorify you throughout all Eternity."[165] Then he instructs them to seal the marriage with a kiss, and the rites are completed as the whole court goes to celebrate a seven-day feast to which all the nobility of Egypt and all the kings of the nation were invited.[166] It is only later that the couple visit Father Jacob and receive an Israelite blessing and his embraces.[167]

An authentic touch is the resentment felt by the proud

Egyptian nobility at the downgrading of a princess. They rally behind the son of Pharaoh, who wanted Asenath for himself. When Pharaoh refused to break the peace and Joseph refused to shed the blood of a new relative, the young man led his furious band in battle against his father and Joseph. In the attack, the brothers of Joseph defended themselves, and the Egyptian prince was slain. Then his father gave obeisance to Levi as the true high priest (an Abraham motif—the king is converted), but he died of grief for his son, whereupon Joseph became pharaoh of Egypt— by no means the first or the last Asiatic or man from Canaan to do so. This romantic and heroic tale is a skillful bit of propaganda, upholding the honor and vindicating the authority of Pharaoh, while gently but firmly supplanting his priesthood with that of Jacob and Levi.

The Mark of Cain

When Cain was cursed because of his sin he went to the land of Nod (Genesis 4:16)—meaning nomadism or wandering; he and his descendants became wanderers on the face of the earth. The parallel with the Lamanites at once springs to mind. Lamanite darkness was ethnic in the broadest sense, being both hereditary and cultural, shifting between "white and delightsome" and "dark and loathsome," along with manners and customs as well as intermarriage (Alma 3:4–10). But inseparable from the cultural heritage of ancient tribes were the markings that members of the society put on themselves, without which they would be considered outcasts. People who marked their foreheads with red after the Lamanite custom "knew not that they were fulfilling the words of God when they began to mark themselves in their foreheads," thus showing that the Lamanite curse had fallen on them (Alma 3:18).

It was the same with the descendants of Cain. Since time immemorial they have been identified throughout the

East with those wandering tribes of metalworkers whose
father was Tubal Cain. "Thubal bore the sins of Cain," says
a midrash, "and followed Cain's trade. For he prepared
weapons for murderers,"[168] a tradition clearly echoed in the
Book of Mormon (Ether 8:15). Tubal is the Sumerian *tibera*,
coppersmith or metalworker.[169] As the sign of their mystery
and their tribe, the wandering smiths or tinkers have
always blackened their faces with soot, a practice still found
among journeying sweeps and some others who work at
the grimy forge.[170] The name by which they were known
was Qenites[171] (cf. Aramaic *qēnā* = smith). The ancient
people of Tubal were also connected with Nukhashshe, a
name that designated those parts of Asia Minor and Syria
where mining and metallurgy are believed to have originated;[172] the same word is the common Semitic root for copper and its alloys, and it is the Egyptian name for the
Ethiopians, usually translated as "the Blacks," *nḥsy*.
According to their own report and universal folklore, these
traveling menders of pots and pans must keep traveling
because they are under a curse. "They are the Gypsies,"
says a very old Judeo-Christian writing, "who carry loads,
and they march on the roads with their backs and necks
breaking under their loads, and they wander round to the
doors of the children of their brethren."[173] They beguile their
outcast condition with wild music and dancing, and they
are the Cainites of old who enticed the righteous Sethians,
called "the Children of God," to join in their revels and so
fall from grace in the days of Jared.[174] Their special mark is
not the blackened face and hands, however, but a tattoo on
the hand or arm, a Tau-sign or a circle and cross. In Genesis
it is the brand of Cain, ancestor of the Kenites, and in
Ezekiel it is the divine mark set on the brows of all just
men.[175] According to a midrash, God placed a letter of the
alphabet on Cain's hand as a mark, so that no one would
slay him,[176] and some of the Jewish doctors maintained that

"the 'Sign of Cain' was the mark on David's brow."[177] Certain it is that "the mark of Cain" goes along with a cursing, a wandering way of life, and a distinctive mark on the body.

No Prejudice

Black persons occasionally turn up in reception scenes such as our Facsimile 3, for example, in the tombs of the Courtiers, of the Engravers, or Setnakht, of Tauser, of Ramses IX, etc., where they represent persons of honor from servants to the gods themselves, for Isis, Osiris, and Horus are all shown at times with black faces. When we see the black man Bak-en-Mut in his own funeral papyrus standing before a black Osiris seated upon the throne, the blackness is no mere whim of the artist, but is meant to be taken seriously, since the black Osiris is wearing not the usual Atef crown, as in countless other such scenes, but only the white crown of the South.[178] In other papyri showing the same scene, the black Osiris is always wearing that white crown alone, making the black connection a positive one.[179] In the drawings and texts, which are numerous, the proportion of black to white seems to follow no pattern but that of a society in which the races mingle freely and equally. If Senusret III has contempt for his black enemies, the great pharaohs of the Eighteenth Dynasty speak with no less contempt of their Asiatic foes.[180] Even among the Egyptian slave population the blacks are far outnumbered by the Asiatics, and no distinction is made between them in the record.[181] The stock representations by the Egyptians of "the four races" (Egyptian, Asiatic, Black, European-Berber) have, according to Heinrich Brugsch, "completely lost . . . any special significance" by the New Kingdom. "The old names still appear on the monuments, but rarely and without the slightest indication of race distinction."[182]

We are fortunate in possessing an impressive gallery of

royal portraits, to say nothing of an even more impressive line of royal mummies, male and female, dating from the earliest dynasties right down to the end. Among them are a few black African types, showing that if black did not prevent one from becoming pharaoh, neither was it a requirement.[183] There was simply no prejudice in the matter. There is a tradition that the most precious gift of Pharaoh to Abraham was a black servant from the king's household, who became inseparably attached to Abraham, and even resembled him like a twin.[184] This recalls Abraham's marriage to Hagar, traditionally a servant or even a daughter of Pharaoh, whose son Ishmael shared equal honors with Isaac, even to receiving the great promise of becoming the father of many nations. When Judah's son refused to accept a Canaanite woman for his wife because of her race, according to the book of *Jubilees*, God smote him. When Judah himself tried to take advantage of the same woman as an inferior, God smote him too.[185]

In the ancient records the blood of Ham is a mixture, always containing more white than black. The mingling of Egyptian and Canaanite is attested in a number of ancient sources,[186] as in Abraham 1:21. Josephus tells us that the countries occupied by Ham stretched "from Syria and Mounts Amanus and Lebanon to the ocean."[187] And while Ham is the ancestor of Pharaoh in Genesis 10:6–20, the line also includes the Philistines, from whom Palestine gets its name.[188] Recent studies of the genealogy of Cain by Johannes Gabriel[189] and Robert North[190] emphasize the claims of such desert tribes as the Kenites and the families of Kenaz and Caleb to belong to the family. Though the Hamites are as conspicuously Asiatic as African,[191] the oldest African stocks as well—Libyans, Tehennu, Berber—were not only white, but often referred to as pale-skinned and redheaded. Joseph Karst detected an extension of "the chain of Hamite people: Kushites, Egyptoids and Libyo-Hamites," in enclaves all over the Mediterranean and the islands clear to Spain.[192] Linguistic evidence intertwines Hamites and Semites the further back in time one goes, their vigorous rivalry being evidenced in the earliest Egyptian hieroglyphics, as shown by Hans Stock.[193] Werner Vycichl finds Semitic traits in the beginning in North Africa, "perhaps due to a wave of Hamitic tribes coming from Asia via the Strait of al-Qantara as the Arabs came later."[194] "The Hamitic invasion," he concludes, "certainly came from the East," though "originally . . . the Hamitic languages were not a single block as were the Semitic."[195]

These few observations, kept to a minimum, should be enough to make it clear that there is no exclusive equation between Ham and Pharaoh, or between Ham and the Egyptians, or between the Egyptians and the blacks, or between any of the above and any particular curse. What was denied was recognition of patriarchal right to the priesthood made by a claim of matriarchal succession.

Olimlah

The one figure in the facsimiles over which the experts have hesitated longest and disagreed most widely is figure 6, which some declared to be a mistake and others an outright forgery. Devéria suggested long ago that it was "an unknown divinity, probably Anubis, but the head has been altered."[196] Yet one professional Egyptologist declared that the artist had "marred the head, which was meant to be the unshaven head of a priest," and another saw in it a dead man's "double, and black figure, who was created at the time of his birth";[197] for yet another it is the monster Amentit, in the very act of seizing his victim. Each expert could justify himself by pointing to one or more parallel compositions. Such a figure appears without a jackal's head in the tombs of the courtiers studied by William Petrie.[198] In some Theban tombs black figures like this one have cat's

faces and others wear masks, and one might be tempted to
see a cat's head on figure 6 were it not that just such male
figures with just such little pointed objects on their heads,
representing cones of perfume, turn up frequently in other
party scenes. But our figure 6 is different from all of those,
and there was no reason on earth for the artist to fake it,
since he made not the slightest attempt to have any of the
other figures resemble characters from the Abraham drama,
and we now know from possessing the original of Facsimile
1 that Reuben Hedlock was on the whole a careful and
accurate copyist.

Next to his blackness, the most striking thing about
Olimlah is his position behind Shulem—who is not his master. The pose occurs quite frequently elsewhere, though we
have not discovered it in any Facsimile 3 parallel. It always
signifies that the person is given support, moral or otherwise, by another, "standing behind him in an attitude of
protection."[199] Ali Radwan has pointed out that at coronation rites every segment of the population under Pharaoh's
sway had to be represented. In our Facsimile 3 the prince,
at the king's wish, sponsors his servant Shulem's presentation to the distinguished visitor Abraham and has
instructed his servant Olimlah to join in with his support as
well.

Here a word on Olimlah's *name* is in order. Since the letter *r* is the weakest sound in Egyptian and the most subject
to shifts and changes, slipping all the way from the weak
vowels *a* and *e* to the sound of *l* (a very frequent exchange),
and since in Egyptian as in Semitic languages in general an
o must be represented by a *w*, it is by no means extravagant
to see in *Ol-im-lah* such a perfectly good Egyptian name as
Wr-imn-ra, "Great is Amon"—a real name,[200] or a name
formed on the very old pattern of Wr-ir-n(m)-Ptah, "Great
is the begotten of Ptah," or Wr-n(i)-Ra, "I magnify Ra."[201]

Any Other Suggestions?

The story of the pioneer Lady is not to be found in histories of Egypt; that is why we have been at pains to tell it at some length. Are there any other stories, then, that might take its place, any other tales of how the land was settled? Surprisingly, there are only two serious competitors, one literary, the other archaeological, that upon examination end up giving the Lady their full support.

First the literary version. The written record refers constantly to the "Followers of Horus" (*šmsw-Hr*), who came from Asia to Egypt along the Road or "Way of Horus," which was the land route along the coast from Canaan. The Pyramid Texts contain many lively little vignettes of life on the march with Horus—preparing the king's camp at evening, setting up his tent, the mess call, etc.[202] The followers are designated by the ideograms of the bow, staff, and boomerang, and the presence of the omnipresent hawk and faithful dog (*wep-wawet*) who go ahead and find out the way.[203] Need we add that Horus and his company advance through virgin territory amid tremendous tempests of wind, thunder, lightning, and meteoric displays?[204] Or that the standard of Isis leads the procession,[205] or that the hero shares his tent with the Vulture Mother of Upper Egypt, the Lady Nekhbet?[206]

Those who have made a special study of the Followers of Horus moving to Egypt along the Way of Horus all insist that the legend is by no means fiction. There was "absolutely nothing mythological" about these pioneers, according to Sethe; and the story of how Horus enters the land and takes possession "contains not the slightest trace of any mythological connections whatever."[207] The Egyptians always looked back with pride on their pioneer ancestors and held them up as examples of solid, old-fashioned virtues to their children: "A son who hearkens to his father is like a Follower of Horus, who succeeds in life because he follows

the rules; he reaches old age and the dignity of an elder."[208]
The familiar hawk, hound, bows, boomerangs, royal litter,
and tent were no mere heraldic symbols, but viewed as
"completely real," and brought out for full-scale dramatization of the event on every Founders' Day, a semiannual
festival mentioned in the very earliest of Egyptian records
as celebrating the year of the "Followers of Horus."[209] What
puzzled scholars initially about this was that the title
✝"Followers of Horus" in these inscriptions was regularly
written with the ideogram of a *ship*. How come, if they
came by land?[210]

The explanation was easily found and not disputed: The
ship recalls the king's sailing upon the Nile to take possession of the country *after* his overland journey (fig. 91). That,
too, was part of the celebration. To commemorate their
coronation, the Thinite kings (i.e., of the first two dynasties)
were carried about in a procession "like Horus in his venerable ship," as the formula went. This can only mean, as
Sethe notes, "a festival procession . . . in which the god's
vessel was carried about."[211] He was carried by followers
wearing the jackal masks of Wep-wawet, the land rover,[212]
and the procession also wound through the mountains, but
the weapon he bore was the Horus spear, a harpoon with a
✝ hawk's-head point, showing conquest by water as well as
land (fig. 92).[213] The oldest historical record of the pharaohs,
the famous Palermo Stone (fig. 93), shows us, in the words
of Alan H. Gardiner, that "every second year saw the occurrence of a 'Following of the Horus,' which, whether as an
actual Royal Progress by river or as a merely reminiscent
ceremony, certainly recalled those historic voyages in which
the king proceeded northwards to bring about the unification of the Two Lands."[214] Earliest of all, the Followers of
Horus turn up on the prehistoric memorial tablets from
royal graves of the First Dynasty at Abydos, where again
the title is always written with the sign of the ship.[215]

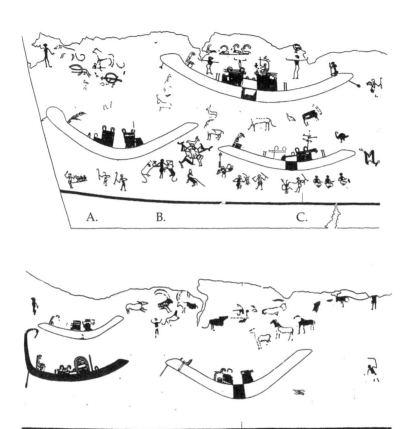

Figure 91. The oldest painted tomb wall discovered in Egypt (c. 3300 B.C.) shows a flotilla of six large boats with steering oars and various-shaped cabins. The spaces around them are filled with wild and domestic animals as well as people, some fighting and others kneeling on the ground. A man prepares to club three captives with his stone mace (A), a ritual of the conquering pharaoh depicted on temple walls for the next three thousand years (see fig. 75B, p. 438). Another man holds two lions by the neck (B) in the familiar pose of the Master of Animals (see fig. 87, p. 527). The double arrow standard of Min rises above one cabin (C; see fig. 94, p. 595, and fig. 104, p. 636).

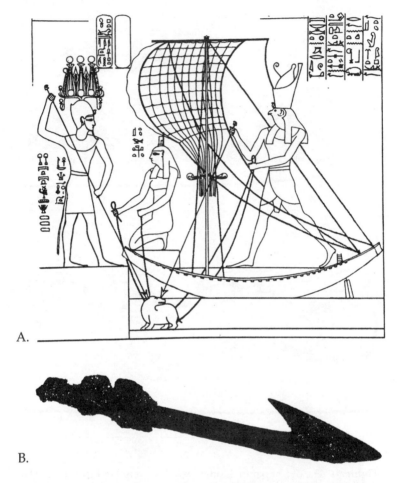

Figure 92. In this scene from the temple of Horus at Edfu, c. 300 B.C., Ptolemy wears the triple Atef on the Khepresh crown and assists Horus and his mother, Isis, in spearing a tiny hippopotamus, the symbol of Seth (A). Their barbed spears have a small Horus head on the other end, showing them to be aspects of the "spear of Horus." The sail catches the wind in the new style of Greek-influenced perspective while everything else is shown in its traditional Egyptian form. The royal sport of hunting hippopotami was very ancient as shown by this copper harpoon dating from c. 3300 B.C. (B).

Figure 93. This black basalt fragment known as the Palermo stone came from a six-foot long slab inscribed on both sides in the Fifth Dynasty, c. 2350 B.C., to record all the preceding gods and kings of lower Egypt and the major events of their reigns. Behind the *rnpt* palm-rib glyph, here symbolizing just one year, a boat sign appears every other year. It was very difficult to polish this hard volcanic stone smooth and then scratch the inscription on it. The Egyptians thought their efforts were worthwhile because they intended this sacred genealogy to last through eternity.

These last were the work of the so-called Naqada II civilization of Egypt, the people who, archaeologists agree, were the first to bring authentic Egyptian civilization to the land. "Where they came from we do not know," wrote Elise J. Baumgartel, "nor how they entered Egypt. They must have had connections with the Sumerian civilisation," that is, through some unknown and remote common source.[216] These, according to Hans A. Winkler, were the "Standard People" whose tribal emblems mounted on standards led them on the march as Followers of Horus.[217] They spoke a West Semitic language akin to the Hamitic of Naqada I. Baumgartel finds that their pottery "may be of Palestinian origin."[218] But were not their relatives of the Naqada I culture the real first settlers in the land? No, they did not live in the valley, but in the high country on either side of it; the valley proper was not inhabited at all until the Naqada II people moved in.[219] The latter were the "Dynastic Race" who greatly exceeded "the original inhabitants in intelligence. . . . Hence the enormous jump from the primitive Predynastic Egypt to the advanced civilization of the Old Empire."[220]

Now it was these Naqada II people who produced a large number of those splendid pots on which are depicted the great ceremonial barges sailing the river with the oversize figure of the dancing goddess looming over all else (fig. 94),[221] from which it would seem that the written and archaeological records alike tend to confirm, and at no point refute, the tradition of the Pioneer Lady and her Royal Son. As a clincher we are confronted with a complication that Werner Kaiser finds disturbing and that has never been explained, namely, that the primitive standards of Horus and his followers seem to be the same as the equally ancient standards of Min.[222]

For a general view of the archaeological evidence, Walter B. Emery's *Archaic Egypt* may serve as a convenient

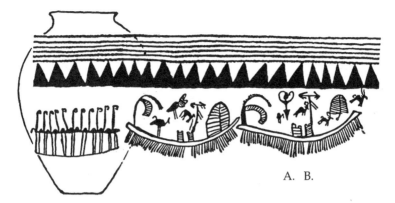

Figure 94. This ten-inch high pot, c. 3500–3000 B.C., was decorated with highly stylized figures, including the famous "dancing goddess" who has her arms lifted above her head, with hands turned in like a ballerina's (A). Marsh birds such as flamingos seem to watch as the many-oared boats move past with their passengers of ostriches, gazelles, and ibex. The double-headed arrow, the thunderbolt of Min, is also recognizable (B).

guide. Four main points may be noted confirming the story of the Lady. First, the dynastic race was a reality, with the sudden appearance of a full-blown Egyptian civilization coming from some as-yet-undiscovered homeland by way of the Wadi Hammamat (fig. 95) to Coptos; also, the occupation was definitely from south to north.[223] Second, in the earliest court/coronation scene, King Narmer, father of Hor-Aha if not Hor-Aha himself (the founder of the First Dynasty), sits enthroned under the outspread wings of a huge vulture (Mut the Mother), while a woman sits facing him at his own level in a booth mounted for carrying in a procession (fig. 96). His tomb at Saqqara was notably smaller than that of his mother, Nit-hotep (Neith has settled). Compared with her tomb, that of Narmer, whom Emery takes to be her husband, "is almost insignificant."[224] Hor-Aha's son was succeeded on the throne by a woman, Meryet-Nit (the Power of Neith); her name was written by the two crossed arrows on a staff (fig. 97).[225] Always "Hathor was . . . a female counterpart of

Figure 95. A 1912 photograph shows the ancient Way of Horus or Wadi Hammamat near the stelae of Ramses IV.

Horus,"[226] and the king was Horus, who belonged to the Bee and the Nebti, the Two Ladies, to satisfy both the North and the South. Third, boats predominate in the graves (fig. 98), large wooden boats; the Queen-Mother Nit-hotep had "a large brick-built boat grave" for a full-sized ship,[227] and Meryet-Nit's shipmaster was found near her with model boats.[228] Zer, the third king, is shown paying ritual visits to the shrines of Buto and Sais by boat.[229] "We know nothing of the origin of Horus," the only clue being his big ship, "as early as the commencement of the First Dynasty."[230] Fourth, the settlement, which brought a completely developed writing system, "immense and intricate structures," and advanced technology and high artistic achievement with it,[231] set foot in the South, and from there moved to the North, taking over the country completely.[232]

Figure 96. The eight-inch high ceremonial stone mace head of King
Narmer is covered with significant images of his kingship. This rollout
drawing shows the king wearing the Red Crown enthroned under a
canopy on a high platform with fan bearers at the bottom. A large vulture, the mother goddess, spreads her wings over her son below. The
kneeling figure seated in a sedan chair before him is in the typical pose
of a woman. The upper right corner features a row of standard bearers
with the same symbols seen in Kheruef's tomb built a thousand years
later (cf. fig. 85 O, p. 503).

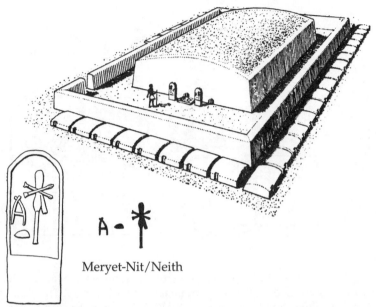

Meryet-Nit/Neith

Figure 97. The tomb of Queen Meryet-Nit is an impressive display of her power. The large mound is surrounded by the smaller graves of her courtiers. Two large stelae inscribed with her name, written with two blunt-nosed crossed arrows on a standard, were erected before the tomb where offerings were placed.

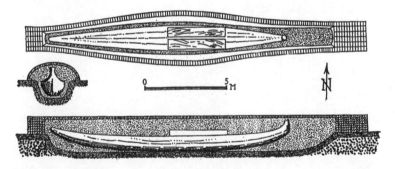

Figure 98. A typical boat grave of this period included this streamlined wooden vessel buried in sand with a brick retaining wall around it. It was placed so that it would carry the deceased from the east to the setting sun in the west.

Notes

1. Henri Gauthier, *Le personnel du dieu Min* (Cairo: BIFAO, 1931), 1; Henri Gauthier, *Les fêtes du dieu Min* (Cairo: BIFAO, 1931), 17, 288–90.

2. Gauthier, *Fêtes du dieu Min*, 17, 288–90.

3. Gauthier, *Personnel du dieu Min*, 2; Alessandra Nibbi, "Remarks on the Two Stelae from the Wadi Gasus," *JEA* 62 (1976): 55.

4. Gauthier, *Personnel du dieu Min*, 3, 7–8; Gauthier, *Fêtes du dieu Min*, 103–4, 194.

5. Gauthier, *Fêtes du dieu Min*, 289.

6. Ibid., 195.

7. Gerald A. Wainwright, "The Origin of the Storm-Gods of Egypt," *JEA* 49 (1963): 13.

8. Gauthier, *Fêtes du dieu Min*, 189–91.

9. Harris Papyrus 6:1–7; 3, plates 25–26, in E. A. Wallis Budge, *Egyptian Hieratic Papyri in the British Museum* (London: Trustees of the British Museum, 1910), 24–25.

10. Gauthier, *Fêtes du dieu Min*, 234–35.

11. Ibid., 236–37.

12. Paul Guiyesse and Eugène Lefébure, *Le Papyrus funeraire de Soutimes* (Paris: Leroux, 1978), plate xvii commentary, p. 10, no. 14.

13. Wainwright, "Origin of the Storm-Gods of Egypt," 19.

14. Eugène Lefébure, "Les huttes de Cham," *BE* 36 (1915): 216–17.

15. Pausanius, *Description of Greece* X, 32, 18.

16. Gauthier, *Fêtes du dieu Min*, 61–63; Lefébure, "Huttes de Cham," 226–27.

17. Joachim Spiegel, *Die Götter von Abydos* (Wiesbaden: Harrassowitz, 1973), 66, 71–72.

18. Gauthier, *Fêtes du dieu Min*, 282.

19. Ibid., 244–46.

20. Gauthier, *Personnel du dieu Min*, 4.

21. Gauthier, *Fêtes du dieu Min*, 142–43.

22. Lefébure, "Huttes de Cham," 220.

23. Gauthier, *Fêtes du dieu Min*, 283.

24. Lefébure, "Huttes de Cham," 211–12.

25. Ibid., 225–26.

26. Ibid.

27. Alan H. Gardiner, *Egyptian Grammar* (Oxford: Oxford University Press, 1957), 503.

28. Eugène Lefébure, "Le Cham et l'Adam Égyptiens," *BE* 35 (1912): 9.

29. Herodotus, *History* II, 99.

30. Gauthier, *Fêtes du dieu Min*, 34.

31. Gauthier, *Personnel du dieu Min*, 77–78.

32. Lefébure, "Huttes de Cham," 234.

33. Gauthier, *Fêtes du dieu Min*, 15; James H. Breasted, *Ancient Records of Egypt*, 5 vols. (Chicago: University of Chicago Press, 1906–1907), 1:58, 65.

34. Hugh W. Nibley, "Tenting, Toll, and Taxing," *Western Political Quarterly* 19 (1966): 609–12; reprinted in *The Ancient State, CWHN* 10 (Salt Lake City: Deseret Book and FARMS, 1991): 46–49.

35. Gauthier, *Personnel du dieu Min*, 84–85; Spiegel, *Götter von Abydos*, 66, 68, 75–76.

36. Gauthier, *Fêtes du dieu Min*, 20.

37. Spiegel, *Götter von Abydos*, 67, 69–70.

38. Constantin E. Sander-Hansen, *Die Texte der Metternichstele* (Copenhagen: Munksgaard, 1956), 35–40.

39. Spiegel, *Götter von Abydos*, 67.

40. Source not found; see preface.

41. Sander-Hansen, *Texte der Metternichstele*, 49.

42. Ibid., 36–37.

43. Spiegel, *Götter von Abydos*, 72, 74.

44. Gauthier, *Fêtes du dieu Min*, 209.

45. Spiegel, *Götter von Abydos*, 66.

46. Theodor Gaster, "The Egyptian 'Story of Astarte' and the Ugaritic Poem of Baal," *Bibliotheca Orientalis* 9 (1952): 82–85; Hugh W. Nibley, "The Arrow, the Hunter, and the State," *Western Political Quarterly* 19 (1966): 338–39; reprinted in *The Ancient State, CWHN* 10:5–6.

47. Gauthier, *Fêtes du dieu Min*, 217–18.

48. Ibid., 221.

49. Ibid., 220.

50. Cf. Lefébure, "Huttes de Cham," 210, 212.

51. Ibid., 226.

52. Gauthier, *Fêtes du dieu Min*, 286; Lefébure, "Huttes de Cham," 219.

53. Spiegel, *Götter von Abydos*, 70–71.

54. Lefébure, "Huttes de Cham," 217 (Louvre C30).

55. Ibid., 216.

56. Ibid., 224.

57. Ibid., 215, 217–18.

58. Ibid., 215–16.

59. Ibid., 234.

60. Ibid., 230–31.

61. Ibid., 219.

62. Lefébure, "Cham et l'Adam Égyptiens," 8, 10–11.

63. Lefébure, "Huttes de Cham," 218, 220.

64. Ibid., 220–21.

65. Ibid., 226.

66. Ibid., 228.

67. Hermann te Velde, *Seth, God of Confusion* (Leiden: Brill, 1967), 48–49.

68. Alan H. Gardiner, *The Library of A. Chester Beatty* (Oxford: Oxford University Press, 1931), 26.

69. Lefébure, "Huttes de Cham," 219.

70. Ibid.

71. Ibid., 218.

72. Ibid., 219.

73. Ibid., 218.

74. Gauthier, *Fêtes du dieu Min*, 201.

75. Ibid., 200.

76. Lefébure, "Cham et l'Adam Égyptiens," 9.

77. Gauthier, *Fêtes du dieu Min*, 89.

78. Lefébure, "Cham et l'Adam Égyptiens," 12.

79. Gauthier, *Fêtes du dieu Min*, 201–3; quotation on 202.

80. Ibid., 203; W. Golenischeff, "Une excursion à Berenice," *RT* 13 (1890): 87–88.

81. Gauthier, *Fêtes du dieu Min*, 230–31.

82. Herodotus, *History* II, 91.

83. Lefébure, "Huttes de Cham," 213.

84. Cf. Lefébure, "Cham et l'Adam Égyptiens," 10–11.

85. Te Velde, *Seth, God of Confusion*, 48–49.

86. Plutarch, *De Iside et Osiride*, 19.

87. Lefébure, "Cham et l'Adam Égyptiens," 7–8.

88. Ibid., 12.

89. Francis L. Griffith, *Stories of the High Priests of Memphis* (Oxford: Clarendon, 1900), 15–29.

90. Ibid., 2.

91. Ibid., 41–66.

92. Sander-Hansen, *Texte der Metternichstele*, 47.

93. Griffith, *Stories of the High Priests of Memphis*, 57–59.

94. Ibid., 61–65.

95. Ibid., 14.

96. Ibid., 16–40.

97. Lefébure, "Huttes de Cham," 219.

98. Spiegel, *Götter von Abydos*, 68.

99. Ibid., 73.

100. Ibid., 69.

101. Ibid., 71.

102. Ibid., 76.

103. Ibid., 68–69; Rudolf Anthes, "Egyptian Theology in the Third Millennium B.C.," *JNES* 18 (July 1959): 207.

104. Sander-Hansen, *Texte der Metternichstele*, 43–44.

105. Lefébure, "Huttes de Cham," 211–12; Hans Bonnet, "Geissel," in *Reallexikon der ägyptischen Religionsgeschichte* (Berlin: de Gruyter, 1952), 465.

106. Lefébure, "Huttes de Cham," 215–16.

107. Siegfried Schott, ed., "Das Buch von der Abwehr des Bösen," in *Urkunden mythologischen Inhalts*, Urkunden des ägyptischen Altertums, vol. 6, part 1 (Leipzig: Hinrichs, 1929), 136.

108. Lefébure, "Huttes de Cham," 219.

109. Sander-Hansen, *Texte der Metternichstele*, 47.

110. Bonnet, *Reallexikon der ägyptischen Religionsgeschichte*, 461.

111. Gauthier, *Personnel du dieu Min*, 69–70.

112. Plutarch, *De Iside et Osiride*, 56; Gauthier, *Fêtes du dieu Min*, 33.

113. Gauthier, *Fêtes du dieu Min*, 34–35; Bonnet, *Reallexikon der ägyptischen Religionsgeschichte*, 580.

114. Gauthier, *Fêtes du dieu Min*, 160–72, 288.

115. Gauthier, *Personnel du dieu Min*, 123; Lefébure, "Huttes de Cham," 226–27.

116. Gauthier, *Personnel du dieu Min*, 114–16.

117. Ibid., 110–11.

118. Ibid., 54.

119. Strabo, *Geography* XVII, 1, 46.

120. Gauthier, *Personnel du dieu Min*, 28.

121. Ibid., 118.

122. Gauthier, *Fêtes du dieu Min*, 8–9.

123. Ibid., 11, 61.

124. Te Velde, *Seth, God of Confusion*, 27–32, 44.

125. Lefébure, "Huttes de Cham," 211, 229.

126. Ibid., 228.

127. Gauthier, *Fêtes du dieu Min*, 227–28, 230–31.

128. Ibid., 239, no. 1.

129. Lefébure, "Cham et l'Adam Égyptiens," 11.

130. Louis Ginzberg, *The Legends of the Jews*, 7 vols. (Philadelphia: Jewish Publication Society, 1909–13), 1:177–78, 318–19.

131. Lefébure, "Huttes de Cham," 230.

132. Strabo, *Geography* XVII, 1, 46; cf. Hugh W. Nibley, "A New Look at the Pearl of Great Price," *IE* 72 (February 1969): 64.

133. Lefébure, "Huttes de Cham," 233.

134. Gauthier, *Fêtes du dieu Min*, 236–37, 266–67.

135. Wolfgang Richter, "Urgeschichte und Hoftheologie," *Biblische Zeitschrift* 10 (1966): 99.

136. Ibid.

137. Ibid., 115; F. M. Theodor de Liagre Böhl, "Babel und Bibel (I)," *JEOL* 16 (1959): 115.

138. *Jubilees* 9:14, in *The Apocrypha and Pseudepigrapha of the Old Testament*, ed. Robert H. Charles, 2 vols. (Oxford: Clarendon, 1976), 2:27.

139. *Jubilees* 10:29–33; Ginzberg, *Legends of the Jews*, 1:172.

140. Emil G. H. Kraeling, "The Earliest Hebrew Flood Story," *Journal of Biblical Literature* 66 (1947): 291; Robert Graves and Raphael Patai, *Hebrew Myths* (New York: Greenwich House, 1983), 121.

141. *Jubilees* 7:13.

142. E. A. Wallis Budge, ed., *The Book of the Cave of Treasures* (London: Religious Tract Society, 1927), 118–19, 121.

143. A. Epstein, "Les Chamites de la table ethnographique selon le Pseudo-Jonathan," *REJ* 24 (1892): 85.

144. Louis I. Newman, *Hasidic Anthology* (New York: Scribner, 1944), 297.

145. Ibid.

146. Victor Aptowitzer, "Les premiers possesseurs de Canaan," *REJ* 82 (1926): 279.

147. Ibid., 280.

148. Ibid., 280–86.

149. Georg Fohrer, "Israels Haltung gegenüber den Kanaanäern und anderen Völkern," *Journal of Semitic Studies* 13 (1968): 64–75.

150. Anthes, "Egyptian Theology," 176–83.

151. Ibid., 180.

152. Diodorus Siculus, *The Library of History* XL, 3, 1–3.

153. Alexandre Moret, *Du caractère religieux de la royauté pharaonique* (Paris: Leroux, 1902), 57.

154. Ibid., 57–59.

155. Nahman Avigad and Yigael Yadin, eds., *A Genesis Apocryphon* (Jerusalem: Hebrew University Press, 1956), col. 20:21–29.

156. Nibley, "A New Look at the Pearl of Great Price," *IE* 73 (April 1970): 80–82; in this volume, pp. 346–51.

157. *Joseph and Asenath,* in Paul Riessler, *Altjüdisches Schrifttum ausserhalb der Bibel* (Heidelberg: Kerle, 1957), 497–538. For an English translation, see C. Burchard, trans., *Joseph and Aseneth,* in James H. Charlesworth, ed., *The Old Testament Pseudepigrapha,* 2 vols. (Garden City, NY: Doubleday, 1985), 2:177–247.

158. *Joseph and Asenath* 8:9–10, in Riessler, *Altjüdisches Schrifttum ausserhalb der Bibel,* 505–6.

159. *Joseph and Asenath* 10:2–13:12, in ibid., 506–12.

160. *Joseph and Asenath* 14:3–15, in ibid., 514–15.

161. *Joseph and Asenath* 15:4, in ibid., 516.

162. *Joseph and Asenath* 15:5–7, in ibid., 516.

163. *Joseph and Asenath* 21:1–9, in ibid., 525–26.

164. *Joseph and Asenath* 21:5, in ibid., 526.

165. *Joseph and Asenath* 21:6–7, in ibid.

166. *Joseph and Asenath* 21:7, in ibid., 526.

167. *Joseph and Asenath* 22:1–13, in ibid., 526–28.

168. Micha J. bin Gorion, *Die Sagen der Juden,* 5 vols. (Frankfurt: Rütten & Loening, 1913–27), 1:160.

169. Zacharie Mayani, *Les Hyksos et le monde de la Bible* (Paris: Payot, 1956), 180.

170. Robert Eisler, *Iēsous Basileus ou Basileusas,* 2 vols. (Heidelberg: Winter, 1929), 2:180.

171. Ibid., 2:180, 217.

172. Mayani, *Hyksos et le monde de la Bible,* 179.

173. Budge, *Book of the Cave of Treasures,* 120–21.

174. Ibid., 87–93; *Le combat d'Adam et Eve,* in J.-P. Migne, *Dictionnaire des Apocryphes* I, Encyclopedie théologique, ser. 3, vol. 23 (Paris: Chez l'editeur, 1856), 349–52.

175. Graves and Patai, *Hebrew Myths,* 96–97.

176. Bin Gorion, *Sagen der Juden,* 1:136, 239–40.

177. Robert North, "The Cain Music," *Journal of Biblical Literature* 83 (1964): 389.

178. Alexandre Piankoff, *Mythological Papyri II,* Bollingen Series 40, vol. 3 (New York: Pantheon, 1957), plate 12.

179. Ibid., plates 20, 24.

180. Alan H. Gardiner, *Egypt of the Pharaohs* (Oxford: Clarendon, 1961), 37.

181. Abd Bakir, *Slavery in Pharaonic Egypt* (Cairo: BIFAO, 1952), 72, 97–99. (Cahier no. 18, in Supplement to *ASAE*.)

182. Heinrich K. Brugsch, *Die Geographie der Ägypter nach den Denkmälern*, Geographie Inschriften altägyptischer Denkmäler, vol. 6 (Leipzig: Hinrichs, 1860), 51.

183. Pierre Montet, *Eternal Egypt* (New York: New American Library, 1964), plates 26–64.

184. Geza Vermes, "Sepher ha-Yashar," cited in *Scripture and Tradition in Judaism* (Leiden: Brill, 1961), 73; Ginzberg, *Legends of the Jews*, 1:203, 292–94.

185. *Jubilees* 41:23–25.

186. René Dussaud, "Cham et Canaan," *RHR* 59 (1909): 221–30.

187. Josephus, *Antiquities* I, 6, 2; cf. Epstein, "Chamites de la table ethnographique," 83–85.

188. Richter, "Urgeschichte und Hoftheologie," 100.

189. Johannes Gabriel, "Die Kainitengenealogie, Gen. 4:17–24," *Biblica* 40 (1959): 409–27.

190. North, "Cain Music," 373–89.

191. Joseph Karst, "Aïa-Kolchis et les Chamites septentrionaux," *Orientalia* 3 (1934): 31–41.

192. Ibid., 33.

193. Hans Stock, "Das Ostdelta Ägyptens in seiner entscheidenden Rolle für die politische und religiöse Entwicklung des alten Reiches," *Die Welt des Orients* (1948): 144–45.

194. Werner Vycichl, "Notes sur la préhistoire de la langue égyptienne," *Orientalia* 23 (1954): 217.

195. Ibid., 218–19.

196. Théodule Devéria, "Fragments de manuscrits funéraires égyptiens consiérés par les Mormons comme les mémoires autographes d'Abraham," *Mémoires et Fragments* (Paris: Leroux, 1896), in *BE* 4 (1896): 201.

197. Nibley, "A New Look at the Pearl of Great Price," *IE* 71 (April 1968): 67–68.

198. William F. Petrie, *Tombs of the Courtiers and Oxyrhynchus* (London: British School of Archaeology in Egypt, 1925), plate 32.

199. Maxence de Rochemonteix, "Le temple d'Apet," *RT* 6 (1885): 25.

200. Hermann Ranke, *Die Aegyptischen Personnennamen*, 2 vols. (Glückstadt, Germany: Augustin, 1935–52), 1:80.

201. Konrad Hoffmann, "Die theophoren Personnennamen des älteren Ägyptens," Untersuchungen zur Geschichte und Altertumskunde Aegyptens, vol. 7 (1915; reprint, Hildesheim: Olms, 1964), 51–52.

202. Pyramid Text 273–74 (§403–5); 690 (§2100), in Raymond O. Faulkner, *Ancient Egyptian Pyramid Texts* (Oxford: Clarendon, 1969), 93, 299; Coffin Text 216, in Adriaan de Buck, ed., *The Egyptian Coffin Texts*, 7 vols. (Chicago: University of Chicago Press, 1935–61), 3:192.

203. Kurt H. Sethe, *Beiträge zur ältesten Geschichte Ägyptens*, vol. 3 in Untersuchungen zur Geschichte und Altertumskunde Aegyptens, 16.

204. Nibley, "Tenting, Toll, and Taxing," 600; in *The Ancient State*, *CWHN* 10:33–34.

205. Werner Kaiser, "Einige Bemerkungen zur ägyptischen Frühzeit," *ZÄS* 85 (1960): 125–27.

206. Émile Massoulard, *Préhistoire et protohistoire d'Égypte* (Paris: Institut d'ethnologie, 1949), 445.

207. Sethe, *Beiträge zur ältesten Geschichte Ägyptens*, 3:3–21.

208. Ibid., 7.

209. Kaiser, "Einige Bemerkungen zur ägyptischen Frühzeit," 118–19.

210. Hans W. Helck, "Gegenstände aus der Umgebung des Königs," *Anthropos* 49 (1954): 972–77.

211. Sethe, *Beiträge zur ältesten Geschichte Ägyptens*, 3:15.

212. Ibid., 16–17.

213. Heinrich Schäfer, "Der Speer des Horus als Ruckenbrett von Mumien und als Amulett," *ZÄS* 41 (1904): 68–70.

214. Gardiner, *Egypt of the Pharaohs*, 414; Coffin Text 12, in de Buck, *Egyptian Coffin Texts*, 1:38–40.

215. Sethe, *Beiträge zur ältesten Geschichte Ägyptens*, 3:15.

216. Elise J. Baumgartel, "Some Notes on the Origin of Egypt," *Archiv Orientalní* 20 (1952): 281.

217. Hans A. Winkler, *Völker und Völkerbewegungen im vorgeschichtlichen Oberägypten im Lichte neuer Felsbilderkunde* (Stuttgart: Kohlhammer, 1937), 6–7.

218. Elise J. Baumgartel, *The Cultures of Prehistoric Egypt* (Oxford: Oxford University Press, 1947), 41.

219. Ibid., 49.

220. D. E. Derry, "The Dynastic Race in Egypt," *JEA* 42 (1956): 85; Reginald Engelbach, "An Essay on the Advent of the Dynastic Race in Egypt and Its Consequences," *ASAE* 42 (1943): 193–221.

221. Wolfhart Westendorf, *Painting, Sculpture, and Architecture of Ancient Egypt* (New York: Abrams, 1969), 15.

222. Kaiser, "Einige Bemerkungen zur ägyptischen Frühzeit," 121–22, 128.

223. Walter B. Emery, *Archaic Egypt* (Baltimore: Penguin, 1961), 38–42.

224. Ibid., 44–47.

225. Ibid., 65.

226. Ibid., 124.

227. Ibid., 49–54; cf.68.

228. Ibid., 66–68.

229. Ibid., 59.

230. Ibid., 120.

231. Ibid., 177, 192, 222–24.

232. Ibid., 99–101, 119–21.

12

The Deseret Connection

Min the Beekeeper

Our concern with Min and his mistress leads to a theme that cannot be evaded, namely, the association or identity of the two with the honeybee. I had thought to spare the reader a somewhat involved discourse, because there is no mention of beekeeping in the Book of Abraham; yet it presents such a remarkable control over Joseph Smith's accounts of what is supposed to have happened away back in the days of what the Jews call "the Separation," i.e., the great migrations from the tower, that to ignore it once detected would be a dereliction of duty.

The garden (*ḥsp*) before Min's beehive house at Coptos[1] hummed with the sound of busy bees, for Min of Coptos, the first ruler of Egypt, was "fond of honey"[2] and was "a god of bees,"[3] whose priests were called *ꜥftyw*, "Bees,"[4] and whose number two priest was the *ꜥft n byt*, "Keeper of the Bees." The mountain behind Coptos was the Egyptian Hymettus, an important source of that wild honey which the Egyptians always favored.[5]

T   In Egypt the bee is, before all else, a sign of royalty. Everyone knows that the oldest title placed before the name of a king was the "insibya," the combined signs of "the sedge and the bee";[6] but the sedge is a later addition, an emblem of temporal political power, according to recent studies, while the bee sign originally stood alone as the supreme symbol of sacral primal kingship in Egypt.[7] Queen Hatshepsut still thinks of herself as leader of the bee people.[8] Why the bee? Eberhard Otto confesses himself entirely at a loss to explain it. It makes no sense whatever, he writes; "I fear that its real meaning, its etymological, temporal, geographical or ethnic origin, will forever remain unknown."[9]

Since the bee symbol is constantly associated with the king of Lower Egypt in the records, it is important, as Hugo Müller cautions, not to suppose it so localized in the beginning;[10] even in later times, Otto reminds us, the bee does not refer to Lower Egypt alone.[11] In hieroglyphic the bee is constantly equated with the Red Crown worn by the first king of Lower Egypt at Sais;[12] but the fact that the oldest representation of that crown comes not from Sais in the Delta, but from Naqada (fig. 99), being "characteristic of the first prehistoric civilization"[13] in the domain of "Min, who was the chief god of Panopolis (Ekhmim), also of Koptos nearly opposite Nakadeh, and was the original form of Amun of Thebes,"[14] led Gerald Wainwright to conclude that "our symbol does not represent the king of Sais himself but only Neith worship, it . . . merely indicates the presence of a primitive Libyan population of Neith worshippers at Nakadeh, just as at Sais."[15] Every indication is that it was not the king himself, but the Lady Neith who was the Bee. It was early recognized that the words for bee, Red Crown, and honey, all of which were read the same way, whether as n.t, bi.t or ḥb.t,[16] all had feminine endings, the crown itself being "personified as a goddess" and at the same time identical with the Bee.[17] "The word bj.t," Kurt Sethe noted, "is to be read as a feminine, with the general meaning of 'the Bee,'"[18] while "the male rulers of Lower Egypt in a later age

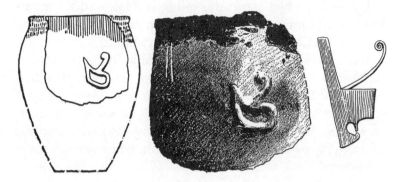

Figure 99. This fragment from a finely burnished pot shows the earliest representation of the Red Crown to survive. It must have been important to the potter to go to the extra effort to make this a raised design rather than simply incising or painting it into the clay, as was commonly done with other decorations. The distinctive protruding coil evokes an insect's antenna as well as the coiling rope of Min's temple (see fig. 89A, p. 561).

of development as successors and descendants of this royal Bee were given the name of bi-ty, 'he who *belongs* to the Bee,' 'the *descendant* of the Bee.'"[19] Likewise the bee symbol of Min = Horus does not tell us that Min is a bee, but that "Min is he who belongs to the Bee, who stands in relationship to the bee," which greatly puzzles Henri Gauthier.[20] In the Leiden Book of Breathings, the succession to the crown is assured when Horus marries the queen bee and takes over the land.[21] "It is noteworthy," wrote Sethe, "that the masculine god Geb wears in representations of his prehistoric form the Red Crown which properly belongs to his wife."[22] In an important formula, Min "unites the power of Horus with that of Seth, who reposes in Thebes and Coptos, and belongs to the Bee."[23]

The bee title and bee crown are par excellence the possession of Neith of Sais, where stood her palace, "the House of the Bee,"[24] but as the Bee Lady she may not be separated from Nut—both women are called the Bee in the Pyramid Texts as mothers of the king.[25] "Tracing the royal bee-title back to them as queen bees" strongly suggests to Sethe a prehistoric matriarchal rule, an idea that he rejects on the grounds that the ancients thought the ruler of the hives was a king.[26] This misunderstanding comes from rhetorical passages of late writers dedicated to asserting the victory of Zeus over the old matriarchal order.[27] Sethe himself insists that "Neith always passed, regardless of all other theological speculations, as the oldest of all gods and the greatest—the Mother of the Gods."[28] At the time of the Pyramid Texts, ⅄ her counterpart "Nut was completely dominant over her husband the Earth-god as well as over Shu and Tefnut. . . . As in the case of Neith, we are confronted with the idea of a female rule."[29] It is as the Bee that Nut rules as "the queen *schlechthin* (supreme)," without regard to a defined territory.[30] "O Nut," says a Pyramid Text, "thou hast appeared at *bi.t*, the Bee, because thou hast power over the gods and their Ka's."[31]

Peter Le Page Renouf found that the N.t crown of the Lady was worn by the high priest of Coptos as well as the king, the crown being inseparable and interchangeable with the Bee.[32] The king wore the crown in the role of the Bee, Müller observed.[33] We have already seen him wearing the horned Hathor mask or her robe and the mask of Maat or the Maat feather to identify himself with those ladies and lay claim to a share of their authority.[34]

It was in the marsh of Khemmis that Horus = Min was born and nursed by the Two Ladies, Khemmis being Akhmim-Panopolis, Min's town or Ham's town, as noted above.[35] Sethe derived the word Khemmis (a Greek derivative) from the Egyptian name for place, *ḥb.t* meaning bee or honey,[36] the place-name being written with a combination of papyrus and bee glyphs. We have already mentioned the *f* possibility that *ḥb.t* could be related to "Egypt," and certainly denotes "that which is forbidden." In the initiation mystery of Her Weben, that damsel calls Isis "her mother of the Bee-swamp-Chemmis."[37] It is significant that besides Horus-Min and the women, only two other characters appear in the primordial bee-swamp drama: "Shu and Tefnut as the 'royal couple of the king' were also born there."[38] Their presence on the scene brings up another important office of the Bee.

The Bee and the Migrations

⚶   The bee is before all creatures the sponsor, inspiration, and guide of the Great Trek. As a creature of the preexistent or pre-diluvian world, and all but sole survivor of the great catastrophes that desolated the earth,[39] the bee is first to arrive on the scene and start things going again in the new world.[40] In the first of all migrations, Adam and Eve were accompanied and guided by the bees as they moved from the Garden into the dark outer world.[41] The bees brought ℘ with them "the primordial creative divine power";[42] their honey, "made by the bees of Paradise," is the food of heaven.[43] When our first ancestors were allowed to bring some of their original blessings from Eden with them, Adam bore the olive, vine, date, pomegranate, and nard, but to Eve was given the greatest blessing, for she was accompanied by her friends from the Garden with their honey[44]—the busy bees whose beneficent labors among the plants and trees made it possible to renew the verdure of the former world in their new one. According to one of the oldest Egyptian ritual sources, when they found the earth barren of life after the flood, the bees got to work restoring the fertility of the woods and fields while busily producing their honey and wax for the benefit of man.[45] They were especially qualified to conduct Adam and Eve into a strange world, because they knew the place from its older times, themselves being the survivors from the other and better age.[46]

The bees led the migration to Egypt in a time of cosmic

upheaval: "Re wept again; the water of his Eye fell to the earth, and there she (the Sun's Eye) was changed into a bee."[47] Much is said in the Egyptian mythological texts of this falling of strange liquid substances from the sky, putting one strongly in mind of Immanuel Velikovsky's specula- tions on such phenomena at a time of world catastrophe,[48] for this was during the tempest of the *Bitiw,* the Bee people.[49] While Re's sweat was the water of the flood, his tears became the bees, "the flies that build."[50] The time of the great weeping that we mentioned earlier[51] was a time of penitence and atonement, for the substances that descended to the afflicted earth were all of a purifying and healing nature. Thus when Horus wept, the water of his eye, on falling to earth, bloomed as myrrh, both sweet-smelling and medicinal, while Geb's nose bled aromatic cedar.[52] The "mighty weeping" of Shu and Tefnut, the flood pair, became the source, the sap or pitch (*sfy*), of divine incense (*sntr*) upon the earth.[53] In the *Book of the Cow,* various effu- sions from the ailing Re form precious mineral substances;[54] he coughed and spat bitumen (*mrḥ.t*) of which Nut made healing ointment.[55] Even Isis and Nephthys became sick, and their sweat fell to earth as precious *tíšps* ointment.[56] When Re became sick again, he drooled *tfwy,* which became papyrus,[57] while his sweat produced linen.[58] Are we to con- clude from this that at a time of great upheavals of nature, civilization was preserved or reestablished by a migrating "culture-hero"? Egyptian ritual texts have a great deal to say about the Wen-nefer, the "Agathos Daimon," who in the beginning brought the blessings of civilized living to benighted humanity.[59] But the wandering hero is always a youth of status inferior to that of the Great Mother; it was the tears of Nut that brought the human race itself into exis- tence or rather revived it upon the earth.[60] In the Hittite ver- sion, the Bee revives the human race after the flood, under the guidance and rule of the Great Mother: When the youthful hero Telepinu lay dead, and all nature with him, the eagle was sent to find him but failed; so the Bee took his place, seeking through the great floods under a dark and tempestuous sky until he found him, brought him to life by stinging his hands and feet, and so revived all life on earth and restored the dominion of the royal pair.[61]

The best-known version of this strange drama is the story of King Solomon and Queen Bilqis, in which the perennial survivors of world catastrophe are not the bees but the ants, the only serious rivals of the bees in nature.[62] Ants living near Los Alamos covered their trails with tunnels of leaves and litter and so shielded themselves from the deadly radiation from above, and the Hopis say that the ants have known the secret of surviving the great destructions by going underground until the dangers from the sky have passed, when they emerge again as first on the spot to greet any newcomers to the new world.[63] In the cycle of Solomon, he and the queen of Sheba both migrate through the terrible deserts of a desolate and blighted world. Their romantic rivalry and marriage is really a duel of male versus female for the throne, as well as a long search for water and a promised land: when the Lady finally arrives at her destination, like the princess who discovered the Nile, she pulls up her skirt and wades in.[64] We must content ourselves with this later version of the "Egyptus" story by observing that it is the ant people rather than the Bee people who help out there, but the fundamental plot is the same. It will be recalled that the first wandering tribes of Greeks to enter the land were the Myrmidons, the ant people, "whose tribal emblem was the ant" and who "claimed to be autochthonous, as ants are."[65]

In the story of the Sun's Eye, the Lady on the way to Egypt gives instructions on how the land is to be purified after the great afflictions. "Has the Bee no esteem?" she asks, and compares it to the *khpr*-beetle (the sacred scarab)

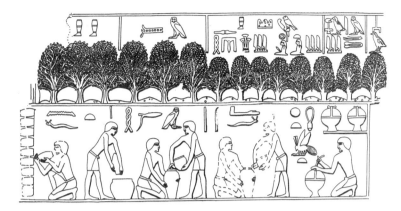

Figure 100. The earliest depiction of collecting honey is from the Room of the Seasons in the Sun Temple of Niussre. Starting from the left, a stacked wall of cylindrical pottery hives is placed in an orchard as shown above. A kneeling worker removes one, which is then emptied into a vessel. Various steps of refining it for different purposes are shown, ending with the sealing of unusual spherical jars.

as the great source and originator of life cycles (fig. 100). "Its proper name is Honey-fly, . . . and the bee keeper summons it with the reed flute, which the goddess had in the beginning. To write the word for honey, picture Nut with the reed in her hand. It is she who purifies the temples of Upper and Lower Egypt when they are founded anew. For the gods will not rest (*ḥtp*—settle down) in their shrines unless they are purified." The god can take many forms, the Lady explains, "but as the King of Egypt, he is called the Honey-fly. It was he who founded the house of the King of Lower Egypt, which is called the First Chapel of Nut."[66] But in this story it is the Lady herself who is the Bee, and her honey is the healing and forgiveness that preceded the settling and building up of the land.[67] As Hathor who discovered the land, she is "the Eye of Re in Letopolis, . . . she of great favor in the chamber of the Bee."[68] The first thing the royal couple beheld upon arriving in Egypt, according to the *Book of the*

Cow, was the Bee, which had preceded them.[69] A venerable Pyramid Text recalls that "in every beautiful place where Re goes, he finds N[eith] there," already awaiting him.[70] The king enters the land as Hathor-Tefnut once did, welcomed by all nature: "The Two daughters of the Bee have born thee, . . . the palms serve thee, the fig-trees bow down to thee."[71]

As usual, the Leiden Book of Breathings is particularly instructive, telling how that Sokar, after crossing the desert with Her Majesty (in the role of Shu = Horus), next crossed the river to Thebes just at dawn of the festival of Mn-b.t, the Establishing of the Bee on the "Day of Apportioning the Islands."[72] "You see the Bee-ceremony of the Leading in of the Two Lady Companions on the night of the Hkr-feast"— feasting following famine.[73] Thoth heralds her arrival as she dons the crown of fresh *hbite*-blossoms from the bee marshes in honor of "Hathor-Mut the Mistress of Karnak. Art thou not the daughter of the Master-builder who built the Tower of Hathor? Hast thou not taken the cymbal to rejoice with the (goddess) at Panopolis [Akhmim = Khemmis = Min's City]? . . . Hast thou not caused men and women to shake [or let down] their hair for her who is in Sistrum-town (Diospolis Parva, [Coptos])?" This last refers to the Lady Tefnut, according to Wilhelm Spiegelberg.[74] The sound of cymbal and sistrum, like the beating of tin pans today, would cause the bees to move. The name of the major road of the West by which the immigrants travel is "the Bee Shines (*hd* = is white) when the White Crown is radiant."[75]

Cave paintings from Altimira show Paleolithic man going after honey, his indispensable source of sweets, to which the ancients at all times paid close attention, marking carefully the swarming and migratory habits of the bees.[76] Min or his priest as *bi.ti* was a cultivator of bees, or perhaps it was his duty to gather wild honey in the desert.[77]

He could have started out as "a god of bees" in his desert home, his popularity explained, Gauthier suggests, by the Egyptian preference for *wild* honey.[78] In a prolonged experiment in bee raising in Palestine, Philip J. Baldensperger discovered one hundred years ago that the bee man must be in a constant state of migration,[79] "traveling like a Beduin through the land, to find a feeding place now in one spot, then in another," success being possible "only by virtue of ceaseless migration (*Wandern*)."[80] The Beduin he describes is ever following the swarms in their search for little garden spots—promised lands in the desert.[81] The ever-perceptive brethren of Basra inform us that all the animals in their journeys through the world seeking livelihood have the Bee for their spokesman; having been on the scene from the beginning, the Bee is in a position to brief and enlighten all the others beginning with an eyewitness account of how God created the earth—for the bees were there even before Adam and Eve.[82] Without them, no garden.

The traditions of the Old World are closely matched by the oldest record of the New, the Maya Book of Chilam Balam, which begins with the settling of the land by bee swarms of the four directions, each of a different color, under the direction of "two gods in the form of large bees who govern all the bees."[83] Coming up from the south, they stirred honey and drank it on the route, and "they swarmed . . . in great numbers" among the trees and plants of their new land.[84] The Bacabs, hailing from the four directions,[85] "were the representatives of the gods. They were the advocates or patrons of the bee-keepers, and it has been thought their name was in some way connected with bees or honey."[86]

Why No Bee Standard?

One particular circumstance has long arrested the attention of scholars, namely, that though banners, standards, and totems are conspicuous at the head of the marching and migrating tribes of old, the standard of the bee is somehow never found among them.[87] "It is a striking thing," writes Otto, "that the 'Bee' is not to be grasped as a numinous entity or even as a 'Symbol.'"[88] Why not? The bee is not the symbol of the people, the land, or the leader because it always remains itself: if others want to identify with it, that can be arranged, but it must always retain its real nature in order to perform its real function. The best-known standard borne by the king on the march is the Wep-wawet emblem of the jackal or hunting dog (the one held by figure 2 in Facsimile 2 of the Book of Abraham), who goes ahead of the host in strange terrain sniffing out the way and scouting ahead.[89] In this capacity he is not the leader but a dependent, specifically designated as the *šms-bí.t*,[90] "the Follower or Attendant of the Bee." As the real leader, the Bee cannot be reduced to a mere emblem of his Upper Egyptian entourage.[91] From the earliest times the most common occurrence of the Bee was in the title *sḏꜣwtj bjtj*, whose pronunciation has never been settled, and whose meaning Hermann Grapow found "unreadable."[92] The real significance of the whole thing is exceedingly ancient and, in the opinion of Otto, ever guarded by the Egyptians as one of their deepest secrets.[93] That we may be dealing with a specific migration of Egyptians and not with some universal "nature myth" is indicated by the conspicuous absence of the bee from extensive lists of fauna preserved in the Babylonian texts, implying, according to Elizabeth D. Van Buren, that bees had to be imported into Babylonia from Egypt, along with "the meaning which the insect had for the Egyptians."[94] "There was never any real apiculture" in Mesopotamia, according to a recent study, and "wild honey or apiculture do not form a part of ancient Chinese civilisation."[95] Hence, incidentally, the prominence of the bee in Maya migration legends suggests Mediterranean rather than Asiatic origins (fig. 101).

Figure 101. Examples of the Maya glyphs for honey (A) and bees (B) show the extreme stylization of their writing system, an indication of long familiarity with the art of collecting honey.

Among the hives in Min's garden stood the bullhead standard on its pole. The ancients often observed that *apes nascuntur ex bubulo corpore putrefacto*, "bees are brought forth from the decayed carcass of an ox," irresistibly suggesting to the Romans the association of the bee (apis) with the Apis-bull of the Egyptians.[96] Let us recall that the primitive shrine of Min was a beehive-shaped house with a bull's skull on a pole standing before the door,[97] and that the Lady on the way to Egypt discoursed on the importance of the Bee: "Has the Bee then, no esteem?" she asks, because she builds her honeycomb in a cave that smells of "the manure of the Cow from which she came forth, which is really the Goddess." Hathor = Tefnut the Cow is herself the Bee Lady.[98] In the tomb of Seti I, the soul is revived by bees that come from the sacred skin of an ox.[99] With the hundreds of golden bees found in the grave of Childerich, king of the Franks, was also found a golden bucranium or ox skull (fig. 102).[100] Though the ancient Germans and Celts thought of themselves on the march as swarming bees, they nonetheless marched not with the Bee, but with the bull standard at their head.[101] The latest study of ancient bees unites the Great Mother as queen bee par excellence with the Bull as her *paredros* (companion) who represents "the prehellenic

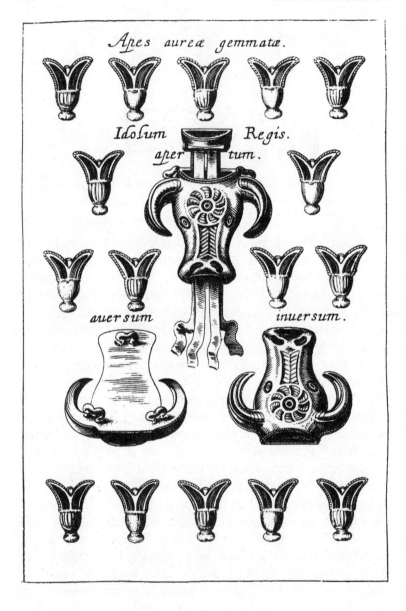

Zeus or [the] primitive Dionysus referred to in the Myce-naean tablettes," confirming the strange but immemorial wedding of the life-giving pair in Egypt.[102]

The Bee and Rites of Resurrection

The issuing of the most tempting and invigorating of food from putrefying corpses was more than a symbol in the mysteries—it was an actual proof of the resurrection. The Bee, "born from the ox" in sacred caves, sets the scene for the mysteries.[103] An inscription from the temple at Denderah, near Coptos, says, "Osiris emulates the Bee in the temple," giving instructions "for knowing the *ḥsp* (sacred garden) of the Bee in the Other World, in the House of Snhty," the last being written with the bee hieroglyph.[104] Osiris appears in both the Pyramid Texts and the Coffin Texts as *bi.ti*, the res-urrected crown and Bee, especially apparent in the tomb of Seti I, with Osiris of the Bees (fig. 103).[105]

Alexandre Moret has written extensively about the important part the sacred skin, or *meskhent*, plays in the Egyptian resurrection rites, in which the skin and the bee go together: The bee born from the skin of the animal is the sign of the resurrection.[106] In the mysteries of Asia Minor, slain victims were revived by the blood of bees, even as the

Figure 102. In 1656 Jean-Jaques Chiflet published this illustrated account of the discovery three years earlier of the tomb of Childerich (d. 482), father of Clovis, who unified middle Europe. Among its wealth of gold jewelry were over three hundred gold bees, their wings set with red gar-nets. The hollow gold ox head may have served as a buckle sewn to his brocaded cloak covered with the bees. The rosette whorl on its forehead is similar to markings found on ancient Near Eastern bull images, inter-preted by some as the hair whorl found on live bulls at that spot. Chiflet, having had a good classical education, commented on the connection between bees and the Apis bull. He also identified the ox head as "Idolum Regis," the image or sign of the king. In 1804 Napoleon used similar golden bees on his coronation robe to claim kinship with the Merovingian dynasty.

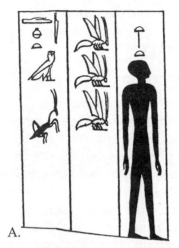 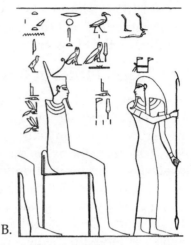

Figure 103. A descending corridor in the tomb of Seti I features this carving of a *šw.t* or shade, symbol of the resurrected soul, followed by three bees and a preying mantis (A). In the great hall of the same tomb Osiris wears the Red Crown with the inscription, "Osiris of the Bees" (B).

king's son Telepinus was restored to life by bee stings on his hands and feet.[107] Glaucus, the son of Minos, was drowned in a great jar of honey and restored to life.[108] Jakob Grimm collected a long list of youthful princes and pretenders drowned in mead or honey, with the idea of resurrection in mind.[109] The Babylonians and Persians embalmed the noble dead in honey, "with about the same lamentation rites as the Egyptians," as Herodotus explains.[110] Everywhere the Bee is the preserver and restorer of life.[111]

But the earlier reports of the power of the Bee to restore life are Egyptian. "You are the daughter mighty with her mother, who appeared as a bee," says a Pyramid Text addressed to Nut; "make the King a spirit within yourself, for he has not died."[112] Here the Lady, the King, and the Bee are fused into one. "O Nut, you have appeared as a bee; you have power over the gods. . . . O Nut, cause the King to be restored, that he may live!"[113] During the awesome "Sem-sleep" of the initiate at the beginning of the mysteries, the candidate calls out that he is "transformed into a bee, in which nothing perishable remains."[114] Those who come to awaken him into a new phase of existence first utter the enigmatic cry of "Bees!"[115] and then say, "Going around [as] a bee, . . . thou seest all the goings round about thy father, . . . the bees (or hornets) giving protection they make him to exist."[116] Commenting on this, Budge remarks, "The beetle [scarab], the mantis, and the bee certainly played a very important part in connection with the resurrection of the deceased."[117]

These themes invaded the Christian church from the first, and Erwin Goodenough has shown how they dominate Jewish symbolism. If Christian legends attribute the building of the first pyx to house the sacred host, symbol of death and resurrection, to the industry of the pious bees,[118] the original shrine of the mysteries at Delphi was also constructed of beeswax by those devoted insects.[119] St. Jerome was puzzled and disturbed by the way the bees invaded the Easter service of the church. "Nothing is harder," he commented in A.D. 384, than to explain why at Easter the Christian congregation must be regaled by bee stories. It is all right for pagan poets to romance about the creatures, he says, "but what has it to do with the deacon, the sacraments of the church, the Easter time, when the Bishop sits silent while the priests carry on a sort of sideshow with the common people, talking to them about the bee?" What is it all about, he asks—you won't find a hint of it in the Old Testament or the New—no mention of bees, or honey, or wax—where does it all come from?[120] As one who had lived in the East, he makes a very good guess at the answer, pointing to Egypt, where the monks of the desert emulated the bees, singing their hymns all day long, gathering the sweets of religion from every bloom of scripture, coming off conquerors in the manner of Denderah, the Bee Lady, and

preparing honey for Christ.[121] To support his theory that the
Eleusinian mysteries came from Crete, Axel W. Persson
observed that the Greeks to this day hold their most solemn
Easter rites in the very bee cave in Crete in which Rhea gave
birth to Zeus,[122] and where Amalthea fed him with milk and
honey even as Amitla fed the infant Abraham.[123]

The most remarkable thesis on the sacred offices of the
bee is found in that minor epic that is an integral part of the
Abraham cycle, the story of Joseph and Asenath, the wedding of Israel and Egypt. The angel who comes to marry
Asenath, the daughter of the high priest of Heliopolis, to
Joseph the son of Jacob, a king and a priest in his own right,
first asks her for a honeycomb, which she orders brought
from the family estate near the temple.[124] Then he has her go
to the pantry and fetch a comb of honey, "white honey like
the dew of heaven."[125] Taking the form of Joseph, the angel
sits on the bed with Asenath while he shares bits of honeycomb with her,[126] saying, "Blessed are they who will eat of
this honey, made by the bees of Paradise. . . . Whoso eateth
thereof will never die. It is the food of heaven."[127] Having
eaten, the bride is told, "The flowers of life will now spring
from thy flesh, thy limbs will flourish, . . . fresh strength will
fill you, and you will never grow old."[128] Then the angel
rubbed the honeycomb and vast numbers of bees issued
forth from it, all white as snow;[129] they alighted on Asenath,
the queen bees gathering on her face and making a honeycomb in her mouth,[130] of which all the bees ate until the
angel dismissed them and they all flew off to heaven.[131]
There were some bees that would have harmed Asenath,
but they had all fallen dead, until the angel stretched his rod
over them and said, "Arise and return to your place!" Then
all the dead bees were resurrected and "flew to the court of
the House of Asenath and lived in the garden there."[132]
When the angel touched the northern corner of the honeycomb with his forefinger, the mark left by the finger turned
to blood.[133]

The Matriarchal Queen Bee

Pierre Somville has pursued the Mediterranean bee cult to its Neolithic hive, which he equates with an archaic matriarchal order in which the bee, always feminine, figures as "the avatar of [the] Goddess" herself.[134]

What might be called the patriarchal takeover was by Jupiter Melissaeus, his name a dead giveaway. It was he who circulated from land to land, establishing kings and princes in whichever region would receive him and his cult in a covenant of hospitality and friendship, ordering "a hospitable throne to be erected in every place in which he rested, to preserve his memory."[135] Jupiter Melissaeus is obviously the wanderer, stranger, interloper, invader—the types with which he himself always has the most sympathy; and his name means not that he *was* the bee, but that he belonged to it or was connected with it. So Erechtheus, who had the male lead in the mysteries, acts only as "the husband of the 'Active Goddess' the Queen-bee."[136] Another missionary for the cause of male rule was Melissaeus the father of Adrasteia and Io, but it turns out that he was really the "Mother-Melissa, the goddess as Queen-bee."[137] It was rank usurpation, but even such chauvinists as Xenophon and Horapollo or the champions of the Emperor of the East, hard-pressed by the female members of his family, never go farther than making a metaphor of the "King-bee": the king is not a bee, but we should compare him with the leader of a hive and respect him *as if* he were such.[138]

We are dealing here with far more than a bit of antiquarian oddity. Among the oldest and holiest shrines found throughout the ancient world and still flourishing far and wide are the cult centers—holy caves, tombs, and springs—of the black virgins. Émile Saillens was able to study upwards of 200 such shrines in France alone, 190 existing as late as the sixteenth century.[139] He traces their origin back to the pre-Roman cults established by merchants and other migrants from the East, deriving the cult ultimately from the Egyptian Isis. One example must suffice: "Apollo, the brother of Diana, entered Gaule with the Romans, but the Celts had an Abellio, and Abellion was the god of the Sun among the Cretans. We have today at the eastern extremity of the Pyrenees a Cape Abeille [bee], near to Banyuls where the image of Our Lady of the Bees reigns. Is this conjunction fortuitous? The bees were the favorite symbol of Diana of the Ephesians," and "this Bee headland faces the rising sun and the distant home of the Phocaeans," those merchants who came from the East long ago.[140]

The bee, by its strange manner of life, is the supreme exponent of both the interdependence and the independence of the sexes, resulting in a perfect deadlock; the ancients were at a loss to determine the sex of the bees,[141] while the church fathers viewed them as an edifying example of total sexlessness.[142] Yet traditions describe the creatures as sex mad.[143]

Aristaeus the Bee Man and the Great Migrations

The earliest traditions of bee wanderings center around the figure of Aristaeus, probably the oldest of all Greek culture heroes.[144] Bacchylides puts him in the Jaredite or even the Enoch tradition, describing him as the son of Uranos and Gaia (e.g., Nut and Geb, respectively), "the Righteous Aristeaus," the only one of all his brethren to escape the great destruction of the human race.[145] In the beginning he traveled through the earth bringing the civilizing blessings of horticulture, and especially bee culture, to a benighted humanity. On the way from the northeast down to Africa, he passed through lands smitten by terrible drought attributed to the dire influence of the Dog Star, Sirius. To bring relief to the blasted lands, Aristaeus sacrificed with all the people on an altar built upon a mountain, to Zeus Ikmaios and to Sirius, thereby functioning as "an atoning priest."[146]

Aristaeus traveled with his mother, Cyrene, daughter of the Most High Zeus (Re, if you will), who was ravaged by Apollo, the sun-god, but gained immortal fame by overcoming a great lion that plagued the land.[147] Arriving in Africa, Aristaeus bestowed there his gifts of honey and olive oil; he also celebrated a super drinking bout with Dionysus, a contest in which the god of wine was the victor.[148] And there at the end of his journey he founded a city and a dynasty: the land was named Cyrene after his mother, and the dynasty was that of the Battids, the original possessors, H. R. Hall would believe, of the *bat* or *bi.t* titles of the rulers of Egypt.[149]

With Dionysus, Aristaeus shares the introduction of the mysteries. The nurse of the babe Dionysus taught Aristaeus the cultivation of honey (the milk and honey motif again); on the other hand, Aristaeus is supposed to have given the gift of honey to his daughter Makris, who herself fed it to the babe Dionysus in a cave on Corcyra, thus inciting the wrath of the great matriarch Hera, who forced her to flee: the "royal jelly," we might say, was not for the male! Later that same cave became the scene of the marriage of Jason and Medaea, the dire confrontation of clashing race and culture, implacable royal ambition, and rampant male and female chauvinism.[150]

But it is resurrection, the basic teaching of the mysteries in which Aristaeus is most involved, as his story is told by Virgil in the *Georgics,* the entire fourth book of which is devoted to the subject.

The reader may recognize our oldest flood motifs there—Aristaeus as Lamech or Gilgamesh visiting the seer at the end of the world to learn why the earth is being destroyed; the blighting of the land by Sirius and the Sun, the strange placing of a flood hero (Proteus, Oceanus, Utnapishtim, Enoch) on a desolate mountain range at the ends of the earth (the Carpathians, the Caucasus), and above all the dominant theme, the quest for resurrection, which takes Aristaeus into the heart of the Orphic mysteries. On ancient coins Aristaeus is shown accompanied by the Dog Star, Sirius, and in his images he usually carries a ram or ram's skin.[151]

Lactantius, discoursing on the false priesthood of the ancients, notes that the first mortal to sacrifice to the gods was Melissaeus, the king of Crete, whose name means not "bee" but belonging to the bee, and whose two daughters, Amalthea and Melissa, fed the infant Jove with goat's milk and honey. Melissa was installed by her father as the first priest (!) of the Great Mother, for which reason the devotees of the Great Mother are called bees (Melissai) to this day. Then Jove traveled through all the earth establishing kings and princes over the people among those who accepted his rule and worship. This he did either as Jupiter Melissaeus, or else there was an earlier Melissaeus (Jove's teacher) who wandered over all the world, setting up the false kingship and priesthood of Jupiter.[152] Scholars see in this myth the obvious supplanting of the old matriarchal rule of Crete by the male dominion of Zeus, the former represented by the bee and the goat,[153] both of which point to the Book of Abraham.

Where Abraham Comes In . . . The Two Migrations

It will be recalled that Abraham's mother was Amitla, long equated by scholars with Amalthea, and that Abraham as a newborn babe was fed milk and honey in a cave, the strange manner of feeding, from two white stones, being paralleled in the case of the infant Horus.[154] Horus's mother, however, was Hathor, the Cow; and Abraham's rivals, both as Pharaoh and Nimrod, sacrifice bulls, while Abraham by divine intervention sacrifices the ram in the thicket as an earnest of redemption and resurrection. All of which is apparently a rich complex of associations that binds the Joseph Smith Abraham to the ancient traditions. Is the Book of Abraham a pagan book, then? On the contrary, the Book of Abraham places the hero in a highly adverse situation vis-à-vis the world, completely surrounded and threatened by the decadent cults of his time, to which his own family subscribes, and from which he struggles to break free. He is trapped in the system and involved in its rites; we read of the prominence of the cult of Sirius and the Sun (Abraham 1:9), of the hierodules and the suffering virgins, of the great drought that dogs Abraham all his days, of the human sacrifices practiced to combat it, of the tension between matriarchy and the patriarchal order with which he has to deal on more than one occasion, of rival claims of priesthood and kingship, with the sacrificial substitutes for the king, and formal dramas of death and resurrection. Even the bees get into the Abraham picture, for the penalty of giving water to a stranger in the cities of the plain was to be covered with honey and stung to death by bees.[155]

If the earliest traditions of migrations of peoples insist on harping on the bees—and even the Hebrew word for the migrating of the hordes is "Bee swarms," *zibariah*[156]—then Joseph Smith puts us right into the picture. For he has told us not of one but of *two* separate migrations taking place shortly after the flood, starting from about the same place, from the Tower, but moving in opposite directions. Both parties toiled through the deserts of a blighted earth under dark and violent skies, moving toward promised lands. And the intimate and peculiar link between the two migrations is the friendly bee. The account of the Jaredite trek makes the bee explicitly a significant item in the baggage of the host: "And they did also carry with them deseret, which, by interpretation, is a honeybee; and thus they did carry with them swarms of bees" (Ether 2:3). Why the odd name, why used in the singular, if they took swarms? Here the bee

is representative and symbolic as well as real and recalls the
bee leaders and migrating swarms of the Maya migrations
in the book of Chumayel. The Latter-day Saints, ever settling and ever on the move, adopted the bee symbol from
the beginning. It caught their imagination, and they saw in it
exactly what the ancients did, the example of a society in
which "men lived together like bees,"[157] of the authority and
order by which they were ruled, and of the industry and
organization with which they gathered the sweets of the
field and enhanced their growth: in the State of Deseret, "our
lovely Deseret," the beehive symbol was everywhere.

When Sirius and the Sun combined their heat to destroy
the world, the wandering Aristaeus sought out the all-wise
Proteus at the ends of the earth, "seeking an oracle concerning the exhausted state of things,"[158] and was told to
make certain chthonian sacrifices, after which vast swarms
of bees came forth and restored fertility in the lands.[159] In
Greece, as elsewhere, the oldest of all religious centers
was established when the Bee maidens, the daughters of
Melissaeus and nurses of Zeus, swarmed at the sacred oak
of Dodona,[160] while sacred doves brought the oracular cult
of Ammon from Egypt.[161] The first oracular shrine in Israel
was founded by Deborah the Bee, where she died on the
migration from Egypt at the sacred Oak of Deborah.[162] The
procession that opened the celebration of the mysteries of
Eleusis was led by a sacred wagon along the Sacred Way (of
the Migration) by priestesses called the Melissai—the Bee
maidens or the Swarm.[163]

The serving maidens at Delphi were a chorus of Bees,
and the high priestess was called "the Bee." A recent archaeological discovery strikingly confirms the many legends that
trace the bee shrines to Egypt. It is the statuette of a singing
girl, found in the Temple of Delos, brought directly from
Neith's cult center at Sais, and inscribed with a supplication
by the girl to be remembered by the maidens "who have

been admitted to the temple of the Bee, . . . who have entered the sanctuary of Neith." "At Delos," write the discoverers, "the importance of the Egyptian cults thoroughly justifies the presence of the statuette."[164]

The Word *Deseret*

The Jaredite story gives us the code name of the migrating bee host in one direction; the Egyptian record gives us the same name for the operation in the other direction. It is the name *Deseret*. Abraham S. Yahuda saw in the word a definite tie between Egypt and Israel. He notes that "tesheret" in Egyptian means "the red one," i.e., the sterile barren land, and that in Genesis 3:19 Adam is made from "red ✝ earth," while in Genesis 3:23 "he was expelled from the 'garden' to till the 'red earth,'"[165] i.e., his first migration was really from the red land to the "black earth" of the land of Egypt, which was "like the garden of the Lord," recalling Eden. Deseret designates the land as the goal of migration—the promised land, quite literally, "the Holy Land."

What did the Egyptians mean by Deseret? We need only take the definitions in the order in which they occur in the *Wörterbuch*.[166] First (speaking of countries and of bees), is anything *red* by nature?[167] The feminine form *dšr.t* designates "Isis as a black-red woman,"[168] the prototype of the black virgins, which still sit in the bee caves all over the Old World; it is also blood or wine and the red jars that contain them;[169] it is the red and angry Eye of Horus; it is the red color of the land, the uniquely red land of Egypt and its deserts;[170] it is the red hair of certain divinities[171] and the red rage of the Lady who protects her son;[172] it is a vengeful goddess;[173] it is the sickness, the redness of the eye or of the sky, that afflicts mankind;[174] and it is blood and the drinking of blood.[175] The "nisbe" form, *dšr.ty* (cf. *bi.ti*), means "belonging to the Red One," and denotes the sun-god;[176] in a bloodthirsty sense it can apply both to the Sun and the Red Crown,[177] and *dšr.t* can mean "the wrath of the Red Crown," while *dšr* denotes also defilement of the waters.[178] *Dšr.t* denotes red vessels of water or wine, the former for ritual cleansing, the latter for breaking and pouring out the wine of wrath of Hathor, who for the celebration goes by the name of *Dšr.t*, "Mistress of the Two Red Jars"—one of purification, the other of vengeance.[179] All of which most forcefully suggests or recalls the coming of the Lady to Egypt, as we have described it above.

As early as the Pyramid Texts, *dšr.t* is the name of the Lady who rests at the mouth of the canyon,[180] and of the Red Crown, the bee crown of Neith, here called "the crown on the head of Re," the mane being also applied to the king who wore it.[181] The crown itself is "personified as a Goddess (Buto)" having the name of *Dšr.t*, a name also borne by the "priest both of the crown and the goddess."[182] Finally, *dšr.t* is the Red Land, the desert country as well as the holy Red Land of Lower Egypt itself, or simply Egypt, which is a red-rock country from one end to the other.[183]

Dsr written with a strong *d*—though often not to be distinguished in writing from the other—has the basic meaning of "opening the way" for someone,[184] be it the god's way to the temple or a migration through the desert or a waterway for the sacred bark on its cruise.[185] *Dsr* is also a special epithet of Ammon-Re as the sun or as a star, and any deity holding his scepter of power is *dsr*. For the commonest meaning of the root is glorious, holy, exalted,[186] either in general or applied to sacred edifices or the Way of the Initiate.[187] The adyton where the Lady spent her first night in Egypt was called *dsr.t*; the name is applied to sacred books, the secret archives,[188] but especially to the holy *land*, and the land of the gods.[189] It can be applied to persons, especially the king as the sacred image or representation of god, *tj.t dsr.t*.[190] It denotes kings and gods, "especially with reference to their position in the Temple, or their seat in the Ship."[191] As an intransitive verb it means to be holy or glorious,[192] designating places as "set apart," "special," and images as removed from vulgar contact, "removed to a sacred place," "concealed in the shrine," e.g., as the concealing of the image of Maat in one's breast from profane eyes[193]—reminding us of the meaning of Egyptus as "that which is forbidden." In this connection it means to honor, praise, exalt, adorn, protect, purify.[194] Of temples it means to make glorious and beautiful, sanctify, dedicate.[195] In the Middle Kingdom it was applied rarely to persons, often to places, and most naturally to a land or country, closely allied to the idea of purity;[196] thus the necropolis of Thebes was called *Tꜣ-ḏsr.t*, the Land Deseret, not as a graveyard but as a name of good omen, the best possible name.[197] The name was applied to wine, honey (mead), and milk as used in ritual.[198] As a goddess, *ḏsr.t* is the Moon's Eye, also a scepter, an offering table, and a gate to the beyond.[199]

In hieroglyphic writing the pictures of the Bee and the Red Crown are often exchanged for each other and are pronounced just alike, whether as *bi.t*, *n.t*, or *ḥb.t*, though it is important to note that none of these titles has as yet been determined with absolute certainty.[200]

While the most common name for the Red Crown is *dšr.t*, "the Red One," that is the only one of its names *not* applied to the Bee as well. Why not, since the epithet seems particularly fitted to the sacred bee as holy, glorious, and red? Alan Gardiner gives a hint when he explains that in the titles, the crown has been "substituted for the bee for superstitious reasons."[201] Otto takes us further, noting with wonder "the absence of the bee among the sacred creatures of ancient Egypt," and that in the bee cult of the Delta "the Bee itself never appears."[202] In the mysteries of Abydos, Osiris himself is the *bity* who "keeps secret that which is to be concealed in the Holy of Holies."[203] The true nature of the bee sign "could no longer be grasped" in historic times.[204] The brother-and-sister pair of the *bity* were Shu and Tefnut, originally anonymous, and in the Pyramid Texts their title is a cryptogram concealing "the Hidden one, the most hidden one of the land."[205] Originally the bee title designated a sacred, prehistoric kingship, "a spiritual entity" existing "before the creation of the cosmos, . . . a holy kingdom stretching back even to the preexistence," etc.[206] If the king as *niswt* was always holy, as *bity* he was super-holy, a condition requiring concealment from the world.

For some such reason the sacred name of the Bee has been withheld from common knowledge. The fact that Pharaoh had "a monopoly on the collection and production of honey," and that a gift of honey was a royal prerogative reserved as the highest honor for high officials, suggests that *dšr.t* as the royal and ritual word for bee was taboo to the vulgar. That bee culture could be not only a monopoly but a trade secret appears in the surprising fact that bee lore, for all its great antiquity, was not worldwide: "There was never any real apiculture" in Mesopotamia, according to Robert J. Forbes's study, and "wild honey or apiculture do not form a part of ancient Chinese civilization."[207] That anything as ancient and elementary as bee culture should be limited to one sector of the ancient world, in which definite contact and exchange between the various peoples practicing it can be clearly established, is definite indication that we are dealing with a single religious tradition and not with a universal primitive expression of biological necessity.

The long researches of Elise Baumgartel (1975) make her conclusions on the subject of Min, the Mother, and the Bee the safest to follow, as well as the latest. The Red Crown was, according to her, "the most ancient and the most exalted, the one that was venerated as a *goddess*," the only crown worn by predynastic kings long before it became the property of the North.[208] "The ancient titles and insignia, all

. . . had their origin in *Upper* Egypt, while nothing comparable is known from Lower Egypt during the early period."[209] That crown was worn by *Min*, who from the beginning was "*bit*, 'the beekeeper,'" and at the same time "'the bull of his mother,'" and "'the king of the gods.'"[210] "He resides at Coptos, and the country east of Egypt to the Red Sea is his kingdom."[211] The first inhabitants of Egypt, the people of Naqada I, who seem to have been matriarchal, "venerated the great goddess and also a young male god who is generally associated with her. He is her *son* and lover."[212] "Min, on the other hand, is the exponent of a *patriarchal* society. . . . While the great goddess has a young lover and is the first of the *cows*, Min is the god of the corn" and, so Baumgartel suggests, would not need the Lady in his rites.[213] Yet it is he who introduces the title "bull of His Mother," from which we assume that *he* is that same Min. His "still unidentified fetish" (the double-arrow of the migration [fig. 104]—Liahona)[214] appears first in the boat pictures on the decorated Naqada II ware (see fig. 94, p. 595),[215] when "the Horus title" also appears, "closely connected with the First Dynasty, the kings of which were called later 'the followers of Horus.'"[216] The various names of the youthful son and consort merely confirm the story at various levels, from Naqada I to full dynastic times.

Of recent years the hitherto exotic name *Essene* has come into common usage, thanks to the Dead Sea Scrolls, which have brought to light the existence of a pious community of desert sectaries whose general way of life can be designated by the generic name of Essene. Many such societies were found throughout the ancient Near East, and the name has been expressly applied to groups in Egypt, Palestine, and Greece, all having in common requirements of chastity and charity in service to God and man.

The word *Essene* first appears in the works of a poet who served at the court of a Ptolemid pharaoh, who

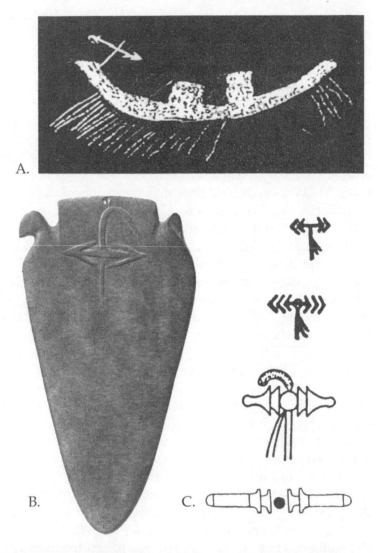

Figure 104. This archaic rock etching from Wadi Hammamat depicts a many-oared boat with two cabins and a standard of Min in the stern (A). The double-headed arrow also appears on this predynastic slate palette from al-Amra (B). The emblem of Min can take a variety of forms, as shown by these examples (C).

remarks in his *Hymn to Zeus* that the god did not become the "Essene" or supreme ruler of the gods by chance, but by merit.[217] Origen, another Alexandrian, informs us that "Essene" means the leader of bees, or, as Geoffrey W. H. Lampe puts it, *"king* (i.e., *queen*) bee."[218] Members of the society that performed the rites of the ever-virgin Artemis (Paul's "Diana of the Ephesians") had to keep pure and unspotted from the world during their year of service, but the high priest and priestess were vowed to perpetual chastity: "The people of Ephesus call them Essenes," writes Pausanius.[219] That is not surprising in view of the fact that Artemis was a bee-goddess, whose emblem of the bee was stamped on all the coins of the city.

Philo compares the Essene societies of Palestine to other such communities in Greece and Persia,[220] and Josephus notes that the Essene community to which he once belonged followed the same order as did the Pythagoreans of the West.[221] Jerome, puzzled by the dedication of Christian congregations to the Easter cult of the bee, can only justify it by appealing to the Essenes of Egypt who imitate Deborah (the name means "bee") in their zeal and gather the honey of Christ.[222] Somville has very recently shown that the cult of the Bee mother was flourishing all around the Mediterranean in prehistoric times,[223] and Saillens has argued that trade alone could account for the presence of the same cult all over Europe,[224] though the legends speak of bee-led immigrations at the dawn of history, seeking not commerce but refuge from storm and starvation—survival.

What ties it all together is Asenath, the queen of the Deseret hive, then and now, as the mother of Ephraim and Manasseh by Joseph, whom she married in the midst of a swarm of bees, bringing her honey and covering her person to do her reverence. Her name is generally explained today as "meaning in Egyptian 'she belongs to, or is the servant of, [the goddess] Neith,'"[225] Neith being the primal Bee mother of the Egyptians. There are other derivations, but since the root meaning of *Essen* is unknown [Syriac *asan*, to gather food supplies, Aramaic *asya, asyyna*, etc., all meaning to cure, heal, revive, associated by Carl Brockelman with "Essene, Therapeut?"],[226] it is not too much to suggest a connection between *Essen, Asse,* and *Asen-ath,* the final *-ath* being the universal Semitic (and Egyptian) feminine singular ending; Asenath herself was undeniably the queen bee when she married Joseph.

Why has the bee been brought back to our consciousness among the more exotic baggage of the restored gospel? The most likely explanation is the least appealing one. Repeated echoes from the remote past keep reminding us that the office and calling of the bee was to bring about the stirrings of life, reviving the biological cycle in a world that had been totally ravaged by cosmic forces of destruction. Is, then, Deseret waiting in the wings, held in reserve against the day, soon to come, when its salutary services will be required again?

From the first the symbol of the bee captivated the imagination of the Latter-day Saints in their migrations and their settlements; the emblematic hive became the seal of the territory and state and adorned every important edifice within the vast expanse of "our lovely Deseret." Finally, by what strange coincidence does the *History of the Church* end with the sign of the bee? After the martyrdom of Joseph and Hyrum Smith, "the bodies . . . were removed . . . at Emma's request, to near the Mansion, and buried side by side, and the bee house then moved and placed over their graves."[227]

Notes

1. Henri Gauthier, *Les fêtes du dieu Min* (Cairo: BIFAO, 1931), 142.

2. Pierre Montet, "Le fruit défendu," *Kemi* 11 (1950): 105.

3. Gauthier, *Fêtes du dieu Min*, 247; see also Eugène Lefébure, "L'abeille en Égypte," *Sphinx* 11 (1908): 1–25.

4. Eugène Lefébure, "Les huttes de Cham," *BE* 36 (1915): 224.

5. Pierre Montet, "Études sur quelques prêtres et fonctionnaires du dieu Min," *JNES* 9 (1950): 24–25.

6. Alan H. Gardiner, *Egyptian Grammar* (Oxford: Oxford University Press, 1957), 51, 73.

7. Eberhard Otto, "Der Gebrauch des Königstitels *bjtj*," *ZÄS* 85 (1960): 145, 152.

8. Adriaan de Buck, *The Egyptian Readingbook* (Leiden: Nederlands Instituut voor het Nabije Oosten, 1963), 50, 53.

9. Otto, "Gebrauch des Königstitels *bjtj*," 143.

10. Hugo Müller, *Die Formale Entwicklung der Titulatur der ägyptischen Könige* (Glückstadt: Augustin, 1938), 44.

11. Otto, "Gebrauch des Königstitels *bjtj*," 146–47.

12. Gardiner, *Egyptian Grammar*, 477, 504.

13. Gerald A. Wainwright, "The Red Crown in Early Prehistoric Times," *JEA* 9 (1923): 26.

14. Ibid., 29.

15. Ibid., 32.

16. Peter Le Page Renouf, "A Second Note on the Royal Title 'Bee,'" *Proceedings of the Biblical Archaeology Society* 14 (1892): 396–402; Peter Le Page Renouf, "Book of the Dead," *Proceedings of the Biblical Archaeology Society* 15 (1893): 227 n. 1; and *The Life-Work of Sir Peter Le Page Renouf*, 4 vols. (Paris: Leroux, 1902–5), 2:442–54. Kurt H. Sethe, "Der Name des Königs von Unterägypten," *ZÄS* 28 (1890): 125–26. W. Max Müller, "Der Name des Königs von Unterägypten," *ZÄS* 30 (1892): 57–59. Eugéne Lefébure, "Un des noms de la royauté septentrionale," *BE* 35 (1912): 321–26. Karl Piehl, "Varia V," *ZÄS* 25 (1887): 39–41. W. Pleyte, "La Guêpe," *ZÄS* 4 (1866): 14–15. Some insisted that the creature was a wasp, Le Page Renouf, "Second Note on the Royal Title 'Bee,'" 396–402; Pleyte, "Guêpe," 14–15; Pierre Lacau, "Suppressions et modifications de signes dans les textes funéraires," *ZÄS* 51 (1913): 57, in spite of the epithet of Melissa's—"honey-bearing." Since there are over twenty thousand species of bees, even experts are not clear on the point.

17. *Wb*, 1:435.

18. Kurt H. Sethe, *Urgeschichte und älteste Religion der Ägypter* (Leipzig: Deutsch-Morgenländische Gesellschaft, 1930), 69–70.

19. Ibid., 70, 6; Otto, "Gebrauch des Königstitels *bjtj*," 143.

20. Henri Gauthier, *Le personnel du dieu Min* (Cairo: BIFAO, 1931), 86.

21. Leiden Papyrus T32, 6/23–25, in Bruno H. Stricker, ed., "De Egyptische Mysteriën: Pap. Leiden T32 (slot)," *OMRO* 37 (1956): 57.

22. Sethe, *Urgeschichte und älteste Religion der Ägypter*, 70.

23. Gauthier, *Fêtes du dieu Min*, 244, 246.

24. Sethe, *Urgeschichte und älteste Religion der Ägypter*, 67.

25. Otto, "Gebrauch des Königstitels *bjtj*," 143; Sethe, *Urgeschichte und älteste Religion der Ägypter*, 69.

26. Sethe, *Urgeschichte und älteste Religion der Ägypter*, 69.

27. See below, note 136. It is noteworthy that they compare the king to the leader of the hive metaphorically, without actually calling him the bee. Thus, according to Chaeremon, "The Egyptians draw a bee to represent the king." Wilhelm Spiegelberg, *Der ägyptische Mythus vom Sonnenauge* (Strassburg: Schultz, 1917), 25 n. 16. "The Egyptians indicate the King by a species of honey-making bee," Ammianus Marcellinus, *Constantius et Gallus* XVII, 4, 11, in Theodor Hopfner, *Fontes Historiae Religionis Aegyptiacae* (Bonn: Marcus and Weber, 1922), 548. Of Cyrus, the model king, Xenophon says, "You seem to me to be a king by nature, no less than the king in a hive of bees." Xenophon, *Cyropaedia* V, 1, 24. See above, pp. 626–28.

28. Sethe, *Urgeschichte und älteste Religion der Ägypter*, 68.

29. Ibid., 69.

30. Adolf Rusch, *Die Entwicklung der Himmelsgöttin Nut zu einer Totengottheit*, Mitteilungen der Vorderasiatisch-Aegyptischen Gesellschaft, vol. 27 (Leipzig: Hinrichs, 1922), 15.

31. Müller, *Formale Entwicklung der Titulatur*, 46; Pyramid Text 444 (§824).

32. Le Page Renouf, "Book of the Dead," 227 n. 1.

33. W. Max Müller, "Der Name des Königs von Unterägyptendes Zeidrens der Biene," *ZÄS* 30 (1892): 57.

34. See above, pp. 432–42.

35. Kurt H. Sethe, "Über einen vermeintlichen Lautwerth des Zeichens der Biene," *ZÄS* 30 (1892): 115.

36. Ibid.

37. Alexandre Piankoff, "Les deux papyrus 'mythologiques' de Her-Ouben au Musée du Caire," *ASAE* 49 (1949): 129–44.

38. Hans Bonnet, *Reallexikon der ägyptischen Religionsgeschichte* (Berlin: de Gruyter, 1952), 131.

39. Otto, "Gebrauch des Königstitels *bjtj*," 147–49.

40. Ibid., 149. The bee was "the primordial creative divine power . . . the most hidden secret of the land."

41. Cf. Sylvain Grébaut, trans., *Livre des mystères du ciel et de la terre* 4, 3, in *PO* 6:429.

42. Otto, "Gebrauch des Königstitels *bjtj*," 149–51.

43. *Joseph and Asenath* 16:14, in Paul Riessler, *Altjüdisches Schrifttum ausserhalb der Bibel* (Heidelberg: Kerle, 1927), 519. For an English translation, see C. Burchard, trans., *Joseph and Aseneth*, in *The Old Testament*

Pseudepigrapha, ed. James H. Charlesworth, 2 vols. (Garden City, NY: Doubleday, 1985), 2:230.

44. Grébaut, *Livre des mystères du ciel et de la terre* 4, 3, in *PO* 6:429.

45. Papyrus Salt 825 2/5–8, in Philippe Derchain, *Le Papyrus Salt 825 (British Museum 10051), rituel pour la conservation de la vie en Égypte* (Brussels: Academie Royale, 1965), 1:137.

46. Jacob Grimm, *Teutonic Mythology*, ed. J. Sallybrass, 4 vols. (London: Bell, 1882–88), 2:695; Friedrich Dieterici, *Thier und Mensch vor dem König der Genien* (1879; reprint, Hildesheim: Olms, 1969), 4.

47. Papyrus Salt 825 2/5–6, in Derchain, *Papyrus Salt 825*, 137.

48. Immanuel Velikovsky, *Worlds in Collision* (New York: Macmillan 1950), 134–38; Immanuel Velikovsky, *Ages in Chaos* (New York: Doubleday, 1952).

49. Albrecht Götze, "Kleinasien," in *Kulturgeschichte des alten Orients* (Munich: Beck, 1933), 135. Cf. Otto, "Gebrauch des Königstitels *bjtj*," 151.

50. Papyrus Salt 825 2/5–6, in Derchain, *Papyrus Salt 825*, 137.

51. See above, p. 470.

52. Papyrus Salt 825 2/2–3, in Derchain, *Papyrus Salt 825*, 137.

53. Papyrus Salt 825 2/4, in ibid.

54. Édouard Naville, "La destruction des hommes par les dieux," *Transactions of the Society of Biblical Archaeology* 4 (1875): 1–19.

55. Papyrus Salt 825 3/1, in Derchain, *Papyrus Salt 825*, 137.

56. Papyrus Salt 825 3/3, in ibid.

57. Papyrus Salt 825 3/2, in ibid.

58. Papyrus Salt 825 2/7, in ibid.

59. Jane Harrison, *Prolegomena to the Study of Greek Religion* (New York: Meridian, 1959), 356.

60. See above, p. 470.

61. Götze, "Kleinasien," 135–36.

62. Adolph Jellinek, *Bet ha-Midrasch*, 6 vols. (1853–77; reprint, Jerusalem: Wahrmann, 1967), 5:22–26. Best known from Thaʿlabi's Arabic text in Rudolf-Ernst Brünnow, *Chrestomathy of Arabic Prose-Pieces* (Berlin: Reuther and Reichard, 1895), 1–22.

63. Frank Waters, *Book of the Hopi* (New York: Viking, 1963), 13–16, and various native informants. Another insect with which the Egyptians seem to have associated the royal progress, if not the migrations, is the ⎸ centipede, represented by the twenty-one litter-bearers of the pharaoh going forth in the land, whose forty-two feet combine to equal those of the questing creature. Victor Loret, "Le mille-pattes et la chaise à porteurs de pharaon," *RdE* 6 (1951): 5–20.

64. Cf. Brünnow, *Chrestomathy of Arabic Prose-Pieces*, 18–19.

65. Robert Graves, *The Greek Myths*, 2 vols. (New York: Braziller, 1959), 1:213.

66. Spiegelberg, *Ägyptische Mythus vom Sonnenauge*, 24–25, lines 15–26.

67. Ibid., 23, 25, e.g., 13–14.

68. Hermann Junker, *Die Onurislegende* (Vienna: Hölder, 1917), 44.

69. *Book of the Cow,* col. 19, in Charles Maystre, "Le livre de la vache du ciel dans les tombeaux de la Vallée des Rois," *BIFAO* 40 (1941): 70.

70. Pyramid Text 470 (§919). Cf. Émile Massoulard, *Préhistoire et protohistoire d'Égypte* (Paris: Institut d'Ethnologie, 1949), 482–83.

71. Pyramid Text 610 (§1719a, 1723c).

72. Leiden Papyrus T32 6/25, in Stricker, "Egyptische mysteriën (slot)," 57.

73. Leiden Papyrus T32 7/2, in ibid., 58.

74. Spiegelberg, *Ägyptische Mythus vom Sonnenauge*, 55.

75. Coffin Text 130, in Adriaan de Buck, *The Egyptian Coffin Text*, 7 vols. (Chicago: University of Chicago Press, 1938), 2:150.

76. Moritz Mainzer, "Jagd, Fischfang und Bienenzucht bei den Juden in der tannäischen Zeit," *Monatsschrift für Geschichte und Wissenschaft des Judentums* 53 (1909): 539–40, 549 n. 3; cf. Deuteronomy 32:13.

77. Cf. Lefébure, "Huttes de Cham," 224.

78. Gauthier, *Fêtes du dieu Min*, 288. See Lefébure," L'abeille en Égypte," 1–25.

79. Philip J. Baldensperger, *The Immovable East* (Boston: Small, Maynard, 1913), 278–79.

80. Gustaf H. Dalman, "Das Land, das mit Milch und Honig fließt," *Mitteilungen des deutschen Palästina-Vereins* (1905): 27; Gustaf H. Dalman, "Nochmals Milch und Honig," *Mitteilungen des deutschen Palästina-Vereins* (1906): 82.

81. Baldensperger, *Immovable East*, 278–79.

82. Cf. Dieterici, *Thier und Mensch*, 4–5.

83. Ralph L. Roy, trans., *The Book of Chilam Balam of Chumayel* (Washington, D.C.: Carnegie Institute, 1933), 64 n. 4; 65 n. 6: "the word for wild bee . . . has the feminine prefix."

84. Ibid., 66.

85. Ibid., 100.

86. Ibid., 171.

87. Victor Loret, "Quelques idées sur la forme primitive de certaines religions égyptiennes," *Revue Égyptologique* 11 (1904): 97; and Victor Loret, "Les enseignes militaires des tribus et les symboles hiéroglyphiques des divinités," *Revue Égyptologique* 10 (1902): 94–101. Massoulard, *Préhistoire et protohistoire d'Égypte*, 482, with plates: most of the earliest standards

were arrow-standards, the most significant being the crossed arrows of Neith and Min. This suggested the Liahona, and it is striking coincidence that Jonathan Shunary, upon first opening the Book of Mormon, identified the word Liahona with a Jewish gematria designating the leader of a swarm of migrating bees in the desert.

88. Otto, "Gebrauch des Königstitels *bjtj*," 144.

89. Hugh W. Nibley, *The Message of the Joseph Smith Papyri: An Egyptian Endowment* (Salt Lake City: Deseret Book, 1975), 188–89.

90. Hermann Kees, "Zum Ursprung der sog. Horusdiener," *Nachrichten von der Gesellschaft der Wissenschaften zu Göttingen* 3 (1927): 204.

91. Ibid., 207.

92. Otto, "Gebrauch des Königstitels *bjtj*," 145; Adolf Erman and Hermann Grapow, *Aegyptische Handwörterbuch* (Berlin: Reuther and Reichard, 1921), 223.

93. Otto, "Gebrauch des Königstitels *bjtj*," 143–52.

94. Elizabeth D. Van Buren, "Mesopotamian Fauna in the Light of the Monuments," *Archiv für Orientforschung* 11 (1936–37): 30–31.

95. Robert J. Forbes, *Studies in Ancient Technology*, 9 vols. (Leiden: Brill, 1966), 5:81, 88.

96. Grimm, *Teutonic Mythology*, 2:696, citing many authors.

97. Discussed by Lefébure, "Huttes de Cham," 220–24; cf. Montet, "Quelques prêtres et fonctionnaires," 24–25.

98. Spiegelberg, *Ägyptische Mythus vom Sonnenauge*, 25.

99. Alexandre Moret, *Mystères égyptiens* (Paris: Colin, 1913), 54, fig. 18.

100. Carl C. Clemen, *Religionsgeschichte Europas*, 2 vols. (Heidelberg: Winter, 1926), 1:339–40; Grimm, *Teutonic Mythology*, 2:696.

101. Clemen, *Religionsgeschichte Europas*, 1:339–40.

102. Pierre Somville, "L'abeille et le taureau," *RHR* 194 (1978): 135.

103. Ludwig Preller, *Griechische Mythologie*, 2 vols., 5th ed. (Berlin: Weidmann, 1964–67), 1:133 (mentioning the bee cave where the pure honey is produced which serves as the first nourishment for the offspring of the gods); Porphyry, *De antro Nympharum*, 1, 7–8, 13; for an English translation, see Thomas Taylor, trans., *On the Cave of the Nymphs in the Thirteenth Book of the Odyssey* (London: Watkins, 1917), 7, 20–25, 33.

104. Victor Loret, "Les fêtes d'Osiris au mois de Khoiak," *RT* 3 (1881): 43–44 (author's translation).

105. Otto, "Gebrauch des Königstitels *bjtj*," 147–48.

106. Moret, *Mystères égyptiens*, 54.

107. Arnobius, *Disputation against the Gentiles* V, 19, in *PL* 5:1120.

108. Apollodorus, *The Library* III, 3, 1.

109. Grimm, *Teutonic Mythology*, 2:696–97.

110. Herodotus, *History* I, 198.

111. Walter H. Robert-Tornow, *De Apium Mellisque apud Veteres Significatione* (Berlin: Weidmann, 1893), 122–26.

112. Pyramid Text 431 (§781).

113. Ibid., 444 (§824).

114. Moret, *Mystères égyptiens*, 53.

115. Eberhard Otto, *Das ägyptische Mundöffnungsritual*, 2 vols. (Wiesbaden: Harrassowitz, 1960), 2:56–57 n. 10.

116. E. A. Wallis Budge, *The Book of Opening of the Mouth*, 2 vols. (London: Paul, Trench, Trübner, 1909), 1:31.

117. Ibid., 1:34.

118. Heinrich Günther, *Die christliche Legende des Abendlandes* (Heidelberg: Winter, 1910), 160. Louis M. O. Duchesne, *Origines du culte chrétien* (Paris: Thorin, 1925), 266–69, a standard sermon on the role of the bee in the Christian mysteries.

119. Pausanius, *Description of Greece* X, 5, 9; Graves, *Greek Myths*, 1:178.

120. Jerome, *Epistle* XVIII, "Ad Praesidium, De Cereo Paschali," 1, in *PL* 30:182–83.

121. Ibid., 4, in *PL* 30:185–86.

122. Source not found; see preface.

123. Hugh W. Nibley, "A New Look at the Pearl of Great Price," *IE* 72 (January 1969): 30.

124. *Joseph and Asenath* 16:4–6, text in Riessler, *Altjüdisches Schrifttum ausserhalb der Bibel*, 519.

125. *Joseph and Asenath* 16:7, in ibid., 518.

126. *Joseph and Asenath* 15, in ibid., 519.

127. *Joseph and Asenath* 14, in ibid.

128. *Joseph and Asenath* 15–16, in ibid.

129. *Joseph and Asenath* 17–18, in ibid.

130. *Joseph and Asenath* 19, in ibid., 519–20.

131. *Joseph and Asenath* 20–21, in ibid., 520.

132. *Joseph and Asenath* 23, in ibid.

133. *Joseph and Asenath* 17, in ibid., 519.

134. Somville, "L'abeille et le taureau," 132.

135. Lactantius, *On False Religion* I, 22, in *PL* 6:248–50.

136. Kruse, "Melissaios," takes notes of the male-chauvinist conquest of Melissaeus, in Pauly-Wissowa, *Real-Enzyclopädie der classischen Altertumswissenschaft* (Stuttgart: Metzler, 1894–1978), 15:1:528–29. The quotation is from Graves, *Greek Myths*, 1:169.

137. Graves, *Greek Myths*, 1:42.

138. References by Olck, "Biene," in Pauly-Wissowa, *Real-Enzyclopädie,* 3:446–50; see Otto, "Gebrauch des Königstitels *bjtj,*" 143.

139. Émile Saillens, *Nos vierges noires, leurs origines* (Paris: Editions Universelles, 1945), 20–23.

140. Ibid., 77.

141. "So herrschte eine grosse Unklarheit über die Sexualität der B[iene]." Olck, "Biene," 432.

142. Duchesne, *Origines du culte chrétien,* 266; Jerome, *Epistle* 13, "Ad Praesidium, De Cereo Paschali," in *PL* 30:182, "quod sine coitu generatur et generant."

143. Eduard Stucken, *Astralymythen der Hebräer, Babylonier und Ägypter* (Leipzig: Pfeiffer, 1896–1907), 207, recounting in particular the Indian Vasu legend.

144. Hiller von Gaertringen, "Aristaios," in Pauly-Wissowa, *Real-Enzyclopädie,* 2:852–56.

145. Ibid., 856.

146. Ibid., 853–54, comparing Aristaeus to Epimenides.

147. Ibid., 853.

148. Ibid., 855–57.

149. Ibid., 856. Herodotus, *History* IV, 155; H. R. Hall, *The Ancient History of the Near East* (London: Methuen, 1927), 97–98.

150. Von Gaertringen, "Aristaios," 854–55.

151. Ibid., 857–58.

152. Lactantius, *On False Religion* I, 22, in *PL* 6:248–50.

153. Kruse, "Melissaios," 528.

154. Nibley, "A New Look at the Pearl of Great Price," *IE* 72 (January 1969): 30.

155. Louis Ginzberg, *Legends of the Jews,* 7 vols. (Philadelphia: Jewish Publication Society, 1909–13), 1:250.

156. Bernhard Beer, *Leben Abraham's nach Auffassung der jüdischen Sage* (Leipzig: Leiner, 1859), 133. See Exodus 23:28.

157. The concept is a favorite with classical writers, listed by Olck, "Biene," 446–48.

158. Virgil, *Georgics* IV, 425–49.

159. Ibid., lines 548–58.

160. C. Julius Hyginus, *Fabularum Liber* (1535; reprint, New York: Garland, 1976), 50 n. 182.

161. Herodotus, *History* II, 55.

162. Genesis 35:8; *Jubilees* 32:30–31.

163. Theodorus Hopfner, "Mysterien," in Pauly-Wissowa, *Real-Enzyclopädie,* 16:2:1226; for other bee swarms of maidens, ibid., 15:1:524–26.

164. Jean Leclant and Hermann Meulenaere, "Une statuette égyptienne a Délos," *Kêmi* 14 (1957): 34–40 (quotations from 36, 40).

165. Abraham S. Yahuda, *The Accuracy of the Bible* (London: Heinemann, 1934), 150–51.

166. *Wb*, vol. 5.

167. Ibid., 5:487–88.

168. Ibid., 489.

169. Ibid.

170. Ibid.

171. Ibid.

172. Ibid., 490.

173. Ibid.

174. Ibid.

175. Ibid., 491.

176. Ibid., 492.

177. Ibid.

178. Ibid.

179. Ibid., 493.

180. Pyramid Text 470 (§910d–911a).

181. *Wb*, 5:493.

182. Ibid., 494.

183. Ibid., 489, 493.

184. Ibid., 609.

185. Ibid., 609–10.

186. Ibid., 610.

187. Ibid., 611.

188. Ibid.

189. Ibid.

190. Ibid.

191. Ibid., 612.

192. Ibid., 613.

193. Ibid., 614.

194. Ibid.

195. Ibid.

196. Ibid., 615.

197. Ibid., 616.

198. Ibid.

199. Ibid., 617.

200. Gardiner, *Egyptian Grammar*, 504.

201. Ibid.

202. Otto, "Gebrauch des Königstitels *bjtj*," 143–44.

203. Ibid., 147.

204. Ibid., 148.

205. Ibid., 148–49.

206. Ibid., 149–50.

207. Forbes, *Studies in Ancient Technology*, 5:81, 88.

208. Elise J. Baumgartel, "Some Remarks on the Origins of the Titles of the Archaic Egyptian Kings," *JEA* 61 (1975): 28–32, esp. p. 28 (emphasis added).

209. Ibid., 32.

210. Ibid., 29.

211. Ibid.

212. Ibid. (emphasis added).

213. Ibid., 30.

214. See Hugh W. Nibley, *Since Cumorah*, 2nd ed. (Salt Lake City: Deseret Book and FARMS, 1988), 251–63.

215. Ibid., 29.

216. Ibid., 30.

217. Callimachus, *Hymn to Zeus*, lines 65–68.

218. Geoffrey W. H. Lampe, ed., *A Patristic Greek Lexicon* (Oxford: Claredon, 1961), 551, citing Origen, *Commentaria in Evangelium Secundum Matthaseum (Commentary on Matthew)* X, 7, in *PG* 13:849. See esp. Hjalmar Frisk, *Griechisches etymologisches Wörterbuch* (Heidelberg: Winter, 1960), 575.

219. Pausanius, *Description of Greece* VIII, 13, 1.

220. Philo, *Quod omnis probus liber sit (Every Good Man Is Free)* XII, 75–88.

221. Josephus, *Antiquities* XV, 371.

222. Jerome, *Epistle* XVIII, "Ad Praesidium, De Cereo Paschali," 4, in *PL* 30:185–86.

223. Somville, "L'abeille et le taureau," 129–46.

224. Saillens, *Nos vierges noires, leurs origines*, 20–23.

225. Nahum M. Sarna, "Asenath," in *Encyclopaedia Judaica*, 3:694.

226. Carl Brockelmann, *Lexicon Syriacum* (Halis Saxonum: Niemeyer, 1928), 35; Marcus Jastrow, *Dictionary of the Targumim, the Talmud Babli and Yerushalmi, and the Midrashic Literature*, 2 vols. (New York: Pardes, 1950), 1:92–93, 95; probably of Asia Minor origin, Frisk, *Griechisches etymologisches Wörterbuch*, 575.

227. Joseph Smith, *History of the Church of Jesus Christ of Latter-day Saints*, 7 vols. (Salt Lake City: Deseret Book, 1950), 6:628–29.

13

Conclusion: A Rough Recapitulation

The first order of business in studying the Book of Abraham is to remove the obstacle that has been diligently erected to prevent anyone from reading it. The Book of Abraham, and especially the explanations of the facsimiles, is routinely put forward as Joseph Smith's supreme indiscretion, his one fatal blunder, so gross and obvious that a casual word from any true scholar should be enough to blow it away. Unfortunately for the critics, they can make no real case against it until they do read it. So there things have stood for a century and a half. During that time knowledge of the world of Abraham, historical or mythical, has grown at an accelerating pace, until now the student who wishes to do justice to the subject must be prepared to open veritable floodgates of comparative study. If he does, he will find that the Book of Abraham is a miraculous performance.

He should note first of all that the book contains many things about Abraham which are not found in the Old Testament but which have striking parallels in the apocryphal Abraham literature, whose importance is being more appreciated every day. The apocryphal literature tells, for example, of idolatry and child sacrifice; of the threat to

648

Abraham's life by his family; of his strange sacrifice on a mountain and his mounting up to the heavens to be shown a wonderful picture, a circular plan of the cosmos, whose 𐤀 key was transmitted by the Holy Ghost in the form of a dove; of how Abraham takes up where Noah leaves off; of how Abraham, on undertaking a dangerous journey, was admonished to remember how God had delivered him from the altar; of how Abraham is sore afflicted at Sarah's plight and prays for her deliverance from Pharaoh's bed or displeasure.

The Book of Abraham also contains important and peculiar details not found in the Bible but occurring in *both* the Hebrew and Egyptian reports, such as Pharaoh's offering human sacrifice in time of drought—the victims being members of his own family; the leading role of the hierodules and the putting to death of royal virgins; the peculiar type of altar on which the sacrifice was made; the victim on the altar praying fervidly for deliverance, in reply to which an angel appears; at the same time the voice of God is heard from heaven, the victim being miraculously delivered by an earthquake that overthrows the altar and kills the priest; after which the liberated victim mounts the throne; how being on the throne he teaches astronomy to the royal court; how he writes an autobiographical account in the first person for the instruction of his posterity; how he examines the records of the fathers to establish his own line; how the king of Egypt had serious doubts about his own divine descent and right to rule; how the king was much concerned with the study of the stars; how Abraham preferred astronomy to astrology, though they were closely related; how cosmology is a fundamental part of basic ritual and doctrine; how Abraham used a circular drawing showing the 𐤀 relationship of ruling powers in the cosmos—a chart represented by Hebrew cabalistic drawings and the Egyptian hypocephalus; how the doctrine of our premortal existence is essential to the creation story; how the cosmic drama begins with a great council of the gods in heaven; how the four canopic figures are like apocalyptic beasts, indicating the four quarters of the earth; how the two opposing halves of the circle show the duality of light vs. dark, peace vs. war, etc.; how Sirius and the Sun were worshiped together as Shagreel, for the relief of drought; how the main theme of the whole Abraham history is the rivalry for the priesthood and kingship, the periodic showdown that is at the heart of the ubiquitous year-rite. All this and much more you will find in the Book of Abraham, the traditions of Canaan and Israel, and the records of the Egyptians.

Facsimile 3 gives us a picture of Abraham at court with king, prince, commoner, and slave all present for a special family night at court—an arrangement recently shown to be typical of Pharaoh's palace life. Facsimile 1 shows the sacrificial scene that is not an embalming scene but a rescue and resurrection, with the man on the couch stirring to life; the altar having the form of a bed—as it really did among the Egyptians; the angel being represented in the form of a hawk; the rites taking place in "Chaldea," where the idolatrous god of Pharaoh was honored by the presence of four local idols, a situation faithfully described in some Egyptian romances; the "idolatrous god of Pharaoh" as a crocodile, as indeed he was—Sobek, the exclusive and primal god of Pharaoh and his family.

So we need not apologize for the Egyptian preoccupation of the Book of Abraham. As is well-known, the patriarchal narratives are closely bound to Egypt: Isaac is the only patriarch who does not go to Egypt, and that only because he was told to confine his domestic intrigues to Abimelech—the very same involvements that Abraham had had with the same king and with Pharaoh. Here are some specifically Egyptian elements found in that book that do not occur in the Old Testament or the Hebrew legends: The woman who discovers Egypt (Sekhmet, Tefnut, Hathor) immediately after the flood (Re and the Sun's Eye, etc.) finds it still under water, and settles her son(s) in it as the king (the Great Cruise). Then there is the frustrated pharaoh always trying to claim a glory that he "diligently imitates" but can never fix in a patriarchal line. We find such oddities as Pharaoh and his son appearing dressed up as Hathor and Maat, as indeed they did on occasion, and Abraham himself dressed up like Osiris with the Atef crown "representing the Priesthood, . . . the grand Presidency in Heaven," with crook and flail as signs of "justice and judgment" (Facsimile 3, figure 1); again, not only living kings but commoners had themselves depicted in such a guise, and the crown and the scepters have been correctly interpreted, to judge by modern research.

That the person being presented to the man on the throne is an unknown, "one of the King's principal waiters," by the Canaanite name of Shulem, is quite in order, the men who commissioned such scenes being in fact very often palace servants, and as such, occasionally Canaanites.

Granted Joseph Smith has turned out an impressive performance, what good is it to us? The argument against the Book of Abraham on which eminent Egyptologists, including James Breasted, were most insistent was that the Egyptians were pagans, worlds removed from the religion of the Hebrews. But for some time now, every year has seen the narrowing of the gap as a steady and growing flow of discoveries and studies brings Egypt, Israel, and early Christianity ever closer and closer together. Even so, what is the religious message? What has the Book of Abraham to teach the modern world in general, and the church in particular? That is, of course, the message of Abraham, for we are commanded to do the works of Abraham (D&C 132:32) and told that there is *no other way for us to go.*

To begin with, Abraham was in the world, a wicked world very much like our own. From childhood to the grave, he was a stranger in his society because he insisted on living by the principles of the gospel and preaching them to others wherever he went, even if it meant getting into trouble. Those principles, teachings, covenants, ordinances, and promises were alien to the world, which was bitterly hostile to them. So Abraham's whole life, as is often stated, was a series of trials or tests, and by example and precept he tells us how to come through victorious. His object? Not to conquer or impress, but to bless all with whom he comes into contact, ultimately shedding the blessing that God gave to him on the whole human race. For that he is first of all the magnanimous, the great-hearted, the ever-hospitable Abraham, who always does the fair and compassionate thing no matter how badly others may behave toward him; he is the friend of God because he is the friend of man, pleading for Sodom and Gomorrah. That is the *moral* pattern for all men to follow.

Only by "doing the works of Abraham" can we hope to establish a better order of things on the earth, that order of Zion lost since the days of Enoch. This takes courage, tact, unfailing faith, and the constant aid of divine revelation. It entails more than human contrivance or human wisdom— Abraham must acquire ever more and more knowledge from above. The guiding principle is intelligence, an awareness of things as they are: the physical world, the structure and nature of the cosmos, and the underlying spiritual realities. For Abraham, everything is a prelude to what lies beyond. Determined to disengage from the absurd and vicious world around him, he is ever moving on, looking for a city made without hands, "whose builder and maker is God" (Hebrews 11:10). He tells us quite frankly that what he wants is peace and happiness for himself and to be a blessing to all mankind (Abraham 1:2). To achieve that required more than philosophical abstractions or convenient arrangements; he would have to go about it God's way, learning first the law of obedience, carrying out specific instructions regarding the building of altars, the bringing of sacrifices, the paying of tithes, the carrying out of explicit ordinances, the bestowal of blessings, the keeping of family records, the making of covenants, prayer and intercession for all mankind, works on behalf of the dead, and marrying for eternal posterity. Indeed, the works of Abraham center around the temple.

Our study of the Book of Abraham has been like rummaging through and poring over a random lot of old plans of some ancient building that has long since fallen into ruin and disappeared under the sands. What good is it to us now? Abraham spent his whole life trying to escape from it; he was determined to find something better. He exerted every faculty of body and mind to carry him toward that state of existence which is man's proper calling and eternal destiny. As Martin Buber puts it, Abraham's life was one long series of separations and departures.[1] There is no thought of returning to the world of Abraham—he was eager to leave it himself. Now that he "hath entered into his exaltation and sitteth upon his throne" (D&C 132:29), why are his past tribulations and the world in which he suffered of particular concern to us? Because they show us the way we still have to go.

We are in a perfect position to "do the works of Abraham" because we find ourselves in his position. The Book of Abraham was given to us along with a notice of eviction from our present quarters. We have been told by the scriptures in no uncertain terms for the past 150 years what experts in many fields are telling us today: that this present dwelling is rapidly becoming unfit for human habitation, that the place is soon going to be torn down, and that it is high time for us to start looking around "for another place of residence," in the manner of Abraham, and to follow his example: *Lekh lekha*—get going!

But where shall we go, and how shall we go about it? To a far greater extent than they realize, the Latter-day Saints are well into the project. Whenever they have settled down, no matter how great their poverty or their need for temporal things, the first order of business, the object and purpose of all their building and planting, has been to get to work on the *temple.* Whether in Kirtland, Far West, Nauvoo, or the valleys of the West, their hearts have been set on activities and observances that, in terms of modern-day progress and success, make no sense at all. The temple and its ordinances seem to be grotesquely out of place and impractical in the present world. The temple is, in fact, a school to wean us away from the things of the world. There the Saints take their bearings on the universe and on the eternities, and there they launch into the work by which all the nations of the earth are to be blessed. "Abraham received all things, whatsoever he received, by revelation and commandment, by my word, saith the Lord, and hath entered into his exaltation and sitteth upon his throne. . . . Go ye, therefore, and do the works of Abraham" (D&C 132:29, 32).

Note

1. See Martin Buber, "Abraham the Seer," *Judaism* 5 (1956): 295–96, 303–4.

Illustration Sources

Except where noted, the illustrations have been drawn or redrawn by Michael Lyon (ML) and computer-enhanced for this volume by David Sterling Lyon (DL), Tyler Moulton (TM), and Jessica Taylor (JT).

Figure 1, p. 38. The four sons of Horus, (A) Facsimile 1, figures 5–8; (B) Facsimile 2, fig. 6, chart from *IE* 72 (August 1969): 86.

Figure 2, pp. 40–41. The four living beings, (A) St. Sabina door panel, Wilhelm Neuss, *Das Buch Ezechiel* (Münster in Westfalia: Aschendorffsche Verlagsbuchhandlung, 1912), 167, fig. 15; (B) metal fan, redrawn (ML) from photograph, courtesy of Coptic Museum, Cairo.

Figure 3, p. 43. The messenger hawk as angel, (A) Facsimile 1, figure 1; (B) Facsimile 2, fig. 7; (C) hypocephalus of the Lady Nestaneteretten. Turin Museum, redrawn (ML); (D) hypocephalus of Châ-Kheper, redrawn (ML), © Louvre.

Figure 4, p. 44. Abraham and angel, illumination from the Apocalypse of Abraham, facsimile edition of the Codex Sylvester, St. Petersburg, 1891.

Figure 5, p. 47. Shield of Achilles, (A) Tabula Iliaca, 1863 drawing by Emiliano Sarti of a fragmentary marble panel, current location unknown; (B) engraving after Sarti drawing from Otto Jahn, *Griechische Bilderchroniken* (Bonn: Marcus, 1873), pl. 2.B, reconstructions (ML).

Figure 6, pp. 48–49. Shield of Achilles, (A) redrawn (ML) from Piotr Bienkowski, "Lo Scudo di Achille," *Mitteilungen des deutschen archäologischen Instituts, Römische Abteilung* 6 (1891), pl. IV; (B) ibid., pl. V.

Figure 7, p. 51. Hephaestus holding the shield, wall painting from the Domus Uboni, Pompeii, computer-enhanced restoration (DL) from a photograph in Paul Hermann, *Denkmäler der Malerei des Altertums* (Munich: Bruckmann, 1904), fig. 139.

Figure 8, p. 52. Facsimile 2.

Figure 9, p. 53. Hypocephalus with stars, redrawn (ML) and grayscale added (JT) from a photograph of Ptolemaic hypocephalus in George Daressy, *Catalogue Général du Musée du Caire, Texts et Dessius Magiques* (Cairo: Institut français d'archéologie orientale, 1903), pl. 13.

Figure 10, pp. 58–61. Egyptian parallels, (A) Iouya psychostasy, redrawn (ML, JT) from Edouard Naville, *Funeral Papyrus of Iouya* (London: Constable, 1908), 22; (B) washing pedestal, redrawn in perspective (ML) from Aylward M. Blackman, "Some Notes on the Ancient Egyptian Practice of Washing the Dead," *JEA* 5 (1918): 121; (C) five-headed serpent; seven-headed dragon, redrawn (ML), courtesy of Oriental Institute Museum; (D) map of the Two Ways, sarcophagus of General Sepi, Cairo Museum, drawing from Pierre Lacau, *Sarcophages antérieurs au Nouvel Empire* (Cairo: Institut français d'archáologie orientale, 1904), pl. 55; (E) Iouya's clapnet, redrawn (ML) from Naville, *Funeral Papyrus,* pl. 14; divine clapnet, redrawn (ML) from Émile Chassinat, *Le temple d'Edfou: Memoirs de la Mission archaeologique francaise au Cairo* (Paris: Librairie de la Société Asiatique, 1897), pl. 150; (F) hell fires, redrawn (ML) from Eugène Lefébure, *Les hypogées royaux de Thèbes, Le tombeau de Séti Ier* (Paris: Leroux, 1886), 2:3: pl. 10; (G.1) Egyptian triple crown, redrawn (ML) from Richard Lepsius, *Denkmäler aus Ägypten und Äthiopien* (Leipzig: Kohlers, 1892),

5:30; (G.2) Persian triple crown, redrawn (ML) from Internet photograph; (G.3) Egyptian crown of justification from Charles H. S. Davis, *The Egyptian Book of the Dead* (New York: Putnam's Sons, 1894), pl. 7; (H) Qa-hedjet embrace, redrawn (ML) from photograph, © Louvre; (I) Khafre statue, Cairo, redrawn (ML) from Ludwig Borchardt, *Statuen und Statuetten von Königen und Privatleuten* (Berlin: Reichsdruckerei, 1911), fig. 15; (J) sun revivifying the dead, Papyrus of Tent-diu-Mut, courtesy of Cairo Museum; (K) Ba and tomb, papyrus of Nefer-weben-f, in Edouard Naville, *Das ägyptische Todtenbuch der XVIII. bis XX. Dynastie*, 3 vols. (Berlin: Asher, 1886), 1: pl. 104.P.c.; (L) chopping block, Papyrus of Ani, redrawn (ML) from E. A. Wallis Budge, *The Papyrus of Ani* (New York: Putname, 1913): 3: pl. 16; (M) lion couches from sarcophagus of Djet-Bastet-iuef-anch, redrawn (ML), from Foto-Pilazaeus-Museum.

Figure 11, p. 62. Stele of Imi-is, Vatican no. 128a, photograph from Walter Wreszinski, "Das Buch von Durchwandeln der Ewigkeit nach einer Stele im Vatikan," *ZÄS* 45 (1908): 111, fig. 5.

Figure 12, p. 65. "Ship of a Thousand," (A) Facsimile 2, figure 4; (B) Khendjer pyramidion, redrawn, reconstructed in perspective (ML), computer graphics (DL), based on original in Cairo Museum.

Figure 13, p. 67. Amduat in tomb of Thutmosis III, drawn (ML) from various photographs, personal visit, with information provided by John Gee, computer graphics (JT).

Figure 14, p. 79. Facsimile 1.

Figure 15, p. 81. Lion-couch scene from tomb of Ramses VI, heavily restored (ML) from original in situ, photographs, and parallels from similar scenes in the cenotaph of Seti I and tomb of Ramses IX.

Figure 16, p. 86. Franklin Spalding, from *IE* 71 (August 1968): 53.

Figure 17, p. 95. Samuel Mercer, courtesy of University of Toronto Library (UTA A78–9941/015).

Figure 18, p. 128. Archibald Sayce, from *Archiv für Orientforschung* 8 (1932–33): 341.

Figure 19, p. 132. W. M. Flinders Petrie (1832), courtesy of Petrie Museum of Egyptian Archaeology.

Figure 20, p. 135. Three bronze hypocephali from W. M. Flinders Petrie, *Abydos*, part I (London: Egypt Exploration Fund, 1902), pls. 76–77.

Figure 21, p. 136. Eduard Meyer, from *ZÄS* 66 (1931): opp. 72, courtesy of Akademie Verlag.

Figure 22, p. 139. James Breasted, from *Bulletin of the American Society of Oriental Research* 61 (1936): 1–4.

Figure 23, p. 142. Friedrich von Bissing, from *Archiv für Orientforschung* 17 (1954–56): 485.

Figure 24, p. 145. Théodule Devéria, from *BE* 4 (1896): frontispiece.

Figure 25, p. 147. John Peters, courtesy of University of Pennsylvania Museum.

Figure 26, p. 148. Arthur Mace, courtesy of Metropolitan Museum of Art, New York.

Figure 27, p. 150. Albert Lythgoe, courtesy of Metropolitan Museum of Art, New York.

Figure 28, p. 151. "Museum Walls," *New York Times*, 29 December 1912, magazine section.

Figure 29, p. 153. E. A. Wallis Budge, courtesy of the Egypt Exploration Society.

Figure 30, p. 183. Theseus and the Bed of Procrustes, Attic red-figure vase, redrawn (ML), courtesy of Kunsthistorisches Museum, Vienna.

Figure 31, p. 185. Heracles and Busiris, Ionian hydria, Österreichisches Museum, Vienna, redrawn (ML) from reconstructed drawing in A. Furtwängler and C. Reichhold, *Die griechische Vasenmalerei* (Munich: Bruckmann, 1900).

Figure 32, p. 196. Abraham in the fire, courtesy of John Rylands University Library of Manchester, Persian translation courtesy of Behzad Tabatawī.

Figure 33, p. 196. Amenophis II and his bow, drawn and slightly restored (ML) from original in Karnak Museum.

Figure 34, p. 240. Bentresh stele, Louvre, from drawing (reversed) in Emmanuel de Rougé, "Étude sur une stèle Égyptienne," *BE* 23 (1910): opp. 144.

Figure 35, p. 242. Tushratta cuneiform letter, © The British Museum.

Figure 36, p. 248. Al-Arish naos, restored drawing (ML) based on photographs and plans in Francis L. Griffith, *The Antiquities of Tell El Yahudiyeh* (London: Kegan Paul, Trübner, 1890), pls. 23–24.

Figure 37, pp. 272–73. Colossus on sledge, from drawing in Percy E. Newberry, *El Bersheh* (London: Egypt Exploration Fund, 1895), 1: pls. 12, 15, translations from 18–19, restoration (ML) and computer graphics (TM) based on John G. Wilkinson's watercolor facsimile c. 1850.

Figure 38, p. 287. Imhotep, © Louvre.

Figure 39, p. 288. Amenhotep, son of Hapu, courtesy of Cairo Museum.

Figure 40, p. 289. Temple of Amenhotep, son of Hapu, (A) perspective reconstruction from Clément Robichon and Alexandre Varille, *Le temple du scribe royal Amenhotep, fils de Hapou* (Cairo: Institut français d'archéologie orientale, 1936), pl. 21; (B) section and plan, ibid., pl. 11.

Figure 41, pp. 306–7. Hatshepsut on throne, redrawn and heavily restored (ML) from Edouard Naville, *The Temple of Deir el Bahari* (London: Egypt Exploration Fund, 1894), part 3, pl. 85.

Figure 42, pp. 308–9. Rekhmire as judge with forty scrolls of the law, heavily restored (ML) and enhanced

(TM); restoration of Rekhmire on lion throne with goose based on parallel scenes in his tomb and that of Ramose.

Figure 43, p. 311. Anen, courtesy of Museo delle Antichità Egizie, Turin.

Figure 44, p. 321. Sacrifice of Isaac from Dura-Europos, redrawn (ML).

Figure 45, pp. 330–31. Ashurbanipal in garden, redrawn (ML), © The British Museum.

Figure 46, pp. 332–33. Isaac and phoenix, Strasbourg bestiary, redrawn (ML) from Otto Schmitt, *Gotische Skulpturen des Straßburger Münsters* (Frankfort am Main, Frankfurter Verlagsanstalt, 1924), 2: pls. 158, 165, 168.

Figure 47, p. 355. The Lady Qudshu in the Stele of Qeh, drawing from E. A. Wallis Budge, *The Gods of the Egyptians* (Chicago: Open Court, 1904), 2:276.

Figure 48, p. 357. Osiris beds, (A) redrawn (ML) from a coffin in the Fitzwilliam Museum, Cambridge; (B) courtesy of Cairo Museum, photograph from Alexandre Moret, *Kings and Gods of Egypt* (New York: Putnam, 1912), opp. 96, pl. 11.

Figure 49, p. 372. Facsimile 3.

Figure 50, p. 385. Khaemhet, Theban Tomb 57, redrawn (ML) from Prisse d'Avennes, *Histoire de l'art égyptien d'après les monuments* (Paris: Bertrand, 1878), 2: pl. 18.

Figure 51, pp. 388–89. Nebamun, Theban Tomb 90, redrawn and restored (ML).

Figure 52, p. 390. Amunuser, Theban Tomb 131, redrawn and restored (ML).

Figure 53, p. 391. Rekhmire, Theban Tomb 100, redrawn and heavily restored (ML).

Figure 54, p. 392. Thanuro, Theban Tomb 101, redrawn and heavily restored (ML).

Figure 55, p. 393. (Name effaced) overseer of horses, Theban Tomb 91, redrawn and heavily restored (ML).

Figure 56, pp. 394–95. Haremheb, Theban Tomb 78.

Figure 57, pp. 396–97. Surer, Theban Tomb 48, redrawn and restored (ML), enhanced (TM).

Figure 58, pp. 398–99. Kheruef, Theban Tomb 192, redrawn and restored (ML).

Figure 59, pp. 400–401. Ramose, Theban Tomb 55, redrawn and restored (ML).

Figure 60, pp. 402–3. Huy, Theban Tomb 40, redrawn and restored (ML) from Nina de G. Davies, *The Tomb of Huy* (London: Egypt Exploration Society, 1926), pl. 20, grayscale (JT) based on watercolor facsimile, Lepsius papers, Berlin.

Figure 61, pp. 404–5. Neferhotep, Theban Tomb 50, redrawn and restored (ML) with grayscale (JT) from a watercolor facsimile by Hoskins.

Figure 62, pp. 406–7. Huya, Amarna Tomb 1, redrawn and restored (ML) from Norman de G. Davies, *El Amarna III* (Boston: Egypt Exploration Fund, 1905), pl. 18.

Figure 63, p. 408. Hekerneheh, Theban Tomb 64, redrawn (ML) from Lepsius, *Denkmäler*, 3: pl. 69a.

Figure 64, p. 409. Stele of Haremheb from Karnak, slightly restored (ML), courtesty of the Egypt Exploration Society.

Figure 65, p. 416. Stele of Apeni, drawing from Henry R. H. Hall, *Hieroglyphic Texts from Egyptian Stelae in the British Museum* (London: British Museum, 1925), pl. 46.

Figure 66, p. 418. Tutankhamun gold shrine, redrawn (ML) from original in Cairo Museum.

Figure 67, p. 421. Anubis masks, (A) redrawn (ML) from Auguste Mariette, *Dendérah* (Paris: Franck, 1870), 4: pl. 31; (B) redrawn (ML) from the MS Barberini, courtesy of Musei Vaticani; (C) redrawn (ML), Foto-Pelizaeus-Museum; (D) redrawn (ML) from original in the Louvre.

Figure 68, p. 423. Stele of Khabekhnet, drawing from Hall, *Hieroglyphic Texts*, pl. 31.

Figure 69, p. 424. Beset mask and statuette, (A) redrawn

(ML) from W. M. Flinders Petrie, *Kahun, Gurob, and Hawara* (London: Paul, Trench, Trübner, 1890), pl. 8, fig. 27; (B) photograph from Henry R. H. Hall, "The Relations of Aegean with Egyptian Art," *JEA* 1 (1914): 203, pl. 34, fig. 2.

Figure 70, p. 426. Imhotep with mother and wife, redrawn and adapted (ML).

Figure 71, p. 427. Ramses II and Anath, courtesy of Brooklyn Museum.

Figure 72, p. 432. Samarian ivory plaque.

Figure 73, p. 434. Hathor mask, drawing (ML).

Figure 74, pp. 436–37. Kerasher version of psychostasy scene; photograph from E. A. Wallis Budge, *The Book of the Dead (Papyrus of Hunefer, Anhai, Kerasher, and Netchemet)* (London: Paul, Trench, Trubner, 1899), pl. 1 (Kerasher section).

Figure 75, p. 438. Maat and Hathor amulets.

Figure 76, p. 445. Amun and crook, redrawn and restored (ML), courtesy of Oriental Institute Museum.

Figure 77, p. 447. Tutankhamun ivory lid, redrawn and slightly restored (ML) from original and photographs, courtesy of the Cairo Museum.

Figure 78, p. 454–55. Temple mural of Amenhotep, son of Hapu, redrawn and restored (ML) from Robichon and Varille, *Le temple du scribe royal Amenhotep*, pl. 34, grayscale (JT) based on Robichon's reconstruction.

Figure 79, p. 469. Belemnite, (A) redrawn and slightly restored (ML) from R. Bullen Newton, "On Some Cretaceous Shells from Egypt," *Geological Magazine* (1898): 394, pl. 15, figs. 2, 4; (B) thunderbolt of Min (c. 2575 B.C.); (C) Roman coin, Charles Daremberg and Edmond Saglio, *Dictionaire des Antiquitiés grecques et romains* (Paris: Hachette, 1877), 1358, fig. 3313.

Figure 80, p. 471. Book of the Cow, (A) reconstruction

drawing (ML) from photographs of tomb; (B) drawing (ML) based on original and photographs of shrine.

Figure 81, p. 472. Elephantine cave, redrawn and restored (ML) from photographs and visit to the site and Hermann Junker, *Das Götterdekret über das Abaton* (Vienna: Hölder, 1913), 37, fig 8; 58, fig. 20.

Figure 82, pp. 492–93. Map of Philae and Bigge, photograph from ibid., 33, 48, map drawn (ML) and captions (JT).

Figure 83, pp. 494–95. Scenes from the isle of Philae, engraving from Jacques-Joseph Champollion-Figeac, *Égypte ancienne* (Paris: Firmin Didot frères, 1839), pls. 4–6, 73.

Figure 84, p. 497. Ivory plaque of Aha from Naqada, redrawn and slightly restored (ML) from photograph, courtesy of Cairo Museum.

Figure 85, pp. 499–503. Tomb of Kheruef, perspective view (ML), courtesy of Oriental Institute Museum.

Figure 86, p. 509. First-Dynasty ivory comb, drawing from W. M. Flinders Petrie, *Tombs of the Courtiers and Oxyrhynkos* (London: British School of Archaeology in Egypt, 1925), pl. 12, fig. 5.

Figure 87, p. 527. Ivory handle of Gebel al-Arak knife, redrawn (ML), © Louvre.

Figure 88, p. 560. (A) Ramses III and the feast of Min, redrawn and restored (ML), courtesy of Oriental Institute Museum; (B) Tutankhamun sickle, drawing (ML), courtesy of Cairo Museum.

Figure 89, p. 561. (A) Temple of Min, redrawn and restored (ML) from Edouard Naville, *Détails relevés dans les ruines quelques temples égyptiens* (Paris: Librarie Orientaliste Paul Geuthner, 1930), pl. 35; (B) alabaster honey pot, drawing (ML).

Figure 90, p. 565. Ramses III and the four birds, redrawn and restored (ML), courtesy of Oriental Institute Museum.

Figure 91, p. 591. Painted tomb, drawing from James E.

Quibéll and F. W. Green, *Hierakonpolis*, part 2 (London: Quariton, 1902), pl. 75.

Figure 92, p. 592. (A) Temple of Horus, Edfu, drawing (ML) from personal visit and various photographs; (B) copper harpoon, courtesy of the British Museum.

Figure 93, p. 593. Palermo stone, photograph from Heinrich Schäfer, *Ein Bruchstück altägyptischer Annalen* (Berlin: Königliche Akademie der Wissenschaften, 1902).

Figure 94, p. 595. Goddess on ship, drawing (ML).

Figure 95, p. 596. Way of Horus, photograph from Jules Couyat and Pierre Montet, *Les inscriptions hiéroglyphiques et hiératiques du Ouadi Hammamat* (Cairo: Institut français d'archäologie orientale, 1912), pl. 1.

Figure 96, p. 597. Mace head of Narmer, redrawn (ML) from James E. Quibéll and F. W. Green, *Hierakonpolis*, part 1 (London: Quariton, 1900), pl. 26.B.

Figure 97, p. 598. Tomb of Queen Meryet-Nit, reconstruction drawing (ML), courtesy of Cairo Museum.

Figure 98, p. 598. Boat grave, illustrations by Walter Emery.

Figure 99, p. 610. Naqada red crown, from Gerald A. Wainwright, "The Red Crown in Early Prehistoric Times," *JEA* 9 (1923): pl. 20. fig. 3; drawing (ML) of red crown from bas-relief of Djoser, Cairo Museum.

Figure 100, p. 615. Beekeeping scene from Abu Gurob, Ägyptisches Museum, Berlin, redrawn and restored (ML) from Ludwig Borchardt and Heinrich Schäfer, "Das Re Heiligtum des Königs Ne-user-r?," *ZÄS* 38 (1900): 94, pl. 5.

Figure 101, p. 619. Maya glyphs for honey and bees, drawings by Hilda M. Ransome.

Figure 102, p. 620. French gold bees, drawing from Jean-Jacques Chifflet, *Anastasis Childerici I* (Antwerp: Ex officina Plantiniana Balthasaris Moreti, 1655), 141.

Figure 103, p. 622. (A) Seti I and bees and (B) Osiris of

the Bees, drawings from Eugène Lefébure, *Les hypogées royaux de Thèbes: première division, le tombeau de Séti Ier* (Paris: Leroux, 1886), pt. 3, pl. 3; pt. 4, pl. 34.

Figure 104, p. 636. Min fetishes, (A) courtesy of Cairo Museum; (B) slate palette, courtesy of the British Museum; (C) courtesy of the Egypt Exploration Society.

ANCIENT EGYPT

and the principal sites mentioned in the text listed from North to South

EGYPTIAN	GREEK	ARABIC	DESCRIPTION	PAGE
		al-Arish	Site of the granite Naos	247
Pr-wsir, Per-Wesir "House of Osiris"	Busiris		City on Delta; early site of human sacrifice	188–89
Ḥm (?), Khem	Letopolis		The city was sacred to Horus; mentioned during 4th Dynasty	57, 615
ʾIwnw, Annu "Sun Pillar"	Heliopolis "City of Sun"	al-Matariya	Sacred university city. Joseph married the daughter of its high priest (Gen. 41:45)	237, 581
		al-Gerza	Type site at point of Delta; "Gerzean" is Naqada II	537, 594
ʾInb·w-ḥd, Inbu-hedj "White Walls"	Memphis	Mit Rahina	An Old Kingdom capital founded by Menes; the site of the Heb-Sed festival	246
Ḥmnw, Khemenu "City of Eight"	Hermopolis "... of Hermes"	al-Ashmunein	Center of the worship of Thoth, god of wisdom	563–64
Ṯni, Tjene	Thinis	al-Barba	Manetho believed pharoahs of 1 and 2 Dynasty were buried here, thus "Thinite Dynasties"	590
ȝbḏw, Abtu	Abydos	al-Arabat	Sacred city where the head of Osiris was enshrined; pilgrimage center	564
		al-Amra	Type site near Abydos; "Amratian" is Naqada I	594
rȝ-ḥnw, Ro-Henu "Way of Hor"		Wadi Hammamat	One entry route of early settlers; later route to Red Sea	595–96
Gbty, Gebti	Coptos	Qifti, Kufi	Early settlement where Wadi Hammamat meets the Nile; later center of Egyptian Christians, thus "Coptic"	537
		Naqada	Neolithic type site, pre-Dynastic burials	496
wȝs.t, Waset "Dominion City"	Thebai, Thebes	Thabūna	A New Kingdom capital sacred to Amon-Ra, the "No-Amon" of Nahum 3:8	299
Nḫn, Nekhen	Hierakono-polis, "Falcon City"	al-Kab	An early capital of Upper Egypt, site of the PerWer "Great House" of Nekhbet	564

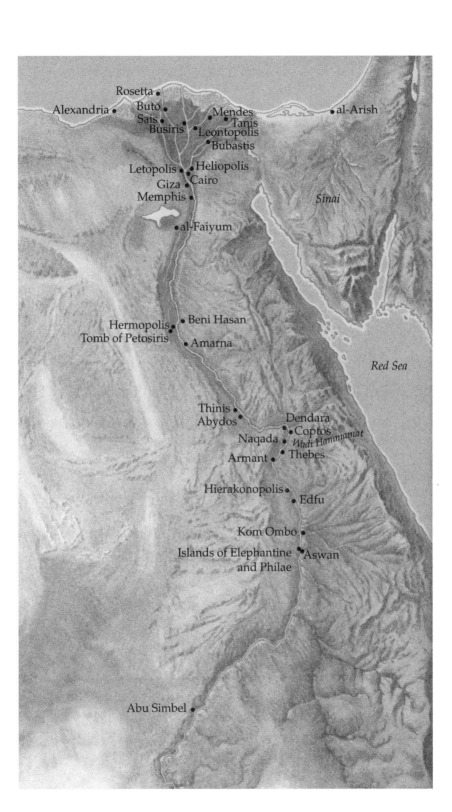

Index of Passages

Index of Subjects

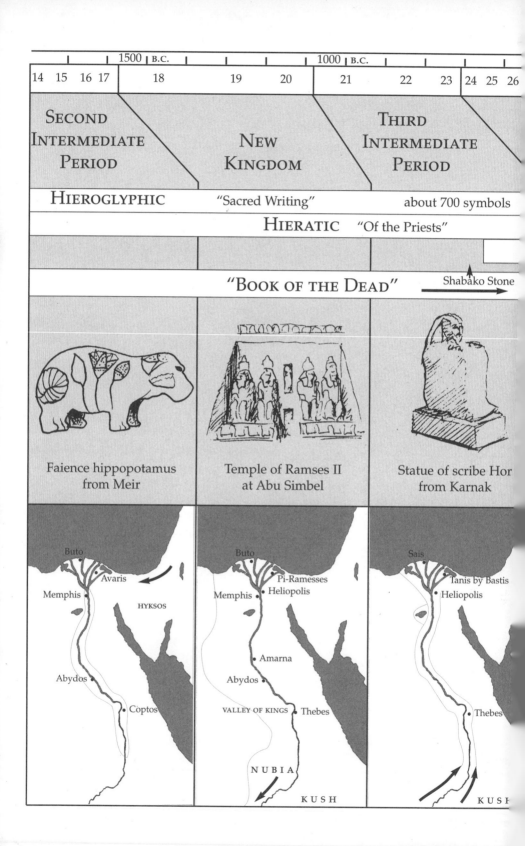

| 14 | 15 | 16 | 17 | 18 | 19 | 20 | 21 | 22 | 23 | 24 | 25 | 26 |

1500 B.C.   1000 B.C.

SECOND INTERMEDIATE PERIOD

NEW KINGDOM

THIRD INTERMEDIATE PERIOD

HIEROGLYPHIC   "Sacred Writing"   about 700 symbols

HIERATIC   "Of the Priests"

"BOOK OF THE DEAD"   Shabako Stone

Faience hippopotamus
from Meir

Temple of Ramses II
at Abu Simbel

Statue of scribe Hor
from Karnak

Buto
Avaris
Memphis
HYKSOS
Abydos
Coptos

Buto
Pi-Ramesses
Heliopolis
Memphis
Amarna
Abydos
VALLEY OF KINGS   Thebes
NUBIA
KUSH

Sais
Tanis by Bastis
Heliopolis
Thebes
KUSH